European human rights law

The Human Rights Act 1998 and the European
Convention on Human Rights

Keir Starmer is a barrister at Doughty Street Chambers
specialising in European human rights law. He has extensive
experience of litigation before the European Court and
Commission of Human Rights.

The Legal Action Group is a national, independent charity
which campaigns for equal access to justice for all members of
society. Legal Action Group:
- provides support to the practice of lawyers and advisers
- inspires developments in that practice
- campaigns for improvements in the law and the
  administration of justice
- stimulates debate on how services should be delivered.

European human rights law

The Human Rights Act 1998 and the European Convention on Human Rights

Keir Starmer

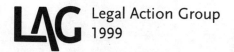

Legal Action Group
1999

This edition published in Great Britain 1999
by LAG Education and Service Trust Ltd
242 Pentonville Road
London
N1 9UN

Reprinted 2000

British Library Cataloguing in Publication Data
A CIP catalogue record for this book is available from the British Library

ISBN 0 905099 77 X

Typeset by Regent Typesetting
Printed in Great Britain by Bell & Bain Ltd, Glasgow

Foreword

by Lord Justice Sedley

The interval of almost two years between the enactment and the coming into force of the Human Rights Act 1998 has provided time for government to reorient its policies and practices, and for courts and lawyers to begin to acquire a new mindset. Both are of critical importance if the new legislation is to be more than window-dressing.

All the signs are that the new human rights regime is going to be taken very seriously indeed. This does not mean an open season in which every doctrine, policy and decision can now be shot down by aggrieved individuals or corporations. Indeed, to the extent that this is attempted, the Act and the Convention risk becoming discredited. What is needed above all is a legal culture in which the new constitutional balance between individual and state is understood, valued and intelligently developed.

In the process of continuing education, which in the years to come will involve judges, lawyers and citizens alike, practising and academic lawyers are going to play a pivotal role. It is they who will have to advise clients and readers both cautiously and imaginatively about their claims; and it is the practitioners who will then have to present clear and educated arguments to judges engaged on the same learning process as themselves.

It is a true pleasure in this situation to be able to welcome and commend Keir Starmer's book. Not the least reason is that it is published by the Legal Action Group, whose already high reputation for accessibility and reliability it will enhance. Beyond this, the text itself is a model of its kind: well organised and clearly written, but without ducking or oversimplifying the problematic issues that we know lie in wait for us.

Particularly useful for practitioners is the book's organisation according to the subject-matter or topics of claims rather than a schematic article-by-article treatment of the Convention. You will find, alongside those issues on which the jurisprudence of the

Convention is relatively well settled, lucid treatments of the major unresolved issues: the relation between the supranational and domestic margins of appreciation; the status of commercial speech under article 10; the relevance of the Convention to environmental protection; the 'horizontal' applicability of rights as between one citizen or corporation and another; the related questions of the positive obligations of states and the role of the courts as 'public authorities'; unlawfully obtained evidence – the fruit of the poisoned tree; access to information; equality under article 14 as a free-standing right, at least in the sense that it is not necessarily dependent on violation of a separate right; the impact of article 8 on immigration and asylum, or on the protection of children; and so on.

This is a volume of real value and importance in the con-stitutional era upon which the United Kingdom is embarking as we leave a century which has witnessed some of the most terrible abuses of human rights in our entire history and embark – with hope, if not with sanguinity – on a new one.

Acknowledgements

This book is based on my work, research and discussions in the field of European human rights law, none of which would have been possible without the help of others. I owe an enormous debt to all of them, including Philip Leach and John Wadham (Liberty), Anne Owers and Kate Akester (Justice), Professor Kevin Boyle and Stuart Weir (Democratic Audit), Murray Hunt, Helen Mountfield and Rabinder Singh (4–5 Grays Inn Square Chambers), Mark Stephens (Stephens Innocent) and Simon McKay (Chadwick Lawrence).

Special thanks are due to those who assisted in the writing of the text itself. They include Michael Ford (Doughty Street Chambers) whose careful comments on chapters 11, 12 and 13 were invaluable; Jonathan Cooper (Justice), whose extensive understanding of the subtleties of Convention jurisprudence added considerably to chapters 4 and 5, and whose sheer enthusiasm kept me going at vital stages of the writing process; Francesca Klug (Human Rights Incorporation Project), one of the driving forces behind the Human Rights Act 1998 and an inspirational colleague, who provided comments on chapters 1, 2, and 5 which added authority to the text (the work on *Hansard* extracts was all hers) and prevented me from slipping into incomprehensible legal jargon – I look forward to our joint work for the Human Rights Act Research Unit; Maryam Samimi (Tooks Court Chambers), who provided important research material for chapter 24, 'Freedom of Expression'; and Iain Byrne, who assisted in the final preparations with calmness and precision.

The team at LAG waited patiently as I broke deadline after deadline for completion of every section of the text. Their commitment to the project has been unswerving.

I would also like to thank my colleagues and the staff at Doughty Street Chambers. They provide the perfect environment for any human rights lawyer, coupling inspiration and stimulation with friendship and humour. My understanding of the Convention owes much to my work with colleagues such as Geoffrey Robertson QC, Edward Fitzgerald QC, Tim Owen and, in particular, Ben Emmerson (with whom I have spent many hours discussing human rights issues and whose expertise I greatly admire and value). Equally, without the support and forbearance of all the staff, including Christine Kings, Michelle Simpson, Justin Hebbs, Richard Bayliss and Paul Friend, I would never have finished the project I took on.

Last, but by no means least, the greatest debt of all is due to Phillippa Kaufmann and Mitchell Woolf. Without them, there would have been no book. Phillippa, a barrister at Doughty Street Chambers, is an acknowledged expert in prison law and public law and (with Tim Owen) wrote the prisoners section of *Halsbury's Laws of England*. She is the author of chapter 16, 'Prisoners', which is the most scholarly treatment of prisoners' rights under the Convention yet written. She also provided invaluable comments and analysis on the rest of the book; not to mention her precious support through the long weekends and evenings spent by me writing and re-writing the rest of the text. Mitchell is a solicitor specialising in human rights law. He wrote chapter 30, 'The Practice and Procedure of the European Court of Human Rights'. He also spent many months at Doughty Street Chambers carrying out vital research for this book with a commitment and dedication second to none. His fingerprint is on every page.

Case references in this book go up to and include June 1999. However, the treatment of cases after January 1999 is more limited than those before that date. Any omissions and errors are, of course, all mine.

Keir Starmer
Doughty Street Chambers
August 1999

Contents

Foreword v
Acknowledgements vii
Table of cases xxiii
Table of statutes lv
Table of statutory instruments lix
Table of conventions lxi
Reference note lxxi

Introduction 1

Part I: Introduction to the Human Rights Act 1998 and the European Convention on Human Rights 5

1   **The Human Rights Act 1998: general principles 7**
     Summary 9
     Timetable for implementation 10
     The rights protected 11
     The position in relation to articles 1 and 13 11
     New legislation 13
     Statutory interpretation: the new rule 14
     Statutory interpretation: the European Community law and New
        Zealand examples 16
     Incorporating the Convention approach to the protection of
        human rights into domestic law 18
     Interpreting the Human Rights Act itself 19
     Declarations of incompatibility 20
     Subordinate legislation 22
     Public authorities 23
     Effect of the HRA on the common law 24
     The obligation to take Strasbourg case-law into account 25
     Case-law from other jurisdictions 27
     The special position of freedom of expression and religion 28
     Remedial orders 29
     Derogations 31

Reservations 32
Applications of the HRA in Scotland, Wales and Northern
  Ireland 32
Safeguards for existing human rights 33
Human Rights Commission 34
Recourse to the Convention before the HRA comes into force 35
The Convention and European Community law 39

2 The Human Rights Act 1998: claims and remedies 41
Introduction 43
The meaning of 'public authority' under the Human Rights
  Act 45
Relevance of Convention case-law to the meaning of public
  authority and the notion of state responsibility 47
The concept of 'victim' under the Human Rights Act 1998 49
'Victim' contrasted with 'sufficient interest' in judicial review
  proceedings 57
Remedies 59
Aggravated and exemplary damages 61
Damages under the Convention: general principles 62
Pecuniary loss under the Convention 63
Non-pecuniary loss under the Convention 65
Costs and expenses under the Convention 72
The special rules applicable to judicial acts 72
The limitation period for claims under the HRA 73
Convention claims in relation to the acts of private individuals 74
Retrospective claims under the Human Rights Act 76

3 Convention rights: overview, structure and summary 77
Introduction 83
Overview 84
Convention rights: checklist 86
Article 2: the right to life 89
Article 3: the prohibition on torture, inhuman and degrading
  treatment and punishment 91
Article 4: the prohibition on slavery and related practices 93
Article 5: the right to liberty 95
Article 6: fair trial 118
Article 7: the prohibition on retrospective criminal offences 123
Article 8: privacy and related matters 125
Article 9: religion and belief 131
Article 10: freedom of expression 134
Article 11: freedom of assembly and association 137
Article 12: the right to marry and found a family 141

Article 13: the right to an effective remedy 142
Article 14: the prohibition on discrimination 145
Article 1 of the first Protocol: the right to property 147
Article 2 of the first Protocol: the right to education 149
Article 3 of the first Protocol: the duty to hold free elections 150

4   **The Convention approach to the protection of human rights 153**
Introduction 155
Principles of interpretation: the Vienna Convention 156
The objects and purpose of the Convention 157
The principle of effectiveness 158
Dynamic interpretation: the Convention as a 'living instrument'
    160
Autonomous meaning 161
Previous Convention case-law 161
Recourse to other human rights instruments 162
Restricting Convention rights 165
The principle of legality 166
The principle of proportionality 169
Restrictions expressly permitted under articles 8(2), 9(2), 10(2)
    and 11(2) 176
Restrictions expressly permitted under other articles 180
Restrictions impliedly permitted under the Convention 182
Restrictions specifically provided for by a valid derogation 185
Restrictions on the political activity of aliens specifically provided
    for by article 16 185
Restrictions on activities aimed at the destruction of Convention
    rights specifically provided for by article 17 186
The margin of appreciation 187
Non-applicability of the margin of appreciation under the
    HRA 190
Waiver of Convention rights 192

5   **Positive obligations under the Convention 193**
Introduction 194
The scope of positive obligations under the Convention 195
Putting in place a legal framework which provides effective
    protection for Convention rights 196
Preventing breaches of Convention rights 199
Providing information and advice relevant to the breach of
    Convention rights 202
Responding to breaches of Convention rights 204
Providing resources to individuals to prevent breaches of their
    Convention rights 205

The relationship between positive and negative obligations   206
Positive obligations under the HRA   207

Part II: The European Convention on Human Rights and criminal law   211

6   The Convention in criminal proceedings: an introduction   213
Introduction   214
Relevant Convention provisions   214
The classification of criminal proceedings   218
Forfeiture and tax proceedings   219
When is an individual 'charged' under the Convention?   221
Substantive challenges to the criminal law   222
Certainty   222
Non-retrospectivity   225
Criminal liability for conduct protected under the Convention   226

7   The pre-trial stage   229
Introduction   231
The right to be brought promptly before a court   231
Function of court before which an accused person is brought   233
Bail   234
Grounds for refusing bail   235
Bail conditions   238
The right to test the legality of arrest or detention before a court: article 5(4) of the Convention and bail   239
Trial within a reasonable time   241
Charge   243
Access to a lawyer   245
Lawyer/client communications   247
Disclosure   248
Public interest immunity   252
Time and facilities for preparation of defence   254
Pre-trial publicity   255

8   Fair trial guarantees in criminal cases   259
Introduction   260
An independent and impartial court   261
The right to a public hearing   264
The right to 'participate effectively' in criminal proceedings   266
Trial in absentia   267
Legal aid   268
Legal representation   269

Interpreters and translations 272
The burden of proof 273
The standard of proof 276
Changing plea 276
Reasons 277
Costs in criminal cases 277
International co-operation in criminal matters 278
Double jeopardy 279
Amicus lawyers, intervening parties and clerks in magistrates'
     courts 280

9   Evidence in criminal cases 281
Introduction 283
Hearsay evidence: general principles 283
Non-compellable witnesses 285
Illness and death 286
Absconding witnesses 288
Fear of reprisals 288
Anonymous witnesses 290
Undercover agents and entrapment 293
Protecting the rights of victims and witnesses in criminal
     proceedings 295
Unlawfully obtained evidence 297
Confession evidence 299
Accomplice evidence 299
Expert evidence 301
Defence evidence 301
The right to silence: freedom from self-incrimination 303
The right to silence: drawing adverse inferences 305
Intimate samples 309

10 Sentence and appeals 311
Sentence: introduction 312
Article 3 issues in sentencing 312
The fair trial guarantees of article 6 in sentencing 312
Non-retrospectivity 312
Sentences for Convention-protected activity 313
Punitive and preventative sentences 313
Victim involvement in sentencing 314
Appeals: introduction 314
Legal aid and legal representation at the appeal stage 316
The right to oral argument at a public hearing in the presence of
     the accused at the appeal stage 317
Proceedings for leave to appeal 318

Loss of time pending appeal   319
Reasons in appeal proceedings   320
New evidence and references back to the Court of Appeal   320

Part III: The European Convention on Human Rights and civil proceedings   323

11   The Convention in civil proceedings: an introduction   325
Introduction   326
Convention rights in civil proceedings   326
The application of article 6(1) in civil proceedings   327
Judicial review and the Convention   328

12   Civil rights and obligations: the scope of article 6(1) of the Convention   331
Introduction   333
The meaning of 'civil' rights and obligations   333
Analysis of Convention case-law   335
The need for a basis in domestic law   344
The need for a 'determination' of rights or obligations   346
The application of article 6(1) where civil rights and obligations
    are determined by bodies other than courts or tribunals   348
Official investigations   350

13   The right to a fair trial in civil proceedings: the content of article 6(1) of the Convention   351
Introduction   353
The 'right of access' to a court   354
Restrictions on instituting proceedings   355
Arbitration clauses   356
Immunities and privileges   357
Limitation periods   361
Security for costs orders   363
Requirement of notice and clarity   364
Legal aid in civil proceedings   365
The right to a tribunal   367
Independence and impartiality   368
Public hearings   369
The right to participate effectively in civil proceedings   371
The right to be present   371
Equality of arms   371
The right to an adversarial hearing   372
Disclosure   373
Evidence and witnesses   374

Burden and standard of proof   375
Expert evidence   375
Reasons   376
Costs   377
The enforcement of judgments   377
Civil appeals   378
Trial within a reasonable period   378

Part IV: The European Convention on Human Rights: specific issues   383

14   **The right to life and physical integrity   385**
Introduction   387
The right to life   387
The duty to protect the right to life by law   388
The obligation to take appropriate measures to protect life   389
Investigation and prosecution   391
Criminal investigations   392
The use of force and the exceptions provided for in article 2(2)   393
The test of absolute necessity   395
Abortion   397
Euthanasia   398
The death penalty   399
The prohibition on torture, inhuman and/or degrading treatment/punishment   399
Torture   401
Inhuman treatment/punishment   402
Degrading treatment/punishment   403
Procedural aspects of article 3   404
State responsibility under article3   404
The protection of physical integrity under article 8   405
Medical care: overview   407
Medical treatment, the right to life and the prohibition on inhuman and degrading treatment   407
Health advice   409
Access to health information   410
Medical records   411
Negligence   411

15   **Police powers   413**
Introduction   415
Positive obligations and policing   415

Police surveillance   416

The obligation that police surveillance be 'prescribed by law'   417

The obligation that police surveillance be necessary and proportionate   422

Fingerprints, photographs and other personal data   424

Search and seizure   426

Agents provocateurs and entrapment   428

Arrest and related issues   429

The application of article 5 to police powers: the threshold issue   431

The pre-conditions of lawful arrest and detention under article 5   434

Grounds for arrest under the Convention   435

The meaning of 'reasonable suspicion'   436

Preventative detention   438

Reasons for arrest   439

Other grounds for arrest under the Convention   440

Arrest and detention outside the UK   440

The exercise of stop and search and similar powers   441

Remedies for police misconduct: overview   443

Ill-treatment and the use of force   444

Handcuffs   445

Racism and other forms of discrimination   446

The burden and standard of proof in misconduct cases   447

Vicarious liability   448

Police immunity in negligence actions   449

Damages in civil actions against the police   451

Fair trial generally   451

16   **Prisoners   453**

Introduction   455

Article 2   455

Article 3   456

Article 4   468

Article 5   469

Article 6   474

Articles 8(2) to 11(2) – general considerations   477

Article 8   478

Article 9   486

Article 10   486

Article 11   489

Article 12   489

Article 14   490
Article 1 of the First Protocol   490
Article 2 of the First Protocol   491

17   Mental health   493
Introduction   494
Detention under article 5 of the Convention   494
Meaning of 'unsound mind'   495
Lawfulness   495
Procedure prescribed by law   496
Emergency admissions   496
Voluntary surrender   497
The meaning of 'detention' under article 5   497
Periodic review   498
The reviewing body   498
The nature of the review   499
Procedural safeguards at review hearings   499
The timing of reviews   500
Release   500
Detention after or as a result of criminal proceedings   502
Conditions of detention: article 3   503
Immigration, asylum, extradition and deportation   505

18   Immigration, asylum, extradition and deportation   505
Introduction   506
Inhuman and degrading treatment: the basis framework   506
The application of article 3 to admission cases   508
The application of article 3 to expulsion cases   509
Expulsion and the right to life   514
Expulsion and fair trial   514
Detention under article 5   515
Private and family life under article 8   517
The application of article 8 to admission cases   518
The application of article 8 to expulsion cases   519
Discrimination   520
Procedural safeguards in admission and expulsion cases   522

19   Family life   523
Introduction   525
The right to 'family life'   525
The meaning of 'family life' under article 8   527
Adoptive relationships and fostering   529
Embryology and surrogacy   529
Lesbian and gay couples   530

Transsexuals 530
Wider family relationships 531
What does the right to family life cover? 532
Marriage 533
Founding a family 534
Children born out of wedlock 535
Divorce and separation 536
Custody and access 537
The enforcement of court orders 537
Maintenance payments 538
Domestic violence 538
Adoption 539
Placing children in care 540
Names 541
Sexual identity: the position of transsexuals 541
Procedural fairness in proceedings concerning family life 543

20 Children 547
Introduction 548
Parental control over children 548
Corporal punishment 549
Protection against abuse 552
The detention of children under article 5(1)(d) of the
    Convention 553
Children in criminal proceedings 554
The emergence of child-specific rights in the criminal
    context 555
The Strasbourg approach 558

21 Education 561
Introduction 562
The scope of the right to education 563
Regulation of the right to education 564
The right to respect for religious and philosophical
    convictions 565
The distinction between basis elementary and higher
    education 568
Private schools 569
Funding 570
Special needs 570
Setting the curriculum 572
Disciplinary matters 573
Corporal punishment 573
Suspension/expulsion 574

Challenging disciplinary measures   576
School uniform requirements   576

22   Housing, planning and the environment   577
Introduction   578
Housing rights under article 8(1)   579
The meaning of 'home' under article 8(1)   579
Restrictions on article 8(1) rights   581
Housing rights under article 1 of Protocol 1   582
The meaning of property/ possessions   582
The test for deprivation and control of property/possessions   584
The overlap with article 8   585
Access and occupation of a 'home'   586
Eviction   586
Peaceful enjoyment and the environment   587
Planning   589
Procedural fairness in housing matters   590
Does the Convention provide a 'right' to housing?   592
Discrimination   593

23   Welfare benefits and entitlements   595
Introduction   596
Welfare benefits and entitlements as property rights   596
Welfare benefits and entitlements and article 8   599
Procedural fairness in the determination of welfare benefits and
    entitlements   600
Discrimination   604

24   Freedom of expression   605
Introduction   606
The scope of article 10   607
The medium of expression   607
Access to information   608
Licensing of broadcasting, television and cinema enterprises
    609
Restrictions on freedom of expression   610
Restrictions imposed by other private individuals   611
Prior restraint   612
Defamation proceedings   613
Public interest defences   613
Fair comment   616
Protection of the judiciary   616
Court reporting and contempt of court   617
Disclosure of journalists' sources and other journalistic
    materials   619

Commercial speech 620
Artistic expression 620
Race hatred 621

25 Protest and public order 623
Introduction 624
Positive obligations under article 11 626
Using the highway as a forum for protest 628
Types of conduct protected by article 11 629
Balancing freedom of assembly and the prevention of
    disorder 630
Orders banning meetings and marches 632

26 Property rights 635
Introduction 636
The 'fair balance' test 636
Compensation 637
Meaning of 'possessions' 637
Deprivation of property 638
Control on the use of property/possessions 640
Peaceful enjoyment of possessions 641
Taxes, other contributions and penalties 641
Procedural rights 642

27 Thought, conscience and religion 643
Introduction 644
The scope of freedom of thought, conscience and religion 645
Manifesting a religion or belief 646
Obeying the law 647
Proselytism 649
Positive obligations under article 9 650
Restricting article 9(1) rights 651
Blasphemy and freedom of expression 652
Religious discrimination 654
Who can raise an article 9 claim? 654
Conscientious objectors 655
The special provision made for freedom of religion in the
    HRA 655

28 Workplace rights 657
Introduction 659
The applicability of article 6(1) in the employment context 659
The special position of public officials 661
Specific workplace rights 665
Slavery, servitude and forced labour 665

The right to form and join a trade union   668
The right not to form and join a trade union   670
Trade union activities   671
Industrial action   672
Excluded groups   673
The protection of other Convention rights in the workplace   673
Privacy at work   674
Security vetting   675
Freedom of thought, conscience and religion   676
Freedom of expression   677
The prohibition on discrimination   680
Contracting out of Convention rights   680
The applicability of the Convention between private
    individuals   680

29   **Discrimination   683**
Introduction   684
The dependent nature of article 14   684
The ambit test   686
The meaning of discrimination   687
Differential treatment   687
Legitimate aim   688
Proportionality   688
Suspect groups   689
Indirect discrimination   689
Positive discrimination   690
Discrimination as degrading treatment   690
Developing article 14 principles   690

**Part V: Pursuing a case to the European Court of Human
Rights   693**

30   **The practice and procedure of the European Court of Human
Rights   695**
Introduction   697
Locus standi   698
Victim status   699
Making a complaint   699
Admissibility   700
Friendly settlement   702
Merits   703
Costs   703
Referral to the Grand Chamber   704
Admissibility: special considerations   705

Striking out of the list   710
Interim relief and urgent applications   710
Legal aid   711
Advisory opinion   712
Binding force and the execution of judgments   712

APPENDICES   715
A   Human Rights Act 1998   717
B   European Convention on Human Rights   741
C   Universal Declaration of Human Rights   757
D   UN Covenant on Civil and Political Rights   761
E   UN Convention on the elimination of all forms of racial
   discrimination   769
F   UN Convention on the elimination of all forms of
   discrimination against women   773
G   UN Convention on the rights of the child   779
H   European Social Charter   793
I   Rules of the European Court of Human Rights   801
J   Rules of the Committee of Ministers   831
K   European Court of Human Rights complaint form   837
L   European Court of Human Rights form of authority   843

Index   847

Table of cases

A and A v Netherlands (1992) 72 DR 118   19.35
A and Others v Denmark (1996) 22 EHRR 458   13.81
A and Others v Spain (1990) 66 DR 188   3.159
A B v Switzerland Appl 20872/92 80B DR 66   16.25, 16.58
A v France (1993) 17 EHRR 462   2.14, 15.25, 15.95
A v Switzerland (1984) 38 DR 219   3.136, 27.37
A v Switzerland (1986) 46 DR 257   18.13
A v UK (1998) 2 FLR 959   4.24, 14.60, 20.1,
    20.11, 20.13, 30.13

A v UK Appl 6840/74 Commission (16 July 1980)   17.34
A, B, C and D v Germany (1979) 18 DR 176   2.19–2.35
A-G Gambia v Momodou Jobe [1984] AC 689   1.28
A-G Hong Kong v Lee Kwong-Kut [1993] AC 951   1.28
A-G v Guardian Newspapers [1987] 1 WLR 1248   1.77
Abas v Netherlands Appl 27943/95 [1997] EHRLR 418   6.15, 9.83
Abbott v UK (1990) 67 DR 290   30.36
Abdulaziz, Cabales and Balkandali v UK (1985) 7 EHRR
    471   2.19–2.35, 2.57,
    3.13, 3.115, 3.170, 3.183, 14.55, 18.3, 18.10, 18.32, 18.35–18.37, 18.46,
    18.47, 19.11, 19.38, 29.5, 29.17, 29.18, 29.21, 29.23
Adam and Khan v UK (1967) 10 Year Book 478   19.35
Adams and Benn v UK Appls 28979/95 and 30343/96
    (1996) 23 EHRR 160 CD   12.8, 24.18
Adegbie v Austria Commission (1997) 90-A DR 31   18.37, 18.38
ADT v UK (1996) EHRLR 555   6.37
Aerts v Belgium [1998] EHRLR 777   13.37, 13.40
Agee v UK (1976) 7 DR 164   12.28
Agneessens v Belgium (1988) 58 DR 63   3.189, 26.8
AGOSI v UK (1987) 9 EHRR 1   6.13
Agrotexim v Greece (1995) 21 EHRR 250   2.19–2.35
Ahmad v UK (1982) 4 EHRR 126   3.131, 27.5, 28.46
Ahmed v Austria (1997) 24 EHRR 278   18.17
Ahmed v UK (1995) 20 EHRR CD 72   2.19–2.35, 28.54
Ahmut Sadik v Greece (1996) 24 EHRR 323   2.19–2.35
Air Canada v UK (1995) 20 EHRR 150   6.16
Airey v Ireland (1977) 8 DR 42   3.47, 5.19, 5.30
Airey v Ireland (1979) 2 EHRR 305   13.33, 13.35–13.37,
    19.30, 19.43, 19.50   xxiii

Airey v UK (1979–80) 2 EHRR 305   13.39
Akdivar v Turkey (1997) 23 EHRR 143   4.89, 30.13, 30.28,
                                                          30.29

Akhtar v UK Commission (12 February 1992)
    (unreported)   18.38
Aksoy v Turkey (1996) 23 EHRR 553   2.58, 3.13, 14.19,
                                                          14.20, 14.45, 14.47,
                                                          15.84, 15.93

Albert and le Compte v Belgium A/58 (1983) 5 EHRR
    533   10.3, 12.41,
                                                          12.45–12.47, 28.3,
                                                          28.4
Alberti v Italy 59 DR 100   9.3
Algar v Spain [1999] EHRLR 212   8.9
Ali v Switzerland (Commission) Appl 24881/94,
    26 February 1997   3.68, 18.28
Allan Jacobsson v Sweden (1990) 12 EHRR 56   3.90, 22.37
Allenet de Ribemont v France (1995) 20 EHRR 557   2.55, 7.79
Alsterland v Sweden (1988) 56 DR 229   12.36, 12.37
Ait-Mouhoub v France [1999] EHRLR 215   13.28
Altun v Germany (1983) 36 DR 209   5.17, 18.11, 18.13
Aminoff v Sweden (1985) 43 DR 120   21.23
Amwr v France (1996) 22 EHRR 533   2.34, 3.29, 15.55
Anderson and Others v UK [1998] EHRLR 218   25.12
Anderson v UK (27 October 1997)   25.5
Andersson and Kullman v Sweden 46 DR 251   5.31
Andersson v Sweden (1992) 14 EHRR 615   19.5, 19.10, 19.56
Andronicou and Constantinou v Cyprus (1997) 25
    EHRR 491   3.9, 13.38, 14.27,
                                                          14.31
Angelini v Sweden (1986) 51 DR 41   3.133, 27.8
Antoniades v UK (1990) 64 DR 232   22.16, 22.23
AP v Austria (1995) 20 EHRR CD 63   5.31
Arrondelle v UK (1980) 19 DR 186   22.32
Arronelle v UK (1982) 26 DR 5   3.117
Arrowsmith v UK (1978) 19 DR 5; (1978) 3 EHRR 110   3.131, 3.132, 10.5,
                                                          25.23, 27.4, 27.5,
                                                          27.11, 27.12
Arrowsmith v UK (1979–80) 1 EHRLR 737   6.37
Artico v Italy A/37 (1980) 3 EHRR 1   1.26, 2.57, 4.12,
                                                          8.29, 8.30, 25.9
Asch v Austria A/203-A (1991) 15 EHRR 597   9.10, 9.11
Ashingdane v UK (1985) 7 EHRR 528   3.63, 3.99, 4.77,
                                                          13.8, 13.15, 16.38,
                                                          16.43, 16.51, 17.6,
                                                          17.12
Assenov v Bulgaria [1999] EHRLR 225   14.56, 15.93
Associacion De Aviadores De La Republica, Mata et al
    v Spain Appl 10733/84 41 DR 211   16.49

Associated Provincial Picture House v Wednesbury
   Corporation [1948] 1 KB 223   1.73, 16.78
Association of General Practitioners v Denmark
   (1989) 62 DR 226   22.15
Association X v UK (1978) 14 DR 31   14.66, 14.76
Atkinson, Crook and the Independent v UK
   Appl 13366/87 (1990) 67 DR 244   8.17, 24.39
Austria v Italy (1963) 6 YB 740   8.42, 8.48, 9.46
Autronic AG v Switzerland (1990) 12 EHRR 485   2.19–2.35, 4.22,
                                       4.45, 24.6, 24.8,
                                       24.18
Axen v Germany (1981) Com Rep 78   13.46
Axen v Germany (1984) 6 EHRR 195   8.13, 10.17, 13.49,
                                       24.39
Ayala v Portugal Appl 223663/94 DR 87B   16.26
Aydin v Turkey (1997) 25 EHRR 251   2.58, 3.180, 5.29,
                                       14.19, 14.20, 14.49
Aytekin v Turkey (Commission) 18 September 1997   14.25, 14.29
Ayuntamiento de M v Spain (1991) 68 DR 209   2.19–2.35

B R and J v Germany (1984) 36 DR 130   19.40
B v Austria   7.34
B v France (1992) 16 EHRR 1   4.17, 19.25, 19.62
B v FRG Appl 55 DR 271   16.26
B v Netherlands (1985) 43 DR 198   12.25
B v UK (1984) 38 DR 213   13.71
B v UK (1988) 10 EHRR 87   19.56
Bader v Austria (1996) 22 EHRR CD 213   24.7
Baegen v Netherlands A/327-B (1995)   9.37
Baggetta v Italy (1987) 10 EHRR 325   2.55
Baggs v UK (1985) 44 DR 13; 52 DR 29   22.32
Bahaddar v Netherlands Commission (22 May 1995)
   (unreported)   18.24
Balfour v UK Commission (Admissibility Decision)
   2 July 1997, noted in [1997] EHRLR 665   28.9
Bamber v UK Appl 33742/96 [1998] EHRLR 110   16.78
Baner v Sweden (1989) 60 DR 128   3.189, 26.8
Baragiola v Switzerland 75 DR 76   9.51
Baraona v Portugal A/122 (1987) 13 EHRR 329   12.5, 12.20, 15.101
Barar v Sweden [1999] EHRLR 332   18.13
Barbera, Messegue and Jabardo v Spain (1988)
   11 EHRR 360   8.22, 8.42, 8.49, 9.1,
                                       9.3, 9.4, 9.48
Barfod v Denmark (1991) 13 EHRR 493   24.18, 24.33, 24.36,
                                     24.37
Barrett v UK (1997) 23 EHRR CD 185   14.13
Barthold v Germany (1985) 7 EHRR 383   4.30, 4.39, 4.61,
                                     4.62, 24.6, 24.33
BB v France [1998] EHRLR 620   14.68, 18.20

BBC v UK (1996) 84-A DR 129   24.43
Beaumartin v France A/296-A (1994) 19 EHRR 485   12.10
Beer and Regan v Germany [1998] EHRLR 478   13.23
Beldjoudi v France (1992) 14 EHRR 801   18.40, 18.41
Belgian Linguistic Case (No 1) (1967) 1 EHRR 241   1.26, 3.186, 3.149,
                                                            3.197
Belgian Linguistic Case (No 2) (1968) 1 EHRR 252   4.78, 21.4, 21.5,
                                                            21.7, 21.9, 21.20,
                                                            21.24, 21.29, 29.4,
                                                            29.6, 29.10, 29.18,
                                                            29.19

Belilos v Switzerland (1988) 10 EHRR 466   1.64, 21.3
Bellet v France A/333-B (1995)   13.32
Bellis v UK (1997) 24 EHRR CD 71   24.10
Bendenoun v France (1994) 18 EHRR 54   6.18, 7.61–7.63
Benham v UK (1996) 22 EHRR 293   6.12, 6.13, 6.19,
                                                            8.26–8.28

Benjamin and Wilson v UK Appl 228212/95 [1998]
    EHRLR 226   16.46, 17.16
Bentham v Netherlands (1986) 8 EHRR 1   3.90, 12.12, 12.12,
                                                            12.34, 13.41

Bentham v UK (1993) 22 EHRR 293   2.70
Berns and Ewert v Luxembourg Appln 13251/87
    (1991) 68 DR 137   7.77, 7.80
Berrehab v Netherlands (1988) 11 EHRR 322   18.33, 18.43, 19.16
Bezicheri v Italy A/164 (1990) 12 EHRR 210   3.77, 7.16, 7.30
BH v UK, Appl 30307/96 [1998] EHRLR 334   7.12
Bizzotto v Greece Appl 76/1995/582/668 [1997]
    EHRLR 178   16.38
Bladet Tromso As and Others v Norway (1997)
    23 EHRR CD 40   24.28, 24.32
Blathwayt v Crawley [1976] AC 397   1.82
Block v Germany (1989) 12 EHRR 247   2.63
Bock v Germany A/150 (1989)   13.81, 13.83
Boner v UK A/300-B (1994) 19 EHRR 246   10.15
Bonisch v Austria A/92 (1985) 9 EHRR 191   9.52, 9.53
Bonnechaux v Switzerland Appl 8224/78 18 DR 100   16.26
Bonzi v Switzerland Appl 7854 12 D & R 185   16.16
Booth-Clibborn v UK (1985) 43 DR 236   3.199
Borgers v Belgium (1991) 15 EHRR 92   1.26, 3.93, 8.1
Boti v Italy (1998) 26 EHRR 241   22.2
Botta v Italy [1998] EHRLR 486   5.21
Bouamar v Belgium (1987) 11 EHRR 1   3.56, 20.16
Boucheras v France (1991) 69 DR 236   17.21
Bouessel du Bourgu v France (1993) 16 EHRR CD 49   27.14
Boughanemi v France (1996) 22 EHRR 228   18.40, 18.42, 19.26
Bowman v UK (1998) 26 EHRR 1   2.19–2.35, 3.200
Boyle and Rice v UK (1988) 10 EHRR 425   1.7, 3.178, 16.58
Boyle v UK (1994) 19 EHRR 179   19.28

Bozano v France (1986) 9 EHRR 297 — 3.21, 3.37, 3.67, 6.6, 15.43, 18.27, 18.29, 30.24

Brady v UK Appl 8575/297 — 16.49

Bramelid and Malmstrom v Sweden (1982) 29 DR 64 — 3.189, 26.8

Brandsetter v Austria (1991) 15 EHRR 378 — 2.68, 9.54, 13.55

Brannigan and McBride v UK (1993) 17 EHRR 539 — 1.60, 3.73, 4.53, 4.82, 7.10

Bricmont v Belgium (1989) 12 EHRR 217 — 9.13, 9.55, 9.56, 10.10

Brincat v Italy (1992) 16 EHRR 591 — 7.7

Brind v UK (1994) 77-A DR 42 — 24.13

Brogan and others v UK A/145-B (1988) 11 EHRR 117 — 1.60, 3.52, 3.72, 3.73, 3.86, 7.5–7.9, 15.2, 15.58, 15.59, 15.61, 15.62

Brown v UK (1985) 8 EHRR 273 — 8.12

Brozicek v Italy A/167 (1989) 12 EHRR 371 — 7.45, 8.40

Bruggemann and Scheuten v Germany (1976) 5 DR 103 — 2.19–2.35, 14.35

Bryan v UK (1995) 21 EHRR 342 — 11.15, 12.43, 12.45–12.47, 22.38

Bucholz v Germany (1981) 3 EHRR 597 — 13.81, 13.83

Buckley v UK (1996) 23 EHRR 101 — 3.118, 4.43, 4.50, 4.51, 4.93, 17.33, 22.8, 22.10, 22.13, 22.25, 22.43

Burghartz v Switzerland (1994) 18 EHRR 101 — 19.58

Burton v UK (1996) 22 EHRR CD 134 — 5.32, 22.45, 22.47

Byrne v UK [1998] 626 — 8.54

C v Germany (1986) 46 DR 176 — 18.13

C v UK (1983) 37 DR 142 — 3.132, 27.11, 27.14, 27.17

C v UK (1987) 54 DR 162 — 28.14

Callaghan and Others v UK (1989) 60 DR 296 — 10.28

Camenzind v Switzerland (Court) 16 December 1997 — 15.38, 15.39

Campbell and Cosans v UK (1982) 4 EHRR 293 — 2.19–2.35, 3.13, 4.78, 14.48, 20.8, 21.3, 21.9, 21.13, 21.15, 21.16, 21.28, 21.41, 21.45

Campbell and Fell v UK (1984) 7 EHRR 165 — 6.13, 6.14, 8.6, 8.14, 8.15, 13.43, 13.45, 13.50, 16.50, 16.52

Campbell v UK (1978) 14 DR 186 — 30.26

Campbell v UK (1988) 57 DR 148 — 14.53, 16.51

Campbell v UK (1992) 15 EHRR 137 — 4.46, 7.52, 16.61, 16.70

Campbell v UK Appl 7819/77 — 16.58

Can v Austria A/96 (Commission Decision) 12 July 1984 — 4.24

Canea Catholic Church v Greece (Court)
  16 December 1997   13.10
Cannon v UK Appln 29335/95 [1997] EHRLR 280   7.58, 7.69, 7.70
Cantoni v France 15 November 1996 (unpublished)   6.28
Caprino v UK (1978) 12 DR 14   3.33, 3.37
Cardot v France (1991) A 220 para 34   30.25, 30.27
Carlin v UK [1998] EHRLR 452   23.8
Casado Coca v Spain (1994) 18 EHRR 1   24.44
Castells v Spain (1992) 14 EHRR 445   3.143, 4.35, 24.29
CC v UK, Appl 32819/96 [1998] EHRLR 335   7.12
CCSU v UK (1987) 50 DR 228   2.19–2.35, 3.163,
                                                          28.36
CFDT v EC (1978) 13 DR 231   1.83, 1.97
CG v Austria (1994) 18 EHRR CD 51   23.11
Chahal v UK (1997) 23 EHRR 413   3.66, 3.68, 3.180,
                                                          3.182, 11.12, 11.13,
                                                          13.21, 18.1, 18.4,
                                                          18.11, 18.21, 18.28,
                                                          18.30, 30.2
Chappell v UK (1987) 53 DR 241   3.131, 3.134, 15.40,
                                                          27.5, 27.18, 27.36
Chare nee Jullien v France (1991) 71 DR 141   14.74
Chartier v Italy Appl 9044/80 33 DR 41   16.26
Cheall v UK (1985) 42 DR 178   28.26–28.27/28
Chester v UK 68 DR 65   16.61
Chinoy v UK (Commission) Appl 15199/89,
  4 September 1991   3.67
Chorherr v Austria A/266-B (Court) 24 September 1998
  (unreported)   25.11, 25.19
Choudhury v UK Appl 17439/90 Commission
  (5 March 1991)   27.22
Choudry v UK Commission (13 May 1996) (unpublished)   18.20
Christians Against Racism and Fascism v UK (1980)
  21 DR 138   2.19–2.35, 3.153,
                                                          25.3–25.5, 25.24,
                                                          30.21
Christie v UK (1993) 78-A DR 119   3.112, 15.21, 15.28
Church of X v UK (1969) 12 Yearbook 306   3.134, 27.36
Clooth v Belgium (1991) 14 EHRR 717   7.20, 7.21, 7.23
Coke and others v UK [1999] EHRLR 130   23.8
Colozza v Italy (1985) 7 EHRR 516   8.21, 8.23
Comninos & National Compania Naviera SA v UK
  (1996) 23 EHRR CD 165   12.39
Company S and I v Sweden (1986) 50 DR 121   12.15
Confederation des Syndicats Medicaux Francais v
  France (1986) 47 DR 225   2.19–2.35
Confederation Francais Democratique du Travail v
  The European Communities and their Member
  States (1978) 12 EHRR 485   2.19–2.35

Corigliano v Italy A/57 (1982) 5 EHRR 334 — 6.21, 7.35

Cossey v UK 24 (1990) 13 EHRR 622 — 3.172, 4.17, 4.70, 19.33, 19.37, 19.61, 19.63

Costello-Roberts v UK (1993) 19 EHRR 105 — 2.14, 3.109, 3.111, 21.40

Costello-Roberts v UK (1995) 19 EHRR 112 — 4.24, 14.52, 14.60, 20.1, 20.10

Couez v France; Benkessiouer v France European Court (24 August 1998) (unreported) — 28.9, 28.13, 28.13

Cremieux v France (1989) 59 DR 67 — 30.27, 30.29

Crociani and Others v Italy Appl 8603/79 and Others, (1989) 22 DR 147, 13.3 — 7.77

Croiciani v Italy (1980) 22 DR 147 — 13.42

Croissant v Germany (1992) 16 EHRR 135 — 8.34, 8.36

Cruz Varas v Sweden (1992) 14 EHRR 1 — 18.1, 18.17, 18.18, 30.13, 30.37

Curran v UK [1998] EHRLR 507 — 6.31

Cybulski v UK (1996) 23 EHRR CD 53 — 8.54

Cyprus v Turkey Comm Report, 10 July 1976 (1976) 4 EHRR 482 — 3.27, 14.49, 14.58, 14.69, 15.94, 16.13

D v FRG (1984) 36 DR 24 — 30.25

D v UK (1997) 24 EHRR 423 — 3.182, 11.13, 14.68, 18.8, 18.20, 18.24, 22.46, 30.37

D'Haeses, Le Compte v Belgium (1983) 6 EHRR 114 — 14.53

Dalban v Romania [1998] EHRLR 641 — 24.32

Darby v Sweden (1991) Comm Rep (unpublished) — 3.133, 27.9, 29.15

Darnell v Uk (1991) 69 DR 306 — 28.14

Daud v Portugal [1998] EHRLR 634 — 8.30, 8.32

Davis v UK Appl 27042/95 [1997] EHRLR 298 — 16.82

De Becker v Belgium B/2 (1960) Commission Report, para 279 — 4.87

De Cubber v Belgium (1984) 7 EHRR 236 — 12.46

De Geouffre de la Pradelle v France A/253-B (1992) — 13.32

De Haes and Gijsels v Belgium (1997) 25 1 — 24.38

De Moor v Belgium A/292-A (1994) 18 EHRR 372 — 8.51, 12.13, 13.68

De Salvador Torres v Spain (1996) 23 EHRR 601 — 10.24

De Santa v Italy, Lapalorcia v Italy, Abenavoli v Italy European Court (2 September 1997) (unreported) — 28.9

De Varga-Hirsch v France Appl 9559/81 33 DR 158 — 16.26

De Wilde, Ooms and Versyp v Belgium (No 2) (1972) 1 EHRR 438; (1971) 1 EHRR 373 — 2.53, 3.19, 3.28, 3.61, 3.75, 3.78, 4.58, 15.53, 16.43, 16.44, 17.11, 30.19, 30.25–30.27, 30.29

Delcourt v Belgium (1970) 1 EHRR 355   3.93, 8.1, 8.2, 8.6,
                                                 8.7, 13.1
Delta v France (1990) 16 EHRR 574   2.60, 9.17, 9.18
Demai v France A/289-C (1994)   13.81
Derbyshire CC v Times Newspapers Ltd [1992] QB 770   1.73
Deumeland v Germany A/100 (1986) 8 EHRR 425   12.6, 23.16–23.18
Deweer v Belgium (1980) 2 EHRR 439   13.12, 30.29
Dhoest v Belgium Appl 10448/83 D & R 5   16.17, 16.32, 16.45
Di Pede v Italy (Court) 26 September 1996   12.37, 13.72, 13.79
Diaz Ruamo v Spain A/285-B (1994) (unreported)   14.22
Diennet v France (1995) 21 EHRR 554   12.13, 13.46
Dobbie v UK Appl 28477/95 [1997] EHRLR 166   13.26
Dombo Beheer BV v Netherlands (1994) 18 EHRR 213 3.96, 13.2, 13.54,
                                                 13.62
Domenichini v Italy Appl 101/1995/607/695 [1997]
    EHRLR 192   16.63
Donnelly v UK (1972) 4 DR 72   30.26–30.29
Doorson v Netherlands (1996) 22 EHRR 330   9.11, 9.18, 9.22,
                                                 9.23, 9.25, 9.29,
                                                 9.36, 15.63
DP v UK (1986) 51 DR 195   22.15, 22.18
DPP v Hutchinson [1990] 2 AC 783   1.38
DPP v Jones and Lloyd [1999] 2 All ER 257   1.76
Draper v UK Appl 8186/78 24 DR 782   16.80
Drozd and Janousek v France and Spain (1992) 14
    EHRR 745   3.45, 8.55, 16.39,
                                                 18.25
DS and ES v UK (1990) 65 DR 245   3.132
Dublin Well Woman Centre Ltd v Ireland (1997) 23
    EHRR CD 125   13.70
Dubowska and Skup v Poland (1997) 24 EHRR CD 75 27.21
Dudgeon v UK (1981) 4 EHRR 149   4.40, 4.63, 4.64,
                                                 4.93, 6.36, 27.9,
                                                 29.22, 29.24, 30.22,
                                                 30.40
Dujardin v France Appl 16734/90 (1991) (unreported)   14.21
Dyer v UK (1984) 39 DR 246; 7 EHRR 469   13.17
E and G Muller-Eberstein v Germany Appl 29753/96,
    27 November 1996   10.26
E v Norway Appl 11701/85 17 EHRR 30   16.47, 17.21
East African Asians v UK (1973) 3 EHRR 76   3.13, 14.53, 14.55,
                                                 15.89, 18.9, 18.35,
                                                 29.17, 29.21
East Berkshire Health Authority ex p Walsh [1985]
    QB 152   2.8
Eckle v Germany (1982) 5 EHRR 1   2.19–2.35, 4.89,
                                                 6.21, 7.35
Editions Periscope v France A/234-B (1992) 14 EHRR 597 12.21

Edwards v UK (1985) 8 EHRR 96	3.199
Edwards v UK (1992) 15 EHRR 417	7.59, 7.68, 7.68
Eggs v Switzerland Appl 7341/76 6DR 170	16.14
Ekbetani v Sweden (1988) 13 EHRR 504	8.19, 10.9, 10.18, 13.49, 13.76
ELH and PBH v UK Appls 32094/96 and 2568/96 [1998] EHRLR 231	16.59
Elliniki Radiophonia Tileorassi [1991] ECR I-2925	1.80
Engel and Others v Netherlands (1976) 1 EHRR 706; (1979–80) 1 EHRR 647; (1976) 1 EHRR 647	3.30, 3.41, 3.49, 6.11, 6.12, 6.34, 8.6, 9.54, 10.3, 13.43, 15.74
Englund v Sweden (1994) 77-A DR 10	28.30
Ensslin, Baader and Raspe v Germany Appl 7572/76 14 DR 64 (1978) 14 DR 112	7.80, 7.81, 8.21, 8.35, 16.11, 16.16, 16.17, 16.19
Eriksson v Sweden (1989) 12 EHRR 183	2.66, 12.18, 19.4, 19.19, 19.56
Erkalo v Netherlands [1999] EHRLR 117	17.21
Erkner and Hofauer v Austria (1987) 9 EHRR 464	26.6
Esbester v UK (1994) 18 EHRR CD 72	3.112
Ettle v Austria (1987)	13.43
Ewing v UK 10 EHRR 143	6.21
Ezelin v France A/202 (1991) 14 EHRR 362	3.156, 25.11, 25.18
F v Switzerland (1988) 10 EHRR 411	4.40, 4.54, 4.55, 4.70, 19.36, 19.43
F v Switzerland (1989) 61 DR 171	8.34
F v UK Appl 18123/91 (1992) 15 EHRR CD 32	8.31
Family H v UK (1984) 37 DR 105	21.11, 21.18
Farrant v UK Appl 7219/75 50 DR 5	16.67
Farrell v UK (1982) 30 DR 96	14.22
Fayed v UK (1994) 18 EHRR 393	12.47, 13.18
Feldbrugge v Netherlands A/99 (1986) 8 EHRR 425	12.6, 13.59, 23.14, 23.16–23.18, 23.20
Ferrantelli and Santangelo v Italy (1996) 23 EHRR 288	9.12
Findlay v UK (1997) 24 EHRR 221	2.61
Firman v Gerogia	18.14
Fischer v Austria (1995) 20 EHRR 349	1.64
Foreign Students v UK (1977) 9 DR 185	21.24
Foti v Italy A/56 (1983) 5 EHRR 313	6.21, 7.35, 7.43
Foucher v France (1997) 25 EHRR 36	7.64
Fox, Campbell and Hartley v UK (1989) 11 EHRR 117; (1990) 13 EHRR 157	3.53, 3.53, 3.69, 3.86, 7.41, 7.43, 15.60, 15.60, 15.62, 15.65, 15.67

Frederiksen v Denmark (1988) 56 DR 237 — 2.19–2.35
Fredin v Sweden (1991) 13 EHRR 784 — 3.90, 22.33, 22.37
Fressoz and Roire v France [1999] EHRLR 339 — 24.42
Friedl v Austria A/305-B Comm Rep (1995) — 15.32, 15.35
Funke v France (1993) 16 EHR 297 — 2.58, 9.61, 15.39

G and E v Norway (1983) 35 DR 30 — 22.11
G v France (1988) 57 DR 100 — 13.63
G v FRG (1989) 60 DR 256 — 25.6
G v Netherlands (1993) 16 EHRR CD 38 — 19.22
G v UK Appl 9370/81 (1983) 35 DR 75 — 6.21, 7.47, 9.47
Galloway v UK [1999] EHRLR 119 — 6.11, 16.25, 16.58
Garland v British Rail Engineering [1982] 1 QB 770 — 1.75
Gaskin v UK (1989) 12 EHRR 36 — 2.60, 8.17, 14.74, 19.18, 19.31, 24.7

Gasus Dosier- und Fordertechnik GmbH v
    Netherlands (1995) 20 EHRR 403 — 22.15, 26.21
Gaygusuz v Austria (1996) 23 EHRR 364 — 18.44, 23.6, 23.23, 29.17

Geyseghem v Belgium [1998] EHRLR 633 — 10.18
Geyseghem v Belgium [1999] EHRLR 337 — 8.24
Giama v Belgium (1980) 21 DR 73 — 18.23
Gillow v UK (1987) 13 EHRR 593 — 2.49
Gillow v UK (1986) 11 EHRR 335 — 3.119, 12.10, 22.9, 22.13, 22.25, 22.26

Ginikanwa v UK (1988) 55 DR 251 — 12.13
Glasenapp v Germany (1986) 9 EHRR 25 — 28.6, 28.49, 28.50
Glazewska v Sweden (1985) 45 DR 300 — 21.7, 21.25
Glimmerveen and Hagenback v Netherlands (1979)
    18 DR 187 — 3.143, 4.85, 4.86, 6.37, 24.48, 24.49
Goddi v Italy (1984) 6 EHRR 457 — 2.54, 7.75, 8.20, 8.32
Golder v UK (1979–80) 1 EHRR 524 — 3.95, 3.99, 3.121, 4.5, 4.9, 4.58, 4.76, 13.6, 13.8, 13.15, 13.79, 15.97, 16.50, 16.53, 16.55

Goodman International and Goodman v Ireland
    (1993) 16 EHRR CD 26 — 8.49
Goodwin v UK (1996) 22 EHRR 123 — 3.145, 4.23, 4.62, 24.1, 24.42, 24.43, 30.41

Govell v UK (Commission) 14 January 1998
    (unreported) Appl 27237/95 — 2.44, 2.60, 3.181, 4.31, 15.23

Grace v UK Appl 11523/85 62 DR 22 — 16.51, 16.54, 16.60, 16.68, 16.69

Gradinger v Austria (1995) A/328-C — 8.57

Graeme v UK (1990) 64 DR 158   21.33

Granger v UK A/174 (1990) 12 EHRR 469   2.57, 8.27, 8.29, 10.13, 10.16

Grare v France (1992) 15 EHRR CD 100   17.33

Greek Case (1969) 12 Yearbook 1   3.13, 14.45, 14.49, 14.50, 14.69

Greek Case (1979–80) 1 EHRR 524   16.10, 16.13

Gregory v UK (1997) 25 EHRR 577   8.9, 8.10

Grepne v UK (1990) 66 DR 268   13.28, 13.70

Grigoriades v Greece [1998] EHRLR 222   28.53

Groppera Radio AG v Switzerland (1990) 12 EHRR 321   3.146, 4.24, 4.30, 24.11

GSM v Austria (1983) 34 DR 119   7.44

Guchez v Belgium (1984) 40 DR 100   12.13

Guenat v Switzerland (1995) 81-A DR 130   15.54

Guenoun v France (1990) 66 DR 181   13.46

Guerra and Others v Italy (1998) 26 EHRR 357   2.62, 3.111, 5.23, 22.2, 22.36, 24.7

Guillot v France (Commission) 24 October 1996 (unreported)   19.58, 19.59

Guincho v Portugal (1984) 7 EHRR 223   13.79, 13.83, 30.29

Gustafson v Sweden (1997) 25 EHRR 623   12.25

Gustafsson v Sweden (1996) 22 EHRR 409   4.22, 28.33

Guzzardi v Italy (1980) 3 EHRR 333   3.24+3.25, 3.27,. 3.58, 3.61, 15.48, 15.64, 15.74, 17.6

H v Belgium (1988) 10 EHRR 339   3.90, 12.13, 12.32, 13.47

H v France (1989) 12 EHRR 74   12.19, 13.65, 13.66, 13.78, 13.83, 14.78

H v Norway Appl 17004/90 (1992) (unreported)   14.34

H v UK (1985) 45 DR 281   13.8

H v UK (1987) 10 EHRR 95   13.81, 19.56, 19.69

H v UK (1993) 16 EHRR CD 44   16.72

H v UK A/136-B, 9 June 1988 (unreported)   2.63

H, W, P and K v Austria (1989) 62 DR 216   3.143

Haase v Germany 11 DR 78   7.55

Habsburg-Lothringen v Austria (1989) 64 DR 210   12.30

Hacisuleymanoglu v Itlay Appl 23241/94 79-B DR 121   16.57

Hadjianastassiou v Greece (1992) 16 EHRR 219   13.69

Haider v Austria Appl 25060/94 83 DR 66   16.78

Hakansson and Sturesson v Sweden A/171 (1991) 13 EHRR 1   12.10, 13.47, 26.16

Halford v UK (1997) 24 EHRR 523   2.65, 15.14, 15.22, 28.40

Hall v UK [1998] EHRLR 215   7.79

Hamer v UK (1979) 24 DR 5   3.169, 16.80, 19.32, 19.34

Hamil v UK Appl 21656/93 [1997] EHRLR 169   9.74
Handyside v. UK (1976) 1 EHRR 737   1.26, 3.143, 4.11,
                                                    4.60, 4.61, 4.64,
                                                    4.66, 4.89, 4.91,
                                                    4.93, 24.1, 24.5,
                                                    30.25
Hardiman v UK Appl 25935/94 [1996] EHRLR 425   7.66
Harman and Hewitt v UK (1989) 67 DR 88   3.112
Harman v UK (1984) 38 DR 53   6.24–6.25
Haseldine v UK (1992) 73 DR 225   28.53
Hashman and Harrup v UK [1999] EHRLR 342   4.32
Hatami v Sweden [1998] EHRLR 618   18.17
Hauschildt v Denmark (1989) 12 EHRR 266   8.7, 8.8, 8.11
Hautanemi v Sweden (1996) 22 EHRR CD 155   2.31
Helmers v Sweden (1993) 15 EHRR 285   13.31, 13.76
Hendricks v Netherlands (1983) 5 EHRR 233   19.44
Hentrich v France (1994) A 296-A para 33   26.21, 30.25
Herczegfalvy v Austria (1992) 15 EHRR 437   3.122, 17.33
Hertel v Switzerland [1999] EHRLR 116   24.33
Hill v Chief Constable of West Yorkshire [1989] AC 53   15.96, 15.98
Hilton v UK (1976) 4 DR 176   30.28
Hilton v UK (1988) 57 DR 108   2.28, 14.53, 28.42,
                                                    30.21
Hilton v UK Appl 5613/72, 3 EHRR 104   16.22
Hippen (P) v Austria (1994) 18 EHRR CD 93   15.82
Hippin v Austria Appl 18764/91 79A DR 23   16.29
Hiro Balani v Spain A/303-B (1995) 19 EHRR 566   8.51, 10.25, 13.68
HLR v France (1997) 26 EHRR 29   18.19
Hoang v France A/243 (1992) 16 EHRR 53   8.27
Hoare v UK [1997] EHRLR 678   6.37, 24.47
Hodgson, Woolf Productions and the NUJ v UK
   Appls 11553/85 and 11658/85 (1987) 10 EHRR 503;
   (1987) 51 DR 136   7.77, 24.41
Hoffman v Austria (1993) 14 EHRR 319   19.46, 27.35, 29.17
Hogben v UK Appl 11653/85 46 DR 231   16.33
Hojemeister v Germany 6 July 1981 (unpublished)   15.50
Hokkanen v Finland (1994) 19 EHRR 139   13.81, 19.30, 19.47,
   19.69., 30.6
Holy Monastries v Greece (1994) 20 EHRR 1   13.7
Hornsby v Greece (1997) 24 EHRR 250   12.2, 12.9, 12.37,
   12.38, 13.73
Howard v UK (1985) 52 DR 198   22.24, 22.25
Huber v Austria (1976) 6 DR 65   3.86
Huber v France (1998) 26 EHRR 457   28.11–28.11
Hughes v UK (1986) 48 DR 258   14.67
Hurtado v Switzerland A/280-A (1994) (unreported) 14.53, 14.69
Hussain and Singh v UK (1996) 22 EHRR 1   10.6, 16.41, 16.45
Huvig v France (1990) 12 EHRR 528   4.35, 15.15, 15.17,
                                                    15.18, 28.40

Ibbotson v UK [1999] EHRLR — 6.31
Imbrechts v Belgium (1991) 69 DR 312 — 13.46
Imbrioscia v Switzerland A/275 (1993) 17 EHRR 41 — 7.48
Informationsverein Lentier v Austria (1993) 17 EHRR 93 — 4.47, 24.12, 24.16
Inze v Austria (1987) 10 EHRR 394 — 3.186, 4.22, 19.40, 29.17
Ireland v UK (1978) 2 EHRR 25 — 2.13, 2.14, 2.54, 3.11, 3.13, 3.53, 6.3, 7.12, 14.41, 14.42, 14.44–14.46, 14.48, 14.49, 14.59, 15.59, 15.64, 15.66, 15.81, 15.85, 15.91, 15.94, 16.9, 16.10, 17.31, 18.3–18.5, 30.5
Iskcon v UK (1994) 76A DR 90 — 3.131, 27.5, 27.16
Islam v UK [1996] 22 EHRR CD 215 — 16.72
Iversen v Norway (1963) 6 Yearbook 278 — 28.22
IZ v Greece (1994) 76-A DR 65 — 12.30

J v Switzerland (1989) 62 DR 269 — 30.26
Jacubowski v Germany (1988) 13 EHRR 212 — 24.44, 24.45
Jaggard and Brown v UK (1996) 24 EHRR 1 — 2.35
James v UK A/98 (1986) 8 EHRR 123 — 3.191, 4.73, 4.93, 12.32, 22.15, 22.18, 22.19, 22.21, 23.9, 26.7, 26.13, 26.15, 26.16
Janowski v Poland [1999] EHRLR 341 — 6.38
Jaramillo v UK — 18.43
Jastrzebski v Poland Appl 25669/94 20 EHRR CD 126 — 16.26
Jaxel v France (1987) 54 DR 70; (1989) 59 DR 42 — 12.13
Jensen v Denmark (1991) 68 DR 177 — 12.36, 12.38
Jersild v Denmark A/298 (1994) — 4.24, 4.43, 4.43, 6.37, 24.1, 24.50
Jespers v Belgium (1981) 27 DR 61 — 7.55, 7.58, 7.63
Jeznach v Poland Appl 27850/95 — 16.26
Johansen v Norway (1985) 44 DR 155 — 3.19, 19.10
Johansen v Norway (1996) 23 EHRR 33 — 19.55, 19.57
John Ryan v UK Appl 32875/96, Comm Dec, 1st July 1998 — 16.31, 16.41
Johnson v UK (1997) 27 EHRR 296 — 2.59, 16.44
Johnson v UK (1999) 27 EHRR 440 — 17.22, 17.23, 17.25, 17.27
Johnston v Chief Constable of the Royal Ulster Constabulary [1986] ECR 1651 — 1.84
Johnston v Ireland (1986) 9 EHRR 203 — 2.23, 3.169, 19.41, 19.42, 27.9
Jordan Abiodun Iye [1994] Imm AR 287 — 1.81
Jordebo Foundation of Christian Schools v Sweden (1987) 61 DR 92 — 12.12, 21.11, 21.26, 21.27

K v Austria A/225-B (1993) Commission Report 3.48, 7.32, 9.66, 24.42

K v Ireland (1984) 38 DR 158 30.24

K v Sweden (1991) 71 DR 94 12.36, 12.38

K v UK (1986) 50 DR 199 18.32, 19.12

K, C and M v Netherlands 80-A DR 87 30.31

K, F and P v UK (1984) 40 DR 298 30.27

Kamasinski v Austria A/168 (1989) 13 EHRR 36 7.46, 7.64, 7.65, 8.30, 8.30, 8.41, 10.18

Kamma v Netherlands (1974) 1 DR 4 4.59

Kanthak v Germany (1988) 58 DR 94 3.118, 22.10

Kaplan v UK (1980) 4 EHRR 64 2.33

Kara v UK [1999] EHRLR 232 28.39

Karakay v France A/289-B (1994) 13.81

Karakuzey v Germany (1996) 23 EHRR CD 92 19.49, 27.15

Karlheinz Schmidt v Germany (1994) 18 EHRR 513 29.17

Kay v UK (Commission), Appln. No. 17821/91,
 1 March 1994 (unreported) 3.62, 17.21

Kaya v Turkey (Court) 19 February 1998 14.17, 14.20

KDP v Germany (1957) 1 Yearbook 222 4.85, 24.48

Kebeline and Others v DPP 1.5

Keegan v Ireland (1994) 18 EHRR 342 2.66, 12.18, 19.13, 19.53

Keenan v UK [1998] EHRLR 648 124.13, 14. 69, 16.4

Kelly v UK (1985) 42 DR 205 30.23

Kelly v UK Appl 17579/90 (1993) (unreported) 14.22, 14.24, 14.25

Kennedy v UK [1999] EHRLR 214 9.12

Kemmache v France A/218 (1991) 14 EHRR 520 7.21, 7.39

Kerkhoven v Netherlands (Commission) 19 May 1992
 (unreported) 19.24

Kerojavi v Finland A/328 (Court) 19 July 1995 [1996]
 EHRR 66 13.60, 23.16

Ketterick v UK (1983) 5 EHRR 465 13.12

Keus v Netherlands (1990) 13 EHRR 700 17.21

K-F v Germany [1998] EHRLR 228 3.37, 15.58

Khan v UK (1986) 48 DR 253 3.132

Khan v UK pending before the Court 9.43

Kilbourn v UK (Commission) 16 May 1985 (unreported) 22.24

Kiss v UK Appl 6224/73 7 DR 55 16.52

Kjeldsen Busk Madsen and Pedersen v Denmark
 (1979–80) 1 EHRR 711 4.10, 21.13, 21.26, 21.28, 21.33, 21.34, 21.36

Klass v Germany A/28 (1978) 2 EHRR 214 2.27, 2.39, 3.179, 4.52, 4.91, 11.12, 15.10, 15.12, 15.26, 15.28–15.29, 28.40, 30.8

KM v UK Appl 28376/95 [1997] EHRLR 299   16.43
Knudson v Norway (1985) 42 DR 247   14.36, 28.45, 28.48
Koendjbiharie v The Netherlands Appl 11497/85 13
   EHRR 820   16.47, 17.21
Kokkinakis v Greece (1980) 19 DR 5   6.37
Kokkinakis v Greece (1993) 17 EHRR 397   3.131, 3.132, 4.61,
                                                  6.23, 27.5, 27.6,
                                                  27.18, 27.19, 27.24,
                                                  27.29
Kolompar v Belgium (1992) 16 EHRR 197   18.29
König v Federal Republic of Germany (1980)
   2 EHRR 469   2.57
König v Germany (1978) 2 EHRR 170   3.90, 12.5, 12.6,
                                                  12.12–12.13, 12.14,
                                                  12.30, 13.80, 23.14,
                                                  30.18
Kontakt-Information-Therapie and Hagen v Austria
   (1988) 57 DR 81   14.42
Kopp v Switzerland (1998) 27 EHRR 91   15.19
Kosiek v Germany (1986) 9 EHRR 329 (Commission
   Decision) 11 May 1984   4.24, 28.49, 28.52
Kostovski v Netherlands A/166 (1989) 12 EHRR 435 9.3, 9.4, 9.23, 9.24,
                                                  9.27
Kotalla v The Netherlands Appl 7994/77 14 DR 238 16.32
Kraska v Switzerland A/254-B (1993) 18 EHRR 188   12.13, 13.3
Krause v Switzerland Appl 7986/77 13 D & R 73   16.16
Kremzow v Austria (1993) 17 EHRR 322   7.74
Kremzow v Austria [1997] ECR I-2629   1.83
Kröcher and Möller v Switzerland 34 DR 24   16.17
Krone-Verlag GmbH and Mediaprint Anzeigen GmbH
   & Co KG v Austria (1997) 23 EHRR CD 152   6.13
Kroon v Netherlands (1995) 19 EHRR 263   18.32, 19.12, 19.14
Kryzycki v Germany (1978) 13 DR 57   3.42, 16.48
Kudla v Poland [1998] EHRLR 630   16.26
Kuhnen v Germany 56 DR 205   3.143, 4.86, 24.49
Kurt v Turkey (1998) 27 EHRR 373   14.17, 14.20

L v Sweden (1988) 61 DR 73   3.83, 3.86, 17.24
Lacin v Turkey (1995) 81-A DR 76   30.21
Lala v Netherlands (1994) 18 EHRR 586   10.18
Lalljee v UK (1986) 8 EHRR 45   18.1, 18.9
Lambert v France [1999] EHRLR 123   15.28
Lamguindaz v UK (1994) 17 EHRR 213   18.40, 18.41
Lamy v Belgium (1989) 11 EHRR 529   7.32
Langborger v Sweden (1989) 12 EHRR 416   13.44
Lant v UK Appl 11046/84 45 DR 236   16.57
Larissis v Greece [1998] EHRLR 505   27.19
Larkos v Cyprus [1998] EHRLR 653   22.28

Laskey v UK (1997) 24 EHRR 39   6.36
Lauko v Slovakia [1999] EHRLR   6.9
Launder v UK [1998] EHRLR 337   18.24
Lawless v Ireland (No 2) (1961) 1 EHRR 15   4.85, 4.87, 24.48
Lawless v UK (1958) YB 308   30.27
LCB v UK (1998) 27 EHRR 212   5.25–5.26,
                                                             14.70–14.72
Le Compte v Belgium (1987) 10 EHRR 29   12.42
Le Compte, Van Leuven and de Meyere v Belgium
    (1982) 4 EHRR 1   3.90, 3.159, 8.6,
                                                             13.45
Leander v Sweden (1987) 9 EHRR 433   3.179, 4.36, 4.93,
                                                             5.24, 8.17, 11.12,
                                                             24.7, 28.42
Lehideut v France A/996 (Court) 23 September 1998   4.84
Leigh, Guardian Newspapers and Observer Ltd v UK
    (1984) 38 DR 307   2.28
Lemon v UK (1982) 28 DR 77   27.22
Lenzing AG v UK [1999] EHRLR 132   13.11
Letellier v France (1991) 14 EHRR 83   7.15, 7.17, 7.18, 7.24
Lindsay v UK (1979) 15 DR 247   3.201
Lindsay v UK (1986) 49 DR 181   29.13, 29.20
Lindsay v UK (1997) 24 EHRR CD 199   2.22, 3.199
Lingens v Austria (1981) 26 DR 171   8.44
Lingens v Austria (1986) 8 EHRR 407   2.55, 3.142, 4.92,
                                                             6.37, 24.26, 24.28
Lithgow v UK (1986) 8 EHRR 329   4.77, 13.7, 13.8,
                                                             26.6, 26.7, 26.14,
                                                             26.15
Litster v Forth Dry Dock and Forth
Estuary Engineering [1990] 1 AC 546   1.20, 1.21
Lobo Machado v Portugal (1997) 23 EHRR 79   13.2
Lockwood v UK 15 EHRR CD 48   16.27
Logan v UK (1996) 22 EHRR CD 178   19.48
Loizidou v Turkey (1996) 23 EHRR 513   2.20, 3.119, 15.70
Lombardo v Italy (1992) 21 EHRR 188   12.27, 23.16, 28.3,
                                                             28.6, 28.9, 28.10,
                                                             28.11
Lombo Machado v Portugal (1997) 23 EHRR 79   13.55
Lopez Ostra v Spain (1994) 20 EHRR 277   2.13, 2.15, 2.67,
                                                             3.111, 5.20, 5.21,
                                                             5.23, 5.33, 5.35,
                                                             22.2, 22.32, 22.34
Loukanov v Bulgaria (1997) 24 EHRR 121   2.35
Lowes v UK Appl 13214/87 59 DR 244   16.77
Luberti v Italy (1984) 6 EHRR 441   16.48, 17.21, 17.23
Ludi v Switzerland A/238 (1992) 15 EHRR 173   9.34, 9.35, 15.42
Luedicke, Delkasam and Koc v Germany (1978)
    2 EHRR 149   8.38–8.44

Lukanov v Bulgaria Appl 21915.93 80A DR 198   3.54, 15.57, 16.26
Lukka v UK (1987) 9 EHRR 552   18.35
Lutz v Germany 24 A/123 (1987) 10 EHRR 182   8.52

M v Bulgaria (1996) 22 EHRR CD 101   27.35
M v UK (1987) 52 DR 266   13.8
M'Naughton Rules Appl 15023/89 (1990) 87 LS Gaz 31   8.46
Mabey v UK (1996) 22 EHRR CD 123   22.9
Machatova v Slovak Republic (1997) 24 EHRR CD 44   12.25, 23.21
Mahamoud v UK [1996] EHRLR 219   13.81
Maillard v France (1998) 27 EHRR 232   28.12
Mairitsch v Austria (1989) 11 EHRR 46   26.20
Malmstrom v Sweden (1983) 38 DR 18   13.9
Malone v UK A/82 (1984) 7 EHRR 14   4.31, 4.35, 4.56,
   15.11, 15.13,
   15.15–15.17, 15.24,
   26.14, 28.40, 29.12
Manoussakis v Greece (1997) 23 EHRR 387   27.25
Mansell v UK Appl 32072/96 [1997] EHRLR 664   16.41
Mantovanelli v France (1997) 24 EHRR 370   13.67
Marckx v Belgium (1979) 2 EHRR 330   3.113, 4.15, 4.17,
   4.22, 5.18, 14.53,
   19.27, 19.30, 19.40,
   26.2, 26.9, 29.11,
   29.20
Markt Intern Verlag & Beermann v Germany
   (1990) 12 EHRR 161   24.22, 24.44, 24.45
Marleasing v La Comercial Internacional de
   Alimentacion [1990] ECR I-4135   1.20
Martin v Switzerland (1995) 81-A DR 136   14.74
Martins Moreira v Portugal (1988) 13 EHRR 577   13.65
Massa v Italy (1993) 18 EHRR 266   28.3, 28.6, 28.10
Masson and van Zon v Netherlands (1996) 22 EHRR 491   12.24
Matadeen v Pointu and Others [1998] 3 WLR 18   1.28
Mathews v UK (1996) 22 EHRR CD 175   3.199
Mathieu-Mohin and Clerfayt v Belgium (1987) 10
   EHRR 1   3.200, 3.202, 4.55,
   4.79
Matznetter v Austria (1969) 1 EHRR 198   7.23
Maxwell v UK (1994) 19 EHRR 97   2.62, 10.15, 10.16
McCallum v UK 13 EHRR 597   16.67
McCann v UK (1995) 21 EHRR 97   2.30, 2.52, 3.8, 3.9,
   14.3, 14.7, 14.14,
   14.15, 14.17, 14.23,
   14.27, 14.27, 14.29,
   14.30, 14.66, 16.7,
   30.2
McCotter v UK Appl 18632/91 15 EHRR CD 98   16.57

McCourt v UK Appl 20433/92 15 EHRR 110 CD   10.7
McDonnell v Ireland (1990) 64 DR 203   30.27
McFeeley v UK (1980) 20 DR 44   3.131, 3.157, 16.21,
                                                                 16.24, 16.34, 16.57,
                                                                 16.58, 16.73, 16.75,
                                                                 16.79, 27.7, 30.22,
                                                                 30.26, 30.27
McGinley and Egan v UK (1998) 27 EHRR 1   5.26, 13.61, 14.72
McGonnell v UK [1999] EHRLR 335   13.44
McLeod v UK [1999] EHRLR 125   15.40
McMichael v UK A/308 (1995) 20 EHRR 205   2.66, 4.50, 13.58,
                                                                 19.66–19.68, 22.43
McVeigh, O'Neill and Evans v UK (1981) 5 EHRR 71   3.50, 15.33, 15.35,
                                                                 15.56, 15.76, 15.78,
                                                                 15.79
Megyeri v Germany (1993) 15 EHRR 584   16.45, 17.14, 17.19
Mellacher v Austria (1989) 12 EHRR 391   3.190, 26.17
Mercier de Brettens v Switzerland (1987) 54 DR 178   30.23
Mersch v Luxembourg (1985) 43 DR 34   2.27
MG v FRGH Appl 13079/87 (1989) (unreported)   25.13
MH v UK Appl 28572/95 [1997] EHRLR 279   9.49
Minelli v Switzerland (1983) 5 EHRR 554   8.53
Minister for Home Affairs v Fisher [1979] 3 All ER 21   1.28
Minister of State for Immigration and Ethnic Affairs v
    Teoh [1995] 183 CLR 273   1.79
Ministry of Transport v Noort [1992] 3 NZLR 260   1.23, 1.24
Minniti v Italy (1987) 59 DR 5   23.16
MK v Austria (1997) 24 EHRR CD 59   9.15
Monnell and Morris v UK A/115 (1988) 10 EHRR 205   3.43, 10.8, 10.9,
                                                                 10.16, 10.19, 10.22,
                                                                 10.26, 13.31, 13.75
Morissens v Belgium (1988) 56 DR 127   28.52, 28.53
Moustaquim v Belgium (1991) 13 EHRR 802   18.41, 18.46, 19.26
Mrs W v Ireland (1983) 32 DR 211   2.20
Mrs W v UK (1983) 32 DR 19   2.30
MS and PS v Switzerland (1985) 44 DR 175   2.27
Muller v Austria (1975) 3 DR 25   23.1, 23.4–23.5
Muller v Switzerland A/133 (1988) 13 EHRR 212   4.24, 4.35, 4.93,
                                                                 6.37, 24.4, 24.6,
                                                                 24.18, 24.46
Munro v UK (1987) 52 DR 158   13.37
Murray v UK (1996) 22 EHRR 29   6.21, 7.49, 7.50,
                                                                 9.67, 9.69,
                                                                 9.71–9.73
Murray (Kevin) v UK Appl 22384/93 [1997] EHRLR 169   9.74
Murray (Sean) v DPP (House of Lords Case)   9.67
Murray and Others v UK (1994) 19 EHRR 193   3.53, 15.31, 15.32,
                                                                 15.60, 15.61, 15.61,
                                                                 15.62, 15.63, 15.67

Muyldermans v Belgium A/214-A (1991) Com Rep   13.53

N v Sweden (1984) 40 DR 203   3.136, 27.37
Naddaf v Germany (1987) 9 EHRR 561   16.6
NATFE v UK (1998) 25 EHRR CD 122   28.35
National & Provincial Building Society v UK (1998)
    25 EHRR 127   4.93, 12.17
National Union of Belgium Police v Belgium
    (1979–80) 1 EHRR 578   3.160, 4.22, 28.31,
    28.32, 29.16
Navarra v Spain (1993) A 273-B   30.26
Neigel v France 17 March 1997 (unreported)
    [1997] EHRLR 424   28.6, 28.7, 28.9,
    28.13
Nelson v UK (1986) 49 DR 170   29.14
Neumeister v Austria (No 1) A/8 (1968) 1 EHRR 91   4.69, 7.14, 7.26,
    7.31, 7.39
Neves e Silva v Portugal A/153 (1989) 13 EHRR 535   2.33, 12.21
New York Times v Sullivan (1964) 376 US 254   24.30
Ng v Canada (1993) 1 IHRR 161   18.14
Nibbio v Italy A/228-A (1992)   13.81
Nicodemo v Italy European Court (2 September 1997)
    (unreported)   28.9
Niderost-Huber v Switzerland (1997) 25 EHRR 709   13.2, 13.55, 13.57
Nielsen v Denmark (1988) 11 EHRR 175   3.31, 3.32, 20.3,
    20.5, 20.19
Niemietz v Germany (1992) 16 EHRR 97   3.109, 3.110, 3.117,
    15.36, 15.40, 28.40
Nordh v Sweden (1990) 69 DR 223   12.25
Norris v Ireland (1985) 44 DR 132   2.31
Norris v Ireland (1988) 13 EHRR 186   2.24, 6.36, 27.9
Nortier v Netherlands (1993) 17 EHRR 273   20.19

O v UK (1998) 13 EHRR 578   2.66
Obermeier v Austria A/179 (1990) 13 EHRR 290   12.27, 13.81, 28.3
Oberschlick v Austria (1991) 19 EHRR 389   2.55, 24.28, 24.30
Observer, The and The Guardian v UK (1991) 14
    EHRR 153   4.63, 24.18, 24.22
Oerlemans v Netherlands A/219 (1991) 15 EHRR 561   12.10
Olsson v Sweden (No 1) A/130 (1988) 11 EHRR 259   3.114, 12.18, 19.6,
    19.7, 19.29, 20.1
Olsson v Sweden (No 2) (1994) 17 EHRR 134   4.24
Omkarananda and the Divine Light Zentrum v
    Switzerland (1981) 25 DR 105   3.131, 12.28, 27.5
Open Door Counselling and Dublin Well Woman v
    Ireland (1992) 15 EHRR 244   2.24, 2.39, 2.55,
    4.40, 24.8
Osman and Another v Ferguson and Another [1993]
    4 All ER 344   15.96

Osman v UK (1999) 1 FLR 198   2.64, 3.7, 3.95, 4.77,
                                                        5.16, 12.33, 13.13,
                                                        14.8, 14.10, 14.62,
                                                        14.63, 15.96, 15.101,
                                                        22.31
Osman v UK Appl 23452/94 (Commission decision
    1.7.97) (unreported)   16.4
Otto-Preminger Institute v Austria (1995) 19 EHRR 34   6.37, 24.6, 27.21,
                                                        27.27, 27.28
Ouinas v France Appl 13756/88 65 DR 265   16.58
Ozturk v Turkey (1984) 6 EHRR 409   6.11, 6.12, 8.39

P v S and Cornwall CC [1996] ECR I-2143   1.83
Panikian v Bulgaria (1997) 24 EHRR CD 63   22.17
Papamichalopoulos v Greece A/330-B (1995)   2.54
Pathan v UK Appl 26292-95 (Commission) 16 January
    1996   19.28
Paton v UK (1980) 19 DR 244   2.29, 14.32–14.34,
                                                        14.36
Pauger v Austria (1997) 25 EHRR 105   23.16
PD and LD v UK (1989) 62 DR 292   21.33
Pelladoah v Netherlands (1994) 19 EHRR 81   8.35
Pelle v France Appl 11691/85 50 DR 263   16.52
Pendragon v UK [1999] EHRLR 223   25.26
Pepper v Hart [1993] AC 593   1.8, 1.9
Perez de Rada Cavanilles v Spain A/1019 (Court)
    28 October 1998   13.26
Perez Mahia v Spain (1987) 9 EHRR 91   7.73
Perin v France Appl 18656/91, 1 December 1992,
    unpublished   6.18
Pfarrmeier v Austria (1995) 22 EHRR 175   6.14
Pfeiffer and Plankl v Austria (1992) 14 EHRR 692   4.98, 16.63
Philis v Greece (1991) 13 EHRR 741; (1990) 66 DR 260   2.60, 4.77, 8.36,
                                                        13.8, 13.7
Piermont v France (1995) 20 EHRR 301   4.84, 25.14
Pierre-Bloch v France (1997) 26 EHRR 202   3.200, 12.31
Piersack v Belgium (1983) 5 EHRR 169   8.6, 8.7, 8.10
Piersack v Belgium (1984) 7 EHRR 251   2.51
Pinder v UK (1984) 7 EHRR 464   13.12
Pine Valley Developments Ltd v Ireland (1993)   2.56
Pine Valley Developments v Ireland (1991) 14 EHRR 319   3.189, 22.31, 22.37,
                                                        26.8, 26.16, 26.17
Platform Artze fur das Leben v Austria (1991) 13
    EHRR 204   2.16, 5.5, 5.16, 5.22,
                                                        24.21, 25.8, 25.11,
                                                        25.14
Poitrimol v France (1993) 18 EHRR 130   8.24
Poku v UK Commission (15 May 1996)   18.20, 30.37

Popescu and Cucu v France Commission (11 September
  1995)   18.13
Porter v UK (1987) 54 DR 207   12.39
Powell and Rayner v UK A/172 (1990) 12 EHRR 355   4.93, 5.6, 5.33, 5.34,
                                                          12.33, 13.10
Prager and Oberschlick v Austria (1995) 21 EHRR 1   24.36, 24.37
Pressos Compania Naviera v Belgium (1996) 21
  EHRR 301   3.189, 26.10
Preston and Another v UK Appl 24193/94 [1997]
  EHRLR 695   7.67
Pretto and Others v Italy A/71 (1983) 6 EHRR 182   4.24, 8.13, 8.18,
                                                          13.50
Price v UK (1988) 55 DR 224   19.27
Priorello v Italy (1985) 43 DR 195   12.30
Pudas v Sweden (1988) 10 EHRR 380   3.90, 12.12, 12.34
Purcell v Ireland (1989) 70 DR 262   24.13

Quaranta v Switzerland A/205 (1991)   8.28
Quinn v France (1995) 21 EHRR 529   2.58, 3.37
Quinn v UK Appl 23496/94 (1996) 23 EHRR CD 41   9.73

R v Goodwin (No 2) [1993] 2 NZLR 390   9.45
R v Governor of HMP Swaleside, ex p Wynter
  (DC) (unreported) 11/5/98   16.52
R v Her Majesty's Inspectorate on Pollution ex p
  Greenpeace (No 2) [1994] 4 All ER 329   2.37, 2.39
R v Khan [1996] 3 WLR 162   1.77
R v Kirifi [1992] 2 NZLR 8   9.45
R v Kirk [1984] ECR 2689   1.83
R v Laugalis (1993) 10 CRNZ   1.24
R v Ministry of Defence ex p Smith [1996] 1 All ER 257   1.78
R v R [1991] 4 All ER 481   6.25
R v Rangi [1992] 1 NZLR 385   1.24
R v Secretary of State for Employment ex p EOC
  [1995] AC 1; [1994] 2 WLR 409   1.80, 2.37
R v Secretary of State for Foreign and Commonwealth
  Affairs ex p World Development Movement [1995]
  2 WLR 409   2.37
R v Secretary of State for Social Services ex p CPAG
  [1990] 2 QB 540   2.37
R v Secretary of State for the Environment and
  Secretary of State for Wales ex p NALGO
  (1992) 5 Admin LR 785   1.74
R v Secretary of State for the Home Department
  ex p Ahmed, Patel and Others 30 July 1998,
  QBCOF 98/0650/4, *Times* 15 October 1998   1.79
R v Secretary of State for the Home Department
  ex p Anderson [1984] QB 778   16.51, 16.69

R v Secretary of State for the Home Department
ex p Brind [1991] 1 AC 969   1.74
R v Secretary of State for the Home Department
ex p Bugdaycay [1987] AC 514; [1987] 1 All ER 940   1.78, 11.11
R v Secretary of State for the Home Department
ex p Leech (No 2) [1994] QB 198   16.2, 16.51, 16.78
R v Secretary of State for the Home Department
ex p Main [1998] 2 All ER 291   16.70
R v Secretary of State for the Home Department
ex p McQuillan   1.78
R v Secretary of State for the Home Department
ex p Norney (1995) 7 Admin LR 861   1.75
R v Secretary of State for the Home Department
ex p Pierson [1997] 3 WLR 492   16.33, 16.41
R v Secretary of State for the Home Department
ex p Simms and O'Brien [1998]2 All ER 491   16.78
R v Secretary of State for Transport ex p Factortame
(No 2) [1990] ECR I-2433   1.84
R v Switzerland (1987) 51 DR 83   13.8
R v UK (1988) 10 EHRR 74   20.2, 20.3
R, S, A, and C v Portugal Appl 9911/82 36 DR 200   16.22
Radio ABC v Austria (1997) 25 EHRR 185   24.13
Radio X, S, W and A v Switzerland (1984) 37 DR 236   24.10
Rai, Allmond and 'Negotiate Now' v UK (1995)
(Commission) 19 EHRR CD 93   4.34, 25.26
Raimondo v Italy A/281 (1994) 18 EHRR 237   12.10
Raninen v Finland (1997) 26 EHRR 563   3.34, 14.61, 15.86,
                                                         15.87, 16.30
Rantzen v Mirror Group Newspapers [1994] QB 670   1.77
Rasmussen v Denmark (1984) 7 EHRR 371   3.184, 18.44, 19.41,
                                                         22.48, 23.2, 23.23,
                                                         29.7, 29.16, 29.23
Rassemblement Jurassien and Unite Jurassienne v
Switzerland (1980) 17 DR 93   3.153, 25.3, 25.10
Raymond v Honey [1983] AC 1   16.51, 16.67
Rayner v UK (1986) 47 DR 5   3.111, 26.20
Rebai v France Appl 26561/95 88B D & R 72   16.23
Reed v UK 5 EHRR 114   16.12
Reed v UK Appl 7630/76 (1979) 19 DR 113   2.34, 16.20, 30.28
Rees v UK (1986) 9 EHRR 56   3.172, 4.17, 4.54,
                                                         4.70, 19.37, 19.60,
                                                         19.61, 19.63
Reinette v France (1989) 63 DR 189   2.20, 15.71
Reid v UK [1998] EHRLR 211   8.12
Rekvenyi v Hungary [1999] EHRLR 114   4.32, 4.35
Remer v Germany Appl 25096/94 82A DR 117   16.26
Remli v France (1996) 22 EHRR 253   8.9, 8.10
Revert v France (1989) 62 DR 309   3.159

Ribitsch v Austria (1995) 21 EHRR 573 — 2.58, 3.13, 14.54, 15.83, 15.92

Ringeisen v Austria (1979–80) 1 EHRR 455 — 3.90, 7.22, 8.4, 12.3, 12.4, 12.10, 23.13, 30.30

Ringeisen v Austria (No 2) (1972) 1 EHRR 504 — 2.53

RO v UK Appl 23094/93 (1994) 18 EHRR CD 212 — 8.50

Robins v UK (1997) 26 EHRR 527 — 12.2, 12.9, 12.37, 13.70, 13.79

Rommelfanger v Germany (1989) 62 DR 151 — 2.78, 4.98, 24.21, 28.56, 28.57

Rookes v Barnard [1964] AC 1129 — 2.46

Roux v UK Appl 12039/86 46 DR 263 — 16.43, 16.47

Rowe and Davis v UK Appl 28910/95 — 7.70

Ruiz-Mateos v Spain (1993) 16 EHRR 505 — 8.58, 12.5, 13.55

Ruiz v Spain [1999] EHRLR 334 — 13.68

S v France (1988) 65 DR 250 — 22.32, 26.20

S v Germany (1983) 39 DR 43 — 8.57, 8.58

S v Switzerland (1988) 59 DR 256 — 12.28

S v Switzerland (1991) 14 EHRR 670 — 2.60, 7.53

S v UK (1986) 47 DR 274 — 22.7, 22.16, 22.25, 22.27, 22.28

S v UK Appl 19085/91 15 EHRR CD 106 — 16.57

Saidi v France A/261-C (1993) 17 EHRR 251 — 9.21

Salabiaku v France A/141-A (1988) 13 EHRR 379 — 3.93, 6.34, 8.1, 8.45, 8.45, 8.47, 13.1

Salesi v Italy [1996] EHRLR 66 — 23.17, 23.19

Sanchez-Reisse v Switzerland (1986) 9 EHRR 71 — 3.79, 16.47

Santa Cruz Ruiz v UK (Commission) 1 July 1998 — 2.70, 3.86

Saunders v UK (1997) 23 EHRR 313 — 2.61, 9.59, 9.64, 9.71, 9.75

Scarth v UK [1999] EHRLR 332 — 13.48

Schenk v Switzerland A/140 (1988) 13 EHRR 242 — 9.1, 9.43

Scherer v Switzerland (1994) 18 EHRR 276 — 3.143, 6.37, 24.47

Schertenlieb v Switzerland Appln 8339/78 (1980) 23 DR 137 — 7.26

Schiesser v Switzerland A/34 (1979) 2 EHRR 417 — 7.11, 7.12

Schmautzer v Austria (1995) 21 EHRR 511 — 6.14

Schmid v Austria Appln 10670/83 (1985) 44 DR 195 — 7.27

Schmidt and Dahlstrom v Sweden (1976) 1 EHRR 632 — 3.160, 4.22, 28.34, 29.9

Schmidt v Germany (1994) 18 EHRR 513 — 3.20, 3.186

Schonenberger and Durmaz v Switzerland (1988) 11 EHRR 202 — 7.52

Schopfer v Switzerland [1998] EHRLR 646 — 8.35

Schouten and Meldrum v Netherlands (1995) 19 EHRR 432 — 12.15, 23.19, 23.20

Schuler-Zdraggen v Switzerland (1995) 21 EHRR 404 — 2.50

Schuler-Zgraggen v Switzerland (1993) 16 EHRR 405   2.55, 13.45, 13.47,
23.16, 23.16, 23.19
Schwabe v Austria A/242-B (28 August 1992)   24.34
Scollo v Italy (1996) 22 EHRR 514   22.22
Scott v Spain (1996) 24 EHRR 391   15.70
SD, DP and T v UK (1996) 22 EHRR CD 148   2.32
Sekanina v Austria A/266-A (1993) 17 EHRR 221   8.54
Selmouni v France (1998) EHRLR 510   15.93
Serves v France [1998] EHRLR 213   9.66
Shahzad v UK [1998] EHRLR 210   9.32
Sheffield and Horsham v UK 1999 27 EHRR 163   4.17, 19.63
Sibson v UK (1993) 17 EHRR 193   28.30
Sidiropulos v Greece (Commission) 11 April 1997,
    Appl 26695/95 (unreported)   3.158
Sigurjonsson v Iceland (1993) 16 EHRR 462   3.159, 4.8, 4.18,
28.29
Silva Pontes v Portugal (1994) 18 EHRR 156   12.2, 12.37, 13.72,
13.79, 13.81
Silver v UK (1983) 5 EHRR 347; (1983) 13 EHRR 582   3.178, 4.31, 4.34,
4.36, 16.54, 16.58,
16.61, 16.62, 16.76
Simpson v AG (Baigent's Case) [1994] 3 NZLR 667   9.45
Simpson v UK (1989) 64 DR 188   12.29, 21.29, 21.32
Singh and Hussein v UK (1996) 22 EHRR 1   3.79, 16.31, 20.19
SM and MT v Austria (1993) 74 DR 179   3.29, 15.55
Smith Kline and French Laboratories v
    Netherlands (1990) 66 DR 70   3.189, 26.8
Smith v UK Appl 25373/94 (1995) 21 EHRR CD 75   6.19
Smith v UK [1998] EHRLR 499   22.10
Societies W, X, Y and Z v Austria (1977) 7 DR 148   3.20
Soderback v Sweden (Commission) 22 October 1997
    (1998) EHRLR 342   19.15, 19.54
Soering v UK (1989) 11 EHRR 439   2.26, 3.182, 4.10,
    4.15, 4.22, 4.24, 4.37, 5.17, 11.10, 11.11, 11.13, 18.1, 18.12, 18.14, 18.14,
    18.16, 18.25, 30.39
Sorabjee v UK   18.43
SP v UK Appl 28915/95 (1997) 23 EHRR 139, CD   1.66, 21.3
Spadea and Scalabrino v Italy (1995) 21 EHRR 482   22.22, 22.29
Sporrong and Lonroth v Sweden (1984) 7 EHRR 256   2.56
Sporrong and Lonroth v Sweden (1982) 5 EHRR 35   3.90, 3.193, 4.74,
12.10, 26.3, 26.11,
26.23
SPRL Anca v Belgium (1984) 40 DR 170   12.11
Staarman v Netherlands (1985) 42 DR 162   19.33
Stan Grek Refineries and Stratis Andreadis v
    Greece (1994) 19 EHRR 293   12.21
Stanford v UK A/282 (1994)   3.97, 8.2, 8.22
Stedman v UK Appl 29107/95 (1997) 23 EHRR CD 168   5.12, 13.26, 22.28,
28.47, 28.57

Steel and Others v UK (Court) 23 September 1998   3.36, 3.47, 3.52,
                                                  3.67, 3.156, 24.17,
                                                  25.3, 25.21
Stephan v UK and Wickramsighe v UK [1998]
    EHRLR 338   12.13
Stevens and Knight v UK [1999] EHRLR 126   23.8
Stevens v UK (1986) 46 DR 245   3.143, 21.47, 24.6
Stewart v UK (10044/82) (1984) 39 DR 162   3.8, 14.22, 14.27
Stewart-Brady v UK (1997) 24 EHRR CD 38   5.7
Stjerna v Finland 24 EHRR 195   19.58, 22.2
Stogmuller v Austria (1969) 1 EHRR 155   4.69, 7.20, 7.27,
                                                  7.36, 13.78, 15.60,
                                                  30.26
Stubbings v UK Appls 22083/93 and 22095/93
    (1996) 23 EHRR 213   5.9, 13.24, 13.27,
                                                  20.14
Stubbings v Webb [1993] 1 AC 498   5.9, 13.24
Sulak v Turkey (1996) 84-A DR 98   21.24, 21.43
Sunday Times v UK (1979) 2 EHRR 245   3.36, 4.2, 4.29, 4.30,
                                                  4.31, 4.33, 4.43,
                                                  4.56, 4.62, 4.91,
                                                  4.96, 6.24, 19.6,
                                                  24.9, 24.15, 24.40,
                                                  30.18
Sunday Times v UK (No 2) (1991) 14 EHRR 229   4.61, 4.62, 24.2
Sunday Times v UK 6 November 1980 (unpublished)   2.49
Sutherland v UK 1 July 1997, [1998] EHRLR 117   2.24, 6.36
SW and CR v UK (1995) 21 EHRR 363   3.105, 4.35, 6.24
Swedish Engine Drivers' Union v Sweden (1979-80)
    1 EHRR 578   4.22, 28.33
Swedish Engine Drivers' Union v Sweden (1976)
    1 EHRR 617   3.177
Szrabjer and Clarke v UK Appl 27004/95 and 270111/95
    [1998] EHRLR 230   16.80, 16.83, 23.7

T v Belgium (1983) 34 DR 158   3.143
T v UK Appl 8231/78 49 DR 5   16.74–16.76
Tand v UK [1998] EHRLR 484   8.22
Talmon v Netherlands [1997] EHRLR 448   28.24
Tanko v Finland Appl 23634/94 (1994) (unreported) 14.66
Taspinar v Netherlands (1985) 44 DR 262   18.43
Tavares v France Appl 16593/90 (1991) (unreported) 14.77
Taylor v UK (1997) 23 EHRR CD 132   13.11
Taylor v UK Appl 31209/96 [1998] EHRLR 90   6.33
Taylor, Crampton, Gibson and King v UK (1994)
    79-A DR 127   14.17
Teixeira de Castro v Portugal 9 Jun 1998   9.31–9.33, 9.35,
                                                  15.42

Tete v France (1987) 54 DR 52   3.199
Thompson and Venables v UK Appl 1998   16.42
Thorgiersen v Iceland (1992) 14 EHRR 843   24.26, 24.31, 24.33,
                                                                     24.35
Thynne, Wilson and Gunnell v UK (1990) 13 EHRR 666   3.78, 10.6, 16.41,
                                                                     16.45
Times Newspapers Ltd v UK (1990) 65 DR 307   2.25, 2.39
Tinnelly and McElduff v UK [1997] EHRLR 663;
    (1998) 27 EHRR 249   7.71, 11.9, 12.22,
                                                                     13.20, 13.22
Togher v UK [1998] EHRLR 637   16.28
Tolstoy Miloslavsky v UK (1995) 20 EHRR 442   13.28, 13.31, 24.18,
                                                                     24.26
Tomasi v France A/241-A (1992) 15 EHRR 1   2.58, 3.13, 7.16,
                                                                     14.41, 14.50, 15.81,
                                                                     15.82, 16.29, 18.4
Tomsett v UK Appl 25985/94 [1997] EHRLR 104   16.44
Toth v Austria A/224 (1991) 14 EHRR 551   7.31
TP and KM v UK and Z v UK [1998] 624   13.19
Traktorer, The Aktiebolag v Sweden (1991) 13 EHRR 309   3.90, 3.189, 26.8
Treholdt v Norway Appl 14610/89 71 DR 168   16.16
Trivedi v UK Appl 31700/96 [1997] EHRLR 521   9.14
Tucht v Germany Appl 9336/81 (1982) (unreported)   28.53
Turner v UK (1997) 23 EHRR CD 181   22.10
TV v Finland 15 EHRR CD 179   16.58
Twenty one detained persons v FRG Appls 3134/67,
    3172/67 and 3188-206/67 6 April 1968,
    11 Yearbook 528   16.37
Tyrer v UK (1978) 2 EHRR 1   1.26, 4.17, 16.11,
                                                                     20.6, 20.10, 30.36

Umlauft v Austria (1995) 22 EHRR 76   6.14
Union Alimentaria SA v Spain (1989) 12 EHRR 24   13.80, 13.82
Unterpertinger v Austria A/110 (1986) 13 EHRR 175   9.7, 9.9, 9.10, 9.11,
                                                                     9.60

V v Netherlands (1984) 39 DR 267   27.15
V v UK Commission Report (4 December 1998)
    (unreported)   10.6, 20.30, 20.31
Vachur v France Appl 20366/92 (1996) 24 EHRR 492   10.11
Valle v France (1994) 18 EHRR 549   13.81
Valsamis v Greece (1996) 24 EHRR 294   21.17, 21.21, 21.38,
                                                                     21.46
Van de Hurk v Netherlands A/288 91994 18 EHRR 481   8.51, 10.25, 13.41,
                                                                     13.68
Van der Heijden v Netherlands (1985) 41 DR 264   2.78, 28.51, 28.57
Van der Leer v Netherlands (1990) 12 EHRR 567   3.40, 3.70, 3.83, 6.6,
                                                                     15.68, 17.8

Van der Mussele v Belgium (1984) 6 EHRR 25 — 2.13, 3.12, 3.17, 3.185, 4.25, 28.19, 28.20, 28.22, 29.11, 29.13

Van Droogenbroeck v Belgium (1982) 4 EHRR 443 — 3.43, 10.6, 16.41, 28.17

Van Marle v Netherlands A/101 (1986) 8 EHRR 483 — 3.189, 12.34, 12.40, 26.8

Van Mechelen and Others v Netherlands (1997) 25 EHRR 647 — 9.6, 9.22, 9.23, 9.27, 9.29, 9.29

Van Oostereijck v Belgium (1980) A 40 para 30–41 — 30.27, 30.28

Van Orshoven v Belgium (1997) 26 EHRR 55 — 8.58, 13.56

Van Raalte v Netherlands (1997) 24 EHRR 583 — 3.186, 18.47, 23.23, 29.17, 29.20

Van Volsem v Belgium Appl 14641/89 (unreported) — 14.53

Vasquez v Queen [1994] 1 WLR 1304 — 1.28

Vearncombe v UK (1987) 59 DR 186 — 22.32

Velosa Bareto v Portugal A/334 [1996] EHRLR 212 — 22.29

Verein Gemeinsam Lernen v Austria (1995) 82-A DR 41 — 21.26, 21.29, 21.30

Vereniging Rechtswinkels Utrecht v Netherlands (1986) 46 DR 200 — 3.131, 16.73, 27.7

Vermeire v Belgium A/270-A (1990) (unreported) — 2.55, 19.40

Vermeulen v Belgium (Court) 20 February 1996 — 13.2

Vernillo v France (1991) A 198 para 27 — 30.26, 30.27, 30.29

Vidal v Belgium 22 April 1992 (unpublished) — 9.56, 9.59

Vijayanathan and Pusparajah v France (1992) 15 EHRR 62 — 2.26

Vilvarajah v UK A/215 (1991) 14 EHRR 248 — 3.182, 11.11, 11.13, 18.1, 18.17, 18.18

Vogt v Germany (1995) 21 EHRR 205 — 4.35, 4.43, 4.44, 24.18, 28.50

W and KL v Sweden (1985) 45 DR 143 — 21.20

W and Others v UK (1984) 37 DR 96 — 21.19, 21.29

W v Sweden (1988) 59 DR 158 — 17.24

W v Switzerland A/254 (1993) 17 EHRR 60 — 7.19, 7.22

W v UK (1983) 32 DR 190 — 14.12

W v UK (1987) 10 EHRR 29 — 4.49, 11.15, 12.18, 12.42, 12.44, 12.45, 19.64, 19.66

W, X, Y and Z v Austria (1977) 7 DR 148 — 28.23

W, X, Y and Z v UK Appl 3435-38/67 (1968) 11 Yearbook 562 — 28.18

Waddington v Miah [1974] 1 WLR 683 — 6.28

Waite and Kennedy v Germany (Commission) 2 December 1997 — 12.27, 13.23

Wakefield v UK 66 DR 251 — 16.28, 16.57

Walsh v UK — 6.33
Walverens v Belgium 5 March 1980 (unpublished) — 3.28, 15.52, 15.53
Warwick v UK (1986) 60 DR 5 — 20.9, 21.41, 21.46
Wasa Liv Omsesidigt, Forsakringbolaget Varlands
    Pensionsstiftelse v Sweden (1988) 58 DR 163 — 3.192, 4.73, 22.20, 23.10, 26.18
Wassink v Netherlands A/185-A (1990) (unreported) — 3.37, 3.86, 17.10, 17.18
Watson v UK Appl 21387/93 [1997] EHRLR 181 — 16.42
Webb v UK Appl 33186/96 (1997) 24 EHRR CD 73 — 10.26
Weber v Switzerland (1990) 12 EHRR 508 — 4.63
Weeks v UK (1987) 10 EHRR 293 — 10.1, 16.41, 16.43, 16.45
Weeks v UK (1988) 13 EHRR 435 — 2.52, 2.57, 3.43, 3.44, 3.78
Welch v UK (1995) 20 EHRR 247 — 1.26, 3.106, 6.31, 6.32, 10.4, 10.6
Wemhoff v Germany (1979–80) 1 EHRR 55 — 4.9, 4.69, 7.13, 7.26, 7.34, 7.38
Weston v UK (1980) 3 EHRR 402 — 3.40
Whitear v UK Appl 28625/95 (Commission)
    17 January 1997 (1997) EHRLR 291 — 19.45
Whiteside v UK (1994) 76A DR 80 — 3.117, 19.51, 22.31
Widmer v Switzerland Appl 20527/92 (1993) (unreported) — 14.38
Wiggins v UK (1978) 13 DR 40 — 3.190, 22.6, 22.8, 22.25
Wille v Liechtenstein (1997) 24 EHRR CD 45 — 15.95
Williams v YUK (1992) Appl 19404/92 (unreported) — 15.35
Windisch v Austria A/186 (1990) 13 EHRR 282 — 9.20,
Winer v UK (1986) 48 DR 154 — 2.29, 5.7, 13.36, 13.37
Wingrove v UK (1996) 14 EHRR 1 — 4.35, 4.93, 24.18, 27.31, 27.33
Winterwerp v Netherlands (1979) 2 EHRR 387 — 3.22, 3.34, 3.37,
    3.39, 3.40, 3.60, 3.62, 3.63, 3.99, 4.68, 6.5, 6.6, 13.9, 15.44, 17.3–17.6, 17.7,
    17.9, 17.10, 17.15, 17.19, 17.21, 18.26
WM v Germany (1997) 24 EHRR CD 79 — 14.13
Wolfgram v Germany (1986) 49 DR 213 — 14.22
Wood v UK (1997) 24 EHRR CD 69 — 22.28
Woodson v North Carolina — 18.14
Worm v Austria (1997) 25 EHRR 454 — 4.93, 7.78, 24.41
Woukam Moudefou v France A/141-B (1988) 13
    EHRR 549 — 7.31, 16.45
Wynne v UK (1994) 19 EHRR 353 — 10.6, 16.41

X and Association Z v UK 38 CD 86 — 24.11
X and Church of Scientology v Sweden (1979) 16 DR 68 — 3.131, 3.132, 27.5, 27.20

X and U v UK (1983) 5 EHRR 601	18.34
X and Y v Germany (1976) 10 DR 224	3.17, 18.1, 22.32, 28.23
X and Y v Germany (1977) 9 DR 219	18.35
X and Y v Ireland 22 DR 51	8.5
X and Y v Netherlands (1975) 1 DR 66	13.33
X and Y v Netherlands (1985) 8 EHRR 235	3.111, 3.123, 5.8, 5.9, 14.49, 19.52, 20.12, 20.13, 22.2
X and Y v Sweden (1977) 7 DR 123	15.50, 15.51
X and Y v Switzerland (1978) 13 DR 241	3.170, 16.59, 19.38
X and Y v Switzerland (8 April 1991) Commission (unreported)	6.37
X and Y v UK (1983) 32 DR 220	19.23, 19.24
X and Y v UK Appl 5302/71	18.9
X Ltd and Y v UK (1982) 28 DR 77	4.35, 6.26, 6.37
X v Austria (1966) 9 Yearbook 112	2.33
X v Austria (1967) 24 CD 20	14.53
X v Austria (1968) 11 Yearbook 322	3.41
X v Austria (1969) 12 Yearbook 206	3.42
X v Austria (1970) 13 Yearbook 798	3.41
X v Austria (1970) 35 CD 151	8.58
X v Austria (1972) 42 CD 145	13.62
X v Austria (1974) 1 DR 44	2.34
X v Austria (1975) 2 DR 87	30.24
X v Austria (1977) 7 DR 87	2.24, 14.36
X v Austria (1978) 14 DR 171	10.27, 12.39
X v Austria (1979) 15 DR 160	7.73
X v Austria (1979) 18 DR 154	3.47, 15.50, 15.51
X v Austria (1979) 3 EHRR 285	22.22
X v Austria (1980) 21 DR 246	12.15
X v Austria (1983) 31 DR 66	13.52
X v Austria (1987) 11 EHRR 112	3.53, 15.60
X v Bedfordshire CC [1995] 3 All ER 353	13.19
X v Belgium (1969) 12 Yearbook 174	14.22
X v Belgium (1975) 7 DR 75	19.17
X v Belgium (1979) 16 DR 82	21.7
X v Belgium (1980) 23 DR 237	12.12
X v Belgium 45 Collection of decisions 20	15.31
X v Commission [1994] ECR I-4737	1.83
X v Denmark (1975) 3 DR 153	28.1
X v Denmark (1976) 5 DR 154	28.45
X v Denmark (1978) 15 DR 128	2.34, 16.16
X v France (1982) 29 DR 228	30.21
X v France (1982) 31 DR 241	3.113, 19.17
X v France (1983) 32 DR 266	12.15
X v France (1991) 14 EHRR 483	2.35, 2.63, 12.19, 13.81

X v FRG (1978) 16 DR 111   3.70, 15.51, 15.52,
                                                         15.66

X v FRG Appl 10565/83 7 EHRR 152   16.2, 16.5
X v FRG Appl 7408/76 10 DR 221   16.15
X v Germany (1956) 1 Yearbook 202   22.44
X v Germany (1963) 6 Yearbook 520   3.45, 3.47, 13.52,
                                                         13.54

X v Germany (1969) 32 Collected Decisions 87   18.13
X v Germany (1969) 32 Collected Decisions 96   18.13
X v Germany (1974) 46 Collected Decisions 22   28.22
X v Germany (1975) 19 Yearbook 276   29.8
X v Germany (1975) 3 DR 92   3.47
X v Germany (1976) 3 DR 104   15.31
X v Germany (1976) 5 Collected Decisions 154   18.13
X v Germany (1978) 14 DR 60   13.71
X v Germany (1979) 17 DR 227   3.122
X v Germany (1980) 18 DR 216   26.9, 28.23
X v Germany (1981) 24 DR 137   3.132
X v Germany (1981) 25 DR 240   13.69
X v Germany (1981) 26 DR 270   22.32
X v Germany (1982) 26 DR 97   28.23
X v Germany (1982) 29 DR 194   3.143
X v Germany (1985) 7 EHRR 141   12.29, 14.77
X v Germany 11 EHRR 46   9.44
X v Germany 13 Yearbook 176   12.15
X v Germany 26 Collection of Decisions p1   12.15
X v Germany 9 Collection of Decisions 53   15.34
X v Greece (Commission) 11 January 1995   12.8
X v Iceland Appl 6825/74 5 DR 86   16.57
X v Ireland (1973) 16 Yearbook 388   14.12
X v Ireland (1976) 7 DR 78   14.67
X v Irteland (1980) 22 DR 51   30.23
X v Italy (1989) 58 DR 100   9.3
X v Netherlands (1962) 5 YB 224   3.70
X v Netherlands (1971) 38 Coll Dec 9   29.8
X v Netherlands (1973) 16 Yearbook 274   29.8
X v Netherlands (1974) 2 DR 118   20.2, 20.3
X v Netherlands (1976) 7 DR 161   28.24
X v Netherlands, Appl 2894/66 (1966) 9 Yearbook 564   7.7, 15.66
X v Norway Appl 3444/67 (1970) 35 CD 37   7.78
X v Sweden (1959) 2 Yearbook 354   13.53
X v Sweden (1972) 43 Collected Decisions 111   18.13
X v Sweden (1979) 16 DR 105   2.32
X v Sweden (1979) 17 DR 74   13.28, 13.30
X v Sweden (1986) 8 EHRR 252   23.1, 23.4–23.5
X v Sweden (1997) 12 DR 192   21.22
X v Sweden (1997) 17 DR 74   13.28
X v Sweden (Commission) 7 Mat 1984   21.29

X v Switzerland (1975) 3 DR 155	12.11
X v Switzerland (1978) 13 DR 248	3.113, 19.20
X v Switzerland Appl 7754/77 11 DR 216	16.38
X v Switzerland Appl 8500/79, 18 DR 28	16.1, 16.37, 16.81
X v UK (1970) 30 CD 70	13.48
X v UK (1974) 14 Yearbook 250	15.66
X v UK (1975) 10 DR 37	16.35
X v UK (1975) 2 DR 50	21.24
X v UK (1975) 3 DR 165	3.201
X v UK (1976) 5 DR 100	27.18
X v UK (1976) 7 DR 115	9.50
X v UK (1977) 10 DR 5	30.28
X v UK (1977) 11 DR 160	21.23
X v UK (1977) 2 Digest 438	13.46
X v UK (1978) 14 DR 197	2.34, 21.20, 21.29, 27.18
X v UK (1978) 16 DR 190	24.9
X v UK (1978) 3 EHRR 63	25.3
X v UK (1979) 20 DR 202	6.13, 16.75
X v UK (1980) 19 DR 244	4.25
X v UK (1980) 21 DR 126	8.33
X v UK (1980) 21 DR 5	6.13, 16.72
X v UK (1980) 21 DR 95	13.40, 16.11
X v UK (1980) 23 DR 228	21.25
X v UK (1981) 24 DR 57	12.36, 16.79
X v UK (1981) 24 DR 98	18.1
X v UK (1981) 25 DR 147	30.33, 30.34
X v UK (1981) 4 EHRR 188	10.1, 10.6, 16.41, 16.43, 17.10, 17.14, 17.15–17.17, 17.29
X v UK (1982) 28 DR 177	22.25
X v UK (1982) 28 DR 5	3.132, 16.21, 16.35, 16.58, 27.18
X v UK (1984) 37 DR 158	6.13
X v UK (1984) 6 EHRR 583	28.3
X v UK (1989) 11 EHRR 49	18.34
X v UK (1998) 25 EHRR CD 89	12.45
X v UK (Commission) 1 December 1986 (unpublished)	21.8
X v UK (Commission) 9 December 1992 (unreported)	29.14
X v UK (Commission) Appl 18187/91 (10 February 1993)	3.131, 27.5
X v UK Appl 10117/82 7 EHRR 140	16.20
X v UK Appl 13477/878 (Commission) 4 October 1989	21.42
X v UK Appl 20657/92, 15 EHRR CD 113	9.26
X v UK Appl 5265/71 3 DR 5	16.20
X v UK Appl 6564/74, 2 DR 105	16.59, 16.80
X v UK Appl 8065/77 14 DR 246	16.58
X v UK Appl 8158/78 21 DR & 95	16.20
X v UK Appl 8233/78 (1979) 3 EHRR 271	7.40

X v UK Appl 8496/79 (1980) 21 DR 168 — 12.14
X v UK Appl 9054/80 30 DR 113; 5 EHRR 260 — 16.57, 16.79
X v UK B/412 ref at para 138; 4 EHRR 188 — 3.78, 3.80, 16.47
X, Y and Z v Germany (1982) 29 DR 224 — 21.35
X, Y and Z v UK (1997) 24 EHRR 143 — 3.113, 4.17, 4.22, 18.32, 19.12, 19.21, 19.25

Y v Sweden (Commission) 7 May 1984 — 21.26
Yagci and Sargin v Turkey A/319 (1995) 29 EHRR 505 — 7.16, 7.19, 30.27
Yanasik v Turkey (1993) 74 DR 14 — 21.24, 21.42, 21.43
Yarrow v UK (1983) 30 DR 155 — 2.33
Young, James and Webster v UK (1981) 4 EHRR 38; (1982) 5 EHRR 201 — 2.55, 2.57, 3.157, 3.159, 4.11, 5.11, 5.12, 24.21, 28.1, 28.29, 28.30, 28.57, 30.13, 30.18

Z v Austria (1988) 56 DR 13 — 24.7
Z v Finland (1998) 25 EHRR 371 — 2.65, 9.38, 14.74
Zamir v UK (1985) 40 DR 42 — 3.36, 3.66, 3.67, 18.36
Zand v Italy (1980) 15 DR 70 — 13.42
Zander v Sweden A/279-B (1994) 18 EHRR 175 — 3.90, 12.10
Zappia v Italy (Court) 26 September 1996 — 12.37, 13.72
Zentralrat Deutscher Sinti und Roma and Rose v Germany (1997) 23 EHRR CD 209 — 2.31
Zimmerman and Steiner v Switzerland (1983) 6 EHRR 17 — 13.83
Zumtobel v Austria (1993) 17 EHRR 116 — 13.47

Table of statutes

Civil Aviation Act 1982
    12.33
Commonwealth Immigrants Act
    1968   18.9
Companies Act 1985 13.18
    ss431(5), 432(2),
    436(3)   9.62
Courts and Legal Services Act 1980
    s108   2.70, 3.86
Crime (Sentences) Act 1997
    ss2, 3, 4   16.31
    s10   16.26
    s28   16.41, 16.43
    s28(1), (2)   16.42
    s30   16.26
    s32   16.47
Criminal Appeals Act 1968
    s2(1)   2.42
Criminal Evidence Act 1984
    15.75
Criminal Justice Act 1988
    ss23, 26   9.14
Criminal Justice Act
    1991   16.42
    s2(2)(b)   16.41
    s34   16.41–16.43
Criminal Justice and Public Order
    Act 1994   7.51, 9.72
    s25   7.12
Crown Proceedings Act 1947
    13.17
Customs and Excise Act 1979
    6.16
Drug Trafficking Offences Act 1986
    3.106,
    6.31–6.33, 10.4
Education Act 1944 1.63, 21.2

European Communities Act 1972
    s2(1)   1.84
    s3   1.84
Fair Employment (Northern Ireland)
    Act 1976   7.71, 12.22,
    13.20
Fair Employment (Northern Ireland)
    Act 1989   12.22, 13.20
Human Rights Act 1998 (HRA)
    1.1–1.5, 1.8, 1.11, 1.17, 1.20,
    1.22, 1.25, 1.27, 1.29, 1.30, 1.31,
    1.32, 1.35, 1.42, 1.43–1.44, 1.45,
    1.53, 1.56, 1.61, 1.65, 1.66, 1.69,
    1.71, 1.73, 2.1, 2.6, 2.7, 2.12,
    2.13, 2.17, 2.37, 2.39, 2.40,
    2.74–2.77, 2.79, 2.81, 3.2, 3.3,
    3.5, 3.174, 3.196, 4.1, 4.13, 4.14,
    4.82, 4.94, 4.95, 4.97, 5.36, 6.1,
    6.22, 6.23, 7.10, 11.1, 11.6, 13.4,
    14.39, 21.2, 22.18, 24.24, 28.1,
    28.4, 29.24, 30.1, 30.30
    s1(1)   1.6, 3.2
    s1(2)   1.6, 1.61
    s2   1.44, 1.44,
    1.47, 3.174,
    5.37
    s2(1)   1.25, 1.44, 2.39
    s3   1.16
    s3(1)   1.1, 1.14, 1.16,
    1.18, 1.36
    s3(2)(c)   1.36
    s4   1.30, 1.32
    s4(2), (4)   1.30
    s4(5)   1.30, 1.33
    s4(6)(a)   1.30
    s4(6)(b)   1.30
    s5(1), (2), (4)   1.34

Human Rights Act 1998 *continued*		Human Rights Act 1998 *continued*	
s6	1.39, 1.41, 2.2–2.4, 2.8	s19	1.11
		s19(1)	1.11
s6(1)	2.2, 2.8, 5.37, 28.4	s20	1.4
		s21(1)	1.36, 1.55
s6(3)	1.40, 2.7	s21(5)	1.4
s6(3)(a)	1.40, 2.7	s22(4)	1.4, 1.5, 2.81
s6(3)(b)	1.40, 2.7, 2.8	s22(6)	1.4
s6(4)	1.40	s57(7)	2.37
s6(5)	1.40, 2.7, 2.8	Sch 1	2.41, 3.2, 5.37
s6(6)	1.39, 2.4	Sch 2, para 1	1.57
ss7–9	1.70, 2.39, 2.47	Sch 2, para 1(1)(b)	1.57
s7	1.35, 1.41, 1.41, 2.3, 2.4, 2.6, 2.18, 2.47, 2.73, 2.75	Sch 2, para 1(4)	1.57
		Sch 2, para 2	1.58
		Sch 2, para 2(a)	1.58
		Sch 2, para 2(b)	1.58
s7(1)(a)	1.37, 1.41, 2.4, 2.69, 2.73, 2.75	Sch 2, para 3	1.58
		Sch 2, para 4	1.58
s7(1)(b)	1.4, 1.5, 1.37, 2.5, 2.75, 2.79	Sch 3, Pt I	1.60
		Sch 3, Pt II	1.63
s7(2)	2.4	Insurance Companies Act 1982	
s7(3)	2.18		12.45
s7(5)	2.73	Interception of Communications Act	
s7(6)	2.6, 2.18	1985	7.67, 15.21–15.23, 28.41
s7(7)	1.4, 1.41, 2.4, 2.39		
s7(8), (11)	2.40	Limitation Act 1980	5.9
s8	1.8, 2.41	Marriage Act 1983	
s8(1)	1.8, 2.40	s1	16.80
s8(2)	2.40	Mental Health Act 1959	
s8(3)	2.43		13.15, 16.35, 16.38
s8(4)	2.43		
s8(6)	2.79	Mental Health Act 1980	
s9(1)	2.69		3.80
s9(3)	2.69, 2.70	Mental Health Act 1983	
s9(4)	2.71		16.44, 17.16
s9(5)	2.71, 2.72	Northern Ireland Assembly Act 1973	
s10	1.55	s1	1.69
s11	1.3, 1.70, 1.71	Northern Ireland Constitution Act	
s11(b)	2.39, 2.47	1973	
s12	1.49, 1.50, 1.52	s21(1)	1.69
s12(2)	1.51	s38(1)(a)	1.69
s12(3)	1.52	Northern Ireland (Emergency	
s13	1.49, 1.54, 27.38	Provisions) Act 1987	
			9.67
s14(3)	1.61	Police Act 1997	15.23
s14(4)(a)	1.61	Police and Criminal Evidence Act	
s16(1)–(4)	1.61	1984	15.75

Police and Criminal Evidence Act
1984 *continued*
s78   1.73
Prevention of Terrorism (Temporary
Provisions) Act 1976
                 15.33, 15.76
Prevention of Terrorism (Temporary
Provisions) Act 1984
                    3.71, 7.8
s12   7.8
Prevention of Terrorism (Temporary
Provisions) Act 1989
                    7.49

Prison Act 1952   16.54
Public Order Act 1936
                  2.23, 25.24
Public Order Act 1986
                    25.24
Town and Country Planning Act 1990
                    12.43
Trade Union and Labour Relations
(Consolidation) Act 1992
s22A   28.35
War Crimes Act 1991 6.29

Table of statutory instruments

Criminal Evidence (Northern Ireland) Order 1988	7.50, 7.51, 9.67, 9.68, 9.69, 9.70, 9.72
Prevention of Terrorism (Supplementary Temporary Provisions) Order 1976	15.33, 15.76
Prison Rules 1964	16.2, 16.54, 16.82
rr33, 34	16.56, 16.62
rr37, 37A	16.56
Rules of the European Court of Human Rights	
rule 17	30.9
rule 24(6)	30.19
rule 28	30.14
rule 38(1)	30.14
rule 40	30.38
rule 41	30.39
rule 42	30.13
rule 47	30.9
rule 47(3)	30.10
rule 49	30.11
rule 54(2)	30.14
rule 59	30.16
rule 59(2)	30.16
rule 60	30.17
rule 60(1)	30.17
rule 61	30.2
rule 62	30.15
rule 62(1)	30.15
rule 62(3)	30.15
rules 63–70	30.14
rule 72	30.19
rule 73	30.19
rule 74	30.19
rule 75	30.17
rule 78	30.19
rules 82–90	30.44
rules 91–96	30.40
rule 93(1)	30.41
rule 93(2)	30.41

Rules of the European Court of Human Rights *continued*
   rule 95   30.42
   rules 97–102   30.2
Rules of the Supreme Court
   Order 53 r3(7)   2.36
Transfer of Undertakings (Protection of Employment)
      Regulations 1981 SI No 1794   1.21

Table of conventions

Convention on the Elimination of All Forms of
   Discrimination against Women   1.73
European Agreement Relating to Persons Participating
   in Proceedings of the European Commission and
   Court of Human Rights
   art 3(2)   7.53
European Convention on Human Rights and
   Fundamental Freedoms 1950   1.2, 1.13–1.16, 1.18,
1.25–1.28, 1.30, 1.31–1.33, 1.35–1.39, 1.41, 1.42–1.44, 1.45–1.48, 1.52,
1.54–1.56, 1.61, 1.64, 1.66–1.70, 1.71, 1.73, 1.83, 2.2–2.6, 2.13–2.15,
2.17, 2.19–2.35, 2.37–2.39, 2.40, 2.51, 2.55–2.57, 2.61, 2.69, 2.74–2.81,
3.1, 3.3, 3.49, 3.84, 3.93, 3.130, 3.141, 3.173–3.175, 3.177–3.179, 3.185,
3.201, 4.2, 4.4, 4.5, 4.6, 4.8, 4.9, 4.10, 4.13–4.22, 4.24, 4.26, 4.29, 4.30,
4.33, 4.37, 4.38, 4.41, 4.42, 4.43, 4.48, 4.59–4.60, 4.73, 4.75, 4.76, 4.78,
4.85, 4.88, 4.90, 4.95–4.98, 4.97, 5.1–5.7, 5.10, 5.11, 5.22, 5.30, 5.32,
5.33, 5.34, 5.36–5.39, 6.2, 6.3, 6.6, 6.22–6.24, 6.34, 6.35, 7.1, 7.9, 7.14,
7.17, 7.26, 8.5, 8.6, 8.43, 8.47, 8.55, 8.56, 9.3, 9.8, 9.23, 9.29, 9.30, 9.42,
9.75, 10.7, 10.8, 11.1, 11.4–11.6, 15.1, 15.4, 19.1, 20.1, 20.2, 20.30,
21.10, 23.1, 24.1, 24.2, 24.14, 24.33, 27.1, 25.1, 28.38, 28.56, 28.57, 29.2,
29.3, 30.1, 30.45
   art 1   1.8, 2.20, 3.173,
   4.83, 4.88, 4.94,
   5.11, 5.36, 18.25,
   19.52
   arts 2–12   1.6, 3.2, 5.36, 11.2,
   18.44, 22.48
   art 2   1.59, 3.3–3.5, 3.6,
3.10, 4.2, 4.25, 5.13–5.15, 5.21, 5.28, 14.1–14.4, 14.6, 14.7, 14.10, 14.11,
14.13, 14.14, 14.17, 14.19, 14.21, 14.22, 14.29–14.34, 14.36, 14.38,
14.39, 14.56, 14.62–14.64, 14.66–14.68, 14.71, 14.75, 14.76, 15.1, 15.2,
15.48, 16.3–16.7, 18.1, 18.24, 21.2, 22.28, 22.46, 30.37
   art 2(1)   1.8, 3.3, 3.4, 4.26,
   14.5, 14.7, 14.8,
   14.22
   art 2(2)   3.3, 3.6, 3.8–3.9,
   14.4, 14.22, 14.23,
   14.28, 14.32

European Convention on Human Rights and Fundamental Freedoms 1950
continued

art 2(2)(a)   3.9, 14.25, 14.27

art 2(2)(b)   3.9, 14.27

art 2(2)(c)   3.9, 14.27

art 3   1.59, 2.14, 2.58, 3.3,
3.10, 3.11–3.14, 3.21, 3.23, 3.44, 3.65, 3.180, 3.183, 4.2, 4.22, 5.13, 5.14,
5.17, 5.28, 5.29, 6.3, 7.2, 9.45, 10.2, 11.10, 11.12, 14.1, 14.3, 14.19,
14.41–14.44, 14.46, 14.48–14.55, 14.57, 14.59, 14.61, 14.64, 14.66,
14.66, 14.68, 14.69, 14.75, 15.1, 15.2, 15.46, 15.81–15.83, 15.85–15.87,
15.89, 15.91–15.93, 15.94, 16.1, 16.2, 16.5, 16.8, 16.11, 16.12, 16.14,
16.17, 16.18, 16.20–16.22, 16.25, 16.26, 16.28, 16.30–16.36, 16.38,
16.43, 17.1, 17.32, 17.33, 18.1, 18.4, 18.5, 18.7–18.9, 18.10, 18.12–18.14,
18.15, 18.16, 18.18, 18.19, 18.20–18.21, 18.22–18.24, 19.50, 20.6–20.8,
20.10–20.12, 20.31, 21.4, 21.39, 21.40, 21.46, 22.28, 22.46, 22.47, 29.21,
30.37

art 4   1.59, 3.3, 3.15, 4.25,
8.57, 16.37, 16.81,
25.1, 28.15, 28.16,
28.19, 28.22

art 4(1)   3.15, 4.2, 15.1

art 4(2)   3.3, 3.15, 3.17, 4.2,
28.23, 28.24

art 4(3)   3.3, 3.18, 4.2

art 4(3)(a)   3.19, 16.37

art 4(3)(b)   3.19, 27.1, 28.18

art 4(3)(c)   3.20

art 4(3)(d)   3.20

art 5   2.48, 2.70, 3.18,
3.19, 3.21, 3.23–3.28, 3.29–3.31, 3.32–3.40, 3.44, 3.52, 3.55, 3.73, 3.85,
4.2, 4.87, 6.4–6.6, 6.22, 6.24, 6.34, 7.2, 7.3, 7.6, 14.10, 15.1, 15.43,
15.46–15.50, 15.52, 15.53, 15.54–15.56, 15.59, 15.71, 15.72, 15.89,
15.100, 16.1, 16.38, 17.1, 17.11, 17.24, 18.2, 20.4, 20.15, 20.19, 28.16

art 5(1)   3.21, 3.22, 3.23,
3.34, 3.36, 3.40, 3.48, 3.58, 4.67, 6.6, 10.23, 15.42, 15.44, 15.46, 15.56,
15.61, 15.69, 16.31, 16.38, 16.48, 17.3, 17.7, 17.27

art 5(1)(a)–(f)   3.3, 3.22, 4.26, 4.67,
15.44, 15.56, 16.48

art 5(1)(a)   3.41–3.43, 3.45,
3.48, 6.5, 10.1,
10.23, 16.38, 16.39,
17.27, 17.29

art 5(1)(b)   3.46, 3.49, 15.74,
15.77

art 5(1)(c)   3.51, 3.52, 3.54,
3.57, 3.66, 3.70, 4.69, 7.5, 7.13, 15.57, 15.58, 15.60, 15.61, 15.61, 15.64,
15.66, 15.69, 15.73, 18.30, 20.17

art 5(1)(d)   3.55–3.57, 16.81,
20.15–20.17

European Convention on Human Rights and Fundamental Freedoms 1950
    continued
    art 5(1)(e)   3.41, 3.58–3.62,
        3.64, 4.68, 6.5, 16.38, 16.43, 17.3, 17.5, 17.6, 17.8, 17.12, 17.13, 17.16,
        17.17, 17.19, 17.20, 17.26, 17.27, 17.29, 17.30
    art 5(1)(f)   3.65–3.68,
                                          18.26–18.30
    art 5(2)–(5)   3.21, 3.23, 15.43,
                                        15.45, 15.46
    art 5(2)   3.3, 3.69, 3.70, 7.41,
                                        7.42, 7.44, 7.46,
                                        15.65, 15.67, 15.68
    art 5(3)   2.53, 3.3, 3.71, 3.73,
        4.53, 4.69, 4.82, 7.5, 7.6, 7.8–7.11, 7.13, 7.14, 7.19, 7.21–7.23, 7.28, 7.33,
        7.34–7.38, 7.39, 15.58
    art 5(4)   2.53, 3.35,
        3.74–3.80, 3.82, 3.83, 3.176, 7.28–7.30, 7.31–7.32, 7.54, 16.40–16.48,
        17.10, 17.13, 17.15, 17.16, 17.18, 17.19, 17.31, 18.29
    art 5(5)   2.48, 2.49,
                                        2.69–2.71, 3.83,
                                        3.85, 3.86, 15.100,
                                        16.48
    art 6   1.26, 2.60–2.61, 3.3,
        3.79, 3.85, 3.87, 3.88, 3.89, 3.97, 3.103, 4.2, 4.19, 4.24, 4.87, 6.7–6.9,
        6.11–6.14, 6.16–6.20, 6.21, 6.22, 6.34, 7.2, 7.4, 7.49, 7.50, 7.61,
        7.67–7.68, 7.70, 7.78, 8.1, 8.2, 8.22, 8.22, 8.36, 8.44, 8.50, 8.56, 8.58, 9.2,
        9.12, 9.13, 9.16, 9.19, 9.24, 9.25, 9.30, 9.32, 9.34, 9.36, 9.37, 9.43–9.45,
        9.50, 9.51, 9.58–9.60, 9.61, 9.63, 9.65, 9.68, 9.70, 9.71, 10.3, 10.6,
        10.8–10.11, 10.16, 10.17, 10.19, 10.25, 10.26, 10.28, 13.73, 13.82, 15.1,
        15.8, 15.41, 15.96, 15.97, 16.42, 16.49, 16.52, 16.53, 18.25, 18.48, 20.19,
        20.21, 20.31, 22.37, 29.6
    art 6(1)   2.55, 3.3, 3.87, 3.88,
        3.90–3.92, 3.93, 3.94, 3.95, 3.99, 3.176, 4.9, 4.24, 4.26, 4.75, 4.76, 4.77,
        6.20, 6.21, 6.32, 7.31, 7.33–7.37, 7.39, 7.40, 7.54, 7.55, 7.60, 7.76, 7.78,
        7.78, 7.79, 8.1, 8.4, 8.7, 8.9, 8.10, 8.11, 8.12, 8.13, 8.14, 8.17, 8.18, 8.51,
        9.8, 9.14, 9.26, 9.70, 11.1, 11.1, 11.3, 11.7, 11.8, 11.14, 11.15, 12.1–12.4,
        12.5, 12.6–12.13, 12.14–12.24, 12.25–12.29, 12.30–12.37, 12.38–12.42,
        12.43, 12.44, 12.45–12.47, 13.1–13.7, 13.9–13.10, 13.13–13.15, 13.18,
        13.21, 13.22, 13.24, 13.26, 13.30–13.32, 13.35, 13.36, 13.38, 13.4, 13.41,
        13.43–13.45, 13.50, 13.52, 13.54, 13.56, 13.58–13.63, 13.65–13.68,
        13.70, 13.72–13.75, 13.78, 13.81, 13.83, 14.8, 14.75, 15.96, 15.97, 16.42,
        16.50–16.53, 17.1, 17.18, 18.48, 19.47, 19.53, 19.64, 19.66–19.69, 20.29,
        22.4, 22.38–22.41, 22.43, 23.1, 23.2, 23.12, 23.13–23.22, 24.39, 24.41,
        26.22, 25.1, 28.2–28.10, 28.11, 28.13–28.14
    art 6(2)   3.87, 3.88, 7.76,
                                        7.78, 7.79, 8.42,
                                        8.44–8.45, 8.46,
                                        8.48, 8.52, 8.53, 9.1,
                                        13.2, 13.54

European Convention on Human Rights and Fundamental Freedoms 1950
continued

art 6(3)	3.3, 3.87, 3.88, 3.101, 6.20, 8.2, 8.29, 10.11, 13.2, 13.54
art 6(3)(a)	7.41, 7.42, 7.44–7.46, 10.24
art 6(3)(b)	7.54–7.56, 7.58, 7.59, 7.60, 7.62, 7.64, 7.65, 7.72, 7.74
art 6(3)(c)	3.96, 4.12, 5.2, 7.47,

7.48, 7.52, 7.53, 8.21, 8.25, 8.27, 8.30, 8.33, 8.34, 8.35, 8.36, 8.38, 9.70,
13.36, 28.22

art 6(3)(d)	8.3, 9.1, 9.4, 9.5, 9.8, 9.10, 9.14, 9.17, 9.20, 9.21, 9.26, 9.56
art 6(3)(e)	8.37–8.41
art 7	1.59, 3.34, 3.103, 3.106, 4.2, 4.35, 6.10, 6.22, 6.24–6.25, 6.26, 6.30–6.32, 6.34, 15.1, 18.48
art 7(1)	3.102, 3.104, 3.107, 6.23, 6.28, 6.29, 6.31, 6.32, 10.4
art 7(2)	3.3, 3.107, 6.29, 6.30
arts 8–12	6.24, 6.35, 10.5
arts 8–11	3.9, 3.36, 4.35, 4.56, 4.57, 4.61, 4.65, 4.66, 6.35, 13.16, 14.27, 16.53, 16.55
art 8	1.79, 2.14, 2.24,

2.65, 3.3, 3.21, 3.23, 3.31, 3.65, 3.108, 3.109–3.112, 3.113, 3.115,
3.117–3.121, 3.123, 3.126, 3.135, 3.138–3.140, 3.148–3.150, 3.166,
3.167, 3.171, 4.2, 4.3, 4.17, 4.49–4.51, 5.5, 5.7, 5.8, 5.13, 5.18, 5.19, 5.21,
5.24, 5.26–5.27, 5.31, 5.33, 5.34, 5.35, 6.36, 6.36, 7.2, 7.52, 7.76, 9.35,
9.36, 9.39, 9.41, 9.75, 11.3, 11.12, 14.10, 14.32, 14.35, 14.36,
14.61–14.63, 14.72–14.73, 14.74, 15.1, 15.6, 15.14, 15.19, 15.21–15.23,
15.25, 15.30, 15.31, 15.33, 15.36, 15.39, 15.40–15.43, 15.46, 15.87,
15.89, 15.95, 16.2, 16.51, 16.56, 16.57, 16.70, 16.71, 16.74, 16.80, 17.1,
17.24, 18.1, 18.10, 18.32, 18.35, 18.36, 18.39, 18.42, 18.43, 18.47,
19.13–19.15, 19.18, 19.20, 19.23, 19.26, 19.30, 19.35, 19.40–19.42,
19.44–19.48, 19.50, 19.51, 19.54–19.56, 19.60, 19.62, 19.64–19.66,
19.68, 20.2, 20.4, 20.10, 20.13, 21.4, 21.39, 21.48, 22.2, 22.3, 22.24,
22.30, 22.34–22.36, 22.39, 22.43, 22.45, 23.11, 24.3, 24.7, 25.9, 26.20,
27.35, 25.1, 28.38–28.42, 28.44, 29.5, 29.22, 29.22

European Convention on Human Rights and Fundamental Freedoms 1950
    continued
    art 8(1)   3.3, 3.118, 3.120,
        5.34, 14.35, 18.31, 19.1, 19.3, 19.28, 22.5, 22.6–22.12, 22.25–22.27,
        22.42, 22.44, 22.45, 28.40
    art 8(2)   3.3, 3.120, 3.121,
        3.125, 3.148, 3.170, 3.179, 4.3, 4.26, 4.29, 4.52, 4.56, 4.57, 5.34, 15.6,
        15.7, 15.31, 15.33, 15.36, 15.37, 16.53, 16.58, 16.66, 17.24, 18.31, 18.39,
        19.3, 19.8, 19.11, 19.29, 19.38, 19.48, 19.55, 19.59, 22.12, 22.13, 22.25,
        22.28, 22.42
    arts 9–11   3.127, 26.14
    art 9   3.3, 3.126, 3.130,
        3.131, 3.133–3.137, 3.138–3.140, 3.171, 4.2, 4.3, 5.12, 15.1, 15.26, 16.73,
        19.49, 21.4, 21.16, 24.3, 27.1, 27.2, 27.4–27.6, 27.8, 27.9, 27.11,
        27.13–27.16, 27.21, 27.22, 27.25, 27.27, 27.29, 27.32, 27.35–27.37, 25.1,
        28.38, 28.44, 28.45, 28.47, 28.48
    art 9(1)   3.3, 27.3, 27.4,
                                              27.8–27.10, 27.12,
                                            27.20
    art 9(2)   3.3, 3.130, 3.137,
                                              3.138, 3.148, 4.3,
                                            4.26, 4.29, 4.56,
                                            4.57, 27.12, 27.13,
                                            27.17, 27.23, 27.24
    art 10   1.53, 2.14, 2.25, 3.3,
        3.48, 3.126, 3.131, 3.135, 3.138, 3.141, 3.143, 3.144, 3.145, 3.147, 3.148,
        3.152, 3.171, 4.2, 4.3, 4.24, 4.39, 4.45, 4.47, 4.83, 5.24, 6.24, 7.76, 7.77,
        7.78, 8.17, 8.44, 10.5, 11.4, 14.72, 15.1, 15.26, 15.95, 16.2, 16.74, 16.76,
        16.78, 21.16, 24.1, 24.3, 24.4, 24.6–24.9, 24.16, 24.17, 24.22, 24.24,
        24.26, 24.28, 24.32, 24.37, 24.42–24.44, 24.46, 24.50, 25.1–25.16, 25.22,
        25.24, 27.1, 27.7, 27.28, 27.30–27.32, 25.1, 28.38, 28.50, 28.51, 28.53,
        28.54, 28.56
    art 10(1)   3.3, 3.146, 4.24,
                                              24.7, 24.11, 24.19,
                                            25.11, 27.29
    art 10(2)   3.3, 3.146, 3.147,
        3.148, 4.3, 4.22, 4.26, 4.29, 4.56, 4.57, 4.62, 7.77, 16.75, 24.11, 24.15,
        24.25, 24.28, 24.48, 24.50, 25.2, 25.11, 25.23, 27.30, 28.49, 28.53
    art 10(2)(b)   20.22
    art 11   3.3, 3.126, 3.135,
         3.138, 3.151, 3.153–3.162, 3.164, 3.165–3.167, 3.171, 4.2, 4.3, 4.18, 4.22,
        4.83, 5.5, 15.1, 15.26, 16.79, 24.3, 24.21, 25.1–25.11, 25.13, 25.14, 25.17,
        25.18, 25.20, 25.24, 25.25, 28.15, 28.25, 28.26, 28.29, 28.30, 28.31,
        28.33–28.35, 28.37, 28.39, 29.9
    art 11(1)   3.3, 25.5, 25.25, 2
                                            8.26, 28.33
    art 11(2)   3.3, 3.148, 3.152,
        3.162–3.164, 4.3, 4.26, 4.29, 4.56, 4.57, 16.53, 25.2, 25.6, 25.25, 28.25,
        28.36

European Convention on Human Rights and Fundamental Freedoms 1950
    continued

art 12   3.3, 3.115,
    3.168–3.171, 4.26, 4.54, 4.70, 15.1, 16.80, 17.1, 19.1, 19.32, 19.35–19.38,
    19.42, 19.43
art 13   1.7, 1.8, 2.41, 3.2,
    3.3, 3.83, 3.84, 3.112, 3.173, 3.174–3.182, 3.184, 4.88, 4.94, 5.4, 5.29,
    11.8–11.12, 11.14, 14.8, 14.19, 21.4, 21.46, 21.47
art 14   1.6, 2.55, 3.2, 3.3,
    3.135, 3.183, 3.184, 4.3, 4.41, 4.83, 5.36, 15.88–15.90, 16.81, 18.2, 18.10,
    18.44–18.46, 18.47, 19.46, 21.4, 21.30, 21.39, 22.48, 23.2, 23.6, 23.11,
    23.23, 27.1, 27.34, 27.35, 25.1, 28.47, 29.2, 29.3–29.10, 29.12, 29.14,
    29.15, 29.18, 29.19, 29.22–29.24
art 14(4)   20.22
art 15   1.59, 3.5, 4.81, 8.57,
                                            14.39
art 15(1)   7.9
arts 16–18   1.6
art 16   4.26, 4.83, 4.84
art 17   4.26, 4.85, 4.86,
                                            4.87, 24.48, 24.49
art 18   4.59
art 26   1.44, 30.4
art 27   30.4
art 27(2)   1.44, 30.4
arts 28, 29   30.12
art 30   30.19
arts 31–33   4.5
art 31   1.44
art 33   30.5
art 34   2.18, 2.19, 2.37,
                                            30.5, 30.7
art 35   4.88, 30.20
art 35(1)   30.25
art 37   30.36
art 38   30.15
art 39   30.37
art 40   30.14
art 41   2.43, 2.46, 2.48,
                                            2.49, 2.51, 2.58,
                                            2.68, 3.83, 3.84,
                                            3.86, 15.100, 30.17
art 43   30.19
art 44(1)   30.19
art 44(2)   30.19
art 45   30.14
art 46(1), (2)   30.45
art 47   30.44

European Convention on Human Rights and Fundamental Freedoms 1950
continued

art 47(1), (2)	30.44
art 50	2.48, 2.49, 2.54, 2.56, 2.57, 3.84
art 53	1.59, 1.71
art 57	3.5, 14.39
art 64	1.62
art 93	7.53

European Convention on Human Rights and
Fundamental Freedoms First Protocol — 4.37, 15.1, 21.6, 27.15

arts 1–3 — 1.6, 3.2

art 1 — 3.3, 3.117,
3.188–3.190, 3.191, 4.19, 4.26, 4.71, 4.72, 13.71, 16.83, 21.31, 21.32,
22.1, 22.14, 22.16–22.19, 22.21, 22.22, 22.24, 22.29, 22.33, 22.37,
23.1–23.4, 23.6–23.8, 23.9, 23.11, 26.1–26.3, 26.5–26.9, 26.11, 26.12,
26.14, 26.19, 26.21, 26.23, 29.8

arts 2–12 — 3.184, 23.23, 28.55

art 2 — 1.63, 3.3, 3.135,
3.194–3.196, 3.197, 4.26, 4.75, 4.78, 5.2, 16.84, 20.8, 21.1, 21.4–21.6,
21.9, 21.10, 21.12, 21.14, 21.15, 21.19–21.22, 21.24, 21.25, 21.26, 21.29,
21.33, 21.41–21.46, 21.48

art 3 — 3.3, 3.198–3.202,
4.26, 4.55, 4.75,
4.79, 5.2, 12.30

European Convention on Human Rights and
Fundamental Freedoms Fourth Protocol — 4.37

arts 2–4 — 18.3

art 2 — 3.25, 15.48, 25.14

European Convention on Human Rights and
Fundamental Freedoms Sixth Protocol — 3.5, 4.26, 4.37, 14.39

art 1 — 1.6, 3.2, 3.3

art 2 — 1.6, 3.3

European Convention on Human Rights and
Fundamental Freedoms Seventh Protocol — 4.37, 8.57, 8.58, 28.6

art 2 — 10.8, 10.9

art 3 — 3.85

art 4 — 8.57

European Convention on Human Rights and
Fundamental Freedoms Eighth Protocol — 30.15

European Convention on Human Rights and
Fundamental Freedoms Eleventh Protocol — 1.44, 4.37, 30.2,
30.15, 30.20, 30.37, 30.44

art 46 — 30.2

art 46(2) — 30.2

European Convention on the Status of Children Born
out of Wedlock — 4.22

European Convention on the Transfer of Sentenced
    Prisoners   16.58
European Convention on Transfrontier Television   4.22
European Extradition Convention   4.22
European Social Charter   4.18, 4.22
International Covenant on Civil and Political Rights   1.73, 4.24, 9.60
    art 14   4.24
    art 14(3)(g)   9.60
    art 19   4.24
    art 19(2)   24.46
    art 21(2)   28.6
    art 24(2)   19.58
    art 26   29.3
International Covenant on the Elimination of All Forms
    of Discrimination against Women 1979   29.1
International Covenant on the Elimination of All Forms
    of Racial Discrimination 1996   1.73, 4.24, 24.50,
    29.1
International Labour Organisation Convention
    Concerning Forced or Compulsory Labour,
    No 29 (1930)   4.25, 28.19
    art 2   28.20
International Labour Organisation Convention, No 87   4.18, 28.27
    arts 3, 5   28.27
International Labour Organisation Convention, No 98   4.18
International Labour Organisation Convention
    Concerning the Abolition of Forced Labour,
    No 105   3.17, 4.25, 28.19
Statute of the Council of Europe
    art 8   30.45
Treaty of European Union (Maastricht Treaty)
    art F2   1.82
    art F2(1)   1.82
    art L   1.83
United Nations Convention Against Torture and Other
    Cruel, Inhuman or Degrading Treatment or
    Punishment   4.24
    art 1   16.12
United Nations Convention on the Rights of the Child
    1990   1.73, 4.24, 20.27
    art 3   1.79
    arts 7, 8   19.58
    art 40(1), (3), (4)   20.27
United Nations Convention Relating to the Status of
    Refugees   4.24
United Nations Guidelines for the Prevention of Juvenile
    Delinquency (the Riyadh Guidelines)   20.28

United Nations Rules for the Protection of Juveniles
    Deprived of their Liberty   20.28
  rule 1   20.28
United Nations Standard Minimum Rules for the
    Administration of Juvenile Justice 1985 (the
    Beijing Rules)   20.23
  rule 1.4   20.23
  rule 1.6   20.23
  rule 5.1   20.24
  rule 6.1   20.24
  rule 6.2   20.24
  rule 18.1   20.25
  rule 19.1   20.25
United Nations Standard Minimum Rules for the
    Treatment of Prisoners   4.24
Universal Declaration of Human Rights
  art 16   19.42
Vienna Convention on the Law of Treaties 1969   1.26, 4.5, 4.9
  art 4   4.5
  art 31   1.26, 4.7
  art 31(1)   1.26, 4.5
  art 32   4.7
  art 32(2)   4.7

Reference note

Note on the European Convention of Human Rights, researching convention case-law and abbreviations used in this book.

The European Convention on Human Rights

The *European Convention for the Protection of Human Rights and Fundamental Freedoms*[1] ('the Convention') is an international treaty of the Council of Europe. It was adopted in 1950, ratified by the UK in 1951 and entered into force in 1953. It is set out in full in appendix B.

The Convention is divided into three sections. Section I describes and defines the rights and freedoms guaranteed under the Convention. Section II establishes the European Court of Human Rights and provides for its operation. Section III deals with miscellaneous provisions such as territorial application,[2] reservations,[3] denunciations,[4] signature and ratification.[5]

Since it was first drafted, the Convention has been amplified by a number of Protocols. One of the most important is Protocol 11, which abolished the European Commission of Human Rights ('the European Commission'). As a result, the Convention is now administered by two bodies: the European Court of Human Rights and the Committee of Ministers of the Council of Europe.

Case-law of the European Convention on Human Rights

At the international level, any individual, non-governmental organisation or group of individuals can petition the European Court of Human Rights in Strasbourg alleging a violation of Convention rights. Three judges of the European Court sitting in Committee determine whether a petition is 'admissible'. And, if so,

1 Cmnd 8969.
2 Article 56.
3 Article 57.
4 Article 58.
5 Article 59.

seven judges of the European Court sitting as a Chamber determine the merits of the petition. Cases involving a serious question affecting the interpretation of the Convention are dealt with by a Grand Chamber of eleven judges.[6] See, generally, chapter 30[7] and appendix I.[8] Under the Human Rights Act 1998, the judgments of the European Court on these issues 'must be taken into account' by any domestic court or tribunal determining a question in connection with a Convention right.[9]

Before November 1998, when it was abolished, it was the function of the European Commission of Human Rights to determine whether a petition was admissible and, if so, to give its opinion of the case on the merits. Its decisions on these issues are still of relevance to the proper interpretation of the Convention and, as with European Court judgments, 'must be taken into account' under the Human Rights Act 1998 by any domestic court or tribunal determining a question in connection with a Convention right.[10]

How the European Court and Commission of Human Rights are referenced in this book

In this book, the European Court of Human Rights is referred to either as 'the European Court' or 'the Court'. Domestic courts are referred to as 'domestic courts' and/or always appear in lower case. The European Commission on Human Rights is referred to as 'the European Commission' or 'the Commission'.

Judgments of the European Court of Human Rights

The official judgments of the European Court of Human Rights are published in English and French in an official series called the *Reports of Judgments and Decisions* or 'RJD'. Before 1996, they were published as 'Series A' and 'Series B'. Series A contained the full text of the European Court's judgments and from 1984 it also contained extracts of the European Commission's decision on the merits. Series B (which is not up-to-date) contained the pleadings, arguments and relevant documentation. References to these reports appear in human rights books, articles and literature as, for example, *Hauschildt v Denmark* (1989) Series A, No 154 or *Hauschildt v Denmark* (1989) A/154. All judgments of the European

---

6 Article 30.

7 'The Practice and Procedure of the European Court of Human Rights'.

8 'The Rules of the European Court of Human Rights'.

9 See chapter 1, 'The Human Rights Act: General Principles'.

10 Ibid.

Court have paragraph numbers.

Most (but not all) judgments of the European Court of Human Rights are also published in the *European Human Rights Reports* ('EHRR'), which are widely available in law libraries. References to these reports appear in human rights books, articles and literature as, for example, *Hauschildt v Denmark* (1989) 12 EHRR 266, denoting volume 12, page 266. These reports also contain the paragraph numbers of the official judgments.

Very recent judgments and some of those not reported in the EHRR series are available from the European Court's website which is: http://www.dhcour.coe.fr. In addition, summaries of some of the more significant European Court judgments are published in the bi-monthly *European Human Rights Law Review* ('EHRLR').

In this book, the EHRR reference is given where a judgment of the European Court is published in that series. Otherwise the Series A or RJD. reference is given, save for very recent cases where the only reference is to the date of the European Court's judgment.

Decisions of the European Commission of Human Rights

All the decisions of the European Commission of Human Rights are published by the Council of Europe. Between 1974 and 1995 most (but not all) were published in a series called the *Decisions and Reports* or 'DR' in numerical volumes. Indexes, by name, number and summaries by article and keyword, are produced at intervals for every 20 to 15 volumes. References to these reports appear in human rights books, articles and literature as, for example, *Jespers v Belgium* (1981) 27 DR 61, denoting volume 27, page 61. They are available in good law libraries or through TSO.

Summaries and extracts of some European Commission decisions are also reported in the EHRR series. In volumes 1 to 14, these appear as part of the ordinary text. From volume 15 (1993) they appear as a separate section at the end of the bound copies of the reports with the abbreviation 'EHRR CD', denoting European Human Rights Reports, Commission Decisions'. Hence, for example, *Quinn v UK* (1996) 23 EHRR CD 41.

Earlier decisions of the European Commission are available in more obscure publications such as the *Collection of Decisions* (sometimes abbreviated to 'CD'), the *Yearbook* (sometimes abbreviated to 'YB') and the *Digest of Strasbourg case-law* (sometimes abbreviated to 'Digest').

More recent decisions and some of those not reported elsewhere are available from the European Commission's website which is:

http://www.dhcomm.coe.fr. In addition, summaries of some of the more significant European Commission decisions are published in the EHRLR (see above).

In this book, the DR reference is given where a decision of the European Court is published in that series. Otherwise the next best reference is given, save for very recent cases where the only reference is to the date of the European Commission's decision.

Precedent

There is no formal doctrine of precedent binding the European Court. As a matter of general practice and practical necessity, before its abolition in 1998, the European Commission regarded the European Court's judgments as the final authority on the interpretation of the Convention.[11] The European Court, for its part, has regard to, and will usually follow, cases it has decided. However, it can depart expressly or impliedly from its previous case-law where it considers it timely or appropriate to do so.[12]

Abbreviations used in case references in this book

EHRR	European Human Rights Reports.
EHRR CD	European Human Rights Reports, section on European Commission Decisions.
DR	Decisions and Reports. Series of reported decisions of the European Commission.
EHRLR	European Human Rights Law Review. Summaries of some European Court and Commission cases from 1996 onwards.
Collection	Collection of Decisions of the European Commission between 1955 and 1974.
CD	Same as Collection.
Yearbook	Yearbook of the European Convention on Human Rights published annually, containing general information, statistics and some cases, but tends to overlap with the DR series and has no index.
YB	Same as Yearbook.
Digest	Digest of Strasbourg case-law. Published in 1982, with looseleaf supplements for decisions up to 1990 and judgments up to 1992.

11 See Reid, *A Practitioner's Guide to the European Convention on Human Rights*, Sweet & Maxwell, 1998 p43.

12 See, for example, the references to the Convention as a 'living instrument' in chapter 4.

Introduction

The Human Rights Act 1998 (HRA) marks the beginning of a new era in the quest to develop and protect human rights in the UK. For centuries the idea had prevailed that UK political and legal institutions were perfectly suited to protecting human rights and required no fundamental change; while the UK had ratified all the major international and regional human rights instruments, none were really needed. And, although domestic courts have increasingly accepted the legitimacy of referring to the European Convention on Human Rights (ECHR), there has been a clear reluctance to develop human rights jurisprudence. Research in 1996 demonstrated that, while the Convention had been referred to in 316 cases between 1975 and 1996, it had influenced the outcome in only 16.[1]

The HRA challenges the old approach. As the White Paper *Rights Brought Home: The Human Rights Bill*[2] noted:

> In this country it was long believed that the rights and freedoms guaranteed by the Convention could be delivered under our common law. In the last two decades, however, there has been a growing awareness that it is not sufficient to rely on the common law and that incorporation is necessary.[3]

In the government's view, the approach which the UK has so far adopted towards the Convention does not sufficiently reflect its importance and has not stood the test of time.[4]

The HRA therefore represents a new beginning and a fundamental shift to a rights-based system of law. Part of a

---

1   'Incorporation by the Back Door?' by Klug F and Starmer K [1996] PL 223.
2   Cm 1997 3782.
3   Ibid para 1.4.
4   Ibid para.1.15.

comprehensive programme of constitutional reform,[5] the Home Secretary has described it as 'the first major Bill on human rights for more than 300 years'.[6] Later he referred to it as 'a key component of our drive to modernise our society and refresh our democracy ... to bring about a better balance between rights and responsibilities'.[7] Its impact on all areas of law and practice will be profound.

The design of the HRA is to give the courts as much space as possible to protect human rights, short of a power to set aside Acts of Parliament.[8] Its key principles are:

1) legislation should be construed compatibly with the Convention as far as possible, but Parliamentary sovereignty should not be disturbed;

2) where the courts cannot reconcile primary legislation with Convention rights, designated courts[9] can make a declaration of incompatibility, which in effect puts Parliament on notice as to their finding;

3) Parliament can then take speedy remedial action;

4) where the courts cannot reconcile delegated legislation with Convention rights, they can disapply it or strike it down;

5) public authorities should comply with Convention rights or face the prospect of legal challenge; and

6) remedies should be available for a breach of Convention rights by a public authority.[10]

Taken together, these principles are intended to ensure a 'dialogue' between the executive, legislature and the courts on human rights protection in the UK.[11]

The model of incorporation established under the HRA thus differs from others models considered by the government – in particular the so-called Canadian, New Zealand and Hong Kong models.

---

5 The other key components of this programme include: devolution in Scotland and Wales, reform of the House of Lords, a referendum on the voting system for the House of Commons, freedom of information and an elected Mayor for London.

6 HC Debs, col 769, 16 February 1998.

7 Ibid cols 782-783.

8 Lord Chancellor, HL Debs, col 1228, 3 November 1997.

9 See para 1.33.

10 Lord Chancellor, HL Debs, col 839, 5 February 1998

11 Home Secretary, HC Debs, col 1141, 24 June 1998.

The Canadian Charter of Rights and Freedoms 1982 enables the courts to strike down any legislation which is inconsistent with the Charter, unless the legislation contains an explicit statement that it is to apply 'notwithstanding' the provisions of the Charter. But legislation which has been struck down may be re-enacted with a notwithstanding clause.

The New Zealand Bill of Rights Act 1990, on the other hand, is an 'interpretative' statute which requires past and future legislation to be interpreted consistently with the rights contained in the Act as far as possible but provides that legislation stands if that is impossible. Its provisions are not as strong as the HRA.

The Hong Kong Bill of Rights Ordinance 1991 distinguishes between legislation enacted before and after the Ordinance took effect. Previous legislation is subordinated to the provisions of the Ordinance, but subsequent legislation takes precedence over it.

The UK government also considered, but rejected, the approach adopted in the European Communities Act 1972 which provides for European Community law to take precedence over domestic law where it has 'direct effect'. The distinguishing characteristic of European Community law is that it is a requirement of membership of the European Union that member states give priority to directly effective EC law in their own legal systems. No such requirement exists under the Convention.

The preamble to the HRA describes it as an Act to 'give further effect' to Convention rights. However, this rather understates the position: as the Lord Chancellor has explained:

> We have sought to protect the rights of individuals against the abuse of power by the state, broadly defined, rather than to protect them against each other. That is the only practical difference between full incorporation of Convention rights into our domestic law and the actual effect of the [HRA]. I hope that we can put to one side ... the meaning of the word 'incorporation' and concentrate on what the [HRA] was designed to achieve, which is a real enhancement of the human rights of people in this country.[12]

In addition, the Home Secretary has frequently referred to the HRA as incorporating the Convention into UK law.[13]

Although the primary purpose of the HRA is to enable individuals to enforce their Convention rights in domestic courts, the government hopes that its impact will be much wider and, in

---

12 HL Debs, col 850, 5 February 1998.
13 See HC Debs, col 771, 16 February 1998.

particular, that it will lead to a change in culture. According to the Lord Chancellor, '[O]ur courts will develop human rights throughout society. A culture of awareness will develop.'[14] Every public authority will know that its behaviour, its structures, its conclusions and its executive actions will be subject to this culture.[15] Each will have to ask itself, 'Have we equipped ourselves to meet our legal obligations?' And that includes courts and tribunals.

Above all else, the HRA represents a new way of thinking about law, politics and the relationship between public authorities and individuals. Its potential is enormous; its effectiveness depends on the combined willingness of all of us to approach decision-making from a human rights perspective.

14   HL Debs, col 1228, 3 November 1997.
15   Home Office Minister, Lord Williams, HL Debs, col 1308, 3 November 1997.

Introduction to the Human Rights Act 1998 and the European Convention on Human Rights

CHAPTER 1

The Human Rights Act 1998: general principles

1.1   Summary

1.4   Timetable for implementation

1.6   The rights protected

1.7   The position in relation to articles 1 and 13
1.9   Use of Hansard

1.11   New legislation

1.14   Statutory interpretation: the new rule

1.20   Statutory interpretation: the European Community law and New Zealand examples

1.25   Incorporating the Convention approach to the protection of human rights into domestic law

1.27   Interpreting the Human Rights Act itself

1.29   Declarations of incompatibility

1.36   Subordinate legislation

1.39   Public authorities

1.42   Effect of the HRA on the common law

1.44   The obligation to take Strasbourg case-law into account

continued

1.48   **Case-law from other jurisdictions**

1.49   **The special position of freedom of expression and religion**

1.55   **Remedial orders**

1.59   **Derogations**

1.62   **Reservations**

1.66   **Application of the HRA in Scotland, Wales and Northern Ireland**

1.70   **Safeguards for existing human rights**

1.72   **Human Rights Commission**

1.73   **Recourse to the Convention before the HRA comes into force**

1.74   Not directly enforceable

1.75   Interpreting legislation

1.76   Common law

1.77   Judicial discretion

1.78   Heightened scrutiny

1.79   The exercise of prerogative powers

1.80   Incorporation via Community law

1.81   Ministerial guidance and public policy

1.82   **The Convention and European Community Law**

Summary

1.1   The Human Rights Act (HRA) incoporates the rights and freedoms set out in the European Convention on Human Rights into UK law.[1] The main principles of the Act can be summarised as follows:

1) All legislation (primary, subordinate and whenever enacted) must be interpreted so as to be compatible with the Convention, 'so far as it is possible to do so'.[2] This is a new rule of construction and goes far beyond the present rule which enables the courts to take the Convention into account in resolving any ambiguity in legislation. Courts should proceed on the basis that Parliament is deemed to have intended that all legislation be compatible with the Convention.

2) Where, even applying the new rule of construction, it is simply not possible to interpret legislation so as to be compatible with the Convention, the courts can strike down subordinate legislation.[3] They have no power to strike down primary legislation, but the House of Lords, Judicial Committee of the Privy Council, Court of Appeal and the High Court (and the High Court of Justiciary in Scotland) may make a 'declaration of incompatibility' – a constitutional innovation – which (in theory) should prompt government action. Such a declaration does not affect the validity, continuing operation or enforcement of the legislation in question, nor does it bind the parties to the proceedings in which it is made. However, it is intended to operate as a clear signal to Parliament that an incompatibility has been found.

3) It is unlawful for public authorities, including all courts and tribunals, to act in a way which is incompatible with the Convention. The definition of 'public authority' is in very wide terms and includes courts, tribunals and 'any person certain of whose functions are functions of a public nature'.

4) Individuals who believe that their Convention rights have been infringed by a public authority may either bring proceedings against that public authority, or rely on their Convention rights in proceedings brought by others. The remedies available for breach of Convention rights are wide and include damages.

---

1   Cmnd 8969 (1950).
2   S3(1).
3   See para 1.36 to 1.38.

1.2   The HRA does not confine Convention issues to a constitutional court. Instead, Convention rights can be called upon as they arise, in ordinary court proceedings. And, in resolving Convention issues, all courts and tribunals must take into account the case-law of the European Court of Human Rights, the European Commission of Human Rights and the Committee of Ministers established under the Convention.

1.3   The HRA is not intended to extinguish existing legal provisions safeguarding human rights in UK law. It is intended to improve upon and supplement them.[4] This is confirmed by s11 which provides that a person may rely on a Convention right without prejudice to any other right or freedom conferred on him/her and that the right to bring civil proceedings against a public authority for acting or proposing to act in a way which is incompatible with Convention rights does not affect the right to make any claim or bring any proceedings which could otherwise have been made or brought. The HRA binds the Crown and extends to Wales, Scotland and Northern Ireland.[5] Nothing in the Act creates a criminal offence.[6]

Timetable for implementation

1.4   Save for the provisions relating to the appointment of judges to the European Court of Human Rights, s20 (powers of ministers to make orders under the Act) and s21(5) (substitution of other sentences for the death penalty), the HRA comes into force on 2 October 2000. In the interim, s22(4) is important. It provides that :

> Paragraph (b) of subsection (1) of section 7 applies to proceedings brought by or at the instigation of a public authority whenever the act in question took place; but otherwise that subsection does not apply to an act taking place before the coming into force of that section.

1.5   In other words, an individual may rely on his/her Convention rights when faced with proceedings brought by a public authority, even where an alleged breach of those rights occurred before the HRA came into force. Since s7(1)(b) includes appeals from the

---

4   See the *Explanatory and Financial Memorandum*.
5   S22(6).
6   S7(7).

decisions of courts and tribunals, s22(4) may have profound implications for cases likely to be on appeal after 2 October 2000.[7]

The rights protected

1.6   The rights protected under the HRA are those set out in articles 2–12 and 14 of the Convention, articles 1–3 of the first Protocol and article 1 of the sixth Protocol as read with articles 16–18 of the Convention.[8] These rights have effect subject to any designated derogation or reservation.[9] They include the right to life (article 2), protection from torture and inhuman or degrading treatment or punishment (article 3), protection from slavery and forced or compulsory labour (article 4), the right to liberty and security of person (article 5), the right to a fair trial (article 6), protection from retrospective criminal offences (article 7), the protection of private and family life (article 8), freedom of thought, conscience and religion (article 9), freedom of expression (article 10), freedom of association and assembly (article 11), the right to marry and found a family (article 12), freedom from discrimination (article 14), the right to property (article 1 of the first Protocol), the right to education (article 2 of the first Protocol), the right to free and fair elections (article 3 of the first Protocol) and the abolition of the death penalty in peacetime (articles 1 and 2 of the sixth Protocol). An overview of these rights is provided in chapter 3.

The position in relation to articles 1 and 13

1.7   Articles 1 and 13 are not included in the schedule to the HRA. Article 1 obliges contracting states to 'secure' Convention rights to 'everyone within their jurisdiction'. And article 13 provides that anyone whose Convention rights are violated shall have an 'effective remedy' before a national authority. In *Boyle and Rice v UK*[10] the European Court confirmed the independent existence of article 13 as a substantive right, the application of which did not depend on the existence of a violation of another right or freedom in the Convention. However, for article 13 to apply the claim that another Convention right had been

---

7   *Kebeline and Others v DPP* [1999] TLR 251.
8   S1(1). And see chapter 3.
9   S1(2). And see paras 1.59 to 1.65.
10 (1988) 10 EHRR 425.

breached must be 'arguable'. Admissibility decisions by the Convention organs, whereby some claims are rejected as manifestly ill-founded,[11] are a guide to arguability but not definitive.

1.8   According to the Lord Chancellor, the HRA gives effect to article 1 by securing to people in the UK the rights and freedoms of the Convention and gives effect to article 13 by establishing a scheme under which Convention rights can be raised and remedied before UK courts.[12] These observations are important because they demonstrate that there is no objection to incorporation of articles 1 and 13 in principle – merely an assertion that they are adequately provided for in the body of the Act itself. Consequently, there is no basis for UK courts to ignore article 13. On the contrary, under s2(1), courts 'must take into account' the case-law of the European Court and Commission of Human Rights under article 13: a point conceded by the government in the House of Lords:

> ... the courts may have regard to article 13. In particular, they may wish to do so when considering the very ample provisions of [section] 8(1) [remedies].[13]

The Lord Chancellor recognised the significance of this statement by adding:

> One always has in mind *Pepper v Hart* when one is asked questions of that kind.[14]

This will be particularly important when courts are considering what relief, remedy or order should be made under s8 where a public authority has acted in a way which is incompatible with the Convention.

Use of Hansard: note

1.9   Since the decision of the House of Lords in *Pepper v Hart*,[15] Parliamentary statements by ministers may in certain circumstances be admissible in order to interpret an Act of Parliament when its meaning is ambiguous, obscure or may lead to absurdity.

1.10   References to Hansard are admissible where:

1) legislation is obscure, ambiguous or leads to an absurdity;

---

11 See chapter 30.
12 HL Debs (committee stage) col 475, 18 November 1997.
13 HL Debs col 477, 18 November 1997.
14 Ibid.
15 [1993] AC 593.

2) the material relied upon consists of one or more statements by a minister or other promoter of the Bill and such other material as is necessary to understand such statements and their effect; and

3) the statements relied upon are clear.

New legislation

1.11   For legislation passed after the HRA becomes law, s19 provides that:

19 (1) A Minister of the Crown in charge of a Bill in either House of Parliament must, before Second Reading of the Bill –

(a) make a statement to the effect that in his view the provisions of the Bill are compatible with the Convention rights ('a statement of compatibility'); or

(b) make a statement to the effect that although he is unable to make a statement of compatibility the government nevertheless wishes the House to proceed with the Bill.

(2) The statement must be in writing and be published in such manner as the Minister making it considers appropriate.

The government intends that this statement should be included alongside the Explanatory and Financial Memorandum which accompanies a Bill when it is introduced into each House of Parliament.[16]

1.12   The government hopes that this new requirement will ensure that all ministers, their departments and officials are fully seized of the gravity of the Convention's human rights obligations. To the same end, the government proposes to strengthen collective government procedures so as to ensure that a proper assessment is made of the human rights implications when collective approval is sought for a new policy.[17] Revised guidance to government departments on these procedures are to be made publicly available.[18]

1.13   This scheme obviously leaves open the possibility that Parliament will pass legislation which is incompatible with the Convention in the future. However, in such a case, the minister will be expected to explain the reasons for doing so to Parliament during the normal course of proceedings on the Bill.[19]

16 White Paper (*Rights Brought Home: The Human Rights Bill* Cm 7382, 1997) para 3.2.

17 Ibid, para 3.4.

18 Ibid.

19 White Paper, para 3.3.

Statutory interpretation: the new rule

1.14   Section 3(1) of the HRA provides that:

3   (1) So far as it is possible to do so, primary legislation and subordinate legislation must be read and given effect in a way which is compatible with the Convention rights.

(2) This section –

(a) applies to primary legislation and subordinate legislation whenever enacted;

(b) does not affect the validity, continuing operation or enforcement of any incompatible primary legislation; and

(c) does not affect the validity, continuing operation or   enforcement of any incompatible subordinate legislation if (disregarding any possibility of revocation) primary legislation prevents removal of the incompatibility.

1.15   What this means is that UK courts must strive to find a construction consistent with the intentions of Parliament and the wording of legislation which is nearest to the Convention rights.[20] Courts should proceed on the basis that Parliament is deemed to have intended its statutes to be compatible with the Convention to which the UK is bound: the only basis for courts concluding that Parliament has failed to carry that intention into effect is where it is impossible to construe a statute so as to be compatible with the Convention.[21]

1.16   The intention underlying s3(1) was expressed by the Lord Chancellor as follows:

We want the courts to strive to find an interpretation of the legislation which is consistent with Convention rights as far as the language of the legislation allows and only in the last resort to conclude that the legislation is simply incompatible with them.[22]

Courts should not 'contort the meaning of words to produce implausible or incredible meanings',[23] but it is important to note that the government rejected an attempt to amend s3 so as to impose an obligation to interpret statutory provisions in accordance with the Convention only where it is 'reasonable' to do so.[24] According to the Home Secretary:

---

20   Lord Chancellor, HL Debs (committee stage) col 535, 18 November 1997.

21   Ibid.

22   Ibid; see also the Home Secretary, HC Debs, cols 421–422, 3 June 1998.

23   Home Secretary, n22.

24   HL Debs cols 533–536, 18 November 1997.

... if we had used just the word 'reasonable' we would have created a subjective test. 'Possible' is different. It means, 'What is the possible interpretation? Let us look at this set of words and the possible interpretations.'[25]

This new rule of construction was described in the White Paper as going:[26]

... far beyond the present rule which enables the courts to take the Convention into account in resolving any ambiguity in a legislative provision. The courts will be required to interpret legislation so as to uphold the Convention rights unless legislation itself is so clearly incompatible with the Convention that it is impossible to do so.[27]

The Lord Chancellor has been equally enthusiastic about its scope,[28] and has indicated that it ought to provide 'a strong form of incorporation'.[29]

1.17   According to Lord Cooke in the Parliamentary debates '... the common law approach to statutory interpretation will never be the same again'.[30] In his view, the Act enjoins a search for possible meanings as distinct from the true meaning, so long as it is 'fairly possible' and not 'strained'.[31] Likewise, at the Committee Stage in the House of Lords, the Lord Chancellor maintained:

... The word possible is the plainest means that we can devise for simply asking the courts to find the construction consistent with the intentions of Parliament ... we want the courts to construe statutes so that they bear a meaning that is consistent with the convention whenever that is possible according to the language of the statutes but not when it is impossible to achieve that.[32]

1.18   Section 3(1) applies to past as well as to future legislation. And to the extent that it affects the meaning of a legislative provision, the courts will not be bound by previous interpretations. They will be able to build a new body of case-law, taking into account the Convention rights.[33] This has major implications for the doctrine of precedent.

---

25 HC Debs cols 421–422, 21 October 1998.

26 *Rights Brought Home: The Human Rights Bill* (Cm 3782, 1997).

27 Ibid at para 2.7.

28 *The Development of Human Rights in Britain under an Incorporated Convention on Human Rights*, [1998] Public Law 221 at p228.

29 HL Debs col 1230, 3 November 1997.

30 HL Debs col 1273, 3 November 1997.

31 HL Debs col 533, 18 November 1997.

32 HL Debs col 535, 18 November 1997.

33 White Paper, para 2.8.

For example, a Crown Court may find itself obliged to disregard previous Court of Appeal or House of Lords authority on the meaning of a statute if this is necessary in order to give effect to Convention rights.

1.19   It is also clear that, having given the courts a new interpretative tool, Parliament intends them to use it. At the third reading, the Lord Chancellor said: '... in 99% of the cases that will arise, there will be no need for judicial declarations of incompatibility.'[34] Similarly, the Home Secretary said: 'We expect that, in almost all cases, the courts will be able to interpret legislation compatibly with the Convention.'[35]

Statutory interpretation: the European Community law and New Zealand examples

1.20   Although the new rule of statutory construction under the HRA is innovative, it is not wholly unique. Courts and tribunals are obliged to interpret the provisions of domestic law so as to be compatible with European Community law, so far as it is possible to do so.[36] And the Lord Chancellor has referred to this body of law to demonstrate the strong interpretative techniques that can be expected under the HRA, citing *Litster v Forth Dry Dock and Forth Estuary Engineering*[37] as an example.[38]

1.21   In *Litster* the issue was whether protection in the Transfer of Undertakings Regulations,[39] limited, on the wording of the regulations, to those employed in a business immediately before the time of the transfer, could be extended to employees unfairly dismissed very shortly before the transfer. The applicants had clearly not been employed in the business immediately before the transfer as those words would normally be interpreted. Nor were the words ambiguous. Yet the House of Lords interpreted the regulations by implying the additional words 'or would have been so employed if they had not been unfairly dismissed' to ensure compatibility with the underlying Community obligation which the Regulations were intended to implement.

34   HL Debs col 840, 5 February 1998.
35   HC Debs col 780, 16 February 1998.
36   See, for example, *Marleasing v La Comercial Internacional de Alimentacion* [1990] ECR I-4135.
37   [1990] 1 AC 546.
38   Note 28.
39   Transfer of Undertakings (Protection of Employment) Regulations 1981.

1.22   The Lord Chancellor has therefore given the clearest possible green light to the courts to read words into legislation under the HRA to ensure compatibility with Convention rights. Such an approach would also be consistent with that adopted by the courts in New Zealand when dealing with a similar (but weaker) provision in the New Zealand Bill of Rights.

1.23   Section 6 of the New Zealand Bill of Rights requires that:

> Wherever an enactment can be given a meaning that is consistent with the rights and freedoms contained in this Bill of Rights, that meaning shall be preferred to any other meaning.

Applying this provision, the New Zealand courts have read words into legislation to achieve conformity with the Bill of Rights. For example, in *Minister of Transport v Noort*[40] the Court of Appeal held that a limited opportunity to consult a lawyer by telephone should be read into drink-driving legislation despite the absence of words to that effect.

1.24   The existing New Zealand decisions also seem to indicate that the only cases where legislation will not be interpreted consistently with the protected rights is where a statutory provision contains a clear limitation of fundamental rights:[41] courts are required to interpret as consistent with the Bill of Rights not only those provisions which are ambiguous in the sense that the language used is capable of two different meanings but also those provisions where there is no ambiguity in that sense, unless a clear limitation is expressed. Anticipating the adoption of similar principles in the UK, the Lord Chancellor has indicated that where there is no ambiguity in the sense that the *language* used is capable of two different meanings, it will be 'possible' to read legislation so as to be compatible with Convention rights unless there is a clear indication that a limitation on the protected rights was intended to make it impossible to read it compatibly.[42]

---

40 [1992] 3 NZLR 260.
41 See *R v Laugalis* (1993) 10 CRNZ; and also *Ministry of Transport v Noort* [1992] 3 NZLR 260; and *R v Rangi* [1992] 1 NZLR 385.
42 Note 28.

Incorporating the Convention approach to the protection of human rights into domestic law

1.25   The HRA introduces another important change in domestic law. Under the Act, courts will not only be required to find an interpretation of legislation which is consistent with Convention rights, but they will also be expected to apply the same techniques of interpretation as the Strasbourg bodies.[43] That is because they are under a duty to have regard to the case-law of the European Court and Commission of Human Rights when determining any question of Convention rights (see below).[44]

1.26   These techniques of interpretation are examined in detail in chapter 4. In brief, domestic courts will be expected to apply the following principles when dealing with Convention rights:

1) As an international treaty, the Convention must be interpreted according to the international law rules on the interpretation of treaties contained in the Vienna Convention on the Law of Treaties.[45] Article 31 of the Vienna Convention requires that all treaties:

> ... shall be interpreted in good faith in accordance with the ordinary meaning to be given to the terms of the treaty in their context and in light of its object and purpose'.

This rule has led the European Court to adopt a teleological approach, ie, one that seeks to realise the objects and purposes of the Convention.

2) The objects and purposes of the Convention include its role as 'an instrument for the protection of individual human beings' and the promotion of 'the ideals and values of a democratic society'.[46] And the European Court has consistently held that 'democracy' is characterised by 'pluralism, tolerance and broadmindedness'.[47]

3) The Convention is intended to guarantee rights that are practical and effective not theoretical and illusory.[48]

4) The Convention is a 'living instrument' and therefore must be

---

43   Note 28 at p228.
44   S2(1).
45   Cmnd 7964.
46   *Belgian Linguistic Case (No 1)* (1979–80) 1 EHRR 241.
47   *Handyside v UK* (1979–80) 1 EHRR 737.
48   *Artico v Italy* (1981) 3 EHRR 1.

interpreted 'in the light of present day conditions'.[49] In *Borgers v Belgium*[50] the Court noted that the evolution of the case-law of the Strasbourg institutions reflected 'the increased sensitivity of the public to the fair administration of justice'. As a general rule, the older a decision of the European Court or Commission of Human Rights, the less reliable a guide it is to the proper interpretation of Convention rights.

5) The terms of the Convention are to be given their 'ordinary meaning'.[51] The European Court is not bound by the domestic approach to the interpretation of the Convention. It can adopt an 'autonomous approach' by which it decides for itself the meaning of Convention words or concepts. So, for example, the mere fact that under domestic law a person has not been charged with an offence will not preclude the application of article 6 of the Convention.[52]

Interpreting the Human Rights Act itself

1.27   Clearly, like any other legislation, the HRA must as far as possible be read and given effect in a way which is compatible with Convention rights. In addition, its status, as a constitutional instrument in a larger package of constitutional reforms, calls for a generous interpretation of its provisions.

1.28   In *Minister for Home Affairs v Fisher*[53] the Privy Council considered the approach that should be taken to legislation which seeks to incorporate human rights into domestic law. Lord Wilberforce observed that the legislation there in question, the Bermuda constitution, was based upon international human rights instruments and had been greatly influenced by the European Convention on Human Rights. It was therefore to be given:

> a generous interpretation avoiding what has been called 'the austerity of tabulated legalism', suitable to give individuals the full measure of the fundamental rights and freedoms referred to.[54]

49   *Tyrer v UK* (1979–80) 2 EHRR 1.
50   (1991) 15 EHRR 92.
51   Vienna Convention article 31(1).
52   See *Welch v UK* (1995) 20 EHRR 247.
53   [1979] 3 All ER 21.
54   See pp23f–24ff.

A similar approach was more recently taken in *Matadeen v Pointu and Others*[55] where Lord Hoffmann explained, in the context of the protection given to human rights by the Mauritius constitution, that the moral and political values underpinning such legislation must be taken into account.[56]

Declarations of incompatibility

1.29   It is a fundamental principle of the HRA that it does not affect the validity, continuing operation or enforcement of any incompatible primary legislation, or any incompatible subordinate legislation if primary legislation prevents the removal of the incompatibility. This reflects the priority afforded to parliamentary sovereignty by the government. In its view, the authority that Parliament derives from its democratic mandate, means that it must remain competent to make any law on any matter of its choosing. To enable courts to set aside Acts of Parliament would be likely to 'draw the judiciary into serious conflict with Parliament'.[57] And on many occasions in the last 20 years the judiciary has emphasised that it does not want the power to strike down legislation: a point reiterated by Lord Bingham in the House of Lords debate on the HRA.[58]

1.30   Where a designated court[59] is satisfied that a provision of primary legislation is incompatible with Convention rights, or that a provision of subordinate legislation is incompatible with the Convention and the primary legislation under which it was made prevents the removal of that incompatibility, it has power under the HRA to make a 'declaration of incompatibility'.[60] Section 4 provides that:

4   (1) Subsection (2) applies in any proceedings in which a court determines whether a provision of primary legislation is compatible with a Convention right.
(2) If the court is satisfied that the provision is incompatible with a Convention right, it may make a declaration of that incompatibility.
(3) Subsection (4) applies in any proceedings in which a court deter-

55   [1998] 3 WLR 18.
56   See also *AG Gambia v Momodou Jobe* [1984] AC 689; *Ag Hong Kong v Lee Kwong-Kut* [1993] AC 951; and *Vasquez v Queen* [1994] 1 WLR 1304.
57   White Paper, para 2.13.
58   HL Debs col 1246, 3 November 1997.
59   S4(5).
60   S4.

mines whether a provision of subordinate legislation, made in the exercise of a power conferred by primary legislation, is compatible with a Convention right.

(4) If the court is satisfied –
  (a) that the provision is incompatible with a Convention right, and
  (b) that (disregarding any possibility of revocation) the primary legislation concerned prevents removal of the incompatibility, it may make a declaration of that incompatibility.

Such a declaration does not affect the validity, continuing operation or enforcement of the provision in respect of which it is made.[61] Nor does it bind the parties to the proceedings in which it is made.[62] However, it is intended to operate as a clear signal to Parliament that an incompatibility has been found.

1.31   The government envisages that a declaration of incompatibility will 'almost certainly' prompt legislative change.[63] A point emphasised by the Lord Chancellor in the House of Lords debate on the Act.[64] The HRA therefore provides a 'fast-track' procedure for amending the law so as to bring it into conformity with the Convention.[65]

1.32   Like all remedies under the Act, a s4 declaration of incompatibility is a discretionary remedy. However, it is the government's intention that courts should generally make declarations of incompatibility when they find an Act to be incompatible with the Convention.[66] The only examples given by the Lord Chancellor where a declaration might *not* be made were where there may be an alternative statutory appeal route which the court thinks ought to be followed or where there is another procedure which courts think an applicant should exhaust before a declaration is granted.[67]

1.33   Designated courts under the HRA – with power to make a declaration of incompatibility – are the House of Lords, the Court of Appeal, the High Court, the Judicial Committee of the Privy Council, the Courts-Martial Appeal Court and, in Scotland, the High Court of Justiciary (sitting otherwise than as a trial court) or the Court of Session.[68] Unfortunately, there is no (formal) procedure by which any other court can alert Parliament to problems of compatibility.

61 S4(6)(a).
62 S4(6)(b).
63 White Paper, para 2.9.
64 HL Debs col 1230, 3 November 1997.
65 See paras 1.55 to 1.58.
66 Lord Chancellor, HL Debs (committee stage) col 546, 18 November 1997.
67 Ibid.
68 S4(5).

1.34   If a court is considering whether or not to make a declaration of incompatibility the Crown has a right to be notified.[69] A minister or person nominated by a minister is then entitled to be joined as a party to the proceedings[70] and, in criminal proceedings, may appeal (with leave) to the House of Lords against any declaration of incompatibility.[71]

1.35   An amendment to ensure that the courts are not inhibited from making a declaration of incompatibility when a case before them turns on the *absence* of legislation – rather than on a specific *provision* of legislation – was rejected by the government during the passage of the HRA through the House of Lords. According to the Lord Chancellor, if individuals believe that their Convention rights have been violated as a result of action by a public authority which is not governed by legislation, the right course is for them to bring legal proceedings against the authority under HRA s7 or to rely on their Convention rights in other legal proceedings to which they and the authority are party. If the court finds in their favour it will be able to grant whatever remedy is within its jurisdiction and appears just and appropriate. The fact that there is no specific legislation for the court to declare incompatible with the Convention does not affect the ability of the person concerned to obtain a remedy. The absence of legislation entails that there is no legislative warrant for acts in breach of the Convention by the public authority.[72] Therefore, there is nothing to stop the courts providing a remedy in such cases.[73]

Subordinate legislation

1.36   Like primary legislation, subordinate legislation[74] must also be read and given effect in a way which is compatible with Convention rights as far as possible.[75] The major difference is that, unlike primary legislation, delegated legislation can be struck down (or simply disapplied) where it is impossible to interpret it so as to be compatible with Convention rights. This is a radical extension of the ultra vires

69   S5(1).
70   S5(2).
71   S5(4).
72   HL Debs (committee stage) col 814, 24 November 1997.
73   Lord Chancellor, HL Debs (committee stage) col 815, 24 November 1997.
74   Defined in HRA s21(1).
75   S3(1).

principle. The only exception is where primary legislation prevents removal of the incompatibility.[76]

1.37　In effect, therefore, subordinate legislation can be challenged in two ways:

1) A direct challenge can be made on the basis that the minister or other responsible body acted unlawfully in making subordinate legislation which is incompatible with Convention rights: the s7(1)(a) route.[77]

2) Alternatively, an indirect challenge can be made in legal proceedings brought by others: the s7(1)(b) route.

See further, chapter 2.

1.38　Where a provision in subordinate legislation is found to be incompatible with Convention rights, the question of severance may arise. Under the present rule, severance of the offending provision is permitted so long as its removal will not result in subordinate legislation that is so different to that originally made that it cannot be assumed that, in such a form, it would ever have been made.[78] The HRA may require this role to be broadened.

Public authorities

1.39　Section 6 of the HRA makes it unlawful for a public authority to act in a way which is incompatible with Convention rights, unless it is required to do so to give effect to primary legislation.[79] In this context, 'act' includes a failure to act;[80] but does not include a failure to legislate or make remedial orders.[81]

1.40　The Act does not define 'public authority'. Section 6(3) expressly includes courts and tribunals[82] and 'any person certain of whose functions are functions of a public nature'[83] and expressly excludes both Houses of Parliament[84] and any person exercising functions in

76 S3(2)(c).
77 See Lord Chancellor, HL Debs col 543, 18 November 1997.
78 *DPP v Hutchinson* [1990] 2 AC 783.
79 See para 2.2.
80 S6(6).
81 See paras 2.2 to 2.6.
82 S6(3)(a).
83 S6(3)(b).
84 But not the House of Lords in its judicial capacity: see s6(4).

connection with proceedings in Parliament. Section 6(5) then provides that in relation to a particular act, 'any person certain of whose functions are functions of a public nature' is not a public authority if the nature of the act in question is private.

1.41 Section 7 complements s6 by providing that anyone who claims that a public authority has acted (or proposes to act) in a way which is incompatible with Convention rights can either bring proceedings against that authority (s7(1)(a)) or rely on Convention rights in any 'legal proceedings' brought by others but only if s/he is (or would be) a 'victim' within the meaning of s7(7). The definition of 'public authority', 'victim' and the operation of s7 are examined in detail in chapter 2.

Effect of the HRA on the common law

1.42 As noted above, courts and tribunals are included within the definition of a 'public authority' under the Act. It follows that they will be acting unlawfully if they fail to develop the law – both statute law and the common law – in a way which is compatible with Convention rights, even where litigation is taking place between private individuals.

1.43 The Lord Chancellor recognised this in debate during the Bill's passage through the House of Lords when he rejected an amendment to exclude courts and tribunals from the definition:

> We also believe that it is right as a matter of principle for the courts to have the duty of acting compatibly with the Convention not only in cases involving other public authorities but also in developing the common law in deciding cases between individuals. Why should they not? In preparing this Bill, we have taken the view that it is the other course, that of excluding Convention considerations altogether from cases between individuals which would have to be justified. The courts already bring Convention considerations to bear and I have no doubt that they will continue to do so in developing the common law ... [section] 3 requires the courts to interpret legislation compatibly with the Convention rights and to the fullest extent possible in all cases coming before them.[85]

In other words, legislation must be read and given effect in a way which is compatible with Convention rights whoever is before the courts *and* the common law must be developed so as to be compatible

85   HL Debs col 783, 24 November 1997.

with the Convention. Notably, the HRA does not protect the common law from the effects of the Convention in the same way as it does primary legislation.

The obligation to take Strasbourg case-law into account

1.44   The HRA does not make decisions of the European Court and Commission of Human Rights binding in domestic law. But it does include a strong provision in relation to the interpretation of Convention rights. Section 2(1) requires that any court or tribunal determining a question in connection with a Convention right 'must take into account':

1) judgments, decisions, declarations and advisory opinions of the European Court of Human Rights;

2) decisions of the European Commission on Human Rights under what were[86] articles 31 (opinion on the merits), 26 (exhaustion of domestic remedies) or 27(2) (admissibility); and

3) decisions of the Committee of Ministers of the Council of Europe whenever made or given, so far as, in the opinion of the court or tribunal, they are relevant to the proceedings in which that question has arisen.[87] What that means is that, where relevant, domestic courts should apply Convention jurisprudence and its principles to the cases before them.[88] According to the Lord Chancellor:

> ... [s2] requires courts in the United Kingdom to take account of the decisions of the Convention institutions in Strasbourg in their consideration of Convention points which come before them. It is entirely appropriate that our courts should draw on the wealth of existing jurisprudence on the Convention.[89]

There is nothing in the Act itself to suggest that the requirement in s2(1) is limited to judgments, decisions or opinions relating to the UK. And, at the Committee Stage, the Lord Chancellor made it

---

86 The Convention was fundamentally amended on 11 November 1998 when Protocol No11 came into force. See paras 30.1 to 30.5.

87 S2(1).

88 Lord Chancellor, HL Debs col 515, 18 November 1997.

89 HL Debs col 1230, 3 November 1997.

clear that s2 was intended to require courts to take account of Strasbourg decisions regardless of the identity of the respondent state.[90]

1.45   The circumstances in which domestic courts might depart from existing Strasbourg decisions are not clear. At the committee stage, the Lord Chancellor said:

> The Bill would of course permit United Kingdom courts to depart from existing Strasbourg decisions and upon occasion it might well be appropriate to do so and it is possible that they might give a successful lead to Strasbourg. For example, it would permit the United Kingdom courts to depart from Strasbourg decisions where there has been no precise ruling on the matter and Commission opinion which does so has not taken into account subsequent Strasbourg case-law.[91]

At the report stage, he added:

> These may also be occasions when it would be right for the United Kingdom courts to depart from Strasbourg decisions. We must remember that the interpretation of the Convention rights develops over the years. Circumstances may therefore arise in which a judgment given by the European Court of Human Rights decades ago contains pronouncements which it would not be appropriate to apply to the letter in the circumstances of today in a particular set of circumstances affecting this country. The [HRA] would allow our courts to use their common sense in applying the European Court's judgment to such a case.[92]

1.46   Clearly, therefore, insofar as domestic courts seek to reconcile inconsistent Strasbourg case-law and/or plug the gaps in Strasbourg jurisprudence, they will be on safe ground, assuming they do so according to the most recently articulated principles of the European Court. In this context it is important to recall that the Convention represents a floor not a ceiling for the protection of human rights.[93] However, any court which simply ignores or declines to follow clear Strasbourg case-law, and thereby restricts Convention rights, runs the obvious risk of appeal and, ultimately, challenge in Strasbourg.

---

90   HL Debs (committee stage) col 513, 18 November 1997.
91   HL Debs (committee stage) col 514, 18 November 1997.
92   HL Debs col 1270, 19 January 1998.
93   Lord Chancellor, HL Debs col 510, 18 November 1997.

1.47   When the case-law of the European Court and Commission is cited under HRA s2, the following points should be borne in mind when assessing the weight to be given to it:[94]

1) The age of the decision. In general, the older a decision is, the less reliable a guide it is to a contemporary construction of Convention rights. The Convention is to be treated as a living instrument.[95]

2) A judgment of the European Court has more authority than a decision of the European Commission, particularly a decision on admissibility. Similarly, a decision of a Chamber of the European Court has more authority than a decision of the Committee of the Court.

3) Caution is needed where the European Court or Commission relied on the 'margin of appreciation' doctrine in concluding that there was no violation of the Convention because the doctrine has no direct application in domestic law.[96]

Case-law from other jurisdictions

1.48   The Convention has been incorporated into the law of other European states for many years. Consequently, there are numerous decisions of their national courts interpreting the Convention. In addition, comparable human rights provisions have been construed and interpreted in common-law jurisdictions such as New Zealand, Canada and India for many years and in the voluminous case-law of the US Supreme Court. These sources are therefore invaluable as a guide to the interpretation of Convention rights, particularly in areas where the European Court has not yet given any, or any definitive, ruling.

94 See Bratza N, Duffy P, *The European Convention on Human Rights in Practitioners' Handbook of EC Law 1998* pp632–633. Judge Bratza QC is a judge of the European Court of Human Rights.
95 See paras 4.16 to 4.18.
96 See paras 4.94 to 4.96.

The special position of freedom of expression and religion

1.49　Sections 12 and 13 of the HRA make special provision for freedom of expression and religion. They were added as late amendments to the Act.

1.50　Section 12 applies in any case where the grant of any remedy or order by a court or tribunal might affect the exercise of the Convention right to freedom of expression. It is not limited to cases where freedom of expression is the only, or the main, issue. But it does not apply in criminal proceedings.

1.51　It prohibits ex parte relief unless the court is satisfied that:

1) the applicant has taken all practicable steps to notify the respondent; or

2) there are compelling reasons why the respondent should not be notified.[97]

According to the Home Secretary, this is intended to ensure that ex parte injunctions are granted 'only in exceptional circumstances'.[98]

1.52　Section 12 also limits the scope for pre-trial injunctions, which can be granted only if the court is satisfied that 'the applicant is likely to establish that publication should not be allowed'.[99] Again, according to the Home Secretary, this is intended to ensure that:

> ... no relief is granted to restrain publication pending a full trial of the issues unless the court is satisfied that the applicant is likely to succeed at trial ... we believe that the courts should consider the merits of an application when it is made and should not grant an interim injunction simply to preserve the status quo ante between the parties ... [100]

In all such cases, the court must have regard to the importance of the Convention right to freedom of expression. And where proceedings relate to material which the respondent claims, or which appears to the court, to be journalistic, literary or artistic material (or to conduct connected with such material) the court must have regard to:

1) the extent to which the material has, or is about to, become available to the public; or the extent to which it is, or would be, in the public interest for the material to be published; and

97 S12(2).
98 HC Debs cols 356, 538 and 539, 2 July 1998.
99 S12(3).
100 Note 98.

2) any relevant privacy code.[101]

The Act does not define 'the public interest' but the Home Secretary indicated that the Strasbourg case-law on this issue would be relevant.[102]

1.53   Article 10 does not, however, take precedence over article 8 either under the Convention or under the HRA. So far as the latter is concerned, an amendment to that effect was rejected by the government.[103]

1.54   Section 13 is less specific. It simply requires that any court or tribunal determining any question arising under the HRA which *might* affect the exercise by a religious organisation (itself or its members collectively) of the Convention right of freedom of thought, conscience and religion must have 'particular regard to the importance of that right'. It is intended to 'reassure' churches and other religious organisations that the Act will not be used to 'intrude upon genuinely religious beliefs or practices'.[104]

Remedial orders

1.55   Section 10 of the HRA provides for the making of remedial orders in respect of legislation which has been declared incompatible with the Convention or which, in view of a finding of the European Court, appears to a minister to be incompatible, so as to remove the incompatibility or possible incompatibility. Remedial orders are statutory instruments,[105] which amend legislation so as to remove any incompatibility with Convention rights. They are to be used only 'to protect human rights, not to infringe them'.[106]

1.56   According to the Lord Chancellor, faced with a declaration of incompatibility Parliament 'generally will' legislate.[107] Where post-HRA legislation has been declared compatible with the Convention during its passage through Parliament, the Lord Chancellor has predicted that:

101 For example, the codes published by Press Complaints Commission, the Broadcasting Standards Commission, the Independent Television Commission and the BBC.

102 HC Debs cols 539–540, 2 July 1998.

103 HC Debs cols 542–543, 2 July 1998.

104 Home Secretary, HC Debs cols 1020–1021, 20 May 1998.

105 S20(1).

106 Lord Chancellor, HL Debs col 1231, 3 November 1997.

107 HL Debs col 1229, 3 November 1997.

> If a Minister's prior assessment of compatibility ... is subsequently found by a declaration of incompatibility by the courts to have been mistaken, it is hard to see how a Minister could withhold remedial action.[108]

And, so far as decisions of the European Court are the trigger for remedial orders, there is no requirement that they involve the UK.

1.57   The rules governing remedial orders are set out in HRA Sch 2. Para 1 provides that:

1   (1) A remedial order may –
    (a) contain such incidental, supplemental, consequential or transitional provision as the person making it considers appropriate;
    (b) be made so as to have effect from a date earlier than that on which it is made;
    (c) make provision for the delegation of specific functions;
    (d) make different provision for different cases.
    (2) The power conferred by sub-paragraph (1)(a) includes –
    (a) power to amend primary legislation (including primary legislation other than that which contains the incompatible provision); and
    (b) power to amend or revoke subordinate legislation (including subordinate legislation other than that which contains the incompatible provision).
    (3) A remedial order may be made so as to have the same extent as the legislation which it affects.
    (4) No person is to be guilty of an offence solely as a result of the retrospective effect of a remedial order.

Clearly, therefore, a remedial order may have retrospective effect,[109] but may not create retrospective criminal liability.[110]

1.58   There are two procedures for making a remedial order: a standard procedure[111] and an emergency procedure.[112] These are set out in HRA Sch 2 paras 2, 3 and 4.[113]

108 Ibid.
109 Para 1(1)(b) .
110 Para 1(4).
111 Sch 2 para 2(a).
112 Sch 2 para 2(b).
113 See appendix A.

Derogations

1.59 Article 15 of the Convention provides that:

(1) In time of war or other public emergency threatening the life of the nation any High Contracting Party may take measures derogating from its obligations under this Convention to the extent strictly required by the exigencies of the situation, provided that such measures are not inconsistent with its obligations under international law.

(2) No derogation from article 2,[114] except in respect of deaths resulting from lawful acts of war, or from articles 3,[115] 4 (paragraph 1)[116] and 7[117] shall be made under this provision.

No derogation is, however, permitted if it would breach other international law obligations.[118]

1.60 The UK has one derogation in place[119] concerning pre-trial detention under prevention of terrorism legislation. The terms of this derogation are set out in HRA Sch 3 Pt I.

1.61 Under the Act, this derogation will have effect in domestic law because Convention rights are subject to designated derogations.[120] If a designated derogation is amended or replaced, it ceases to be a designated derogation.[121] Future derogations become designated derogations by means of an order laid before Parliament. If any such order is not approved by a resolution passed by each House within 40 days, it ceases to have effect, save that it is capable of interim effect.[122] Designated derogations cease to have effect after five years, unless renewed.[123]

---

114 The right to life.

115 The prohibition on torture, inhuman and degrading treatment and punishment.

116 The prohibition on slavery.

117 The prohibition on retrospective application of the criminal law.

118 See article 53 of the Convention.

119 Arising from the case of *Brogan v UK* (1989) 11 EHRR 117 and deemed valid in *Brannigan v UK* (1994) 17 EHRR 539

120 S1(2).

121 S14(3).

122 S14(4)(a) and s16(3) and (4).

123 S16(1) and (2).

Reservations

1.62   Article 64 of the Convention allows a state to enter a reservation when it ratifies the Convention if any law in force in that state is not in conformity with a Convention provision.

1.63   The UK has entered a reservation in respect of article 2 of the First Protocol to the Convention (the right to education) in the following terms:

> ... in view of certain provisions of the Education Acts in the United Kingdom, the principle affirmed in the second sentence of article 2 is accepted by the United Kingdom only in so far as it is compatible with the provision of efficient instruction and training, and the avoidance of unreasonable public expenditure.[124]

Whether this reservation will withstand challenge in Strasbourg is not clear.

1.64   In *SP v UK*,[125] which involved the schooling arrangements of a dyslexic child, the European Commission took the view that in light of developments in the case-law of the Convention,[126] questions may arise as to whether the reservation is valid and, if valid, whether it is applicable to law which entered into force subsequent to the making of the reservation.[127] However, on the facts of that case, it did not need to resolve the issue.

1.65   Under the HRA this reservation and any future reservations designated by an order made by the Secretary of State have effect in domestic law. Like designated derogations they are subject to periodic review, but, unlike designated derogations, they are not subject to the requirement of periodic renewal.

Application of the HRA in Scotland, Wales and Northern Ireland

1.66   The HRA extends to Scotland, Wales and Northern Ireland. In Scotland, the position with regard to Acts of the Westminster Parliament will be the same as in England and Wales. All courts will be required to interpret the legislation in a way which is compatible

---

124 See HRA Sch 3 Part II.
125 Appl 28915/95 (1997) 23 EHRR CD 139.
126 See *Belilos v Switzerland* (1988) 10 EHRR 466, paras 52–59.
127 See *Fischer v Austria* (1995) 20 EHRR 349.

with the Convention as far as possible. If a provision is found to be incompatible, the Court of Session (sitting otherwise than as a trial court) or the High Court will be able to make a declaration to that effect, but this will not affect the validity or continuing operation of the provision.

1.67 The position is different, however, in relation to Acts of the Scottish Parliament. The Scottish Parliament has no power to legislate in a way which is incompatible with the Convention. It is, therefore, possible to challenge such legislation and actions in the Scottish courts on the ground that the Scottish Parliament or Executive has incorrectly applied its powers.

1.68 Similarly, the Welsh Assembly has no power to make subordinate legislation or to take executive action which is incompatible with the Convention. And, again, it is possible to challenge such legislation and action in the courts on the ground that the Assembly has exceeded its powers.

1.69 In Northern Ireland, as in Scotland, the position with regard to Acts of the Westminster Parliament will be the same as in England and Wales. In addition, Orders in Council made under Northern Ireland Constitution Act 1973 s38(1)(a) or the corresponding provisions of the Northern Ireland Act 1998 are included in the definition of 'primary legislation' under the Act[128] and, therefore, immune from challenge. However, Acts of the Parliament of Northern Ireland, Measures of the Assembly established under Northern Ireland Assembly Act 1973 s1 and Acts of the Northern Ireland Assembly are all included in the definition of 'subordinate legislation' under the HRA[129] and can be challenged in the courts insofar as they are incompatible with Convention rights.

Safeguards for existing human rights

1.70 Section 11 of the HRA safeguards existing human rights by providing that:

> A person's reliance on a Convention right does not restrict –
> (a) any other right or freedom conferred on him by or under any law having effect in any part of the United Kingdom; or
> (b) his right to make any claim or bring any proceedings which he could make or bring apart from sections 7 to 9.

128 S21(1).
129 Ibid.

This is an important provision in a number of respects. Its purpose was clarified in debate in the House of Lords by the Lord Chancellor:

> Convention rights are, as it were, a floor of rights; and if there are different or superior rights or freedoms conferred by or under any law having effect in the United Kingdom, this is a Bill which only gives and does not take away.[130]

The HRA cannot, therefore, be used to read down or restrict human rights insofar as they are already recognised in domestic law. This may be important in the context of public interest litigation.[131] It also complements article 53 of the Convention itself, which provides that:

> Nothing in this Convention shall be construed as limiting or derogating from any of the human rights and fundamental freedoms which may be ensured under the laws of any High Contracting Party or under any other agreement to which it is a Party.

In addition, s11 makes it clear that individuals can continue to rely on human rights instruments other than the Convention in domestic proceedings to the extent permitted under common law.[132] These instruments will therefore be relevant to the interpretation of the Convention and the HRA[133] and be important in their own right. Finally, s11 may be relevant to questions such as aggravated and exemplary damages under the HRA.[134]

Human Rights Commission

1.72   No provision has been made for a Human Rights Commission. The government claims not have closed its mind to such a body at some stage in the future,[135] but wants to consider more closely how any such body would work with existing bodies such as the Commission for Racial Equality, the Equal Opportunities Commission and the newly created Disability Rights Commission. In the meantime, the Government has proposed a Parliamentary Committee on Human Rights.[136]

130 HL Debs col 510, 18 November 1997.
131 See paras 2.20 to 2.23.
132 See paras 4.21 to 4.25.
133 See para 4.21.
134 See paras 2.29 to 2.31
135 White Paper, para 3.11.
136 White Paper, para 3.6.

Recourse to the Convention before the HRA comes into force

1.73 Before the HRA comes into force, the existing rules governing recourse to the Convention in domestic law will prevail. These rules will also continue to apply to other international human rights instruments ratified by the UK, including the *International Covenant on Civil and Political Rights*, the *International Convention on the Elimination of All Forms of Racial Discrimination*, the *Convention on the Elimination of All Forms of Discrimination against Women*, the *Convention on the Rights of the Child* and the various ILO Conventions.[137] They can be summarised as follows (paras 1.74 to 1.82):

Not directly enforceable

1.74 Like any other treaty obligations which have not been embodied in domestic law by statute, the Convention and other human rights instruments are not part of domestic law. Therefore the courts have no power to enforce Convention rights directly. If domestic law conflicts with the Convention the courts must enforce the domestic law (*R v Secretary of State for the Home Department ex p Brind*;[138] *R v Secretary of State for the Environment and Secretary of State for Wales ex p NALGO*[139]). With this limitation, however, the Convention and other human rights instruments can be relevant in a variety of circumstances.

Interpreting legislation

1.75 They may be deployed for the purpose of resolving an ambiguity in primary or subordinate legislation (for the general principle, see *Garland v British Rail Engineering*[140]).

---

135 White Paper, para 3.11.
136 White Paper, para 3.6.
137 These instruments will also be directly relevant under the HRA itself: see chapter 4.
138 [1991] 1 AC 969.
139 (1992) 5 Admin LR 785.
140 [1982] 1 QB 770.

In *ex p Brind*, Lord Bridge held that:

> ... it is already well settled that, in construing any provision in domestic legislation which is ambiguous in the sense that it is capable of a meaning which either conforms to or conflicts with the Convention, the courts will presume that Parliament intended to legislate in conformity with the Convention, not in conflict with it. (747H–748A).

Particular weight will be attached to the Convention where the court is considering legislation which has been enacted to comply with Convention obligations (*R v Secretary of State for the Home Department ex p Norney*[141]).

Common law

1.76   The Convention and other human rights instruments can be used where the common law is developing and uncertain or where it is certain but incomplete; the Convention also reflects certain co-extensive rights already recognised in the common law.

This principle was first stated in *Derbyshire CC v Times Newspapers Ltd*[142] where Butler-Sloss LJ held that:

> ... where the law is clear and unambiguous, either stated as the common law or enacted by Parliament, recourse to article 10 is unnecessary and in appropriate. ... But where there is ambiguity, or the law is otherwise unclear or so far undeclared by an appellate court, the English court is not only entitled but, in my judgment obliged to consider the implications of article 10. (830 B-C)

It was affirmed by the House of Lords in *DPP v Jones and Lloyd*[143] where the Lord Chancellor said:

> If, contrary to my judgment, the common law of trespass is not as clear as I have held it to be, then at least it is uncertain and developing, so that regard should be had to the Convention in resolving the uncertainty and in determining how it should develop.

---

141 (1995) 7 Admin LR 861.
142 [1992] QB 770.
143 [1999] 2 All ER 257.

Judicial discretion

1.77　The Convention and other human rights instruments may also be used when a court is considering how to exercise a judicial discretion (see *Attorney-General v Guardian Newspapers*;[144] *Rantzen v Mirror Group Newspapers*[145].

This use of the Convention is particularly important in criminal cases. In *R v Khan (Sultan)*,[146] the House of Lords held that a trial judge may have regard to the Convention as a material consideration in exercising the discretion conferred by Police and Criminal Evidence Act 1984 s78 to admit or exclude evidence.

Heightened scrutiny

1.78　Although it is not necessary for a decision-maker exercising an administrative discretion conferred by statute to exercise that discretion in accordance with the Convention or other human rights instruments (*ex p Brind*), where fundamental rights or freedoms are at stake (including Convention rights), domestic courts will require a stricter justification of the exercise of public powers than would satisfy the *Wednesbury* perversity test.[147] In *R v Ministry of Defence ex p Smith*,[148] Sir Thomas Bingham accepted as an accurate distillation of the principles laid down by the House of Lords in *R v Secretary of State for the Home Department ex p Bugdaycay*[149] and *ex p Brind* the submission that:

> The court may not interfere with the exercise of an administrative discretion on substantive grounds save where the court is satisfied that the decision is unreasonable in the sense that it is beyond the range of responses open to a reasonable decision-maker. But in judging whether the decision-maker has exceeded this margin of appreciation the human rights context is important. The more substantial the interference with human rights, the more the court will require by way of justification before it is satisfied that the decision is reasonable in the sense outlined above.[150]

144 [1987] 1 WLR 1248.
145 [1994] QB 670.
146 [1996] 3 WLR 162.
147 *Associated Provincial Picture Houses Ltd v Wednesbury Corporation* [1948] 1 KB 223.
148 [1996] 1 All ER 257.
149 [1987] AC 514.
150 At p263d.

See also *Sedley J* in *R v Secretary of State for the Home Department ex p McQuillan:*[151]

> Once it is accepted that the standards articulated in the European Convention are standards which both march with those of the common law and inform the jurisprudence of the European Union, it becomes unreal and potentially unjust to continue to develop English public law without reference to them.[152]

The excercise of prerogative powers

1.79   Ratification of the Convention and other human rights instruments may give rise to an expectation that the executive will act in accordance with its obligations insofar as it exercises prerogative powers.

In *R v Secretary of State for the Home Department ex p Ahmed, Patel and Others*,[153] Lord Woolf MR quoted with approval the following passage of the judgment of Mason CJ and Deane J in the High Court of Australia in *Minister of State for Immigration and Ethnic Affairs v Teoh*,[154] which concerned article 3 of the UN Convention on the Rights of the Child:

> ... ratification by Australia of an international convention is not to be dismissed as a merely platitudinous or ineffectual act, particularly when the instrument evidences internationally accepted standards to be applied by courts and administrative authorities in dealing with basic human rights affecting the family and children. Rather, ratification of the convention is a positive statement by the executive government to this country to the world and to the Australian people that the executive government and its agencies will act in accordance with the convention. That positive statement is an adequate foundation for a legitimate expectation, absent statutory or executive indications to the contrary, that administrative decision-makers will act in conformity with the convention ...

Adopting this approach, Lord Woolf accepted in the context of article 8 of the European Convention of Human Rights that:

> ... the entering into a treaty by the Secretary of State could give rise to a legitimate expectation on which the public in general are entitled to rely. Subject to any indication to the contrary, it could be a representation that the Secretary of State would act in accordance

---

151 [1995] 4 All ER 400.
152 At p422.
153 30 July 1998, QBCOF 98/0650/4, *The Times* 15 October 1998.
154 [1995] 183 CLR 273.

with any obligations which he accepted under the treaty. This legitimate expectation could give rise to a right to relief, as well as additional obligations of fairness, if the Secretary of State, without reason, acted inconsistently with the obligations which this country had undertaken.[155]

See also Hobhouse LJ at § 42E–F.

Incorporation via Community law

1.80   The Convention may be incorporated into domestic law via Community law (*Elliniki Radiophonia Tileorassi;*[156] see also *R v Secretary of State for Employment ex p EOC*[157]).

Ministerial guidance and public policy

1.81   Finally, recourse to the Convention and other human rights instruments is permissible where they are referred to (albeit not incorporated) in ministerial guidance (*Jordan Abiodun Iye;*[158] it is also a relevant source of public policy (*Blathwayt v Cawley*[159]).

The Convention and European Community Law

1.82   There is some scope for enforcing Convention rights through European Community Law. Article F2 of the Maastricht Treaty on the European Union establishes a clear commitment to Convention rights by providing that:

> The Union shall respect fundamental rights, as guaranteed by the European Convention for the Protection of Human Rights and Fundamental Freedoms signed in Rome on 4 November 1950 and as they result from the constitutional traditions common to the Member States, as general principles of Community law.

In addition, article F2(1) includes a commitment by states to exercise powers relating to asylum and immigration in conformity with the European Convention on Human Rights.

---

155 At pp23F-24A.
156 [1991] ECR-I 2925.
157 [1995] AC 1.
158 [1994] Imm AR 287.
159 [1976] AC 397 at p425H-426A.

1.83   Although these commitments are non-justiciable in themselves,[160] they add considerable weight to the relevance of the Convention in the interpretation of European Community legislation[161] and to its significance in reviewing administrative and legislative measures at both the domestic[162] and the European level.[163] In *Kremzow v Austria*[164] the European Court of Justice observed that:

> As the Court has consistently held, fundamental rights form an integral part of the general principles of Community law whose observance the Court ensures. For that purpose, the Court draws inspiration from the constitutional traditions common to the Member States and from the guidelines supplied by international treaties for the protection of human rights on which the Member States have collaborated or of which they are signatories. The [European] Convention [on Human Rights] has special significance in that respect. As the Court has also held, it follows that measures are not acceptable in the Community which are incompatible with the observance of the human rights thus recognised and guaranteed.

However, measures taken by the institutions of the European Union cannot themselves be challenged in Strasbourg under the Convention.[165]

1.84   European Community law is directly enforceable in UK law.[166] Where there is a conflict with domestic law, Community law takes precedence.[167] And judgments of the European Court of Justice are binding.[168] Consequently, when domestic courts and tribunals apply Community law they are obliged to strive for a result compatible with Convention rights. Hence, where Convention rights are part of Community law, UK legislation can be disapplied if it contravenes the Convention.[169]

---

160 See article L.
161 See, for example, *P v S and Cornwall County Council* [1996] ECR I-2143.
162 *R v Kirk* [1984] ECR 2689.
163 *X v Commission* [1994] ECR I–4737.
164 [1997] ECR I–2629.
165 See *CFDT v EC* (1978) 13 DR 231.
166 European Communities Act 1972 s2(1).
167 *R v Secretary of State for Transport ex p Factortame (No 2)* [1990] ECR I-2433.
168 European Communities Act 1972, s3.
169 *Johnston v Chief Constable of the Royal Ulster Constabulary* [1986] ECR 1651.

CHAPTER 2

Human Rights Act 1998: claims and remedies

2.1 Introduction

2.7 The meaning of 'public authority' under the Human Rights Act

2.12 Relevance of Convention case-law to the meaning of public authority and the notion of state responsibility

2.18 The concept of 'victim' under the Human Rights Act 1998

2.20 Territorial reach

2.21 Person's entitled to bring proceedings

2.22 Those directly affected

2.23 No need for detriment or prejudice

2.24 Those at risk

2.26 The risk of serious and irreparable harm

2.27 Surveillance cases

2.29 Indirect victims

2.31 Representative actions

2.33 Companies

2.34 Limitations

2.35 Death

2.36 'Victim' contrasted with 'sufficient interest' in judicial review proceedings

continued

2.40   **Remedies**

2.45   **Aggravated and exemplary damages**

2.48   **Damages under the Convention: general principles**

2.55   **Pecuniary loss under the Convention**

2.57   **Non-pecuniary loss under the Convention**
2.58   Wrongful detention and police misconduct cases
2.60   Fair trial cases
2.65   Privacy cases
2.66   Child-care cases
2.67   Environmental issues

2.68   **Costs and expenses under the Convention**

2.69   **The special rules applicable to judicial acts**

2.73   **The limitation period for claims under the HRA**

2.75   **Convention claims in relation to the acts of private individuals**

2.81   **Retrospective claims under the Human Rights Act**

Introduction

2.1 In addition to the creation of a new rule of statutory interpretation,[1] the Human Rights Act 1998 (HRA) makes it unlawful for any public authority, including a court or tribunal to act in a way which is incompatible with Convention rights. This is a radical development in UK law, underpinned by special provisions about claims and remedies under the HRA.

2.2 Section 6 of the HRA provides that:

6 (1) It is unlawful for a public authority to act in a way which is incompatible with a Convention right.

(2) Subsection (1) does not apply to an act if –
   (a) as the result of one or more provisions of primary legislation, the authority could not have acted differently; or
   (b) in the case of one or more provisions of, or made under, primary legislation which cannot be read or given effect in a way which is compatible with the Convention rights, the authority was acting so as to give effect to or enforce those provisions

(3) In this section 'public authority' includes –
   (a) a court or tribunal, and
   (b) any person certain of whose functions are functions of a public nature, but does not include either House of Parliament or a person exercising functions in connection with proceedings in Parliament.

(4) In subsection (3) 'Parliament' does not include the House of Lords in its judicial capacity.

(5) In relation to a particular act, a person is not a public authority by virtue only of subsection (3)(b) if the nature of the act is private.

(6) An 'act' includes a failure to act but does not include a failure to –
   (a) introduce in, or lay before, Parliament a proposal for legislation; or
   (b) make any primary legislation or remedial order.

2.3 Section 7 complements s6 by providing that:

7 (1) A person who claims that a public authority has acted (or proposes to act) in a way which is made unlawful by section 6(1) may –
   (a) bring proceedings against the authority under this Act in the appropriate court or tribunal, or
   (b) rely on the Convention right or rights concerned in any legal proceedings,
   but only if he is (or would be) a victim of the unlawful act.

(2) In subsection (1)(a) 'appropriate court or tribunal' means such

---

1 Examined in chapter 1.

court or tribunal as may be determined in accordance with rules; and proceedings against an authority include a counterclaim or similar proceeding.

(3) If the proceedings are brought on an application for judicial review, the applicant is to be taken to have a sufficient interest in relation to the unlawful act only if he is, or would be, a victim of that act.

If the proceedings are made by way of a petition for judicial review in Scotland, the applicant shall be taken to have title and interest to sue in relation to the unlawful act only if he is, or would be, a victim of that act.

2.4   Section 6 of the HRA, therefore, makes it unlawful for a public authority to act in a way which is incompatible with Convention rights, unless it is required to do so to give effect to primary legislation.[2] In this context, 'act' includes a failure to act;[3] but does not include a failure to legislate or make remedial orders.[4] And s7 provides that anyone who claims that a public authority has acted (or proposes to act) in a way which is incompatible with Convention rights can bring proceedings against that authority (s7(1)(a)) – so long as s/he is (or would be) a 'victim' within the meaning of s7(7). Proceedings can be brought only in an 'appropriate court or tribunal' which means such court or tribunal as may be determined by rules yet to be made.[5]

2.5   Alternatively, anyone may rely on Convention rights in any 'legal proceedings' brought by others: for example, as part of a defence to criminal or civil proceedings (s7(1)(b)). Legal proceedings in this context includes, but is not limited to, proceedings brought by or at the instigation of a public authority and an appeal against the decision of a court or tribunal.[6]

2.6   It is envisaged that Convention points will normally be taken in the context of proceedings instituted against individuals or already open to them. But, if none is available, it will be possible for people to bring cases on Convention grounds alone.[7] Introducing the HRA in the House of Lords, the Lord Chancellor explained that under s7 individuals will be able to rely on the Convention when acting as

2   Paras 1.39 to 1.41.
3   S6(6).
4   Paras 1.55 to 1.57.
5   S7(2).
6   S7(6).
7   White Paper (Cm 7382, 1997) para 2.3.

claimant in civil proceedings, or in seeking judicial review, or on appeal. He emphasised that individuals will also be able to bring proceedings against public authorities purely on Convention grounds even if no other cause of action is open to them.[8]

The meaning of 'public authority' under the Human Rights Act

2.7   The HRA does not define 'public authority'. However, s6(3) expressly includes:

1) courts and tribunals[9] and

2) 'any person certain of whose functions are functions of a public nature'.[10]

And expressly *excludes* both Houses of Parliament[11] and any person exercising functions in connection with proceedings in Parliament. Section 6(5) then provides that in relation to a particular act, 'any person certain of whose functions are functions of a public nature' is not a public authority if the nature of the act in question is private.

2.8   According to the Lord Chancellor during the passage of the Bill through the House of Lords:

> [Section 6(1)] refers to a 'public authority' without defining the term. In many cases it will be obvious to the courts that they will be dealing with a public authority. In respect of government departments, for example, or police officers, or prison officers, or immigration officers, or local authorities, there can be no doubt that the body in question is a public authority. Any clear case of that kind comes in under [s6(1)]; and it is then unlawful for the authority to act in a way which is incompatible with one or more of the Convention rights. There is no exemption for private acts such as is conferred by [s6(5)] in relation to [s6(3)(b)].
>
> [Section 6(3)(b)] provides further assistance on the meaning of public authority. It provides that 'public authority' includes 'any person certain of whose functions are functions of a public nature'. That provision is there to include bodies which are not manifestly public authorities, but some of whose functions only are functions of a public nature. It is relevant to cases where the courts are

---

8   HL Debs col 1232, 3 November 1997.

9   S6(3)(a).

10   S6(3)(b).

11   But not the House of Lords in its judicial capacity: see s6(4).

not sure whether they are looking at a public authority in the full-blooded [s6(1)] sense with regard to those bodies which fall into the grey area between public and private. The Bill reflects the decision to include as 'public authorities' bodies which have some public functions and some private functions.[12]

The extent to which this classification cuts through the old public/private law divide remains to be seen. However, the Lord Chancellor's assertion that even the private acts of obvious public authorities are caught by HRA s6 may require some modification of the existing principles.[13]

2.9   The inclusion of 'any person certain of whose functions are functions of a public nature' is intended to expand, rather than restrict, the meaning of 'public authority'. According to the Home Secretary:

> When we were drawing up the Bill, we noted that the Convention had its origins in a desire to protect the individual against the abuse of power by the state, rather than to protect one individual against the actions of another ... we wanted a realistic and modern definition of the state so as to provide a correspondingly wide protection against the abuse of human rights. Accordingly, liability under the Bill would go beyond the narrow category of central and local government and the police – the organisations that represent a minimalist view of what constitutes the state.[14]

The current test in judicial review proceedings, therefore, is only a starting point.[15]

2.10   In debate, Railtrack, which has statutory public powers and functions, was given as an example of a body with a mixture of public and private functions.[16] When carrying out its functions relating to safety, it would qualify as a public authority. But when carrying out its functions as, for instance, a property developer by engaging in private transaction such as the disposal or acquisition of land, it would not so qualify.[17] Similarly, a private security company would be exercising public functions in relation to the management of a contracted-out prison but would be acting privately when, for example, guarding commercial premises. Doctors in general practice

12 HL Debs col 811, 24 November 1997.
13 For example, the distinction between private and public law matters in *R v East Berkshire Health Authority ex p Walsh* [1985] QB 152.
14 HC Debs cols 406 and 408, 17 June 1998.
15 See Home Secretary, ibid.
16 See Lord Williams, HL Debs col 758, 24 November 1997.
17 Ibid.

would be public authorities in relation to their NHS functions, but not in relation to their private clients.[18]

2.11   In effect, therefore, a threefold classification emerges:

1) Obvious public authorities, all of whose acts are caught by s6.

2) Hybrid bodies, whose public functions are caught by s6.

3) Private bodies with no public functions, which are not caught by s6 at all, but in relation to which the 'horizontal application' of the HRA might be relevant.[19]

In each case, Convention case-law will be relevant to the appropriate classification.

Relevance of Convention case-law to the meaning of public authority and the notion of state responsibility

2.12   It is clear that the government intended the meaning of public authority under the HRA to correspond with the notion of state responsibility under the Convention. In the House of Commons the Home Secretary said:

> The principle of bringing rights home suggested that liability in domestic proceedings should lie with bodies in respect of whose actions the United Kingdom Government was answerable in Strasbourg ... As a minimum, we must accept what Strasbourg has developed and is developing.[20]

2.13   This is likely to add a dynamic aspect to the interpretation of 'public authority' under the Act because the Strasbourg bodies have developed the doctrine of state responsibility under the Convention according to the following principles:[21]

1) States cannot escape liability under the Convention simply by asserting that an individual or body entrusted with public functions acted ultra vires. States are strictly liable for the conduct of their subordinates and cannot shelter behind their inability to ensure that their will is respected.[22]

18 These examples were given by the Lord Chancellor in debate at the House of Lords Committee Stage n12.
19 See paras 2.58 to 2.62.
20 Note 14.
21 See further, chapter 4.
22 *Ireland v UK* (1979–80) 2 EHRR 25 at para 159.

2) States cannot absolve themselves from responsibility by delegating their obligations to private bodies or individuals.[23]

3) State responsibility attaches to the acts of private individuals if the state has facilitated or colluded in such acts.[24]

4) States can be responsible for the acts of private individuals under the doctrine of 'positive obligations'.[25]

2.14   The first of these principles was articulated in *Ireland v UK*[26] in the context of a practice of ill-treatment including five interrogation techniques found to breach article 3. It was followed in *A v France*[27] where state liability under article 8 was triggered by a police officer recording a telephone conversation without authority and in breach of French law. And, in the context of a complaint under article 10 of the Convention, the Commission observed that:

> ... the responsibility of a state under the Convention may arise for acts of all its organs and servants. As in connection with international law generally, the acts of persons acting in an official capacity are imputed to the state. In particular, the obligations of a Contracting Party under the Convention can be violated by a person exercising an official function vested in him, even where his acts are performed without express authorisation and even outside or against instructions.[28]

2.15   The second principle was applied in *Costello-Roberts v UK*.[29] There the European Court found that corporal punishment by the headmaster of an independent school engaged state responsibility under the Convention.[30] And the third principle was applied in *Lopez-Ostra v Spain*[31] where the state was held responsible for pollution caused by a private waste treatment plant on the basis that (through a local council) it had granted permission for the plant to be built and had subsidised its construction.[32]

---

23 *Van Der Mussele v Belgium* (1984) 6 EHRR 163.
24 *Lopez-Ostra v Spain* (1995) 20 EHRR 277.
25 See chapter 5.
26 (1979–80) 2 EHRR 25 at para 159.
27 (1993) 17 EHRR 462.
28 *Wille v Liechtenstein* (1997) 24 EHRR CD 45 at 48.
29 (1995) 19 EHRR 112.
30 Ibid at para 28.
31 (1995) 20 EHRR 277.
32 Ibid at para 52.

2.16   A good example of state responsibility for the acts of private individuals is *Platform Artze für das Leben v Austria*.[33] There the European Court accepted, in principle, that the state was under a duty to protect demonstrators from the acts of private individuals – namely, counter-demonstration.[34]

2.17   Transposing these principles into the HRA, liability for breach of Convention rights may be very wide indeed. According to the Home Secretary:

> Under the Convention, the Government are answerable in Strasbourg for any acts or omissions of the state about which an individual has complaint under the Convention. The Government has a direct responsibility for core bodies, such as central Government and the police, but they also have a responsibility for other public authorities, in so far as the actions of such authorities impinge on private individuals.
>
> The [HRA] had to have a definition of a public authority that went at least as wide and took account of the fact that, over the past 20 years, an increasingly large number of private bodies, such as companies or charities, have come to exercise public functions that were previously exercised by public authorities ... it was not practicable to list all the bodies to which the [HRA's] provisions should apply. Nor would it have been wise to do so. What was needed instead was a statement of principle ... [s56] therefore adopts a non-exhaustive definition of a public authority.[35]

By hitching the definition of a public authority to the notion of state responsibility under the Convention, the government has given practical effect to the requirement that the HRA, like the Convention, be interpreted as a 'living instrument'.[36]

The concept of 'victim' under the Human Rights Act 1998

2.18   For the purposes of s7, a person is a victim of an unlawful act only if s/he would be a victim for the purposes of article 34 of the Convention if proceedings were brought in the European Court of Human Rights.[37] And where an applicant relies on his/her Con-

33 (1991) 13 EHRR 204.
34 See chapter 5.
35 HC Debs col 775, 16 February 1998.
36 See paras 4.16 to 4.18.
37 S7(6).

vention rights by bringing judicial review proceedings, s/he will be taken to have a 'sufficient interest' only if s/he is, or would be, a victim within this meaning.[38]

2.19   Article 34 of the Convention does not define the meaning of a 'victim'. However, a number of important principles have emerged from the extensive case-law of the Court and Commission. These are examined below (paras 2.20 to 2.35).

Territorial reach

2.20   The Convention applies to all persons within the jurisdiction of contracting states.[39] Jurisdiction may extend beyond a state's national territory where a state exercises its authority abroad, for example where its servants or agents detain an individual abroad[40] or where a state exercises de facto control over another state's territory.[41] In addition, the authorised agents of the state, including diplomatic or consular agents and the armed forces not only remain under its jurisdiction abroad but bring any other person or property 'within the jurisdiction' of the state to the extent that they exercise authority over such person or property.[42] However, taking part in the activities of the European Union or Council of Europe is insufficient to trigger jurisdiction.[43]

Persons entitled to bring proceedings

2.21   Any person, non-government organisation or group of individuals may bring proceedings under the Convention. In this context, 'person' includes a corporate body.[44] However, public authorities cannot bring proceedings under the Convention.[45]

---

38   S7(3).
39   Article 1.
40   *Reinette v France* (1989) 63 DR 189.
41   *Loizidou v Turkey* (1996) 23 EHRR 513.
42   *Mrs W v Ireland* (1983) 32 DR 211 at para 14.
43   *Confederation Francais Democratique du Travail v the European Communities and their Members States* (1978) 13 DR 231.
44   *Autronic AG v Switzerland* (1990) 12 EHRR 485.
45   *Ayuntamiento de M v Spain* (1991) 68 DR 209.

Those directly affected

2.22 As a general rule, only those 'directly affected' by an act or omission can claim to be victims under the Convention. The European Court is not concerned with abstract compliance with the Convention. Subject to the exceptions set out below, representative actions are not permitted.[46]

No need for detriment or prejudice

2.23 There is no requirement that a victim show detriment in the sense of prejudice.[47] Detriment is relevant only to the question of compensation or 'just satisfaction' and, even in that context, it is a very broad concept.[48]

Those at risk

2.24 Those 'at risk' of being affected by an act or omission qualify as victims. The following cases demonstrate the scope of this rule.

> In *Campbell and Cosans v UK*[49] children attending a school where corporal punishment was practised were treated as 'victims' under the Convention, even though they had not been punished.

> In *Norris v Ireland*[50] the Court accepted that the applicant was a victim under article 8 where he complained that legislation penalising homosexual conduct in private violated his rights under article 8. The fact that the risk of prosecution in the applicant's case was 'minimal' was irrelevant since there was no stated policy on the part of the prosecuting authorities not to enforce the legislation.

> In *Sutherland v UK*[51] the applicant, who complained that the age of consent for lawful homosexual activities (18) violated his article 8 rights and was discriminatory (the heterosexual age of consent being 16), had never been prosecuted nor had the domestic authorities shown any interest in his sexual activities. Nonethe-

---

46 *Lindsay v UK* (1997) 24 EHRR CD 199.
47 *Johnston v Ireland* (1987) 9 EHRR 203; *Eckle v Germany* (1983) 5 EHRR 1.
48 See para 2.25.
49 (1982) 4 EHRR 293.
50 (1988) 13 EHRR 186.
51 European Court (1 July 1997), [1998] EHRLR 117.

less, the Commission found that, in view of the distress he felt in having to choose between engaging in a sexual relationship and breaking the law, he was 'directly affected' by the legislation in question and therefore could claim to be a victim under the Convention.

In *Open Door Counselling and Dublin Well Woman v Ireland*[52] the Court accepted that two women were victims under the Convention on the basis that they belonged to a class of women of child-bearing age which *might* be adversely affected by an injunction imposed on the dissemination of information by an abortion centre. Similarly in *Bruggemann and Sceuten v Germany*[53] the Commission accepted that a woman who is not pregnant but who challenges legislation on abortion on the basis that it affects her sexual relations could claim to be a 'victim' under the Convention. On the other hand, the Commission refused to entertain an application from a man who considered it his duty as a citizen to challenge abortion legislation even though he was not affected by it in any way.[54]

2.25   In *Times Newspapers Ltd v UK*[55] the Commission accepted in principle[56] that:

> ... a newspaper publisher could in certain circumstances be regarded as a victim of a violation of article 10 of the Convention even though no defamation proceedings had been brought against any of its newspapers, for example where the law of defamation was at the same time too vague to allow the risk of proceedings to be predicted.[57]

However, not every newspaper is 'directly affected' by a court decision (to which it was not a party) which merely opened the possibility that on some future date in unknown circumstances it might be prosecuted for contempt of court.[58]

52   (1993) 15 EHRR 244.
53   (1976) 5 DR 103.
54   *X v Austria* (1977) 7 DR 87.
55   (1990) 65 DR 307.
56   But not on the facts.
57   Note 55 at p312.
58   *Leigh, Guardian Newspapers and Observer Ltd v UK* (1984) 38 DR 75.

The risk of serious and irreparable harm

2.26 The risk of serious and irreparable harm warrants a more generous approach to the concept of 'victim' under the Convention. In such cases, the Strasbourg bodies are willing to consider a complaint on the basis that a violation of the Convention is 'possible'. In *Soering v UK*[59] the Court held that the mere prospect of a prolonged period on death row was enough to bring the applicant within the meaning of 'victim' under the Convention.[60]

Surveillance cases

2.27 A sophisticated approach to the concept of 'victim' is needed in cases involving invasion of privacy such as surveillance and the maintenance of secret files because it is frequently difficult, if not impossible, for individuals to know and/or prove that they are or have been subject to such measures. In *Klass v Germany*[61] the Court held that all users or potential users of the postal and telecommunication services were 'directly affected' by legislation which provided for secret surveillance and would therefore qualify as victims.[62] And the applicants in the case were not deprived of their victim status merely because the government made a retrospective statement to the effect that they had not been subject to surveillance.[63]

2.28 In *Hilton v UK*[64] the Commission sought to narrow the application of the rule in *Klass v Germany* on the basis that the category of persons likely to be affected by security checks was significantly narrower than all users of postal and telecommunications services; in such cases, there must be a 'reasonable likelihood' that some measure has been taken in relation to the alleged victim.[65]

---

59 (1989) 11 EHRR 439.
60 The limits of this approach were examined in *Vijayanathan and Pusparajah v France* (1993) 15 EHRR 62.
61 (1979–80) 2 EHRR 214.
62 See also *MS and PS v Switzerland* (1985) 44 DR 175.
63 The position may, however, be different where there is a statutory duty to notify those concerned of any surveillance measures taken against them after the event: *Mersch v Luxembourg* (1985) 43 DR 34.
64 (1986) 57 DR 108.
65 Ibid at 119.

Indirect victims

2.29   Indirect victims can bring proceedings under the Convention where they have suffered some injury themselves and the direct victim is unable to bring a complaint.[66] In *Abdulaziz, Cabales and Balkandali*[67] the applicants who were lawfully settled in the UK were allowed to claim under article 8 when their husbands were refused permission to join them. And in *Paton v UK*[68] a prospective father who claimed that his wife proposed to have an abortion without his consent was considered by the Commission to be a 'victim' under the Convention such that he could raise a right to life claim.

2.30   A further category of 'indirect' victims are those affected by the death of another. A good example is *McCann v UK*[69] where the relatives of three IRA suspects killed by members of the SAS in Gibraltar brought claims under article 2 (the right to life) before the Court. Similarly in *Mrs W v UK*[70] the applicant was an 'indirect victim' in relation to the death of her husband and unmarried brother, who were killed by terrorists in Northern Ireland. The Commission also considered her to be a 'direct victim' by reason of the 'continuing situation in respect of her own security'.[71]

Representative actions

2.31   Representative actions can take two forms under the Convention. First, unincorporated bodies, such as professional associations, non-government organisations and/or trade unions[72] can act on behalf of their members, but only if they identify those members 'directly affected' by the measure in question and provide evidence of their authority to represent them.[73] Second, in respect of certain rights under the Convention, an unincorporated association can itself

---

66   *Winer v UK* (1986) 48 DR 154.

67   (1985) 7 EHRR 471.

68   (1980) 19 DR 244.

69   (1995) 21 EHRR 97.

70   (1983) 32 DR 190.

71   Ibid para 8.

72   For example *CCSU v UK* (1987) 50 DR 228; but see the limitations imposed by *Ahmed v UK* (1995) 20 EHRR CD 72.

73   *Confederation des Syndicats Medicaux Francais v France* (1986) 47 DR 225; see also *Zentralrat Deutscher Sinti und Roma and Rose v Germany* (1997) 23 EHRR CD 209.

be a 'victim'. So, for example, in *Christians Against Racism and Fascism v UK*[74] the applicant association – a broad alliance of religious groups – was considered a 'victim' when its planned procession was banned under the (then) Public Order Act 1936. Similarly, a church body or association with religious or philosophical aims is capable of possessing and exercising the right to freedom of religion since an application by such a body is in reality lodged on behalf of its members: *Hautanemi v Sweden*.[75]

2.32 Claims can also be brought in a representative capacity where a victim lacks legal capacity. However, unless the representative is a custodial parent or legal guardian, evidence of the person's authority to act as representative will be needed.[76] In *SD, DP and T v UK*[77] a claim was brought by a solicitor, supported by a letter of authority from the guardian *ad litem* appointed by the court to safeguard the interests of the children applicants in domestic proceedings. In the particular context of protecting children (and drawing on the UN *Convention on the Rights of the Child*), the Commission held that this was a valid exercise of the right of individual petition: the mother being disinterested and the local authority being the subject of the complaint.

Companies

2.33 Where the interests of a company are affected, it is, in principle, the company that is the 'victim' under the Convention. However, where a shareholder's interests are affected by measures taken against a company, s/he might be a 'victim' under the Convention;[78] and the chair and managing director of a company will usually have standing to challenge measures taken against their company.[79]

---

74 (1980) 21 DR 138.
75 (1996) 22 EHRR CD 155; however in *Norris v Ireland* (1985) 44 DR 132 the Commission did not regard the National Gay Federation as a victim of the law prohibiting homosexual acts.
76 *X v Sweden* (1979) 16 DR 105.
77 (1996) 22 EHRR CD 148.
78 *Agrotexim v Greece* (1996) 21 EHRR 250; but see also *Neves e Silva v Portugal* (1991) 13 EHRR 535; *Yarrow v UK* (1983) 30 DR 155 and *X v Austria* (1966) 9 Yearbook 112.
79 *Kaplan v UK* (1982) 4 EHRR 64.

Limitations

2.34   The fact that an individual is acquitted in criminal proceedings may preclude him/her from being a 'victim' under the Convention,[80] but not if there is a risk of further prosecution.[81] Similarly, a favourable decision in civil proceedings will deprive an individual of 'victim' status only if it either expressly or in substance acknowledges a breach of the Convention and affords proper redress: for example, the lifting of a deportation order.[82] In *Amwr v France*[83] a favourable decision came after the applicants had been deported to Syria and was thus of no effect. However, where the law is amended before a case reaches the Strasbourg bodies – for example to reinforce the status of a child born out of wedlock – an applicant may cease to be a 'victim'.[84]

Death

2.35   Where an applicant dies during proceedings under the Convention, his/her claim can be continued by a spouse or other close relative so long as s/he has a legitimate interest in the outcome; examples include the parents of an AIDS sufferer,[85] the wife of a man wrongly arrested and detained,[86] the father of someone convicted of sadomasochistic activities[87] and the widow and children of a man convicted of disturbing the peace in the course of distributing election leaflets, who had a 'moral interest' in continuing the proceedings.[88]

---

80 *X v Austria* (1974) 1 DR 44 and *Reed v UK* (1979) 19 DR 113.

81 *Bowman v UK* (1998) 26 EHRR 1.

82 Appln No 7706/76, 4 Digest 409; for other examples of this general rule see *Frederiksen v Denmark* (1988) 56 DR 237; *X v UK* (1978) 14 DR 197 and A, B, C and *D v Germany* (1979) 18 DR 176.

83 (1996) 22 EHRR 533.

84 *X v Denmark* (1978) 15 DR 128; this decision has, however, been subject to considerable criticism: see Harris et al, *Law of the European Convention on Human Rights*, Butterworth 1995 p636.

85 *X v France* A/234-C (unreported) where the Court awarded the whole of the non-pecuniary compensation which would have been paid to the applicant for not being able to live independently and in better psychological condition for the remaining part of his life.

86 *Loukanov v Bulgaria* (1997) 24 EHRR 121.

87 *Jaggard and Brown v UK* (1997) 24 EHRR 39.

88 *Ahmut Sadik v Greece* (1997) 24 EHRR 323; the case was ultimately rejected as inadmissible.

'Victim' contrasted with 'sufficient interest' in judicial review proceedings

2.36 Applicants in judicial review must show a 'sufficient interest' in a case in order to have standing to seek judicial review.[89] Where the applicant is clearly affected by the decision or measures under challenge, no difficulty arises. Where the applicant is not so affected, the following factors will be relevant in determining whether s/he (or it) has 'sufficient interest':

1) the importance of maintaining the rule of law;

2) the importance of the issue raised;

3) the likely existence of any other responsible challenger;

4) the nature of the breach of duty against which relief is sought; and

5) the expertise and experience of the applicant body.

2.37 Thus public interest groups such as the Child Poverty Action Group,[90] the Joint Council for the Welfare of Immigrants,[91] Greenpeace,[92] the World Development Movement,[93] the Equal Opportunities Commission[94] and trade unions have been able to bring judicial review proceedings in their own name on behalf of a class of unspecified individuals who might be affected by the measure in question. However, as noted above, where an applicant relies on Convention rights in judicial review proceedings under the HRA, s/he will be taken to have a 'sufficient interest' only if s/he is, or would be, a victim for the purposes of article 34 of the Convention.[95]

2.38 The result is a mismatch. On the one hand, the Convention approach is broader, particularly in relation to those 'at risk' of a breach of their Convention rights. On the other hand, the Convention approach is narrower in that it is more restrictive of representative actions and/or public interest litigation.

2.39 The effect of this mismatch remains to be seen. However, in some respects it is mitigated by the following factors:

90 *R v Secretary of State for Social Services ex p CPAG* [1990] 2 QB 540.

91 *R v Secretary of State for Social Security ex p JCWI* [1997] 1 WLR 275.

92 *R v Her Majesty's Inspectorate on Pollution ex p Greenpeace (No 2)* [1994] 4 All ER 329.

93 *R v Secretary of State for Foreign and Commonwealth Affairs ex p World Development Movement* [1995] 1 WLR 386.

94 *R v Secretary of State for Employment ex p EOC* [1994] 2 WLR 409.

95 S57(7).

1) The Strasbourg bodies do not prohibit representative actions. But they do insist that the body bringing the proceedings genuinely represents individuals who are 'directly affected' by a breach of the Convention and that it has permission to act on their behalf. And the concept of being 'directly affected' is broadly construed where important issues of human rights are at stake: see *Open Door Counselling and Dublin Well Woman v Ireland*[96] and *Times Newspapers Ltd v UK*[97].

2) In some public interest litigation, the body seeking to bring judicial review proceedings is, in truth, an association of interested individuals, who might well qualify as 'victims' under the Convention. In *R v Inspectorate of Pollution ex p Greenpeace (No 2)*[98] the applicant persuaded the court that it was, at least in part, an association of victims as well as a representative body.

3) The European Court in *Klass v Germany*[99] held that:

> ... the procedural provisions of the Convention must, in view of the fact that the Convention and its institutions were set up to protect the individual, be applied in a manner which serves to make the system of individual applications efficacious.[100]

The same principle, by analogy, applies to proceedings under the HRA by the combined effect of ss2(1) and 7(7).

4) Section 11(b) of the HRA provides that:

> A person's reliance upon a Convention right does not restrict ... his right to make any claim or bring any proceedings which he could make or bring apart from sections 7 to 9.

Therefore it will be difficult for domestic courts to shut out claims that could have been made before the HRA was enacted; for example judicial review proceedings based on fundamental common law rights, bolstered by the Convention.[101] And the idea that a public interest group can rely on the Convention indirectly, but not directly, in judicial review proceedings is likely to lead to undesirable anomalies.

5) In debate, the Lord Chancellor recognised that there is 'flexible

---

96 (1993) 15 EHRR 244.
97 (1990) 65 DR 307.
98 [1994] 4 All ER 329.
99 (1979–80) 2 EHRR 214.
100 Para 34.
101 See para 1.78.

Strasbourg jurisprudence on the victim test'.[102] He also asserted that 'there is nothing in our Bill which would prevent pressure groups – interest groups – from assisting and providing representation for victims who wish to bring cases forward ... interest groups will plainly be able to provide assistance to victims who bring cases under the Bill, including ... the filing of amicus briefs.'[103]

Remedies

2.40   Section 8(1) of the HRA provides that:

> In relation to any act (or proposed act) of a public authority which the court finds is (or would be) unlawful, it may grant such relief or remedy, or make such order, within its powers as it considers just and appropriate.

This includes an award of damages. But damages may be awarded only by a court or tribunal which has power to award damages, or to order the payment of compensation, in civil proceedings.[104] This means that criminal courts will not have power to award damages where they find, during the course of a trial, that a violation of an individual's Convention rights has occurred.[105] If the existing powers to grant relief in tribunals are inadequate, rules may be made to extend their powers.[106] But nothing in the HRA creates a criminal offence.[107]

2.41   What remedy is appropriate will depend on the facts of the case and, according to the Government's White Paper[108] 'on a proper balance between the rights of the individual and the public interest'.[109] In some cases the right course may be for the decision of the public authority in the particular case to be quashed. In other cases, the only appropriate remedy may be an award of damages.[110]

102 HL Debs col 809, 5 February 1998.
103 HL Debs col 810, 5 February 1998.
104 S8(2).
105 A point made by the Lord Chancellor at HL Debs col 854, 24 November 1997.
106 S7(11).
107 S7(8).
108 *Rights Brought Home: The Human Rights Bill* Cmnd 3782.
109 Ibid para 2.6.
110 Ibid.

The overriding requirement is that a remedy be effective. Introducing [section 8] of the Bill, the Lord Chancellor declared:

> I cannot conceive of any state of affairs in which an English court, having held an act to be unlawful because of its infringement of a Convention right, would under clause 8(1) be disabled from giving an effective remedy.[111]

This should largely mitigate against the exclusion of article 13 from Schedule 1 of the Act.[112] The notion of an effective remedy under article 13 is examined in chapter 3.[113]

2.42   In relation to criminal proceedings, the powers of a court to quash an indictment, to stay proceedings, to allow a submission of no case to answer and to exclude evidence may be of particular significance. In the Court of Appeal, it seems likely that a conviction following a trial in which the appellant's article 6 rights (the right to a fair trial) have been violated will be deemed 'unsafe' within s2(1) of the Criminal Appeals Act 1968 (an example of the interpretation of domestic legislation so as to give effect to Convention rights).[114]

2.43   Section 8(3) restricts the power of the courts to award damages by providing that:

> No award of damages is to be made unless, taking account of all the circumstances of the case, including –
> (a) any other relief or remedy granted, or order made, in relation to the act in question (by that or any other court), and
> (b) the consequences of any decision (of that or any other court) in respect of that act,
> the court is satisfied that the award is necessary to afford just satisfaction to the person in whose favour it is made.

In deciding whether to make such an award and in calculating the amount, courts will be required to take into account the principles applied by the European Court in relation to the award of compensation under article 41 of the Convention.[115] The Government's intention is that 'people will be able to receive compensation from a domestic court equivalent to what they would have received in Strasbourg'.[116]

---

111 HL Debs col 479, 18 November 1997.
112 See paras 1.7 to 1.8.
113 Paras 3.173 to 3.182.
114 *Archbold* (1999) para 16–25.
115 S8(4).
116 See White Paper, para 2.6.

2.44   The failure of the European Court to articulate the principles it
         applies when awarding compensation is likely to prove a real imped-
         iment to the effective operation of this requirement in domestic pro-
         ceedings. The cases referred to below provide some indication of the
         Court's approach, but inevitably depend to a great extent on the facts
         of each individual case.

Aggravated and exemplary damages

2.45   To date, the European Court has not awarded aggravated or
         exemplary damages. In most cases, they have not been sought. And
         where they have been sought, the Court has ignored the claim with-
         out comment. So far as aggravated damages are concerned, it could
         be argued that the Court's broad approach to non-pecuniary loss in
         effect recognises their legitimacy, particularly where it has made
         awards to compensate for frustration, distress and feelings of help-
         lessness.[117]

2.46   The question of exemplary damages is perhaps different. They are
         not intended to be compensatory; their function[118] is to punish
         'oppressive, arbitrary or unconstitutional action by servants of the
         government'.[119] By insisting that there must be a causal link between
         breach and compensation,[120] the European Court has declined to
         interpret article 41 so as to cover such damages. That is in keeping
         with its role as an international supervisory body; as Karen Reid, a
         member of the Secretariat of the European Commission of Human
         Rights, has pointed out, the Court's emphasis is on making public
         and binding findings applicable to human rights standards, not
         awarding damages.[121]

2.47   Domestic courts have a different role. And s11(b) specifically pro-
         vides that a person's reliance on a Convention right does not restrict
         'his right to make any claim ... which he could make or bring apart
         from sections 7 to 9'. Arguably, therefore, exemplary damages can be
         awarded in cases brought against public authorities under s7 of HRA
         according to the usual domestic rules (oppressive, arbitrary or
         unconstitutional action).

---

117 See para 2.55.
118 In the present context.
119 *Rookes v Barnard* [1964] AC 1129.
120 See paras 2.46 to 2.52.
121 Reid *A Practitioner's Guide to the European Convention on Human Rights* Sweet
    & Maxwell, 1998 p398.

Damages under the Convention: general principles

2.48   Article 41[122] of the Convention provides that:

> If the Court finds that there has been a violation of the Convention or the protocols thereto, and the internal law of the High Contracting Party concerned allows only partial reparation to be made, the Court shall, if necessary, afford just satisfaction to the injured party.

Article 5(5) provides a separate (and additional) requirement that anyone deprived of his/her liberty contrary to article 5 shall have an *enforceable* right to compensation.[123] And domestic courts will have to give effect to this provision.

2.49   Unlike a claim for compensation under article 5(5), just satisfaction cannot be claimed by an applicant as of right under article 41: it is a matter for the European Court's discretion, having regard to what is equitable.[124] And the Court will not raise the issue of just satisfaction of its own motion.[125]

2.50   Just satisfaction is awarded under three heads: pecuniary loss, non-pecuniary loss and costs and expenses. A comprehensive schedule of the Court's awards on an article by article basis is set out in Reid, *A Practitioner's Guide to the European Convention on Human Rights*.[126] Interest is payable on Convention awards.[127]

2.51   The principles upon which the European Court operates are not clear. In most cases it tends simply to recite that it has made an assessment 'on an equitable basis'. The most useful starting point is the Court's recognition that the purpose of an award under article 41 is to put the applicant as far as possible in the position s/he would have been in had the violation of the Convention not taken place.[128]

2.52   On some occasions the European Court has held that no award of damages is necessary because the finding of a violation constituted 'just satisfaction'. However, it has never set out the basis for this

---

122 Formerly article 50.

123 See paras 3.84 to 3.86.

124 *Sunday Times v UK* (article 50) 6 November 1980 (unreported).

125 Note 121 at p397.

126 Ibid at pp399–401 and 403–420; see also Mowbray 'The European Court of Human Rights' Approach to Just Satisfaction' [1997] *Public Law* 647–659.

127 See *Schuler-Zdraggen v Switzerland* (1995) 21 EHRR 404.

128 *Theory and Practice of the European Convention on Human Rights* Van Dijk and Van Hoof Kluwer,1998 p250; see also *Piersack v Belgium* (article 50) (1984) 7 EHRR 251 at para 12.

approach or the circumstances in which it is applicable. The fact that the applicant has criminal convictions does not seem to be a determinative factor.[129] But the fact that the applicants are terrorist suspects invariably is.[130]

2.53   Where the breach of the Convention is technical, damages might not be awarded. For example, in *De Wilde, Ooms and Versyp v Belgium (No 2)*,[131] where the Court found a violation of article 5(4) of the Convention because the three applicants were unable to challenge the lawfulness of their detention as vagrants, the Court awarded no damages on the basis that, even if they had been able to take proceedings in order to test the lawfulness of their detention, the applicants would not have been released any sooner. However, this is not an absolute rule. In *Ringeisen v Austria (No 2)*,[132] the Court held that withholding damages where pre-trial detention was taken into account upon sentence would deprive article 5(3) of much of its effectiveness.

2.54   The European Court has no power to issue directions to a state to take steps or measures to rectify a breach of the Convention. For example, in *Ireland v UK*[133] it refused the request of the Irish government to direct that criminal proceedings be brought against those responsible for ill-treatment. However, where restitutio in integrum is possible, for example, the return of property wrongly seized, the Court will allow a period for the state to take the necessary step and award compensation if it fails to do so.[134]

Pecuniary loss under the Convention

2.55   Pecuniary loss under the Convention has much the same meaning as in domestic law. Causation is usually the issue, but, broadly speaking, so long as causation is established, the European Court will award damages for any pecuniary damage proved. The following are examples:

---

129 See *Weeks v UK* (1988) 13 EHRR 435 and *Govell v UK* (Commission) 14 January 1998 (unreported).
130 *McCann and Others v UK* (1995) 21 EHRR 97.
131 (1972) 1 EHRR 438.
132 (1972) 1 EHRR 504.
133 (1978) 2 EHRR 25.
134 *Papamichalopoulos v Greece* (article 50) A/330-B (1995) (unreported).

1) In *Young, James and Webster v UK*,[135] the Court awarded £17,626, £45,215 and £8,706 to the three applicants for the violation of their article 11 rights (dismissal from employment under a closed shop agreement) for loss of past and future earnings, loss of pension rights and loss of travel privileges.

2) In *Lingens v Austria*,[136] the Court held that the applicant was entitled to recover a fine and costs awarded against him by the Austrian court which convicted him of criminal defamation. It also awarded him a sum to represent the loss of opportunity and additional printing costs of having to publish the judgment of the domestic courts against him in his journal, *Profil*. This was essentially a loss of profit award. Similarly, in *Oberschlick v Austria*[137] where a journalist had been convicted of defamation and fined, the Court awarded a sum to compensate him for the fine and the costs awarded against him in the domestic proceedings.

3) In *Baggetta v Italy*[138] the European Court awarded a sum to compensate the applicant for his inability to assume his duties in the public service during the prolongation of his criminal proceedings and also a sum for the prolonged uncertainty of the outcome of the criminal proceedings and their financial repercussions.

4) In *Vermeire v Belgium*[139] the applicant was awarded a sum equivalent to the amount he would have inherited if he had been legitimate.

5) In *Open Door Counselling and Dublin Well Woman v Ireland*[140] one of the applicants was awarded £25,000 for loss of income due to the discontinuance of abortion counselling services while an injunction was in place: the Court awarded this sum even though it was not substantiated, on the basis that the discontinuance 'must have resulted in loss of income'.[141]

6) In *Schuler-Zgraggen v Switzerland*[142] the applicant was awarded about £10,000 representing interest on late payment of invalidity

135 (1982) 5 EHRR 201.
136 (1986) 8 EHRR 407.
137 (1991) 19 EHRR 389.
138 (1987) 10 EHRR 325.
139 A/270-A (1990) (unreported).
140 (1992) 15 EHRR 244.
141 Para 87.
142 (1993) 16 EHRR.

benefits which had originally been denied to her in breach of articles 14 and 6(1) of the Convention.

7) In *Allenet de Ribemont v France*[143] compensation was awarded for a reduction in business opportunities attributable to adverse comments by public officials.

2.56 Property cases have led to very high awards. In *Sporrong and Lonnroth v Sweden*[144] the Court awarded about £100,000 where a planning restriction prevented development for 20 years. In *Pine Valley Developments Ltd v Ireland*[145] £1,200,000 IR was awarded to reflect the value that land would have been worth had the applicant not been prevented from developing it contrary to the Convention.

Non-pecuniary loss under the Convention

2.57 Non-pecuniary loss under the Convention also has much the same meaning as in domestic law. It has been awarded in respect of anxiety, distress, loss of employment prospects, feelings of injustice, deterioration of way of life and other varieties of harm and suffering. In such cases, the Court has often taken the view that matters such as pain and distress are not susceptible to positive proof and has, in effect, presumed loss.[146] Examples include:

1) *König v Federal Republic of Germany* (article 50)[147] where the Court awarded damages for the 'permanent and deep anxiety' caused to the applicant by prolonged civil proceedings.[148]

2) *Artico v Italy*[149] where the Court awarded compensation for the sensation of 'confusion and neglect' caused by a failure to provide adequate legal representation.

3) *Weeks v UK*[150] where the Court awarded £8,000 to a life sentence prisoner because of the 'frustration and helplessness' he must have felt at being unable to argue for his early release.

143 (1995) 20 EHRR 557.
144 (1984) 7 EHRR 256.
145 A/246-B (1993) (article 50) (unreported).
146 *Abdulaziz, Cabales and Balkandali v UK* A/94 (1985) 7 EHRR 471; and see generally Harris, O'Boyle and Warbrick *Law of the European Convention on Human Rights* at p687.
147 A/36 (1980) 2 EHRR 469.
148 Ibid para 19.
149 (1980) 3 EHRR 1.
150 (1988) 13 EHRR 435.

4) *Gillow v UK*[151] where the Court awarded £10,000 for the 'stress and anxiety' caused when the authorities refused the applicants a permit to live in their house in Guernsey.

5) *Young, James and Webster v UK*[152] £2,000, £6,000 and £3,000 awarded for the 'harassment, humiliation and stress' in finding other employment after dismissal for not joining a trade union.[153]

The issue at stake is often important and the examples set out below are intended to give some indication of the approach adopted and the level of compensation awarded for non-pecuniary loss across a range of issues.

Wrongful detention and police misconduct cases

2.58   Where there has been wrongful imprisonment and/or police misconduct, damages are available under article 41 and awards have been comparatively high.[154] The following are examples:

1) In *Tomasi v France*[155] the Court awarded £75,075[156] to the applicant in respect of police assaults in custody amounting to a violation of article 3 and for delay in criminal proceedings brought against him. This did not include a sum for excessive pre-trial detention for which the applicant had already been compensated in domestic proceedings.

2) In *Funke v France*[157] the applicant was awarded £5,877[158] for infringement of the fair trial guarantee against self-incrimination[159] and for invasion of his privacy by an unlawful police search.

3) In *Ribitsch v Austria*[160] the applicant was awarded £6,287[161] in relation to a finding that he had been punched and kicked in police custody contrary to article 3 of the Convention.

---

151 (1987) 13 EHRR 593.
152 (1982) 5 EHRR 201.
153 This was in addition to the pecuniary award set out above.
154 See generally chapter 15.
155 (1992) 15 EHRR 1.
156 1999 value: £88,572.
157 (1993) 16 EHRR 297.
158 1999 value: £6,825.
159 See paras 9.60 to 9.74.
160 (1996) 21 EHRR 573.
161 1999 value: £7,095.

4) In *Quinn v France*[162] the applicant was awarded about £1,000[163] for wrongful imprisonment of 11 hours. There were no aggravating features; the authorities simply failed to act sufficiently swiftly after a court order that he be released.

5) In *Aksoy v Turkey*[164] the applicant was awarded £25,040 for serious ill-treatment in custody over a 14-day period contrary to article 3. This sum was awarded to the father of the applicant (who had died) in view of the seriousness of the violations and the anxiety and distress that he must have suffered as a father.[165]

6) In *Aydin v Turkey*[166] the applicant was awarded £25,000 for serious ill-treatment in custody, including rape, contrary to article 3 and a failure to investigate her claims properly.

2.59   The conduct of the applicant will have a bearing on the sum awarded. In *Johnson v UK*[167] the Court awarded the applicant £10,000 compensation for non-pecuniary loss in circumstances where the imposition of a hostel residence condition delayed his release from Rampton Hospital from June 1989 until January 1993. In doing so, it observed that:

> While it is true that the applicant spent an excessive amount of time in a maximum security psychiatric hospital after it was conclusively shown that he was no longer suffering from mental illness, it must also be noted that the delay in his release cannot be attributed entirely to the authorities. In the first place, some period of deferment of release was inevitable having regard to the need to locate a hostel suited to the applicant's situation. Secondly, the applicant's negative attitude towards his rehabilitation did not facilitate their task and after October 1990 he refused to co-operate further with the authorities in finding a suitable hostel.[168]

The case was, therefore, not one of straightforward false imprisonment.

162 (1996) 21 EHRR 529.
163 10,000 francs.
164 (1996) 23 EHRR 553.
165 Ibid para 113.
166 (1998) 25 EHRR 251.
167 (1998) 27 EHRR 296.
168 Ibid para 77.

Fair trial cases

2.60   Assessing non-pecuniary loss in fair trial cases is obviously difficult and the European Court has often stated that it is unwilling to speculate on the outcome of a case. However, it has frequently awarded substantial sums to cover the loss of a real opportunity to advance a practical and effective case, and to procure a different outcome in the proceedings. The following are examples:

1) In *Goddi v Italy*[169] the Court awarded 5,000,000 lira[170] to the applicant whose trial had proceeded despite the non-attendance of his lawyer.

2) In *Delta v France*[171] the applicant was awarded about £12,000 where his conviction was based on hearsay evidence contrary to article 6 of the Convention. This award was not based on the assumption that he would have been acquitted had the evidence been excluded, the Court being unwilling to speculate on the likely outcome.

3) In *S v Switzerland*[172] the applicant was awarded about £1,000 for not being able to communicate freely with his lawyers for about seven months while in pre-trial detention.

4) In *Philis v Greece*[173] the applicant who had not been able to sue in person for his professional fees was awarded about £3,000 for the feelings of frustration that this must have caused.

2.61   Sometimes, however, no award is made, even where fair trial provisions have been breached. For example, in *Saunders v UK*[174] no award was made to the applicant who had been convicted in breach of the prohibition on self-incrimination implied into article 6.[175] Although the Court claimed not to be speculating about the outcome of the trial had the evidence in question not been adduced, it made its position fairly clear:

> [The Court] cannot speculate as to whether the outcome of the trial would have been any different had use not been made of the transcripts by the prosecution and, like the Commission, underlines

---

169 (1984) 6 EHRR 457.
170 1999 value: £3,516.
171 (1993) 16 EHRR 574.
172 (1992) 14 EHRR 670.
173 (1991) 13 EHRR 741.
174 (1997) 23 EHRR 313.
175 See paras 9.60 to 9.74.

that the finding of a breach of the Convention is not to be taken to carry any implications as regards that question.

A similar result followed in *Findlay v UK*[176] where the procedural rules in court martial proceedings were found to be in breach of article 6 of the Convention.

2.62   Although seeking to analyse the Court's approach is precarious in the absence of reasons, it appears that the Court is reluctant to award damages where to do so would effectively undermine a conviction because, as it stated in the *Findlay* case, 'it has no jurisdiction to quash convictions pronounced by national courts'.[177] However, even if compensation is not awarded in respect of the conviction itself, it might in appropriate cases be awarded for feelings of 'isolation and confusion' caused by a fair trial breach: see *Granger v UK*[178] where £1,000 was awarded when no lawyer was appointed to assist the applicant with his appeal.

2.63   A finding of excessive delay in criminal or civil proceedings also usually leads to an award. The following are examples:

1) In *H v UK*[179] £12,000 was awarded for unreasonable delay in childcare proceedings.

2) In *Bock v Germany*[180] the Court awarded the applicant DM10,000[181] where his divorce proceedings had taken nine years.

3) In *X v France*[182] the applicant's parents were awarded about £18,000 for delay in civil proceedings for negligence in which their son attempted to obtain compensation for becoming HIV positive.[183]

2.64   Where access to the courts is denied altogether, the Court's reluctance to speculate about the possible outcome of proceedings will not necessarily preclude it from awarding compensation for non-pecuniary loss. For example, in *Osman v UK*[184] the applicants were awarded £10,000 each for being denied the opportunity to bring proceedings against the police for failing to take adequate measures to prevent the death of their husband and father respectively.

---

176 (1997) 24 EHRR 221.
177 Ibid para 88; see also *Maxwell v UK* (1995) 19 EHRR 97.
178 (1990) 12 EHRR 469.
179 A/136-B, 9 June 1988 (unreported).
180 (1990) 12 EHRR 247.
181 Approximately £10,000 at the time.
182 (1992) 14 EHRR 483.
183 He subsequently died.
184 (European Court) 28 October 1998; [1999] 1 FLR 193.

Privacy cases

2.65 The Court has been particularly sensitive to the need for compensation for non-pecuniary loss in privacy cases where pecuniary damage will often be difficult to establish. For example:

1) In *Gaskin v UK*[185] the applicant, who had been denied access to some of his social services files, was awarded £5,000[186] in recognition that he had 'suffered some emotional distress and anxiety'.[187]

2) In *Z v Finland*[188] the Court awarded 200,000 FIM (approx £22,000) where the applicant's HIV status was disclosed when her name was published as part of a court judgment contrary to article 8 of the Convention.

3) In *Halford v UK*[189] the applicant, the former Assistant Chief Constable of Merseyside, was awarded £10,000 for the interception of her telephone calls by other police officers for use against her in sex discrimination proceedings. No actual financial loss was established, but the sum was awarded to reflect the serious nature of the breach.

4) In *Govell v UK*[190] the Council of Ministers awarded the applicant £1,000 where the Commission had found that the installation of a secret listening device in his home was not 'prescribed by law' because the guidelines were unpublished, despite the fact that, by the time of the award, the applicant was serving a long prison sentence for drug-related offences.

Child-care cases

2.66 Awards in child-care cases also tend to be comparatively high, again often reflecting the degree of anxiety and distress presumed by the Court. The following are examples:

1) In *O v UK*[191] the applicants were awarded £5,000 for procedural deficiencies in wardship proceedings.

---

185 (1990) 12 EHRR 36.
186 1999 value.
187 Note 185 para 58.
188 (1998) 25 EHRR 371.
189 (1997) 24 EHRR 523.
190 (Commission) 14 January 1998 (unreported) Appl 27237/95.
191 (1991) 13 EHRR 578.

2) In *Eriksson v Sweden*[192] the applicant was prevented from challenging an order restricting her contact with her daughter and requiring that her daughter remain at a foster home. She was awarded about £18,000[193] and her daughter was awarded about £9,000.[194]

3) In *Keegan v Ireland*[195] the Court awarded the applicant £10,000 for the trauma and anxiety he had suffered when the authorities refused to recognise his claim over his natural child and denied him the opportunity to challenge the child's adoption in court.

4) In *McMichael v UK*[196] £8,000 was awarded where the applicants had been denied access to certain documents during custody and access proceedings, partly on the basis that the Court took the view that it 'cannot be certain that no practical benefit would have accrued to them if the procedural deficiency had not existed'.

Environmental issues

2.67   The case-law of the Court and Commission on environmental issues is fairly recent and is developing.[197] However, to date, awards have been made to compensate for non-pecuniary loss. For example, in *Lopez Ostra v Spain*[198] the Court awarded about £16,000 for the distress caused by the emission of toxic fumes from a waste management plant near the applicant's house and the inconvenience caused to her by having to move. And in *Guerra and Others v Italy*[199] the Court awarded about £3,000 to the applicants to compensate them for the fact that the authorities had not provided them with sufficient information about a pesticide factory to enable them to assess the risks of living in its vicinity.

192 (1990) 12 EHRR 183.
193 1999 value £22,830.
194 1999 value £11,415.
195 (1994) 18 EHRR 342.
196 A/308 (1995) 20 EHRR 205.
197 See chapter 22.
198 (1995) 20 EHRR 277.
199 (1998) 26 EHRR 357.

Costs and expenses under the Convention

2.68   To be entitled to costs and expenses under article 41, an applicant must show that they were: (a) actually incurred, (b) necessarily incurred, and (c) are reasonable. However, when legal aid payments have been made under the Council of Europe's legal aid scheme the Court will assume, in the absence of proof to the contrary, that the applicant is under an obligation to pay his/her lawyer additional fees in respect of the Convention proceedings.[200]

The special rules applicable to judicial acts

2.69   Special rules apply where an individual claims that a judicial act has violated (or might violate) his/her Convention rights. Section 9(1) provides that:

> (1) Proceedings under s7(1)(a) in respect of a judicial act may be brought only –
> (a) by exercising a right of appeal;
> (b) on an application (in Scotland a petition) for judicial review; or
> (c) in such other forum as may be prescribed by rules.

This does not affect any rule of law which prevents a court being the subject of judicial review.[201] Furthermore, in respect of a judicial act done in good faith, damages may not be awarded otherwise than to compensate a person to the extent required by article 5(5) of the Convention.

2.70   Article 5(5) contains a very specific guarantee for breaches of article 5 by providing that everyone 'who has been the victim of arrest or detention in contravention of the provision of this article shall have an enforceable right to compensation'. It does not require proof of bad faith on the part of the authorities. In *Santa Cruz Ruiz v UK*,[202] the Commission found a breach of article 5(5) where the applicant had been imprisoned by magistrates for failing to make payments under a maintenance order. No claim could be brought domestically because s108 of the Courts and Legal Services Act 1980 provides immunity for magistrates except where they act beyond their jurisdiction and in bad faith. Section 9(3) of the HRA sweeps

---

200 See, for example *Brandstetter v Austria* (1993) 15 EHRR 378.
201 S9(3).
202 (Commission) 1 July 1998.

away that rule. However, not every error of a magistrates' court will take it outside its jurisdiction. In *Bentham v UK*,[203] the European Court found that a Divisional Court's ruling that a magistrates' court's finding of culpable neglect in proceedings for non-payment of the (then) community charge could not be sustained on the evidence before it, did not clearly amount to a ruling that it had exceeded its jurisdiction.[204]

2.71 Any award of damages required by article 5(5) in respect of a judicial act is to be made against the Crown. And the appropriate person (ie, the minister responsible for the court concerned or a person or government department nominated by him/her),[205] if not a party to the proceedings, is joined.[206]

2.72 In this context, judicial act means a judicial act of a court and includes an act done on the instructions, or on behalf, of a judge. And judge includes a member of a tribunal, a justice of the peace and a clerk or other officer entitled to exercise the jurisdiction of a court.[207]

The limitation period for claims under the HRA

2.73 The limitation period for bringing proceedings against a public authority under s7 is short. Section 7(5) provides that:

> Proceedings under subs(1)(a) must be brought before the end of –
> (a) the period of one year beginning with the date on which the act complained of took place; or
> (b) such longer period as the court or tribunal considers equitable having regard to all the circumstances
> but that is subject to any rule imposing a stricter time limit in relation to the procedure in question.

2.74 Where a person does not bring proceedings against a public authority but merely seeks to rely on his/her Convention rights in legal proceedings brought by others, no limitation period is imposed by the HRA.

---

203 (1996) 22 EHRR 293.
204 Ibid para 46.
205 S9(5).
206 S9(4).
207 S9(5).

Convention claims in relation to the acts of private individuals

2.75   Although most of the provisions in the HRA focus on the acts or omissions of public authorities, the acts of private individuals do not fall outside its scope for three reasons. First, because the European Court and Commission have developed an elaborate doctrine of 'positive obligations' under the Convention according to which state authorities can be held liable, in certain circumstances, for not providing effective protection against the acts of private individuals. This doctrine is examined in detail in chapter 5. By analogy, where a public authority has failed to provide effective protection against the acts of private individuals in similar circumstances, s7 will be triggered and proceedings may be brought against that authority;[208] alternatively the public authority's omission can be relied upon in other legal proceedings.[209]

2.76   The second reason why the acts of private individuals do not fall outside the scope of the HRA is that, as noted above, courts and tribunals are included within the definition of a 'public authority' under the Act. It follows that they will be acting unlawfully if they fail to develop the law – both statute law and the common law – in a way which is compatible with Convention rights, even where litigation is taking place between private individuals.

2.77   The Lord Chancellor recognised this in debate during the HRA's passage through the House of Lords when he rejected an amendment to exclude courts and tribunals from the definition:

> We also believe that it is right as a matter of principle for the courts to have the duty of acting compatibly with the Convention not only in cases involving other public authorities but also in developing the common law in deciding cases between individuals. Why should they not? In preparing this Bill, we have taken the view that it is the other course, that of excluding Convention considerations altogether from cases between individuals which would have to be justified. The courts already bring Convention considerations to bear and I have no doubt that they will continue to do so in developing the common law ... Clause 3 requires the courts to interpret legislation compatibly with the Convention rights and to the fullest extent possible in all cases coming before them.[210]

208 S7(1)(a).
209 S7(1)(b).
210 HL Debs col 783, 24 November 1997.

2.78   In other words, legislation must be read and given effect in a way which is compatible with Convention rights whoever is before the courts *and* the common law must be developed so as to be compatible with the Convention. In *Rommelfanger v Germany*[211] the Commission recognised the duty of the courts in some cases to protect the Convention rights of private individuals before them. And in this respect, the consistent case-law of the Commission that state responsibility is engaged under the Convention where a court's jurisdiction is invoked in relation to Convention rights is also obviously important.[212]

2.79   The third reason why the acts of private individuals do not fall outside the scope of the HRA is that s7(1)(b) provides that, in addition to proceedings against a public authority, Convention rights may be relied upon in 'any legal proceedings'. As noted above,[213] this includes proceedings brought by or at the instigation of a public authority[214] but does not *exclude* proceedings between private individuals. Hence the courts or tribunals may be called upon to protect Convention rights in ordinary civil litigation between two private parties. However, in this respect, an unlawful act or omission of a public authority must be identified before s7(1)(b) comes into play by reason of the 'victim' requirement: Convention rights are not made directly enforceable against private individuals by this route.

2.80   Against this background, it is clearly important to identify the right party to proposed litigation where a breach of Convention rights is claimed. Under the doctrine of positive obligations, public authorities owe duties to individuals to protect them from the acts of others; no duty is directly imposed on those others to respect Convention rights. In other cases, the parties to litigation may well be private individuals, but the basis for the claim that Convention rights should be protected is that courts and tribunals, as public authorities, are under a duty to protect Convention rights of the parties before them; again no duty is directly imposed on others to respect Convention rights. However, it is obvious that courts and tribunals can give effect to their duty only by imposing duties on private individuals, albeit indirectly.

211 (1989) 62 DR 151.
212 See, for example *Van der Heijden v Netherlands* (1985) 41 DR 264. See further paras 4.94 to 4.96.
213 See paras 2.1 to 2.6.
214 S8(6).

Retrospective claims under the Human Rights Act

2.81   No proceedings may be brought against a public authority in respect
of an act or omission taking place before the coming into force of the
HRA.[215] The position is different, however, in respect of proceedings
brought by or at the instigation of a public authority; in that case an
act or omission may be challenged as incompatible with Convention
rights whenever the act or omission took place.[216]

215 S22(4).
216 S22(4).

CHAPTER 3

Convention rights: overview, structure and summary

3.1   Introduction

        Overview

        Convention rights: checklist

3.4   Article 2: the right to life

3.4   Is article 2 engaged?

3.8   Does article 2(2) apply?

3.9   Has article 2(2) been complied with?

3.10   Article 3: the prohibition on torture, inhuman and degrading treatment and punishment

3.10   Is article 3 engaged?

3.14   Do any implied restrictions apply?

3.15   Article 4: the prohibition on slavery and related practices

3.15   Is article 4 engaged?

3.18   Do any of the exemptions in article 4(3) apply?

3.21   Article 5: the right to liberty

3.21   The scheme of article 5

3.23   Is article 5 engaged?

3.26   *Period of detention*

3.27   *Curfews*

3.28   *Voluntary surrender*

continued

3.29   *Ability to leave*

3.30   *Status of individual concerned*

3.31   *Children*

3.33   Is detention 'lawful'?

3.34   *Lawful under domestic law*

3.36   *The requirements of the Convention*

3.37   *The prohibition on arbitrary detention*

3.38   Have the procedural requirements of domestic law been complied with?

3.41   Is detention permitted under article 5(1)(a)–(f)?

3.41   *Article 5(1)(a): detention following conviction*

3.46   *Article 5(1)(b): arrest and detention to enforce court orders or obligations prescribed by law*

3.51   *Article 5(1)(c): arrest on 'reasonable suspicion'*

3.55   *Article 5(1)(d): the detention of children*

3.58   *Article 5(1)(e): detention of persons of unsound mind and others*

3.65   *Article 5(1)(f): detention pending deportation or extradition*

3.69   Have reasons been given for detention as required under article 5(2)?

3.71   In the criminal context: have the pre-trial rights in article 5(3) been complied with?

3.73   If not, does the UK derogation apply?

3.74   Are habeas corpus proceedings available?

3.84   Is there an enforceable right to compensation for wrongful detention?

3.87   **Article 6: fair trial**

3.87   The scheme of article 6

3.89   Do the proceedings involve the determination of a criminal charge?

3.90   If not, do the proceedings involve the determination of a civil right or obligation?

3.92   In either case, have the fair trial requirements of article 6(1) been met?

3.94   Are any further guarantees required to ensure a fair trial?

3.99   Are there any relevant implied limitations?

3.100   In the criminal context: has the presumption of
         innocence been respected?

3.101   In the criminal context: have the minimum guarantees of
         article 6(3) been complied with?

3.102   Article 7: the prohibition on retrospective criminal offences

3.103   Do the proceedings relate to a criminal offence or criminal
         penalty?

3.104   If so, has there been retrospective application of the
         criminal law?

3.107   If so, can retrospective application be justified under article
         7(2)?

3.108   Article 8: privacy and related matters

3.109   Is article 8 engaged?

3.109   Private life

3.112   Secret surveillance by the security services

3.113   Family life

3.117   The home

3.121   Correspondence

3.123   Positive obligations under article 8

3.125   Can the reason for any restriction be found in article 8(2)?

3.127   If so, is the restriction 'in accordance with law'?

3.129   If so, is it 'necessary in a democratic society'?

3.130   Article 9: religion and belief

3.131   Is article 9 engaged?

3.136   Conscientious objectors

3.137   Can the reason for any restriction be found in article 9(2)?

3.139   If so, is the restriction 'prescribed by law'?

3.140   If so, is the restriction 'necessary in a democratic society' ?

3.141   Article 10: freedom of expression

3.143   Is article 10 engaged?

3.146   Is any restriction in truth a licensing restriction?

continued

3.147   If not, can the reason for any restriction be found in article 10(2)?

3.149   If so, is the restriction 'prescribed by law'?

3.150   If so, is the restriction 'necessary in a democratic society'?

3.151   Article 11: freedom of assembly and association

3.153   Is article 11 engaged?

3.153   Freedom of assembly

3.157   Freedom of association

3.160   Trade unions

3.162   Is any restriction limited to the army, police and civil servants?

3.164   If not, can the reason for any restriction be found in article 11(2)?

3.166   If so, is the restriction 'prescribed by law'?

3.167   If so, is the restriction 'necessary in a democratic society'?

3.168   Article 12: the right to marry and found a family

3.169   Is article 12 engaged?

3.171   If so, do the age requirements and domestic rules
conform to the Convention?

3.173   Article 13: the right to an effective remedy

3.175   Is article 13 applicable?

3.178   If so, is there an 'arguable' breach of that right?

3.179   If so, is the remedy in question 'effective'?

3.183   Article 14: the prohibition on discrimination

3.184   Is there a substantive Convention right in issue?

3.185   If so, is there different treatment?

3.186   If so, does it have a legitimate aim?

3.187   Are the means employed to achieve the aim proportionate?

3.188   Article 1 of the first Protocol: the right to property

3.189   Is article 1 of Protocol 1 engaged?

3.190   If so, does the measure in question amount to
deprivation or control of property?

3.191   If deprivation: is it in the public interest and has a 'fair balance' been struck?

3.192   If control: does it have a legitimate aim and is it proportionate?

3.193   If neither deprivation nor control: does the measure in question nonetheless interfere with peaceful enjoyment of possessions?

3.194   Article 2 of the First Protocol: the right to education

3.195   Is article 2 of Protocol 1 engaged?

3.196   If so, does the reservation apply?

3.197   Are there any relevant implied limitations?

3.198   Article 3 of the First Protocol: the duty to hold free elections

3.199   Is article 3 of Protocol 1 engaged?

3.200   If so, what principles apply?

3.202   Are there any relevant implied limitations?

Introduction

3.1   Convention rights are not dealt with on an article by article basis in this book. Instead, they are dealt with on an issue by issue basis, bringing together the Convention case-law according to the subject-matter. However, the structure of Convention rights is important and this chapter, therefore, analyses the structure of all of the articles of the Convention which are applicable in the UK and summarises their scope and effect.

3.2   The rights protected under the Human Rights Act 1998 (HRA) are those set out in:

1) articles 2–12 and 14 of the Convention itself;

2) articles 1–3 of the First Protocol; and

3) article 1 of the Sixth Protocol.[1]

They are not set out in identical form and do not enjoy equal protection.[2] Although not included in Schedule 1 of the HRA, article 13 is relevant to its application.[3]

3.3   This chapter provides an overview of the Convention rights incorporated into UK law by the HRA. It starts by identifying the scope of each of the relevant Convention articles. A checklist for each article is then provided because the Court adopts a structured approach to Convention rights and, broadly speaking, each case progresses through this checklist. Finally, a summary of the rights in question is provided. For convenience of reference, in the overview section, the material is organised to correspond with the checklist.

---

1   S1(1).
2   See paras 4.2 to 4.3.
3   See paras 1.7 to 1.8.

Overview

Convention

Article 2   1) The right to life.

2) The circumstances when deprivation of life does not breach article 2(1).

Article 3   The prohibition on torture, degrading and inhuman treatment or punishment.

Article 4   1) The prohibition on slavery and servitude.

2) The prohibition on forced or compulsory labour.

3) The exclusion from article 4(2) of:

a) Work done whilst in detention or on conditional release from detention.

b) Military service and work done by conscientious objectors.

c) Work needed to deal with an emergency or a calamity threatening the life or well-being of the community.

d)   Normal civic obligations.

Article 5   1) The right to liberty and security of person. Exceptions:

a) Detention after conviction.

b) Detention for non-compliance with a court order or to secure an obligation prescribed by law.

c) Arrest in the criminal context.

d) Detention of children.

e) Detention of the mentally ill, alcoholics, drug addicts, vagrants and to prevent the spread of infectious diseases.

f) Detention to prevent unlawful entry and pending extradition and expulsion.

2) The right to reasons for arrest.

3) The preconditions of a lawful arrest in the criminal context, the right to bail and the right to trial within a reasonable period.

4) Habeas corpus.

5) The right to compensation for wrongful detention.

Article 6   ·1) The right to a fair trial in criminal and civil proceedings.

> 2) The presumption of innocence.
> 3) Minimum rights in criminal cases:
>   a) Information about charge.
>   b) Adequate time and facilities.
>   c) Legal aid and legal representation.
>   d) Witnesses.
>   e) Interpretation.

Article 7
1) The prohibition on retrospective criminal offences.
2) Exceptions for crimes recognised under international law.

Article 8
1) The right to privacy, family life, home and correspondence.
2) Permitted restrictions on article 8(1) rights.

Article 9
1) Freedom of thought, conscience and religion.
2) Permitted restrictions on article 9(1) rights.

Article 10
1) Freedom of expression.
2) Permitted restrictions on article 10(1) rights.

Article 11
1) Freedom of assembly and association.
2) Permitted restrictions on article 11(1) rights.

Article 12   The right to marry.

Article 13   The right to an effective remedy.

Article 14   The prohibition on discrimination.

First Protocol
Article 1   The right to property.

Article 2   The right to education.

Article 3   Election rights.

Sixth Protocol
Article 1   Abolition of death penalty.

Article 2   Exclusions from article 1 in times of war or imminent threat of war.

Convention rights: checklist

Whenever a convention issue arises, it can be analysed on a check-list basis. The first task is to identify the Convention right engaged; the next, to progress through the checklist.

Article 2   – Is article 2 engaged?
             – Does article 2(2) apply?
             – Has article 2(2) been complied with?

Article 3   – Is article 3 engaged?
             – Do any implied restrictions apply?

Article 4   – Is article 4 engaged?
             – Do any of the exemptions in article 4(3) apply?

Article 5   – Is article 5 engaged?
             – Is detention 'lawful'?
             – Have the procedural requirements of domestic law been complied with?
             – Is detention permitted under articles 5(1)(a)–5(1)(f)?
             – Have reasons been given for detention in accordance with article 5(2)?
             – In the criminal context, have the pre-trial rights in article 5(3) been complied with?
             – If not, does the UK derogation apply?
             – Are habeas corpus proceedings available?
             – Is there an enforceable right to compensation for wrongful detention?

Article 6   – Do the proceedings involve the determination of a criminal charge?
             – If not, do the proceedings involve the determination of a civil right or obligation?
             – In either case, have the fair trial requirements of article 6(1) been met?
             – Are any further guarantees required to ensure a fair trial?
             – Are there any relevant implied limitations to the article 6 requirements?
             – In the criminal context: has the presumption of innocence been respected?
             – In the criminal context: have the minimum guarantees of article 6(3) been complied with?

Article 7	– Do the proceedings relate to a criminal offence or criminal penalty?
	– If so, has there been retrospective application of the criminal law?
	– If so, can retrospective application be justified under article 7(2)?
Article 8	– Is article 8 engaged?
	– Can the reason for any restriction be found in article 8(2)?
	– If so, is the restriction 'in accordance with law'?
	– If so, is the restriction 'necessary in a democratic society'?
Article 9	– Is article 9 engaged?
	– Can the reason for any restriction be found in article 9(2)?
	– If so, is the restriction 'prescribed by law'?
	– If so, is the restriction 'necessary in a democratic society'?
Article 10	– Is article 10 engaged?
	– Is any restriction in truth a licensing restriction?
	– If not, can the reason for any restriction be found in article 10(2)?
	– If so, is the restriction 'prescribed by law'?
	– If so, is the restriction 'necessary in a democratic society'?
Article 11	– Is article 11 engaged?
	– Is any restriction limited to the army, police and civil servants?
	– If so, can that restriction be justified?
	– If not, can the reason for any restriction be found in article 11(2)?
	– If so, is the restriction 'prescribed by law'?
	– If so, is the restriction 'necessary in a democratic society'?
Article 12	– Is article 12 engaged?
	– If so, do the age requirements and domestic rules conform to the Convention?
Article 13	– Is article 13 applicable?

	– If so, is there an 'arguable' breach of that right? – If so, is the remedy in question 'effective'?
Article 14	– Is there a substantive Convention right in issue? – If so, is there different treatment? – If so, does it have a legitimate aim? – If so, are the means employed to achieve the aim proportionate?
Article 1 of Protocol 1	– Is article 1 of Protocol 1 engaged? If so, does the measure in question amount to deprivation or control of property? If deprivation: is it in the public interest and has a 'fair balance' been struck? If control: does it have a legitimate aim and is it proportionate? If neither deprivation nor control: does the measure in question nonetheless interfere with with peaceful enjoyment of possessions?
Article 2 of Protocol 1	– Is article 2 of Protocol 1 engaged? If so, does the reservation apply? Are there any relevant implied limitations?
Article 3 of Protocol 1	– Is article 3 of Protocol 1 engaged? If so, what principles apply? Are there any relevant implied limitations?

Article 2: the right to life

Is article 2 engaged?

3.4　Article 2(1) provides that:

> Everyone's right to life shall be protected by law. No one shall be deprived of his life intentionally save in the execution of a sentence of a court following his conviction of a crime for which this penalty is provided by law.

The fundamental nature of the right to life is obvious and in peace time derogation from article 2 is not possible.

3.5　The death penalty is not prohibited under article 2, but in this respect article 2 has been supplemented by Optional Protocol No 6 which provides that:

(1) The death penalty shall be abolished. No one shall be condemned to such penalty or executed.

(2) A State may make provision in its law for the death penalty in respect of acts committed in time of war or of imminent war; such penalty shall be applied only in the instances laid down in the law and in accordance with its provisions. The State shall communicate to the Secretary General of the Council of Europe the relevant provisions of that law.

(3) No derogation from the provisions of this be made under article 15 of the Convention. Protocol shall be made under Article 15 of the Convention.

(4) No reservation may be made under [article 57] of the Convention in respect of the provisions of this Protocol.

The UK ratified Optional Protocol No 6 on 27 January 1999 and the HRA gives it effect in domestic law.

3.6　Article 2 imposes two duties on the state (and its officials). First, not to deprive anyone of his/her life save in the limited circumstances prescribed by article 2(2) (see below). Second, to take reasonable measures to protect life.

3.7　The duty to take reasonable measures to protect life includes a duty to put in place 'effective criminal law provisions to deter the commission of offences against the person backed up by law-enforcement machinery for the prevention, suppression and sanctioning of breaches of such provisions.'[4] It may also include, in

4　*Osman v UK* (Court) 28 October 1998 at para 115; [1999] 1 FLR 193; noted at [1999] EHRLR 228.

certain well-defined circumstances, a positive obligation on the authorities to take preventative operational measures to protect an individual whose life is at risk from the criminal acts of another individual.[5]

Does article 2(2) apply?

3.8   Article 2(2) provides that:

> Deprivation of life shall not be regarded as inflicted in contravention of this article when it results from the use of force which is no more than absolutely necessary:
>
> (a) in defence of any person from unlawful violence;
> (b) in order to effect a lawful arrest or to prevent the escape of a person lawfully detained;
> (c) in action lawfully taken for the purpose of quelling a riot or insurrection.

The fundamental nature of the right to life dictates that these provisions are not only 'exhaustive' but must also be 'narrowly construed.'[6] Moreover, article 2(2) is not intended to be a list of situations in which intentional killing is justified; rather it sets limits on the use of force which may result – as an unintended consequence – in the deprivation of life.[7]

Has article 2(2) been complied with?

3.9   Even when the use of force is permitted under article 2(2), it must be no more than 'absolutely necessary' for the achievement of one of the purposes defined in article 2(2)(a), (b) or (c). The use of the term 'absolutely necessary' indicates that a stricter and more compelling test of necessity must be employed from that normally applicable when determining whether state action is 'necessary in a democratic society' under articles 8 to 11 of the Convention. In particular, the force used must be strictly proportionate to the achievement of the aims set out in sub-paragraphs 2(a), (b) and (c) of article 2.[8]

---

5   Ibid; see further chapter 16.
6   *Stewart v UK* (10044/82) 39 DR 162; *McCann v UK* (1995) 21 EHRR 97.
7   *McCann v UK* n6.
8   *McCann v UK* n6 at para 149; *Andronicou and Constantinou v Cyprus* (1997) 25 EHRR 491 at para 171; see further chapter 14.

Article 3: the prohibition on torture, inhuman and degrading treatment and punishment

Is article 3 engaged?

3.10 Article 3 provides that:

> No one shall be subjected to torture or to inhuman or degrading treatment or punishment.

It is one of the strongest rights under the Convention in the sense that it is expressed in unqualified terms[9] and in peace time derogation from article 2 is not possible.

3.11 Article 3 covers three separate categories of prohibited treatment or punishment: (1) torture; (2) inhuman treatment/punishment; and (3) degrading treatment/punishment. In each case conduct must 'attain a minimum level of severity' before article 3 is breached.[10] The assessment of this minimum is relative; it depends on all the circumstances of the case, such as the duration of the treatment, its physical or mental effects and, in some cases, the sex, age and state of health of the victim.

3.12 The guidelines given by the European Court in *Ireland v UK*[11] provide a useful starting point in assessing whether conduct reaches the threshold of severity required to breach article 3. The guidelines define the three separate categories of prohibited treatment or punishment as follows:

1) *Torture*

Deliberate inhuman treatment causing very serious and cruel suffering.

2) *Inhuman treatment/punishment*

Treatment/punishment that causes intense physical and mental suffering.

3) *Degrading treatment/punishment*

Treatment/punishment that arouses in the victim a feeling of fear, anguish and inferiority capable of humiliating and debasing the victim and possibly breaking his or her physical or moral resistance.

---

9 But see para 3.14.
10 *Ireland v UK* (1979–80) 2 EHRR 25 at para 162.
11 Note 10.

3.18   However, since the Convention is a 'living instrument' to be interpreted according to 'notions currently prevailing in democratic states',[12] these guidelines should not be applied too rigidly. In some cases, conduct found by the Court and Commission to fall below the threshold of severity for article 3 many years ago, may have to be reconsidered in future cases.

3.19   The European Court and Commission have found many forms of conduct to be *capable* of breaching article 3, including: serious assaults[13] (particularly assaults in custody);[14] the application of psychological interrogation techniques;[15] prison conditions;[16] rape;[17] corporal punishment;[18] extradition or expulsion where torture or ill-treatment might be a consequence;[19] and even the threat of torture so long as it is 'sufficiently real and immediate' to cause mental anguish.[20] In addition both the Court and the Commission have recognised that the institutionalisation of certain practices can amount to degrading treatment contrary to article 3. So, for example, in the *East African Asians* cases[21] the Commission found a violation of article 3 on the basis that the practice of refusing to allow British passport holders who had been expelled from Uganda, Tanzania and Kenya to take up residence in the UK amounted to institutionalised racism. This is possibly subject to the qualification introduced by the European Court in *Abdulaziz, Cabales and Balkandali v UK*[22] that degradation must be intentional to violate article 3.

Do any implied restrictions apply?

3.14   Although expressed in unqualified terms, some limits are inherent in the application of article 3. While torture and most forms of inhuman treatment/punishment cannot be justified in any circumstances, it is clear that degrading treatment can be justified in some

---

12 *Van der Mussele v Belgium* (1984) 6 EHRR 163; see further paras 4.16 to 4.18.
13 See, for example: The *Greek* Case (1969) 12 Yearbook 1; *Tomasi v France* (1993) 15 EHRR 1; *Ribitsch v Austria* (1996) 21 EHRR 573.
14 See chapter 15.
15 *Ireland v UK* (1979–80) 2 EHRR 25.
16 See chapter 16.
17 *Aksoy v Turkey* (1997) 23 EHRR 553.
18 See chapter 20.
19 See chapter 18.
20 *Campbell and Cosans v UK* (1982) 4 EHRR 293.
21 (1981) 3 EHRR 76.
22 (1985) 7 EHRR 471.

clearly-defined circumstances. For example, most if not all punishment is degrading and both the Commission and Court have drawn a distinction between ordinary prison conditions and those which fall below an acceptable standard.[23]

Article 4: the prohibition on slavery and related practices

Is article 4 engaged?

3.15 Article 4 provides that:

(1) No one shall be held in slavery or servitude.

(2) No one shall be required to perform forced or compulsory labour.

In peace time derogation is possible from article 4(2) but not from article 4(1).

3.16 Slavery and servitude are to be distinguished from forced or compulsory labour. Slavery and servitude relate primarily to the status of an individual and his/her condition in life, whereas forced or compulsory labour is a much broader concept concerned with work exacted under threat of a penalty.[24]

3.17 When considering cases under article 4(2), the European Court has adopted the definition of 'forced or compulsory labour' provided by the relevant Conventions of the International Labour Organisation (ILO).[25] The European Commission for its part has paid particular attention to ILO Convention No 105 which sets out five categories of forced labour: (a) political coercion or education or as a punishment for holding or expressing political views or views ideologically opposed to the established political, social or economic system; (b) mobilising and using labour for purposes of economic development; (c) labour discipline; (d) punishment for having participated in strikes; (e) and racial, social or religious discrimination. Tested against this criteria, an obligation to carry out legal aid work does not violate article 4(2).[26] Nor does an obligation on young advocates to undertake free legal representation for poor defendants.[27]

---

23 See chapter 16.
24 See para 16.37 and paras 28.16 to 28.24.
25 See, for example: *Van der Mussele v Belgium* n12.
26 *X and Y v Germany* (1976) 10 DR 224.
27 See, for example: *Van der Mussele v Belgium* n12; see further chapter 28.

Do any of the exemptions in article 4(3) apply?

3.18   Article 4(3) provides that:

> For the purpose of this article the term 'forced or compulsory labour' shall not include:
>
> (a) any work required to be done in the ordinary course of detention imposed according to the provisions of article 5 of this Convention or during conditional release from such detention;
>
> (b) any service of a military character or, in case of conscientious objectors in countries where they are recognised, service exacted instead of compulsory military service;
>
> (c) any service exacted in case of an emergency or calamity threatening the life or well-being of the community;
>
> (d) any work or service which forms part of normal civic obligations.

3.19   Article 4(3)(a) permits forced or compulsory labour only where it is in the ordinary course of detention and complies with article 5, which in the view of the Court in *De Wilde, Ooms and Versyp v Belgium*[28] implies that the work is aimed at rehabilitation. Article 4(3)(b) does not give conscientious objectors the right to exemption from military service; the words 'in countries where they are recognised' leaves states a choice whether or not to recognise conscientious objectors and, if so recognised, to provide some sub-stitute service for them.[29]

3.20   There have been few cases under articles 4(3)(c) and 4(3)(d). The main purpose of article 4(3)(d) is to cover obligations which all citizens have, such as to assist someone who is helpless, to fill in tax documents,[30] to observe safety requirements and other similar activities.[31] In *Schmidt v Germany*[32] the European Court found a violation of article 4(3)(d) where male citizens were required either to serve in the fire brigade or to pay a financial contribution in lieu of such service.

---

28   (1979–80) 1 EHRR 373.

29   *Johansen v Norway* (1985) 44 DR 155.

30   *Societies W, X, Y and Z v Austria* (1977) 7 DR 148.

31   *Law and Practice of the European Convention on Human Rights and the European Social Charter* Gomien et al Council of Europe Publishing, 1996 p124.

32   (1994) 18 EHRR 513.

33   See, for example, *Bozano v France* (1987) 9 EHRR 297, which concerned 'disguised extradition' designed to circumvent proper court procedures.

Article 5: the right to liberty

The scheme of article 5

3.21   Article 5 has two limbs. First it guarantees liberty and security of person: para 5(1). Second it provides a set of procedural rights for detainees: paras 5(2)–5(5). In this context, liberty and security of person are very closely linked; the European Court and Commission rarely distinguish between the two. At most, the reference to security of person underlines the prohibition on arbitrary detention in article 5.[33] It does not refer to physical or bodily integrity independent of liberty.[34]

3.22   The scheme of article 5(1) is to set up a positive right to liberty with limited exceptions and an overriding requirement that any deprivation of liberty must be 'in accordance with a procedure prescribed by law' and 'lawful'. It provides that:

> Everyone has the right to liberty and security of person. No one shall be deprived of his liberty save in the following cases and in accordance with the procedure prescribed by law:
>
> (a) the lawful detention of a person after conviction by a competent court;
>
> (b) the lawful arrest or detention of a person for non-compliance with the lawful order of a court or in order to secure fulfilment of any obligation prescribed by law;
>
> (c) the lawful arrest or detention of a person effected for the purpose of bringing him before the competent legal authority on reasonable suspicion of having committed an offence, or when it is reasonably considered necessary to prevent his committing an offence or fleeing after having done so;
>
> (d) the detention of a minor by lawful order for the purpose of educational supervision or his lawful detention for the purpose of bringing him before the competent legal authority;
>
> (e) the lawful detention of persons for the prevention of the spreading of infectious diseases, of persons of unsound mind, alcoholics or drug addicts or vagrants;

---

34 Issues of physical or bodily integrity therefore fall to be considered by reference to other provisions such as article 3 (the prohibition on ill-treatment etc) or article 8 (privacy).

35 *Winterwerp v Netherlands* (1979–80) 2 EHRR 387 at para 37.

(f) the lawful arrest or detention of a person to prevent his effecting an unauthorised entry into the country or of a person against whom action is being taken with a view to deportation or extradition.

The exceptions provided for in paras 5(1)(a)–5(1)(f) are to be narrowly construed and represent an exhaustive definition of the circumstances in which a person may lawfully be deprived of his/her liberty.[35]

Is article 5 engaged?

3.23   Not every restriction on a person's liberty amounts to detention. A threshold issue therefore has to be determined; namely whether there has been a deprivation of liberty within the meaning of article 5. If not, neither the substantive provisions of paragraph 5(1) nor the procedural aspects of paragraphs 5(2)–5(5) will apply.[36]

3.24   The starting point under the Convention is the 'concrete situation' of the person concerned. Relevant to this assessment will be a whole range of criteria such as the type of interference with liberty concerned, its duration, effect and manner of implementation.[37]

3.25   Article 5 is not, in principle, concerned with mere restrictions on liberty of movement; such restrictions are governed by article 2 of the Fourth Protocol to the Convention.[38] However, the difference between deprivation of and restriction upon liberty is 'merely one of degree or intensity, and not one of nature or substance.'[39]

Period of detention

3.26   The period of detention is relevant, but not definitive. The objective is more important. If the objective is to detain, article 5 applies. If there is some other objective, the action of the person(s) detaining will have to be carefully examined to see whether, in effect, it

---

36 Nonetheless, article 3 and/or article 8 might still be relevant.

37 *Guzzardi v Italy* (1981) 3 EHRR 333 at para 92. See also: J L Murdoch 'Article 5 of the European Convention on Human Rights: The protection of liberty and security of person' *Human Rights Files No 12*, 1994, Council of Europe Press, p11.

38 Article 2 of the Fourth Protocol provides:

> Everyone lawfully within the territory of a state shall, within that territory, have the right to freedom of movement and freedom to choose his residence.

This provision has not (yet) been ratified by the UK.

39 *Guzzardi v Italy* n37 at para 93.

amounts to a deprivation of liberty within the meaning of article 5. This issue is examined in detail in chapter 15.[40]

Curfews

3.27   Instructions or orders confining individuals to a specific area, such as curfews, are particularly difficult to categorise. In *Cyprus v Turkey*,[41] the Commission held that orders imposed by the occupying military authorities confining individuals to their homes amounted to a 'deprivation of liberty' within the meaning of article 5, while the imposition of a night curfew did not.[42] The European Court adopted a similar approach in *Guzzardi v Italy*[43] where it found that the applicant had been deprived of his liberty when he was confined by a court order to stay within a small area on an island and had limited social contact.

Voluntary surrender

3.28   The mere fact that a person has voluntarily surrendered to detention will not automatically exclude article 5 protection. In *De Wilde, Ooms and Versyp v Belgium*[44] where the applicants had given themselves up to the police under Belgian vagrancy laws, the Court held that:

> The right to liberty is too important in a 'democratic society' within the meaning of the Convention for a person to lose the benefit of the protection of the Convention for the single reason that he gives himself up to be taken into detention.[45]

Similarly in *Walverens v Belgium*[46] the Commission was prepared to overlook the fact that the applicant's attendance at a police station was technically voluntary where, in reality, he felt constrained from leaving.[47]

Ability to leave

3.29   As a general rule, an ability to leave the area of confinement will usually exclude the application of article 5. So, for example, in *SM and*

40   Paras 15.46 to 15.55.
41   Comm Report, 10 July 1976.
42   Ibid para 235.
43   Note 37.
44   Note 28.
45   Ibid para 65.
46   Commission (5 March 1980); unreported.
47   See para 3.26.

MT v Austria,[48] the Commission found no deprivation of liberty where the applicants, who were Lebanese, were confined to the transit area of Vienna airport but free to leave at any time. However, there are exceptions. In *Amwr v France*[49] the applicants, fleeing from the regime in Somalia via Syria, argued that their article 5 rights had been infringed when, having arrived at Paris-Orly airport, they were held for 20 days in the transit area and a nearby hotel (part of which had been converted as a holding area). The French government argued that although the transit area was 'closed on the French side' it was 'open to the outside', so that the applicants could have returned of their own accord to Syria. The European Court disagreed. In its view the mere fact that it was possible for the applicants to leave voluntarily did not automatically exclude the application of article 5. Since Syria could not offer protection comparable to that of France, the possibility of returning there was 'theoretical' and thus irrelevant for article 5 purposes.

Status of individual concerned

3.30   Sometimes the status of the individual concerned will also affect the question of whether there has been a deprivation of liberty. In *Engel v Netherlands*[50] the applicants, all members of the armed forces, made complaints relating to a disciplinary regime under which they were subjected to 'strict arrest' (confinement to a cell), 'aggravated arrest' (confinement to designated but unlocked premises) and 'light arrest' (confinement to military premises while off-duty). The European Court found that only 'strict arrest' came within the meaning of article 5 because it was the only form of detention which deviated from 'normal conditions' of military life.

Children

3.31   The Court and Commission have been prepared to accept that parents and schools can deprive children of their liberty without raising an article 5 issue. In *Nielsen v Denmark*[51] a 12-year-old boy was admitted by his mother to a psychiatric hospital against his will. He was not mentally ill and tried to escape several times during his confinement at the hospital (over five months). The Commission found

---

48   (1993) 74 DR 179.
49   (1996) 22 EHRR 533.
50   (1979–80) 1 EHRR 647.
51   (1989) 11 EHRR 175.

this to be a 'deprivation of liberty', but the Court, by a bare majority, disagreed. In its view the exercise of parental rights under article 8 of the Convention inevitably involved imposing restrictions on children which could not legitimately be placed on adults. However, in an important passage the Court emphasised that:

> ... the rights of the holder of parental authority cannot be unlimited and that it is incumbent on the State to provide safeguards against abuse.[52]

On the facts, the Court was satisfied that the mother's decision was based on what appeared to her to be sound medical advice and that she was acting in what she perceived to be the interests of her son's health.

3.32   The *Nielsen* case is important in another respect in the context of arrest and detention because the Danish government contended before the Court that article 5 did not apply to a deprivation of liberty resulting from the acts of private individuals rather than state authorities (or public officials). In so far as it found that the state has a responsibility to ensure that private individuals cannot subject others to arbitrary detention, the Court implicitly rejected this. It follows that the mere fact that an arrest is carried out by a private individual (for example, a member of a private security firm) will not necessarily preclude the application of article 5.

Is detention 'lawful'?

3.33   The requirement in article 5 that every arrest and/or detention be 'lawful' has three aspects. First, every arrest and/or detention must be lawful under the applicable domestic law.[53] Second, every arrest and/or detention must conform with the general requirements of the Convention. Third, arrest and/or detention must not be 'arbitrary'. Each of these will be examined briefly.

Lawful under domestic law

3.34   Whether an arrest and/or detention is lawful under the applicable domestic law will depend in the first place on whether there is a clear legal basis for the deprivation of liberty on the facts of each case. When applying this test, the European Court and Commission of Human Rights – as international supervisory bodies – have been

---

52 Ibid at para 72.
53 This may include EC law: see *Caprino v UK* (1978) 12 DR 14.

slow to interfere with the findings of domestic courts that an arrest and/or detention is lawful.[54] However, both bodies have retained ultimate power to review the interpretation and application of domestic law on the basis that it remains their function to determine whether article 5 has been breached. On this basis, in *Winterwerp v Netherlands*[55] the European Court was prepared to examine whether an order for the applicant's detention on the basis that he was of 'unsound mind' was based on reliable evidence about his mental condition and was otherwise supported by the facts. However, (so far) the Strasbourg bodies have declined to review the facts upon which a conviction is based. So long as a prison sentence was lawful (in domestic law terms) when imposed, the fact that it is later overturned will not mean that article 5(1) has been breached.

3.35   Under the HRA, the approach of domestic courts and tribunals to the question of lawfulness will be different. That is because, as the European Court and Commission have long recognised, their task is to scrutinise every arrest and/or detention for compliance with domestic law.[56] Where an arrest and/or detention is unlawful in domestic law, it is automatically in breach of article 5.[57] This will have an impact on damages since article 5(5) provides that anyone who has been arrested and/or detained in breach of article 5 has 'an enforceable right' to compensation.[58]

The requirements of the Convention

3.36   In addition, the term 'lawful' in article 5(1) has been held to require that the domestic law upon which an arrest and/or detention is based must be accessible and precise.[59] This, in effect, imports into article 5 the principle derived from articles 8–11 that any restriction on Convention rights must be 'prescribed by law'.[60] According to this principle domestic law must be adequately accessible, in the sense that a citizen must have an indication that is adequate in the circumstances of the legal rules applicable in a given case, and that the law

54 See chapter 4.
55 (1979) 2 EHRR 387.
56 *Wassink v Netherlands* A/185-A (1990), unreported, at para 24.
57 See *Raninen v Finland* (1998) 26 EHRR 563 at para 46.
58 See further paras 3.84 to 3.86.
59 *Steel and Others v UK* (Court) 23 September 1998 noted at [1999] EHRLR 109; see also *Zamir v UK* (1985) 40 DR 42 at paras 90–91.
60 This doctrine is examined in detail in chapter 4 see paras 4.29 to 4.36.

must be formulated with sufficient precision to enable the citizen to foresee – if need be with appropriate advice – the consequences of his/her actions.[61]

The prohibition on arbitrary detention

3.37 The term 'lawful' in article 5 prohibits arbitrary arrest and/or detention; for example, where there has been an abuse of power or bad faith in the process. So, for example, in *Bozano v France*[62] the applicant was sentenced in his absence to life imprisonment in Italy. He was subsequently arrested in France but an extradition request from Italy was refused because the French courts do not recognise trials in absentia. About a month after his release the applicant was again arrested in France but this time the French police took him to a pre-arranged rendezvous with Swiss police at the border. The Swiss courts thereafter extradited the applicant to Italy where he began serving his sentence. In relation to the action of the French police, the European Court found a violation of article 5 because the applicant's arrest and detention was 'a disguised form of extradition' designed to get round an adverse court decision and was therefore arbitrary. There is also authority to the effect that arrest and/or detention is 'arbitrary' if, although properly motivated, it is not proportionate to the legitimate aim being pursed.[63]

Have the procedural requirements of domestic law been complied with?

3.38 The requirement in article 5 that arrest and/or detention be 'in accordance with the procedure prescribed by law' clearly overlaps with the requirement that arrest and/or detention be 'lawful'. It involves consideration of how the decision to deprive an individual of his/her liberty has been taken, rather than why.

3.39 Where there is no procedure prescribed by law, or those effecting an arrest or ordering detention fail to adhere to procedural steps or safeguards laid down in domestic law there will be a breach of article 5. And domestic law must itself be in conformity with the Con-

---

61 See *Sunday Times v UK* (1979–80) 2 EHRR 245.
62 (1987) 9 EHRR 297.
63 See *The Law of the European Convention on Human Rights* Harris et al Butterworths, 1995 p106. See further: *Winterwerp v Netherlands* n35 and *Caprino v UK* (1981) 22 DR 5 at para 67. Where there is a short delay before release see *Quinn v France* (1996) 21 EHRR 529 and *K-F v Germany* [1998] EHRLR 228.

vention, including the general principles expressed or implied there-in.[64]

3.40   The term 'procedure' includes the procedure followed by a court when ordering detention and the rules governing the legality of an arrest.[65] So, for example, in *Van der Leer v Netherlands*[66] the European Court found a violation of article 5 where the domestic court failed to hear from the applicant before confining her to a psychiatric hospital for six months. Although domestic law provided for the making of such an order without a hearing in certain circumstances, the domestic court had not established that it was following this procedure. In *Winterwerp v Netherlands*[67] an argument that a full court rather than a single judge should have ordered the applicant's detention failed. And in *Weston v UK*,[68] the European Commission held that an arrest pursuant to a bench warrant issued by a judge within his jurisdiction was 'in accordance with a procedure prescribed by law' under article 5(1).

Is detention permitted under article 5(1)(a)–(f)?

Article 5(1)(a): detention following conviction

3.41   Article 5(1)(a) allows 'the lawful detention of a person after conviction by a competent court'. A 'conviction' means a 'finding of guilt' in respect of an offence.[69] And a 'competent court' is one with jurisdiction to try the case.[70] These definitions are broad enough to legitimise detention ordered outside the criminal justice system – for example, detention ordered by a military court – so long as the body ordering detention is independent of the executive and the parties and provides 'adequate judicial guarantees'.[71] Detention is not limited to imprisonment; it can include detention in a mental institution so long it is based on a 'conviction', but detention in such circumstances is primarily considered under article 5(1)(e).[72]

---

64   *Winterwerp v Netherlands* n35.
65   Harris et al n63, p104.
66   (1990) 12 EHRR 567.
67   Note 35.
68   (1981) 3 EHRR 402.
69   See Harris et al, n63, p110.
70   *X v Austria* (1968) 11 Yearbook 322 at p348; *X v Austria* (1970) 13 Yearbook 798 at p804.
71   *Engel v Netherlands* (1979–80) 1 EHRR 647.
72   See paras 3.58 to 3.64.

3.42   Article 5(1)(a) does not require a 'lawful conviction', only 'lawful detention'. On the basis of this distinction, the European Commission has refused to consider applications from prisoners who claim that they have been wrongly convicted.[73] By the same logic, the fact that a conviction is overturned on appeal will not affect the 'lawfulness' of detention pending appeal.[74] And the same applies to acquittal following a re-trial.[75]

3.43   To satisfy article 5(1)(a) detention must not only follow conviction in point of time, but must also 'result from, follow upon or occur by virtue of the conviction'.[76] The European Court found this requirement satisfied in *Weeks v UK*[77] where the applicant, who had been given a discretionary life sentence, was recalled to prison after his release on licence.[78] However, in that case, the Court indicated that article 5(1)(a) would be breached if a decision not to release or to re-detain were based on grounds which were inconsistent with the objectives of the sentencing court.[79] In *Monell and Morris v UK*[80] the European Court found that an order that time spent in prison pending an unmeritorious appeal should not form part of the sentence being served came within the scope of article 5(1)(a). This demonstrates the flexibility of the Court's approach where it considers the objective – speedy appeals by discouraging unmeritorious cases – legitimate.[81]

3.44   So far as sentence is concerned, article 5(1)(a) provides very little scope for challenge. In *Weeks v UK*[82] the Court held that:

> It is not for the Court, within the context of article 5, to review the appropriateness of the original sentence ...[83]

Therefore the only question in most cases will be whether the court imposing a sentence has followed the procedure required under

73 *Krzycki v Germany* (1978) 13 DR 57.
74 Ibid.
75 *X v Austria* (1969) 12 Yearbook 206 at p236.
76 *Monnell and Morris v UK* (1988) 10 EHRR 205 at para 40.
77 (1988) 10 EHRR 293.
78 See also *Van Droogenbroeck v Belgium* (1982) 4 EHRR 443.
79 Para 49; the position of life sentence prisoners generally is examined in chapter 16.
80 Note 76.
81 The case of *Monell and Morris v UK* n76 is examined further in chapter 10 at paras 10.19 to 10.21.
82 Note 77.
83 Ibid at para 50.

domestic law. An exceptionally severe sentence may, however, raise an issue under article 3.[84]

3.45   Conviction in another country can provide the basis for detention within the meaning of article 5(1)(a), whether or not that country is a party to the European Convention on Human Rights.[85] Accordingly, it is not contrary to the Convention for the UK to enforce a sentence passed abroad. However, delicate issues arise where it is alleged that a conviction abroad has been secured without regard to the article 6 requirements of a fair trial. The position adopted by the majority of the European Court in *Drozd and Janousek v France and Spain*[86] was that states receiving prisoners from abroad were not required to ensure that article 6 had been observed in the trial process because such a requirement would thwart the current trend towards increasing co-operation between states in the administration of justice. However, a number of judges dissented in strong terms from this position and it is clear that the position would be different if there had been a 'flagrant denial of justice' abroad.[87] Equally the position might be different where a conviction abroad has been secured without 'respect for the rule of law'.[88]

Article 5(1)(b): arrest and detention to enforce court orders or obligations prescribed by law

3.46   There are two limbs to article 5(1)(b). The first limb authorises arrest or detention 'for non-compliance with the lawful order of a court'. The second limb authorises arrest or detention 'in order to secure the fulfilment of an obligation prescribed by law'.

3.47   The first limb is designed to permit various forms of civil detention to enforce court orders including injunctions, maintenance orders, custody orders etc. Specific examples include detention for failure to pay a fine,[89] for refusal to undergo a psychiatric examination,[90] for refusal to undergo a blood test in affiliation proceedings[91]

---

84   This is implicit in the Court's judgment in *Weeks v UK* n77 at para 47.
85   *X v Germany* (1963) 6 Yearbook 494 at p576; *Drozd and Janousek v France and Spain* (1992) 14 EHRR 745.
86   Note 85.
87   Majority judgment at para 110.
88   *X v Germany* (1963) 6 Yearbook 494.
89   *Airey v Ireland* (1977) 8 DR 42.
90   *X v Germany* (1975) 3 DR 92.
91   *X v Austria* (1979) 18 DR 154.

and for refusing to be bound over to keep the peace and be of good behaviour.[92]

3.48   To authorise arrest or detention, an order of the court must be 'lawful' (a specific requirement of article 5(1)(a)) and 'in accordance with a procedure prescribed by law' (a general requirement under article 5(1)).[93] It must also not conflict with other provisions of the Convention; so, for example, in *K v Austria*[94] the Court found a breach of article 5(1)(b) where the applicant was imprisoned for failure to give evidence in court in circumstances that infringed freedom of expression under article 10.[95]

3.49   The second limb of article 5(1)(b) justifies arrest or detention only to enforce compliance with a 'specific and concrete obligation';[96] a general obligation to obey the law is not sufficient.[97] Whether the person concerned must have been given an opportunity to comply with the obligation before a power of arrest or detention arises depends on the facts. The general rule was set out by the European Court in a strong statement of principle in *Engel and Others v Netherlands*:[98]

> The court considers that the words 'secure the fulfilment of any obligation prescribed by law' concern only cases where the law permits the detention of a person to compel him to fulfil a specific and concrete obligation which he has until then failed to satisfy. A wide interpretation would entail consequences incompatible with the notion of the rule of law from which the whole Convention draws its inspiration.[99]

3.50   Nonetheless, the Commission has taken the (somewhat narrower) view that very special circumstances can justify arrest or detention even where the person concerned has not been given an opportunity to comply with the obligation in question.[100] However, so far, such circumstances have been confined to the exercise of special police powers under anti-terrorist legislation.[101]

---

92 *Steel and Others v UK* note 59.

93 See paras 3.33 to 3.40.

94 A/225-B (1993) Commission Report, unreported.

95 See *The Law of the European Convention on Human Rights* Harris et al Butterworths, 1995 p112.

96 *Engel and Others v Netherlands* (1979–80) 1 EHRR 647.

97 Ibid; preventative detention is dealt with at para 15.64.

98 Note 96.

99 Ibid at para 69.

100 See *McVeigh, O'Neill and Evans v UK* (1983) 5 EHRR 71.

101 See paras 15.72 to 15.79.

Article 5(1)(c): arrest on 'reasonable suspicion'

3.51   Three grounds for arrest are included in article 5(1)(c) of the Convention. They are:

1) the existence of a reasonable suspicion that the person arrested has committed an offence;

2) when it is reasonably considered necessary to prevent the person arrested committing an offence;

3) when it is reasonably considered necessary to prevent the person arrested fleeing after having committing an offence.

These are considered in detail in chapter 15.[102]

3.52   The term 'offence' in article 5 has been widely defined by the European Commission and Court and does not necessarily correspond to its domestic meaning.[103] *Brogan and Others v UK*[104] concerned the exercise of a statutory power of arrest of any person 'concerned in the commission, preparation or instigation of acts of terrorism', where the definition of 'terrorism' was the 'use of violence for political ends'. Although no criminal offence with the same definition existed, the Court held that the prohibited conduct was 'well in keeping with the idea of an offence'.[105] Similarly, in *Steel and Others v UK*[106] the Court took the view that, despite its classification as non-criminal in domestic law, 'breach of the peace must be regarded as an "offence" within the meaning of article 5(1)(c)' bearing in mind 'the nature of the proceedings in question and the penalty at stake'.[107]

3.53   What amounts to 'reasonable suspicion' will obviously vary according to the facts. In *Fox, Campbell and Hartley v UK*[108] the European Court held that:

> [H]aving a 'reasonable suspicion' presupposes the existence of facts or information which would satisfy an objective observer that the person concerned may have committed the offence in question.[109]

It is not necessary to show that an offence has been committed. Nor

---

102   Paras 15.43 to 15.63.
103   For a discussion of autonomous meanings, see para 4.19.
104   (1989) 11 EHRR 117.
105   Ibid at para 51. See also *Ireland v UK* (1979–80) 2 EHRR 25 at para 196.
106   Note 59.
107   Ibid at para 49.
108   (1991) 13 EHRR 157.
109   Ibid at para 36.

is it necessary to show that, if an offence has been committed, the arrested person is responsible.[110] The honesty and bona fides of a suspicion constitute one indispensable element of its reasonableness,[111] but 'honest belief' alone is not enough; there must be an objective basis justifying arrest and/or detention.[112]

3.54   An arrest to prevent a person fleeing after having committing an offence – the third ground set out above – justifies arrest only where there are reasonable grounds for believing that an offence has been committed.[113] It therefore overlaps with the other grounds of arrest/detention under article 5(1)(c) to such an extent that it is widely considered to be redundant.

Article 5(1)(d): the detention of children

3.55   Article 5 protects the liberty and security of children as well as adults. However, their freedom of movement and liberty is subject to wider restrictions.[114] Article 5(1)(d) provides two grounds of detention applicable only to children. The upper age for minors in Europe varies, but in 1972 the Council of Europe recommended that this age be fixed at 18.[115]

3.56   The first ground permits the detention of a child for the purpose of educational supervision pursuant to a 'lawful order'. In this context the word 'lawful' connotes compliance with domestic law[116] and the reference to 'order' means an order of the court or an administrative authority. It is intended to underpin a general obligation that children attend school. Since it is the *purpose* of detention under article 5(1)(d) that is crucial, temporary detention at a police station or even at a prison can be justified so long as it is a preliminary to a regime of supervised education.[117] However, in *Bouamar v Belgium*[118] the Court held that the Belgian authorities could not invoke the 'educational supervision' provision in article 5(1)(d) to justify the isolated confinement of a 16-year-old child in a remand

---

110 *X v Austria* (1987) 11 EHRR 112.
111 *Murray v UK* (1994) 19 EHRR 193 at para 61.
112 *Fox, Campbell and Hartley v UK* (1990) 13 EHRR 157.
113 *Lukanov v Bulgaria* (1997) 24 EHRR 121 at para 80 of Commission Report.
114 See paras 20.2 to 20.5.
115 Resolution (72) 29.
116 Both substantive and procedural.
117 *Bouamar v Belgium* (1989) 11 EHRR 1 at para 50.
118 Note 117.

prison on nine different occasions for periods of seven to 14 days, totalling 119 days in all because:

> ... the detention of a young man in a remand prison in conditions of virtual isolation and without the assistance of staff with educational training cannot be detention of a child for the purpose of bringing him/her regarded as furthering any educational aim.[119]

3.57   The second limb of article 5(1)(d) provides for the before a 'competent legal authority'. This does not authorise detention pending criminal proceedings, which is governed by article 5(1)(c).[120] It is intended to provide for situations in which it is necessary to detain a child to 'secure his removal from harmful surroundings';[121] for example, detention pending a court order placing a child in care.[122]

Article 5(1)(e): detention of persons of unsound mind and others

3.58   Article 5(1)(e) covers five separate categories of detention, namely:

1) detention to prevent the spread of infectious diseases;

2) detention of persons of unsound mind;

3) detention of alcoholics;

4) detention of drug addicts; and

5) detention of vagrants.

There are two reasons why the Convention permits the detention of individuals falling into these categories: (a) self-protection and (b) protection of the public.[123] However, in each case, detention will be justified under article 5(1)(e) only if it is 'lawful' and 'in accordance with a procedure prescribed by law'.[124]

3.59   The meaning of the terms underpinning each of the five categories in article 5(1)(e) is 'autonomous'; ie, the definition in domestic law is not conclusive.[125] So far, the case-law of the European Court and Commission has been mainly concerned with the definition of 'persons of unsound mind' and 'vagrants'. There are no cases

119 Ibid at para 52.
120 See paras 3.51 to 3.54.
121 See the *Travaux preparatoires*: 3 TP 724.
122 *Law of the European Convention on Human Rights* Harris et al, Butterworth, 1995, p121.
123 *Guzzardi v Italy* (1981) 3 EHRR 333.
124 For the meaning of these phrases see paras 4.29 to 4.36.
125 See para 4.19.

in which the terms 'infectious diseases', 'alcoholics' or 'drug addicts' have been defined.

3.60   In *Winterwerp v Netherlands*[126] the Court took the view that the term 'persons of unsound mind' was not susceptible to a definitive interpretation because its meaning was continually being evolved by advances in medical understanding and treatment and by changes in societal attitudes. However, as a bare minimum, the Court emphasised that article 5(1)(e) cannot permit detention of an individual merely because his/her 'views or behaviour deviate from norms prevailing in a particular society'.[127]

3.61   A similar approach has been adopted to the meaning of 'vagrants'. In *De Wilde, Ooms and Versyp v Belgium*[128] the European Court did not define this term, preferring to approach the case on the basis that the definition in the Belgian Criminal Code, namely 'persons who have no fixed abode, no means of subsistence and no regular trade or profession', was not irreconcilable with article 5(1)(e). However, in *Guzzardi v Italy*,[129] the Court rejected the suggestion that the anti-social behaviour of suspected mafia members, who lacked any identifiable source of income, brought them within the meaning of 'vagrants' for the purposes of article 5(1)(e).

3.62   In *Winterwerp v Netherlands*[130] the Court gave specific content to the requirement that detention be 'lawful' and 'in accordance with a procedure prescribed by law' under article 5(1)(e) in the context of mental disorder. In particular:

1) The medical disorder relied upon to justify detention must be established by objective medical expertise. Recall of a restricted patient not backed up by medical evidence is not permitted.[131]

2) The nature or degree of the disorder must be sufficiently extreme to justify detention.

3) The detention should last only as long as the medical disorder (and its required severity) persist. Implicit in this requirement is the right to periodic review.[132]

---

126 (1979–80) 2 EHRR 387.
127 Ibid at para 37.
128 (1979–80) 1 EHRR 373.
129 (1981) 3 EHRR 333.
130 Note 126.
131 *Kay v UK* Commission (1 March 1994), unreported.
132 See further paras 17.13 to 17.22.

3.63   In *Ashingdane v UK*[133] the European Court added the requirement that the detention of a person of unsound mind is lawful only if effected in a hospital, clinic or other appropriate institution authorised for that purpose.[134] However, in 'emergency cases' these safeguards do not necessarily apply. In particular, there is no need for objective medical evidence before an individual is detained on an emergency basis.[135]

3.64   Although the Court has not articulated similar principles in relation to the other categories of detention provided for by article 5(1)(e), an analogous approach is likely in most cases.

Article 5(1)(f): detention pending deportation or extradition

3.65   Immigration, asylum, extradition and deportation are dealt with in chapter 18 below. Broadly speaking, there is no right under the Convention to enter or remain in a particular country,[136] but article 5(1)(f) provides certain safeguards for those detained to prevent them entering the country illegally and those detained pending a decision on their deportation or extradition.

3.66   So far the Court and Commission have taken a fairly narrow approach to article 5(1)(f). In *Chahal v UK*[137] the European Court recalled that:

> Article 5(1)(f) does not demand that the detention of a person against whom action is being taken with a view to deportation be reasonably considered necessary, for example to prevent his committing an offence or fleeing; in this respect article 5(1)(f) provides a different level of protection from article 5(1)(c).
>
> Indeed, all that is required under this provision is that 'action is being taken with a view to deportation'. It is therefore immaterial, for the purposes of article 5(1)(f), whether the underlying decision to expel can be justified under national or Convention law.[138]

It follows that a subsequent finding that a deportation or extradition decision was unlawful is unlikely to affect the legality of detention under article 5(1)(f).

---

133 (1985) 7 EHRR 528.
134 But that does not require the state to provide any particular level of treatment so as to ensure that an individual is detained no longer than absolutely necessary; see chapter 17.
135 *Winterwerp v Netherlands* n126; see also *X v UK* (1982) 4 EHRR 188.
136 Subject to article 3 and article 8 considerations: see chapter 18.
137 (1997) 23 EHRR 413.
138 Ibid at para 112; see also *Zamir v UK* (1985) 40 DR 42.

3.67 Nonetheless, in keeping with the other sub-paragraphs of article 5(1), detention under article 5(1)(f) must be 'lawful' and 'in accordance with a procedure prescribed by law';[139] among other things, this imports the requirement that the legal provisions relied upon to justify detention be accessible and precise.[140] In *Chinoy v UK*[141] the Commission found no breach of the lawfulness criteria where evidence from tape recordings allegedly made in breach of French law were used in extradition proceedings in England because their use was not contrary to English law and not arbitrary.[142] However in *Bozano v France*[143] the Court found a violation of article 5(1)(f) because the applicant's arrest and detention was 'a disguised form of extradition' designed to get round an adverse court decision and was therefore arbitrary.[144]

3.68 In addition, any deprivation of liberty will be justified only for as long as deportation or extradition proceedings are in progress. Where deportation or extradition is impossible, article 5(1)(f) will not apply.[145] Equally, if the proceedings are not prosecuted with due diligence, detention will cease to be justified under article 5(1)(f). The Strasbourg bodies will, therefore, examine whether the duration of deportation or extradition proceedings has been excessive.[146]

Have reasons been given for detention as required under article 5(2)?

3.69 Article 5(2) provides that:

> Everyone who is arrested shall be informed promptly, in a language which he understands, of the reasons for his arrest and of any charge against him.

What this means is that anyone arrested must be told 'in simple, non-technical language' that s/he can understand 'the essential legal and factual grounds for his arrest'.[147]

---

139 For the meaning of these phrases see paras 4.29 to 4.36.

140 *Steel and Others v UK* note 59; see also *Zamir v UK* note 59 at paras 90–91.

141 Commission (4 September 1991), unreported.

142 See *A Practitioner's Guide to the European Convention on Human Rights* Reid Sweet and Maxwell, 1998, p191.

143 Note 33.

144 For a fuller analysis of this case, see para 3.37.

145 *Ali v Switzerland* Commission (26 February 1997) pending before the Court.

146 *Chahal v UK* note 137 at para 113.

147 *Fox, Campbell and Hartley v UK* (1991) 13 EHRR 157 at para 40.

3.70   The purpose of this provision is to enable anyone who has been arrested to challenge the lawfulness of his/her detention.[148] No special form is required[149] and the reasons for arrest need not be in writing.[150] Most cases have concerned arrest and/or detention in the criminal context (ie, where article 5(1)(c) is in play) and the principles derived from those cases are considered in detail in chapter 15.[151] However, the duty applies in the non-criminal context as well: in *Van der Leer v Netherlands*[152] the European Court found a breach of article 5(2) where the applicant became aware of a court order confining her to a psychiatric hospital only by accident ten days after it was made.

In the criminal context: have the pre-trial rights in article 5(3) been complied with?

3.71   Article 5(3) provides that:

> Everyone arrested or detained in accordance with the provisions of paragraph 1(c) of this article shall be brought promptly before a judge or other officer authorised by law to exercise judicial power and shall be entitled to trial within a reasonable period or to release pending trial. Release may be conditioned by guarantees to appear for trial.

3.72   According to the European Court's interpretation, this provision guarantees three separate rights:

1) The right to be brought promptly before a judge or other officer authorised by law to exercise judicial power. Bringing a person before a magistrates' court will suffice. An alternative to bringing a detainee before a court is prompt release.[153]

2) The right to be released on bail, save where continued detention can be justified on the facts.

3) The right to be tried within a reasonable period.

---

148 Ibid; and *X v Germany* (1978) 16 DR 111.
149 *X v Netherlands* (1966) 9 Yearbook 474 at 480; and *X v UK* (1974) 14 Yearbook 250 at 276.
150 *X v Netherlands* (1962) 5 YB 224 at 228; and *X v FRG* (1978) 16 DR 111 at p113.
151 See paras 15.65 to 15.68.
152 (1990) 12 EHRR 567.
153 *Brogan and Others v UK* (1989) 11 EHRR 117 at para 58.

The case-law on these rights is complex and is examined in detail in chapter 7.[154]

If not, does the UK derogation apply?

3.73 Derogation from article 5 is permitted. The UK has entered one derogation arising from the case of *Brogan and Others v UK*[155] in 1988 in which the Court held that the detention of the applicants under the Prevention of Terrorism (Temporary Provisions) Act 1984 for more than four days constituted a breach of article 5(3)[156] of the Convention, because they had not been brought promptly before a judicial authority.[157] The then government entered a derogation following the judgment in order to preserve the Secretary of State's power under the Act to extend the period of detention of persons suspected of terrorism connected with the affairs of Northern Ireland for a total of up to seven days. The validity of the derogation was subsequently upheld by the European Court in *Brannigan and McBride v UK*[158] in 1993.

Are habeas corpus proceedings available?

3.74 Article 5(4) provides that:

> Everyone who is deprived of his liberty by arrest or detention shall be entitled to take proceedings by which the lawfulness of his detention shall be decided speedily by a court and his release ordered if a detention is not lawful.

Although on its face, article 5(4) covers all forms of arrest and/or detention, the case-law of the European Court and Commission has confined its application to the following situations:

1) Where the initial decision to deprive an individual of his/her liberty was not taken by a court.

2) Where the justification for detention is based upon circumstances which may change over time and there is accordingly a need to test the continued legitimacy of detention.

---

154 See paras 7.5 and 7.27.
155 (1989) 11 EHRR 117.
156 The terms of article 5(3) are set out above.
157 See chapter 7.
158 (1994) 17 EHRR 539.

3.75   Where detention follows conviction and sentence for a criminal offence, it is generally the case that article 5(4) rights are incorporated in the sentencing process, including any appellate proceedings that might be taken. This is so whenever the sentence is imposed for the purposes of retribution and deterrence. The sentence itself constitutes the lawful authority for the prisoner's detention throughout its duration.[159]

3.76   However, where detention in the criminal context has a preventative component, then as soon as the protection of the public becomes the sole basis for detention, the punitive element having been served, article 5(4) is engaged. This is because detention in the preventative phase is justified by reference to the prisoner's dangerousness, a characteristic which is susceptible to change over time. The application of this principle to those serving discretionary life sentences and to children detained at Her Majesty's Pleasure is examined in detail in chapter 16.[160]

3.77   In addition, pre-trial detention must be reviewed at short intervals because the circumstances justifying a refusal of bail may vary over time and because the Convention assumes that pre-trial detention will be of strictly limited duration:[161] see chapter 7.[162] For similar reasons, article 5(4) confers a right of periodic review on the mentally ill who have been detained in a psychiatric institution. However, the intervals for review can be somewhat longer than those required for pre-trial detention: see chapter 17.[163]

3.78   Article 5(4) requires that the body whose task it is to determine the lawfulness of detention is independent of the executive and the parties. The procedure which it follows must be one which has 'a judicial character and gives to the individual concerned guarantees appropriate to the kind of deprivation of liberty in question, of [a] judicial procedure the forms of which may vary from one domain to another'.[164] What is required is a review not only of the procedure which has been followed but also of whether detention complies substantively with domestic law and the general principles of the Convention. Judicial review proceedings in England and Wales

---

159 *De Wilde, Ooms and Versyp v Belgium* (1979–80) 1 EHRR 373 at para 76.
160 See paras 16.43 to 16.46.
161 *Bezicheri v Italy* (1990) 12 EHRR 210.
162 See paras 7.13 to 7.16.
163 See paras 17.20 to 17.22.
164 *De Wilde, Ooms and Versyp v Belgium* note 159 paras 76–78; *X v UK (1982)* 4 EHRR 188, para 53.

do not necessarily meet this standard of review; particularly where a detention decision can be challenged only on the basis of irrationality.[165] And, to be effective, the reviewing body must have the power to take a legally binding decision to release the person detained.

3.79 Although article 5(4) proceedings may not be subject to all the requirements of a fair trial under article 6 of the Convention, there are certain minimum requirements. In *Sanchez-Reisse v Switzerland*,[166] the European Court held that the equality of arms principle applies in habeas corpus proceedings such that an adversarial procedure was required. This has disclosure implications.[167] Where questions arise involving the assessment of character or personal attitudes it may be essential for the proper and fair examination of the issues that the detained person be given an opportunity to participate in an oral hearing. And in *Singh and Hussein v UK*[168] the Court considered that where disputed issues of fact arose, the possibility should exist for having witnesses examined and cross-examined to establish their credibility.

3.80 Finally, the requirement that a challenge to the lawfulness of detention be heard speedily has two aspects. First, it requires that a person must have access to a remedy speedily upon detention.[169] Second, once the remedy has been triggered, it must be processed speedily.

3.81 Whether the condition of a speedy determination has been met is a question which depends on the circumstances of the particular case. Relevant factors are the diligence shown by the national authorities or whether delay is attributable to matters for which state responsibility is engaged or for which the detainee is to blame. It is for the state to justify any delay which, without more, appears to violate the need for speediness.

3.82 Where the review under article 5(4) is not completed until appellate or judicial review proceedings have been completed, the period ends with that final determination.

---

165 *Weeks v UK* (1988) 10 EHRR 293; *Thynne, Wilson and Gunnell v UK* (1991) 13 EHRR 666.

166 (1987) 9 EHRR 71.

167 See para 7.32.

168 (1996) 22 EHRR 1.

169 *X v UK* (1981) 4 EHRR 188 ref at para 138 where a delay of six months before a patient recalled under the Mental Health Act was entitled to apply to the MHRT was found to violate article 5(4); see further chapter 17.

3.83   A person who absconds remains entitled to a remedy under article 5(4) because s/he is still deprived of his/her liberty in law.[170] However, where release has been ordered, article 5(4) no longer applies, even if release is conditional, eg, on licence.[171] In such cases any claim for wrongful arrest/detention will have to be founded on article 13, article 41 or article 5(5).

Is there an enforceable right to compensation for wrongful detention?

3.84   Remedies under the Convention usually operate at two levels. Article 13 requires that everyone whose Convention rights have been violated 'shall have an effective remedy' before a national body.[172] This can, but need not include compensation.[173] At another level, article 41[174] provides for 'just satisfaction' where the European Court has found a violation of Convention rights and domestic law provides no, or no effective, remedy.[175] Again, this can, but need not include compensation.[176]

3.85   Article 5(5) is different. It contains a very specific guarantee for breaches of article 5 which is without parallel in the Convention[177] by providing that:

> Everyone who has been the victim of arrest or detention in contravention of the provisions of this article shall have an enforceable right to compensation.

What is required, therefore, is a right to compensation in domestic law for any breach of article 5.

3.86   Although there has not been much case-law in Strasbourg under article 5(5), the following principles have emerged:

1) The fact that arrest/detention is lawful in domestic law will not

---

170 *Van der Leer v Netherlands* n152.
171 *L v Sweden* (1988) 61 DR 62.
172 See paras 3.173 to 3.182.
173 See paras 3.179 to 3.182.
174 Formerly article 50; see paras 2.46 to 2.52.
175 Ibid.
176 See para 2.50.
177 Article 3 of the Seventh Protocol provides a similar remedy for miscarriages of justice which may involve a breach of article 6. However, the UK has not (yet) ratified the Seventh Protocol.

affect the right to compensation under article 5(5) if it is unlawful under the Convention.[178]

2) However, any arrest/detention which is unlawful in domestic law will automatically be unlawful under the Convention and thus give rise to a claim under article 5(5).[179]

3) Article 5(5) provides a *right* to compensation; an ex gratia payment is insufficient.[180]

4) A rule that compensation is payable only on proof of damage is not contrary to article 5(5).[181] However, in this context, damage includes both pecuniary and non-pecuniary damage, and under the Convention non-pecuniary damage includes 'moral' damage, eg, distress, pain and suffering.[182]

5) Article 5(5) does not require proof of bad faith on the part of the authorities. In *Santa Cruz Ruiz v UK*,[183] the Commission found a breach of article 5(5) where the applicant had been imprisoned by magistrates for failing to make payments under a maintenance order. No claim could be brought domestically because s108 of the Courts and Legal Services Act 1980 provides immunity for magistrates except where they act beyond their jurisdiction *and* in bad faith. However, an error within jurisdiction does not necessarily give rise to a claim under article 5(5): see *Bentham v UK*.

6) Article 5(5) and article 41 of the Convention are not mutually exclusive. In principle, the disposition of a claim under article 5(5) does not preclude the possibility of a further award under article 41 but, in practice, the European Court will rarely, if ever, find compensation appropriate under article 41 where an award has been made under article 5(5).

178 See *Brogan and Others v UK* n153 and *Fox, Campbell and Hartley v UK* (1991) 13 EHRR 157.

179 *L v Sweden* (1989) 61 DR 62.

180 Harris et al n122, p159.

181 *Wassink v Netherlands* A/185-A (1990) at para 38 (unreported).

182 See the Commission's observations in *Huber v Austria* (1976) 6 DR 65 at p.69; see also para 2.55.

183 (Commission) 1 July 1998, noted at [1998] EHRLR 208.

Article 6: fair trial

The scheme of article 6

3.87   Article 6 provides that:

(1) In the determination of his civil rights and obligations or of any criminal charge against him, everyone is entitled to a fair and public hearing within a reasonable time by an independent and impartial tribunal established by law. Judgment shall be pronounced publicly but the press and public may be excluded from all or part of the trial in the interests of morals, public order or national security in a democratic society, where the interests of juveniles or the protection of the private life of the parties so require, or to the extent strictly necessary in the opinion of the court in special circumstances where publicity would prejudice the interests of justice.

(2) Everyone charged with a criminal offence shall be presumed innocent until proved guilty according to law.

(3) Everyone charged with a criminal offence has the following minimum rights:

(a) to be informed promptly, in a language which he understands and in detail, of the nature and cause of the accusation against him;

(b) to have adequate time and facilities for the preparation of his defence;

(c) to defend himself in person or through legal assistance of his own choosing or, if he has not sufficient means to pay for legal assistance, to be given it free when the interests of justice so require;

(d) to examine or have examined witnesses against him and to obtain the attendance and examination of witnesses on his behalf under the same conditions as witnesses against him;

(e) to have the free assistance of an interpreter if he cannot understand or speak the language used in court.

Article 6(1) applies to both criminal and civil proceedings, whereas articles 6(2) and 6(3) apply only to criminal proceedings.

3.88   Articles 6(2) and 6(3) are supplementary to article 6(1). They are not intended to be an exhaustive list of the requirements of fairness in criminal proceedings; rather they represent irreducible minimum guarantees. On that basis, the European Court and Commission have frequently read other rights into article 6 in the criminal context, and read guarantees similar to those in article 6(3) into civil proceedings.

Do the proceedings involve the determination of a criminal charge?

3.89   The question whether proceedings involve the determination of a criminal charge can be assessed by reference to three criteria:

1) the classification of the proceedings in domestic law;

2) the nature of the offence or conduct in question; and

3) the severity of any possible penalty.

The first criterion is not as important as the second and third, unless the proceedings are classified as criminal in domestic law. If so, that classification is conclusive and article 6 applies. In contrast, the fact that proceedings are classified as civil in domestic law is merely a starting point. See chapter 6.[184]

If not, do the proceedings involve the determination of a civil right or obligation?

3.90   Outside the criminal sphere, article 6(1) applies only to the determination of 'civil rights and obligations'. This covers all proceedings between private individuals and some, but not all, proceedings between private individuals and public authorities. Although the case-law of the European Court and Commission is by no means clear, the key distinction is between decisions of an essentially administrative character which have a direct bearing on the determination and/or substantive content of a private right or obligation (within the definition) and those which do not (outside the definition). On that basis, article 6(1) has been applied to: the decision of a regional property transactions commission;[185] a decision to withdraw permission to run a medical clinic and to practise medicine;[186] a decision not to grant the applicant a licence to run a petrol station;[187] a decision to revoke the applicant's taxi licence;[188]

---

184   Paras 6.11 to 6.12.
185   *Ringeisen v Austria* (1979–80) 1 EHRR 455.
186   *Konig v Germany* (1979–80) 2 EHRR 170.
187   *Bentham v Netherlands* (1986) 8 EHRR 1.
188   *Pudas v Sweden* (1988) 10 EHRR 380.

disputes concerning expropriation permits;[189] the grant of licences to sell alcohol;[190] building regulation decisions;[191] the grant of dumping permits;[192] withdrawal of a permit to work a gravel pit;[193] and disciplinary proceedings in the medical[194] and legal[195] professions.

3.91   Article 6(1) also requires that there be a dispute 'contestation' concerning the particular right or obligation in question. And there must be a direct link between the dispute and the right or obligation in question. The underlying principles and case-law are examined in chapter 12. The classification of welfare benefits is examined in chapter 23.

In either case, have the fair trial requirements of article 6(1) been met?

3.92   Article 6(1) requires (as a minimum):

1) a fair and public hearing;

2) an independent and impartial tribunal;

3) trial within a reasonable period;

4) public judgment (with some exceptions); and

5) a reasoned decision.

These requirements have generated a great deal of case-law. In the criminal context, this is examined in chapter 8 and in the civil context it is examined in chapter 13.

3.93   The object and purpose of article 6(1) is 'to enshrine the fundamental principle of the rule of law'.[196] Therefore, it is to be interpreted broadly:

> ... a restrictive interpretation of article 6(1) – notably in regard to observance of the fundamental principle of the impartiality of the courts – would not be consonant with the object and purpose of the provision, bearing in mind the prominent place which the right to a

189 *Sporrong and Lonroth v Sweden* (1983) 5 EHRR 35.
190 *Tre Traktorer AB v Sweden* (1991) 13 EHRR 309.
191 *Allan Jacobsson v Sweden* (1990) 12 EHRR 56.
192 *Zander v Sweden* (1994) 18 EHRR 175.
193 *Fredin v Sweden* (1991) 13 EHRR 784.
194 *Le Compte, van Leuven and de Meyere v Belgium* (1982) 4 EHRR 1.
195 *H v Belgium* (1988) 10 EHRR 339.
196 *Salabiaku v France* (1991) 13 EHRR 379.

fair trial holds in a democratic society within the meaning of the Convention.[197]

Consistent with this approach, the evolution of the case-law of the Strasbourg institutions reflects 'the increased sensitivity of the public to the fair administration of justice'.[198]

Are any further guarantees required to ensure a fair trial?

3.94 Article 6(1) lists the minimum requirements of a fair trial. Other rights have been read into the Convention to ensure that the right to a fair trial is practical and effective. Among the most important are:

1) the right of access to a court;

2) equality of arms; and

3) the right to participate effectively in proceedings.

3.95 The European Court first recognised the right of access to a court in *Golder v UK*.[199] In the context of a rule prohibiting prisoners from bringing defamation proceedings, the Court held:

> In civil matters one can scarcely conceive of the rule of law without there being a possibility of access to the courts ... The principle whereby a civil claim must be capable of being submitted to a judge ranks as one of the universally recognised fundamental principles of law; the same is true of the principle of international law which forbids the denial of justice. Article 6(1) must be read in light of these principles.[200]

In *Osman v UK*[201] the European Court found that the rules governing police immunity from negligence proceedings violated the applicants' right of access to a court.

3.96 The principle of equality of arms requires a fair balance between the parties and applies to both criminal and civil cases. In the civil context, the Court has held that:

> ... 'equality of arms' implies that each party must be afforded a reasonable opportunity to present his case – including his evidence – under conditions that do not place him at a substantial disadvantage vis-à-vis his opponent.[202]

---

197 *Delcourt v Belgium* (1979–80) 1 EHRR 355.
198 *Borgers v Belgium* (1993) 15 EHRR 92 at para 24.
199 (1979–80) 1 EHRR 524.
200 Ibid at para 35.
201 Court (28 October 1998); noted at [1999] EHRLR 228. See further chapter 15.
202 *Dombo Beheer BV v Netherlands* (1994) 18 EHRR 213 at para 33.

Legal aid and legal representation fall to be considered on this basis in civil proceedings. They are specifically provided for in criminal proceedings.[203]

3.97   The right to participate effectively is a broad right extending beyond mere presence. In *Stanford v UK*[204] the Court held that:

> ... article 6, read as a whole, guarantees the right of an accused to participate effectively in a criminal trial. In general this includes, inter alia, not only his right to be present, but also to hear and follow the proceedings.[205]

The issue in that case was poor acoustics in the court room.

3.98   The case-law on the application of these rights is examined in the criminal context in chapter 8 and in the civil context in chapter 13.

Are there any relevant implied limitations?

3.99   Rights which have been read into article 6(1) can, by implication, be restricted. So, for example, some restrictions can be placed on access to the courts by prisoners[206] and by those who are mentally ill.[207] However, a restriction will not be compatible with article 6(1) unless: (a) the aim of the restriction is legitimate; and (b) there is a reasonable relationship of proportionality between the means employed and the aim sought to be achieved.[208] See further, chapter 4.[209]

In the criminal context: has the presumption of innocence been respected?

3.100   The presumption of innocence covers issues such as pre-trial publicity, the burden and standard of proof in criminal cases, adducing evidence of previous convictions and costs in criminal cases. These are examined in chapter 8.

---

203 See article 6(3)(c), and chapter 8.

204 A/282 (1994), unreported.

205 Ibid at para 26; see also *T and V v UK*, Commission, noted at [1998] EHRLR 484.

206 *Golder v UK* (1979–80) 1 EHRR 524.

207 *Winterwerp v Netherlands* (1979–80) 2 EHRR 387.

208 *Ashingdane v UK* (1985) 7 EHRR 528.

209 Paras 4.76 to 4.77.

In the criminal context: have the minimum guarantees of article 6(3) been complied with?

3.101 Article 6(3) deals with a number of specific rights in criminal cases, including:

1) Information about charge.
2) Adequate time and facilities to prepare a defence.
3) Legal aid and legal representation.
4) The right to call and cross-examine witnesses.
5) Interpretation.

As noted above, these rights are not intended to be an exhaustive list of the requirements of fairness in criminal proceedings, they are minimum guarantees. They are examined in chapter 8.

Article 7: the prohibition on retrospective criminal offences

3.102 Article 7(1) provides that:

> No one shall be held guilty of any criminal offence on account of any act or omission which did not constitute a criminal offence under the national or international law at the time when it was committed. Nor shall a heavier penalty be imposed than the one that was applicable at the time the criminal offence was committed.

Do the proceedings relate to a criminal offence or criminal penalty?

3.103 The meaning of 'criminal offence' under article 7 is consistent with the meaning of 'criminal charge' under article 6.[210] In some cases, therefore, it will include proceedings classified as civil in domestic law; eg, contempt of court proceedings. Save in this respect, article 7 has no application in civil cases. However, where Convention rights are in issue in any proceedings, the requirement that any interference be 'prescribed by law'[211] demands certainty.[212]

---

210 See para 3.89.
211 See paras 4.29 to 4.36.
212 See paras 4.32 to 4.36.

If so, has there been retrospective application of the criminal law?

3.104   Two separate principles emerge from article 7(1):

1) The law in question must have existed at the time of the act in question for the conviction to be based on it.

2) No heavier penalty for the infringement of the law may be imposed than was in force at the time the act was committed.

3.105   The first principle has two limbs. First, it prohibits the retrospective application of the criminal law. Second, it requires certainty in the criminal law; 'clarification' and development is permitted, but only where consistent with the essence of the offence in question and where any change in the law is reasonably foreseeable.[213] These requirements are examined in detail in chapter 6.[214]

3.106   The second principle was considered in *Welch v UK*[215] where a new provision of the Drug Trafficking Offences Act 1986 relating to confiscation orders came into force after the applicant's arrest but before his trial. The European Court held that a confiscation order was a penalty and that article 7 had, therefore, been breached.

If so, can retrospective application be justified under article 7(2)?

3.107   Article 7(2) provides that:

This article shall not prejudice the trial and punishment of any person for any act or omission which, at the time when it was committed, was criminal according to the general principles of law recognised by civilised nations.

It is intended to exclude from article 7(1) challenge, laws which were passed at the end of the Second World War to punish war crimes, treason and collaboration with the enemy.[216]

---

213 See *SW* and *CR v UK* (1996) 21 EHRR 363.
214 See paras 6.22 to 6.26
215 (1995) 20 EHRR 247.
216 See paras 6.27 to 6.31.

Article 8: privacy and related matters

3.108 Article 8 provides that:

(1) Everyone has the right to respect for his private and family life, his home and his correspondence.

(2) There shall be no interference by a public authority with the exercise of this right except such as is in accordance with the law and is necessary in a democratic society in the interests of national security, public safety or the economic well-being of the country, for the prevention of disorder or crime, for the protection of health or morals, or for the protection of the rights and freedoms of others.

It thus protects four distinct interests: private life, family life, the home and correspondence.

Is article 8 engaged?

Private life

3.109 The notion of 'private life' in article 8 is a broad one and is not susceptible to exhaustive definition.[217] It includes the idea of an 'inner circle' in which individuals may live their personal lives as they choose without interference from the state. On that basis, the European Court and Commission have reviewed cases involving the interception of communications, secret surveillance and the collection and retention of personal data, including medical records. In so far as these issues involve the police, they are dealt with in chapter 15.

3.110 However, the European Court has held that it would be too restrictive to limit article 8 to the notion of an 'inner circle': it also covers the right to develop one's own personality and to create and foster relationships with others.[218] This interpretation has provided the basis for an examination of issues relating to sex, sexuality and sexual orientation from an article 8 perspective. And on the basis that most people develop relationships worthy of protection in their working lives, the Court has been unwilling to interpret article 8 so as to exclude activities of a business or professional nature.[219]

---

217 *Niemietz v Germany* (1993) 16 EHRR 97; *Costello-Roberts v UK* (1995) 19 EHRR 112.
218 *Niemietz v Germany* note 217.
219 Ibid.

3.111   The notion of 'private life' in article 8 also covers physical integrity. So, for example, the Court and Commission have considered issues such as corporal punishment,[220] physical abuse[221] and medical treatment from an article 8 perspective. It also encompasses environmental issues such as noise pollution,[222] pollution from waste treatment plants[223] and toxic emissions.[224] These are examined in chapter 22.

Secret surveillance by the security services

3.112   The principles set out in chapter 15 relating to secret surveillance by the police apply equally to secret surveillance by the security services.[225] The case of *Harman and Hewitt v UK*[226] prompted the government to place the activities of MI5, MI6 and GCHQ on a statutory footing. And (so far) the European Commission has rejected challenges under articles 8 and 13 to the current legislative schemes.[227]

Family life

3.113   Protection of private life and of family life under article 8 are closely related. In *Marckx v Belgium*[228] the European Court held that the term 'family life' encompasses:

> ... at least the ties between near relatives, for instance those between grandparents and grandchildren, since such relatives may play a considerable part in family life.

Blood relationships are a starting point, but the Strasbourg bodies have recognised that financial and emotional ties are sufficient to establish family life within the meaning of article 8. Relationship between parents and illegitimate[229] or adopted children[230] are covered and in *X v Switzerland*[231] the European Commission found that living

220 *Costello-Roberts v UK* n217.
221 *X and Y v Netherlands* (1986) 8 EHRR 235.
222 *Rayner v UK* (1986) 47 DR 5.
223 *Lopez Ostra v Spain* (1995) 20 EHRR 277.
224 *Guerra and Others v Italy* (1998) 26 EHRR 357.
225 See paras 15.9 to 15.29.
226 (1989) 67 DR 88.
227 *Esbester v UK* (1994) 18 EHRR CD 72; *Christie v UK* (1993) 78-A DR 119.
228 (1979–80) 2 EHRR 330 para 45.
229 Ibid.
230 *X v France* (1982) 31 DR 241.
231 (1978) 13 DR 248.

in the same household in a situation of financial dependency and with a genuinely close relationship was sufficient to constitute family life for article 8 purposes. By the same token, a de facto relationship between a man and a woman short of marriage can constitute family life, depending on the strength of the ties between them. Important in this context are 'whether the couple live together, the length of their relationship and whether they have demonstrated their commitment to each other by having children or by any other means'.[232]

3.114 Generally speaking, the European Court and Commission favour 'vertical' family relationships (minor children, parents, grandparents) over 'horizontal' ones (siblings, nieces and nephews etc).[233] But a claim based (indirectly) on a sibling relationship succeeded in *Olsson v Sweden*.[234]

3.115 The right to family life under article 8 is closely connected to the right to marry and found a family under article 12. However, article 12 protects single actions – marrying or having or adopting children – whereas article 8 protects a continuing condition.[235] Although the Commission has held that an intention to marry cannot found a claim to family life under article 8, in *Abdulaziz, Cabales and Balkandali v UK*[236] the European Court made it clear that 'this does not mean that all intended family life falls entirely outside its ambit'.[237]

3.116 The right to family life under article 8 is considered in more detail below in chapters 16,[238] 17,[239] 18,[240] 19[241] and 20.[242]

The home

3.117 The home is protected by article 8 and article 1 of the First Protocol (the right to property).[243] So far as article 8 is concerned, the right pro-

232 *X, Y and Z v UK* (1997) 24 EHRR 143.
233 *Short Guide to the European Convention on Human Rights* Gomien D Council of Europe Press, 1991, p65.
234 (1989) 11 EHRR 259.
235 *Short Guide to the European Convention on Human Rights* n233 p66.
236 (1985) 7 EHRR 471.
237 Ibid at para 62.
238 See paras 16.57 to 16.59.
239 See para 17.1.
240 See paras 18.31 to 18.43.
241 See paras 19.3 to 19.69.
242 See paras 20.6 to 20.14.
243 See chapter 26.

tected is a right to occupy an existing home without interference and to enjoy its comforts. Harassment by others[244] and noise nuisance[245] can violate this aspect of article 8. And, in this respect, no distinction is to be drawn between residential and business premises.[246]

3.118   A home need not be lawfully established to come within the scope of article 8. In *Buckley v UK*[247] the European Court defined 'home' as a continuous residence with no intention to establish home elsewhere. How far this principle extends is unclear; in *Kanthak v Germany*[248] the Commission left open the question whether a search of the applicant's camping car came within the scope of article 8(1).

3.119   The extent to which article 8 protects the right to set up a home is unclear. In *Gillow v UK*[249] the European Court held that the notion of 'home' was capable of covering a place where the applicants intended to live. However, in that case, the applicants had owned the home for 18 years and were, in reality, seeking to return to it. More recently, the Court has held that denial of access to land upon which the applicant wished to build a home did not come within the meaning of article 8; but such circumstances may raise an issue of property rights.[250]

3.120   Searches of residential or business premises raise issues under article 8(1) and, therefore, require justification under article 8(2). This and related issues are examined in chapter 15.[251] Other issues arising under this aspect of article 8 are examined in Chapter 22.

Correspondence

3.121   The scope of article 8 in its application to correspondence is wide. It encompasses letters, telephone calls, faxes and (presumably) other forms of communication such as e-mail. Most complaints to the European Court and Commission have come from prisoners and these are examined in chapter 16.[252] Broadly speaking, prisoners have the right to communicate with their lawyers without interference;[253]

---

244   *Whiteside v UK* (1994) 76A DR 80.
245   *Arrondelle v UK* (1982) 26 DR 5.
246   *Niemietz v Germany* n217.
247   (1996) 23 EHRR 101; see further chapter 22.
248   (1988) 58 DR 94.
249   (1986) 11 EHRR 335.
250   *Loizidou v Turkey* (1997) 23 EHRR 513.
251   See paras 15.36 to 15.40.
252   See paras 16.60 to 16.68.
253   *Golder v UK* (1979–80) 1 EHRR 524.

interference with non-legal correspondence is permitted, but must be justified under article 8(2).

3.122   In *X v Germany*[254] the Commission found that the right to respect for correspondence did not include a right to the perfect functioning of the postal service which, by its very nature, involves a certain risk of inefficiency. In that case the applicant complained because his mail was not being forwarded in accordance with his instructions. However, different considerations may apply where a system of interception is set up for intercepting mail from specific groups such as prisoners or those detained in mental hospitals.[255]

Positive obligations under article 8

3.123   The primary duty of the state and public authorities under article 8 is to refrain from interfering with an individual's right to respect for his/her private and family life, home and correspondence. However, the European Court and Commission have extrapolated from the underlying principles of article 8 an important secondary duty, namely a duty to take action to ensure that article 8 rights are protected effectively. This obligation was most clearly articulated in *X and Y v Netherlands*[256] where the Court held that:

> [article 8] does not merely compel the state to abstain from ... interference: in addition to this primarily negative undertaking, there may be positive obligations inherent in an effective respect for private and family life ... These obligations may involve the adoption of measures designed to secure respect for private life even in the sphere of the relations of individuals between themselves.[257]

In that case the positive obligation required was to protect mentally handicapped children from sexual assault by enabling their parents to file criminal complaints in respect of assaults upon them.

3.124   The circumstances in which positive obligations arise under the Convention and the measures necessary to fulfil them are not straight-forward. They are therefore examined separately in chapter 5.

---

254 (1979) 17 DR 227.
255 See *Herczegfalvy v Austria* (1993) 15 EHRR 437.
256 (1986) 8 EHRR 235.
257 Ibid at para 23.

Can the reason for any restriction be found in article 8(2)?

3.125   A restriction on article 8 rights will be compatible with the Convention only if it is aimed at protecting one of the interests listed in article 8(2), namely:

1) national security;
2) public safety;
3) the economic well-being of the country;
4) the prevention of disorder or crime;
5) the protection of health or morals; and
6) the protection of the rights and freedoms of others.

This list in intended to be exhaustive and in each case the interest in question is to be narrowly construed.[258]

3.126   In addition all restrictions must also be: (a) 'in accordance with law' and (b) 'necessary in a democratic society'. These principles, which essentially define the appropriate balance between the exercise of individual rights and the public interest (if any) in restricting such exercise, are fundamental to the operation of articles 8, 9, 10 and 11.[259]

If so, is the restriction 'in accordance with law'?

3.127   A restriction will be 'in accordance with law'[260] only if (a) it has some basis in domestic law and (b) it is sanctioned by legal rules which are accessible to potential victims and reasonably clear.

3.128   These requirements are dealt with in detail in chapter 4.[261]

If so, is it 'necessary in a democratic society'?

3.129   A restriction will be 'necessary in a democratic society' only if:

1) there is a pressing social need for restriction; and
2) the restriction in question is proportionate to the aim of responding to that need; in other words it does not go further than is needed, bearing in mind the objective in question.

These requirements are also dealt with in detail in chapter 4.[262]

258 See paras 4.57 to 4.59.
259 See paras 4.29 to 4.36 and 4.60 to 4.66.
260 This has the same meaning as 'prescribed by law' in articles 9–11.
261 Paras 4.29 to 4.36.
262 Paras 4.37 to 4.55 and 4.60 to 4.66.

Article 9: religion and belief

3.130   Article 9 provides that:

(1) Everyone has the right to freedom of thought, conscience and religion; this right includes freedom to change his religion or belief and freedom, either alone or in community with others and in public or private, to manifest his religion or belief, in worship, teaching, practice and observance.

(2) Freedom to manifest one's religion or beliefs shall be subject only to such limitations as are prescribed by law and are necessary in a democratic society in the interests of public safety, for the protection of public order, health or morals, or for the protection of the rights and freedoms of others.

It has two limbs. First, it protects freedom of thought, conscience and religion. Second, it protects freedom to manifest one's religion or belief. This is significant because whereas the latter is qualified by article 9(2), the former is not. Freedom of thought is, therefore, an absolute right. This means that any action by the state to coerce or compel people's thinking, or to make them reveal their beliefs, is contrary to the Convention and cannot be justified by considerations relating to the public interest.[263]

Is article 9 engaged?

3.131   The Strasbourg bodies have deliberately adopted a broad approach to freedom of thought, conscience and religion. Thus article 9 protection has been extended to Druidism,[264] pacifism,[265] and veganism;[266] and to the Muslim religion,[267] the Krishna consciousness movement,[268] Jehovah's Witnesses,[269] the Divine Light Zentrum[270] and the Church of Scientology.[271] However, article 9 protection does not

---

263 *Human Rights in Europe* Robertson A H Manchester University Press, 1993 p145.

264 *Chappell v UK* (1987) 53 DR 241.

265 *Arrowsmith v UK* (1978) 19 DR 5.

266 *X v UK* Commission (10 February 1993), unreported.

267 *Ahmad v UK* (1982) 4 EHRR 126.

268 *Iskcon v UK* (1994) 76A DR 90.

269 *Kokkinakis v Greece* (1994) 17 EHRR 397.

270 *Omkarananda and the Divine Light Zentrum v Switzerland* (1981) 25 DR 105.

271 *X and Church of Scientology v Sweden* (1979) 16 DR 68.

extend beyond 'the sphere of private, personal beliefs' to cover the espousal of purely idealistic or political goals, such as those of a prisoners' support group[272] or IRA prisoners claiming 'special category status';[273] but article 10 (freedom of expression) may be applicable in those cases.

3.132   A much narrower approach has been taken to the question of manifesting religion or belief. In this respect, the European Court and Commission have sought to distinguish between conduct which directly expresses religion or belief (protected) and conduct which is merely motivated by religion or belief (not protected). So, for example, trying to convince one's neighbour[274] and eating Kosher food[275] have been found to be manifestations of religion or belief; and in *X v UK*[276] the Commission accepted that the applicant had established that his religion required that high caste Sikhs not clean floors. On the other hand, distributing pacifist leaflets,[277] advertising a religious artefact promulgated by the Church of Scientology,[278] marriage for Muslims,[279] non-payment by Quakers of taxes used for defence purposes[280] and the wish to have one's ashes scattered on one's own land[281] have not been found to be manifestations of religion or belief.

3.133   Freedom of religion includes freedom to change one's religion. And in *Angelini v Sweden*[282] the Commission held that this is a guarantee against indoctrination of religion by the state. However, the maintenance of an established church is not, of itself, a violation of article 9.[283]

3.134   The rights conferred under article 9 may be exercised by an individual, by a church body or by an association with religious and philosophical objects.[284] However, it may be more difficult for a

272 *Vereniging Rechtswinkels Utrecht v Netherlands* (1986) 46 DR 200.
273 *McFeeley v UK* (1980) 20 DR 44.
274 *Kokkinakis v Greece* n269.
275 *DS and ES v UK* (1990) 65 DR 245.
276 (1982) 28 DR 5.
277 *Arrowsmith v UK* (1980) 19 DR 5.
278 *X and Church of Scientology v Sweden* n271.
279 *Khan v UK* (1986) 48 DR 253.
280 *C v UK* (1983) 37 DR 142.
281 *X v Germany* (1981) 24 DR 137.
282 (1986) 51 DR 41.
283 *Darby v Sweden* (1991) Commission, unreported.
284 *Chappell v UK* (1987) 53 DR 241.

church body or association than for an individual to establish that its activities amount to a manifestation of religion or belief.[285]

3.135 Article 9 clearly overlaps with a number of other rights, including article 8 (family life), article 10 (freedom of expression), article 11 (freedom of association), article 14 (discrimination) and article 2 of the First Protocol (education). These issues are examined below in chapters 21,[286] 24,[287] 27,[288] and 29.[289]

Conscientious objectors

3.136 A series of complaints before the European Commission have concerned the question of conscientious objection to military service. So far, all such complaints have been rejected on the basis that article 4[290] specifically envisages compulsory military service.[291] Thus, in countries where compulsory military service exists, article 9 does not require substituted civilian service[292] and where such substituted service does exist, a person cannot resist it by invoking article 9.[293]

Can the reason for any restriction be found in article 9(2)?

3.137 A restriction on article 9 rights will be compatible with the Convention only if it is aimed at protecting one of the interests listed in article 9(2), namely:

1) public safety;

2) public order;

3) health or morals; or

4) the rights and freedoms of others.

This list is intended to be exhaustive and in each case the interest in question is to be narrowly construed.[294]

---

285 *Church of X v UK* (1969) 12 Yearbook 306.
286 See paras 21.12 to 21.23.
287 See paras 24.4 to 24.9.
288 See paras 27.5 to 27.20.
289 See paras 29.11 to 29.18.
290 See paras 3.15 to 3.20.
291 See, *European Human Rights* Clements L, Sweet & Maxwell, 1994, p168.
292 *A v Switzerland* (1984) 38 DR 219.
293 *N v Sweden* (1984) 40 DR 203.
294 See paras 4.57 to 4.59.

3.138   The structure of article 9 is therefore similar to that of article 8 and the same general principles apply. However, there are two important differences:

1) As noted above, only the *manifestation* of religion or belief is subject to the limitations set out in article 9(2).

2) Unlike articles 8, 10 and 11, 'the interests of national security' do not justify restriction on the right to manifest one's religion or belief.

If so, is the restriction 'prescribed by law'?

3.139   The general principles applicable to article 8 apply to article 9: see above. They are examined in chapter 4.[295]

If so, is the restriction 'necessary in a democratic society' ?

3.140   The general principles applicable to article 8 apply to article 9: see above. They are also examined in Chapter 4.[296]

Article 10: freedom of expression

3.141   Article 10 provides:

(1) Everyone has the right to freedom of expression. This right shall include freedom to hold opinions and to receive and impart information and ideas without interference by public authority and regardless of frontiers. This article shall not prevent states from requiring the licensing of broadcasting, television or cinema enterprises.

(2) The exercise of these freedoms, since it carries with it duties and responsibilities, may be subject to such formalities, conditions, restrictions or penalties as are prescribed by law and are necessary in a democratic society, in the interests of national security, territorial integrity or public safety, for the prevention of disorder or crime, for the protection of health or morals, for the protection of the rights of others, for preventing the disclosure of information received in confidence, or for maintaining the authority and impartiality of the judiciary.

295 Paras 4.29 to 4.36.
296 Paras 4.37 to 4.55 and 4.60 to 4.66.

Article 10 enjoys a special position under the Convention. It is not only one of the cornerstones of democracy, but is also a prerequisite for the enjoyment of many of the other rights and freedoms enshrined in the Convention.[297] It has given rise to a great deal of case-law, which is examined in detail in chapter 24.

3.142   Safeguards afforded to the press are particularly important. While the press must not overstep the bounds set, it is incumbent on the press to impart information and ideas on political matters as in other areas of public interest.[298]

Is article 10 engaged?

3.143   Attempts to try and confine the meaning of 'expression' in article 10 have not been successful. The medium of expression is unimportant: article 10 clearly covers words, pictures, video, cinema and even conduct intended to convey an idea or information.[299] The subject-matter is more important, but as the European Court observed in the landmark case of *Handyside v UK*:[300]

> Freedom of expression constitutes one of the essential foundations of [a democratic] society, one of the basic conditions for its progress and for the development of every man ... It is applicable not only to 'information' or 'ideas' that are favourably received or regarded as inoffensive or as a matter of indifference, but also to those that offend, shock or disturb the State or any sector of the population. Such are the demands of that pluralism, tolerance and broadmindedness, without which there is no 'democratic society'.

That said, political speech tends to attract greater protection than, for example, pornography[301] and racist speech is virtually unprotected.[302]

3.144   A number of cases in Strasbourg have involved public sector employees who have complained that their article 10 rights have been infringed by reason of special restrictions attached to their posts. On a related theme, several cases have raised article 10 issues in the context of access to, or dismissal from, employment. These are examined in chapter 28.

---

297 *Short Guide to the European Convention on Human Rights* Gomian D. Council of Europe Press, 1991, p72.
298 *Lingens v Austria* (1986) 8 EHRR 407.
299 *Stevens v UK* (1986) 46 DR 245.
300 (1979–80) 1 EHRR 737.
301 Contrast the approach in *Castells v Spain* (1992) 14 EHRR 445 to that in *Scherer v Switzerland* (1994) 18 EHRR 276.

3.145   In addition to pure freedom of expression, article 10 also protects freedom to hold opinions and to receive and impart 'information and ideas'. No limit is placed on the definition of 'information and ideas', but article 10 does not impose any general duty on the state to provide information. However, it does protect individuals from being compelled to disclose information.[303]

Is any restriction in truth a licensing restriction?

3.146   Licensing of broadcasting, television or cinema enterprises is permitted under article 10(1) and, therefore, does not need to be justified under article 10(2).[304] However, only the technical means of broadcasting, not the information imparted may be licensed under article 10(1).

If not, can the reason for any restriction be found in article 10(2)?

3.147   A restriction on article 10 rights, other than a licensing restriction, will be compatible with the Convention only if it is aimed at protecting one of the interests listed in article 10(2), namely:

1) national security;
2) territorial integrity;
3) public safety;
4) the prevention of disorder or crime;
5) the protection of health or morals;
6) the protection of the rights of others;
7) preventing the disclosure of information received in confidence; or
8) maintaining the authority and impartiality of the judiciary.

This list in intended to be exhaustive and in each case the interest in question is to be narrowly construed.[305]

---

302 *Glimmerveen and Hagenback v Netherlands* (1979) 18 DR 187; *X v Germany* (1982) 29 DR 194; *T v Belgium* (1983) 34 DR 158; *Kuhnen v Germany* 56 DR 205; *H, W, P and K v Austria* (1989) 62 DR 216.

303 *Goodwin v UK* (1996) 22 EHRR 123; see further chapter 24.

304 See *Groppera Radio AG v Switzerland* (1990) 12 EHRR 321.

305 See paras 4.57 to 4.59.

3.148   The structure of article 10 is, therefore, similar to that of article 8 and the same general principles apply. However, there are two important differences:

1) The special position of freedom of expression under the Convention has led to heightened scrutiny by the European Court and Commission of any restrictions upon it.

2) The list of permitted restrictions under article 10(2) is somewhat longer and more specific than those in articles 8(2), 9(2) and 11(2) and uniquely includes reference to 'duties and responsibilities'.[306]

If so, is the restriction 'prescribed by law'?

3.149   The general principles applicable to article 8 apply to article 10: see above. They are examined in chapter 4.[307]

If so, is the restriction 'necessary in a democratic society'?

3.150   The general principles applicable to article 8 apply to article 10: see above. They are also examined in chapter 4.[308]

Article 11: freedom of assembly and association

3.151   Article 11 provides that:

(1) Everyone has the right to freedom of assembly and freedom of association with others, including the right to join trade unions for the protection of his interests.

(2) No restriction shall be placed on the exercise of these rights other than such as are prescribed by law and are necessary in a democratic society in the interests of national security or public safety, for the prevention of disorder or crime, for the protection of health or morals or for the protection of the rights of others. This article shall not prevent the imposition of lawful restrictions on the exercise of these rights by members of the armed forces, of the police or of the administration of the State.

Article 11 thus protects three interests: (a) freedom of assembly, (b) freedom of association, and (c) freedom to form and join trade

---

306 In practice, however, these words have added little.
307 Paras 4.29 to 4.36.
308 Paras 4.37 to 4.55 and 4.60 to 4.66.

unions.

3.152   The first is closely linked to article 10 (freedom of expression). And the second and third are closely linked to each other. In each case, article 11(2) permits special restrictions on members of the armed forces, the police and public servants.

Is article 11 engaged?

Freedom of assembly

3.153   Freedom of assembly under article 11 has been broadly interpreted by the European Court and Commission. It includes marches as well as static assemblies and covers both public and private events.[309] It also confers a right to hold meetings, marches and demonstrations on the public highway.[310] And organisers as well as participants can claim article 11 protection.[311]

3.154   Article 11 protects only 'peaceful' assembly, but, in this respect, peaceful intentions are sufficient. The mere fact that violence breaks out at an assembly will not automatically preclude the application of article 11.[312] And in many cases, state authorities will come under a positive duty to ensure that an assembly can take place without interference by others. The extent of this duty is examined in chapters 5 and 25.

3.155   Notice requirements and/or the imposition of conditions on an assembly do not necessarily breach article 11; so long as the aim is to protect peaceful assemblies. And where the circumstances are such that it is not practicable for an assembly to proceed peacefully, a blanket ban can be imposed.[313]

3.156   Criminal sanctions imposed for participation in an assembly can breach article 11; in *Steel and Others v UK*,[314] the European Court found that, on the facts, an arrest for breach of the peace was a disproportionate measure to the otherwise legitimate aim of preventing disorder and crime. Equally, indirect sanctions against participants, such as disciplinary measures, can breach article 11.[315]

---

309 *Christians Against Racism and Fascism v UK* (1980) 21 DR 138.
310 *Rassemblement Jurassien and Unite Jurassienne v Switzerland* (1980) 17 DR 93.
311 *Christians Against Racism and Fascism v UK* n309.
312 Ibid.
313 Ibid.
314 Court (28 September 1998); noted at [1999] EHRLR 109.
315 *Ezelin v France* (1992) 14 EHRR 362.

Freedom of association

3.157 Freedom of association under article 11 implies the right of individuals to come together to further their common interests. It does not include the right to share the company of others: see *McFeeley v UK*[316] which concerned a prisoner's claim to a right of association with others. Nor does it include the right to belong to a particular association. The Strasbourg bodies have taken the view that associations are free to regulate their own membership and activities. However, the right to freedom of association can include a right not to belong to a particular association: see *Young, James and Webster v UK.*[317]

3.158 Preventing individuals from forming an association and preventing a particular individual from joining an association are clear breaches of article 11. Registration or licensing schemes are not prohibited, so long as they do not impair the activities of an association. But a refusal to register a particular association might well violate article 11.[318]

3.159 The term 'association' in article 11 presupposes a voluntary grouping with a common goal.[319] The non-voluntary and public nature of most (but not all)[320] professional regulatory bodies therefore excludes them from article 11 protection.[321]

Trade unions

3.160 The right to form and join trade unions is clearly an aspect of freedom of association under article 11. How far it extends beyond the formal act of forming or joining a trade union to more substantial matters such as trade union activity is not clear. Broadly speaking, the European Court and Commission have been reluctant to extend protection to trade union activity unless it can be shown to be indispensable to the protection of members' interests. This limited protection stems from the phrase 'for the protection of his interests' in article 11. It has been held to require that trade unions be 'heard' in

---

316 (1980) 20 DR 44.
317 (1982) 4 EHRR 38.
318 *Sidiropulos v Greece* (Commission) 11 April 1997, (unreported).
319 *Young, James and Webster v UK* n317.
320 See *Sigurjonsson v Iceland* (1993) 16 EHRR 462.
321 See *Le Compte, Van Leuven and de Meyere v Belgium* (1982) 4 EHRR 1 (doctors); *Revert v France* (1989) 62 DR 309 (architects); and *A and Others v Spain* (1990) 66 DR 188 (lawyers).

the collective bargaining process, but not that they be 'consulted'.[322] And the right to strike, which is not expressly guaranteed, has not been considered indispensable to the exercise of article 11 rights.[323] See chapter 28.

3.161   When interpreting article 11, the Strasbourg bodies have frequently taken other international instruments into account, in particular those promulgated by the International Labour Organisation.[324]

Is any restriction limited to the army, police and civil servants?

3.162   Article 11(2) makes special reference to the army, police and civil servants. The effect is to exclude these groups from much of the protection of article 11(2) such that any restriction on their article 11 rights will survive article 11 challenge so long as: (a) it is imposed in accordance with domestic law, and (b) it is not arbitrary.

3.163   So, for example, in *CCSU v UK*[325] the European Commission refused to review the decision to remove the applicants' trade union rights against the requirement that it be 'necessary in a democratic society' because they were civil servants employed at GCHQ and thus came within the exception to article 11(2).

If not, can the reason for any restriction be found in article 11(2)?

3.164   A restriction on article 11 rights, other than one applying solely to the army, police or civil servants, will be compatible with the Convention only if it is aimed at protecting one of the interests listed in article 11(2), namely:

1) national security;

2) public safety;

3) the prevention of disorder or crime;

4) the protection of health or morals; or

5) the protection of the rights of others.

322 *National Union of Belgian Police v Belgium* (1979–80) 1 EHRR 578.
323 *Schmidt and Dahlstrom v Sweden* (1976) 1 EHRR 632.
324 See paras 4.21 to 4.25.
325 (1987) 50 DR 228.

This list is intended to be exhaustive and in each case the interest in question is to be narrowly construed.[326]

3.165   The structure of article 11 is, therefore, similar to that of article 8 and the same general principles apply.

If so, is the restriction 'prescribed by law'?

3.166   The general principles applicable to article 8 apply to article 11: see above. They are examined in chapter 4.[327]

If so, is the restriction 'necessary in a democratic society'?

3.167   The general principles applicable to article 8 apply to article 11: see above. They are also examined in chapter 4.[328]

Article 12: the right to marry and found a family

3.168   Article 12 provides that:

> Men and women of marriageable age have the right to marry and to found a family, according to the national laws governing the exercise of this right.

Is article 12 engaged?

3.169   The right to marry under article 12 has been interpreted as 'a right to form a legal relationship, to acquire a status' the essence of which is 'the formation of a legally binding association between a man and a woman'.[329] It does not imply the right to divorce.[330] The extent of the right to found a family is less clear.

3.170   In *X and Y v Switzerland*[331] the European Commission took the view that, since the applicants were married, they had already founded a family; this approach was followed in *Abdulaziz, Cabales and Balkandali v UK*[332] where the European Court held that 'family'

---

326 See paras 4.57 to 4.59.
327 Paras 4.29 to 4.36.
328 Paras 4.37 to 4.55 and 4.60 to 4.66.
329 *Hamer v UK* (1979) 24 DR 5.
330 *Johnston v Ireland* (1987) 9 EHRR 203.
331 (1978) 13 DR 241.
332 (1985) 7 EHRR 471.

comes into existence upon lawful marriage. In *X and Y v Switzerland* the Commission held that article 12 could not provide the basis for conjugal visits in prison on the basis that interferences with family life permitted under article 8(2) could not amount to a violation of article 12. In a non-prison context, the position is different. In *Abdulaziz, Cabales and Balkandali v UK* the Court observed that 'it is scarcely conceivable that the right to found a family ... should not encompass the right to live together.'[333]

If so, do the age requirements and domestic rules conform to the Convention?

3.171   Unlike articles 8, 9, 10 and 11 which are subject to fairly wide-ranging restrictions, the right to marry under article 12 is subject only to the requirement that: (a) individuals seeking to marry are 'of marriageable age'; and (b) they comply with marriage rules in domestic law.

3.172   Domestic law can prescribe the procedural requirements for legally valid marriages, but must not have the effect of impairing the very essence of the right to marry.[334] So far, the European Court has maintained that preventing transsexuals from marrying does not have that effect.[335]

Article 13: the right to an effective remedy

3.173   Article 13 provides that:

> Everyone whose rights and freedoms as set forth in this Convention are violated shall have an effective remedy before a national authority notwithstanding that the violation has been committed by persons acting in an official capacity.

It complements article 1 of the Convention which requires Contracting States to secure Convention rights to everyone in their jurisdiction and reflects the basic principle that Convention rights are intended to be given effect in domestic law.

3.174   Article 13 is not included among the Convention rights which are

---

333 Ibid para 62.
334 *Cossey v UK* (1991) 13 EHRR 622.
335 See *Rees v UK* (1987) 9 EHRR 56 and *Cossey v UK* (1991) 13 EHRR 622. And see para 19.37.

to be given effect in UK domestic law under the HRA.[336] According to the Lord Chancellor, the 1998 Act gives effect to article 13 by establishing a scheme under which Convention rights can be raised before UK courts.[337] And, in any event, HRA s2 requires courts and tribunals to take the case-law of the European Court and Commission into account, including their case-law on article 13, when determining any question which arises in connection with a Convention right.[338]

Is article 13 applicable?

3.175 Article 13 is not free-standing. It can be considered only if one of the substantive rights or freedoms protected by the Convention is in issue.

3.176 In addition, article 13 has no application where article 5(4) or article 6(1) are in play. Article 5(4) requires a specific remedy of release in cases of wrongful detention; and article 6(1) guarantees everyone a fair trial (and hence determination) of any criminal charge against him/her and of his/her civil rights and obligations. These requirements are stricter than article 13.

3.177 The European Court has imposed a further restriction on article 13 by insisting that it cannot require a domestic remedy for a violation stemming directly from legislation. If this were otherwise it would be tantamount to requiring that the Convention be directly incorporated. By the same token, neither article 13 nor the Convention generally obliges states to implement the Convention in domestic law in any particular manner.[339]

If so, is there an 'arguable' breach of that right?

3.178 Despite its wording, it is not a precondition of article 13 that there be an actual breach of some other Convention right before it comes into play. What is required is that anyone with an 'arguable claim' be entitled to *seek* an effective remedy.[340] In this context, an 'arguable claim' is a claim which is not wholly unsubstantiated on the facts and gives rise to a prima facie issue under the Convention.[341]

336 See paras 1.7 to 1.8.
337 HL Debs (Committee stage), col 475 18 November 1997.
338 See paras 1.44 to 1.47.
339 *Swedish Engine Drivers' Union v Sweden* (1979–80) 1 EHRR 617.
340 *Silver v UK* (1983) 5 EHRR 347.
341 *Boyle and Rice v UK* (1988) 10 EHRR 425.

If so, is the remedy in question 'effective'?

3.179   To be effective a remedy must involve the determination of a claim and provide the possibility of redress. However, the requirement of effectiveness has to be read in the context of the complaint. In cases of secret surveillance, the Strasbourg bodies have accepted that article 13 requires a remedy that is only 'as effective as it can be'.[342] This approach has been justified on the basis that the Convention is to be read as a whole and, therefore, where surveillance can be justified under article 8(2), the remedy required under article 13 should not undermine it, for example, by requiring disclosure of the surveillance measures taken.[343]

3.180   On the other hand, where fundamental rights are at stake, the effectiveness requirement is likely to be more strictly construed. In *Chahal v UK*[344] the Court held that the requirement of a remedy which is 'as effective as it can be' is not appropriate in respect of a complaint that a person's deportation will expose him/her to a real risk of treatment in breach of article 3. In such cases, given the irreversible nature of the harm that might occur if the risk of ill-treatment materialised and the importance the Court attaches to article 3, the notion of an effective remedy under article 13 requires independent scrutiny of the claim that there exist substantial grounds for fearing a real risk of treatment contrary to article 3. Similarly in *Aydin v Turkey*,[345] which involved an allegation of rape and ill-treatment in custody, the Court took the view that without prejudice to any other remedy available in domestic law, article 13 imposed an obligation on states to carry out a thorough and effective investigation of incidents of torture.[346]

3.181   The notion of a remedy under article 13 is not restricted to judicial remedies. However, where no judicial remedy is available, the independence, powers and binding authority of the body in question will be relevant to the question of whether it is capable of providing an effective remedy. In *Govell v UK*[347] the European Commission took the view that a police complaint in a bugging case did not constitute an effective remedy for article 13 purposes because

---

342 *Leander v Sweden* (1987) 9 EHRR 433.

343 *Klass v Germany* (1979–80) 2 EHRR 214.

344 (1997) 23 EHRR 413.

345 (1998) 25 EHRR 251.

346 See paras 14.19 to 14.21.

347 Commission (14 January 1998); noted at [1999] EHRLR 121.

the Police Complaints Authority was not a sufficiently independent body.

3.182   Whether judicial review proceedings in domestic law provide an effective remedy as required by article 13 will depend on the context and level of scrutiny. In *Soering v UK*[348] the European Court found that it did.[349] But in *Chahal v UK*[350] it found that it did not. The most recent decision, *D v UK*,[351] supports *Soering* but only on the basis that the domestic courts subject decisions on life expectancy to 'anxious scrutiny' in judicial review proceedings. See, further, chapter 11, where this issue is examined in detail.

Article 14: the prohibition on discrimination

3.183   Article 14 provides that:

> The enjoyment of the rights and freedoms set forth in this Convention shall be secured without discrimination on any ground such as sex, race, colour, language, religion, political or other opinion, national or social origin, association with a national minority, property, birth or other status.

The list of the prohibited grounds of discrimination is illustrative, not exhaustive. Discriminatory treatment is capable of amounting to ill-treatment under article 3; but the threshold is a high one.[352]

Is there a substantive Convention right in issue?

3.184   Article 14, like article 13, is not free-standing. It does not provide a general right to freedom from discrimination. It can be invoked only in relation to one of the other Convention rights set out in articles 2 to 12 and the First Protocol. However, no breach of another Convention right need be established: the test for the application of article 14 is whether the facts in issue 'fall within the ambit' of one or more of the other Convention provisions.[353]

---

348 (1989) 11 EHRR 439.
349 This case was followed in *Vilvarajah v UK* (1992) 14 EHRR 248.
350 Note 344.
351 (1997) 24 EHRR 423.
352 *Abdulaziz, Cabales and Balkandali v UK* (1985) 7 EHRR 471.
353 *Rasmussen v Denmark* (1985) 7 EHRR 371.

If so, is there different treatment?

3.185 Discrimination under the Convention requires like to be compared to like; in other words it depends upon individuals who are in similar situations being treated differently.[354] In *Van der Mussele v Belgium*[355] a trainee barrister claimed that he had been treated less favourably than apprentices in other professions because, unlike them, he was obliged to work for free by providing unpaid legal representation. The Court rejected his claim on the basis that there were fundamental differences between the various professions and accordingly like was not being compared to like.

If so, does it have a legitimate aim?

3.186 Not every difference in treatment is discriminatory. The essential question is whether a 'reasonable and objective justification' can be shown for the difference in question.[356] Although a 'margin of appreciation'[357] is allowed when determining whether a difference in treatment can be justified, 'very weighty reasons' will be needed to justify discrimination on grounds of race or sex.[358]

Are the means employed to achieve the aim proportionate?

3.187 Even where some difference in treatment can be justified, the measure in issue still has to be proportionate to the legitimate aim pursued;[359] in other words the Strasbourg bodies will examine whether it goes further than is really necessary bearing in mind the objective in question. The concept of proportionality is dealt with in detail in chapter 4.[360]

---

354 *Fredin v Sweden* (1991) 13 EHRR 784.

355 (1984) 6 EHRR 163.

356 *Belgian Linguistics Case* (1979–80) 1 EHRR 241.

357 This concept is examined in paras 4.88 to 4.97.

358 *Schmidt v Germany* (1994) 18 EHRR 513; *Inze v Austria* (1988) 10 EHRR 394; and *Van Raalte v Netherlands* (1997) 24 EHRR 503.

359 *Belgian Linguistics Case* n356.

360 Paras 4.37 to 4.55.

Article 1 of the first Protocol: the right to property

3.188 Article 1 of the First Protocol provides that:

> Every natural or legal person is entitled to the peaceful enjoyment of his possessions. No one shall be deprived of his possessions except in the public interest and subject to the conditions provided for by law and by the general principles of international law.
>
> The preceding provision shall not, however, in any way impair the right of a state to enforce such laws as it deems necessary to control the use of property in accordance with the general interest or to secure the payment of taxes or other contributions or penalties.

In effect, therefore, article 1 of Protocol 1 guarantees the right to peaceful enjoyment of possessions, but reserves to the state power to: (a) deprive individuals of their possessions, and (b) to control the use of property, subject to certain qualifications.[361]

Is article 1 of Protocol 1 engaged?

3.189 The terms 'possessions' in the first paragraph of article 1 of the first Protocol has been interpreted broadly. It includes all property and chattels and also acquired rights with economic interests such as shares,[362] patents,[363] fishing rights,[364] alcohol licences,[365] planning consents,[366] the ownership of a debt[367] and, in some circumstances, even 'goodwill'.[368] In *Pressos Compania Naviera v Belgium*[369] the European Court construed possessions so as to include a claim for negligence, which had been removed by retrospective legislation. Welfare benefits and other similar benefits can also constitute possessions: see chapter 23.

---

361 See chapter 26.
362 *Bramelid and Malmstrom v Sweden* (1982) 29 DR 64.
363 *Smith Kline and French Laboratories v Netherlands* (1990) 66 DR 70.
364 *Baner v Sweden* (1989) 60 DR 128.
365 *The Traktorer Aktiebolag v Sweden* (1991) 13 EHRR 309.
366 *Pine Valley Developments v Ireland* (1992) 14 EHRR 319.
367 *Agneessens v Belgium* (1988) 58 DR 63.
368 *Van Marle v Netherlands* (1986) 8 EHRR 483.
369 (1996) 21 EHRR 301.

If so, does the measure in question amount to deprivation or control of property?

3.190   Article 1 of Protocol 1 distinguishes between deprivation and control of property. Deprivation of property is permitted only if it is in the 'public interest' and in accordance with general principles of international law. Control of property is permitted in a wider range of circumstances and reflects an assumption that some form of control over the enjoyment of possessions is inevitable in democratic societies. The right of an individual to live in his/her own house amounts to a deprivation of property;[370] whereas rent control legislation merely controls property.[371] See, further, chapter 22.

If deprivation: is it in the public interest and has a 'fair balance' been struck?

3.191   In *James v UK*[372] the European Court held that the public interest requires:

1) that any deprivation of property must be for a legitimate purpose; and

2) the achievement of that purpose must strike a 'fair balance' between the demands of the general interest of the community and the need to protect individual rights – ie, not impose an excessive burden on the latter.

Although article 1 of the first Protocol does not expressly guarantee a right to compensation, deprivation of property without compensation is likely to be justifiable only in exceptional circumstances.

If control: does it have a legitimate aim and is it proportionate?

3.192   The principles to be applied when assessing whether control of property complies with the Convention are similar but less strict. In particular:

1) the measure in question must have a legitimate aim, in the sense of not being 'manifestly without reasonable foundation'; and

370   *Wiggins v UK* (1978) 13 DR 40.
371   *Mellacher v Austria* (1990) 12 EHRR 391.
372   (1986) 8 EHRR 123.

2) there must be a reasonable relationship of proportionality between the means employed and the achievement of that aim.[373]

Again there must be a 'fair balance' between the demands of the general interest of the community and the need to protect individual rights.

If neither deprivation nor control: does the measure in question nonetheless interfere with peaceful enjoyment of possessions?

3.193 Where a measure falls short of deprivation or control, the European Court will consider whether a 'fair balance' has been struck between the demands of the general interest of the community and the requirements of the protection of the individual's fundamental rights.[374] A fair balance will not be achieved where measures impose 'an individual and excessive burden' on those affected. See, further, chapter 26.

Article 2 of the first Protocol: the right to education

3.194 Article 2 of the first Protocol provides that:

No person shall be denied the right to education. In the exercise of any functions which it assumes in relation to education and to teaching, the state shall respect the right of parents to ensure such education and teaching in conformity with their own religious and philosophical aims.

It is dealt with in detail in chapter 21.

Is article 2 of Protocol 1 engaged?

3.195 Article 2 enshrines the right to education. It does not oblige the state to provide education; rather it restricts state interference in education. Hence the requirement that states respect the right of parents to ensure that their children are educated in accordance with their religious and philosophical convictions.

373 *Wasa Liv Omsesidigt, Forsakringbolaget Valands Pensionsstiftelse v Sweden* (1988) 58 DR 163.
374 *Sporring and Lonroth v Sweden* (1983) 5 EHRR 35 at para 69.

If so, does the reservation apply?

3.196   The UK has entered a reservation in respect of the right to education in the following terms:

> ... in view of certain provisions of the Education Acts in the United Kingdom, the principle affirmed in the second sentence of article 2 is accepted by the United Kingdom only in so far as it is compatible with the provision of efficient instruction and training, and the avoidance of unreasonable public expenditure.

Under the HRA this reservation has effect in domestic law.[375] See further chapter 21.

Are there any relevant implied limitations?

3.197   The Court has recognised that article 2 of Protocol 1 'by its very nature calls for regulation':[376] see further, chapter 4.[377]

Article 3 of the First Protocol: the duty to hold free elections

3.198   Article 3 of the First Protocol provides that:

> The High Contracting Parties undertake to hold free elections at reasonable intervals by secret ballot, under conditions which will ensure the free expression of the opinion of the people in the choice of the legislature.

Is article 3 of Protocol 1 engaged?

3.199   Article 3 of the First Protocol applies only to the election of the 'legislature'. And metropolitan county councils, such as the (former) Greater London Council, are not part of the legislature.[378] In *Lindsay v UK*[379] the European Commission left open the question of whether the European Parliament constituted part of the legislature; in *Tete v*

---

375   See paras 1.62 to 1.65.
376   *Belgian Lingustic Case* (No 2) (1968) 1 EHRR 252.
377   Para 14.78.
378   *Edwards v UK* (1986) 8 EHRR 96; *Booth-Clibborn v UK* (1985) 43 DR 236.
379   (1979) 15 DR 247.
380   (1987) 54 DR 52.

France[380] it tended to the view that it was not (yet); but more recently it has admitted the case of *Mathews v UK.*[381]

If so, what principles apply?

3.200   To date the European Court has considered only one case under article 3 of the First Protocol: *Mathieu-Mohin and Clerfayt v Belgium.*[382] There it set out the following general principles:

1) the importance of free elections is such as to impose positive duties on the state;[383]

2) the rights protected are the right to vote and the right to stand for election;

3) these rights are not absolute and can be subject to implied limitations, so long as any such limitations do not impair the very essence of the right.

3.201   Article 3 of the First Protocol does not apply to referenda.[384] And it does not oblige states to introduce any particular electoral system: proportional representation with single transferable vote is not contrary to the Convention.[385]

Are there any relevant implied limitations?

3.202   In *Mathieu-Mohin and Clerfayt v Belgium*[386] the European Court read into article 3 of Protocol 1 the right to vote and the right to stand for election. However, these rights are not absolute and can be restricted by implication: see further, chapter 4.[387]

3.203   Restrictions on electoral campaigning may raise issues under article 10 (freedom of expression). In *Bowman v UK,*[388] the European Court found that a statutory limitation on election expenditure operated, for all practical purposes, as a total barrier on the applicant's ability to publish information with a view to influencing voters.

---

381 (1996) 22 EHRR CD 175. For the merits decision, see: [1998] EHRLR 340.
382 (1988) 10 EHRR 1. But see *Bowman v UK* (1998) 26 EHRR 1 and *Pierre-Bloch v France* [1998] EHRLR 216 on election expenses.
383 For a general discussion of positive duties see chapter 5.
384 *X v UK* (1975) 3 DR 165.
385 *Lindsay v UK* (1979) 15 DR 247.
386 Note 382.
387 Para 4.78.
388 (1998) 26 EHRR 1.

Although the aim of the provision – securing equality between candidates – was legitimate, the restriction was disproportionate.[389]

---

389 Ibid para 47.

CHAPTER 4

The Convention approach to the protection of human rights

4.1	**Introduction**
4.5	**Principles of interpretation: The Vienna Convention**
4.9	**The objects and purpose of the Convention**
4.11	**The principle of effectiveness**
4.16	**Dynamic interpretation: the Convention as a 'living instrument'**
4.19	**Autonomous meaning**
4.20	**Previous Convention case-law**
4.21	**Recourse to other human rights instruments**
4.22	Council of Europe instruments
4.24	UN human rights instruments
4.26	**Restricting Convention rights**
4.29	**The principle of legality**
4.30	The first rule: identifying and establishing the legal basis for restrictions
4.31	The second rule: accessibility
4.32	The third rule: certainty
4.37	**The principle of proportionality**
4.43	'Relevant and sufficient' reasons

continued

4.46   Less restrictive alternatives
4.48   Procedural fairness
4.52   Safeguards against abuse
4.54   The 'very essence' test

4.56   Restrictions expressly permitted under articles 8(2), 9(2), 10(2) and 11(2)
4.57   The requirement of a legitimate aim
4.60   The meaning of the phrase 'necessary in a democratic society'
4.63   Pressing social need
4.65   The principle of proportionality in the context of articles 8–11

4.67   Restrictions expressly permitted under other articles
4.67   The restrictions on the right to liberty expressly provided for in articles 5(1)(a)-5(1)(f)
4.70   The restrictions on the right to marry expressly provided for in article 12
4.71   The restrictions on the right to property expressly provided for in article 1 of the First Protocol

4.75   Restrictions impliedly permitted under the Convention
4.76   Implied restrictions on the right to a fair trial under article 6(1)
4.78   Implied restrictions on the right to education under article 2 of the First Protocol
4.79   Implied restrictions on election rights under article 3 of the First Protocol

4.81   Restrictions specifically provided for by a valid derogation

4.83   Restrictions on the political activity of aliens specifically provided for by article 16

4.85   Restrictions on activities aimed at the destruction of Convention rights specifically provided for by article 17

4.88   The margin of appreciation

4.94   Non-applicability of the margin of appreciation under the HRA

4.98   Waiver of Convention rights

Introduction

4.1 The Convention approach to the protection of human rights and, in particular, the European Court's rules and techniques for interpreting the Convention will become an important part of domestic law under the Human Rights Act 1998 (HRA). Key to this approach is the principle of effectiveness: that the Convention must be interpreted so as to make its safeguards 'practical and effective' not 'theoretical or illusory'. This principle (examined below) has been the springboard for (among other things) the development of implied rights (for example, the right of access to a court),[1] positive obligations (see chapter 5) and extended state responsibility.[2]

4.2 Also important is the Convention approach to the restriction of human rights. Broadly speaking, the European Court recognises three distinct categories of Convention rights and its approach to their protection varies from one category to another. The categories are:

1) *Absolute rights*: ie, those which cannot be restricted in any circumstances (even in times of war or other public emergency) and which are not to be balanced with any general public interest. These are articles 2, 3, 4(1)[3] and 7.

2) *Derogable but (otherwise) unqualified rights*: ie, those in relation to which the government can enter a derogation (see chapter 1), but which otherwise are not to be balanced with any general public interest. These are articles 4(2) and (3),[4] 5 and 6.

3) *Qualified rights*: ie, those which although set out in positive form are subject to limitation or restriction clauses which enable the general public interest to be taken into account.[5] These are Articles 8, 9, 10 and 11.

4.3 The operation of the limitation or accommodation clauses under articles 8, 9, 10 and 11 is crucial. It is the settled case-law of the European Court and Commission that a limitation or restriction on

---

1   See paras 13.6 to 13.7.
2   See paras 2.12 to 2.17.
3   The prohibition on slavery.
4   The prohibition of forced or compulsory labour.
5   However, as the European Court of Human Rights pointed out in *Sunday Times v UK* (1979–80) 2 EHRR 245, it is not faced with a choice between two conflicting principles (an individual's right and the general public interest), but with a principle that is subject to a number of exceptions (para 65).

the rights under these articles can only be justified if the person or body imposing the limitation or restriction can show:

1) That the limitation or restriction in question is 'prescribed by law'.

2) That the limitation or restriction pursues one of the aims specifically listed in articles 8(2), 9(2), 10(2) or 11(2) as the case may be.

3) That the limitation or restriction is 'necessary in a democratic society'. To satisfy this test, the person or body imposing the limitation or restriction on the rights set out in articles 8, 9, 10 or 11 must show that the limitation or restriction fulfils a pressing social need and that it is proportionate to the aim of responding to that need.

4) That the limitation or restriction is not discriminatory under article 14.

4.4   This chapter examines the principles for interpreting the Convention first, and then deals with the rules governing the restriction of Convention rights.

Principles of interpretation: The Vienna Convention

4.5   The European Convention on Human Rights is an international treaty and, as such, its interpretation is governed by rules of international law. These are set out in the *Vienna Convention on the Law of Treaties* (1969).[6] Strictly speaking this Convention does not have retrospective effect,[7] but the European Court has accepted that the rules set out in articles 31 to 33 give expression to general principles of international law and, therefore, apply to the interpretation of the European Convention.[8]

4.6   Article 31(1) of the Vienna Convention provides that:

> A treaty shall be interpreted in good faith in accordance with the ordinary meaning to be given to the terms of the treaty in their context and in light of its objects and purpose.

This has been the springboard for the adoption by the European Court

---

6   Cmnd 7964.
7   See article 4.
8   See *Golder v UK* (1979–80) 1 EHRR 524 at paras 29–30 and 34–36.

and Commission of a teleological approach to the interpretation of the European Convention, ie, one that seeks to realise its objects and purpose.

4.7   The text, preamble, annexes and related agreements and instruments of the contracting parties are relevant to its interpretation.[9] Recourse may also be had to 'supplementary means of interpretation' such as the preparatory work (travaux préparatoires) and the circumstances of its conclusion. These can be used so as to confirm the meaning resulting from article 31 (above) or to determine the meaning when such interpretation leaves the meaning 'ambiguous or obscure' or where it 'leads to a result which is manifestly absurd or unreasonable'.[10]

4.8   The travaux préparatoires of the European Convention are published in *The Collected Edition of the Travaux Preparatoires of the European convention on Human Rights*.[11] However, since the Convention is to be interpreted as a 'living instrument'[12] recourse to the travaux préparatoires will be rare and, where necessary, will be ignored.[13]

The objects and purpose of the Convention

4.9   Even before the Vienna Convention came into force, the European Court recognised the principles enshrined in it, in particular the requirement that the Convention be interpreted in light of its objects and purpose. In the early case of *Wemhoff v Germany*[14] the Court held that:

> ... given that it is a law-making treaty, it is also necessary to seek the interpretation that is most appropriate in order to realise the aim and achieve the object of the treaty, and not that which would restrict to the greatest possible degree the obligations undertaken by the parties.[15]

See also *Golder v UK*[16] where the Court justified its interpretation of

9 Article 32(2).
10 Article 32.
11 Council of Europe.
12 See paras 4.16 to 4.18.
13 See *Sigurjonsson v Iceland* (1993) 16 EHRR 462.
14 (1979–80) 1 EHRR 55.
15 Ibid para 8.
16 Note 8.

article 6(1) of the Convention so as to include a 'right of access' to a court as well as fair trial in pending proceedings[17] on the basis that this accorded with the objects and purpose of the Convention, including the rule of law referred to in the preamble.

4.10   The objects and purpose of the Convention include:

1) 'The maintenance and further realisation of human rights' (preamble); and, more generally, 'the protection of human rights';[18]

2) the maintenance and promotion of 'the ideas and values of a democratic society';[19] and

3) the rule of law.[20]

So far as the second of these is concerned, for the European Court and Commission, 'pluralism, tolerance and broadmindedness' are the hallmarks of a democratic society.[21] And in *Young, James and Webster v UK*[22] the Court recognised that:

> Although individual interests must on occasion be subordinate to those of a group, democracy does not simply mean that the views of a majority must always prevail: a balance must be achieved which ensures the fair and proper treatment of minorities and avoids any abuse of a dominant position.[23]

The principle of effectiveness

4.11   The object and purpose of the Convention as an instrument for the protection of human rights require that its provisions be interpreted and applied so as to make its safeguards 'practical and effective' not 'theoretical and illusory'.

4.12   In *Artico v Italy*[24] the Italian government argued that it had fulfilled its obligations under article 6(3)(c) of the Convention – the right to free legal assistance if no means to pay and the interests of justice so require – by appointing a lawyer to represent the applicant at his

---

17 See paras 13.6 to 13.7.
18 *Soering v UK* (1989) 11 EHRR 439 at para 87.
19 *Kjeldsen Busk Madson and Peterson v Belgium* (1979–80) 1 EHRR 711 at para 53.
20 Note 8 at para 34.
21 *Handyside v UK* (1979–80) 1 EHRR 737.
22 (1982) 4 EHRR 38.
23 Ibid at para 63.
24 (1981) 3 EHRR 1.

criminal trial and could not be called upon to ensure that the lawyer was present and prepared on the first day of the hearing. The European Court disagreed. In an important passage of its judgment it held that:

> ... the Convention is intended to guarantee not rights that are theoretical or illusory but rights that are practical and effective ... mere nomination does not ensure effective assistance since the lawyer appointed for legal aid purposes may die, fall seriously ill, be prevented for a protracted period from acting or shirk his duties. If they are notified of the situation, the authorities must either replace him or cause him to fulfil his obligations. Adoption of the Government's restrictive interpretation would lead to results that are unreasonable and incompatible with both the wording of [article 6(3)(c)] and the structure of article 6 taken as a whole; in many instances free legal assistance might be worthless.[25]

4.13   This has far-reaching implications for the enforcement of Convention rights under the HRA. Courts and tribunals, as public authorities, will be under a duty to ensure that the exercise of Convention rights is practical and effective. Such a duty may include the necessity to explore Convention issues even when they are not raised by the parties before the court.

4.14   The principle of effectiveness also has important ramifications for liability under the HRA. To ensure that Convention rights are practical and effective, the European Court has developed both a sophisticated notion of state responsibility and the doctrine of positive obligations. These are examined in chapter 2[26] and chapter 5 respectively.

4.15   In *Soering v UK*[27] the European Court made the connection between the objects and purpose of the Convention and the principle of effectiveness:

> In interpreting the Convention regard must be had to its special character as a treaty for the collective enforcement of human rights and fundamental freedoms ... Thus, the object and purpose of the Convention as an instrument for the protection of individual human beings require that its provisions be interpreted and applied so as to make its safeguards practical and effective.[28]

---

25 Ibid at para 33.
26 Paras 2.12 to 2.17.
27 Note 18.
28 Ibid at para 87.

And the Court has subsequently relied upon the principle of effectiveness when considering the scope of positive obligations[29] and interpreting the meaning of a 'victim' under the Convention.[30]

Dynamic interpretation: the Convention as a 'living instrument'

4.16 When interpreting the Convention, the European Court and Commission have adopted an evolutive and dynamic, rather than a static and historical, approach. This means that the Convention is to be interpreted in light of 'present day conditions', not those prevailing when it was drafted. Therefore, as a general rule, the older a decision of the Court or Commission, the less reliable a guide it is to the interpretation of Convention rights.

4.17 There are numerous examples throughout the European Court and Commission case-law of the application of the 'living instrument' principle. In *Tyrer v UK*[31] the Court expressly took into account developments in penal policy throughout Europe since the Convention was drafted when considering whether birching as a punishment was compatible with the Convention. And in *Marckx v Belgium*[32] the Court approached the case on the basis that although a distinction between legitimate and illegitimate children may have corresponded to opinions held in the 1950s, it was nonetheless incompatible with a proper interpretation of article 8 of the Convention in the late 1970s. More recently, the Court has reviewed its approach to the rights of transsexuals three times within a 12-year period on the basis that there might have been scientific and societal developments since its last consideration of the issue.[33] Each time, the Court has made it clear that while the interests of legal certainty supported the principle that it should follow its own decisions, it was free to depart from an earlier decision if there were cogent reasons for doing so. And the need to ensure that the Convention was inter-

---

29 See chapter 5.

30 See *Marckx v Belgium* (1979–80) 2 EHRR 330 and paras 2.18 to 2.35.

31 (1981) 2 EHRR 1.

32 Note 30.

33 Transsexuals' rights were first considered by the Court in *Rees v UK* (1986) 9 EHRR 56 and then reviewed in *Cossey v UK* (1981) 13 EHRR 622, *B v France* (1993) 16 EHRR 1, *X, Y and Z v UK* (1997) 24 EHRR 143 and *Sheffield and Horsham v UK* (1999) 27 EHRR 163.

preted as a 'living instrument' in light of present-day conditions was one such reason.[34]

4.18 One of the most dynamic examples of the Court's interpretation of the Convention as a living instrument is *Sigurjonsson v Iceland*,[35] where, in resisting an argument that the right of association under article 11 of the Convention included a negative right not to join an association, the Icelandic government drew attention to the travaux préparatoires of the Convention showing that such a right was deliberately omitted. Drawing on the *European Social Charter and International Labour Organisation Conventions 87 and 98*, the Court ignored the travaux preparatoires on the basis that the Convention had to be interpreted as a living instrument and there was a growing measure of common ground at the domestic and international level that the right not to join an association was inherent in article 11.

Autonomous meaning

4.19 Legal terms in the Convention are to be given an 'autonomous' interpretation. Concepts such as 'civil rights and obligations' and 'criminal charge' in article 6 and 'possessions' in article 1 of Protocol 1 have a Convention meaning which is independent of the meaning which might be accorded to them in the domestic legal system of a Convention state.

Previous Convention case-law

4.20 There is no formal doctrine of precedent under the Convention. The European Court will usually follow its previous decisions, but it is not bound to do so and it has frequently recognised that the principle of dynamic interpretation[36] requires it to reconsider existing principles in light of any developments since they were first articulated.

---

34 See *Cossey v UK* n33 at para 35.
35 Note 13.
36 See paras 4.16 to 4.18.

Recourse to other human rights instruments

4.21   Other human rights instruments are becoming increasingly relevant in Convention case-law. The European Court will examine both Council of Europe and other international instruments for a number of purposes, including:

1) to assist in the proper interpretation of the provisions of the Convention itself;

2) to define the scope of the margin of appreciation; and

3) as evidence of present-day standards when considering how to interpret the Convention as a 'living instrument'.

Examples of their use are set out below.

Council of Europe instruments

4.22   The European Court's recourse to Council of Europe instruments includes:

1) *National Union of Belgium Police v Belgium*[37] where the European Court used the *European Social Charter* as a basis for its analysis of the right to collective bargaining under article 11.[38]

2) *Schmidt and Dalstrom v Sweden*[39] where scope of any right to strike under article 11 of the Convention was determined by reference to the *European Social Charter*.

3) *Marckx v Belgium*: where the Court examined the *European Convention on the Status of Children Born out of Wedlock* to determine whether illegitimate children were protected under the European Convention.

4) *Inze v Austria*:[40] where the Court looked again at the *European Convention on the Status of Children Born out of Wedlock* to determine whether laws restricting the hereditary rights of illegitimate children violated the European Convention.

5) *Soering v UK*:[41] where the Court took the *European Extradition Convention* into account when considering whether the appli-

---

37   (1979–80) 1 EHRR 578.
38   See also *Swedish Engine Drivers' Union v Sweden* (1979–80) 1 EHRR 617.
39   (1979–80) 1 EHRR 632.
40   (1988) 10 EHRR 394.
41   Note 18 at para 56.

cant's extradition to Virginia where he might face a 'death row' situation violated article 3 of the European Convention.

6) *Autronic AG v Switzerland:*[42] where the Court took into account the *European Convention on Transfrontier Television* when assessing whether a refusal to grant the applicant a licence to receive and retransmit programmes from a Soviet telecommunications satellite was 'necessary' in a democratic society under article 10(2) of the European Convention.

7) *Gustafsson v Sweden:*[43] where the court referred to the *European Social Charter* as evidence of the widespread international recognition of the right to collective bargaining.

8) *X, Y and Z v UK:*[44] where the Court considered a Resolution of the Parliamentary Assembly recommending that Member States allow transsexuals to alter their birth certificates as evidence of a development in social attitudes towards transsexuals relevant to the interpretation of the European Convention as a 'living instrument'.[45]

4.23 European Union materials may also be relevant. For example, in *Goodwin v UK*[46] the Court relied upon a resolution of the European Parliament.

UN human rights instruments

4.24 The Court's recourse to UN human rights instruments includes:

1) *Pretto v Italy:*[47] where the Court examined the *International Covenant on Civil and Political Rights* to assist in determining the scope of the obligation under article 6(1) of the European Convention to pronounce judgments in public.

2) *Can v Austria:*[48] where the Commission interpreted article 6 European Convention so as to conform with article 14 of the *International Covenant on Civil and Political Rights and the UN Standard Minimum Rules for the Treatment of Prisoners.*

---

42 (1990) 12 EHRR 485
43 (1996) 22 EHRR 409.
44 Note 33.
45 However, the Court concluded that, for the time being at least, UK law does not breach the Convention: see chapter 19.
46 (1996) 22 EHRR 123.
47 (1983) 6 EHRR 182.
48 (Commission Decision) 12 July 1984; (1986) 8 EHRR 121.

3) *Kosiek v Germany:*[49] where the Commission interpreted article 10 of the European Convention by reference to the *International Covenant on the Elimination of All Forms of Racial Discrimination.*

4) *Muller v Switzerland:*[50] where the Court relied upon the wording of article 19 of the *International Covenant on Civil and Political Rights* to confirm its view that article 10 of the European Convention protects artistic expression.

5) *Soering v UK:*[51] where the Court took the *UN Convention Relating to the Status of Refugees* and the *UN Convention Against Torture and Other Cruel, Inhuman or Degrading Treatment or Punishment* into account when considering whether the applicant's extradition breached the European Convention.

6) *Groppera Radio AG v Switzerland:*[52] where the Court referred not only to the wording of article 19 of the *International Covenant on Civil and Political Rights* but also to its drafting history to confirm that the third sentence of article 10(1) of the European Convention permits regulation only of the technical aspects of broadcasting, not the content of broadcasts.

7) *Jersild v Denmark:*[53] where the Court examined the *International Covenant on the Elimination of All Forms of Racial Discrimination,* including its 'objects and purpose', when considering the extent to which racist speech should be protected under the European Convention.

Recently, the European Court has been willing to attach considerable weight to the UN *Convention on the Rights of the Child.*[54]

4.25   Finally, both the European Court and Commission have held that, as a general rule, the words 'forced or compulsory labour' in article 4 of the European Convention must be interpreted in line with the definitions contained in the Conventions of the International Labour

49 (1986) 9 EHRR 328 (Commission Decision) 11 May 1984.
50 (1991) 13 EHRR 212.
51 Note 18 at para 86.
52 (1990) 12 EHRR 321.
53 (1995) 19 EHRR 1.
54 See *Olsson v Sweden* (No 2) (1994) 17 EHRR 134; *Costello-Roberts v UK* (1995) 19 EHRR 112; and *A v UK* (1998) 2 FLR 959; (1999) 27 EHRR 611.

Organisation:[55] see *Van der Mussele v Belgium*.[56] And in *X v UK*[57] the Commission used article 4 of the *American Convention on Human Rights* to aid its interpretation of article 2 of the European Convention (the right to life).

Restricting Convention rights

4.26 Permitted restrictions on Convention rights fall into six categories:[58]

1) Restrictions expressly permitted under articles 8(2), 9(2), 10(2) and 11(2).

2) Restrictions expressly permitted under other articles. These fall into three sub-groups:
   - the restrictions on the right to liberty expressly provided for in articles 5(1)(a)–5(1)(f);
   - the restrictions on the right to marry expressly provided for in article 12; and
   - the restrictions on the right to property expressly provided for in article 1 of the first Protocol.

3) Restrictions impliedly permitted under the Convention. Again these fall into three sub-groups:
   - implied restrictions on the right to a fair trial under article 6(1);
   - implied restrictions on the right to education under article 2 of the First Protocol; and
   - implied restrictions on election rights under article 3 of the first Protocol.

4) Restrictions specifically provided for by a valid derogation.

5) Restrictions on the political activity of aliens under article 16.

6) Restrictions on activities aimed at the destruction of Convention rights under article 17.

4.27 The rules governing each of these categories are different and they are considered separately below. However, there are two principles common to all six categories, namely:

---

55 See, in particular, ILO *Convention Concerning Forced or Compulsory Labour*, No 29 (1930) and ILO *Convention Concerning the Abolition of Forced Labour*, No 105 (1957).

56 (1984) 6 EHRR 163.

57 (1980) 19 DR 244.

58 The restriction on the right to life in article 2(1) ceases to apply to the UK because it has now ratified the sixth Optional Protocol: see para 3.5.

1) All restrictions must be 'lawful': this is frequently referred to as 'the principle of legality'.

2) All restrictions must be 'proportionate': this is frequently referred to as 'the principle of proportionality'.

4.28   These requirements have acquired special meaning under the Convention and it is therefore convenient to examine them first.

The principle of legality

4.29   The principle of legality is derived from the use of the phrases 'in accordance with law' in article 8(2) and 'prescribed by law' in articles 9(2), 10(2) and 11(2) and the use of the word 'lawful' elsewhere in the Convention. What it means is this:

1) First, the legal basis for any restriction on Convention rights must be identified and established. This is essentially a matter of domestic law.

2) Second, the law or rule in question must be 'accessible'; ie, those likely to be affected by a restriction on their Convention rights must be able to find out what the law or rule says.

3) Third, the law or rule in question must be formulated with sufficient clarity to enable those likely to be affected by it to understand it and to regulate their conduct so as to avoid breaking the law.[59]

Each rule is important and they are analysed separately below.

The first rule: identifying and establishing the legal basis for restrictions

4.30   This rule is based on the rule of law and implies that measures which restrict Convention rights should be subject to effective control. Legislation is obviously a sufficient basis in law for a restriction; so too is delegated legislation,[60] the common law[61] and/or European Community law.[62] The rules of a professional body, such as the Bar Council or Law Society, may even suffice, if validly made, so long as they are available to those bound by them.[63]

---

59 *Sunday Times v UK* (1979–80) 2 EHRR 245.
60 *Barthold v Germany* (1985) 7 EHRR 383.
61 *Sunday Times v UK* n59.
62 *Groppera Radio AG v Switzerland* n52.
63 *Barthold v Germany* n60.

The second rule: accessibility

4.31   This rule is intended to act as a brake on the exercise of arbitrary power by providing that a restriction cannot be justified, even if it is authorised in domestic law unless the applicable law or rule is published in a form accessible to those likely to be affected. Materials such as prison orders and instructions,[64] Home Office guidelines[65] and internal police guidelines[66] are unlikely to fulfil this requirement unless they are published. And it is not enough to identify some published legal provision as providing the basis for a restriction if, in truth, that provision is interpreted according to unpublished criteria.[67] However, the mere fact that an individual has to consult a lawyer for effective access to the law or rule in question is not, in itself, a breach of the accessibility rule.[68]

The third rule: certainty

4.32   The purpose of the third rule is two-fold: (a) to enable individuals likely to be affected by a restriction on their rights to understand the circumstances in which any such restriction may be imposed; and (b) to enable such individuals to foresee with a reasonable degree of accuracy the consequences of their actions. Again the mere fact that an individual has to consult a lawyer to properly understand the law or rule in question is not a breach of the certainty rule.[69]

4.33   Absolute certainty is not required. In *Sunday Times v UK*[70] the European Court held that, while an individual should, in principle, be able to foresee the consequences of his/her actions:

> Those consequences need not be foreseeable with absolute certainty; experience shows this to be unattainable ... whilst certainty is highly desirable, it may bring in its train excessive rigidity and the law must be able to keep pace with changing circumstances. Accordingly, many laws are inevitably couched in

---

64   *Silver v UK* (1983) 5 EHRR 347.
65   *Malone v UK* (1985) 7 EHRR 14.
66   *Govell v UK* (14 January 1998); noted at [1999] EHRLR 121.
67   *Silver v UK* note 64.
68   *Sunday Times v UK* note 59.
69   Ibid. See also *Rekvenyi v Hungary* [1999] EHRLR 114 concerning a prohibition on 'political activities' and *Hashman and Harrup v UK* [1999] EHRLR 342: 'bind overs' too vague.
70   Ibid.

terms which, to a greater or lesser extent, are vague and whose interpretation and application are questions of practice.[71]

Applying this principle, the Court concluded that the common law relating to contempt of court was formulated with sufficient precision to satisfy the requirements of the Convention.

4.34   The fact that a law or rule provides the person or body responsible for the measure in question a certain discretion will not necessarily offend the certainty rule, so long as the limits of that discretion are clear.[72] There must be 'sufficient indication of the circumstances in which the discretion will be exercised'[73] either in the empowering provision itself or within supplementary regulations and guidance. A public statement setting out the approach that will be adopted to the exercise of an otherwise over-broad discretion may suffice in some cases.[74]

4.35   Although the degree of certainty required varies according to the measure or restriction in question, the field of application and the categories of individuals likely to be affected, the following principles provide some general guidance:

1) In criminal cases there is an overlap between the certainty rule under articles 8–11 and the prohibition on retrospective application of the criminal law under article 7.[75]

2) The fact that a statutory provision is capable of more than one construction does not necessarily breach the certainty rule.[76]

3) Similarly, the fact that the common law is susceptible to change over time does not breach the certainty rule provided that:

   – the development of the law was reasonably foreseeable;[77] and

   – in the criminal context, that the development of the law is consistent with the essence of the offence. This implies that the constituent elements of an offence cannot be changed to the detriment of the accused.[78]

   – On that basis the removal of immunity enjoyed by husbands

---

71 Ibid at para 49.
72 *Silver v UK* n64.
73 Ibid.
74 *Rai, Allmond and 'Negotiate Now' v UK* (1995) (Commission) 19 EHRR CD 93.
75 See paras 6.22 to 6.26.
76 *Castells v Spain* (1992) 14 EHRR 445 and *Vogt v Germany* (1996) 21 EHRR 205. But see *Rekvenyi v Hungary* note 69.
77 *SW and CR v UK* (1996) 21 EHRR 363.
78 *X Ltd and Y v UK* (1982) 28 DR 77: see further paras 6.22 to 6.26.

from criminal liability for raping their wives was held by the European Court not to offend the certainty rule.[79]

4) In some areas of law, a degree of flexibility is inevitable. So, for example, in *Wingrove v UK*[80] the European Court accepted that the offence of blasphemy, by its very nature, did not lend itself to precise definition. A similar approach was taken in *Muller v Switzerland*[81] to obscenity.

5) In other areas, there may be a tension between the foreseeability requirement and the purpose of the measure in question. Police surveillance is an example. In *Malone v UK*[82] the European Court accepted that:

> ... the requirement of foreseeability cannot mean that an individual should be enabled to foresee when the authorities are likely to intercept his communications so that he can adapt his conduct accordingly.[83]

> What is required in such circumstances is detailed rules setting out the basis upon which activities such as secret surveillance can be carried out; not a requirement that the subject be put on notice when a particular measure is aimed at him/her.[84]

4.36   Instructions and administrative practices which elucidate the law can be relevant to whether a measure is prescribed by law.[85]

The principle of proportionality

4.37   Inherent in the whole of the Convention is the need to find a fair balance between the protection of individual rights and the interests of the community at large.[86] The principle of proportionality is concerned with defining that 'fair balance'. Although the word proportionality does not appear in the text of the Convention or its Protocols, 'the principle of proportionality' is the defining characteristic of the Strasbourg approach to the protection of human rights.

---

79 *SW and CR v UK* n77.
80 (1997) 24 EHRR 1.
81 (1991) 13 EHRR 212.
82 (1985) 7 EHRR 14.
83 Ibid at para 67.
84 *Huvig v France* (1990) 12 EHRR 528: see further paras 15.9 to 15.25.
85 *Silver v UK* n64; *Leander v Sweden* (1987) 9 EHRR 433.
86 See the Court's observations in *Soering v UK* n18 at para 89.

4.38   According to the consistent case-law of the European Court and Commission a fair balance between the protection of individual rights and the interests of the community at large can be achieved only if restrictions on individual rights are strictly proportionate to the legitimate aim they pursue. In other words, even where it is clear that there is a legitimate purpose for restricting a Convention right, the authorities must still show that the actual restriction employed does not go beyond what is strictly necessary to achieve that purpose.

4.39   The case of *Barthold v Germany*[87] demonstrates the principle of proportionality in operation. There proceedings had been brought against the applicant, a veterinary surgeon, for breaking professional conduct rules prohibiting advertising and unfair competition. The nub of the allegation against the applicant was that he had made disparaging remarks about a number of professional colleagues and highlighted the efficiency of his own practice in a newspaper interview. As a result of the proceedings against the applicant an injunction was imposed upon him prohibiting him from repeating the same or similar statements. The European Court accepted that the aim of the injunction – protection of the rights of others – was legitimate, but concluded that the injunction issued did 'not achieve a fair balance between the two interests at stake' because it went further than was necessary to protect that aim. In particular, the approach taken by the authorities to advertising and unfair competition was so strict that it risked:

> ... discouraging members of the liberal professions from contributing to public debate on topics affecting the life of the community if even there is the slightest likelihood of their utterances being treated as entailing, to some degree, an advertising effect.[88]

As a result it was disproportionate and breached article 10 (free speech) of the Convention.

4.40   Other examples of the European Court's general approach include:

1) *Dudgeon v UK*[89] where the Court held that any justification for the criminalisation of all homosexual conduct between males regardless of age or consent was outweighed by the serious detrimental effects it had on homosexuals.

---

87   Note 60.
88   Ibid at para 58.
89   (1982) 4 EHRR 149.

2) *F v Switzerland*[90] where the applicant was subject to a temporary prohibition on remarrying following his third divorce. The Court recognised that the stability of marriage was a legitimate aim, but considered the prohibition to be a disproportionate means of achieving that aim.

3) *Open Door Counselling and Well Woman v Ireland*[91] where the Court found that an injunction preventing the dissemination of information about abortion was disproportionate to the aim of protecting morals because it was framed in absolute terms.

4.41 The principle of proportionality has a very wide field of application. Not only is it relevant to the consideration of all six categories of restrictions on Convention rights set out above, but it is also relevant to: (a) the scope of positive obligations under the Convention: see chapter 5;[92] and (b) the prohibition on discrimination under article 14 of the Convention: see chapter 29.[93]

4.42 In some cases, it will be obvious that a measure is disproportionate. In others, a more sophisticated approach is needed, taking into account the following factors:

1) whether 'relevant and sufficient' reasons have been advanced in support of it;

2) whether there was a less restrictive alternative;

3) whether there has been some measure of procedural fairness in the decision-making process;

4) whether safeguards against abuse exist; and

5) whether the restriction in question destroys the 'very essence' of the Convention right in issue.

These will be examined in turn

'Relevant and sufficient' reasons

4.43 The burden is on the state to demonstrate that a particular measure is proportionate and the European Court will examine whether the reasons advanced to establish proportionality are 'relevant and

---

90 (1988) 10 EHRR 411.
91 (1993) 15 EHRR 244.
92 Paras 5.1 to 5.6.
93 Para 29.17.

sufficient'.⁹⁴ In *Jersild v Denmark*⁹⁵ the Court summarised its approach in the following terms:

> The Court will look at the interference complained of in the light of the case as a whole and determine whether the reasons adduced by the national authorities to justify it are relevant and sufficient and whether the means employed were proportionate to the legitimate aim pursued.⁹⁶

In so doing the Court has to satisfy itself that the national authorities applied Convention standards in the decision-making process and 'that they based their decisions on an acceptable assessment of the relevant facts'.⁹⁷ It is not enough for the responsible authorities to show good faith.⁹⁸

4.44   In *Vogt v Germany*⁹⁹ the applicant had been dismissed from her post as a teacher because of her active membership of the German Communist Party. The reason advanced by the German government to justify this measure was that, in light of the country's experience under the Weimar Republic, it considered membership of the Communist Party to be incompatible with the applicant's duty of political loyalty as a teacher. The European Court held that this reason was 'relevant' but not 'sufficient' to justify the applicant's dismissal because dismissal was an extreme measure; teaching did not intrinsically involve any security risks and membership of the Communist Party was lawful.

4.45   Where no evidence is adduced in support of the reasons given for a restriction, a breach of the Convention is almost inevitable. In *Autronic AG v Switzerland*¹⁰⁰ the government claimed to have refused an application to receive programmes from a Soviet telecommunications satellite on the basis that it had a duty to protect confidential information which might be transmitted from the satellite. Yet it produced no evidence that the equipment used by the applicant was capable of receiving such information. For that and other reasons the European Court found a breach of article 10.

---

94   See, for example, *Buckley v UK* (1997) 23 EHRR 101 at para 77.
95   (1995) 19 EHRR 1.
96   Ibid at para 31.
97   *Jersild v Denmark* n95 at para 31; see also *Vogt v Germany* (1996) 21 EHRR 205 at para 52.
98   *Sunday Times v UK* n59 at para 59.
99   Note 97.
100 Note 42.

Less restrictive alternatives

4.46   A restriction is unlikely to be considered proportionate where a less restrictive, but equally effective, alternative exists. So, for example, in *Campbell v UK*,[101] the European Court considered that the blanket opening of all prisoners' mail to check whether any of it contained prohibited material was disproportionate because the lesser measure of opening only those letters reasonably considered to contain such material would have sufficed.

4.47   Similarly, in *Informationsverein Lentier v Austria*[102] the Court held that refusing the applicant a broadcasting licence on the basis that only a public monopoly could ensure objectivity and impartiality in reporting breached article 10. Although the government's objective was legitimate, it could be achieved by other less restrictive means; the Court cited a licensing scheme with specific conditions as to objectivity and impartiality as an example.

Procedural fairness

4.48   Where a decision to restrict Convention rights involves a public authority exercising a discretion, the principle of proportionality can require procedural fairness to ensure that the rights of those affected by such a decision are properly taken into account. This aspect of proportionality was first recognised in a series of child-care cases, but is now of much wider application.

4.49   In *W v UK*[103] the applicants complained that local authority procedures for determining parental access to children in care breached their family life rights under article 8. Setting out the general Convention principles applicable to the determination of this issue the European Court observed:

> It is true that article 8 contains no explicit procedural requirements, but this is not conclusive of the matter. The local authority's decision-making process clearly cannot be devoid of influence on the substance of the decision, notably by ensuring that it is based on the relevant considerations and is not one-sided and, hence, neither is nor appears arbitrary. Accordingly, the Court is entitled to have regard to that process to determine whether it has been conducted

---

101 (1993) 15 EHRR 137.
102 (1994) 17 EHRR 93.
103 (1988) 10 EHRR 29.

in a manner that, in all the circumstances, is fair and affords due respect to the interests protected by article 8.[104]

4.50   A similar statement of principle was adopted in *McMichael v UK*[105] where confidential documents were not disclosed to the applicants in care proceedings relating to their son:

> Whilst article 8 contains no explicit procedural requirements, the decision-making process leading to measures of interference must be fair and such as to afford due respect to the interests safeguarded by article 8.[106]

The application of this principle was then broadened in *Buckley v UK.*[107]

4.51   In *Buckley v UK* the applicants, who lived in caravans, complained that a local authority decision to remove them from their land breached article 8. On the question of procedural fairness the Court held:

> Whenever discretion capable of interfering with the enjoyment of a Convention right such as the one in issue in the present case is conferred on national authorities, the procedural safeguards available to the individual will be especially material in determining whether the respondent State has, when fixing the regulatory framework, remained within its margin of appreciation. Indeed it is settled case law that, whilst article 8 contains no explicit procedural requirements, the decision-making process leading to measures of interference must be fair and such as to afford due respect to the interests safeguarded to the individual by article 8.[108]

The character of the interests protected by article 8 is obviously a factor in the requirement of procedural fairness, but not the only factor, and the requirement is, in principle, of broad application.

Safeguards against abuse

4.52   Closely linked to the question of procedural fairness is the question of safeguards against abuse. In *Klass v Germany*[109] the European Court made the following observations in the context of intercepting mail and telephone tapping:

104 Ibid at para 62.
105 (1995) 20 EHRR 205.
106 Ibid at para 87.
107 (1997) 23 EHRR 101.
108 Ibid at para 76.
109 (1979–80) 2 EHRR 214.

... the values of a democratic society must be followed as faithfully as possible in the supervisory procedures if the bounds of necessity, within the meaning of article 8(2), are not to be exceeded. One of the fundamental principles of a democratic society is the rule of law ... [which] implies, inter alia, that an interference by the executive authorities with an individual's rights should be subject to an effective control which should normally be assured by the judiciary, at least in the last resort, judicial control offering the best guarantees of independence, impartiality and a proper procedure.[110]

Viewed in this way, the existence of safeguards against abuse can be seen as part of the 'compromise between the requirements for defending democratic society and individual rights'.[111]

4.53   Non-judicial safeguards are also relevant. One of the factors which influenced the European Court in *Brannigan v UK*,[112] when considering whether the measures taken in derogation of article 5(3) of the Convention – pre-trial detention under prevention of terrorism legislation[113] – were proportionate, was the existence of safeguards against arbitrary detention. These included the remedy of habeas corpus, the right to consult a solicitor on arrest or, if extended on reasonable grounds, after 48 hours (such extension being susceptible to judicial review) and regular independent review of the legislation in question.[114]

The 'very essence' test

4.54   On several occasions, the European Court has held that restrictions on Convention rights 'must not restrict or reduce the right in such a way or to such an extent that the very essence of the right is impaired'.[115] This has mainly been in the context of article 12, which sets out the right to marry 'according to the national laws governing the exercise' of that right; the logic being that national laws can regulate but not extinguish the right to marry.

4.55   A broader link between the 'very essence' test and proportionality was made in *F v Switzerland*[116] where the Court held that to impose a

---

110 Ibid at para 55.
111 Ibid at para 59.
112 (1994) 17 EHRR 539.
113 See paras 7.5 to 7.10.
114 Paras 64–65.
115 See, for example, *Rees v UK* (1987) 9 EHRR 56 at para 50 and *F v Switzerland* (1987) 10 EHRR 411 at para 40.
116 Note 115.

temporary prohibition on the applicant remarrying following his third divorce 'affected the very essence of the right to marry' and was 'disproportionate to the legitimate aim pursued'.[117] It was also recognised in *Mathieu-Mohin and Clerfayt v Belgium*[118] where the Court held that, in order to comply with article 3 of Protocol 1, conditions imposed on voting and the right to stand for election should not 'curtail the rights in question to such an extent as to impair their very essence' and should be proportionate.[119]

Restrictions expressly permitted under articles 8(2), 9(2), 10(2) and 11(2)

4.56　Articles 8–11 of the Convention are in common form. The first paragraph of each article sets out a positive right; the second paragraph then sets out the specific circumstances in which that right can be restricted. As noted above, under each article, a restriction will be compatible with the Convention only if:

1) It is 'in accordance with law'[120]/'prescribed by law'.[121] These phrases mean the same thing[122] and are considered above under the heading 'the principle of legality'.

2) The aim of the restriction is legitimate.

3) The restriction is 'necessary in a democratic society'.[123]

Each of these requirements is analysed below.

The requirement of a legitimate aim

4.57　Restrictions on the rights protected in articles 8–11 will be compatible with the Convention only if they are aimed at protecting one of the interests listed in article 8(2), 9(2), 10(2) and 11(2) respectively. The interests protected are broadly the same and generally include:

1) national security;

2) public safety;

117　Ibid at para 40.
118　(1988) 10 EHRR 1.
119　Ibid.
120　Article 8(2).
121　Articles 9(2), 10(2) and 11(2).
122　*Malone v UK* (1985) 7 EHRR 14.
123　*Sunday Times v UK* (1979–80) 2 EHRR 245.

3) the protection of health or morals;

4) the prevention of disorder or crime; and

5) the protection of the rights of others.

4.58   In each case, the list is intended to be exhaustive: there is no scope for states to infer grounds for restriction which are not explicitly stated.[124] In addition, there is a rule of strict interpretation. Not only may the listed criteria alone justify any restrictions; these criteria, in turn, must be understood in such a way that the language is not extended beyond its ordinary meaning.[125]

4.59   A legitimate ground for restriction cannot be used as a pretext for a measure which is really aimed at another improper purpose. Article 18 of the Convention provides that:

> The restrictions permitted under this Convention to the said rights and freedoms shall not be applied for any purpose other than those for which they have been prescribed.

It is not a free-standing provision and can be invoked only in conjunction with another Convention article.[126]

The meaning of the phrase 'necessary in a democratic society'

4.60   The adjective 'necessary' in the phrase 'necessary in a democratic society' is not defined in the Convention itself. However, the European Court has held that it is not synonymous with 'indispensable' or as flexible as 'reasonable' or 'desirable'.[127] Rather, it implies the existence of a 'pressing social need'.[128]

4.61   The requirement that any restriction on the rights protected under articles 8–11 be 'necessary in a democratic society' can therefore be broken down into four parts:

1) Is there a pressing social need for some restriction?

2) If so, does the restriction in question correspond to that need?

3) If so, is it a proportionate response to that need?

---

124 See *De Wilde, Ooms and Versyp v Belgium* (1979–80) 1 EHRR 373 and *Golder v UK* (1979–80) 1 EHRR 524.

125 *Sunday Times v UK* n123.

126 *Kamma v Netherlands* (1974) 1 DR 4.

127 *Handyside v UK* n21 at para 48.

128 Ibid.

4) In any event, are the reasons advanced by the authorities for the restriction 'relevant and sufficient'?[129]

As the last question implies, it is for the authorities to establish both that a pressing social need justifying restriction exists and that the measures actually adopted are proportionate to that need.[130]

4.62   There is no standard of proof as such, but in some cases the European Court has insisted that the importance of the Convention right in issue dictates that the necessity for a restriction be 'convincingly established'. See, for example, in the context of free speech: *Barthold v Germany;*[131] *Sunday Times v UK* (No 2);[132] and *Goodwin v UK.*[133] And in *Sunday Times v UK*[134] the Court emphasised that:

> The Court is faced not with a choice between two conflicting principles, but with a principle of freedom of expression that is subject to a number of exceptions which must be narrowly interpreted. ... It is not sufficient that the interference belongs to that class of the exceptions listed in article 10(2) which has been invoked; neither is it sufficient that the interference was imposed because its subject-matter fell within a particular category or was caught by a legal rule formulated in general or absolute terms: the Court has to be satisfied that the interference was necessary having regard to the facts and circumstances prevailing in the specific case before it.[135]

In other words, whether or not a restriction is 'necessary in a democratic society' is to be decided on a case by case basis without resort to generalisations and against the background of a presumption against restriction.

Pressing social need

4.63   The European Court has not further defined the phrase 'pressing social need', but it is clear from its case-law that unless the reasons advanced by the authorities in support of a restriction demonstrate a real need for its imposition, a 'pressing social need' is unlikely to be

---

129 See *Barthold v Germany* (1985) 7 EHRR 383 and the Commission decision in *Sunday Times v UK* (No 2) (1991) 14 EHRR 229 at para 68.
130 See *Handyside v UK* n21 at para 50 and also *Kokkinakis v Greece* (1994) 17 EHRR 397.
131 Note 129 at para 58.
132 Note 129 at para 50.
133 (1996) 22 EHRR 123 at para 40.
134 Note 123.
135 Ibid at para 65.

made out. The following cases give some indication of the Court's approach:

1) In *Dudgeon v UK*[136] the Court held that although some degree of regulation of sexual conduct by the criminal law could be ffljustified as necessary in a democratic society, the failure to prosecute homosexual conduct in private between consenting males over the age of 21 made it impossible for the government to maintain that there was a pressing social need for the criminalisation of all homosexual conduct between males regardless of age or consent.

2) In *Weber v Switzerland*[137] the applicant was fined for disclosing confidential information about a judicial inquiry. The Court held that although the proceedings against the applicant pursued a legitimate aim – protection of the authority and impartiality of the judiciary – the measure taken against him could not be justified as necessary because the confidential information in question was already in the public domain when disclosed by the applicant.

3) In *The Observer and The Guardian v UK*[138] the Court accepted the government's argument that there was a legitimate aim for restricting publication of the *Spycatcher* book, but found that once the book was in the public domain, the injunction in question was no longer necessary.

4.64　The character of a 'democratic society' is important to the question of 'necessity'. In *Handyside v UK*[139] the European Court referred to pluralism, tolerance and broadmindedness as the hallmarks of a democratic society.[140] On that basis, ideas that offend, shock or disturb are protected. And in *Dudgeon v UK*,[141] part of the Court's reasoning was that:

> Although members of the public who regard homosexuality as immoral may be shocked, offended or disturbed by the commission by others of private homosexual acts, this cannot on its own warrant the application of penal sanctions when it is consenting adults alone who are involved.[142]

136 (1982) 4 EHRR 149.
137 (1990) 12 EHRR 508.
138 (1992) 14 EHRR 153.
139 Note 21.
140 Ibid at para 49.
141 Note 136.
142 Ibid at para 60.

In other words, it will be difficult, if not impossible, to establish a pressing social need to protect intolerance and narrowmindedness.

The principle of proportionality in the context of articles 8–11

4.65　The principle of proportionality is examined in detail above.[143] Although it applies to all restrictions it has special relevance to restrictions on Convention rights under articles 8–11.

4.66　　The link between the requirement that restrictions on Convention rights under articles 8–11 be 'necessary in a democratic society' and the principle of proportionality was first made in *Handyside v UK*[144] where the European Court reasoned that since democracy demanded 'pluralism, tolerance and broad-mindedness', a restriction could not be 'necessary in a democratic society' unless it was 'proportionate to the legitimate aim pursued'.[145] Proportionality has been regarded as an aspect of the 'necessity' test ever since.

Restrictions expressly permitted under other articles

The restrictions on the right to liberty expressly provided for in articles 5(1)(a)–5(1)(f)

4.67　The scheme of article 5(1) is to set up a positive right to liberty with limited exceptions.[146] In addition to the clear requirements that any detention be 'lawful' and fall within one of the exceptions provided for in article 5(1)(a)–(f), the European Court has added a requirement of proportionality.

4.68　　So, for example, in *Winterwerp v Netherlands*[147] the Court held that to justify detention under article 5(1)(e), which permits detention of 'persons of unsound mind', it was not enough simply to show that the individual concerned was a person of unsound mind; it had also to be established that s/he suffered from a mental disorder '... of a

143　See paras 4.37 to 4.55.
144　Note 21.
145　Ibid at para 49.
146　See paras 3.21 to 3.22.
147　(1979–80) 2 EHRR 387.

kind or degree warranting compulsory confinement'. Moreover, the lawfulness of continued confinement depends on 'the persistence of such disorder'.[148]

4.69   Similarly, the Court has established that 'detention on remand' – authorised by article 5(1)(c) – will not comply with the Convention if enquiries reveal there is no longer any reasonable suspicion that the suspect has committed an offence.[149] Similarly, in the context of article 5(3), the Court will examine whether bail conditions go beyond what is strictly necessary.[150]

The restrictions on the right to marry expressly provided for in article 12

4.70   Article 12 of the Convention protects the right to marry providing such marriage is 'according to the national laws governing the exercise of this right'. No express limitation is put on the content of national laws governing marriage, but the Court has implied proportionality so as to restrict the extent to which national laws can inhibit marriage.[151] And any law which destroys the 'very essence'[152] of the right to marry will be incompatible with article 12.[153]

The restrictions on the right to property expressly provided for in article 1 of the First Protocol

4.71   Article 1 of Protocol 1 guarantees the right to peaceful enjoyment of possessions, but reserves to the state power to: (a) deprive individuals of their possessions, and (b) to control the use of property, subject to certain qualifications.[154]

4.72   The European Court's approach to article 1 of Protocol 1 is to enquire first whether a measure amounts to a deprivation or control of property and, if not, to examine whether it nonetheless interferes with an individual's right to peaceful enjoyment of his/her pos-

---

148 Ibid at paras 39–43.

149 *Wemhoff v Germany* (1979–80) 1 EHRR 55 at paras 5 and 12–17.

150 Ibid at para 15; *Neumeister v Austria* (1979–80) 1 EHRR 91 at paras 12–14; and *Stogmuller v Austria* (1979–80) 1 EHRR 155.

151 See *F v Switzerland* (1988) 10 EHRR 411.

152 See paras 4.54 to 4.55.

153 *F v Switzerland* n151; *Rees v UK* (1987) 9 EHRR 56; *Cossey v UK* (1991) 13 EHRR 622.

154 See chapter 26.

sessions.[155] At each stage it has imported the principle of proportionality.

4.73   So far as deprivation is concerned, the Court has interpreted the requirement that deprivation be 'in the public interest and subject to the conditions provided for by law and by the general principles of international law' as meaning that:

1) the measure in question must pursue 'a legitimate aim in the public interest'; and

2) there must be 'a reasonable relationship of proportionality between the means employed and the aim sought to be realised'.[156]

Similarly, in determining whether a measure controlling the use of property complies with the Convention, the Court will consider whether there is 'a reasonable relationship of proportionality between the means employed and the aim sought to be realised'.[157]

4.74   Even where a measure falls short of deprivation or control, proportionality is relevant. In *Sporring and Lonroth v Sweden*[158] the Court held that in approaching any question relating to interference with peaceful enjoyment of possessions it had to 'determine whether a fair balance had been struck between the demands of the general interest of the community and the requirements of the protection of the individual's fundamental rights'.[159] A fair balance will not be achieved where measures impose 'an individual and excessive burden' on those affected.

Restrictions impliedly permitted under the Convention

4.75   The Court is very slow to imply restrictions into the Convention. Where express restrictions are provided for, there is no scope for implied restrictions. However, where the European Court has read implied rights into the Convention, it has also read in implied restrictions. The implied restrictions permitted under article 6(1) and article

---

155 See paras 3.188 to 3.193.

156 *James v UK* (1986) 8 EHRR 123.

157 *Wasa Liv Omsesidigt, Forsakringbolaget Valands Pensionsstiftelse v Sweden* (1988) 58 DR 163.

158 (1983) 5 EHRR 35.

159 Ibid at para 69.

3 of Protocol 1 (below) are examples of this. The Court has also read implied restrictions into article 2 of Protocol 1 where, in the test, there are no restrictions at all.

Implied restrictions on the right to a fair trial under article 6(1)

4.76 In *Golder v UK*[160] the European Court held that article 6(1) of the Convention[161] did not just guarantee the right to a fair trial in legal proceedings which are already pending, but also guaranteed a right of access to the courts because:

> In civil matters one can scarcely conceive of the rule of law without there being a possibility of access to the courts ...[162]

However, it added that, as this is 'a right which the Convention sets forth ... without ... defining it, there is room, apart from delimiting the very content of any right, for limitations permitted by implication'.[163]

4.77 The scope of such implied limitations was considered in *Ashingdane v UK*[164] where the European Court held that a limitation on the right of access to a court:

> ... will not be compatible with article 6(1) if it does not pursue a legitimate aim and if there is not a reasonable relationship of proportionality between the means employed and the aim sought to be achieved.[165]

More recently, in *Osman v UK*,[166] the Court held that while the rules governing police immunity in negligence actions in England and Wales pursued a legitimate aim – the avoidance of defensive policing and diversion of resources – they were disproportionate because they provided blanket immunity without regard to the merits of the case.[167]

---

160 Note 8.
161 See paras 3.87 to 3.99.
162 Note 8 para 34.
163 Ibid para 38.
164 (1985) 7 EHRR 528.
165 Ibid at paras 57–60; see also *Lithgow v UK* (1986) 8 EHRR 329 and *Philis v Greece* (1991) 13 EHRR 741.
166 Court (28 October 1998); [1999] 1 FLR 193; noted at [1999] EHLR 228.
167 See paras 15.96 to 15.99.

Implied restrictions on the right to education under article 2 of the First Protocol

4.78   In the first case it heard under article 2 of Protocol 1, *Belgian Linguistics Case (No 2)*,[168] the European Court held that:

> ... the right to education guaranteed by the first sentence of article 2 of the [First] Protocol by its very nature calls for regulation by the State.[169]

This 'may vary in time and place according to the needs and resources of the community and of individuals' but:

> It goes without saying that such regulation must never injure the substance of the right to education nor conflict with other rights enshrined in the Convention.[170]

In *Campbell and Cosans v UK*[171] the refusal of a school to provide education for the applicants' children unless they agreed to the regime of corporal punishment was found to violate both limbs of this qualification.

Implied restrictions on election rights under article 3 of the First Protocol

4.79   Article 3 of Protocol 1 requires states to 'hold free elections at reasonable intervals by secret ballot under conditions which will ensure the free expression of the opinion of the people in the choice of the legislature'.[172] In *Mathieu-Mohin and Clerfayt v Belgium*[173] the European Court read into this provision the right to vote and the right to stand for election. However, it added:

> The rights in question are not absolute. Since article 3 recognises them without setting forth in express terms, let alone defining them, there is room for implied limitations ...[174]

4.80   States therefore enjoy a margin of appreciation when imposing conditions on voting and standing for election but, it is for the Court to determine in the last resort:

168 (1979–80) 1 EHRR 252.
169 Ibid at para 5.
170 Ibid.
171 (1982) 4 EHRR 293.
172 See paras 3.198 to 3.202.
173 Note 118.
174 Ibid at para 52.

1) 'that the conditions do not curtail the rights in question to such an extent that they impair their very essence and deprive them of their effectiveness';
2) 'that they are imposed in pursuit of a legitimate aim'; and
3) 'that the means employed are not disproportionate'.[175]

Restrictions specifically provided for by a valid derogation

4.81   Article 15 permits states to derogate from their obligations under the Convention 'in time of war or other public emergency threatening the nation', but only 'to the extent strictly required by the exigencies of the situation'. This last requirement involves a determination of whether the circumstances are such that article 15 is engaged and, if so, whether the measures taken in derogation of Convention obligations are proportionate to the need for them.

4.82   The UK has one derogation in place.[176] A challenge to its validity in *Brannigan v UK*[177] failed on the basis that the measures taken in derogation of the UK's obligations under article 5(3) of the Convention were proportionate. The HRA takes effect subject to this derogation.[178]

Restrictions on the political activity of aliens specifically provided for by article 16

4.83   Article 16 provides that:

> Nothing in articles 10, 11 and 14 shall be regarded as preventing the High Contracting Parties from imposing restrictions on the political activities of aliens.

It does not sit well with the general obligation in article 1 that Convention rights are to be secured to 'everyone with the jurisdiction' of a contracting state and the Parliamentary Assembly of the Council of Europe has called for its abolition.[179]

175 Ibid at para 52.
176 See paras 7.9 to 7.10.
177 (1994) 17 EHRR 539.
178 See paras 1.59 to 1.61.
179 Recommendation 799 (1977), 25 January 1977.

4.84   In *Piermont v France*,[180] the only case considered by the European Court on article 16, the term 'alien' was given a very narrow interpretation. There the applicant, a member of the German Green Party and an MEP, had been expelled from French Polynesia when she took part in an anti-nuclear demonstration. The Court held that her status as a national of a Member State of the European Union and MEP prevented France raising article 16 against her.

Restrictions on activities aimed at the destruction of Convention rights specifically provided for by article 17

4.85   Article 17 provides that:

> Nothing in this Convention may be interpreted as implying for any state, group or person any right to engage in any activity or perform any act aimed at the destruction of any of the rights and freedoms set forth herein or at their limitation to a greater extent than is provided for in the Convention.

Its purpose, in so far as it refers to groups or individuals, is to make it impossible for extremists to take advantage of the provisions of the Convention to perform acts aimed at destroying the Convention rights of others.[181]

4.86   In *Glimmerveen and Hagenbeek v Netherlands*[182] article 17 was successfully invoked to justify the prosecution of the applicants for possessing leaflets likely to incite racial hatred and their exclusion from local elections. The same result followed in *Kuhnen v Germany*[183] where the applicant was convicted for publishing pamphlets advocating fascism and racism.

4.87   Article 17 is subject to two important limitations:

1) It can be applied only to those rights which are capable of being exercised so as to destroy the rights of others: it cannot be used to restrict rights designed to protect the individual such as those in articles 5 and 6 of the Convention.[184]

---

180 (1995) 20 EHRR 301.

181 *Lawless v Ireland* (No 2) (1979–80) 1 EHRR 15; see also *KDP v Germany* (1957) 1 Yearbook 222 and *Glimmerveen and Hagenbeek v Netherlands* (1979) 18 DR 187 at p195.

182 Note 181.

183 (1988) 56 DR 205.

184 *Lawless v Ireland* (No 2) n181 at para 7.

2) Any measures taken under article 17 must be strictly proportionate to the threat to the rights of others.[185]

The margin of appreciation

4.88 One of the fundamental principles of international law relating to the Convention is that the role of the domestic authorities in the protection of human rights is different from the role of the international supervisory bodies, such as the European Court. Primarily, it is the duty of the domestic authorities to secure and protect Convention rights. This duty is reflected in:

1) article 1 which obliges contracting states to secure Convention rights to everyone within their jurisdiction;

2) article 13 which requires an effective remedy 'before a national authority' for anyone who claims that his/her Convention rights have been violated; and

3) article 35 which precludes the European Court considering any case unless and until domestic remedies have been exhausted.

4.89 The role of the European Court is different. It is primarily concerned with supervision and its role is therefore subsidiary to that of the domestic authorities:[186] it has no role unless the domestic system for protecting human rights breaks down. This is often referred to as the principle of subsidiarity.

4.90 One of the consequences of the fact that the domestic authorities and the European Court have different roles is that initially it is for the domestic authorities to assess whether a restriction on Convention rights is compatible with the Convention; ie, whether there is a legitimate aim for any given restriction, whether it corresponds to a 'pressing social need' and whether it is 'necessary' and 'proportionate'.[187] The European Court's role is, in effect, to consider whether the assessments made by the domestic authorities are true to the Convention. And, in performing that task, the Court has been reluctant simply to substitute its own assessment for that of the domestic authorities. Instead it is prepared to extend some leeway to

---

185 *De Becker v Belgium* B/2 (1960) Commission Report, para 279; *Lehideut v France* A/996 (Court) 23 September 1998.

186 *Handyside v UK* n21 at para 48; *Eckle v Germany* (1983) 5 EHRR 1 at para 66; and *Akdivar v Turkey* (1997) 23 EHRR 143 at para 65.

187 See paras 4.26 to 4.82.

the domestic authorities because it considers that they are, generally speaking, in a better position to make the assessments in question. In other words, it affords the domestic authorities 'a margin of appreciation'.

4.91   Hence, in *Sunday Times v UK*,[188] the European Court stated;

> It is in no way [the Court's] task to take the place of the competent national courts but rather to review ... the decisions they delivered in the exercise of their power of appreciation ...[189]

And, somewhat more broadly, in *Klass v Germany*:[190]

> It is certainly not for the Court to substitute for the assessment of the national authorities any other assessment of what might be the best policy in this field ...[191]

Because, as the Court recognised in *Handyside v UK*[192] and has repeatedly emphasised:

> By reason of their direct and continuous contact with the vital forces of their countries, state authorities are in principle in a better position than the international judge to give an opinion on the ... 'necessity' of a 'restriction' or 'penalty' ... it is for the national authorities to make the initial assessment of the reality of the pressing social need implied in the notion of 'necessity' in this context.[193]

4.92   However, the domestic authorities do not enjoy an unlimited discretion and they are not free to adopt whatever measures they deem appropriate.[194] In *Lingens v Austria*[195] the European Court held that:

> In exercising its supervisory jurisdiction, the Court cannot confine itself to considering the impugned court decisions in isolation; it must look at them in the light of the case as a whole ... The Court must decide whether the interference at issue was 'proportionate to the legitimate aim pursued' and whether the reasons adduced ... to justify it are 'relevant and sufficient' ...[196]

---

188 Note 123.
189 Ibid at para 59.
190 Note 109.
191 Ibid at para 49.
192 Note 21.
193 Ibid at para 48.
194 *Klass v Germany* (1979–80) 2 EHRR 214.
195 (1986) 8 EHRR 407.
196 Ibid at para 40.

According to the European Court, therefore, 'the domestic margin of appreciation goes hand in hand with European supervision'.[197]

4.93   The scope of the margin of appreciation varies according to the context. However, the following guidelines are usually followed:

1) On issues such as national security,[198] morals,[199] planning policy,[200] tax[201] and choice of social and economic policy[202] a fairly wide margin of appreciation is allowed.

2) On the other hand, the particular importance attached to some rights dictates a narrow margin of appreciation. For example, in the context of legislation criminalising homosexual conduct between consenting adults, the Court noted in *Dudgeon v UK*[203] that:

> The present case concerns a most intimate aspect of private life. Accordingly, there must exist particularly serious reasons before interferences on the part of public authorities can be legitimate ...[204]

Similarly in free speech cases concerning political debate or matters of public interest, the need for a restriction must be 'convincingly established'[205] because where such issues are in play 'there is little scope ... for restrictions'.[206]

3) In addition, where there is a general consensus in Europe about how particular issues are to be dealt with, or the right in issue has 'an objective character',[207] only a narrow margin of appreciation is permitted on the basis that in such cases there is less scope for subtle national differences.

---

197 *Handyside v UK* note 21 at para 47.

198 See, for example, *Leander v Sweden* (1987) 9 EHRR 433.

199 *Handyside v UK* note 21; *Muller v Switzerland* (1991) 13 EHRR 212; and *Wingrove v UK* (1997) 24 EHRR 1.

200 See, for example, *Buckley v UK* (1997) 23 EHRR 101.

201 See, for example, *National Provincial Building Society v UK* (1998) 25 EHRR 127.

202 See, for example, *Powell and Rayner v UK* (1990) 12 EHRR 355 and *James v UK* n156.

203 Note 136.

204 Ibid at para 52.

205 See para 4.62.

206 *Wingrove v UK* (1997) 24 EHRR 1.

207 For example, contempt of court: see *Worm v Austria* (1998) 25 EHRR 454.

Non-applicability of the margin of appreciation under the HRA

4.94   As noted above, there is an integral link between the principle of subsidiarity and the margin of appreciation doctrine. Articles 1 and 13 of the Convention – which underpin the principle of subsidiarity[208] – have been left out of the schedule of rights incorporated into domestic law by the HRA.[209] The reason for this, as explained by the Lord Chancellor,[210] is because the Act gives effect to article 1 by securing Convention rights to people in the UK and gives effect to article 13 by establishing a scheme under which Convention rights can be raised in domestic courts.[211]

4.95   Domestic Courts and tribunals are part of the system for the domestic protection of human rights. They are specifically recognised under the HRA as public authorities and, as a result, it is unlawful for a court or tribunal to act in a way which is incompatible with Convention rights.[212] In other words, domestic courts and tribunals do not have the same role as the European Court, ie, supervising the domestic system for protecting human rights; they are part of that very system. As such, there can be no question of applying the margin of appreciation in their own decision-making.

4.96   When the European Court applies a margin of appreciation it is not affording a discretion to the domestic legislature and executive, it is affording a discretion to the 'domestic authorities', which include domestic courts and tribunals. As noted above, in the case of *Sunday Times v UK*[213] 'It is in no way [the Court's] task to take the place of the competent national courts' (emphasis added)[214] but rather to review the decision they make. In other words, part of the reason why the European Court affords the domestic authorities a margin of appreciation is because it expects the domestic courts and tribunals to have closely scrutinised every case before it reaches Strasbourg. And because, in principle, they are better placed to assess whether there is a 'pressing social need' for a restriction and whether it is 'necessary' etc, the European Court will not lightly interfere with

---

208 See paras 4.88 to 4.89.
209 See paras 1.7 to 1.8.
210 HL Debs (committee stage) col 475, 18 November 1997.
211 See paras 1.7 to 1.8
212 See paras 1.39 to 1.43.
213 (1979–80) 2 EHRR 245.
214 Ibid at para 59.

their assessment. If domestic courts allow a margin of appreciation to the legislature and executive in the cases before them, part of the rationale for applying the margin of appreciation at the international level falls away.

4.97   However, notwithstanding the fact that the margin of appreciation is not applicable in domestic law, nothing in the Convention precludes domestic courts and tribunals from affording *some* discretionmaking bodies when reviewing their actions. The extent of any such deference will depend on the circumstances of the case and relevant factors will probably include:

1) The importance of the right at stake.

2) The seriousness of the interference with that right.

3) The relative specialist knowledge or experience of the body under review on the one hand and the court or tribunal on the other.

4) Wether the body under review is elected or is otherwise accountable to the electorate.

5) Wether the aim of the measure under review is to promote other human rights, including social and economic rights.

6) Wether heightened scrutiny is needed because the applicants are particularly vulnerable or unpopular.

7) Wether the context is one in which there are fairly constant standards throughout democratic societies, especially in the states which are parties to the Convention.[215]

Nonetheless, even where some discretion is afforded to the decision-making body, domestic courts and tribunals must comply with their responsibility under the HRA to act compatibly with Convention rights, which includes a duty to give judgments consistent with the Convention. And this entails a stricter approach than the traditional *Wednesbury* test because: (a) it involves an assessment of the merits of the measure in question; (b) 'proportionality' is a more demanding test than 'perversity'; and (c) under the Convention it is for the state – or relevant public authority – to justify a measure which interferes with Convention rights, not for the individual to establish that the measure in question is unlawful.

---

215 See Singh R, Hunt M and Demetriou M, 'Is there a role for the margin of appreciation in national law after the Human Rights Act?' [1999] EHRLR 14; and Pannick D, 'Principles of interpretation of Convention rights under the Human Rights Act and the discretionary area of judgement' [1998] PL 545.

Waiver of Convention rights

4.98   In some circumstances, Convention rights can be waived. However, there are strict limits. In particular:

1) Waiver must be unequivocal and, where procedural rights are concerned, must accord with the minimum guarantees commensurate with the importance of such rights.[216]

2) Waiver must not conflict with an important public interest.[217] And this may preclude waiver of fair trial rights under article 6.[218]

3) In some cases, it may be necessary for the courts to protect individuals from unreasonable restrictions on their Convention rights, even where such restrictions have been agreed, for example in a contract of employment.[219]

Arbitration clauses in contracts are dealt with elsewhere.[220]

---

216 *Pfeiffer and Plankl v Austria* (1992) 14 EHRR 692.
217 Ibid at paras 38–39.
218 Reid *A practitioner's guide to the European Convention on Human Rights,* Sweet & Maxwell, 1998, p93.
219 *Rommelfanger v Germany* (1989) 62 DR 151.
220 See paras 3.12–3.13.

CHAPTER 5

Positive obligations under the Convention

5.1   Introduction

5.6   The scope of positive obligations under the Convention

5.7   Putting in place a legal framework which
        provides effective protection for Convention rights

5.13   Preventing breaches of Convention rights

5.14   Positive obligations where fundamental rights are at stake

5.18   Positive obligations where intimate interests are at stake

5.22   Positive obligations where Convention rights cannot be
        effectively protected by the legal framework in place

5.23   Providing information and advice relevant to the breach of
        Convention rights

5.28   Responding to breaches of Convention rights

5.30   Providing resources to individuals to prevent breaches of
        their Convention rights

5.33   The relationship between positive and negative obligations

5.36   Positive obligations under the HRA

Introduction

5.1 The European Convention on Human Rights is mainly concerned with setting limits on the ability of state authorities to interfere with individual rights. The scheme of the Convention is therefore to spell out a number of rights and then to set out the circumstances (if any) in which those rights can be restricted. In this sense the Convention defines the negative obligations of state authorities, ie, obligations to refrain from certain action.

5.2 However, the Convention is also concerned with positive obligations ie, obligations on state authorities to take positive steps or measures to protect the Convention rights of individuals. The most straightforward of these obligations arise where, by very definition, a Convention right requires the provision of resources. The right to free legal assistance in criminal cases under article 6(3)(c), the right to education under article 2 of Protocol 1 and the duty to hold elections under article 3 of Protocol 1 are obvious examples.

5.3 Other positive obligations arise more discreetly. Their foundation lies in the recognition that the acts of private individuals can threaten human rights just as much as the acts of state authorities. Since, under the Convention, no liability can be imposed on private individuals as a matter of international law, the European Court and Commission have chosen to impose positive obligations on states and state authorities to take steps to protect individuals from the actions of other individuals.

5.4 The theoretical basis for imposing such positive obligations on state authorities is the combined effect of three inter-related principles:

1) First, the principle that, under article 1 of the Convention, states should *secure* Convention rights to everyone within their jurisdiction.

2) Second, the principle that the Convention rights so secured must be practical and effective not 'theoretical and illusory'.[1]

3) Third, the principle that, under article 13, effective remedies should be provided for arguable breaches of Convention rights.

5.5 The classic example of the translation of these principles into positive obligations is *Plattform Ärzte für das Leben v Austria*.[2] In that case the applicants, a group of anti-abortion protesters, complained

---

1   See the principle of effectiveness analysed in paras 4.11 to 4.15.
2   (1991) 13 EHRR 204.

to the European Court that they had been unable to exercise their right of peaceful assembly because every time they organised a rally or march, they were attacked by counter-demonstrators. The Austrian government responded by claiming that since it, as a state, had not interfered with the applicants' rights, it could not be responsible for any breach of article 11 of the Convention. The Court disagreed. As a matter of principle, it held that:

> ... a demonstration may annoy or give offence to persons opposed to the ideas or claims that it is seeking to promote. The participants must however be able to hold the demonstration without having to fear that they will be subjected to physical violence by their opponents; such a fear would be liable to deter associations or other groups supporting common ideas or interests from openly expressing their opinions on highly controversial issues affecting the community. In a democracy the right to counter-demonstrate cannot extend to inhibiting the exercise of the right to demonstrate.
>
> Genuine, effective freedom of peaceful assembly cannot, therefore, be reduced to a mere duty on the part of the state not to interfere; a purely negative conception would not be compatible with the object and purpose of article 11. Like article 8, article 11 sometimes requires positive measures to be taken, even in the sphere of relations between individuals, if need be.[3]

What was needed was effective policing to enable the applicants to exercise their right to peaceful assembly free from the attacks of counter-demonstrators.[4]

The scope of positive obligations under the Convention

5.6 How state authorities go about protecting individuals from the actions of other individuals is largely a matter for their discretion.[5] The European Court has been careful not to make unreasonable demands, recognising that 'regard must be had to the fair balance that has to be struck between the competing interests of the individual and of the community as a whole'.[6] Ultimately most cases turn

---

3   Ibid at para 32.
4   On the facts, the Court held that the policing provided by the Austrian authorities was sufficient to discharge this duty.
5   For the application of the margin of appreciation to the doctrine of positive obligations see paras 4.88–4.97.
6   *Powell and Rayner v UK* (1990) 12 EHRR 355.

on the character of the Convention right engaged and the serious-ness of the breach in issue. As a result, positive obligations may encompass a wide range of duties. Broadly speaking, the Court has recognised five duties which may be imposed on state authorities:

1) a duty to put in place a legal framework which provides effective protection for Convention rights;

2) a duty to prevent breaches of Convention rights;

3) a duty to provide information and advice relevant to the breach of Convention rights;

4) a duty to respond to breaches of Convention rights;

5) a duty to provide resources to individuals to prevent breaches of their Convention rights.

The scope of these duties and the circumstances in which they apply will vary from case to case. Therefore, each of these requires further examination. However, it is important to note at the outset that they do not represent an exhaustive list of all possible obligations; in each case appropriate steps must be taken to protect Convention rights properly.

Putting in place a legal framework which provides effective protection for Convention rights

5.7   The duty to put in place a legal framework which provides effective protection for Convention rights in many respects represents the minimum obligation of contracting states under the Convention. Broadly speaking the European Court and Commission have been content to leave it to the domestic authorities to decide how best to set up the required legal framework. So, for example, in a number of cases against the UK, the Commission has accepted that the avail-ability of civil remedies for defamation or malicious prosecution can be sufficient to protect privacy rights under article 8.[7] However, there are some circumstances where breach of a Convention right is so serious that the Court has insisted that criminal law sanctions must be put in place.

5.8   In *X and Y v Netherlands*,[8] the perpetrator of a sexual assault on

---

7   See *Stewart-Brady v UK* (1997) 24 EHRR CD 38 and *Winer v UK* (1986) 48 DR 154.

8   (1986) 8 EHRR 235.

the second applicant had not been prosecuted because under Dutch law the fact that the victim was a 16-year-old woman with a mental disorder prevented her from initiating a criminal 'complaint'. The government argued that since it was possible to bring civil proceedings for compensation, its obligations under article 8 had been fulfilled. The Court disagreed. In its view:

> ... the protection afforded by the civil law in the case of wrongdoing of the kind inflicted on Miss Y is insufficient. This is a case where fundamental values and essential aspects of private life are at stake. Effective deterrence is indispensable in this area and it can be achieved only by criminal-law provisions; indeed, it is by such provisions that the matter is normally regulated.[9]

Since Dutch law was defective in this respect, state responsibility was engaged.

5.9   In *Stubbings v UK*[10] the applicants attempted to extend the reach of the decision in *X and Y v Netherlands*[11] by arguing that the widespread problem of child sexual abuse, which was only beginning to be properly understood, demanded new measures for the protection of minors. Their complaint was that the House of Lords' interpretation of the Limitation Act 1980 in *Stubbings v Webb*,[12] restricting the scope for extending the limitation period in civil proceedings based on child sexual abuse, effectively deprived them of a remedy against their abusers contrary to article 8 of the Convention.

5.10   The European Court began its analysis by reiterating that '[sexual abuse] is unquestionably an abhorrent type of wrongdoing, with debilitating effects on its victims. Children and other vulnerable individuals are entitled to State protection, in the form of effective deterrence, from such grave types of interference with essential aspects of their private lives'. However, in its view:

> In the instant case ... such protection was afforded. The abuse of which the applicants complained is regarded most seriously by the English criminal law and subject to severe maximum penalties. Provided sufficient evidence could be secured, a criminal prosecution could have been brought ...
> In principle, civil remedies are also available provided they are brought within the statutory time-limit ... article 8 does not necessarily require that States fulfil their positive obligation to

---

9 Ibid at para 27.
10 (1996) 23 EHRR 213.
11 Note 8.
12 [1993] AC 498.

secure respect for private life by the provision of unlimited civil remedies in circumstances where criminal law sanctions are in operation.'[13]

Where the law provides no remedy for Convention breaches the position will be different.

5.11   In *Young, James and Webster v UK*[14] the government argued that it was not responsible for the applicant's dismissal by British Rail for non-membership of a trade union. Rather than analyse the extent to which the state was responsible for running British Rail, the European Court approached the case on the basis that since article 1 of the Convention imposed a duty on the state to 'secure' Convention rights to everyone within its jurisdiction:

> ... if a violation of one of those rights and freedoms is the result of non-observance of that obligation in the enactment of domestic legislation, the responsibility of the State for that violation is engaged.

Notwithstanding the fact that the immediate cause of the applicants' dismissal was an agreement between British Rail and the railway unions, the Court took the view that:

> ... it was the domestic law in force at the relevant time that made lawful the treatment of which the applicants complained. The responsibility of the Respondent State for any resultant breach of the Convention is thus engaged ...[15]

In effect, therefore, the Court extended state responsibility into the sphere of relations between private individuals because it was responsible for legislation which allowed others to breach the applicants' Convention rights.

5.12   The principle articulated in *Young, James and Webster v UK*[16] was applied in *Stedman v UK*[17] which involved an allegation that the applicant had been dismissed because of her religious beliefs contrary to article 9 of the Convention. Adopting the reasoning of the European Court in *Young, James and Webster v UK*, the Commission held that it was irrelevant that the dismissal was the act of a purely private company if the dismissal was lawful in domestic law. On the

13 Ibid at para 64.
14 (1982) 4 EHRR 38.
15 Ibid at para 49.
16 Note 14.
17 (1997) 23 EHRR CD 168.

facts, however, it found that the applicant had not been dismissed as a result of her religious beliefs.

Preventing breaches of Convention rights

5.13   In some circumstances, providing a legal framework which provides effective protection for human rights will not be enough, and more specific steps are needed. The European Court has never defined the circumstances in which such positive obligations arise and, so far, has refused to develop any 'general theory of positive obligations'.[18] However, its case-law reveals that the duty to prevent breaches of Convention rights may arise in at least the three following situations:

1) Where fundamental rights, such as those in articles 2 and 3, are at stake.

2) Where intimate interests, such as those protected in article 8, are at stake.

3) Where Convention rights cannot be effectively protected by the legal framework in place.

Positive obligations where fundamental rights are at stake

5.14   The fundamental nature of the rights protected by article 2 (the right to life) and article 3 (the prohibition on torture and inhuman treatment/punishment) demand special protection. After the event remedies for breach are not sufficient; reasonable preventative measures are called for.

5.15   The positive duty to protect the right of life under article 2 requires that reasonable steps be taken by the state (and its officials) to protect life. This includes a duty to put in place 'effective criminal law provisions to deter the commission of offences against the person backed up by law-enforcement machinery for the prevention, suppression and sanctioning of breaches of such provisions.'[19] It may also include, in certain well-defined circumstances, a positive obligation on the authorities to take preventative operational measures to protect individuals whose lives are at risk from the criminal acts of other individuals.[20]

18   *Plattform Ärzte für das Leben v Austria* n2.
19   *Osman v UK* [1999] 1 FLR 193; noted at [1999] EHRLR 228.
20   Ibid; see further paras 14.5 to 14.13.

5.16   In *Osman v UK*[21] the European Court held that such obligations arise where it can be established that:

> ... the authorities knew or ought to have known at the time of the existence of a real and immediate risk to the life of an identified individual or individuals from the criminal acts of a third party and that they failed to take measures within the scope of their powers which, judged reasonably, might have been expected to avoid that risk.[22]

In that case, an argument that the police failed to take adequate steps to prevent a teacher, who was infatuated with the second applicant, attacking him and killing his father failed on the facts.

5.17   In *Soering v UK*[23] the European Court held that the absolute prohibition on torture and inhuman treatment/punishment would render the UK government responsible for a breach of article 3 if it extradited the applicant to another state in circumstances where there were substantial grounds for believing that he would be in danger of being subject to such treatment/punishment.[24] The fact that the state was not itself responsible for the treatment/punishment in question was irrelevant. In the earlier case of *Altun v Germany*[25] the Commission recognised that this principle applied even where the danger does not emanate from public authorities for whom the receiving State is responsible.

Positive obligations where intimate interests are at stake

5.18   Many of the cases on positive obligations have involved article 8, which protects a number of intimate interests under the umbrella of 'private and family life'. These have mainly turned on the question of whether or not the state has put in place a legal framework which effectively protects Convention rights. So, for example, the European Court's decision in *Marckx v Belgium*[26] that the non-existence in Belgian law of measures to safeguard the integration of all children, including illegitimate children, into their families, breached article 8, effectively called for legislative reform.

21 Note 19.
22 Note 19 at para 116.
23 (1989) 11 EHRR 439.
24 See paras 18.11 to 18.25.
25 (1983) 36 DR 209; see also *HLR v France* (1997) 26 EHRR 29.
26 (1979–80) 2 EHRR 330.

5.19   In *Airey v Ireland*[27] what was in issue was not the existence of a satisfactory legal framework for the protection of Convention rights, but the applicant's access to it. The applicant there complained that her rights under article 8 had been breached because she was unable to divorce her alcoholic and violent husband because she could not afford legal representation and no legal aid was available to her. Having recognised that protection of family life included the right to separate, the European Court held that:

> Effective respect for private or family life obliges Ireland to make this means of protection effectively accessible, when appropriate, to anyone who may wish to have recourse thereto.[28]

In other words, some positive step was needed to enable the applicant to realise her legal right to separate from her husband.

5.20   The principle of effectiveness also underpinned the European Court's decision in *Lopez Ostra v Spain*.[29] On the basis that '... severe environmental pollution may affect individuals' well-being and prevent them from enjoying their homes in such a way as to affect their private and family life adversely, without, however, seriously endangering their health',[30] the Court held that a positive obligation was imposed on the authorities to take appropriate measures to protect the applicants' right to live their lives free from the adverse affects of severe pollution.[31] By opposing the applicants' legal action to close the waste-treatment plant, the Spanish authorities had failed in that duty and prolonged the applicants' exposure to pollution.

5.21   A different result followed in *Osman v UK*[32] where, in addition to their argument under article 2,[33] the applicants also advanced an argument under article 8. The nub of their complaint was that the police had failed to bring to an end the campaign of harassment, vandalism and victimisation, which the second applicant's teacher had waged against their property. The European Court accepted that an obligation on the police to take preventative measures could arise under article 8, but found that, on the facts, the police had done all they could reasonably have been expected to do.

---

27 (1979–80) 2 EHRR 305.
28 Ibid at para 33.
29 (1995) 20 EHRR 277.
30 Ibid at para 51.
31 Note 29 at para 55.
32 Note 19. But see the limits set in *Botta v Italy* [1998] EHRLR 486 concerning disabled access to beach facilities.
33 See paras 14.5 to 14.13.

Positive obligations where Convention rights cannot be effectively protected by the legal framework in place

5.22   The circumstances in which a positive obligation is imposed on state authorities to take some action on the basis that Convention rights cannot be effectively protected by the legal framework in place are inevitably diverse. The basis for the European Court's decision in *Plattform Ärzte für das Leben v Austria*[34] was a recognition that effective protection for the right of peaceful assembly required immediate police action on the streets. Legal proceedings after the event were no substitute for the practical exercise of the right in issue. And remedies such as preventative injunctions were of limited use without police enforcement.

Providing information and advice relevant to the breach of Convention rights

5.23   In a number of recent cases, the European Court has recognised that in many situations, individuals can protect their Convention rights only if they have access to relevant information. In *Guerra v Italy*[35] the Court took the principles it had established in *Lopez Ostra v Spain*[36] a step further and established a positive obligation to provide information to those affected by environmental pollution. The facts in that case were similar: the applicants lived near a chemical factory which was classified as 'high risk'. However, their complaint was framed more broadly. They claimed that the authorities had failed properly to respect their right to family life and home by failing to provide them with information about the risks of living near to the factory and how to proceed in the event of an accident.

5.24   Although the Commission had proceeded on the basis that the applicants had a right to the information they sought under article 10, the Court rejected this. In its view, article 10 'basically prohibits a government from restricting a person from receiving information that others wish or may be willing to impart to him'.[37] However, the Court found a breach of article 8 on the basis that, once the

---

34   Note 2.
35   (1998) 26 EHRR 357.
36   Note 29.
37   Note 35 at para 53; see also *Leander v Sweden* (1987) 9 EHRR 433 and paras 24.7 to 24.9.

authorities became aware of essential information about the dangers inherent in the running of the factory, they delayed for several years before passing that information to the applicants and therefore prevented them from assessing the risks they and their families ran by continuing to live in the vicinity of the factory.

5.25   In *LCB v UK*[38] the applicant, the daughter of a man who had been present during nuclear testing at Christmas Island in the late 1950s when he was serving in the RAF, complained that the authorities had failed to advise her parents to monitor her health prior to her diagnosis with leukaemia. The European Court approached the case on the basis that:

> ... the State could only have been required of its own motion to take these steps in relation to the applicant if it had appeared likely at that time that any such exposure of her father to radiation might have engendered a real risk to her health.[39]

From an analysis of the facts known at the time, the Court concluded that the authorities could not reasonably have been expected to have established any link between the exposure of the applicant's father to radiation and the likelihood that his children might develop leukaemia. No obligation, therefore arose.

5.26   The position was different in *McGinley and Egan v UK*,[40] where the applicants had themselves been exposed to radiation in the same tests as the applicant's father in *LCB v UK* and claimed under article 8, that they should have been provided with information sufficient to enable them to assess the possible consequences of the tests for their health.

5.27   The European Court held that article 8 was applicable because:

> ... given the fact that exposure to high levels of radiation is known to have hidden, but serious and longlasting, effects on health, it is not unnatural that the applicants' uncertainty as to whether or not they had been put at risk in this way caused them substantial anxiety and distress ...
> ... since the [radiation level records] contained information which might have assisted the applicants in assessing radiation levels in the areas in which they were stationed during the tests, and might indeed have served to reassure them in this respect, they had an interest under Article 8 in obtaining access to them.[41]

---

38   (1999) 27 EHRR 212.
39   Ibid at para 38.
40   (1999) 27 EHRR 1.
41   Ibid at para 99.

In those circumstances the Court took the view that a positive obligation under article 8 arose. As a matter of principle:

> Where a Government engages in hazardous activities, such as those in issue in the present case, which might have hidden adverse consequences on the health of those involved in such activities, respect for private and family life under article 8 requires that an effective and accessible procedure be established which enables persons to seek all relevant and appropriate information.[42]

On the facts, however, the Court found no breach of this positive obligation because the applicants could have sought access to the relevant documents in proceedings before the Pension Appeal Tribunal but had failed to do so.

Responding to breaches of Convention rights

5.28   Where fundamental rights are in issue, such as those under articles 2 and 3, the European Court has imposed an obligation on states to respond diligently to any breaches. The payment of compensation is insufficient; an efficient investigation must be carried out, backed up with criminal prosecutions where appropriate.

5.29   This duty is particularly strict where it is suggested that police officers or other public officials may be responsible for the breach. Its scope was examined by the Court in *Aydin v Turkey*[43] where the applicant complained that, during her detention by the security forces in Turkey, she was raped and subjected to other forms of ill treatment amounting to torture under article 3 of the Convention. The Court held that:

> Given the fundamental importance of the prohibition of torture and the especially vulnerable position of torture victims, Article 13 imposes, without prejudice to any other remedy available under the domestic system, an obligation on states to carry out a thorough and effective investigation of incidents of torture.

Accordingly it formulated the following principle:

> ... where an individual has an arguable claim that he or she has been tortured by agents of the state, the notion of an effective remedy, entails, in addition to the payment of compensation where appropriate, a thorough and effective investigation capable of

42 Note 40 at para 101.
43 (1998) 25 EHRR 251.

leading to the identification and punishment of those responsible and including effective access for the complainant to the investigatory procedure.[44]

Having regard to this principle, the Court found a breach of the Convention because the Turkish authorities had carried out an incomplete enquiry to determine the veracity of the applicant's complaint.[45]

Providing resources to individuals to prevent breaches of their Convention rights

5.30   As noted above, some articles of the Convention by their very nature impose a duty on the state to provide resources such as free legal assistance etc. In *Airey v Ireland*[46] this principle was extended on the basis that the right there in issue – family life – could not be effectively protected without the provision of resources, legal aid in divorce proceedings, by the state. And the principle is one of general application.

5.31   On several occasions applicants have argued that the right to family life under article 8 of the Convention imposes a positive obligation on state authorities to provide them with financial assistance to enable one of two parents to stay at home and take care of their children. So far, the Commission has rejected such arguments. In *Andersson and Kullman v Sweden*[47] the Commission rejected a complaint that the decision of the Swedish social services to terminate family allowance payments and replace them with free crêche places to enable the second applicant to work breached article 8. And in *AP v Austria*[48] it rejected a complaint that failure to make long-term parental leave payments to enable a father to stay at home and look after his children breached article 8.

5.32   There may be circumstances in which a local authority comes under a positive obligation under the Convention to provide housing to those within its catchment area. However, they are likely to arise only in exceptional cases. In *Burton v UK*[49] the Commission rejected an argument that, in failing to provide an individual suffering from

44   Ibid at 103.
45   See further paras 14.5 to 14.13.
46   Note 27.
47   46 DR 251.
48   (1995) 20 EHRR CD 63.
49   (1996) 22 EHRR CD 134.

cancer with a place where she could live out her days in a caravan according to her Romany gypsy background, a local authority had failed in its obligations under article 8.

The relationship between positive and negative obligations

5.33   The boundaries between a state's positive and negative obligations do not lend themselves to precise definition. In many situations the applicable principles are the same. As the European Court observed in *Powell and Rayner v UK*:[50]

> In both contexts regard must be had to the fair balance that has to be struck between the competing interests of the individual and of the community as a whole; and in both contexts the State enjoys a certain margin of appreciation in determining the steps to be taken to ensure compliance with the Convention. Furthermore, even in relation to the positive obligations flowing from the first paragraph of article 8, in striking the required balance the aims mentioned in the second paragraph may be of a certain relevance.[51]

That case and *Lopez Ostra v Spain*[52] provide striking examples of the inter-relationship between the two types of obligations.

In *Powell and Rayner v UK*[53] the applicants, who lived near Heathrow Airport, complained that the excessive noise from the airport breached their rights under article 8 to respect for their private life and home As a preliminary issue, the government argued that the complaint disclosed no direct 'interference by a public authority' because Heathrow Airport and the aircraft using it were not and never had been owned, controlled or operated by the government or any agency of the government. The European Court disagreed. In its view:

> Whether the present case be analysed in terms of a positive duty on the State to take reasonable and appropriate measures to secure the applicants' rights under paragraph (1) of article 8 or in terms of an 'interference by a public authority' to be justified in accordance with paragraph (2), the applicable principles are broadly similar.[54]

50   Note 6.
51   Ibid at para 41.
52   Note 29.
53   Note 6.
54   Ibid at para 41.

State responsibility was therefore engaged, although, on the facts, it found no breach of the Convention.[55]

5.35   A similar approach was taken in *Lopez Ostra v Spain*[56] where the European Court found that state responsibility was engaged where the local authority had failed to take adequate steps to curtail pollution emitted from a privately run waste-treatment plant on the two-fold basis that:

1) Although the local authority was not directly responsible for the plant, it had given permission for it to be built and subsidised its construction.[57]

2) In any event, under article 8, the local authority was under a positive obligation to take such measures as were necessary for the protection of the applicants' private and family life.[58]

In that case the Court found that the measures taken by the local authority were inadequate.

Positive obligations under the HRA

5.36   Positive obligations do not just operate at the international level; they also arise under the HRA for three reasons:

1) First, because articles 2–12 and 14 of the Convention are incorporated into UK law under the Act: see chapter 1.[59] In so far as the European Court has imposed positive obligations on public authorities to ensure the effective protection of those Convention rights, the same obligations are incorporated into UK law under the Act.

2) Second, because the HRA is intended to 'secure' Convention rights in domestic law in accordance with the obligation set out in article 1 of the Convention: see the Lord Chancellor's comments at the Committee stage in the House of Lords.[60] And article 1 provides a springboard for positive obligations.

3) Third, because courts and tribunals are public authorities under

---

55 See paras 22.30 to 22.36.
56 Note 29.
57 Ibid at para 52.
58 Ibid at para 55.
59 Para 1.6.
60 HL (committee stage), col 475, 8 November 1997.

the Act. They must, therefore, protect Convention rights effectively.

5.37   The significance of the inclusion of courts and tribunals within the definition of 'public authority' under the Act has been widely recognised. As Professor Wade has noted:

> ... a court cannot lawfully give a judgment in any case in which Convention rights are in issue except in accordance with those rights set out in Schedule 1 of the [Act]. In other words ... the court must recognise and apply the Convention rights, and it must also, under [s2] follow the case-law and jurisprudence of the Strasbourg institutions, which extend to the award of compensation and costs. There is nothing to confine those provisions to cases brought against public authorities.[61]

That this was the intention behind the inclusion of courts and tribunals in s6(1) has been confirmed by both the Lord Chancellor and Lord Williams of Mostyn during the Committee stages in the Lords.

5.38   An amendment was proposed by Lord Wakeham, chair of the Press Complaints Commission, to disapply the obligation to act compatibly with the Convention 'where the public authority is a court or tribunal and the parties to the proceedings before it do not include a public authority'.[62] Its purpose was to prevent the Convention being used by the courts in disputes between private individuals and, in particular, 'to stop the development of a common law of privacy'.[63]

5.39   The Lord Chancellor, responding at the end of the debate on the amendment, said:

> We ... believe that it is right as a matter of principle for the courts to have the duty of acting compatibly with the Convention not only in cases involving other public authorities but also in developing the common law in deciding cases between individuals. Why should they not? In preparing this Bill, we have taken the view that it is the other course, that of excluding Convention considerations altogether from cases between individuals, which would have to be justified. We do not think that that would be justifiable; nor, indeed, do we think it would be practicable.[64]

---

61 *Human Rights and the Judiciary* Judicial Studies Board Annual Lecture 1998, p5.
62 HL Debs, col 771, 24 November 1997.
63 Ibid col 772.
64 Ibid col. 783.

And later:

> Clause 3 requires the courts to interpret legislation compatibly with convention rights and to the fullest extent possible in all cases coming before them.[65]

In other words, legislation must be read and given effect in a way which is compatible with Convention rights *whoever* is before the courts *and* the common law must be developed so as to be compatible with the Convention, including the positive obligations inherent in the effective protection of Convention rights.

---

65 Lord Chancellor, HL (committee stage), col 783, 24 November 1997.

The European Convention on Human Rights and criminal law

CHAPTER 6

The Convention in criminal proceedings: an introduction

6.1   Introduction

6.2   Relevant Convention provisions
6.3   Article 3
6.4   Article 5
6.5   Article 6
6.8   Article 7

6.9   The classification of criminal proceedings

6.13   Forfeiture and tax proceedings

6.18   When is an individual 'charged' under the Convention?

6.21   Substantive challenges to the criminal law

6.22   Certainty

6.27   Non-retrospectivity

6.32   Criminal liability for conduct protected under the Convention

Introduction

6.1   Although domestic law already conforms to the minimum standards of the Convention in many respects, in others it does not. Accordingly there will be considerable scope for challenging both substantive criminal law and criminal procedure under the Human Rights Act (HRA). Such challenges can be mounted at every level: in the magistrates' court, the Crown Court, the Court of Appeal and the House of Lords.

Relevant Convention provisions

6.2   All Convention rights are relevant to criminal proceedings.[1] However, the articles set out below are of special application. They are examined in detail in chapter in chapter 3.

Article 3

6.3   Article 3 provides:

> 1. No one shall be subjected to torture or to inhuman or degrading treatment or punishment.

In *Ireland v UK*[2] the European Court indicated that ill-treatment must attain a minimum level of severity if it is to fall within the scope of article 3. The assessment of this minimum is relative; it depends on all the circumstances of the case, such as the duration of the treatment, its physical or mental effects and, in some cases, the sex, age and state of health of the victim. In the same case, the Court defined the following three categories of ill-treatment:

1) *Torture*

    Deliberate inhuman treatment causing very serious and cruel suffering.

2) *Inhuman treatment*

    Treatment that causes intense physical and mental suffering.

3) *Degrading treatment*

    Treatment that arouses in the victim a feeling of fear, anguish and inferiority capable of humiliating and debasing the victim and possibly breaking his or her moral resistance.

1   See: 'Substantive challenges to the criminal law', paras 6.21 to 6.37
2   (1978) 2 EHRR 25.

Article 5

6.4 Article 5 provides that:

1. Everyone has the right to liberty and security of person. No one shall be deprived of his liberty save in the following cases and in accordance with the procedure prescribed by law:

   (a) the lawful detention of a person after conviction by a competent court;

   (b) the lawful arrest or detention of a person for non-compliance with the lawful order of a court or in order to secure fulfilment of any obligation prescribed by law;

   (c) the lawful arrest or detention of a person effected for the purpose of bringing him before the competent legal authority on reasonable suspicion of having committed an offence, or when it is reasonably considered necessary to prevent his committing an offence or fleeing after having done so;

   (d) the detention of a minor by lawful order for the purpose of educational supervision or his lawful detention for the purpose of bringing him before the competent legal authority;

   (e) the lawful detention of persons for the prevention of the spreading of infectious diseases, of persons of unsound mind, alcoholics or drug addicts or vagrants;

   (f) the lawful arrest or detention of a person to prevent his effecting an unauthorised entry into the country or of a person against whom action is being taken with a view to deportation or extradition.

2. Everyone who is arrested shall be informed promptly, in a language which he understands, of the reasons for his arrest and of any charge against him.

3. Everyone arrested or detained in accordance with the provisions of paragraph 1(c) of this article shall be brought promptly before a judge or other officer authorised by law to exercise judicial power and shall be entitled to trial within a reasonable period or to release pending trial. Release may be conditioned by guarantees to appear for trial.

4. Everyone who is deprived of his liberty by arrest or detention shall be entitled to take proceedings by which the lawfulness of his detention shall be decided speedily by a court and his release ordered if the detention is not lawful.

5. Everyone who has been the victim of arrest or detention in contravention of the provisions of this article shall have an enforceable right to compensation.

The scheme of article 5 is to set up a positive right to liberty and security with limited exceptions and an over-riding requirement that any deprivation of liberty must be in accordance with a procedure prescribed by law. The exceptions provided for in articles 5(1)(a) to 5(1)(e) are to be narrowly construed and represent an exhaustive definition of the circumstances in which a person may be lawfully deprived of his liberty.[3] The phrase 'in accordance with the procedure prescribed by law' refers to conformity with national law and procedure.[4] Nevertheless, it remains the function of the European Court and Commission to determine whether article 5 has been violated, and these bodies, therefore, have the ultimate power to interpret and apply national law.[5] There is also a more general requirement under the Convention to respect a fair and proper procedure – that is, that ' any measure depriving a person of his liberty should issue from and be executed by an appropriate authority and should not be arbitrary'.[6] In *Van der Leer v Netherlands*,[7] the European Court found a violation of article 5(1) where a judge had failed to hear from a patient or her representative and gave no reason for not doing so.

Article 6

6.5   Article 6 provides that:

1. In the determination of his civil rights and obligations or of any criminal charge against him, everyone is entitled to a fair and public hearing within a reasonable time by an independent and impartial tribunal established by law. Judgment shall be pronounced publicly but the press and public may be excluded from all or part of the trial in the interests of morals, public order or national security in a democratic society, where the interests of juveniles or the protection of the private life of the parties so require, or to the extent strictly necessary in the opinion of the court in special circumstances where publicity would prejudice the interests of justice.

2. Everyone charged with a criminal offence shall be presumed innocent until proved guilty according to law.

---

3   *Winterwerp v Netherlands* (1979) 2 EHRR 387 at para 37.
4   Ibid.
5   *Bozano v France* (1986) 9 EHRR 297, and *Van der Leer v Netherlands* (1990) 12 EHRR 567.
6   Note 3.
7   (1990) 12 EHRR 567.

3. Everyone charged with a criminal offence has the following minimum rights:
   (a) to be informed promptly, in a language which he understands and in detail, of the nature and cause of the accusation against him;
   (b) to have adequate time and facilities for the preparation of his defence;
   (c) to defend himself in person or though legal assistance of his own choosing or, if he has not sufficient means to pay for legal assistance, to be given it free when the interests of justice so require;
   (d) to examine or have examined witnesses against him and to obtain the attendance and examination of witnesses on his behalf under the same conditions as witnesses against him;
   (e) to have the free assistance of an interpreter if he cannot understand or speak the language used in court.

6.6   In most cases the applicability of article 6 will not be in issue: it clearly applies to ordinary criminal proceedings in the magistrates' court and the Crown court, and to any appeal[8] from those courts. The only question in such cases is likely to be *when* article 6 applies (in particular, whether fair trial guarantees apply at the police station prior to charge).[9]

6.7   Where the position is less clear cut, the meaning of 'criminal charge' in article 6 of the Convention will be important. This is considered below.

Article 7

6.8   Article 7 provides:

1. No one shall be held guilty of any criminal offence on account of any act or omission which did not constitute a criminal offence under the national or international law at the time when it was committed. Nor shall a heavier penalty be imposed than the one that was applicable at the time the criminal offence was committed.

2. This article shall not prejudice the trial and punishment of any person for any act or omission which, at the time when it was committed, was criminal according to the general principles of law recognised by civilised nations.

8   See chapter 10.
9   See paras 6.18 to 6.20.

The classification of criminal proceedings

6.9   Since the Convention distinguishes between criminal and civil proceedings, the classification of each is important. In the leading case
of *Engel v Netherlands*,[10] the Court made it clear that 'criminal charge'
is an autonomous concept. In other words, the Strasbourg institutions will decide for themselves whether any given proceedings
involve the determination of a 'criminal charge' within the meaning
of article 6; they will not be bound by the approach taken in domestic
law. In particular, the Court has emphasised that although there is
nothing in the Convention to prevent decriminalisation, this cannot,
of itself, limit the operation of the fundamental guarantee of a fair
trial in article 6.[11]

6.10   For the European Court and Commission, the question of
whether proceedings involve the determination of a 'criminal charge'
can be assessed by reference to three criteria: (a) the classification of
the proceedings in domestic law, (b) the nature of the offence or conduct in question, and (c) the severity of any possible penalty.[12] The
first criterion is not as important as the second and third,[13] unless the
proceedings are classified as criminal in domestic law. If so, that classification is conclusive and article 6 applies. In contrast, the fact that
proceedings are classified as civil in domestic law is merely 'a starting point'.[14]

6.11   When assessing the second criterion – the nature of the offence
in question – the Court and Commission take into account factors
such as how the offence is regarded in other Council of Europe states
and whether the offence applies to the population as a whole or only
to an identifiable sub-group.[15] This has proved a useful technique for
distinguishing between disciplinary proceedings applicable to those
under a specific regime and criminal offences. However, prison
disciplinary proceedings do involve the determination of a criminal

---

10 (1979–80) 1 EHRR 706.
11 *Ozturk v Turkey* (1984) 6 EHRR 409. See *Lauko v Slovakia* [1999] EHRLR 105:
'preventative and educational' sanction still criminal.
12 *Engel v Netherlands* (1979–80) 1 EHRR 706.
13 *Ozturk v Turkey* n11 at para 50.
14 *Benham v UK* (1996) 22 EHRR 293.
15 In *Benham v UK* n14, one key factor leading the Court to conclude that proceedings for non-payment of the community charge were criminal was the fact
that liability to pay and the procedure upon non-payment were of general
application to all citizens.

charge within the meaning of article 6.[16] Examples of offences or conduct where the nature has *not* been considered to be criminal include the imposition of a fine[17] or imprisonment[18] to enforce an injunction, decisions in extradition cases,[19] a decision to classify a prisoner as category A[20] and restrictions placed on the applicant's activities in running an insurance business.[21]

6.12   The severity of the penalty has been determinative in a number of cases. Where a penalty has a deterrent purpose or carries the risk of imprisonment, a finding that article 6 applies is likely. So, for example, in a series of cases against Austria involving minor traffic offences – which are treated as administrative matters in domestic law – the European Court has been influenced by the fact that, although the level of fines was generally low, they were intended to be deterrent and could result in the deprivation of liberty in cases of non-payment.[22] And in *Campbell and Fell v UK*,[23] loss of remission was a key factor in the Court's conclusion that prison disciplinary proceedings attracted article 6 protection.

Forfeiture and tax proceedings

6.13   The classification of forfeiture and tax proceedings under the Convention has caused particular difficulties. And it is clear that, to some extent, the approach of the Strasbourg institutions has been influenced by policy considerations. In the first case to be considered by the European Court, *AGOSI v UK*,[24] which involved seizure of the applicant company's krugerrands by customs and excise and forfeiture after High Court proceedings, the Court simply held, without any elaboration, that:

16 *Campbell and Fell v UK* (1985) 7 EHRR 165.
17 *Krone-Verlag GmbH and Mediaprint Anzeigen GmbH & Co KG v Austria* (1997) 23 EHRR CD 152.
18 Appl 12827/87, 4 July 1988, unpublished.
19 *X v UK* (1984) 37 DR 158.
20 X v UK (1979) 20 DR 202; see chapter 16. Mandatory drugs tests in prison are not criminal: *Galloway v UK* [1999] EHRLR 119.
21 *X v UK* (1980) 21 DR 5.
22 See: *Schmautzer v Austria* (1996) 21 EHRR 511; *Pfarrmeier v Austria* (1996) 22 EHRR 175; *Umlauft v Austria* (1996) 22 EHRR 76.
23 (1985) 7 EHRR 165.
24 (1987) 9 EHRR 1.

None of the proceedings complained of can be considered to have been concerned with the determination of a criminal charge against the applicant.[25]

6.14   The issue arose again in *Air Canada v UK*[26] with similar results. In that case, customs and excise had seized one of the applicant company's aircraft because a large quantity of drugs was found on the plane and the company had been penalised on several previous occasions for breaches of security in regard to other drug-smuggling activities.[27] On the payment of a penalty later the same day, the company regained the aircraft. However, the European Court was not persuaded that the forfeiture was in effect the determination of a criminal charge under article 6. In its view the absence of a criminal charge, the fact that the criminal courts were not involved and the fact there was no threat of criminal proceedings in the event of non-compliance all pointed against the proceedings being criminal.

6.15   Similarly, the European Court and Commission have repeatedly held that ordinary measures taken to enforce tax payments do not involve the determination of a criminal charge within the meaning of article 6. In *Abas v the Netherlands*[28] the Commission took the view that an investigation by the Inspector of Direct Taxes, who investigated taxes on earnings, did not attract the application of article 6 and consequently that the applicant's obligation to answer his questions did not constitute an infringement of the right to silence. Although the applicant was subject to a legal obligation to provide information to the tax inspector, in default of which he could have been fined or imprisoned, the Commission considered that the functions performed by the tax inspector were 'essentially investigative'. The Commission also emphasised that if article 6 applied to tax investigations generally, it would unduly hamper their effective functioning.

6.16   However, where penalties are imposed in tax cases, closer scrutiny is required. In *Perin v France*,[29] the Commission considered that proceedings in which tax penalties of 30% and 50% of the amount due were imposed were criminal proceedings within the meaning of article 6. In *Bendenoun v France*,[30] the Court reached the same

25 Ibid at para 66.
26 (1995) 20 EHRR 150.
27 The power of seizure in such circumstances arose under the Customs and Excise Act 1979.
28 Appl 27943/95 [1997] EHRLR 418.
29 Appl 18656/91, 1 December 1992, unreported.
30 (1994) 18 EHRR 54.

decision in relation to tax surcharges amounting to almost half a million francs: the penalty imposed was not intended as pecuniary compensation but as punishment to deter re-offending.

6.17   Lesser penalties, however, have not been enough to classify tax proceedings as criminal. In *Smith v UK*,[31] the Commission took the view that a surcharge of 10% for 'wilful refusal or culpable neglect' to pay the community charge, which could not be converted into a term of imprisonment,[32] was not a 'criminal charge' within the meaning of article 6.

When is an individual 'charged' under the Convention?

6.18   The right to a fair trial under article 6(1) applies to the determination of a criminal 'charge' and the specific provisions of article 6(3)[33] apply to everyone 'charged' with a criminal offence. The question of when an individual is charged is, therefore, crucial to the determination of *when* article 6 begins to apply. And, like classification of criminal proceedings, this is an autonomous concept.[34]

6.19   In *Eckle v Germany*,[35] the European Court defined a 'charge' for the purposes of article 6(1) as 'the official notification given to an individual by the competent authority of an allegation that he has committed a criminal offence'.[36] In some instances, however, the Court has recognised that it may 'take the form of other measures which carry the implication of such an allegation and which likewise substantially affect the situation of the suspect':[37] an approach endorsed in the case of *Corigliano v Italy*.[38]

6.20   According to this approach, an arrest in the UK probably amounts to a 'charge' within the meaning of the Convention: a conclusion drawn by the Commission in *Ewing v UK*.[39] The argument advanced, but not resolved by the Commission, in *G v UK*[40] that article 6 applies

31 (1996) 21 EHRR CD 74.
32 Unlike the position in *Benham v UK* n7.
33 See chapters 8 and 9.
34 See paras 6.9 to 6.12.
35 (1983) 5 EHRR 1.
36 Ibid at para 73.
37 *Foti v Italy* (1983) 5 EHRR 313.
38 (1983) 5 EHRR 334.
39 (1998) 10 EHRR 141.
40 (1983) 35 DR 75.

only when it is clear that a trial will take place (ie when the applicant is formally charged) is clearly unsustainable in light of the Court's judgment in *Murray v UK*.[41] There the Court held that article 6 applied during police questioning prior to charge.[42]

Substantive challenges to the criminal law

6.21 Once the HRA comes into force, practitioners will be able to rely on the Convention in criminal proceedings in a number of ways. Chapters 7, 8, 9 and 10 deal with procedural matters arising under articles 5, 6 and 7. But, in addition, the Convention will provide a basis for substantive challenges to the criminal law in the following circumstances:

1) where the definition or scope of a criminal offence is so vague and imprecise that it violates the principle of certainty inherent in the Convention and specifically required by article 7;

2) where the act or conduct penalised in criminal proceedings did not constitute a criminal offence at the time it was committed (the principle of non-retrospective application of the criminal law); and

3) where a criminal offence amounts to an unjustifiable interference with exercise by the defendant of his/her Convention rights (for example, free speech).

Before the HRA comes into force, the Convention can be used as an aid to the proper interpretation or development of the law but not as a yardstick for compliance.[44]

Certainty

6.22 On its face, article 7(1)[45] deals simply with the principle that the criminal law should not be applied retrospectively. However, consistent with its short title in the Convention – 'no punishment without law' – the Strasbourg institutions have interpreted this provision broadly. As the European Court pointed out in *Kokkinakis v Greece*:[46]

41 (1996) 22 EHRR 29.
42 See paras 9.67 to 9.74.
44 See paras 1.73 to 1.82.
45 Set out para 6.8.
46 (1994) 17 EHRR 397.

> ... article 7(1) of the Convention is not confined to prohibiting the retrospective application of the criminal law to an accused's disadvantage. It also embodies, more generally, the principle that only the law can define a crime and prescribe a penalty ... and the principle that the criminal law must not be extensively construed to an accused's detriment, for instance by analogy; it follows from this that an offence must be clearly defined in law. This condition is satisfied where the individual can know from the wording of the relevant provision and, if need be, with the assistance of the court's interpretation of it, what acts and
> omissions will make him liable.[47]

6.23 This formulation of the principle of legality overlaps with the rule under article 5 that deprivations of liberty be 'lawful' and with the more general rule that any restriction on the exercise of Convention rights under articles 8 to 12 must be 'prescribed by law':[48] a point emphasised by the European Court in *SW and CR v UK*:[49]

> ... when speaking of ' law' article 7 alludes to the very same concept as that to which the Convention refers elsewhere when using the term, a concept which comprises written as well as unwritten law and implies qualitative requirements, notably those of accessibility and foreseeability.[50]

Thus in *Sunday Times v UK*,[51] the applicant newspaper challenged contempt of court proceedings on the basis that the uncertainty of the law violated article 10[52] of the Convention; and in *Harman v UK*[53] the applicant challenged the same provisions on the same basis, albeit under article 7 of the Convention.[54]

6.24 However, absolute certainty is not required: reasonable certainty is enough. In the context of a challenge to a development in the common law removing the immunity enjoyed by husbands from criminal liability for raping their wives,[55] the European Court noted;

> However clearly drafted a legal provision may be, in any system of law, including criminal law, there is an inevitable element of

47 Ibid at para 52.
48 See paras 4.29 to 4.36.
49 (1996) 21 EHRR 363.
50 Ibid at para 34/32.
51 (1979–80) 2 EHRR 245.
52 Freedom of speech.
53 (1984) 38 DR 53.
54 The case was declared admissible and then settled by the UK government.
55 Prior to July 1990, a husband had enjoyed immunity from criminal liability for raping his wife: *R v R* [1991] 4 All ER 481.

judicial interpretation. There will always be a need for elucidation of doubtful points and for adaptation to changing circumstances. Indeed, in the United Kingdom, as in the other Convention States, the progressive development of the criminal law through judicial law-making is a well entrenched and necessary part of legal tradition. Article 7 cannot be read as outlawing the gradual clarification of the rules of criminal liability through judicial interpretation from case to case, provided that the development is consistent with the essence of the offence and could be reasonably foreseen.[56]

On the facts, the European Court held that the decisions of the Court of Appeal and then the House of Lords did no more than continue a perceptible line of case-law development dismantling the immunity of a husband from prosecution for rape upon his wife.[57] Consequently there was no breach of article 7.

6.25   An indication of the limits within which the common law must operate so as to conform with the principle of reasonable certainty was given by the Commission in *X Ltd and Y v UK*.[58] What article 7 precludes is the extension of existing offences to cover facts which previously did not attract criminal liability:

> This implies that constituent elements of an offence such as e.g. the particular form of culpability required for its completion may not be essentially changed, at least not to the detriment of the accused, by the case-law of the courts.[59]

On the other hand, no objection can be taken where the courts merely clarify the existing elements of an offence and adapt them to new circumstances which can reasonably be brought under the original concept of the offence.

6.26   It is also clear from the case-law of the European Court and Commission that the mere fact that legal advice may be needed to appreciate the precise definition or scope of a criminal offence will not necessarily take it outside the reasonable certainty test. So, for example, in *Cantoni v France*[60] the Court concluded that, with legal advice, inconsistent case-law on the meaning of 'medicinal product' could be clarified; no article 7 issue therefore arose.

---

56 *SW and CR v UK* (1995) 21 EHRR 363 at para 36/34.
57 Ibid at para 43/41.
58 (1982) 28 DR 77.
59 Ibid at para 9.
60 15 November 1996 (unpublished). But see *Hashman and Harrup v UK* [1999] EHRLR 342: 'bind overs' too vague.

Non-retrospectivity

6.27   The principle of non-retrospective application of the criminal law, provided in article 7(1), has given rise to very little case-law before the European Court and Commission. It is reflected in UK law, where, in the absence of express words in a statute to the contrary, there is a presumption that the penal provisions in legislation are not intended to have retrospective effect.[61]

6.28   The War Crimes Act 1991, which gives courts retroactive jurisdiction in relation to a number of offences committed in Germany or a place under German occupation during the Second World War, is protected from challenge under article 7(1) by the qualification in article 7(2):

> This article shall not prejudice the trial and punishment of any person for any act or omission which, at the time when it was committed, was criminal according to the general principles of law recognised by civilised nations.

The travaux preparatoires indicate that article 7(2) was intended 'to make it clear that article 7 does not affect laws which, under the very exceptional circumstances at the end of the Second World War, were passed to punish war crimes, treason and collaboration with the enemy, and does not aim at any legal or moral condemnation of those laws'.[62]

6.29   The retrospective imposition of heavier penalties than those in place when an offence was committed – also prohibited by article 7(1) – has caused greater difficulties. In *Welch v UK*,[63] the applicant was convicted of drug offences committed in 1986. In addition to a sentence of imprisonment, the trial judge imposed a confiscation order pursuant to the Drug Trafficking Offences Act 1986, the operative provisions of which came into force in January 1987. This, the applicant complained, constituted the imposition of a retrospective criminal penalty contrary to article 7.

6.30   The European Court took the view that the concept of a penalty in article 7(1) is, like the notion of civil rights and obligations and criminal charge in article 6(1), an autonomous Convention concept:[64] to render the protection offered by article 7 effective, the Court must

---

61   *Waddington v Miah* [1974] 1 WLR 683.
62   See: *Law of the European Convention on Human Rights* Harris D J, O'Boyle M and Warbrick C, Butterworths, 1995, p282.
63   (1995) 20 EHRR 247.
64   See paras 6.9 to 6.12.

remain free to go behind appearances and assess for itself whether a particular measure amounts in substance to a penalty. Factors relevant to this assessment are whether the measure in question was imposed following conviction of a criminal offence, the nature and purpose of the measure in question, its characterisation under national law, the procedure involved in the making and implementation of the measure and its severity.[65] Since the imposition of a confiscation order under the 1986 Act was conditional upon a conviction for one or more drug trafficking offences and taking into account the fact that the 1986 Act was introduced to overcome the inadequacy of the existing powers of forfeiture, the European Court concluded that there had been a violation of article 7 in *Welch v UK*.

6.31　　The decision in *Taylor v UK*[66] went the other way. There the applicant was convicted in 1994 of drug trafficking between 1990 and 1993. He was imprisoned and a confiscation order made in relation to trafficking dating back to 1974. The Commission distinguished *Welch v UK* on the basis that the applicant, when committing offences between 1990 and 1993 was aware of the possibility that a confiscation order could be made because the Drug Trafficking Offences Act 1986 had come into force by then. On that basis the complaint was declared inadmissible.

Criminal liability for conduct protected under the Convention

6.32　　Subject to article 7 and the procedural requirements of articles 5 and 6, Convention states are free, in principle, to apply the criminal law to acts which are not carried out in the normal exercise of one of the rights protected under the Convention. This proposition was first advanced by the European Court in the context of military disciplinary proceedings in *Engel v Netherlands*[67] and affirmed in the context of ordinary criminal proceedings in *Salabiaku v France*.[68] On that basis, the criminalisation and punishment of activities such as drug trafficking is unlikely to raise any substantive Convention issue.

6.33　　The position is different, however, where criminal offences overlap with Convention rights; particularly those contained in articles 8

65　Note 63 at para 28.
66　Appl 31209/96 [1998] EHRLR 90. See also *Curran v UK* [1998] EHRLR 507 concerning changes in CICB claims. Also *Ibbotson v UK* [1999] EHRLR concerning a requirement to register under the Sex Offenders Act 1997.
67　(1979–80) 1 EHRR 647.
68　(1991) 13 EHRR 379 at para 27.

to 11.[69] In such cases, the Strasbourg institutions take the view that the existence and prosecution of offences for Convention-protected activity must be justified; ie must be shown to be legitimate, necessary and proportionate.[70] The tension between sexual activity classified as criminal in Convention states and the Convention-protected right of privacy provides a classic example.

6.34   In *Norris v Ireland*[71] the European Court held that maintaining in force legislation prohibiting homosexual acts committed in private between consenting adult men constituted an interference with the applicant's right to respect for his private life under article 8.[72] On the question of whether such legislation was 'necessary in a democratic society', the Court noted that the authorities had refrained from enforcing the law in respect of private homosexual acts between consenting adult males for many years. There was no evidence that this had been injurious to moral standards in Ireland or that there had been any demand for stricter enforcement of the law. In light of this, the Court took the view that the Irish government could not maintain that there was a 'pressing social need' to make such acts criminal offences. Although persons who regarded homosexuality as immoral might be offended by private homosexual acts, this could not on its own warrant the application of penal sanctions when only consenting adults were involved. The Court, therefore, found that there had been a breach of article 8.

6.35   A like result followed in *Sutherland v UK*[73] where the applicant complained that fixing the minimum age for lawful homosexual activities at 18, rather than 16 (the minimum age for heterosexual activities), violated his right to respect for his private life and was discriminatory. The Commission agreed. It noted that the body of medical opinion supported the proposition that sexual orientation in both sexes was fixed at 16 and that men aged 16–21 were not in need of special protection from homosexual 'recruitment'. In its opinion the argument advanced by the government – that 'society's claimed entitlement to indicate disapproval of homosexual conduct and its preference for a heterosexual lifestyle' justified the measures in question – did not constitute either an objective or a reasonable justification for an inequality of treatment under the criminal law between homosexuals and heterosexuals.

69 For an overview of Convention rights under articles 8 to 12, see chapter 3.
70 For an explanation of these concepts see chapter 4.
71 (1991) 13 EHRR 186.
72 Following its judgment in *Dudgeon v UK* (1982) 4 EHRR 149.
73 Appl 25186/94, 1 July 1997, [1998] EHRLR 117.

6.36   On the other hand, in *Laskey v UK*[74] the applicants complained that their prosecution and convictions for assault and wounding in the course of consensual sado-masochistic activities between adults was in breach of article 8. However, the European Court accepted the government's assertion that a state is entitled to punish acts of violence and that the criminal law can legitimately be used to deter certain forms of behaviour on public health and moral grounds. It held that:

> ... one of the roles which the state is unquestionably entitled to undertake is to seek to regulate, through the operation of the criminal law, activities which involve the infliction of physical harm. This is so whether the activities in question occur in the course of sexual conduct or otherwise.[75]

In deciding whether to prosecute, the state was entitled to have regard not only to the actual seriousness of the harm caused, but also to the potential for harm inherent in the acts in question.[76]

6.37   Other cases where the question of criminal liability for conduct protected by the Convention has arisen include: *ADT v UK*[77] (gross indecency): *X Ltd and Y v UK*[78] and *Otto-Preminger Institute v Austria*[79] (blasphemy); *Kokkinakis v Greece*[80] (proselytism); *Arrowsmith v UK*[81] (sedition); *X and Y v Switzerland;*[82] *Scherer v Switzerland*[83] and *Hoare v UK*[84] (obscenity); *Muller v Switzerland*[85] (limits of artistic licence); *Lingens v Austria*[86] (criminal libel); *Glimmerveen Hogerback v Netherlands*[87] and *Jersild v Denmark*[88] (race hatred).

6.38   Janowski v Poland,[89] which concerned a prosecution for insulting municipal guards in Poland split the Commission and the European Court. The Commission found a breach of article 10, but (in a majority judgment) the Court did not. In its view, a state can (within reason) legitimately protect its public officials from verbal abuse in public. Had the Court found that the applicants' exchanges had formed part of an open discussion on a matter of public interest, the result may well have been different.

74 (1997) 24 EHRR 39.	82 (8 April 1991) Commission; unreported.
75 Ibid at para 43.	83 (1994) 18 EHRR 276.
76 Note 74 para 46.	84 [1997] EHRLR 678.
77 [1996] EHRLR 555.	85 (1991) 13 EHRR 212.
78 (1982) 28 DR 77.	86 (1986) 8 EHRR 407.
79 (1994) 19 EHRR 34.	87 (1980) 18 DR 187.
80 (1980) 19 DR 5.	88 (1995) 19 EHRR 1.
81 (1979–80) 1 EHRR 737.	89 [1999] EHRLR 341.

CHAPTER 7

The pre-trial stage

7.1	Introduction
7.5	**The right to be brought promptly before a court**
7.9	Arrest and detention under the Prevention of Terrorism legislation
7.11	**Function of court before which an accused person is brought**
7.13	**Bail**
7.17	**Grounds for refusing bail**
7.18	Fear of absconding
7.21	Interference with the course of justice
7.23	The commission of further offences
7.24	The preservation of public order
7.25	**Bail conditions**
7.28	**The right to test the legality of arrest or detention before a court: article 5(4) of the Convention and bail**
7.31	Equality of arms under article 5(4)
7.32	Disclosure under article 5(4)
7.33	**Trial within a reasonable time**
7.41	**Charge**

continued

7.47   **Access to a lawyer**

7.52   **Lawyer/client communications**

7.54   **Disclosure**

7.68   **Public interest immunity**

7.72   **Time and facilities for preparation of defence**

7.76   **Pre-trial publicity**

Introduction

7.1   This chapter deals with the rights and freedoms guaranteed under the Convention from arrest until trial. Issues up to and including arrest are dealt with in chapter 15 (Police powers) and matters such as conditions of detention are dealt with in chapter 16 (Prisoners). The trial process itself is dealt with in chapter 8 (Fair trial guarantees in criminal cases) and chapter 9 (Evidence in criminal cases).

7.2   At the pre-trial stage, article 5 (the right to liberty and security) and article 6 (fair trial) are the most important Convention rights in issue. However, issues also arise under article 3 (the prohibition on torture, degrading and inhuman treatment) and article 8 (privacy).

7.3   Broadly speaking article 5 provides safeguards against arbitrary pre-trial detention. So, for example, unless pre-trial detention can be fully justified by the authorities, article 6 requires an accused person to be released pending trial. And to ensure that this safeguard is effective, anyone held on remand must have access to a court to test the lawfulness of his/her detention.

7.4   Article 6 is concerned with the substantive and procedural requirements of a fair trial. It applies at an early stage and provides the basis for pre-trial disclosure, access to a lawyer and the provision of 'adequate time and facilities' for the preparation of a defence.

The right to be brought promptly before a court

7.5   Pre-trial detention is governed by article 5(3) of the Convention. This requires that everyone arrested under article 5(1)(c), on suspicion of having committed an offence, be brought promptly before a judge or other judicial officer. Bringing a person before a magistrates' court will suffice. However, the mere fact that a detained person is not charged or brought before a court does not, in itself, amount to a violation of article 5(3) so long as s/he is released 'promptly'.[1]

7.6   The assessment of 'promptness' has to be made in light of the object and purpose of article 5 as a whole, which is to prohibit arbitrary arrest and detention and to ensure 'judicial control of interferences by the executive with the individual's right to liberty'.[2] Neither the European Court nor the European Commission has

---

1   *Brogan and Others v UK* (1989) 11 EHRR 117 at para 58.
2   Ibid.

defined the word 'promptly' by reference to a firm minimum period. However, both have indicated that the scope for flexibility in interpreting the notion of 'promptness' in article 5(3) is very limited.

7.7   In a very early case,[3] the Commission took the view that four days did not exceed the requirements of the Convention. However, in light of the European Court's decision in the subsequent case of *Brogan and Others v UK*,[4] such a period may now be considered too long in ordinary criminal proceedings. Without specifying what period would have satisfied the requirements of promptness, the European Court found against the Italian government in *Brincat v Italy*,[5] where the applicant was arrested on blackmail charges and detained for four days before being brought before a public prosecutor.

7.8   In *Brogan and Others v UK*[6] the four applicants were arrested under the Prevention of Terrorism Act 1984[7] and held without being produced before a court for various periods, the shortest of which was four days and six hours. They were then released without charge. The European Court accepted that the special circumstances prevailing in Northern Ireland and the difficulties encountered by the authorities in investigating terrorist offences permitted a longer than usual period of initial detention. Nonetheless, in its view, even the shortest period fell outside the strict constraints permitted by the notion of 'promptness' in article 5(3). To permit the special circumstances to justify such a lengthy period of detention without an appearance before a court would 'impair the very essence of the right to prompt judicial control' protected by article 5(3).

Arrest and detention under the Prevention of Terrorism legislation

7.9   The challenge under article 5(3) in *Brogan and Others v UK*[8] was to the power of the Secretary of State to authorise an extension of detention without charge from 48 hours to seven days for those suspected of involvement in terrorism connected with the affairs of Northern Ireland. Following the European Court's judgment, on 6 December 1988 the Home Secretary informed Parliament that, against the

---

3   *X v Netherlands*, Appl 2894/66 (1966) 9 Yearbook 564.
4   (1989) 11 EHRR 117.
5   (1993) 16 EHRR 591.
6   Note 4.
7   S12.
8   Note 4.

background of terrorist offences in Northern Ireland, the Government did not believe that the minimum period should be reduced. Subsequently, the UK entered a derogation under article 15(1) of the Convention, 'to the extent that the exercise of [powers to authorise extensions of detention] may be inconsistent with the obligations imposed by the Convention'.[9]

7.10   The validity of this derogation was subsequently challenged but upheld by the European Court in the case of *Brannigan and McBride v UK*.[10] The HRA sets out the text of this derogation[11] and article 5(3) will have effect in domestic law subject to its terms. However, its effect in domestic law is time-limited. If not withdrawn earlier, it will expire five years after the HRA comes into force unless both Houses of Parliament agree that it should be renewed, and similarly thereafter.[12]

Function of court before which an accused person is brought

7.11   The function of the court before which an accused person is brought is extremely important. In *Schiesser v Switzerland*[13] the European Court emphasised that in order to comply with the requirements of article 5(3) a court must: review the circumstances militating for and against detention, decide 'by reference to legal criteria, whether there are reasons to justify detention' and order release of the accused person if no such reasons exist.

7.12   For these tasks to be properly performed, a personal appearance by the accused person is necessary[14] and the court must be able to take a binding decision about his/her release. In *Ireland v UK*[15] the European Court made it clear that merely advising that there should be release, even if such advice is invariably followed, is not sufficient. The Commission has found a breach article 5(3) in two cases which challenged the statutory prohibition on bail for those with previous convictions for very serious offences if arrested for the same or a sim-

---

9   See paras 1.59 to 1.61.
10   (1994) 17 EHRR 539.
11   See Appendix A schedule 3.
12   Para 1.61.
13   (1979–80) 2 EHRR 417.
14   *Schiesser v Switzerland* Note 13 at para 31.
15   A/25 (1979–80) 2 EHRR 25.

ilar very serious offence, introduced by s25 of the Criminal Justice and Public Order Act 1994 (now repealed).[16]

Bail

7.13   Article 5(3) of the Convention provides that everyone arrested under article 5(1)(c) on suspicion of having committed an offence is entitled to 'trial within a reasonable time or to release pending trial'. Despite this wording, in *Wemhoff v Germany*[17] the European Court made it clear that under article 5(3) trial within a reasonable time and release pending trial are not alternatives. Unless good reasons can be established for refusing bail, there is a right to be released pending trial. And where bail is refused, pre-trial detention must not be prolonged beyond a reasonable time.

7.14   As the European Court observed in *Neumeister v Austria (No 1)*,[18] the purpose of article 5(3) is to require the provisional release of a person once his/her continuing detention ceases to be reasonable.[19] It follows that, under the Convention, the passage of time provides a basis for making further applications for bail.

7.15   The task of any court considering bail is to:

> ... examine all the facts arguing for or against the existence of a genuine requirement of public interest justifying, with due regard to the principle of the presumption of innocence, a departure from the rule of respect for individual liberty and set them out in their decisions on applications for release.'[20]

Only where there are 'relevant' and 'sufficient' reasons, should bail be refused.[21] And, in all cases, reasons should be given: a point emphasised in *Tomasi v France*[22] and, in *Yagci and Sargin v Turkey*[23] where the European Court was very sceptical about what it called 'stereotyped' reasons for refusing bail.

---

16   *CC v UK* and *BH v UK Commission* (30 June 1998); noted at [1991] EHRLR 210.
17   (1979–80) 1 EHRR 55.
18   (1979–80) 1 EHRR 91.
19   Ibid at para 7.
20   *Letellier v France* (1992) 14 EHRR 83 at para 35.
21   Wemhoff v Germany note 17.
22   (1993) 15 EHRR 1.
23   (1995) 20 EHRR 505.

7.16   In *Bezicheri v Italy*[24] the Court held that, since new issues might arise after the first consideration of bail, an opportunity to take proceedings to review the lawfulness of pre-trial detention had to be provided at reasonable intervals. Given the nature of pre-trial detention, the Court took the view that such intervals should be short; on the facts, an interval of one month was considered reasonable.

Grounds for refusing bail

7.17   The European Court and Commission have identified four grounds upon which pre-trial detention may be justified under the Convention:

1) fear of absconding;
2) interference with the course of justice;
3) the prevention of crime; and
4) the preservation of public order.

The mere fact that there are reasonable grounds for suspecting that a person has committed an offence is not enough. According to the European Court in *Letellier v France*:[25]

> The persistence of reasonable suspicion that the person arrested has committed an offence is a condition sine qua non for the validity of the continued detention, but, after a certain lapse of time, it no longer suffices.'[26]

Fear of absconding

7.18   Fear of absconding cannot be gauged solely on the basis of the severity of the sentence risked: at most, this is a factor to be taken into account when assessing whether any of the four valid grounds for refusing bail are made out. As the European Court stressed in *Letellier v France*,[27] fear of absconding:

> ... must be assessed with reference to a number of other relevant factors which may either confirm the existence of a danger of absconding or make it appear so slight that it cannot justify detention pending trial.[28]

24 (1990) 12 EHRR 210.
25 (1992) 14 EHRR 83.
26 Ibid at para 35.
27 Note 25.
28 Ibid at para 43.

7.19   In *W v Switzerland*[29] the Court emphasised that regard must also be had to the character of the person involved and his/her background, assets and links with the community. And in *Yagci and Sargin v Turkey*[30] and *Mansur v Turkey*[31] the Court found a violation of article 5(3) where the applicants were refused bail on the basis of a statutory presumption that those charged with serious offences were likely to abscond.

7.20   In each case, a general statement that the accused will abscond or engage in the prohibited activity is not enough; supporting evidence must be provided.[32] In *Stogmuller v Germany*[33] the European Court held that:

> There must be a whole set out circumstances ... which give reason to suppose that the consequences and hazards of flight will seem to him to be a lesser evil than continued imprisonment.[34]

Presumably, there must also be an opportunity for the defence to test such evidence as is adduced to justify pre-trial detention.

Interference with the course of justice

7.21   Interference with the course of justice can cover a wide range of conduct. However, general and abstract references to the possibility that there might be interference with the course of justice will not satisfy the strict requirements of article 5(3).[35] Moreover, in *Kemmache v France*[36] the European Court made it clear that where bail is withheld on this basis, pre-trial detention can be justified only so long as a real risk of such conduct persists. Once the risk subsides, release on bail should be ordered.

7.22   Where in the normal course of a criminal investigation evidence is collated and witness statements are taken, the risk of interference with the course of justice diminishes such that, as time passes, pre-trial detention on this basis becomes harder and harder to justify under article 5(3) of the Convention.[37] And where an accused person

29 (1994) 17 EHRR 60.
30 (1995) 20 EHRR 505.
31 (1995) 20 EHRR 535.
32 *Clooth v Belgium* (1992) 14 EHRR 717.
33 (1979–80) 1 EHRR 155.
34 Ibid at para 15.
35 *Clooth v Belgium* n32 at para 44.
36 (1992) 14 EHRR 520.
37 *W v Switzerland* (1994) 17 EHRR 60.

had previously been on bail without interfering with the course of justice, pre-trial detention will be extremely difficult to justify.[38]

The commission of further offences

7.23   The fear that an accused might commit further offences while on bail was recognised as a valid basis for pre-trial detention in *Matznetter v Austria*.[39] However, before pre-trial detention can be authorised on this basis, account must be taken of the background and personal circumstances of the accused.[40] Previous convictions which are not comparable, either in nature or seriousness, with the charges preferred against an accused, are not sufficient to justify a fear that further offences will be committed within the meaning of article 5(3).[41] And where medical reports suggest that further offences might committed by reason of the accused's psychiatric disposition, pre-trial detention will only be justified under article 5(3) of the Convention if appropriate therapeutic care is provided.[42]

The preservation of public order

7.24   The fourth ground upon which bail can be refused under the Convention – the preservation of public order – is unfamiliar to lawyers in the UK. The European Court has never really given a satisfactory definition of what 'public order' means in this context, but in *Letellier v France*[43] it accepted that:

> ... by reason of their particular gravity and public reaction to them, certain offences may give rise to a social disturbance capable of justifying pre-trial detention, at least for a time. In exceptional circumstances this factor may therefore be taken into account for the purposes of the Convention, in any event, in so far as domestic law recognises ... the notion of disturbance to public order caused by an offence.[44]

From this it seems that preservation of public order can only provide a very limited basis for pre-trial detention. It applies only in excep-

38 *Ringeisen v Austria* (1979–80) EHRR 455.
39 A/10 (1969) 1 EHRR 198 at para 9.
40 *Clooth v Belgium* (1991) 14 EHRR 717 at para 40.
41 Ibid.
42 Note 40.
43 (1992) 14 EHRR 83.
44 Ibid at para 51.

tional cases, where the offence charged is particularly grave such that a disruptive public reaction is likely. And, even then, pre-trial detention on this basis alone, should last only for a short period. Most significantly, where preservation of public order is not recognised in domestic law, it cannot provide a free-standing Convention-based justification for pre-trial detention.

Bail conditions

7.25   The approach of the European Court and Commission to the question of bail conditions is straightforward. If no 'relevant' and 'sufficient' reasons are advanced for refusing bail, an accused person should be released unconditionally. Where 'relevant' and 'sufficient' reasons for refusing bail do exist, an accused person should nonetheless be released on bail if the reasons for refusing bail can be met by the imposition of bail conditions.

7.26   So, for example, in *Wemhoff v Germany*,[45] the European Court held that where danger of absconding is the sole justification for refusing someone bail:

> ... his release pending trial must be ordered if it is possible to obtain from him guarantees that will ensure [his appearance at trial].[46]

However, a court considering bail is under a strict duty to make a careful assessment of the information it has about the personal circumstances and resources of an accused person so as not to set too high a surety or recognisance.[47] Setting the amount of a surety by reference to the losses allegedly caused by the person charged with an offence would violate the Convention.[48]

7.27   Sureties are not the only conditions that can be imposed. The surrender of a passport has been approved by the European Court;[49] and restrictions on movement have been approved by the European Commission.[50]

---

45   (1979–80) 1 EHRR 55.
46   Ibid at para 15.
47   *Schertenleib v Switzerland* (1980) 23 DR 137 at 196.
48   *Neumeister v Austria (No 1)* (1979–80) 1 EHRR 91.
49   *Stogmuller v Germany* (1979–80) 1 EHRR 155.
50   *Schmid v Austria* (1985) 44 DR 195.

The right to test the legality of arrest or detention before a court: article 5(4) of the Convention and bail

7.28 Article 5(4) of the Convention is also relevant to the question of pre-trial detention. It overlaps with article 5(3) and provides important procedural guarantees which will apply to any application for release pending trial, including ordinary bail proceedings.

7.29 Article 5(4) of the Convention provides that anyone who has been arrested or is detained has the right to take proceedings to test the lawfulness of his/her detention. Proceedings must be before a court and must be determined speedily. In addition, release must be ordered if the detention is not lawful.

7.30 Article 5(4) can be used where there is a question mark over the lawfulness of arrest and/or detention; or where it is clear that the initial basis for detention was lawful, but circumstances have changed. The significance of this is clear from the European Court's judgment in *Bezicheri v Italy*.[51] There the applicant had been arrested and remanded in custody and, having failed in his first application for release pending trial, he made a second application one month later. However, it took the investigating judge five and half months to consider this second application. The Court held that this violated article 5(4). Since new issues relevant to the question of bail might arise as time passed, the Court emphasised that:

> ... the nature of detention on remand calls for short intervals; there is an assumption in the Convention that detention on remand is to be of strictly limited duration ... because its raison d'etre is essentially related to the requirements of an investigation which is to be conducted with expedition.[52]

The fact that the original decision refusing bail could have been appealed was irrelevant.

Equality of arms under article 5(4)

7.31 Article 5(4) is also important in a number of other respects: in particular because it imports the principle of 'equality of arms'[53] at a very early stage in criminal proceedings. The early judgment of the

51 (1990) 12 EHRR 210.
52 Ibid at para 21.
53 See further chapter 8.

European Court in *Neumeister v Austria* (No 1)[54] to the effect that the 'equality of arms' principle could not be read into article 5(4) has clearly now been overruled. In *Woukam Moudefou v France*[55] the Commission considered that the 'fundamental procedural guarantees' required by article 5(4) included the provision of legal assistance and representation to make an application for release on bail effective. And in *Toth v Austria*[56] the European Court found a breach of article 5(4) because, in its view, proceedings in which the applicant's release pending trial was considered were not 'truly adversarial';[57] unlike prosecuting counsel, neither the applicant nor his lawyer had been present at an appeal against a decision to remand him in custody. The Court also made it clear that where appeal procedures exist in relation to decisions about pre-trial detention, the procedural guarantees at first instance apply with equal force on appeal.

Disclosure under article 5(4)

7.32   The case of *Lamy v Belgium*[58] dealt with the question of access to documents at an early stage. It overlaps with issues of disclosure[59] and may have considerable impact on UK law and practice (particularly in the magistrates' courts). The applicant was arrested under a warrant alleging fraud charges. Four days later he challenged his detention at first instance and, having failed to secure his release, he appealed the next day to the Court of Appeal. He complained to the European Court on the basis that he had not had access to the investigation file at either stage. At the heart of his complaint was the submission that 'truly adversarial proceedings' were not possible where the prosecution authorities could make submissions based on the full facts of the case but the defence only had access to the limited (and somewhat vague) information contained in the arrest warrant. Despite a rule in Belgium that the defence has no right of access to documents until at least 30 days after arrest, the European Court found a violation of article 5(4). In its view:

> Access to the documents was essential for the applicant at this crucial stage in the proceedings, when the court had to decide

---

54   (1979–80) 1 EHRR 91.
55   (1991) 13 EHRR 549.
56   (1992) 14 EHRR 551.
57   Ibid at para 84.
58   (1989) 11 EHRR 529.
59   See paras 7.54 to 7.67.

whether to remand him in custody or to release him. Such access would, in particular, have enabled counsel for [the applicant] to address the court on the matter of the co-defendants' statements and attitude. In the court's view, it was therefore essential to inspect the documents in question in order to challenge the lawfulness of the arrest warrant effectively.

The appraisal of the need for a remand in custody and the subsequent assessment of guilt are too closely linked for access to documents to be refused in the former case when the law requires it in the latter case.

Whereas Crown counsel was familiar with the whole file, the procedure did not afford the applicant an opportunity of challenging appropriately the reasons relied upon to justify a remand in custody. Since it failed to ensure equality of arms, the procedure was not truly adversarial.[60]

Since the Commission has established that adequate time and facilities must be allowed for article 5(4) applications,[61] not only must documents relevant to pre-trial detention be disclosed at an early stage, but also a reasonable period must be given to the applicant and his/her lawyer to study them.

Trial within a reasonable time

7.33 The right to trial within a reasonable time is guaranteed under article 5(3) of the Convention for those held in pre-trial detention. It overlaps with article 6(1), which provides a more general right to trial within a reasonable time in relation to the determination of any criminal charge. But the two regimes are not the same. Because it applies to exclusively to those who are deprived of their liberty before a determination of their guilt or innocence, article 5(3) requires a stricter timetable than that envisaged under article 6(1) for those released on bail.

7.34 Under article 5(3), the starting point for calculating whether there has been trial within a reasonable time is arrest or initial detention. It ends with the finding of guilt or innocence and sentencing at first instance.[62] Detention after conviction and sentence is not covered by article 5(3), but will usually be covered by article 6(1).[63]

60 *Lamy v Belgium* n58 at para 29.
61 *K v Austria* A/255-B (1993); unreported.
62 *B v Austria* (1990) 13 EHRR 20.
63 *Wemhoff v Germany* (1979–80) 1 EHRR 55.

7.35   The reasonable time guarantee in article 6(1) of the Convention begins to run as soon as a person is 'charged' within the meaning of the Convention.[64] In *Eckle v Germany*,[65] the European Court defined a 'charge' for the purposes of article 6(1) as 'the official notification given to an individual by the competent authority of an allegation that he has committed a criminal offence'.[66] In some instances, however, the Court has recognised that it may 'take the form of other measures which carry the implication of such an allegation and which likewise substantially affect the situation of the suspect':[67] an approach endorsed in the case of *Corigliano v Italy*.[68] Unlike the position under article 5(3), the period covered by article 6(1) covers the whole of the proceedings in issue, including appeal proceedings.

7.36   The purposes of article 5(3) and article 6(1) also differ. The purpose of article 5(3) is to ensure that no one spends too long in pre-trial detention. The purpose of article 6(1) is to prevent an accused person from remaining 'too long in a state of uncertainty about his fate'.[69]

7.37   In determining whether there has been trial within a reasonable time, the European Court has been reluctant to apply established or rigid criteria under article 5(3) or article 6(1). It has preferred to take a case by case approach. Relevant factors are extremely diverse and have included matters such as the actual length of any pre-trial detention, the relationship between any such detention and the likely penalty, the effect on the person detained,[70] the complexity of the case, the conduct of the accused, the progress of any investigations and the efficiency of the judicial authorities.

7.38   However, in *Wemhoff v Germany*[71] the European Court emphasised that, when pre-trial detention is in issue, a checklist approach is inappropriate. In each case:

> The Court must judge whether the reasons given by the national authorities to justify continued detention are relevant and sufficient

64 *Eckle v Germany* (1983) 5 EHRR 1.
65 Ibid.
66 Note 64 at para 73.
67 *Foti v Italy* (1983) 5 EHRR 313.
68 (1983) 5 EHRR 334.
69 *Stogmuller v Austria* (1979–80) 1 EHRR 155.
70 It has been suggested that detention on remand may never exceed the prison sentence likely to be incurred: S Trechsel in *The European System for the Protection of Human Rights* (Macdonald, Matscher and Petzold eds), Martinus Nijhoff Publishers, 1993.
71 (1979–80) 1 EHRR 55.

to show that detention was not unreasonably prolonged and contrary to article 5(3) of the Convention.[72]

Any time lost because an accused person has exercised legal remedies and/or rights of appeal provided for in domestic law will not exonerate the state unless such exercise amounts to an abuse of process.

7.39 Although the facts of the cases heard by the European Court have inevitably varied greatly, as a general rule delays of less than two years are unlikely to violate article 5(3) and the longest period found to be acceptable under article 6(1) has been just over seven years in *Neumeister v Austria (No 1)*[73], justified in the Court's view by its extraordinary complexity. However, the Court made it clear that seven years was an exceptionally long period which in most cases would be considered as having exceeded the reasonable time guarantee laid down in article 6(1) and found that the total of two years and four months spent by the applicant in pre-trial detention violated the stricter requirements of article 5(3). Where a person is detained on two separate occasions pending trial, these periods should be treated as cumulative when calculating time under article 5(3).[74]

7.40 In *X v UK*[75] the Commission took the view that an undertaking by the prosecution, on conditions, not to seek a trial on certain counts on an indictment is tantamount to dropping those charges. As a result, it held that the applicant could not bring a complaint of failure to determine criminal charges within a reasonable time under article 6(1) in respect of any period after such an undertaking had been given, nor of a failure to record a verdict on such charges.

Charge

7.41 The Convention does not lay down any procedure for charging an individual with criminal offences. However, both article 5(2) and article 6(3)(a) require certain information to be given at an early stage. Article 5(2) provides:

> Everyone who is arrested shall be informed promptly, in a language which he understands, of the reasons for his arrest and of any charge against him.

72 Ibid at para 12.
73 (1979–80) 1 EHRR 91.
74 *Kemmache v France* (1992) 14 EHRR 520.
75 (1981) 3 EHRR 271.

In *Fox, Campbell and Hartley v UK*[76] the European Court interpreted this as meaning that anyone who is arrested must be told:

> ... in simple, non-technical language that he can understand, the essential legal and factual grounds for his arrest, so as to be able, if he sees fit, to apply to a court to challenge its lawfulness.[77]

7.42   Where criminal proceedings are initiated, the requirements of article 5(2) are supplemented by those of article 6(3)(a) which provides that everyone charged with a criminal offence has the right:

> ... to be informed promptly, in a language which he understands and in detail, of the nature and cause of the accusation against him.

7.43   As noted above, the word 'charged' in this context means 'the official notification given to an individual by the competent authority of an allegation that he has committed a criminal offence'[78] or in certain circumstances the taking of 'other measures which carry the implication of such an allegation and which likewise substantially affect the situation of the suspect'.[79]

7.44   Since the purpose of article 6(3)(a) is to provide an accused with the information s/he needs to begin preparing a defence, the information required by it is 'more specific and more detailed' than the information needed under article 5(2), the purpose of which is to enable an arrested person to challenge the legality of his/her detention.[80] However, the question of precisely how much information must be given at the early stages of criminal proceedings is not clear.

7.45   In *Brozicek v Italy*[81] the European Court took the view that, in the context of charges of resisting police, assault and wounding, the following details were sufficient to fulfil the obligation under article 6(3)(a): a list of the offences of which the applicant had been accused, the place and date of those offences, extracts from the relevant articles of the criminal code and the victims' details. However, it may be that in cases where the offences charged involved less specific acts, more information will be required.

76   (1991) 13 EHRR 157.
77   Ibid at para 40.
78   Note 76 at para 73.
79   *Foti v Italy* (1990) 5 EHRR 313.
80   *GSM v Austria* (1983) 34 DR 119.
81   (1990) 12 EHRR 371.

7.46   Neither article 5(2) nor article 6(3)(a) expressly requires charges or information to be made in writing at an early stage. However in *Kamasinski v Austria*[82] the European Court recognised that a defendant not conversant with the national language might in fact be put at a disadvantage if s/he were not also provided with a written translation of a charge or indictment in a language s/he understood. On the facts, however, the Court accepted that oral translation of the indictment was sufficient.

Access to a lawyer[83]

7.47   Although article 6(3)(c) guarantees everyone charged[84] with a criminal offence the right to legal assistance,[85] it is silent on the question of when this right crystallises. In early cases before the Commission, the UK government argued that article 6(3)(c) should only apply when it was clear that a trial would take place, ie the point at which a person is actually charged or informed that s/he will be prosecuted.[86] However, that position is no longer sustainable.

7.48   In *Imbrioscia v Switzerland*[87] the European Court made it clear that there is nothing in article 6(3)(c) to prevent it from applying to pre-trial proceedings. In that case, the Court took the view that the manner in which it applied during investigatory questioning depended on the 'special features of the proceedings and the circumstances of the case'.[88] It is implicit in the Court's judgment in *Imbrioscia* that if the accused requests access to a lawyer (or a lawyer applies for access to his/her client), save in exceptional circumstances, the state authorities should prevent such access.

7.49   The question of access to a lawyer during police questioning was more directly addressed by the European Court in *Murray v UK*.[89] In that case, which primarily concerned the question of drawing adverse

---

82 (1991) 13 EHRR 36.
83 Legal aid and legal representation are dealt with in chapter 8 (fair trial guarantees) at paras 8.25 to 8.36.
84 The word 'charged' in this context does not necessarily correspond to its meaning in UK law. See paras 6.9 to 6.12.
85 With some exceptions.
86 *G v UK* (1983) 35 DR 75.
87 (1994) 17 EHRR 441.
88 Ibid at para 38.
89 (1996) 22 EHRR 29.

inferences from silence,[90] the applicant, who had been arrested under the Prevention of Terrorism (Temporary Provisions) Act 1989, was denied access to a lawyer for 48 hours during which period he was interviewed on 12 occasions. The Court began by observing that there was no dispute that article 6 applies even at the stage of preliminary investigations by the police.[91] While there may be some flexibility about precisely when it begins to apply, the Court held that where, under domestic law, consequences can flow from the attitude of an accused person during police questioning, 'article 6 will normally require the accused to benefit from the assistance of a lawyer' at that stage.[92]

7.50   However, this right may be subject to restriction for good cause. The question, in each case, is whether the restriction, in light of the entire proceedings, has deprived the accused of a fair hearing.[93] In *Murray v UK*[94] the Court maintained that where adverse inferences can be drawn from silence during police questioning, 'it is of paramount importance for the rights of the defence that an accused has access to a lawyer at the initial stages of police interrogation'.[95] Despite the government's assertion that access to a lawyer had been denied to prevent interference with the course of police investigations, the Court held that:

> ... under the [Criminal Evidence (Northern Ireland) Order 1988], at the beginning of police interrogation, an accused is confronted with a fundamental dilemma relating to his defence. If he chooses to remain silent, adverse inferences may be drawn against him in accordance with the provisions of the Order. On the other hand, if the accused opts to break his silence during the course of interrogation, he runs the risk of prejudicing his defence without necessarily removing the possibility of inferences being drawn against him.
>
> Under such conditions the concept of fairness enshrined in article 6 requires that the accused has the benefit of the assistance of a lawyer already at the initial stages of police interrogation. To deny access to a lawyer for the first 48 hours of police questioning, in a situation where the rights of the defence may well be irretrievably prejudiced, is – whatever the justification for such

90 See paras 9.60 to 9.74.
91 *Murray v UK* note 89 para 62.
92 Ibid at para 63.
93 Note 89 at para 62.
94 Note 89.
95 Note 89 at para 66.

denial – incompatible with the rights of the accused under article 6.[96]

7.51   Since the provisions relating to adverse inferences in the Criminal Justice and Public Order Act 1994 were modelled on those in the Criminal Evidence (Northern Ireland) Order 1988, it will be very difficult (if not impossible) to justify the denial of access to a lawyer before questioning in any criminal proceedings.

Lawyer/client communications

7.52   Lawyer/client communications are protected by article 6(3)(c) and article 8. In general they must be private, confidential and not subjected to restrictions. In *Schönenberger and Durmaz v Switzerland*[97] the European Court rejected the Swiss government's claim that it had intercepted a letter from a lawyer to his client advising him of his right to remain silent because the advice jeopardised the proper conduct of pending criminal proceedings.[98]

7.53   The notion of privacy and confidentiality was developed by the European Court in *S v Switzerland*[99] where almost all communications between the applicant and his lawyer were overseen or intercepted. The European Court noted that, unlike some national laws and international instruments,[100] the European Convention did not expressly guarantee the right of a person charged with a criminal offence to communicate with defence counsel out of hearing of a third person. However, expressly drawing on article 93 of the *Standard Minimum Rules for the Treatment of Prisoners* (which have been annexed to a Council of Europe resolution[101]) and article 3(2) of the *European Agreement Relating to Persons Participating in Proceedings of the European Commission and Court of Human Rights*, the Court held that:

> ... an accused's right to communicate with his advocate out of the hearing of a third person is one of the basic requirements of a fair trial in a democratic society and follows from article 6(3)(c) of the Convention. If a lawyer were unable to confer with his client and receive confidential instructions from him without such

96 Note 89 at para 66.
97 (1989) 11 EHRR 202.
98 See also *Campbell v UK* (1993) 15 EHRR 137.
99 (1992) 14 EHRR 670.
100 See, for example, article 8(2)(d) of the *American Convention on Human Rights*.
101 Resolution (73)5 of the Committee of Ministers.

surveillance, his assistance would lose much of its usefulness, whereas the Convention is intended to guarantee rights that are practical and effective.[102]

The Court accepted that confidentiality could be restricted if, for example, there was a real risk of collusion between a client and his/her lawyer. However, the mere risk of collaboration between defence counsel is not enough.[103]

Disclosure

7.54   The Convention contains no explicit right to disclosure in criminal proceedings. However, the European Court and Commission have read such a right into the fair trial guarantees under article 6(1) and the more specific requirement under article 6(3)(b) that everyone charged with a criminal offence 'have adequate time and facilities for the preparation of his defence'. In addition, as noted above,[104] article 5(4) can require speedy access to documents where the defendant is being held in custody.

7.55   The question of disclosure was first considered in detail[105] by the Commission in *Jespers v Belgium*[106] where the applicant complained that a 'special folder' held by the public prosecutor's department had not been properly disclosed to him in violation of articles 6(1) and 6(3)(b). The Commission began its analysis by observing the requirement of 'equality of arms' between the prosecution and the defence. Noting the considerable resources and powers available to the investigating and prosecuting authorities, the Commission took the view that equality of arms could be achieved in criminal proceedings only if: (a) the authorities were under a duty to 'gather evidence in favour of the accused as well as evidence against him'[107] and (b) the defence had access to relevant material before trial.[108]

7.56   In particular, the Commission emphasised that the 'facilities' which everyone charged with a criminal offence should enjoy under article 6(3)(b) included:

102 Note 99 at para 48.
103 Note 99 at para 49.
104 See para 7.32.
105 Disclosure was considered in general terms in Appln 1816/63, 7 Yearbook 205 and in *Haase v Germany* (1978) 11 DR 78.
106 (1981) 27 DR 61.
107 Ibid at para 55.
108 Note 106 at para 56.

> ... the opportunity to acquaint himself, for the purposes of preparing his defence, with the results of investigations carried out throughout the proceedings.[109]

7.57 For the Commission this right was to be applied broadly. It mattered little by whom, and when, investigations had been ordered or under whose authority they were carried out. And the duty to permit a defendant to have access to the results of investigations applied at all stages, not just in relation to preliminary investigations.[110]

7.58 Despite the qualification of the word 'facilities' in article 6(3)(b) by the word 'adequate', the Commission in *Jespers* insisted that the accused must be provided with facilities 'which assist or may assist him in his defence'.[111] This means that a defendant must:

> ... have at his disposal, for the purposes of exonerating himself or of obtaining a reduction in his sentence, all relevant elements that have been or could be collected by the competent authorities.[112]

A point recently confirmed in *Cannon v UK*.[113] If the 'element' in question is a document, access to that document is a necessary 'facility' if 'it concerns acts of which the defendant is accused, the credibility of testimony etc'.[114] And, in the Commission's view, where the applicant had been given no access at all to the 'special folder' in question, it was unrealistic, and unfair, to expect him to specify which documents he wished to see.[115]

7.59 The Commission's starting-point was adopted by the European Court in *Edwards v UK*.[116] In that case, the applicant complained that article 6(3)(b) had been violated because of the failure of the police at his trial for robbery and burglary to disclose (a) the fact that one of the victims, who had made a statement that she thought she would be able to recognise her assailant, had failed to identify the applicant from a police photograph album and (b) the existence of fingerprints which had been found at the scene of the crime.

7.60 Recognising that the guarantee of adequate facilities in article 6(3)(b) is a specific aspect of the wider right to a fair trial under article 6(1), the Court held that:

109 Note 106 at para 56.
110 Note 106 at para 56.
111 Note 106 at para 57.
112 Note 106 at para 58.
113 Appln 29335/95, 17 January 1997 (unreported).
114 Note 106 at para 58.
115 Note 106 at para 60.
116 (1993) 15 EHRR 417.

... it is a requirement of fairness under article 6(1) ... that the prosecution authorities disclose to the defence all material evidence for or against the accused and that the failure to do so in the present case gave rise to a defect in the trial proceedings.[117]

Since, however, following an independent police inquiry the case had been referred back to the Court of Appeal which had specifically considered the question of non-disclosure and concluded that the applicant's conviction should not be quashed,[118] the European Court found no violation of the Convention.

7.61   The European Court re-examined the question of disclosure in *Bendenoun v France*,[119] a case involving very special facts. The applicant, a company director, was involved in three sets of proceedings – customs, tax and criminal proceedings – which all, more or less, progressed in parallel. In the customs proceedings, the applicant was given access to all documents. In the tax proceedings, in which he was challenging a supplementary tax assessment, he was denied access to a customs report, which the authorities refused to disclose. But in the criminal proceedings, the same report was available to his lawyer throughout the investigatory stages. The applicant complained to the European Court on the basis that the non-disclosure of the customs file in the tax proceedings violated the principle of equality of arms under article 6 of the Convention.

7.62   The Court considered that the tax proceedings involved 'criminal charges' within the meaning of article 6(3)(b),[120] but found no violation of the Convention. The Court noted that the authorities had disclosed all those documents from the file which had been relied upon in the proceedings and that the rest of the file had not been before the domestic court dealing with the tax matter. While the Court accepted that, in itself, this did not necessarily preclude the possibility that disclosure should be made, it held that it did put the applicant under an obligation to specify why he wanted further documents.[121]

7.63   The extent to which the Court's approach in *Bendenoun* qualifies the Commission's approach in *Jespers* is unclear. Clearly the Court came to its decision on the basis that, since the applicant was seeking

---

117 Ibid at para 36.
118 The Court of Appeal had expressly referred to article 6(1)when considering the question of non-disclosure.
119 (1994) 18 EHRR 54.
120 See paras 6.13 to 617.
121 Note 119 at para 62.

documents not relied upon by the prosecution, he had to specify, at least in general terms, why he wanted them. However, the Court was undoubtedly influenced by the fact that, having already had access to the same documents in the file in the parallel criminal proceedings, the applicant was in a perfectly good position to do so. It may be that where a defendant has no way of knowing what further documents are held by the authorities, the broader approach favoured by the Commission should prevail.

7.64   In some cases, disclosure to a defendant's lawyer might suffice for article 6(3)(b) purposes. In *Kamasinski v Austria*[122] the Court found no incompatibility between the Austrian Code of Criminal Procedure, which restricted the right to inspect and make copies of the court file to the defendant's lawyer, and the Convention. The Austrian Code made an exception for unrepresented defendants and this issue arose in *Foucher v France*[123] where the applicant and his father were charged with having used insulting and threatening words and behaviour towards public service employees. The applicant decided to conduct his own case, and sent his mother to the police court registry to consult the case file and procure copies of the relevant documents. This was refused to her on the ground that copies could not be issued to individuals. The applicant met with similar refusal when he went in person to the registry. At the hearing, both defendants argued that the proceedings were unlawful due to the denial of access to the case file and documents. The court of first instance accepted this submission, but it was overturned on appeal.

7.65   The European Court recognised that the principle in *Kamasinski* did not apply on the facts. It cited with approval the decision of the first-instance court that 'the defendants should have been allowed access to their case file in order to prepare their defence [as] the value of such access is sufficiently demonstrated by the use legal representatives make of it...'[124] Since such access had been denied to the applicant, article 6(3)(b) had been violated.

7.66   In *Hardiman v UK*[125] the European Commission held that there was no duty to disclose a co-defendant's prison psychiatric reports prepared for the trial judge. Given the practice of not referring to such reports unless a medical issue arose and bearing in mind that the co-defendant had not been cautioned before meeting the psychi-

---

122 (1991) 13 EHRR 36.
123 (1998) 25 EHRR 234.
124 Ibid at para 36.
125 Appl 25935/94 [1996] EHRLR 425.

atrist and did not have a solicitor present, the Commission found that non-disclosure was not unfair or arbitrary.

7.67   In *Preston and Another v UK*,[126] it came to light during the applicants' trial that their telephone conversations had been intercepted pursuant to a warrant issued under the Interception of Communications Act 1985. The applicants applied for disclosure of the records, but the Court of Appeal and House of Lords took the view that such disclosure would breach the terms of the 1985 Act. The European Commission rejected the applicants' complaints under article 6 on the basis that they had failed to show how access to the records of their telephone conversations by the police prior to their arrest had any effect thereafter on the proceedings or in what respect the material was used to their detriment in preparing the prosecution case, other than to provide the prosecuting authorities with a starting point from which to gather admissible evidence against them.

Public interest immunity

7.68   The European Court has yet to decide whether withholding material from the defence in criminal proceedings on grounds of public interest immunity can be compatible with article 6 of the Convention. The issue arose in *Edwards v UK*[127] where the applicant complained that the police report into his case which led to its reference back to the Court of Appeal[128] had not been disclosed to him. When the applicant's lawyers asked the police for disclosure of the report, this was refused on the grounds of public interest immunity. The fact that the applicant's lawyers did not then apply to the Court of Appeal for an order that the report be disclosed was fatal in the judgment of the majority in the European Court. In their view:

> It is no answer to the failure to make such an application that the Crown might have resisted by claiming public interest immunity since such a claim would have been for the Court to determine.[129]

However, as Judge Pettiti (dissenting) pointed out, the European Court's silence in *Edwards* is not to be understood as approval of the principle of public interest immunity. He took the view that:

---

126 Appl 24193/94 [1997] EHRLR 695.
127 (1993) 15 EHRR 417.
128 The Carmichael Report.
129 *Edwards v UK* n126 at para 38.

... once there are criminal proceedings and an indictment, the whole of the evidence, favourable or unfavourable to the defendant, must be communicated to the defence in order to be the subject of adversarial argument in accordance with article 6 of the Convention.[130]

On examination of the competing arguments for and against disclosure, Judge Pettiti decided that the report should not have been protected by any immunity, and should have been disclosed. He concluded by remarking that 'Under the European Convention an old doctrine such as that of "public interest immunity" must be revised in accordance with article 6'.[131]

7.69   Public interest immunity was one of a number of issues considered by the European Commission in *Cannon v UK*.[132] There the applicant complained that during her trial for blackmail, the prosecution made an ex parte application for non-disclosure of certain information relating to two principal prosecution witnesses on public interest immunity grounds, viz they were police informants. She also complained that further information, which came to light after her trial but before her appeal, was not disclosed to her. For the Commission, the role of the domestic courts in ensuring a fair trial was pivotal. In its judgment, the Court of Appeal's conclusion that disclosure would have made no difference to the verdict was not unfair nor was it arbitrary.

7.70   However, the Commission in *Cannon v UK* did not explicitly address the general issue of public interest immunity nor the particular complaint that ex parte applications for non-disclosure on public interest immunity grounds were incompatible with article 6. These issues were considered by the Commission in *Rowe and Davis v UK*,[133] where the applicants alleged that article 6 prohibits the withholding of relevant evidence from a defendant on the grounds of public interest, and that the ex parte procedure affords the defence insufficient opportunity to make informed representations and is in breach of the audi alteram partem principle.

7.71   Although the question of public interest immunity has arisen in the context of civil proceedings before the European Court and Commission, no ruling directly addressing the issue has yet been

130 Ibid at p 433.
131 Ibid at p 435.
132 Appl 29335/95 [1997] EHRLR 280.
133 Appl 28910/95.

given. However, in *Tinnelly & Sons Ltd v UK*,[134] in the context of a challenge under the Fair Employment (Northern Ireland) Act 1976, the Commission found it difficult to reconcile the 'cumbersome procedure' used by the executive (including the use of public interest immunity certificates) with the notion of effective access to court. In the same case, albeit not specifically on the question of public interest certificates, the European Court noted that in other contexts it had been possible to modify judicial procedures in such a way as to safeguard national security concerns about the nature and sources of intelligence information and yet accord the individual a substantial degree of procedural justice.[135]

Time and facilities for preparation of defence

7.72   Article 6(3)(b) guarantees the right to everyone charged with a criminal offence to have adequate time and facilities for the preparation of his/her defence. In a series of cases before the European Court and Commission, applicants have complained that this provision has been breached by the late production of prosecution evidence or a late change of counsel. Since every case is to be determined on its facts, no hard and fast rules apply about how much time is needed. The following cases provide a rough guide.

7.73   In *X v Austria*[136] the Commission found that a period of 17 days (including ten working days) was sufficient to enable the applicant and his lawyer to prepare for trial, even in a 'fairly complex' case. Similarly, in *Perez Mahia v Spain*[137] the Commission rejected as inadmissible the applicant's complaint that he did not have adequate time and facilities to prepare his defence. His lawyer had been appointed ten days before the hearing, had been given access to the court file and was in a position to deal with the witnesses at trial.

7.74   In *Kremzow v Austria*[138] the position was less clear cut. The Commission found that three weeks to respond to a document prepared by the Attorney-General violated article 6(3)(b). However, the European Court disagreed. In its view, since the document had only 49 pages, three weeks was sufficient.

134 8 April 1997 (merits) [1997] EHRLR 663.
135 *Tinnelly & Sons Ltd v UK*, Judgment 19 July 1998, para 78.
136 (1979) 15 DR 160.
137 (1987) 9 EHRR 91.
138 (1994) 17 EHRR 322.

7.75   Nonetheless, where there is a very late change of lawyer and it is clear that s/he has not had time to properly prepare a case, the domestic authorities are under a duty to take positive measures to ensure that his/her obligations to the defendant are properly fulfilled. Where a lawyer receives instructions on the day of trial, an adjournment may well be needed.[139]

Pre-trial publicity

7.76   Pre-trial publicity raises a number of issues under the Convention. So far the European Court and Commission have only been concerned with the inter-relationship between article 6(1) (fair trial), article 6(2) (the presumption of innocence) and article 10 (freedom of expression). However, it is conceivable that issues under article 8 (privacy) will also arise in the future.

7.77   As a general principle both the European Court and Commission have accepted that pre-trial publicity can adversely affect the fairness of criminal proceedings, particularly where such publicity is instigated or encouraged by those in authority. For that reason press freedom can be restricted under article 10(2), either to protect the rights of others or to maintain the authority and impartiality of the judiciary. In *Hodgson, Woolf Productions and the NUJ v UK*[140] the Commission made it clear that the need to ensure a fair trial and protect members of the jury from exposure to prejudicial influences corresponds to a 'pressing social need'[141] capable of justifying restrictions on press freedom under article 10 of the Convention, so long as any such restrictions are 'proportionate'. Similarly in *Crociani and Others v Italy*[142] the Commission accepted that press freedom:

> ... may be limited by the state's obligation to ensure that every person charged with a criminal offence has a fair trial and not what is sometimes referred to as a 'press trial'.[143]

And on several occasions the Commission has accepted that public comment which creates an atmosphere of animosity or a virulent press campaign can prejudice a fair trial.[144]

139 *Goddi v Italy* (1984) 6 EHRR 457, para 31.
140 (1988) 10 EHRR 503.
141 For a definition of this expression see paras 4.63 to 4.64.
142 (1980) 22 DR 147.
143 Ibid at para 21.
144 *Berns and Ewert v Luxembourg* (1991) 68 DR 137.

7.78   However, the Strasbourg bodies have maintained that neither article 6(1) nor article 6(2) can prevent either the press or public authorities (in this context usually the police or other investigating agencies) from informing the public about criminal investigations that are in progress. In *Worm v Austria*,[145] the European Court remarked that:

> There is a general recognition of the fact that the courts cannot operate in a vacuum. Whilst the courts are the forum for the determination of a person's guilt or innocence on a criminal charge, this does not mean that there can be no prior or contemporaneous discussion of the subject-matter of criminal trials elsewhere, be it in specialised journals, in the general press or amongst the public at large.
>
> Provided that it does not overstep the bounds imposed in the interests of the proper administration of justice, reporting, including comment, on court proceedings contributes to their publicity and is thus perfectly consonant with the requirement under article 6(1) of the Convention that hearings be public. Not only do the media have the task of imparting such information and ideas; the public has a right to receive them.

In the context of that case, where the applicant (a journalist) had been penalised for publishing a highly critical article about the criminal trial of the former Vice-Chancellor in Austria in which he stated that he was guilty, the Court added:

> ... public figures are entitled to the enjoyment of the guarantees of a fair trial set out in article 6, which in criminal proceedings include the right to an impartial tribunal, on the same basis as every other person. This must be borne in mind by journalists when commenting on pending criminal proceedings since the limits of permissible comment may not extend to statements which are likely to prejudice, whether intentionally or not, the chances of a person receiving a fair trial or to undermine the confidence of the public in the role of the courts in the administration of criminal justice.[146]

This passage tends to suggest, at least from an article 10 perspective,[147] the test is whether a publication is likely to prejudice a fair trial, not whether it actually does so.

---

145 (1998) 25 EHRR 454.

146 Ibid at para 50.

147 From an article 6(1) perspective see *X v Norway* Appl 3444/67 (1970) 35 CD 37, which may now have to be reconsidered.

7.79   Discretion and circumspection in relation to pre-trial publicity are, therefore, required. In *Allanet de Ribemont v France*[148] an announcement by the Minister of Justice and a senior police officer, soon after his arrest that the applicant was one of the instigators of the murder of an MP was found by the European Court to have overstepped the mark and violated both article 6(1) and 6(2) of the Convention.[149]

7.80   Whether the case is to be heard by a judge or a jury is relevant to the question of prejudice. Rejecting claims by applicants who had been described as 'bandits', 'criminals' and 'gangs of murderers' in the press, the Commission in *Ensslin and Others v Germany*[150] remarked that they had been 'tried by professional judges and not by a jury, which by its nature is more easily influenced'.[151]

7.81   The Commission has also stressed the need to consider each case in its entirety, which will usually mean waiting until criminal proceedings have concluded.[152] And in *Ensslin and others v Germany*,[153] it drew a sharp distinction between assertions of guilt and more general statements about the general character of the accused such as his/her dangerousness, previous convictions and reaction upon arrest.[154]

---

148 (1995) 20 EHRR 557.
149 Although, in fact, the criminal proceedings were subsequently dropped against the applicant. See *Hall v UK* [1998] EHRLR 215 on coroners' statement.
150 (1978) 14 DR 64.
151 Ibid at para 15.
152 *Berns and Ewert v Luxembourg* (1991) 68 DR 137.
153 Note 150.
154 Note 150 at at para 15.

CHAPTER 8

Fair trial guarantees in criminal cases

8.1   Introduction

8.4   An independent and impartial court

8.13   The right to a public hearing

8.19   The right to 'participate effectively' in criminal proceedings

8.23   Trial in absentia

8.25   Legal aid

8.30   Legal representation

8.37   Interpreters and translations

8.42   The burden of proof

8.48   The standard of proof

8.50   Changing plea

8.51   Reasons

8.52   Costs in criminal cases

8.55   International co-operation in criminal matters

8.57   Double jeopardy

8.59   Amicus lawyers, intervening parties and clerks in magistrates' courts

Introduction

8.1   Article 6 of the Convention guarantees the right to a fair and public hearing in the determination of any criminal charge. The object and purpose of this provision is 'to enshrine the fundamental principle of the rule of law'.[1] It is to be interpreted broadly. For the European Court:

> ... a restrictive interpretation of article 6(1) – notably in regard to observance of the fundamental principle of the impartiality of the courts – would not be consonant with the object and purpose of the provision, bearing in mind the prominent place which the right to a fair trial holds in a democratic society within the meaning of the Convention.[2]

Consistent with this approach, the evolution of the case-law of the Strasbourg institutions reflects 'the increased sensitivity of the public to the fair administration of justice'.[3]

8.2   The principle of 'equality of arms' underpins article 6 and provides the basis for a number of specific rights set out in article 6(3), including the right to legal representation. However, 'it is only one feature of the wider concept of fair trial'.[4] Similarly, article 6(3) is not intended as an exhaustive list of the rights of the defence. It merely exemplifies the minimum guarantees which must be afforded to a defendant in criminal proceedings. The European Court and Commission have frequently read further rights into the Convention; for example, the right to an oral hearing or the right to participate effectively in criminal proceedings.[5]

8.3   Issues relating solely to evidence, such as the article 6(3)(d) right to examine prosecution witnesses, are dealt with in chapter 9 (Evidence in criminal cases). The fair trial guarantees of article 6 apply to children. Additional guarantees may also apply and these are dealt with in chapter 20.

---

1   *Salabiaku v France* (1991) 13 EHRR 379.
2   *Delcourt v Belgium* (1979–80) 1 EHRR 355.
3   *Borgers v Belgium* (1993) 15 EHRR 92 at para 24.
4   *Delcourt* (1979–80) 1 EHRR 355 at para 26.
5   Which may require the provision of a court-room with good acoustics: *Stanford v UK* (1994); see also *T and V v UK* [1998] EHRLR 484.

An independent and impartial court

8.4   The right guaranteed by article 6(1) is to a fair and public hearing 'by an independent and impartial tribunal established by law'. The requirement of independence has been interpreted to mean that the courts must be independent of both the executive and the parties.[6]

8.5   This independence must be institutional and functional. However, the Convention does not require trial by jury in criminal matters.[7] Nor does it prescribe any particular structure for judicial bodies. But, where jurors or lay judges are involved in the determination of guilt or innocence, the European Court's case-law on the independence and impartiality of judges applies equally to them.

8.6   To ascertain whether a court or tribunal meets the requirements of independence, regard must be had to the manner of appointment of its members and the duration of their term of office,[8] the existence of guarantees against outside pressures[9] and the question whether the body presents 'an appearance of independence'.[10] However, the fact that the members of a court or tribunal are appointed by the executive is not, in itself, incompatible with the Convention.[11] Nor does a judge's independence depend on appointment for life.[12] The executive may issue guidelines to members of a court or tribunal about the performance of their functions, so long as any such guidelines are not, in reality, instructions.[13]

8.7   The requirement of impartiality overlaps with that of independence. In order to determine whether this requirement is met, the European Court has developed a test that is both subjective and objective:

> Whilst impartiality normally denotes absence of prejudice or bias, its existence or otherwise can, notably under [article] 6(1) of the Convention, be tested in a variety of ways. A distinction can be drawn in this context between a subjective approach, that is

6 *Ringeissen v Austria* (1979–80) 1 EHRR 455 at para 95.

7 *X and Y v Ireland* (1981) 22 DR 51 at p 73.

8 *Le Compte, Van Leuven and De Meyere v Belgium* (1982) 4 EHRR 1.

9 *Piersack v Belgium* (1983) 5 EHRR 169 at para 27.

10 *Delcourt v Belgium* (1979–80) 1 EHRR 355 at para 31; *Campbell and Fell v UK* (1985) 7 EHRR 165 at para 78.

11 *Campbell and Fell* note 10 at para 79.

12 *Engel and Others v Netherlands* (1979–80) 1 EHRR 647.

13 *Campbell and Fell* note 10 at para 79.

endeavouring to ascertain the personal conviction of a given judge in a given case, and the objective approach, that is determining whether he offered guarantees sufficient to exclude any legitimate doubt in this respect.[14]

For subjective impartiality to be made out, proof of actual bias is needed: the European Court has repeatedly emphasised that 'the personal impartiality of a judge is presumed until there is proof to the contrary'.[15]

8.8   The test of objective impartiality is less strict and has been fashioned on the maxim *justice must not only be done: it must be seen to be done*.[16] It requires a determination of whether, quite apart from a judge's personal conduct, there are 'ascertainable facts which may raise doubts as to his impartiality'.[17] If there is a legitimate reason to fear a lack of impartiality, the judge must withdraw. And, while not determinative, the standpoint of the defendant is important in this assessment.[18]

8.9   The procedure for determining impartiality is as important as the test itself. Once a defendant has raised the issue, it must be investigated unless it is 'manifestly devoid of merit'.[19] The refusal of a French court to take note of the applicant's complaint that a juror had made a racist remark outside court led to a finding that article 6(1) had been violated in *Remli v France*.[20] It was not sufficient for the court to assert that it had no jurisdiction to enquire into events outside its precinct. However, article 6(1) does not require the rule governing the secrecy of jury deliberations in the UK to be breached.[21]

8.10   On the other hand, where a court in domestic proceedings has conducted an inquiry into an allegation of bias and satisfied itself that the defendant had a fair trial, the European Court and Commission will be very reluctant to intervene. In *Gregory v UK*[22] a note was passed from the jury after it had retired to consider its verdict stating 'Jury showing racial overtones. One member to be excused'. The trial

---

14 *Piersack v Belgium* (1983) 5 EHRR 169 at para 30.
15 *Hauschildt v Denmark* (1990) 12 EHRR 266 at para 47.
16 Quoted and adopted by the European Court in *Delcourt v Belgium* (1979–80) 1 EHRR 355.
17 *Hauschildt v Denmark* n15 at para 48.
18 Ibid at para 48.
19 *Remli v France* (1996) 22 EHRR 253 at para 48. Failure to challenge a judge at first instance does not amount to waiver: *Algar v Spain* [1999] EHRLR 212.
20 (1996) 22 EHRR 253.
21 *Gregory v UK* (1997) 25 EHRR 577 at para 44.
22 Note 21.

judge showed the note to the prosecution and defence and subsequently warned the jury to try the case according to the evidence and put aside prejudice. In the European Court's view, that was sufficient for article 6(1) purposes. It found significant the fact that defence counsel had not pressed for discharge of the jury or for asking them in open court whether they were capable of continuing and returning a verdict on the evidence alone.[23] The European Court distinguished the case from *Remli v France*[24] on the basis that:

> In that case, the trial judges failed to react to an allegation that an identifiable juror had been overheard to say that he was a racist. In the present case, the judge was faced with an allegation of jury racism which, although vague and imprecise, could not be said to be devoid of substance. In the circumstances, he took sufficient steps to check that the court was established as an impartial tribunal within the meaning of article 6(1) of the Convention and he offered sufficient guarantees to dispel any doubts in this regard.[25]

Much of the case-law on impartiality has concerned the position of judges who perform more than one function in a criminal prosecution. For example, in *Piersack v Belgium*[26] the European Court found a violation of the Convention where the judge who tried the applicant had previously been a member of the department which had investigated the applicant's case and initiated the prosecution against him.

8.11   Similarly, a number of cases have concerned judges who have taken decisions concerning key issues – for example, bail, legal representation and disclosure – prior to trial. As a general rule, so long as any pre-trial involvement is limited to case supervision, there will be no breach of article 6(1). However, any decision which involves a determination, or near determination, of the merits will be vulnerable to challenge. In *Hauschildt v Denmark*[27] the European Court found a violation of the Convention where the judge who tried the applicant had previously found a 'particularly confirmed suspicion of guilt' during a succession of bail applications.

8.12   The mere fact that a judge has had some previous involvement with the accused is not sufficient to breach article 6(1). In *Brown v*

---

23 Ibid at para 46.
24 Note 20.
25 *Gregory v UK* at para 49. See also *Reid v UK* [1998] EHRLR 211 for civil proceedings.
26 (1983) 5 EHRR 169.
27 (1990) 12 EHRR 266.

UK^{28} the Commission rejected a complaint where one of the judges in the Criminal Division of the Court of Appeal who refused the applicant leave to appeal against conviction had previously granted an injunction preventing him from drawing monies from his bank account. In the Commission's view:

> having regard to the difference between the two decisions the fact that [the judge] had granted the injunction could ... not be held to make him biased, or make him appear biased, when deciding the application for leave to appeal.

Arguably the Commission adopted the wrong test (it specifically referred to the need for evidence of bias), but it is doubtful whether the outcome would have been different if the proper test had been applied.

The right to a public hearing

8.13   The purpose of the right to a public hearing, enshrined in article 6(1), is 'to protect litigants from the administration of justice in secret with no public scrutiny'.[29] In the European Court's view, publicity is conducive to fairness and provides one of the means by which the public's confidence in the courts may be maintained.[30]

8.14   However, in article 6(1), the right to a public hearing is not unqualified:

> The press and public may be excluded from all or part of the trial in the interest of morals, public order or national security in a democratic society, where the interest of juveniles or the protection of the private life of the parties so require, or to the extent strictly necessary in the opinion of the court in special circumstances where publicity would prejudice the interests of justice.

In the case of *Campbell and Fell v UK*[31] the European Court accepted that prison disciplinary proceedings could be conducted inside a prison with no public access for 'reasons of public order and security'.

8.15   However, the Court's judgment in *Campbell and Fell* cannot justify the general exclusion of the public in ordinary criminal proceedings purely on the basis of concerns about public order or security. As the Court noted in that case:

28   (1986) 8 EHRR 272. But see also *Algar v Spain* n19, a court decision going the other way.
29   *Pretto v Italy* (1984) 6 EHRR 182.
30   *Axen v Germany* (1984) 6 EHRR 195.
31   (1985) 7 EHRR 165.

... ordinary criminal proceedings – which may well concern dangerous individuals or necessitate the production of a prisoner before the court – nearly always take place in public, notwithstanding the attendant security problems, the possible propagation of malicious allegations and the wishes of the accused.[32]

8.16 On the facts, however, it was persuaded by the government's arguments that prison disciplinary proceedings occasioned difficulties of greater magnitude than those that arise in ordinary criminal proceedings.

8.17 The matter arose in a different way in *Atkinson, Crook and the Independent v UK*,[33] where the applicants, two journalists and a national newspaper, complained that their article 10 rights were infringed by the decision of a trial judge in criminal proceedings to hold sentencing proceedings in camera. They relied on the principle enunciated by the Court in *Gaskin v UK*[34] and *Leander v Sweden*[35] that 'the right to freedom to receive information basically prohibits a government from restricting a person from receiving information that others wish or may be willing to impart to him'. However, the Commission found that this principle did not apply with the same force in the context of court proceedings. Since article 6(1) makes express reference to the possibility that criminal proceedings may in certain specified circumstances take place in camera, the rights of the defendant and the interests of justice must each be given particular weight.

8.18 The requirement that 'judgment shall be pronounced publicly' has not been interpreted literally. Although not a criminal case, one of the questions in the case of *Pretto and Others v Italy*[36] was whether depositing a judgment in the domestic court's registry, with written notification of its operative provisions to the parties, but without a reading in open court, was enough to comply with article 6(1). Taking into account the various practices in the contracting states, the European Court held that it was. Whether the same practice in criminal proceedings would escape challenge is questionable. As the Court emphasised in *Pretto*, '... in each case the form of publicity to be given to a judgment must be assessed in the light of the special features of the proceedings in question and by reference to the object

---

32 Ibid at para 87.
33 (1990) 67 DR 244.
34 (1990) 12 EHRR 36.
35 (1987) 9 EHRR 433.
36 (1984) 6 EHRR 182.

and purpose of article 6(1).'[37] If no measure at all were taken to publish a judgment, article 6(1) would undoubtedly be violated.[38]

The right to 'participate effectively' in criminal proceedings

8.19   On several occasions the European Court has recognised the right of a defendant to participate effectively in criminal proceedings. Fundamental to such effective participation is presence:

> ... it flows from the notion of a fair trial that a person charged with a criminal offence should, as a general principle, be entitled to be present at the trial hearing.[39]

Consequently, the state is under a positive duty to take steps to ensure that defendants can exercise this right.

8.20   Effective notification of a hearing to both the defendant and his/her lawyer is one such step.[40] In addition, it was implicitly recognised in *Goddi v Italy*[41] that where a defendant is held in custody and the authorities have notice that he wishes to be present at a hearing in criminal proceedings, they should take steps to get him there.[42]

8.21   However, the right to be present at trial is not absolute. In *Ensslin and Others v Germany*,[43] the applicants were unable to attend some parts of their trial because, as a result of their hunger strike, they were medically unfit to do so. The Commission recognised that 'under article 6(3)(c), a criminal trial may not take place without the defence having the opportunity to present its arguments adequately'[44] but nonetheless held that:

> In the circumstances, the judge was able to make use of the only means at his disposal for preventing the proceedings from grinding to a halt, without however placing the defence at any disadvantage, their lawyers being present and having practically unlimited opportunities for contact with their clients.[45]

---

37 Ibid at para 26.
38 *Campbell and Fell v UK* (1984) 7 EHRR 165.
39 *Ekbetani v Sweden* (1991) 13 EHRR 504.
40 *Goddi v Italy* (1984) 6 EHRR 457.
41 Ibid.
42 Note 40 at para 29.
43 (1978) 14 DR 64.
44 Ibid at para 21.
45 Note 43 at para 22.

In addition, the right to be present at trial can be waived. But only where waiver is unequivocal. Therefore, it is for the state authorities to show that an absent defendant was aware of the proceedings against him/her and that adequate steps have been taken to trace him/her.[46]

8.22 The right to participate effectively is a broad right extending beyond mere presence. To treat a defendant in a way which lowered his/her physical and mental resistance during the hearing would violate the requirement of a fair hearing.[47] And in the context of a complaint by an applicant with hearing difficulties, the European Court has recognised that:

> ... article 6, read as a whole, guarantees the right of an accused to participate effectively in a criminal trial. In general this includes, inter alia, not only his right to be present, but also to hear and follow the proceedings.[48]

The Court accepted that poor acoustics was 'undoubtedly a matter which could give rise to an issue under article 6'[49] but in circumstances where the applicant had failed to raise the matter in the domestic proceedings found no violation on the facts.

Trial in absentia

8.23 Subject to the safeguards mentioned above, trial in absentia does not violate the Convention. However, where a defendant subsequently re-emerges, s/he may be entitled to a rehearing of the case on the merits. In *Colozza v Italy*,[50] the European Court disapproved of a rule in Italy restricting retrial to cases where a defendant could establish that his/her absence was not an attempt to evade justice.

8.24 Moreover, where a defendant chooses to be absent, counsel must nonetheless be permitted to attend the trial. Absence of the accused does not deny him/her the benefit of the fundamental (but not absolute) right to legal representation.[51]

---

46 *Colozza v Italy* (1985) 7 EHRR 516.
47 *Barbera, Messegue and Jabardo v Spain* (1989) 11 EHRR 360; see also *T and V v UK* [1998] EHRLR 484 where the Commission expressed the right to participate effectively in very broad terms.
48 *Stanford v UK* (1994) at para 26.
49 Ibid at para 29.
50 (1985) 7 EHRR 516.
51 *Poitrimol v France* (1993) 18 EHRR 130. See also *Geyseghem v Belgium* [1999] EHRLR 337.

Legal aid

8.25   Article 6(3)(c) guarantees a right to legal aid in criminal proceedings subject to two conditions. First, that the accused lacks 'sufficient means' to pay for legal assistance. Second, that 'the interests of justice' require legal aid to be granted. Few issues have arisen before the European Court or Commission concerning the first condition, although, it seems, the level of proof required from a defendant that s/he lacks resources should not be set too high.[52]

8.26   As to the second condition, a number of factors are relevant. The complexity of the case is obviously important. In *Benham v UK,*[53] where the applicant was imprisoned for non-payment of the community charge, one of the reasons that influenced the European Court to hold that legal aid should have been granted was the fact that the proceedings were 'not straightforward'. The test for culpable negligence in particular was hard to understand.[54]

8.27   Closely related to the complexity of the case, is the ability of the defendant to present the case adequately without assistance. In *Granger v UK*[55] the European Court, in finding a violation of article 6(3)(c) in relation to appeal proceedings in Scotland, noted that 'the applicant ... was not in a position fully to comprehend the pre-prepared speeches he read out'.[56] And in *Hoang v France*[57] the Court took the view that where there are complex issues to be argued, the defendant does not have the legal training essential to present and develop appropriate arguments and only an experienced counsel would have the ability to prepare the case, the interests of justice require that a lawyer be officially assigned to the case.[58]

8.28   The seriousness of any possible sanction is also relevant to the question whether legal aid should be granted. In *Benham v UK,*[59] both the European Court and Commission held that, 'where the deprivation of liberty is at stake, the interests of justice in principle call for legal representation'.[60]

---

52 *Law of the European Convention on Human Rights,* Harris, O'Boyle and Warbrick, Butterworths, 1995, p261.
53 (1996) 22 EHRR 293.
54 Ibid at para 62.
55 (1990) 12 EHRR 469.
56 Ibid at para 47.
57 (1993) 16 EHRR 53.
58 Ibid at paras 40–41.
59 Note 53.
60 Note 53 at para 61. See also: *Quaranta v Switzerland* A/205 (1991) para 31; unreported.

8.29 Where factors relevant to the question of legal aid may alter, any refusal of legal aid must be reviewed. In *Granger v UK*,[61] where the degree of complexity involved in one of the issues for determination only really became clear during the hearing, the European Court held that:

> ... some means should have been made available to the competent authorities, including the High Court of Justiciary in the exercise of its overall responsibility for ensuring the fair conduct of the appeal proceedings, to have the refusal of legal aid reconsidered.[62]

And, although all the factors are important, the Court has consistently emphasised that it is not necessary to prove that the absence of legal assistance had caused actual prejudice in order to establish a violation of article 6(3) of the Convention.[63] Such a requirement would in large measure deprive the provision of its substance.

Legal representation

8.30 Legal representation must be 'practical and effective'.[64] The mere nomination of a lawyer is not enough. In *Artico v Italy*[65] both the European Court and Commission emphasised that:

> ... article 6(3)(c) speaks of 'assistance' and not of 'nomination'. Again, mere nomination does not ensure effective assistance, since the lawyer appointed for legal aid purposes may die, fall seriously ill, be prevented for a protracted period from acting or shirk his duties. If they are notified of the situation, the authorities must either replace him or cause him to fulfil his obligations.[66]

However, the point at which the authorities must intervene where a defendant is unhappy about his/her legal representation is unclear. In *Kamasinski v Austria*[67] the applicant complained about the non-attendance of his legal aid lawyer at the indictment hearing, the brevity of his pre-trial visits and of a general failure by his lawyer to acquaint himself with the prosecution evidence prior to trial.

---

61 (1990) 12 EHRR 469.
62 Ibid at para 47.
63 *Artico v Italy* (1981) 3 EHRR 1.
64 Ibid; see further paras 4.12 to 4.15
65 Note 63.
66 Note 63 at para 33.
67 (1991) 13 EHRR 36.

Although it accepted that 'mere nomination' is not enough, the European Court approached the case on the basis that 'a State cannot be responsible for every shortcoming on the part of a lawyer appointed for legal aid purposes'. In its judgment:

> It follows from the independence of the legal profession of the State that the conduct of the defence is essentially a matter between the defendant and his counsel, whether counsel be appointed under a legal aid scheme or be privately financed. The Court agrees with the Commission that the competent authorities are required under article 6(3)(c) to intervene only if a failure by legal aid counsel to provide effective representation is manifest or sufficiently brought to their attention in some other way.[68]

Taking into account the fact that the applicant's lawyer had visited him nine times and had filed both written and telephone motions, the Court concluded that there was nothing on the facts of the case in *Kamasinski* to put the authorities on notice of ineffective legal representation.

8.31   A similarly narrow approach was taken by the Commission in *F v UK*.[69] In that case, the applicant was on trial in Scotland for attempted murder. His counsel had to withdraw on the eve of the trial and the applicant met his replacement for the first time on the morning of the trial. Against the applicant's wishes, his new counsel failed to apply for an adjournment to ensure adequate preparation of the case. However, the Commission took the view that the responsibility of the state was not engaged in such circumstances.

8.32   However, where it is clear that counsel before the court has not had the time and facilities to properly prepare a case, the domestic authorities are under a duty to take measures of a positive nature to ensure that his/her obligations to the defendant are properly fulfilled. An adjournment in such circumstances would usually be called for.[70]

8.33   While manifest failure to represent the defendant effectively is a violation of the Convention, nothing in article 6(3)(c) gives the defendant the right to insist that his/her case be run in an unethical way. In *X v UK*[71] the Commission made it clear that:

> ... an accused person cannot require counsel to disregard principles

---

68   Ibid at para 65. See also *Daud v Portugal* [1998] EHRLR 634 on state responsibility for effective representation.

69   (1992) 15 EHRR CD 32.

70   *Goddi v Italy* (1984) 6 EHRR 457 at para 31. See also *Daud v Portugal* n68 above.

71   (1980) 21 DR 126.

of his professional duty in the presentation of his defence. If such an insistence results in the accused having to conduct his own defence, any consequent 'inequality of arms' can only be attributable to his own behaviour.[72]

8.34   In the first instance it is for the authorities responsible for granting free legal assistance to ensure that defence counsel is capable of effectively defending the case.[73] And choice of counsel by the defendant is not unlimited. Although the Commission has consistently maintained that article 6(3)(c) 'does not provide the right for a legally aided applicant to choose his legal representative',[74] this rule has been mitigated by the Court. In *Croissant v Germany*[75] it held that:

> It is true that article 6(3)(c) entitles 'everyone charged with a criminal offence' to be defended by counsel of his choosing. Nevertheless, and notwithstanding the importance of a relationship of confidence between lawyer and client, this right cannot be considered to be absolute. It is necessarily subject to certain limitations where free legal aid is concerned and also where, as in the present case, it is for the courts to decide whether the interests of justice require that the accused be defended by counsel appointed by them. When appointing defence counsel the national courts must certainly have regard to the defendant's wishes ... However, they can override those wishes when there are relevant and sufficient grounds for holding that this is necessary in the interests of justice.[76]

The position appears to be more generous in relation to privately-paid lawyers: in such cases the defendant's choice should usually be respected. Whether this distinction survives scrutiny under article 14 (the prohibition on discrimination) remains to be seen.

8.35   Even where a lawyer is willing to act for a defendant, the relevant authorities can, in some circumstances, prevent him/her from doing so. In *Ensslin and Others v Germany*,[77] where the defence lawyers were precluded from defending the applicants because they were themselves heavily implicated in the criminal association of the applicants, the Commission held that:

> the right to defend one's case with the assistance of defence counsel of one's choice, secured in article 6(3)(c), is not an absolute right: it

---

72 Ibid at para 6.
73 *F v Switzerland* (1989) 61 DR 171.
74 See, for example, Appln 9728/82 (1983) 6 EHRR 345.
75 (1993) 16 EHRR 135.
76 Ibid at para 29.
77 (1978) 14 DR 64.

is limited by the State's right to make the appearance of barristers before the courts subject to regulations and the obligation on defence counsel not to transgress certain principles of professional ethics.[78]

Similarly lawyers have been precluded from representing clients for refusing to wear robes, showing disrespect to the court or appearing as a witness in the case.[79]

8.36   Finally, the right to defend oneself under article 6(3)(c) is also not absolute. In *Philis v Greece*[80] the Commission found that 'a requirement to be represented by a lawyer in proceedings before a higher court is not incompatible with article 6 of the Convention'. And in *Croissant v Germany*[81] the Court similarly held that:

> The requirement that a defendant be assisted by counsel at all stages of the Regional Court's proceedings – which finds parallels in the legislation of other Contracting States – cannot, in the Court's opinion, be deemed incompatible with the Convention.[82]

Interpreters and translations

8.37   Article 6(3)(e) guarantees to everyone charged with a criminal offence the right 'to have the free assistance of an interpreter if he cannot understand or speak the language used in court'. The object of this provision is to prevent any inequality between a defendant who is not familiar with the language used in court and a defendant who does speak and understand the language.

8.38   Unlike the analogous provision under article 6(3)(c) (legal assistance),[83] this guarantee is not subject to any conditions whatsoever. In *Luedicke, Delkasam and Koc v Germany*[84] the European Court took the view that the term 'free' in article 6(3)(e) had to be given an unqualified meaning, denoting neither a conditional remission or temporary exemption, nor a suspension, but a 'once and for all' exemption or exoneration. Once it is established that a defendant

---

78 Ibid at para 20. See also *Schopfer v Switzerland* [1998] EHRLR 646.
79 *Law of the European Convention on Human Rights*, Harris, O'Boyle and Warbrick, Butterworths 1995, pp259–260. But see *Pelladoah v Netherlands* (1994) 19 EHRR 81: unduly formalistic conditions should not be imposed.
80 (1990) 66 DR 260.
81 (1993) 16 EHRR 135.
82 Ibid at para 27.
83 See above paras 8.30 to 8.36.
84 (1979–80) 2 EHRR 149.

cannot understand or speak the language used in court, then the services of an interpreter must be provided free of cost, irrespective of the defendant's financial status.

8.39   In *Luedicke, Delkasam and Koc*, the European Court took the view that to impose the costs of an interpreter where a defendant was convicted '... would deprive article 6(3)(e) of much of its effect, for it would leave in existence the disadvantages that ... article 6(3)(e) is specifically designed to attenuate'.[85] Moreover, any such approach might have a chilling effect on the exercise of the right.[86]

8.40   The European Court has also accepted that, in principle, article 6(3)(e) applies at an early stage and provides a basis for seeking translation of prosecution material. In *Luedicke, Delkasam and Koc*[87] the Court extended this principle to cover 'those documents or statements in the proceedings ... which it is necessary for [the accused] to understand in order to have the benefit of a fair trial'. And in *Brozicek v Italy*[88] the Court held that documents constituting an accusation should be provided in a language which an accused person understands.

8.41   In *Kamasinski v Austria*[89] the European Court adopted a more restrictive approach. Although it accepted that article 6(3)(e) applied to documentary material disclosed before trial, it took the view that it did not require written translation of all such documentation. The charge did not require written translation; verbal interpretation was sufficient. Nor was written translation required of all documentary evidence, official documents, or even the judgment. But, it seems, to some extent, the Court was influenced by the fact that defence counsel was competent in the applicant's mother-tongue. Where this is not the case the approach adopted in *Luedicke, Delkasan and Koc* should be followed.

The burden of proof

8.42   Article 6(2) of the Convention guarantees the right to everyone charged with a criminal offence to be 'presumed innocent until

---

85 Ibid at para 42.
86 *Ozturk v Germany* A/73 (1984) 6 EHRR 409.
87 Note 84.
88 (1990) 12 EHRR 371.
89 (1991) 13 EHRR 36.

proven guilty according to law'. It flows from this that the burden of proof in criminal proceedings is on the prosecution.[90]

8.43   However, this principle is subject to two qualifications. First, where the defendant is seeking to establish a specific defence, the burden of proof may be transferred from prosecution to defence. Second, within limits, rules under which presumptions of law or fact operate against a defendant are not incompatible with the Convention.

8.44   The first qualification was addressed by the Commission in *Lingens v Austria*[91] which involved a provision in the Austrian penal code making it a criminal offence to damage someone's reputation subject to a special defence if the accused proves the truth of the statement.[92] The Commission reasoned that this did not violate article 6(2) because;

> The offence as conceived in the applicable provisions of the Penal Code ... can ... be committed by a true statement: what exculpates is not the objective truth of a defamatory statement, but ability to prove its truth.[93]

It follows that this qualification to the usual rule about the burden of proof will apply only where the prosecution has discharged the burden of proving an offence and it is then open to the defence to avoid criminal liability. Even then, the Commission carefully assessed the purpose behind the 'legal technique of a defence' – the protection of a private prosecutor from allegations, the truth of which cannot be proven by their author – before concluding that article 6(2) had not been violated.

8.45   The second qualification to the general rule that the prosecution bears the burden of proving the case was addressed by the European Court in *Salabiaku v France*.[94] In that case, the applicant, who had been caught with 10 kgs of cannabis in his luggage at an airport, claimed to have no knowledge of the drugs. He was convicted under a provision in French law whereby a person who is in possession of drugs in such circumstances is presumed to be guilty of smuggling them unless s/he can prove that it was impossible to know about

---

90 See: *Austria v Italy* (1963) 6 yearbook 740 at p782; *Barbera, Messegue and Jabardo v Spain* (1989) 11 EHRR 360 at para 77.

91 (1981) 26 DR 171.

92 The case was subsequently considered by the European Court under article 10, but not article 6: (1986) 8 EHRR 407.

93 Note 91 at para 4.

94 A/141-A (1991) 13 EHRR 379.

them. The Court found that, as applied in the applicant's case, this provision was not contrary to article 6(2) on the basis that since presumptions of fact or of law operate in every legal system, the Convention does not prohibit such presumptions in principle. The Court emphasised, however, that:

> Article 6(2) does not ... regard presumptions of fact or of law provided for in the criminal law with indifference. It requires States to confine them within reasonable limits which take into account the importance of what is at stake and maintain the rights of the defence.[95]

On the facts of *Salabiaku* the presumption flowing from possession did not exceed such reasonable limits because the applicant was not left entirely without a means of defence. He could rely on extenuating circumstances or force majeure.

8.46   It appears that the M'Naughton rules, which require a defendant to show that s/he was suffering from a defect of reason, do not violate article 6(2).[96] In the Commission's opinion they concern the presumption of sanity not of innocence and are neither arbitrary nor unreasonable.

8.47   The extent to which the European Court endorsed strict liability offences in *Salabiaku v France*[97] is unclear. Although not formally part of its reasoning, the Court stated that:

> ... the Contracting States may, under certain conditions, penalise a simple or objective fact as such, irrespective of whether it results from criminal intent or from negligence.[98]

The Court did not explain what it meant by 'certain conditions'. However, it seems to follow from the rest of its judgment that a strict liability offence which left no defence whatsoever would violate the Convention. And, presumably, where the conduct in question involves the exercise of a Convention right (for example, freedom of expression or assembly) any rule of strict liability would be subject to scrutiny for compliance with the requirement of proportionality.[99]

---

95 Ibid at para 28.
96 Appl 15023/89 (1990) 87 LS Gaz 31.
97 Note 94.
98 Note 94 at para 27.
99 See paras 4.37 to 4.55.

The standard of proof

8.48   Neither the European Court nor the Commission has ever clearly stated that in criminal proceedings the standard of proof required under the Convention is beyond reasonable doubt. But such an assumption appears to underpin their case-law. In *Austria v Italy*[100] the Commission stated as a matter of general principle that the presumption of innocence under article 6(2) requires that:

> ... the onus to prove guilt falls on the Prosecution and any doubt is to the benefit of the accused. ... In their judgment, [the judges] can find him guilty only on the basis of direct or indirect evidence sufficiently strong in the eyes of the law to establish his guilt.[101]

8.49   In *Barbera, Messegue and Jabardo v Spain*,[102] the European Court endorsed the rule that 'any doubt should benefit the accused' but did not elaborate upon this requirement. Some guidance can also be gleaned from the Court's reasoning in *Goodman International and Goodman v Ireland*[103] where it rejected a suggestion that the function of a Tribunal of Inquiry set up by the Irish Parliament involved the determination of criminal charges because, inter alia, the tribunal had not stated that the burden of proof throughout the proceedings would be that for a criminal trial, 'beyond reasonable doubt'.

Changing plea

8.50   In *RO v UK*[104] the applicant, who was serving a sentence, applied to withdraw his plea of guilty nine months after the original plea. The trial judge denied the application and he was sentenced to eight years' imprisonment which was increased on appeal to life. The applicant complained that, in breach of article 6, his guilt was determined not by reference to evidence, but by his initial guilty plea which he could not challenge. The Commission considered that a rule which militates against changes of pleas which are unequivocal and voluntary cannot be said to compromise the fairness of proceedings as such, and, therefore, it is necessary to consider the

---

100   (1963) 6 Yearbook 740.
101   Ibid at p784.
102   (1989) 11 EHRR 360 at para 77.
103   (1993) 16 EHRR CD 26.
104   (1994) 18 EHRR CD 212.

impact of the refusal to permit the change of plea on proceedings as a whole. It recalled that the applicant was fully represented and only applied to change his plea nine months later. The Court of Appeal had accepted that the judge had all the material necessary to try the case. The Commission therefore rejected the case as inadmissable.

Reasons

8.51 Article 6(1) obliges domestic courts to give reasons for their judgments.[105] The extent of the reasons that must be given will vary according to the nature of the decision in question. There is no need for courts to give detailed answers to every argument raised during the course of a hearing, but failure to address an important aspect of the case will breach article 6(1). A decision which on its face shows that it was made on a basis not open to the judge cannot be said to be a reasoned decision.[106] And proper reason should always be given where bail is refused: see chapter 7.

Costs in criminal cases

8.52 No 'right' to costs or expenses can be read into the Convention.[107] However, the presumption of innocence under article 6(2) is an important factor where a successful defendant is ordered to pay costs or is refused reimbursement of his/her costs upon acquittal, or where criminal proceedings are discontinued.

8.53 The key question is whether a costs decision amounts to a determination of guilt. If so, the presumption of innocence will be violated. Where there has been no determination on the merits, simply voicing suspicions about guilt in relation to a costs decision is not necessarily a violation of article 6(2), but judges must not overstep the mark. A violation was established in *Minelli v Switzerland*,[108] where the domestic court ordered the applicant to pay part of the private prosecutor's and court costs on the basis that, had the case progressed to trial, he would 'very probably' have been convicted.

---

105 *Van de Hurk v Netherlands* (1994) 18 EHRR 481 at para 61; *Hiro Balani v Spain* (1995) 19 EHRR 566 at para 27.
106 *De Moor v Belgium* (1994) 18 EHRR 372.
107 *Lutz v Germany* (1988) 10 EHRR 182.
108 (1983) 5 EHRR 554.

8.54   Where a defendant is acquitted, the rule is stricter still: judges are not free to voice suspicions about guilt and costs should normally be awarded.[109] On that basis a series of cases against the UK have recently been admitted by the Commission.[110]

International co-operation in criminal matters

8.55   Where a contracting party to the Convention co-operates with another country in the administration of criminal justice, questions of compliance with fair trial guarantees may arise. Most cases have involved extradition or deportation decisions.[111] However, the responsibility of a contracting state where it receives prisoners from other countries was considered by the European Court in *Drozd and Janousek v France and Spain*.[112]

8.56   In that case, the applicants were tried and convicted of armed robbery in the Andorra. Having lost their appeal they elected to serve their sentences in France, in accordance with a special provision of Andorran law. When they reached France, the applicants complained about various features of the criminal justice process in Andorra and argued that the French authorities bore some responsibility for ensuring that their convictions were fair before agreeing to co-operate with the Andorran legal authorities. The European Court rejected this argument. In its view, the Convention does not require the contracting parties to impose its standards on third states or territories. To require a contracting state to review the criminal justice process in other countries for compliance with article 6 would thwart the current trend towards strengthening international co-operation in the administration of justice. However, where there has been a flagrant denial of justice, contracting states are obliged to refuse their co-operation.[113]

---

109 *Sekanina v Austria* (1993) 17 EHRR 221. Where the defendant remains silent during police questioning and declines to reveal his/her defence until trial: see *Byrne v UK* [1998] 626.

110 Appls 22613/93 and 221614/93; and *Cybulski v UK* (1997) 23 EHRR CD 53.

111 These are dealt with in chapter 18 (Immigration, asylum, extradition and deportation).

112 (1992) 14 EHRR 745.

113 Ibid at para 110.

Double jeopardy

8.57 The government has indicated its intention to sign, ratify and incorporate Protocol 7 to the Convention which proves a number of additional fair trial guarantees in criminal trials. Article 4 of Protocol 7 provides that:

(1) No one shall be liable to be tried or punished again in criminal proceedings under the jurisdiction of the same state for an offence for which he has already been finally acquitted or convicted in accordance with the law and penal procedure of that state.

(2) The provisions of the preceding paragraph shall not prevent the reopening of the case in accordance with the law and penal procedure of the State concerned, if there is evidence or new or newly discovered facts, or if there has been a fundamental defect in the previous proceedings, which could affect the outcome of the case.

(3) No derogation from the Article shall be made under Article 15 of the Convention.

The question under article 4 is not the narrow one of whether an individual is tried for two offences which contain the same elements, but whether s/he is tried for two offences which are 'based on the same conduct'.[114] However, the protection provided by article 4 is confined to prosecutions in the same jurisdiction[115] and does not prevent separate disciplinary and criminal proceedings in respect of the same allegation.

8.58 Whether freedom from double jeopardy is also guaranteed under article 6 of the Convention is questionable. The Commission left the matter open in *X v Austria*[116] where it observed that the mere fact that express protection against double jeopardy was provided by Protocol 7 did not necessarily mean that such protection was not inherent in article 6. Subsequently it has adopted a more restrictive approach, suggesting in *S v Germany*,[117] where statements made by the applicant in one criminal trial were used against him in another jurisdiction, that article 6 guarantees 'neither expressly nor by way of implication the principle of ne bis in idem'.[118] The issue has yet to be determined by the European Court.

---

114 *Gradinger v Austria* (1995) A/328-C; unreported.
115 *S v Germany* (1983) 39 DR 43.
116 (1970) 35 CD 151.
117 (1983) 39 DR 43.
118 Ibid at p47

Amicus lawyers, intervening parties and clerks in magistrates' courts

8.59   The right to an adversarial hearing means that the defendant in criminal proceedings must be allowed to know and to comment upon all the evidence adduced and all legal submissions made by others[119] 'with a view to influencing the courts' decision'. Where non-parties or legal advisers have any involvement in a case, this principle requires disclosure of their submissions, and any advice provided by them, to the defendant, if the purpose of their involvement is to 'advise' or 'influence' the court in any way.[120] It also requires that the defendant be afforded an opportunity to comment upon any submissions or advice given. [121] This has clear implications for amicus lawyers, intervening parties and clerks in magistrates' courts.[122]

119 *Ruiz-Mateos v Spain* (1993) 16 EHRR 505.
120 *Van Orshoven v Belgium* (1997) 26 EHRR 55.
121 Ibid.
122 See further paras 13.55 to 13.58.

CHAPTER 9

Evidence in criminal cases

9.1	Introduction
9.4	Hearsay evidence: general principles
9.7	Non-compellable witness
9.12	Illness and death
9.17	Absconding witnesses
9.19	Fear of reprisals
9.23	Anonymous witnesses
9.30	Undercover agents and entrapment
9.36	Protecting the rights of victims and witnesses in criminal proceedings
9.42	Unlawfully obtained evidence
9.46	Confession evidence
9.49	Accomplice evidence
9.52	Expert evidence
9.55	Defence evidence
9.60	The right to silence : freedom from self-incrimination

continued

9.67   The right to silence: drawing adverse inferences

9.75   Intimate samples

Introduction

9.1   Under the Convention, evidential issues in criminal proceedings are usually resolved by reference to articles 6(2) and 6(3)(d) of the Convention. The former enshrines the presumption of innocence; the latter provides that everyone charged with a criminal offence shall be entitled:

> to examine or have examined witnesses against him and to obtain the attendance and examination of witnesses on his behalf under the same conditions as witnesses against him.

However, the European Court and Commission have repeatedly stressed that neither article 6(2) nor article 6(3)(d) requires Convention states to adopt specific rules concerning the admissibility, relevance or probity of evidence.[1] These are matters for regulation under domestic law.

9.2   Consequently, the Court and Commission have not seen it as their task to decide whether particular matters should have been admitted into evidence etc. Instead, they have confined themselves to reviewing whether the proceedings in question, considered as whole, including the way in which the evidence was taken, were fair.[2] So, for example, the Commission has taken the view that where domestic law provides for a conviction on the basis of circumstantial evidence, so long as the trial was fair, no issue arises under article 6.[3] Weight is also for the domestic courts.[4]

9.3   The concept of a witness is autonomous under the Convention.[5] What matters is not whether someone formally gives evidence at a hearing, but whether his/her evidence in some shape or form is taken into account by the court.[6]

Hearsay evidence: general principles

9.4   Article 6(3)(d) of the Convention specifically provides that everyone charged with a criminal offence shall be entitled to 'examine or have

---

1   *Schenk v Switzerland* (1991) 13 EHRR 242 at para 46; *Barbera, Messegue and Jabardo v Spain* (1989) 11 EHRR 360.
2   *Barbera, Messegue and Jabardo* n1 at para 68.
3   *Alberti v Italy* (1989) 59 DR 100.
4   *Alberti v Italy* (1989) 59 DR 100.
5   See para 4.19.
6   *Kostovski v Netherlands* (1990) 12 EHRR 434.

examined witnesses against him'. From this the Strasbourg bodies have derived a number of general principles, including:

1) All the evidence should be produced in the presence of the accused.[7]

2) The hearing of witnesses should be adversarial.[8]

3) The accused should be given an adequate and proper opportunity to challenge and question a witness against him/her, either at the time the witness was making a statement or at some later stage of the proceedings.[9]

However, these are general principles. They form the framework within which evidential issues fall to be determined, but they are not inflexible.

9.5   Nothing in article 6(3)(d) – or the general principles referred to above – prevents a court from relying on hearsay evidence. But where hearsay evidence is admitted, there must be counterbalancing factors which preserve the rights of the defence.[10] In practice, this means that the Strasbourg bodies will balance the reasons advanced by the authorities for relying on hearsay evidence against the inevitable infringement of the accused's right to challenge and question all the witnesses against him/her. Relevant factors in this balancing exercise include the opportunities (if any) afforded to the defence to challenge the evidence in question prior to trial, whether the defence requested the attendance of the witness in question and the impact of the evidence on the trial. Although the context is always important, as a general rule, any conviction based solely or mainly on hearsay evidence is likely to violate article 6(3)(d).

9.6   In *Van Mechelen and Others v Netherlands*,[11] which concerned hearsay evidence given by anonymous police officers, the European Court set out a further general principle:

> Having regard to the place that the right to a fair administration of justice holds in a democratic society, any measures restricting the rights of the defence should be strictly necessary. If a less restrictive measure can suffice then that measure should be applied.[12]

This clearly has important ramifications for UK law and practice in the criminal sphere.

---

7   *Barbera, Messegue and Jabardo* n1 at para 78.
8   *Barbera, Messegue and Jabardo* n1 at para 78.
9   *Kostovski v Netherlands* n6 at para 41.
10   Ibid.
11   (1998) 25 EHRR 647.
12   Ibid at para 58.

Non-compellable witnesses

9.7 Most Convention states have rules relating to compellability which effectively excuse some witnesses from giving evidence. Typical categories include spouses, co-habitees and family members. The compatibility of these rules with the Convention was first considered in *Unterpertinger v Austria*.[13] There the applicant had been convicted of assaulting his former wife and step-daughter on the basis of their written statements because they had taken advantage of a provision in the Austrian code of criminal procedure, which made them non-compellable witnesses.

9.8 The European Court found that the provision in question was 'manifestly *not* incompatible with article 6(1) and 3(d) of the Convention' because:

> ... it makes allowance for the special problems that may be entailed in a confrontation between someone 'charged with a criminal offence' and a witness from his own family and is calculated to protect such a witness by avoiding his being put in a moral dilemma ...[14]

This does not mean that *any* conviction based on the hearsay evidence of a non-compellable witness will survive challenge under the Convention.

9.9 In *Unterpertinger* itself, the European Court scrutinised the impact of the statements of the applicant's former wife and step-daughter on the hearing. It noted that the domestic court:

> ... did not treat these simply as items of information but as proof of the truth of the accusations made by the women at the time ...[15]

And that, although there was other evidence,[16] the applicant's conviction was based 'mainly' on the woman's evidence. In such circumstances, the rights of the defence had not been sufficiently safeguarded. In other words, making certain wintnesses non-compellable is not, in principle, a breach of the Convention; but only if their evidence is very carefully confined when used against a defendant.

---

13 (1991) 13 EHRR 175.
14 Ibid at para 30.
15 Note 13 at para 33.
16 Medical reports, the divorce file and evidence from the applicant's sister-in-law.

9.10   The European Court distinguished *Unterpertinger* in the subsequent case of *Asch v Austria*[17] where the applicant's co-habitee refused to give evidence at his trial for assaulting her, with the result that her statement to the police was read to the court. Influenced by the fact that the statement of the applicant's co-habitee 'did not constitute the only item of evidence on which the first instance court based its decision'[18] the Court found no violation of article 6(3)(d).

9.11   While the impact of the hearsay evidence in *Asch* was considered by reference to a weaker test than that used in *Unterpertinger* – not the *sole* evidence (rather than not the *main* evidence) against the accused – it has not been followed in the Court's subsequent case-law. In the context of hearsay evidence from anonymous witnesses, the Court has maintained that even when 'counterbalancing' procedures are found to compensate for the handicaps under which the defence labour, a conviction should not be based either solely or to a decisive extent on anonymous statements.[19]

Illness and death

9.12   The European Court's approach to hearsay evidence caused by the death or serious illness of a witness has been fairly straightforward. Both can justify reliance on hearsay evidence so long as counterbalancing factors preserve the rights of the defence.[20] In *Ferrantelli and Santangelo v Italy*,[21] where the applicants complained that there had been no confrontation with a witness who had died, the Court found no breach of article 6 because the authorities were not responsible for the death and the hearsay evidence of the witness was corroborated by other evidence.

9.13   Where poor health is in issue, the existence of alternatives which avoid recourse to hearsay evidence usually weigh heavily in the Court's determination. In *Bricmont v Belgium*,[22] where the Prince of Belgium had brought charges against the applicants for forgery but had not given evidence, on medical grounds, the Court found a breach of article 6 on the basis that:

---

17 A/203-A (1993) 15 EHRR 597.
18 Ibid at para 30.
19 *Doorson v Netherlands* (1997) 22 EHRR 330.
20 *Ferrantelli and Santangelo v Italy* (1997) 23 EHRR 288.
21 Note 20. See also *Kennedy v UK* [1999] EHRLR 214.
22 (1990) 12 EHRR 217.

In the circumstances of the case, the exercise of the rights of the defence – an essential part of the right to a fair trial – required in principle that the applicants should have an opportunity to challenge any aspect of the complainant's account during a confrontation or an examination, either in public or, if necessary, at his home.[23]

9.14 Different circumstances prevailed in *Trivedi v UK*[24] where the applicant, a doctor, was convicted of false accounting on the basis of a number of prescriptions he had dispensed to an elderly patient. At trial, the prosecution served a report suggesting that, because of a deterioration in that patient's intellect, he would never be able to give evidence. The trial judge, therefore, allowed the statements which the patient had made to the police to be read under ss23 and 26 of the Criminal Justice Act 1988. The Commission rejected the applicant's complaint that his rights under article 6(1) and 6(3)(d) had been violated, on the basis that the trial judge conducted a thorough inquiry into the matter, the evidence was not the only evidence against the applicant, defence counsel had had the opportunity to comment on the statements to the jury and they had been directed by the judge to attach less weight to the statements because they were hearsay.

9.15 A similar approach was taken in *MK v Austria*[25] where the applicant, charged with unlawful sex with a young boy, wanted the boy called to establish his consent. The domestic court refused this request because the boy was in intensive psychiatric care. Under Austrian law, a victim of a sexual offence who is a minor is generally required to give evidence except where, in the expert opinion of a child psychiatrist, the hearing of the victim could lead to irreparable harm, even if the questioning were carried out with the utmost care.

9.16 The expert, who examined the boy, gave evidence at the applicant's trial, including hearsay evidence of the boy's account of his sexual relationship with the applicant. Recalling that the interests of witnesses and victims are in principle protected by the Convention,[26] the Commission found no violation of article 6. It recognised that it would have been preferable if the boy had been heard in person but, in light of the reasons for his non-attendance, the fact that the expert could be examined by the applicant's lawyer and the existence of other evidence, the overall proceedings had been fair.

23 Ibid at para 81.
24 Appl 31700/96 [1997] EHRLR 521.
25 (1997) 24 EHRR CD 59.
26 See further paras 9.36 to 9.41.

Absconding witnesses

9.17   Where witnesses abscond, compliance with article 6 can be an issue. In *Delta v France*[27] the applicant's conviction for robbery on the underground was based solely on the written statements of the victim and her friend taken soon after the offence, but in the absence of the applicant. At trial the prosecution summonsed the two witnesses but they failed to appear. Although the applicant had not specifically requested that the witnesses be present (at least at first instance),[28] the European Court found a breach of article 6(3)(d). Their evidence was decisive and the applicant had not been able to test their reliability or credibility.

9.18   In *Delta* the court took no steps to ensure the attendance of the witnesses when they failed to appear. In contrast, in *Doorson v Netherlands*[29] repeated, but unsuccessful attempts were made to bring one of the witnesses before the first-instance court and he was brought by force to the Court of Appeal, but absconded before giving evidence. In those circumstances, the European Court found that it was open to the domestic courts to have regard to his police statement; particularly since it was corroborated by other evidence.[30]

Fear of reprisals

9.19   A genuine fear of reprisals can, in some circumstances, justify reliance on hearsay evidence in criminal proceedings. However, the general principles of article 6 remain unaffected: resort to hearsay evidence can be justified only if there are counterbalancing procedures which preserve the rights of the defence. And neither the seriousness of the crime, nor the depth of any fear of reprisals, can justify limiting the need for such counterbalancing factors.

9.20   While 'the collaboration of the public is undoubtedly of great importance for the police in their struggle against crime'[31] and can justify relying on the evidence of anonymous informers in the course of police investigations:

---

27 (1993) 16 EHRR 574.
28 On appeal, the applicant did insist they attend.
29 (1996) 22 EHRR 330.
30 Ibid at para 80.
31 *Windisch v Austria* (1991) 13 EHRR 281.

... the subsequent use of their statements by the trial court to found a conviction is another matter. The right to a fair administration of justice holds so prominent a place in a democratic society that it cannot be sacrificed.[32]

In *Windisch v Austria*[33] the European Court held that an opportunity to cross-examine police officers who took statements from two witnesses who did not attend trial was insufficient to safeguard the rights of the defence. Since the applicant's conviction was based 'to a large extent' on the hearsay evidence, article 6(3)(d) had been violated.

9.21   A similar position was adopted in *Saidi v France*[34] where the applicant was convicted of drug trafficking on the basis of hearsay evidence from three anonymous identification witnesses. The French government sought to justify this on the basis that drug addicts would not come forward as witnesses unless their anonymity was preserved. The European Court emphatically rejected this:

> The Court is fully aware of the undeniable difficulties of the fight against drug-trafficking – in particular with regard to obtaining and producing evidence – and of the ravages caused to society by the drug problem, but such considerations cannot justify restricting to this extent the rights of the defence.[35]

Since the identification evidence constituted the sole basis for the applicant's conviction, article 6(3)(d) had been violated.

9.22   The fear of reprisals relied upon to justify recourse to hearsay evidence does not, as a general rule, have to be linked to any specific threat from the defendant. In *Doorson v Netherlands*[36] there was never any suggestion that the two witnesses, whose hearsay evidence was admitted at trial, had ever been threatened by the applicant. However, in the European Court's judgment, that did not make the decision to rely on their evidence unreasonable per se:

> Regard must be had to the fact, as established by the domestic courts and not contested by the applicant, that drug dealers frequently resorted to threats or actual violence against persons who gave evidence against them.[37]

---

32 Ibid at para 30.
33 Note 31.
34 (1994) 17 EHRR 251.
35 Ibid at para 44.
36 Note 29.
37 Ibid at para 71.

However, the position may be different where the witness is a police officer.[38]

Anonymous witnesses

9.23   The Convention does not rule out the use of anonymous witnesses: the European Court has recognised that the life, liberty and privacy of witnesses can be at stake in some cases.[39] However, there must be counterbalancing procedures which enable the reliability of the evidence to be challenged. And the European Court is acutely aware of the dangers of convicting on the evidence of such witnesses:

> If the defence is unaware of the identity of the person it seeks to question, it may be deprived of the very particulars enabling it to demonstrate that he or she is prejudiced, hostile or unreliable. Testimony or other declarations inculpating an accused may well be designedly untruthful or simply erroneous and the defence will scarcely be able to bring this to light if it lacks the information permitting it to test the author's reliability or cast doubt on his credibility.[40]

The counterbalancing procedures needed to ensure a fair trial will vary from case to case. Whether the accused or his/her lawyer was present when the witness was questioned, whether s/he could ask questions and whether the trial judge was aware of the identity of the witness will be key factors. Any measures restricting the right of the defence must be 'strictly necessary' and 'if a less restrictive measure can suffice then that measure should be applied'.[41] And, even where there are sufficient counterbalancing procedures, a conviction should not be based either *solely* or to a *decisive extent* on evidence from anonymous witnesses.[42]

9.24   The counterbalancing procedures were insufficient to protect the right of the defence in *Kostovski v Netherlands*,[43] where the evidence of two anonymous witnesses was taken by examining magistrates and then presented in hearsay form at the applicant's trial. The

---

38 See: *Van Mechelen and Others v Netherlands* (1998) 25 EHRR 647, discussed at para 9.29.
39 *Doorson v Netherlands* n29.
40 *Kostovski v Netherlands* (1990) 12 EHRR 434 at para 42.
41 *Van Mechelen and Others* n38 at para 58.
42 *Doorson v Netherland* n29 at para 76.
43 Note 40.

defence had not been present at the hearing before the examining magistrates but had been permitted to ask written questions of one of the witnesses, and the police and examining magistrates were available for cross-examination at trial. Threats of reprisals were real and the witnesses were in real danger.[44] Nonetheless, the European Court found the procedure 'irreconcilable with the guarantees contained in article 6'.[45]

9.25   More stringent counterbalancing procedures produced a different result in *Doorson v Netherlands*.[46] There, anonymous witnesses were questioned by an investigating magistrate in the presence of the applicant's counsel who was able to ask the witnesses (through the magistrate) whatever questions he considered to be in the interest of the defence, except those that might lead to the disclosure of the identity of the witness, and all the questions were answered. In the circumstances the European Court found that:

> ... the 'counterbalancing' procedure followed ... must be considered
> sufficient to have enabled the defence to challenge the evidence of
> the anonymous witnesses and attempt to cast doubt on the
> reliability of their statements ...[47]

And since the applicant's conviction was not based solely or to a decisive extent on the evidence of the anonymous witnesses, article 6 had not been breached.

9.26   Similarly in *X v UK*[48] the use of screens in court to shield witnesses from the defendant, public and press were approved by the Commission. The witnesses were journalists, at the applicant's trial for murder in Northern Ireland, who had recorded the events surrounding the murder. They could be seen by the judge and by both prosecution and defence counsel, they could be heard by everyone and their evidence did not involve identification of the applicant, the main issue in the trial. In the circumstances, the Commission found that there was no breach of article 6(1) or 6(3)(d).

9.27   However, even stringent counterbalancing procedures are unlikely to be enough where the anonymous witnesses are police officers. Following *Kostovski* the Dutch authorities introduced new procedures in cases involving the use of anonymous witnesses. In

---

44   Ibid at para 44.
45   Note 40 at para 44.
46   Note 29.
47   Ibid at para 75.
48   (1993) 15 EHRR CD 113.

accordance with this procedure, the statements of anonymous witnesses in *Van Mechelen and Others v Netherlands*,[49] who were police officers, had been taken down by a judge, who had himself ascertained the identity of the police officers concerned, made a written report concerning their reliability and credibility and found their reasons for wanting to remain anonymous sufficient. At trial, the investigating judge, a registrar and the anonymous witnesses, who were in one room, were connected by a sound link to the applicant, their lawyers and the advocate-general, who were in another room and there was no restriction on the questions that could be put to the witnesses.[50]

9.28   Nonetheless the European Court was not persuaded that the rights of the defence had been respected. Not only was the defence unaware of the identity of the witnesses, but it was also prevented from observing their demeanour under direct questioning, and thus from testing their reliability.[51] The opinion of the investigating judge on the reliability and credibility of the witnesses was no substitute for allowing the defence to question the witnesses in its presence and make its own assessment of their reliability and credibility.

9.29   The Court's judgment in *Van Mechelen* makes it clear that only the most exceptional circumstances can justify the use of anonymous witnesses who are police officers. In its view:

> ... the balancing of the interests of the defence against arguments in favour of maintaining the anonymity of witnesses raises special problems if the witnesses in question are members of the police force of the State. Although their interests – and indeed those of their families – also deserve protection under the Convention, it must be recognised that their position is to some extent different from that of a disinterested witness or a victim. They owe a general duty of obedience to the State's executive authorities and usually have links with the prosecution; for these reasons alone their use as anonymous witnesses should be resorted to only in exceptional circumstances. In addition, it is in the nature of things that their duties, particularly in the case of arresting officers, may involve giving evidence in open court.[52]

In such cases, presumptions about the risk of reprisals – based, for example, on the seriousness of the offence – are not enough. Depart-

---

49   (1998) 25 EHRR 647.
50   Save, of course, for any question tending to reveal their identity.
51   N49 at para 59.
52   N49 at para 56.

ing from its approach in *Doorson v Netherlands*,[53] which involved ordinary civilian witnesses,[54] the European Court in *Van Mechelen* maintained that efforts should have been made to assess whether there was an actual threat to police officers or their families.[55]

Undercover agents and entrapment

9.30 The use of undercover agents in criminal cases raises two issues under the Convention: fair trial and privacy. So far as the first is concerned, the European Court's case-law has established that, subject to two qualifications, the use of undercover agents in the investigation of crime is not incompatible with article 6. The first qualification is that the use of undercover agents must be restricted and adequate safeguards must be observed to prevent abuse. The second is that the actions of undercover agents must not exceed passive surveillance: prosecution for an offence incited by an undercover agent will breach article 6.

9.31 The leading case is *Teixeira de Castro v Portugal*.[56] There, two undercover agents, posing as drug addicts, visited the applicant at home and asked him to supply them with heroin. The applicant had no heroin at his house and so the two agents took him to another address where he purchased heroin for them. He was then arrested, prosecuted and convicted.

9.32 Relying on article 6, the applicant argued that he had not had a fair trial because he had been incited to commit an offence, which, but for the intervention of the undercover agents, he would never have committed. The European Court agreed. In its view:

> ... the two police officers did not confine themselves to investigating [the applicant's] criminal activities in an essentially passive manner, but exercised an influence such as to incite the commission of the offence.[57]

Even the obvious public interest in fighting drug-trafficking could not justify using evidence obtained as a result of police incitement.[58]

---

53 (1996) 22 EHRR 330.
54 See para 9.22.
55 Note 49 at para 61.
56 (1999) 28 EHRR 101
57 Ibid at para 38.
58 Note 56 at para 36.

9.33   The Court in *Teixeira de Castro* was partly influenced by the lack of safeguards. In particular, it noted that the activities of the undercover agents had not been ordered and supervised by a judge. In the Court's opinion, this indicated that the applicant was not suspected of any crime before he came into contact with them and weakened the Government's argument that he was predisposed to committing offences.

9.34   Even where safeguards against abuse are in place and the role of undercover agents does not exceed that of passive surveillance, article 6 issues can arise if the agents are not called to give evidence at trial. In *Ludi v Switzerland*[59] the authorities sought to justify reliance on the hearsay evidence of an undercover agent on the basis that if his identity were revealed in the course of his evidence, he would be unable to continue his work as an undercover agent and unable to protect the identity of his informers. In light of the applicant's argument that he wanted to clarify the extent to which he had been influenced by the agent, the European Court found a breach of article 6. The agent was a police officer and even if his true identity were not known, the applicant knew his physical appearance.

9.35   The European Court also considered the article 8 (privacy) implications of using undercover agents in *Ludi v Switzerland.*[60] The applicant argued that the undercover agent in question had abused his relationship of trust to gain access to the applicant's home and private life. Although the Commission thought this an interference with the applicant's article 8 rights,[61] the European Court disagreed. In its view, by engaging in criminal activities such as drug dealing, the applicant must have known that he might encounter undercover agents. In other words, he voluntarily assumed the risk of interference with his private life. Whether, on the other hand, article 8 is violated where undercover agents exceed their role of passive surveillance and incite criminal offences was raised, but not resolved, in *Teixeira de Castro v Portugal.*[62]

59   (1993) 15 EHRR 173.
60   Ibid.
61   Albeit a justifiable interference.
62   Note 56.

Protecting the rights of victims and witnesses in criminal proceedings

9.36   By recognising that in some circumstances the right of an accused to
challenge all the witnesses against him/her must yield to the need to
protect witnesses from reprisals or identification, the Strasbourg
bodies have, to some extent, sought to balance the right to a fair trial
with the rights of victims and witnesses. This was made explicit by
the European Court in *Doorson v Netherlands*[63] where it made the
following observations:

> It is true that article 6 does not explicitly require the interests of
> witnesses in general, and those of victims called upon to testify in
> particular, to be taken into consideration. However, their life, liberty
> or security of person may be at stake, as may interests coming
> generally within the ambit of article 8 of the Convention. Such
> interests of witnesses and victims are in principle protected by
> other, substantive provisions of the Convention, which imply that
> Contracting States should organise their criminal proceedings in
> such a way that those interests are not unjustifiably imperilled.
> Against this background, principles of fair trial also require that in
> appropriate cases the interests of the defence are balanced against
> those of witnesses or victims called upon to testify.[64]

9.37   The same approach has been adopted towards victims and witnesses
in sexual offences cases. In *Baegen v Netherlands*[65] where the applicant had been able to confront, but not question, the complainant in
a rape trial, the Commission had regard to:

> ... the special features of criminal proceedings concerning rape and
> other sexual offences. Such proceedings are often conceived of as an
> ordeal by the victim, in particular when the latter is unwillingly
> confronted with the defendant. In the assessment of the question
> whether or not in such proceedings an accused received a fair trial,
> account must be taken of the right to respect for the victim's
> private life. Therefore, the Commission accepts that in criminal
> proceedings concerning sexual abuse certain measures may be
> taken for the purpose of protecting the victim, provided that such
> measures can be reconciled with an adequate and effective exercise
> of the rights of the defence.[66]

63   (1996) 22 EHRR 330.
64   Ibid at para 70.
65   A/327-B (1995); unreported. See also *Shahzad v UK* [1998] EHRLR 210
(decided before *Teixeira de Castro*).
66   Ibid at para 77.

Since, in that case, the applicant had not used his opportunity to put written questions to the complainant, applied to the court to hear her, or submitted to blood or other tests, the Commission rejected his claim that, in breach of article 6, he had not been able to test her credibility.

9.38   The issue of protecting the rights of victims and witnesses in criminal proceedings arose in another way in *Z v Finland*,[67] where the rights and interests of an innocent third party had to be balanced, not with the right of the defendant to a fair trial, but with the public interest in the prosecution of crime. The applicant had been married to a man who was being tried on several counts of attempted manslaughter. The allegation against him was that he had engaged in sexual acts knowing that he was HIV positive. When the applicant's former husband declined to give evidence himself, the prosecuting authorities seized her medical files and ordered her medical adviser to give evidence in an attempt to establish the date upon which he knew he was HIV positive. In its reasoned judgment convicting the applicant's former husband, the domestic court identified the applicant and referred to her medical files, but ordered that the judgment remain confidential for ten years. The Court of Appeal in Finland upheld the ten-year confidentiality order, but disclosed the applicant's name and medical condition in its judgment, which it faxed to the press.

9.39   It was undisputed before the European Court that the measures complained of constituted interference with the applicant's right to respect for her private and family life under article 8 of the Convention. Moreover the European Court, like the Commission, accepted the Finnish government's claim that the aim of the measures was legitimate; ie to prevent crime and protect the rights of others. The question was, therefore, whether they could be justified as 'necessary in a democratic society'.[68]

9.40   The European Court recognised that respecting medical confidentiality is a 'vital principle', crucial to privacy and also to preserving confidence in the medical profession and in the health services in general.[69] As a result:

> ... any state measures compelling communication or disclosure of such information without the consent of the patient call for the most careful scrutiny on the part of the Court ...[70]

---

67 (1998) 25 EHRR 371.
68 For consideration of this concept, see paras 4.60 to 4.62.
69 Note 67 at para 95.
70 Note 67 at para 96.

The public interest in the investigation and prosecution of crime and the public interest in the publicity of court proceedings can outweigh medical confidentiality,[71] but only in limited circumstances and where safeguards exist to protect the rights and interests of patients.

9.41   Important factors for the European Court in the Z case were:

1) The fact that disclosure could be compelled only in serious cases: under Finnish law medical advisers can be compelled to give evidence without the informed consent of their patients only in relation to offences where a sentence of at least six years is prescribed.

2) Although the applicant had not addressed the domestic court herself, her views were made known and taken into account.

3) The applicant's medical advisers were questioned in camera and there was a ten-year confidentiality order in relation to the reasoned judgment.

4) All those involved in the proceedings were under a duty to treat the information derived from the applicant's medical advisers as confidential. Breach of their duty in this respect could lead to civil and/or criminal liability under Finnish law.

Taking all these factors into account, the Court found no violation of article 8 in relation to the seizure of the applicant's medical files and the order compelling her legal advisers to give evidence, but found a violation in relation to the ten-year confidentiality order (which the Court thought was too short) and disclosure of the applicant's name in the Court of Appeal judgment.

Unlawfully obtained evidence

9.42   Subject to the rule about evidence obtained by ill-treatment,[72] the use of unlawfully obtained evidence in criminal proceedings is not absolutely ruled out under the Convention. The practice of the European Court is to examine the way in which the evidence was obtained, the seriousness of any Convention breach and the impact of the evidence at trial.

9.43   In *Schenk v Switzerland*[73] the applicant's telephone conversations with the man he had allegedly commissioned to kill his wife were

71 Note 67 at para 97.
72 See below para 9.46.
73 (1991) 13 EHRR 242.

secretly recorded. Subsequently, they were used as evidence against him at trial. Before the European Court, the Swiss government conceded that the recordings had been obtained unlawfully because they had not been ordered by the investigating judge. However, the Court refused to accept that a breach of article 6 automatically followed. What mattered was overall fairness. Relevant to that question were the following factors:

1) the applicant had been aware of the unlawfulness of the recordings and had been able to challenge their authenticity in court;

2) the applicant had obtained an investigation of and could have examined the persons allegedly involved in the making of the recording; and

3) the recording was not the only evidence on which the applicant's conviction was based.

In the circumstances, the European Court found no violation of article 6. However, it might have reached a different conclusion if the recording had been the only, or main, evidence against the applicant, or there were doubts as to its authenticity.[74]

9.44   The fact that evidence obtained by a ruse was not the only evidence on which the applicant's conviction was based was also an important factor in *X v Germany*.[75] There the applicant and his co-defendant were arrested in Italy. An Italian undercover police officer, posing as a remand prisoner who spoke no German, was placed in the cell with them. In the Commission's view the use at trial of evidence of the applicant's conversations with his co-defendant did not breach article 6. If the applicant spoke freely to his co-defendant in the company of a third party it was his own responsibility if this was used against him.

9.45   Although the European Court has not gone so far as the courts in New Zealand, which have developed a rule of prima facie exclusion of evidence obtained in breach of the Bill of Rights Act,[76] as noted in chapter 8[77] its case-law is evolving so as to reflect the increased sensitivity of the public to the fair administration of justice. And, in some respects, the Court already appears to have identified certain categories of evidence which cannot be relied upon at trial. These include

---

74 See *Law of the European Convention on Human Rights* Harris, O'Boyle and Warbrick, Butterworths,1995 p210. The pending case of *Khan v UK* before the Court may clarify this issue.

75 (1989) 11 EHRR 84.

76 See *R v Kirifi* [1992] 2 NZLR 8; *R v Goodwin* No 2 [1993] 2 NZLR 390 and *Simpson v AG* (Baigent's Case) [1994] 3 NZLR 667.

evidence obtained in breach of fundamental rights, such as article 3 and evidence which, of itself, breaches article 6 (for example, where an undercover agent or agent provocateur incites criminal offences[78]). Reliance on unlawfully obtained evidence therefore runs the risk of exclusion at trial under the Convention.

Confession evidence

9.46   Evidence obtained by maltreatment cannot be used in criminal proceedings. In *Austria v Italy*[79] the Commission considered, obiter, that the Convention would be violated if a trial court admitted, as evidence, confessions obtained by torture or ill-treatment.

9.47   In *G v UK*[80] the European Commission saw early access to a lawyer as an important safeguard as to the reliability of confession evidence and implied that a confession obtained during incommunicado detention would require very close scrutiny. As for the requirement that domestic procedures exists whereby the validity of confession evidence can be examined, the Commission considered that the existence of the voir-dire procedure in UK law, and the fact that the burden of proving that a statement was voluntary fell on the prosecution, were sufficient.

9.48   The European Court was also concerned about confessions obtained during incommunicado detention in *Barbera, Messegue and Jabardo v Spain*.[81] It expressed 'reservations' about the use of such confessions, particularly where the authorities could not clearly demonstrate that the applicants had waived their right to legal assistance.[82]

Accomplice evidence

9.49   The Commission has found that nothing in the Convention precludes a court from hearing as a witness for the prosecution a person who is guilty of the same offence alleged against the accused.[83] And

---

77   Para 8.1.
78   See paras 9.30 to 9.35.
79   (1963) 6 Yearbook 740.
80   (1984) 35 DR 75.
81   (1989) 11 EHRR 360.
82   Ibid at para 87.
83   Appl 1599/62 v Austria.

in *MH v UK*[84] it found inadmissible a complaint that the admission of the guilty plea of the applicant's co-defendant violated the applicant's right to a fair trial under article 6 of the Convention.

9.50   Different considerations apply where evidence is adduced from an accomplice who has been granted immunity from prosecution. In *X v UK*[85] the applicant was convicted of armed robbery on the evidence of a 'super-grass' witness who had been granted immunity from prosecution in relation to numerous offences. The Commission recognised that the use of such evidence may put in question the fairness of criminal proceedings, but, on the facts, was influenced by the 'numerous elements in the proceedings as a whole and concerning [the witness'] evidence in particular' which indicated that the applicant had a fair hearing. It highlighted that:

1) before trial, prosecuting counsel disclosed to the applicant's counsel the agreement between the DPP and the witness;

2) the jury was told of the agreement and everything that was known about the witness;

3) the applicant's counsel did not object to the witness giving evidence;

4) the applicant did not give evidence or call any witnesses;

5) the judge made it plain to the jury that unless it was satisfied that the witness was telling the truth it could not convict; and

6) the jury convicted the applicant on one count, but not two others.

In the circumstances, there was no breach of article 6. Where no such safeguards exist, the position may well be different.

9.51   In *Baragiola v Switzerland*[86] the Commission emphasised that domestic courts must adopt a 'critical approach' when assessing the evidence of accomplices who stood to lose the benefit of sentence reductions if they went back on their previous statements to the police or retracted their confessions. In that case, the facts that the applicant could challenge accomplice evidence and that his conviction was not solely based on their evidence were crucial to the Commission's determination that there had been no violation of article 6.

---

84 Appl 28572/95 [1997] EHRLR 279.
85 (1976) 7 DR 115.
86 (1993) 75 DR 76.

Expert evidence

9.52 The role of expert witnesses in criminal proceedings has raised difficulties under the Convention. In *Bönisch v Austria*[87] a court-appointed expert had drafted reports which set the criminal proceedings against the applicant in motion and, at trial, his duty was essentially to explain his findings to the court. In those circumstances, the European Court took the view that he was to be treated as a prosecution witness. In such circumstances, the principle of equality of arms required there to be equal treatment between the hearing of the court-appointed expert and the defence expert.

9.53 Such equal treatment had not been afforded in *Bönisch* for two reasons. First, the expert instructed by the defence had been treated as a mere witness rather than an expert, unlike to the court-appointed expert. Second, the court-appointed expert had been able to attend throughout the hearings and had even been able to put questions to the accused and his witnesses, and comment on their evidence. No such facilities were afforded to the defence expert.

9.54 No breach of the Convention was found in *Brandstetter v Austria*[88] where the court-appointed expert was employed by the same institute as the expert on whose opinion an indictment had been based. In the European Court's view this alone did not justify fears that he would be unable to act with proper neutrality.

Defence evidence

9.55 Equality of treatment between the prosecution and the defence does not necessarily require the attendance and examination of every witness the defence wish to call.[89] Normally it is for the domestic courts to decide whether it is necessary or relevant to call a witness. However, the European Court recognised in *Bricmont v Belgium*[90] that:

> There are exceptional circumstances which could prompt the Court to conclude that the failure to hear a person as a witness was incompatible with article 6 ...[91]

---

87 (1987) 9 EHRR 191.
88 (1993) 15 EHRR 378.
89 *Engel and Others v Netherlands* at para 91; *Bricmont v Belgium* (1990) 12 EHRR 217 at para 89.
90 (1990) 12 EHRR 217.
91 Ibid at para 89.

9.56   Failure by the domestic courts to give reasons for not calling defence witnesses (or allowing them to be called) may amount to 'exceptional circumstances'. In *Bricmont*, the Commission took a robust line:

> article 6(3)(d) is a specific right and ... a court must give the reasons for which it decides not to summon those witnesses whose examination has been expressly requested. A court does not have a discretion so extensive that it may deprive article 6(3)(d) of all substance by refraining from demonstrating the irrelevance of the matters on which the examination of witnesses is proposed.[92]

But the European Court declined to follow. Although, in *Vidal v Belgium*,[93] it re-examined the question of reasons for not calling witnesses.

9.57   In that case the applicant, a former prison officer, was charged with providing a gun to a prisoner to assist his escape. The prisoner asserted that the applicant gave him the gun and a note written and signed by the applicant was found on the prisoner when he was caught trying to escape. However, the applicant maintained that the note was given to a different prisoner in the context of a gambling debt. During the course of investigations, another prisoner claimed to the prison governor that, consistent with the applicant's assertion, the gun in question had indeed been brought into the prison by a third party. However, he refused to testify at the applicant's criminal trial unless he was released on licence and his family protected against reprisals. Despite a defence application, in common with three others witnesses, he was not called to give evidence and the applicant was convicted.

9.58   Before the European Court, the applicant argued that his article 6 rights had been breached because he had been deprived of his only means of establishing his innocence. The Court agreed. While it accepted that its function did not permit it to assess the relevance of the evidence as such, nor to form a view on the applicant's guilt or innocence, it found that:

> ... the complete silence of the judgment of [the domestic court] on the point in question is not consistent with the concept of a fair trial which is the basis of article 6.[94]

9.59   From *Vidal*, it is clear that special care is needed where the evidence the defence wishes to adduce is the only means of proving a disput-

92 Commission Report in *Bricmont v Belgium*; note 89.
93 A/235-B (22 April 1992); unreported.
94 Ibid at para 34.

ed point. In *Unterpertinger v Austria*,[95] the European Court was influenced in its finding that the use of hearsay evidence from non-compellable witnesses violated article 6 by the fact that the domestic court had refused to admit evidence that the applicant sought to adduce to undermine the witnesses' credibility.[96]

The right to silence: freedom from self-incrimination

9.60   Article 6 of the European Convention was based on the 1949 version of the UN Human Rights Committee's draft of the International Covenant on Civil and Political Rights which, at that stage, did not expressly set out any prohibition on self-incrimination. Later, the UN draft was amended and article 14(3)(g) of the Covenant now provides that 'in the determination of any criminal charge against him' everyone shall be entitled 'not to be compelled to testify against himself or to confess guilt'. Although no corresponding amendment has ever been made to article 6, it is now clearly accepted that it implicitly includes this prohibition.

9.61   The issue of the right to silence first came before the European Court in *Funke v France*[97] which involved French powers of compulsory questioning. There, the applicant was convicted of an offence of failing to produce bank statements relevant to investigations into customs offences that might have been committed by him. Although no prosecution was actually brought against him, the Court held that by attempting to compel him to produce incriminating evidence, the applicant's right to silence had been infringed.[98] Underpinning the Court's decision was its recognition that the fair trial requirements of article 6 include:

> ... the right of anyone charged with a criminal offence ... to remain silent and not to contribute to incriminating himself.[99]

9.62   Three years later the Court expanded on this principle in *Saunders v United Kingdom*,[100] which involved English powers of compulsory

---

95 (1991) 13 EHRR 175.
96 Ibid at para 33.
97 (1993) 16 EHRR 297.
98 Ibid at para 44.
99 Ibid.
100 (1997) 23 EHRR 313.

questioning. The applicant, a director at Guinness, had been questioned – under threat of punishment akin to contempt of court or a fine if he refused to answer – by DTI inspectors exercising their powers of compulsory questioning under the Companies Act 1985.[101] Having completed their investigations, the DTI inspectors notified the Secretary of State that they had found evidence of possible criminal offences and passed transcripts of the applicant's answers to their questions to the CPS. The applicant was subsequently charged with several counts of false accounting and conspiracy. When the applicant denied any wrongdoing at trial, the prosecution sought to prove the case against him using the evidence provided by the DTI inspectors. Despite the applicant's objections, the court admitted this evidence on the basis of s431(5) of the Companies Act 1985 which provides that:

> ... an answer given by a person to a question put to him in the exercise of powers conferred by this section ... may be used in evidence against him.[102]

The applicant was subsequently convicted.

9.63   The European Court, finding for the applicant, stressed that the right not to incriminate oneself was a generally recognised international standard which lay at the heart of the notion of a fair trial under article 6. It also took a broad approach to the concept of incriminating statements so as to include apparently 'neutral' statements which might nonetheless be deployed to support a prosecution case.

9.64   From this it is clear that where answers are given in the course of compulsory questioning, the use made of them afterwards will be the key issue. In the *Saunders* case the prosecution had employed the applicant's answers to the DTI inspectors in an incriminating manner in order to cast doubt on his honesty and to establish his involvement in the unlawful share support operation. Accordingly, the European Court considered that there had been an infringement of his right not to incriminate himself. And the public interest in combating fraud could not be invoked to justify the use of answers obtained under powers of compulsory questioning in a non-judicial investigation to incriminate the applicant at his trial.

9.65   The position was different in *Abas v the Netherlands*.[103] Although

---

101   Ss 432(2) and 436(3).
102   Note 100.
103   Appl 27943/95 [1997] EHRLR 418.

the applicant in that case had been under a legal obligation to provide information to a Dutch tax inspector (in default of which he
could have been fined or imprisoned), no criminal proceedings were
pursued against him. In the circumstances, the Commission took the
view that the applicant's right not to incriminate himself was not
infringed. And to subject ordinary tax investigations to the requirements of article 6 would, in the Commission's view, unduly hamper
their effective functioning.

9.66   Similarly in *K v Austria*[104] the Commission found no violation of
article 6 where the applicant (a witness) had refused to give evidence
in criminal proceedings because he himself was facing other
criminal proceedings.

The right to silence: drawing adverse inferences

9.67   The case-law of the European Court and Commission on the question of drawing adverse inferences from silence is less extensive. In
John Murray v United Kingdom,[105] the European Court examined the
provisions of the Criminal Evidence (Northern Ireland) Order 1988.
The applicant had been arrested in a house in which an IRA informer
had been held captive. He was taken to Castlereagh police station,
where his access to a solicitor was delayed for 48 hours pursuant to
the Northern Ireland (Emergency Provisions) Act 1987. He was cautioned under the 1988 Order and then interviewed 12 times. He
remained silent throughout. At his trial he elected not to give
evidence. The trial judge (sitting without a jury) exercised his discretion under the 1988 Order to draw adverse inferences from the applicant's silence and convicted him of aiding and abetting the false
imprisonment of the informer.

9.68   Although it recognised that 'the right to remain silent under
police questioning and the privilege against self-incrimination are
generally recognised international standards which lie at the heart of
article 6',[106] the European Court carefully confined its judgment to the
facts of the case, emphasising that it was not its role to examine
whether, in general, the drawing of inferences under the 1988 Order
was compatible with the notion of a fair hearing under article 6. In

---

104 A/255-B (1993). But see also *Serves v France* [1998] EHRLR 213 concerning a
fine for refusing to take the oath as a witness.
105 (1996) 22 EHRR 29 (not to be confused with *Sean Murray v DPP* – the House
of Lords case).
106 Ibid at paras 44–45.

its view, it was self-evident, on the one hand, that it was incompatible with immunity from self-incrimination to base a conviction solely or mainly on the accused's silence or on a refusal to answer questions or to give evidence at trial. On the other hand, the Court deemed it equally obvious that such immunity could not and should not prevent the accused's silence, in situations which clearly called for an explanation from him, being taken into account in assessing the persuasiveness of the evidence adduced by the prosecution. Wherever the line between these two extremes is to be drawn, it follows from this understanding of the right to silence that it is not an absolute right.

9.69   In *Murray v UK*, the European Court noted that the applicant was, in fact, able to remain silent and that he remained a non-compellable witness. It also observed that:

> In Northern Ireland, where trial judges sit without a jury, the judge must explain the reasons for the decision to draw inferences and the weight attached to them. The exercise of discretion in this regard is subject to review by the appellate court.
>
> In the present case, the evidence presented against the applicant by the prosecution was considered by the Court of Appeal to constitute a 'formidable' case against him ...[107]

In the circumstances, the Court took the view that 'having regard to the weight of the evidence against the applicant', the drawing of inferences from his refusal, at arrest, during police questioning and at trial, to provide an explanation for his presence in the house in which the informer was held was 'a matter of common sense' and could not be regarded as unfair or unreasonable. The substantive challenge to the 1988 Order, therefore, failed.

9.70   However, the Court went on to find that the adverse inferences drawn in the applicant's case significantly contributed to a violation of article 6(1) and 6(3)(c) which arose from the delayed access to a solicitor at the police station. In the Court's view:

> [T]he scheme contained in the [1988] Order is such that it is of paramount importance for the rights of the defence that an accused has access to a lawyer at the initial stages of police interrogation. It observes in this context that, under the Order, an accused is confronted with a fundamental dilemma relating to his defence. If he chooses to remain silent adverse inferences may be drawn against him in accordance with the provisions of the Order. On the other hand, if the accused opts to break his silence during the

---

107 Ibid at paras 51 to 52.

course of interrogation, he runs the risk of prejudicing his defence without necessarily removing the possibility of inferences being drawn against him.[108]

Under such conditions the concept of fairness enshrined in article 6 requires that an accused person has the benefit of the assistance of a lawyer at the initial stage of police interrogation. To deny access to a lawyer for the first 48 hours of police questioning, in a situation where the rights of the defence may well be irretrievably prejudiced, is – whatever the justification for such denial – incompatible with the rights of the accused under article 6.[109]

9.71   At the heart of the distinction drawn by the European Court and the Commission between powers of compulsory questioning and the power to draw inferences from silence is the question, or definition, of 'compulsion'. In the *Saunders* case, the Commission emphasised that:

> [T]he privilege against self-incrimination is an important element in safeguarding an accused from oppression and coercion during criminal proceedings. The very basis of a fair trial presupposes that the accused is afforded the opportunity of defending himself against the charges brought against him. The position of the defence is undermined if the accused is under compulsion, or has been compelled to incriminate himself. ... Whether a particular applicant has been subject to compulsion to incriminate himself and whether the use made of the incriminating material has rendered criminal proceedings unfair will depend on an assessment of each case as a whole.[110]

Similarly, in *John Murray*, the Court drew a distinction between 'proper' compulsion (permitted under article 6) and 'improper' compulsion (not permitted). However difficult it may be to draw the distinction in practice, the following general conclusions can be tentatively drawn.

9.72   Most (if not all) of the powers of compulsory questioning violate the Convention in so far as they permit the use in criminal pro-ceedings of statements or documents obtained by the use of such powers. Whether those statements or documents are incriminating on their face is irrelevant if they are used to support the prosecution case. However, the legitimacy of drawing adverse inferences from

108 Ibid at para 66.
109 Legislation has now been enacted to deal with this problem.
110 Note 100 at para 62.

silence during police questioning or failing to testify at trial – for example, under the 1988 Criminal Evidence (Northern Ireland) Order or the 1994 Criminal Justice and Public Order Act – is less clear-cut. In *Murray v UK* the Court based its decision primarily on the strength of the evidence against the applicant. Since this constituted a 'formidable case against him' it called 'as a matter of common sense' for an explanation.[111] However the Court has emphasised the need for safeguards such as the right to legal advice, before adverse inferences can be drawn from failure to answer police questions. In addition, the Court in *Murray v UK* was clearly influenced by the fact that the domestic court gave a fully reasoned judgment, setting out the nature of the influence drawn, which was subject to scrutiny in the Northern Ireland Court of Appeal. No such safeguard exists under the Criminal Justice and Public Order Act 1994. In his partly concurring opinion in the Commission, Sir Nicholas Bratza (now a judge of the European Court) said:

> In reaching the view that there has been no violation of the Convention I attach considerable importance to the fact that adverse inferences under the 1988 Order are drawn by a judge sitting without a jury. Not only is a judge, by his training and legal experience, likely to be better equipped than a lay juryman to draw only such inferences as are justified from a defendant's silence, but, as pointed out by the Commission, a judge in Northern Ireland gives a reasoned judgment as to the grounds on which he decides to draw inferences in any particular case: whether the inferences have been properly drawn in all the circumstances and whether proper weight has been given to them by the trial judge is then subject to review by the Court of Appeal in Northern Ireland. The same safeguards against unfairness do not appear to me to exist in the case of a jury trial. When it is a jury which must decide, without giving reasons, what adverse inferences, if any, to draw against the accused from his silence and what weight to attach to such inferences in arriving at a verdict, the risk of unfairness occurring appears to me to be substantially increased, however carefully formulated a judge's direction to the jury might be.[112]

9.73   A series of further cases, recently admitted for consideration by the Commission, may help to clarify matters. In *Quinn v UK*,[113] which

---

111 Note: under the 1988 Order and the 1994 Act, so long as there is a prima facie case, there is no *requirement* for the prosecution evidence to reach such a high threshold before adverse inferences are drawn.

112 Note 105 at 53.

113 Appl 23496/94 (1997) 23 EHRR CD 41.

concerns adverse inferences drawn from silence during questioning, the applicant is seeking to distinguish his case from that of *John Murray v UK*[114] on the basis that the situation when he was being questioned was not one which 'clearly called for an explanation'. Like *Murray* he had been denied access to a lawyer before being questioned, but unlike *Murray* he had given evidence.

9.74   The issues in *Hamil v UK*[115] and *Kevin Murray v UK*[116] are narrower. In *Hamil* inferences were drawn from the applicant's failure to give evidence at trial even though he had given an explanation for his presence and behaviour before and after his arrest. And in *Kevin Murray* inferences were drawn from the applicant's refusal to answer police questions and to give evidence even though he too had given an explanation to the police upon arrest.

Intimate samples

9.75   The use in evidence of fingerprints, intimate and non-intimate samples does not, of itself, infringe the right not to incriminate oneself. That right is primarily concerned with respecting the will of an accused person to remain silent. In the *Saunders* case, the European Court took the view that:

> [I]t does not extend to the use in criminal proceedings of material which may be obtained from the accused through the use of compulsory powers but which has an existence independent of the will of the suspect such as, inter alia, documents acquired pursuant to a warrant, breath, blood and urine samples and bodily tissues for the purpose of DNA testing.

However, the Court did not consider the *means* by which such evidence is obtained. And it may be that in some cases the exercise of police powers to obtain samples will violate other rights under the Convention.[117] See further chapter 15.

---

114 Note 105.
115 Appl 21656/93 [1997] EHRLR 169.
116 Appl 22384/93 [1997] EHRLR 169.
117 For example, article 8 privacy rights.

CHAPTER 10

Sentence and appeals

10.1   Sentence: introduction

10.2   Article 3 issues in sentencing

10.3   The fair trial guarantees of article 6 in sentencing

10.4   Non-retrospectivity

10.5   Sentence for Convention-protected activity

10.6   Punitive and preventative sentences

10.7   Victim involvement in sentencing

10.8   Appeals: introduction

10.12   Legal aid and legal representation at the appeal stage

10.17   The right to oral argument at a public hearing in the presence of the accused at the appeal stage

10.19   Proceedings for leave to appeal

10.22   Loss of time pending appeal

10.25   Reasons in appeal proceedings

10.27   New evidence and refences back to the Court of Appeal

Sentence: introduction

10.1   Article 5(1)(a) justifies detention after conviction and, broadly speaking, the European Court and Commission have been reluctant to examine cases which only concern sentence. Article 5(1)(a) requires that detention under a criminal sentence must result from, follow and depend upon, a criminal conviction; though it may serve preventative as well as punitive purposes, provided the need for prevention is found to exist at the time of sentence.[1] The Convention issues arising where deportation is ordered are considered in chapter 18.

Article 3 issues in sentencing

10.2   Article 3 issues concerning the 'inhumanity' of unduly severe sentences will only arise in very extreme cases. These are dealt with in chapter 16, along with other article 3 issues relating to prisoners.[2]

The fair trial guarantees of article 6 in sentencing

10.3   Article 6 continues to apply to the sentencing process but the presumption of innocence does not. It deals only with proof of guilt and not with the kind or level of punishment.[3] Consequently, when sentencing, a judge may take into account factors which are inadmissible at trial,[4] including previous convictions.[5]

Non-retrospectivity

10.4   Article 7(1) prohibits a court from imposing a heavier penalty than the one which was applicable at the time that the offence was committed. This was found to have been violated in *Welch v UK*[6] in relation to retroactive confiscation orders under the Drug Trafficking Offences Act 1986.[7]

---

1   *X v UK* (1982) 4 EHRR 188; *Weeks v UK* (1989) 10 EHRR 293.
2   Paras 16.31 to 16.34
3   *Engel and others v Netherlands* (No.1) (1979–80) 1 EHRR 647 at para.90.
4   *Engel and others v Netherlands* (No.1) (1979–80) 1 EHRR 647 at para.90.
5   *Albert and le Compte v Belgium* A/58 (1983) 5 EHRR 533.
6   (1995) 20 EHRR 247.
7   See chapter 6, paras 6.27 to 6.31.

Sentences for Convention-protected activity

10.5 Special considerations may also arise where an individual is being punished for conduct which is covered by articles 8 to 12 of the Convention. The rules restricting the exercise of rights under those articles – in particular the requirement of proportionality – must not be infringed by the imposition of too severe a sentence. So, for example, in *Arrowsmith v UK*[8] the Commission carefully scrutinised the applicant's sentence for sedition for compliance with article 10.[9]

Punitive and preventative sentences

10.6 The case-law of the European Court and Commission distinguishes between three types of sentence:

1) Punitive sentences imposed on principles of retributive proportionality as punishment for the crime committed. Typically these involve fixed-term sentences 'to a period of imprisonment imposed by the court as appropriate to the case'.[10] The sentence orders detention for the period merited as punishment and there is no right under the Convention to parole or release before the pre-determined period. This analysis has also been applied to the mandatory life sentence.[11]

2) Preventative sentences based purely or predominantly on some characteristic in the offender – such as mental disorder[12] or youth, dangerousness and unpredictability.[13] Such sentences are imposed both for preventative and therapeutic or rehabilitative objectives. Continuing detention must therefore be justified by reference to these purposes, and periodic review by a court or independent tribunal is required of detention under any measure of preventative detention which is premised upon some characteristic in the offender susceptible to change with the passage of time.[14]

---

8   (1978) 19 DR 5.
9   Ibid at para 99 see further paras 6.32 to 6.37.
10 *Van Droogenbroeck v Belgium* (1982) 4 EHRR 433.
11 *Wynne v UK* (1995) 19 EHRR 333.
12 As in the case of restriction order patients whose position was analyses in *X v UK* (1982) 4 EHRR 188.
13 As in *Weeks v UK* note 1.
14 *X v UK* (1982) 4 EHRR 188; *Thynne, Wilson and Gunnell v UK* (1991) 13 EHRR 666; and *Hussain and Singh v UK* (1996) 22 EHRR 1; see further chapter 16.

3) Mixed sentences, which have a partly retributive and partly preventative purpose. UK sentences identified as having this dual nature are the discretionary life sentence (which has an initial tariff stage followed by an indeterminate period of preventative detention)[15] and the sentence of detention during Her Majesty's Pleasure imposed on juveniles convicted of murder.[16] In each case the European Court has clearly held that detention in the post-tariff stage must be reviewed by a court or independent tribunal to determine whether detention is still justified on grounds of continuing dangerousness – which is the only justification under the Convention for continued detention at that stage. Moreover, the Convention requires a judicial fixing of the tariff to accord with article 6, since the tariff is, in effect, a sentence within a sentence.[17]

Victim involvement in sentencing

10.7   Attempts by the victims of crime or their relatives to argue for the right to participate in the sentencing process on the basis that the commission of a criminal offence by the defendant has infringed their Convention rights have all failed. In *McCourt v UK*[18] the applicant complained that, in breach of her right to private and family life, she had not been able to participate in the sentencing process of the person convicted of the murder of her daughter. However, the Commission declared her application manifestly ill-founded.

Appeals: introduction

10.8   There is no right to appeal under the Convention itself. This is provided for by article 2 of Protocol 7 (which has not yet entered force). However, where a right of appeal is provided in domestic law, article 6 applies. This was established by the European Court in *Delcourt v Belgium*:[19]

---

15 *Thynne, Wilson and Gunnell v UK* (1991) 13 EHRR 666.
16 *Hussein and Singh v UK* (1996) 22 EHRR 1.
17 *T and V v UK* (Commission); noted at [1998] EHRLR 484.
18 (1993) 15 EHRR CD 110.
19 (1979–80) 1 EHRR 355.

A criminal charge is not really 'determined' as long as the verdict of acquittal or conviction has not become final. Criminal proceedings form an entity and must, in the ordinary way, terminate in an enforceable decision ...

... The Convention does not, it is true, compel the Contracting States to set up courts of appeal or of cassation. Nevertheless, a State which does institute such courts is required to ensure that persons amenable to the law shall enjoy before these courts the fundamental guarantees in article 6.[20]

And, since the consideration of an application for leave to appeal constitutes part of the determination of a criminal charge, article 6 applies at that stage.[21]

10.9 The additional guarantees of article 2 of Protocol 7 cannot be read as intending to limit the applicability of article 6 in criminal appeals.[22] However, the manner of application of article 6 to appeal proceedings does depend on the special features of the proceedings involved. Account has to be taken of the entirety of the proceedings and the role of the appellate courts in the overall process.[23]

10.10 This means that some of the article 6 guarantees, such as the right to an oral hearing and the right of the accused to be present, are less strictly applied in appeal proceedings, particularly where the only issues raised are points of law. However, the extent to which an appeal court can cure defects in the proceedings below is limited. So, for example, a public appeal hearing will not rectify a non-public trial.

10.11 On a practical note, although reasonable time limits may be applied to appeal proceedings,[24] the relevant authorities bear the burden of keeping an applicant informed about such matters. In *Vachur v France*[25] the applicant was not given a time limit for filing his appeal, nor was he informed of the date of the appeal hearing. As a matter of general principle, the European Court held that states must ensure that everyone charged with a criminal offence – including those who appeal – benefits from the safeguards provided by article 6(3). Putting the onus on a convicted appellant to find out when an allotted period of time starts to run, or expires, is not compatible with the 'diligence' which the contracting states must exercise

---

20 Ibid at para 25.
21 *Monnell and Morris v UK* (1988) 10 EHRR 205.
22 *Ekbatani v Sweden* (1991) 13 EHRR 504 at para 26.
23 *Monnell and Morris* note 21.
24 *Bricmont v Belgium* (1986) 48 DR 106.
25 (1997) 24 EHRR 482.

to ensure that the rights guaranteed by article 6 are enjoyed in an effective manner.[26]

Legal aid and legal representation at the appeal stage

10.12   The case-law of the European Court has established that it will normally be in the interests of justice for a person to receive representation on an appeal where a substantial prison sentence is involved and there is a real issue to be considered.

10.13   In *Granger v UK*[27] the applicant had been convicted of three charges of perjury in relation to his evidence at a murder trial. He was sentenced to five years' imprisonment. He had received legal aid at trial. The applicant wished to appeal against his conviction, but was refused legal aid because the Supreme Court Legal Aid Committee of the Law Society of Scotland was not satisfied that he had substantial grounds for appealing. The applicant's counsel had previously advised against an appeal, but his solicitor disagreed and prepared statements for the applicant to read out. At the appeal the applicant presented his case in person, but was unsuccessful.

10.14   The European Court declined to assess whether the Legal Aid Committee's analysis of the applicant's prospects of success was sound. Whether the interests of justice required grant of legal aid had to be determined in light of the case as a whole and in the applicant's case personal liberty was at stake. In reality, he had been unable to present his own case, or to deal with the legal arguments raised during the proceedings. Given the importance and complexity of the issue involved, the Court took the view that the competent authorities, including the domestic court, should have reconsidered the refusal of legal aid.[28]

10.15   In *Maxwell v UK*[29] a similar approach was taken. There, the applicant's request for legal aid to conduct an appeal against his conviction for assault was refused by the Scottish Legal Aid Board because it was not satisfied that he had substantial grounds for appeal. The European Court accepted that the legal issues in the appeal were not particularly complex, but recognised that without the services of a

26   Ibid at para 28.
27   (1990) 12 EHRR 469.
28   Ibid at paras 46–47.
29   (1995) 19 EHRR 97.

lawyer the applicant was unable to address the court competently and thus to defend himself effectively. The issue at stake was extremely important for him because he had been sentenced to five years, the appeal court had wide powers and its decision was final. In the circumstances, he should have been granted legal aid for his appeal.[30]

10.16   A narrower approach was taken in *Monnell and Morris v UK*,[31] which pre-dated *Granger* and *Maxwell*. There the European Court held that the interests of justice could not be taken to require the automatic grant of legal aid whenever a convicted person, with no objective likelihood of success, wished to appeal after having received a fair trial at first instance in accordance with article 6.[32]

The right to oral argument at a public hearing in the presence of the accused at the appeal stage

10.17   The European Court has firmly established that it is not necessary for every stage of criminal proceedings to be held in public. The important underlying principle in article 6 is that there should be a fair trial. In *Axen v Germany*[33] the Court found no breach of article 6 where the first-instance trial had been held in public and an appeal involved only points of law. The Court also held that it was not necessary for the appeal judgment to be read out in public; handing a written copy to the applicant was sufficient.

10.18   However, a pre-condition of any departure from the applicant's right to be present in appeal proceedings is that there has been an oral hearing at first instance at which s/he has been entitled to be present. Beyond that, the right to be present depends on the role of appellate courts and the particular facts of the case. Where the appellate court may hear issues of fact as well as of law, there may well be a need for an oral hearing in the applicant's presence. Thus in *Ekbetani v Sweden*[34], where the nub of the applicant's appeal was that he had not committed the act in question and the appeal court assessed his credibility, the European Court found that he should have been present. But each case will turn on its facts and the Court

---

30   Ibid at para 38. See also: *Boner v UK* (1995) 19 EHRR 246.
31   (1987) 10 EHRR 205.
32   Ibid at para 70.
33   (1984) 6 EHRR 195.
34   (1991) 13 EHRR 504.

has recognised the difficulties that attach to the attendance of prisoners.[35]

Proceedings for leave to appeal

10.19   The procedure normally followed by the Court of Appeal in England and Wales when dealing with applications for leave to appeal was scrutinised by the European Court in *Monnell and Morris v UK*.[36] In that case, the applicants complained under article 6 because they were not present when their application for leave to appeal was determined and no oral argument was heard.

10.20   The European Court rejected their complaint. It noted that on an application for leave to appeal, the Court of Appeal does not re-hear the case on the facts, and no witnesses are called, even though the grounds of appeal involve questions of fact as well as law. The issue for decision is whether the applicant has demonstrated the existence of arguable grounds which would justify hearing an appeal. In the Court's view the limited nature of this issue did not, in itself, call for oral argument at a public hearing or the personal appearance of the applicants before the Court of Appeal.[37]

10.21   Even an order that the applicants lose time against their sentence as a result of their unsuccessful appeal[38] did not persuade the European Court that there should have been oral argument at a public hearing in the presence of the applicants. In its view:

> ... the basis on which loss of time was ordered against [the applicants] was, in line with the stated policy and practice of the Court of Appeal, the unmeritorious character of their own applications for leave to appeal. The nature of the issue to be decided for the ordering of loss of time was not such that their physical attendance was essential to assist the Court of Appeal in its determination.[39]

The principle of equality of arms was respected since the prosecution did not appear and the applicants' interests were sufficiently safe-

---

35   *Kamasinki v Austria* (1991) 13 EHRR 36 at para 107. See also *Lala v Netherlands* (1994) 18 EHRR 586 and *Geyseghem v Belgium* [1998] EHRLR 633: heavier emphasis on right to be present.

36   (1988) 10 EHRR 205.

37   Ibid at para 58.

38   See paras 10.22 to 10.24.

39   Note 36 at para 61.

guarded by receipt of legal advice as to their prospects of appeal and the opportunity of making written submissions.

Loss of time pending appeal

10.22 In *Monnell and Morris v UK*[40] the European Court recognised that an order made by the Court of Appeal that part of the time spent by the applicants in custody after conviction should not count towards their sentences effectively imposed an additional period of imprisonment on them. Moreover, it was imposed for reasons unconnected with the facts of the offence or with the character or criminal record of the applicants; it was ordered in line with the stated policy of deterring clearly unmeritorious appeals.

10.23 However, in the Court's view this did not take it outside the ambit of article 5(1)(a) of the Convention.[41] While the loss of time ordered by the Court of Appeal was not treated under domestic law as part of the sentence as such, it did form part of the period of detention which resulted from the overall sentencing procedure that followed conviction. The power to order loss of time was a component of the machinery existing in UK law to ensure that criminal appeals were considered within a reasonable period. As such it was an inherent part of the criminal process following conviction of the offender and pursued a legitimate aim under paragraph 5(1)(a). The Court found that there was a sufficient and legitimate connection between the conviction of each of the applicants and the loss of time order. It accordingly held that the deprivation of liberty was not contrary to article 5(1).

10.24 The matter arose in a different way in *De Salvador Torres v Spain*[42] where the first-instance court found no aggravating circumstances when convicting and sentencing the applicant for fraud. On appeal, the Supreme Court disagreed. It found that, on the facts established by the first instance court and uncontested by the applicant, he had taken advantage of his position as head administrator of a public institution, thus aggravating the offence. It therefore increased his sentence. The European Court rejected the applicant's complaint that his rights under article 6(3)(a) had been violated on the basis that the public nature of the applicant's position was an intrinsic element of

40 Note 36.
41 See para 10.1.
42 (1997) 23 EHRR 601.

the original accusation of embezzlement of public funds and he must have been aware that the appeal court might find this to be an aggravating factor in the lesser offence, for the purposes of determining his sentence.

Reasons in appeal proceedings

10.25   As a general rule, article 6 requires courts to give reasons for their decisions. Although this does not necessarily mean that a detailed answer must be given to every point raised,[43] if an issue is decisive, there should be a 'specific and express outcome'.[44]

10.26   However, the extent to which the right to reasons applies in appeal proceedings will vary according to the issue to be determined. In *Webb v UK*[45] the applicant complained that the Privy Council failed to give reasons for refusing her application for special leave to appeal against her conviction in Bermuda. Drawing on the European Court's reasoning in *Monnell and Morris v UK*,[46] the Commission noted that an appeal to the Privy Council was limited to points of 'great and general importance' or a 'grave injustice'. In such circumstances, very limited reasoning may satisfy the requirements of article 6 because:

> ... it must be apparent to litigants who have been refused leave that they have failed to satisfy the Privy Council that their case involves [such a point] ...[47]

On that basis, the applicant's rights had not been violated.

New evidence and references back to the Court of Appeal

10.27   The European Court has yet to deal with the question of new evidence which emerges post-conviction. However, in a very early case the Commission took a robust line:

43   *Van der Hurk v Netherlands* (1994) 18 EHRR 481.
44   *Hiro Balani v Spain* (1995) 19 EHRR 565 para 28.
45   Appl 33186/96 (1997) 24 EHRR CD 73.
46   Note 36.
47   Note 45 at p 74. For a similar approach involving the Constitutional Court in Germany, see: *E and G Muller-Eberstein v Germany* Appl 29753/96, 27 November 1996 (Commission).

... article 6 does not apply to proceedings for re-opening a trial given that someone who applies for his case to be re-opened and whose sentence has become final, is not someone 'charged with a criminal offence' within the meaning of the said article.[48]

And in the civil context, the Commission has adopted a similar approach. In *X v Austria*,[49] it declined to read a right to a rehearing into article 6 where facts, discovered after the final determination of a case, cast doubt on the impartiality of one of the expert witnesses.

10.28   However, where a procedure is provided for referring a case back to an appeal court which has the power to uphold or overturn a conviction,[50] article 6 applies.[51] It does not, however, guarantee any particular outcome. In *Callaghan and Others v UK*,[52] the Commission rejected the proposition that a retrial before a jury should be ordered where fresh evidence has come to light. Article 6 was satisfied if the Court of Appeal, after hearing the fresh evidence and submissions by counsel, determined whether the applicants' convictions were safe and satisfactory. Moreover, the presumption of innocence does not apply in such proceedings.[53]

48 Appl 864/60, 9 CD 17; Appl 1237/61, 5 Yearbook 101.
49 (1978) 14 DR 171.
50 For example, by the Criminal Cases Review Commission.
51 *Callaghan and Others v UK* (1989) 60 DR 296.
52 Ibid.
53 *Callaghan and Others v UK* note 51 at para 2.

PART III

The European Convention on Human Rights and civil proceedings

The Convention in civil proceedings: an introduction

11.1   Introduction

11.4   Convention rights in civil proceedings

11.7   The application of article 6(1) in civil proceedings

11.8   Judicial review and the Convention
11.9   Judicial review and article 13
11.14   Judicial review and article 6(1)

Introduction

11.1   The Convention will have a profound impact in civil proceedings for two reasons:

1) First, where 'Convention rights' are engaged in civil proceedings, they will have to be protected according to the Convention rules: see chapter 4.

2) Second, article 6(1) guarantees a fair trial in the determination of 'civil rights and obligations'. It is an independent and free-standing right.

Under the Human Rights Act 1998 (HRA), Convention rights, including article 6(1), are incorporated into UK law, making both limbs applicable.

11.2   At the outset it is, therefore, important to distinguish between 'Convention rights' and 'civil rights and obligations'. 'Convention rights' are those rights protected under the Convention itself; whereas 'civil rights and obligations' are those rights and obligation recognised in domestic law, the determination of which is decisive for private rights and obligations.[1] This includes all private litigation and some litigation between individuals and public authorities.

11.3   Although 'Convention rights' and 'civil rights and obligations' will frequently overlap, they are distinct. Where a Convention right is not properly recognised in domestic law, an issue of Convention compliance may arise under the article that protects that right (eg, privacy rights under article 8), but no article 6(1) issue arises. On the other hand, where a private right is recognised in domestic law, article 6(1) will apply to its determination irrespective of whether it corresponds to a Convention right.

Convention rights in civil proceedings

11.4   Where civil proceedings engage Convention rights, decisions reached by the courts which are incompatible with their protection will breach the Convention. So, for example, in the *Spycatcher* litigation, the European Court found that the domestic courts had acted in breach of article 10. By extending injunctions prohibiting publication of a biography by a former secret service agent after it had

---

1   See chapter 12.

been published elsewhere and imported into the UK, they had gone beyond what was 'necessary in a democratic society'.[2]

11.5   What is required, therefore, is for a domestic court to identify whether a Convention right is engaged in proceedings before it and, if so, to apply the Convention principles applicable to the protection of that right. An overview of Convention rights is provided in chapter 3 above, and the Convention principles applicable to their protection are set out in chapter 4 above. In most cases, a restriction on a Convention right will be justified only if it:

1) is 'prescribed by law';

2) pursues a 'legitimate aim'; and

3) is proportionate.[3]

11.6   Under the HRA, individuals will be able to brings civil proceedings against a public authority which has breached (or threatens to breach) their Convention rights. Alternatively, they will be able to rely on their Convention rights in other legal proceedings, including proceedings brought by others.[4] Whenever they do so, domestic courts will be under a duty to interpret legislation[5] and develop the common law compatibly with the Convention.[6]

The application of article 6(1) in civil proceedings

11.7   Turning to the second route by which the Convention is relevant to civil proceedings – the determination of 'civil rights and obligations', article 6(1) provides that:

> In the determination of his civil rights and obligations ... everyone is entitled to a fair and public hearing within a reasonable time by an independent and impartial tribunal established by law.

There are three pre-conditions to its application:

1) First, the rights or obligations in question must be 'civil' in nature.

2) Second, those rights must have a basis in domestic law.

3) Third, there must be a 'determination' of the rights or obligations in question.

2   The proper approach to the protection of Convention rights is dealt with in chapter 4..

3   See paras 4.56 to 4.66

4   See chapter 2.

5   So far as it is possible to do so: see chapter 1.

6   See paras 1.42 to 1.43.

The first two pre-conditions are examined in chapter 12 below, and the third is examined in chapter 13.

Judicial review and the Convention

11.8   Judicial review proceedings are relevant to both the enforcement of Convention rights required by article 13 of the Convention and to the fair determination of civil rights and obligations under article 6(1). However, the applicable principles are different and require separate examination.

Judicial review and article 13

11.9   Article 13 requires that anyone whose Convention rights have been breached 'shall have an effective remedy' before a national authority.[7] The extent to which judicial review proceedings are capable of providing such a remedy has been considered by the European Court in a number of cases.

11.10   In *Soering v UK*[8] the Court found no breach of article 13 where judicial review proceedings were available to challenge a decision to extradite the applicant to Virginia. The applicant complained that judicial review was not a sufficient check on a decision to extradite him to Virginia where he might be exposed to the 'death row phenomenon' contrary to article 3 of the Convention. The Court rejected this, observing that:

> Although the Convention is not considered to be part of United Kingdom law ... English courts can review the 'reasonableness' of an extradition decision in the light of the kind of factors relied on by [the applicant] before the Convention institutions ...[9]

In other words, rather than consider the compatibility of judicial review proceedings with article 13 of the Convention in general, the European Court looked at the practicalities to determine whether the rules governing the High Court's jurisdiction precluded the applicant from advancing any of the arguments he relied upon. Since they did not, there was no breach of article 13.

11.11   The inability of the High Court to examine the merits of a decision in judicial review proceedings was addressed more directly

7   See paras 3.173 to 3.182.
8   (1989) 11 EHRR 439.
9   Ibid at para 121.

in *Vilvarajah v UK*.[10] There, the applicant complained that judicial review was not an effective remedy to challenge decisions refusing him asylum. On the basis that, where it could be established that there was a serious risk of inhuman or degrading treatment, any decision refusing asylum would be struck down as 'unreasonable', the European Court found no breach of article 13. As in *Soering v UK*[11] the Court was influenced by the government's argument that such cases were subjected to 'anxious scrutiny' by the domestic courts in accordance with the decision in *R v Secretary of State ex p Bugdaycay*.[12]

11.12   A different result followed in *Chahal v UK*[13] where it was accepted by all parties that the scope of judicial review proceedings was more limited where a deportation decision was ordered on the ground of national security. The government argued that, despite this limitation, judicial review as a remedy was as effective as it could be, given the necessity of relying on secret sources of information: an argument that had, in the past, been accepted in relation to the compatibility of secret surveillance measures with article 8.[14] The European Court disagreed. In its view:

> The requirement of a remedy which is 'as effective as it can be' is not appropriate in respect of a complaint that a person's deportation will expose him or her to a real risk of treatment in breach of article 3, where the issues concerning national security are immaterial.
>
> In such cases, given the irreversible nature of the harm that might occur if the risk of ill-treatment materialised and the importance the Court attaches to article 3, the notion of an effective remedy under article 13 requires independent scrutiny of the claim that there exist substantial grounds for fearing a real risk of treatment contrary to article 3.[15]

Article 13 was therefore breached.[16]

11.13   The approach taken in *Soering v UK*[17] and *Vilvarajah v UK*[18] was adopted by the European Court in the subsequent case of *D v UK*[19]

---

10   (1992) 14 EHRR 248.
11   Note 8.
12   [1987] 1 All ER 940.
13   (1997) 23 EHRR 413.
14   See: *Klass v Germany* (1979) 2 EHRR 214; *Leander v Sweden* (1987) 9 EHRR 433.
15   Note 13 paras 150 and 151.
16   See also, *Tinnelly v UK* (1998) 27 EHRR 249.
17   Note 8.
18   Note 10.
19   (1997) 24 EHRR 423.

which concerned the expulsion of the applicant, an AIDS sufferer, to St Kitts. It accepted that, unlike the position in *Chahal v UK*,[20] the High Court was not precluded from reviewing the factual basis underlying the impugned decision.[21] Again the Court was influenced by the government's argument that, where it could be established that there was a serious risk of inhuman or degrading treatment, any decision refusing asylum would be struck down as 'unreasonable'.

Judicial review and article 6(1)

11.14   The requirements of article 6(1) of the Convention are stricter than those of article 13. In particular, the Court has consistently held that a fair determination of civil rights and obligations requires an examination on the merits.

11.15   When an administrative body which does not comply with article 6(1) takes a decision affecting civil rights and obligations, there must be scope for review or appeal to a court or tribunal which does.[22] And where factual issues are in dispute, that means that the reviewing body must have power to determine them. Hence a breach of article 6(1) was found in *W v UK*[23] where, in judicial review proceedings, the High Court had no jurisdiction to consider the merits of a local authority decision restricting the applicant's access to his child. On the other hand, where the only issue is one of law or policy, judicial review proceedings may satisfy article 6(1), particularly where the initial decision was taken by a quasi-judicial body with fact-finding functions, such as a planning inspector.[24]

---

20   Note 13.
21   Note 19 at para 72.
22   See paras 12.41 to 12.46
23   (1988) 10 EHRR 29.
24   *Bryan v UK* (1996) 21 EHRR 342; see further chapter 12.

CHAPTER 12

Civil rights and obligations: the scope of article 6(1) of the Convention

12.1   Introduction

12.2   The meaning of 'civil' rights and obligations

12.9   Analysis of Convention case-law

12.10   Property rights

12.12   Licensing

12.13   Professional disciplinary tribunals

12.15   Tax proceedings

12.18   Family proceedings

12.19   Claims for compensation from public authorities

12.22   Legal rights to compensation

12.23   Discretionary and ex gratia payments, including compensation for criminal injuries

12.26   Welfare benefits and related issues

12.27   Employment disputes: the distinction between private employees and public servants

12.28   Immigration and nationality cases

12.29   Education

12.30   Election rights

12.32   The need for a basis in domestic law

continued

12.34   The need for a 'determination' of rights or obligations

12.41   The application of article 6(1) where civil rights and obligations are determined by bodies other than courts or tribunals

12.47   Official investigations

Introduction

12.1 Article 6(1) of the Convention guarantees a fair trial in the 'determination' of 'civil rights and obligations'. As noted above in chapter 11 there are three pre-conditions to its application in civil proceedings:

1) the rights or obligations in question must be 'civil' in nature;

2) those rights must have a basis in domestic law; and

3) there must be a 'determination' of the rights or obligations in question.

Each is important and will be analysed in turn.

The meaning of 'civil' rights and obligations

12.2 The meaning of 'civil' rights and obligations in article 6(1) has given rise to a great deal of case-law. It clearly includes all rights and obligations determined in ordinary civil litigation between private individuals – tort, contract, family law, employment law, property law etc – up to and including the assessment of damages[1] any award of costs[2] and the enforcement of a judgment.[3] It also includes some, but not all, litigation between private individuals and public authorities. The dividing line is therefore important.

12.3 For the European Court, the central question is whether the proceedings in question are *decisive* for *private* rights and obligations.[4] The personal, economic or individual characteristics of any dispute are therefore vital. Where such characteristics predominate, the proceedings are likely to be covered by article 6(1), irrespective of whether they are classified in domestic law as private or public law proceedings.

12.4 It is not necessary that both parties should be private persons. So, for example, in *Ringeisen v Austria*[5] the European Court found that article 6(1) was applicable where the applicant sought to challenge the decision of a public authority, the Regional Real Property Transactions Commission, on the basis that its decision – whether

---

1 *Silva Pontes v Portugal* (1994) 18 EHRR 156.
2 *Robins v UK* (1998) 26 EHRR 527.
3 *Hornsby v Greece* (1997) 24 EHRR 250: see further paras 13.74 to 13.75.
4 *Ringeisen v Austria* (1979–80) 1 EHRR 455 at para 94.
5 Note 4.

or not to approve the transfer of certain plots of land to him – directly affected the private law relationship between the applicant and the vendor. As the Court observed:

> Although it was applying rules of administrative law, the Regional Commission's decision was to be decisive for the relations in civil law ... between [the applicant] and [the vendor].[6]

12.5   As noted above, whether the rights and obligations in question are classified as public or private law rights in domestic law is relevant, but not decisive:[7] the phrase 'civil rights and obligations' has an autonomous Convention meaning. It is not to be interpreted solely by reference to domestic law, the status of the parties to the proceedings, the legislation giving rise to the rights and obligations in question or the nature of the tribunal established to hear and determine disputes about those rights and obligations.[8] As the European Court observed in *Konig v Germany*:[9]

> Whether or not a right is to be regarded as civil ... must be determined by reference to the substantive contents and effects of the right – and not its legal classification – under the domestic law of the State concerned.[10]

Constitutional or public law proceedings are, therefore, included within article 6(1) where the outcome is decisive for private rights and obligations; even where proceedings are brought to challenge legislation.[11]

12.6   It follows that the mere fact that one party to litigation is the state will not exclude the application of article 6(1). Nor is the question whether it 'acted as a private person or in its sovereign capacity' conclusive.[12] In borderline cases, however, the existence of a 'uniform European notion' in relation to the subject-matter of the right or obligation in question can be influential.[13]

12.7   That does not mean that domestic law is irrelevant. It defines private law rights and therefore provides the legal framework in which the Convention test is to be applied. And article 6(1) extends

6   Note 4 at para 94.
7   *Konig v Germany* (1979–80) 2 EHRR 170.
8   *Baraona v Portugal* (1991) 13 EHRR 329.
9   Note 7.
10   Note 7 at para 89.
11   *Ruiz-Mateos v Spain* A/262 (1993) 16 EHRR 505.
12   *Konig v Germany* n7.
13   See *Feldbrugge v Netherlands* (1986) 8 EHRR 425 and *Deumeland v Germany* (1986) 8 EHRR 448.

only to rights and obligations which can be said, on arguable grounds at least, to be recognised in domestic law.[14]

12.8   The Commission has found that 'civil rights' can include rights arising under directly applicable European community law.[15] However, in *Adams and Benn v UK*,[16] article 6(1) was not applied because the European community law right contended for by the applicants – freedom of movement – was a right of a public law nature. In the Commission's opinion it lacked the personal, economic or individual characteristics of the private law sphere. In light of the emphasis placed on the free movement of workers in European community law, this was a surprising decision.

Analysis of Convention case-law

12.9   What follows is an analysis of the European Court's case-law on the meaning of civil rights and obligations arranged according to subject matter. In determining whether a given right or obligation comes within article 6(1) it is often useful to consider analogous cases, bearing in mind that, in certain categories of case, there is now a presumption that article 6(1) applies. The recent case-law of the Court has tended to include rather than exclude the application of article 6(1) – for example, on costs[17] and the enforcement of judgment[18] – and some of the its older case-law, along with some of the case-law of the Commission, should be treated with caution.

Property rights

12.10   Most proceedings which have a bearing on property rights are considered decisive of private rights and obligations and hence article 6(1) applies to them. *Ringeisen v Austria*[19] is an example. Other examples include:

1) *Hakansson and Sturesson v Sweden*,[20] which involved a decision by the County Agricultural Board in Sweden to withhold a permit

14 See paras 12.32 to 12.33.
15 *X v Greece* (Commission) 11 January 1995, unreported.
16 (1997) 23 EHRR CD 160.
17 *Robins v UK* n2.
18 *Hornsby v Greece* n3.
19 Note 4.
20 (1991) 13 EHRR 1.

needed for the retention of agricultural land for more than two years.

2) *Zander v Sweden*,[21] where the applicant, whose land was adjacent to a waste-tip, challenged a licensing authority's decision granting a licence to a third party to dump without any conditions to safeguard the applicant's water from pollution.

3) *Sporrong and Lonroth v Sweden*,[22] which involved a challenge by landowners to expropriation permits issued by the government at the behest of the local authority and orders prohibiting construction issued by the local administrative board.

4) *Raimondo v Italy*,[23] where the applicant's property was confiscated on the basis that he was a mafia suspect.

5) *Oerlemans v Netherlands*,[24] which involved a challenge by the applicant to a designation order made by the Minister of Cultural, Recreational and Public Works classifying his land as a protected natural site and prohibiting some farming activities on it.

6) *Gillow v UK*[25] where the applicants were refused permission to live in their house in Guernsey under local housing legislation.

Entitlement to compensation for breaches of property rights is also a 'civil right': see *Beaumartin v France*.[26]

12.11   Finally, once registered, patent rights are 'civil rights' within the meaning of article 6(1).[27] The same will apply to other intellectual property rights. Likewise, bankruptcy decisions affect civil rights and obligations because they deprive individuals of the right to manage their own property and affairs.[28]

Licensing

12.12   Article 6(1) is applicable to most licensing decisions because they affect the right to engage in commercial activity. The following cases are examples:

21   (1994) 18 EHRR 175.
22   (1983) 5 EHRR 35.
23   (1994) 18 EHRR 237.
24   (1993) 15 EHRR 561.
25   (1989) 11 EHRR 335.
26   (1995) 19 EHRR 485.
27   *X v Switzerland* (1975) 3 DR 155.
28   *S.P.R.L. Anca v Belgium* (1984) 40 DR 170.

1) *Konig v Germany*,[29] where proceedings before the Tribunal for the Medical Profession in Germany led to the withdrawal of the applicant's licence to run a medical clinic.[30]

2) *X v Belgium*,[31] where, as a result of the applicant's conviction for keeping a brothel, the local authority terminated her licence to run a public house.

3) *Benthem v Netherlands*,[32] where an Administrative Litigation Division of the Council of State revoked a decision to issue the applicant with a licence to run a petrol station.

4) *Pudas v Sweden*,[33] which involved a challenge by the applicant to the revocation of his licence to run a taxi service by the County Administrative Board in Sweden.

5) *Jordebo Foundation of Christian Schools v Sweden*[34] which involved a decision of the local school board to refuse the application permission to run a private school. In the Commission's opinion:

> ... the private character of the right to run a school does not change because of the administrative supervision to which the school is subject.[35]

Any suggestion by the European Court in *Konig v Germany*[36] that article 6(1) applies only to decisions to continue licences and not to decisions to grant them has been overruled by its subsequent decision in *Benthem v Netherlands*.[37]

Professional disciplinary tribunals

12.13 Closely allied to the right to engage in commercial activity is the right to practise a profession. Article 6(1) will therefore be applicable to hearings before professional disciplinary tribunals where the outcome is capable of affecting pecuniary interests, such as the ability to continue working. Examples include:

29 (1979–80) 2 EHRR 170.
30 See further paras 12.13 to 12.14.
31 (1980) 23 DR 237.
32 (1985) 8 EHRR 1.
33 (1988) 10 EHRR 380.
34 (1987) 61 DR 92.
35 Ibid at para 87.
36 (1979–80) 2 EHRR 170.
37 Note 32.

1) *Konig v Germany*[38] which involved the revocation of the applicant's permission to practise as a doctor in proceedings before the Tribunal for the Medical Profession in Germany.[39]

2) *Guchez v Belgium*[40] where the applicant challenged the decisions of the disciplinary board and Board of Appeal of the Architects' Association in Belgium which suspended him from practising as an architect for one year for 'canvassing custom' and 'profit-seeking'.

3) *H v Belgium*[41] which involved an application to be reinstated as an advocate before the Council of the Ordre des Avocats in Antwerp after being struck off the Bar roll.

4) *Ginikanwa v UK*[42] where a barrister was disbarred from practice by the Bar Disciplinary Tribunal, a decision upheld by the judges sitting as Visitors to the Inns of Court.

5) *De Moor v Belgium*[43] which involved the refusal of the Belgian Bar Council to enrol the applicant as a pupil barrister.

In *Jaxel v France*[44] the Commission admitted a case, which was later discontinued after a friendly settlement,[45] where the applicant, the managing director of a property company, complained about the decision of the Prefect of the Moselle banning him from all professional activity in law or property.

12.14   A more restrictive approach has been adopted towards police officers. In *X v UK*[46] the Commission held that police disciplinary proceedings did not involve the determination of a civil right or a criminal charge. It observed that, in contradistinction to *Konig v Germany*,[47] police officers are specially selected and trained by the state to perform tasks on its behalf related to law and order. In the exercise of their functions, the police are exclusively subordinated to

38 (1979–80) 2 EHRR 170. See *Stephan v UK* and *Wickramsighe v UK* [1998] EHRLR 338: GMC proceedings not criminal.
39 See also *Kraska v Switzerland* (1994) 18 EHRR 188 and *Diennet v France* (1996) 21 EHRR 554.
40 (1984) 40 DR 100.
41 (1987) 10 EHRR 339.
42 (1988) 55 DR 251.
43 (1994) 18 EHRR 372.
44 (1987) 54 DR 70 and (1989) 59 DR 42.
45 For the friendly settlement rules, para 30.15.
46 (1980) 21 DR 168.
47 (1979–80) 2 EHRR 170.

governmental authorities and do not enter into contractual relationships of a private nature. As a result, whatever the proper legal categorisation of their employment, police officers have no 'civil right' within the meaning of article 6(1) to continue to perform their functions. This conclusion has not been tested before the European Court, which has broadened the scope for applying article 6(1) in relation to public officials generally: see chapter 28.

Tax proceedings

12.15 The Commission had consistently held that article 6(1) does not apply to tax proceedings.[48] In *X v Austria*[49] it extended this principle to other fiscal matters related to tax proceedings on the basis that:

> Whereas ... the fiscal advantages in question [the right to tax reimbursements] have repercussions on the trader's business, they find their basis in specific provisions of public law supporting an economic policy ... the granting or refusal of such reimbursements will not affect any of the trader's rights to perform his private activity and to enter into contracts with third persons; it will only affect the terms of sale or the finding of new outlets.[50]

On that basis, the Commission has ruled numerous cases inadmissible and the European Court has not had the opportunity to address the issue. However, in *Schouten and Meldrum v Netherlands*,[51] which involved contribution payments under a Dutch health insurance scheme,[52] the Court appears, without deciding the issue, to have endorsed the Commission's approach.

12.16 The limits of this approach were explored in *Editions Periscope v France*,[53] where the Court held that article 6(1) did apply to proceedings for damages for losses sustained as a result of the unlawful deprivation of certain tax concessions. It reasoned that:

> ... the subject-matter of the applicant's action was 'pecuniary in nature and ... the action was founded on an alleged infringement of rights which were likewise pecuniary rights. The right in question

---

48 See *X v Germany* 26 Collection of Decisions p1; *X v Germany* 13 Yearbook 176; *X v France* (1983) 32 DR 266; and *Company S and T v Sweden* (1986) 50 DR 121.

49 (1980) 21 DR 246.

50 Ibid at p 247.

51 (1995) 19 EHRR 432.

52 For welfare benefits generally, see chapter 23.

53 (1992) 14 EHRR 597.

was therefore a 'civil right', notwithstanding the origin of the dispute and the fact that the administrative courts had jurisdiction.[54]

In effect, the Court treated the applicant's case as a claim for compensation against a public authority (see below).

12.17   Similarly, in *The National & Provincial Building Society and Others v UK*,[55] the European Court held that restitution proceedings for taxes paid under regulations later declared invalid, involved the determination of the applicants' 'civil rights' within the meaning of article 6(1). This conclusion was not affected by the fact that 'the rights asserted ... had their background in tax legislation ...'.[56] The same applied to parallel judicial review proceedings despite their public law nature.[57]

Family proceedings

12.18   Although family proceedings often involve public authorities, the outcome is usually decisive for private rights and obligations and thus article 6(1) applies. In *W v UK*[58] the European Court rejected the government's argument that once a child is taken into care, all rights are vested in the local authority and no 'rights or obligations' subsist in the parents. It therefore applied article 6(1). Similar results followed in *Olsson v Sweden*,[59] which also involved care proceedings; *Eriksson v Sweden*,[60] which entailed a fostering decision; and *Keegan v Ireland*,[61] which related to an adoption decision: see further chapter 19.

Claims for compensation from public authorities

12.19   Where an individual claims compensation from a public authority for an unlawful act, article 6(1) will usually apply so long as there is a right to such compensation. So, for example, article 6(1) was held to apply in *X v France*[62] where the applicant, who was diagnosed as HIV

---

54   Ibid at para 40.
55   (1998) 25 EHRR 127.
56   Ibid at para 97.
57   Note 55 at para 98.
58   (1988) 10 EHRR 29.
59   (1989) 11 EHRR 259.
60   (1990) 12 EHRR 183.
61   (1994) 18 EHRR 342.
62   (1992) 14 EHRR 483.

positive, brought proceedings against the French Minister of Health for failing to bring into force rules governing the supply of blood products. Similarly, in *H v France*[63] the Court had no doubt that article 6(1) applied in medical negligence proceedings against a Strasbourg hospital.

12.20   Article 6(1) also applies to civil actions against the police. In *Baraona v Portugal*[64] the applicant claimed damages for the losses he incurred as a result of the wrongful issue of an arrest warrant against him. By the same token, it applies to proceedings against a public official for unlawful conduct in refusing to grant a manufacturing licence.[65]

12.21   Article 6(1) also applies to claims for compensation from public authorities based on contract. In *Stan Grek Refineries and Stratis Andreadis v Greece*[66] the European Court held that article 6(1) applied to the applicants' claim for damages for breach of a contract between them and the state.

Legal rights to compensation

12.22   A clearly defined right to compensation – or some other pecuniary benefit[67] – is a 'civil right' within the meaning of article 6(1). So, for example, in *Tinnelly and McElduff v UK*[68] the European Court held that the requirements of a fair trial under article 6(1) applied in proceedings for compensation for religious discrimination before the Fair Employment Tribunal in Northern Ireland. It observed that:

> ... in submitting their complaints in accordance with the procedures laid down in the [Fair Employment (Northern Ireland) Acts of 1976 and 1989], the applicants were seeking a ruling that they had been denied the opportunity to compete for and obtain work on the basis of their abilities and competitiveness alone and to be given security clearance for this purpose without regard to their religious beliefs or political opinions. Had it been established that they were indeed the victims of unlawful discrimination, the county court ... were ultimately empowered ... to assess the extent of the applicants' loss and order financial reparation in their favour ...[69]

63 (1990) 12 EHRR 74.
64 (1991) 13 EHRR 329.
65 *Neves e Silva v Portugal* (1991) 13 EHRR 535.
66 (1994) 19 EHRR 293.
67 See chapter 23.
68 (1999) 27 EHRR 249.
69 Ibid at para 61.

The fact that the contracts in issue were public procurement contracts and that the applicants' offers were never accepted did not prevent their rights being classified as 'civil rights' under article 6(1).

Discretionary and ex gratia payments, including compensation for criminal injuries

12.23   Where the payment of compensation is discretionary or payments are made on a purely ex gratia basis the position is different. Article 6(1) will not apply on the basis that the individual has no 'right' to the compensation or payment in question.

12.24   In *Masson and van Zon v Netherlands*,[70] the European Court rejected the applicant's claim that the procedure for determining whether he should have been awarded compensation after his acquittal in criminal proceedings breached article 6(1). The relevant Dutch legislation provided that a competent court 'may' award former suspects compensation when they were acquitted, in equitable cases. In the Court's view:

> The grant to a public authority of such a measure of discretion indicates that no actual right is recognised in law.[71]

Nor, apparently, could any such right be derived from the Convention itself, which is directly applicable in the Netherlands.[72]

12.25   Similarly, article 6(1) does not apply to purely ex gratia criminal injuries compensation schemes,[73] to the allocation of resources under a non-legislative natural disaster fund[74] or to discretionary hardship awards.[75] However, where a statute defines in clear terms the pre-conditions for a criminal injuries compensation claim, an applicant who arguably fulfils those conditions has a right to compensation and hence article 6(1) applies.[76]

Welfare benefits and related issues

12.26   The application of the Convention to welfare benefits and related issues is dealt with in detail in chapter 23 below. As a general rule,

70   (1996) 22 EHRR 491.
71   Ibid at para 51.
72   Note 70 at para 49.
73   See *B v Netherlands* (1985) 43 DR 198.
74   *Nordh v Sweden* (1990) 69 DR 223.
75   See *Machatova v Slovak Republic* (1997) 24 EHRR CD 44.
76   *Gustafson v Sweden* (1998) 25 EHRR 623.

article 6(1) applies to all welfare benefits cases but does not necessarily apply to the payment, rather than receipt, of benefits.

Employment disputes: the distinction between private employees and public servants

12.27 Disputes relating to private law relations between private employers and employees come within the scope of article 6(1).[77] However, disputes relating to the recruitment, employment and retirement of public servants are as a general rule outside the scope of article 6(1).[78] The applicable rules are examined in detail in chapter 28.[79]

Immigration and nationality cases

12.28 The European Court has yet to determine whether decisions relating to immigration and nationality involve the determination of civil rights and obligations under article 6(1). The case-law of the Commission suggests not: see *Agee v UK*[80] on deportation on security grounds; *Omkaranda and the Divine Light Zentrum v Switzerland*[81] on expulsion; *P v UK*[82] on asylum proceedings; and *S v Switzerland*[83] on nationality proceedings. And this is so even where the decision in question clearly affects the exercise of civil rights and obligations.[84] The underlying basis for these decisions is that no 'right' exists in domestic law for those without citizenship to remain in the UK.

Education

12.29 In two cases the Commission has held that the right to education is a public law right. As a result, in *Simpson v UK*[85] it found article 6(1) inapplicable to procedures set up to deal with the schooling of children with special educational needs. And in *X v Germany*[86] it came

---

77 See *Waite and Kennedy v Germany* (Commission) 2 December 1997 and *Obermeier v Austria* (1991) 13 EHRR 290.

78 *Lombardo v Italy* (1996) 21 EHRR 188 at para 17.

79 See paras 28.2 to 28.14.

80 (1976) 7 DR 164.

81 (1981) 25 DR 105.

82 (1987) 54 DR 211.

83 (1988) 59 DR 256.

84 See, for example, *Agee v UK* n80 at para 28.

85 (1989) 64 DR 188.

86 (1985) 7 EHRR 141.

to the same conclusion in respect of the applicant's claim that she had been denied university admission to study dentistry.

Election rights

12.30   In *Konig v Germany*,[87] which concerned a professional disciplinary hearing,[88] the European Court observed that:

> ... even adopting a wide interpretation [of the concept of civil rights] there are some rights conferred by the Convention that cannot be classified as civil rights (e.g. the right to free elections – article 3 of the First Protocol).[89]

For many years the Commission has taken this to mean that all election rights are political not 'civil' in nature. Accordingly it has found article 6(1) inapplicable in proceedings to have the legality of a local election reviewed in *Priorello v Italy*[90] and *IZ v Greece*;[91] and to the applicant's challenge to a prohibition on his standing for the office of head of state in *Habsburg-Lothringen v Austria*.[92]

12.31   The Court has now endorsed this approach. In *Pierre-Bloch v France*[93] it held that the right to stand for election to the French National Assembly was a political not a civil right. Accordingly article 6(1) did not apply to proceedings whereby the applicant was removed from his seat for election expenditure irregularities, even though 'in the proceedings in question the applicant's pecuniary interests were also at stake'.[94]

The need for a basis in domestic law

12.32   Article 6(1) is intended to regulate the form and conduct of proceedings relating to rights and obligations which are recognised in domestic law. It does not require a state to provide legal remedies where none already exist.[95] The European Court has frequently emphasised that:

87   (1979–80) 2 EHRR 170.
88   See paras 2.12 to 2.13.
89   Note 87 at para 89.
90   (1985) 43 DR 195.
91   (1994) 76-A DR 65.
92   (1989) 64 DR 210.
93   (1998) 26 EHRR 202.
94   Ibid at para 51.
95   Although other Convention articles may require the recognition of such remedies see chapter 5.

Article 6(1) extends only to contestations (disputes) over (civil) rights and obligations which can be said, at least on arguable grounds, to be recognised under domestic law; it does not in itself guarantee any particular content for (civil) 'rights and obligations' in the substantive law of the contracting states.[96]

In other words, for article 6(1) to apply, an individual must establish that s/he has an arguable claim in domestic law to the civil right or obligation in question.

12.33   Difficult issues arise in relation to restrictions, immunities and privileges. Where these are broad-based and strictly applied, it has been argued that their effect is to extinguish civil rights and obligations in domestic law and thus exclude the applicability of article 6(1). In some cases, the European Court has acceded to this argument. For example, in *Powell and Rayner v UK*,[97] which concerned the statutory exclusion of liability in trespass and nuisance for aircraft under the Civil Aviation Act 1982, the Court found that article 6(1) did not apply on the basis that:

> ... the effect of [the statutory provision] is to exclude liability in nuisance with regard to the flight of aircraft in certain circumstances, with the result that the applicants cannot claim to have a substantive right under English law to obtain relief for exposure to aircraft noise in those circumstances. To this extent there is no 'civil right' recognised under domestic law to attract the application of article 6(1).[98]

However, where restrictions, immunities and privileges apply to what is otherwise a recognised civil right, such as the right to sue for negligence, different considerations apply. These are dealt with in chapter 13.[99] And it may be that *Powell and Rayner v UK*[100] will have to be reconsidered in light of the Court's decision in *Osman v UK*,[101] which concerned the extent of police immunity from negligence actions.[102]

---

96 See *H v Belgium* (1988) 10 EHRR 339 at para 40 and *James v UK* (1986) 8 EHRR 123 at para 81.
97 (1990) 12 EHRR 355.
98 Ibid at para 36.
99 Paras 13.14 to 13.24.
100 Note 97.
101 (Court) 28 October 1998 noted at [1999] EHRLR 228.
102 See chapter 4 and paras 15.96 to 15.99.

The need for a 'determination' of rights or obligations

12.34   Article 6(1) does not apply whenever civil rights and obligations are in issue, but only when they are being 'determined'. In most cases, this requirement causes little difficulty because the European Court has held that, as a matter of principle, the word 'determination' should not be construed technically: it must be given a substantive rather than formal meaning. Moreover, the dispute in question need not relate to the actual existence of a right, it is enough if the dispute merely relates to the scope of the right, or the manner in which it may be exercised; and this covers questions of fact and of law.[103] The dispute must, however, be genuine (ie, not hypothetical) and of a serious nature.[104] And too tenuous or remote a connection between the proceedings and any effect they may have on civil rights and obligations will preclude the application of article 6(1).[105]

12.35   Consequently, article 6(1) applies not only where the determination of civil rights and obligations is the primary object of the proceedings in question, but also where the proceedings determine such rights and obligations indirectly. The application of article 6(1) to professional disciplinary proceedings is an example. The purpose of such proceedings is (usually) to determine whether an individual has breached professional rules of conduct and, if so, to administer an appropriate sanction. However, the outcome of the proceedings can be, and often is, determinative of civil rights and obligations, such as the right to engage in commercial activity and/or the right to practise a profession. In such circumstances, article 6(1) applies.[106]

12.36   In a series of decisions, the Commission held that article 6(1) does not apply to proceedings which are ancillary to, rather than determinative of, civil rights and obligations; for example, decisions on interim relief,[107] the enforcement of judgments,[108] and the award of costs.[109] However, these decisions are now of doubtful validity in light of subsequent decisions of the European Court.

---

103 See *Benthem v Netherlands* n32.
104 Ibid and *Van Marle v Netherlands* A/101 (1986) 8 EHRR 483.
105 *Pudas v Sweden* (1988) 10 EHRR 380 at para 31.
106 See paras 12.13 to 12.14.
107 *X v UK* (1981) 24 DR 57; *Alsterland v Sweden* (1988) 56 DR 229.
108 *K v Sweden* (1991) 71 DR 94; *Jensen v Denmark* (1991) 68 DR 177.
109 *Alsterland v Sweden* n107.

12.37 In *Robins v UK*[110] the Commission, following the approach it had adopted in the cases referred to above, held that costs proceedings after the conclusion of civil litigation were not covered by article 6(1).[111] However, when the case reached the Court, it departed from the Commission's approach. In its view:

> ...article 6(1) of the Convention requires that all stages of legal proceedings for the 'determination of ... civil rights and obligations', not excluding stages subsequent to judgment on the merits, be resolved within a reasonable time.[112]

The legal costs, which formed the subject matter of the proceedings in question, were incurred during the resolution of a dispute between neighbours which undoubtedly involved the determination of civil rights and obligations.[113]

12.38 Similarly the European Court's decision in *Hornsby v Greece*[114] clearly overrules the Commission's decision in *K v Sweden*[115] and *Jensen v Denmark*.[116] In that case the Court held that the enforcement of a court's judgment was an integral part of the 'trial' for article 6(1) purposes.[117]

12.39 On the other hand, the Commission recently affirmed its decision in *Porter v UK*[118] that a refusal of leave by the House of Lords does not constitute a determination of civil rights and obligations.[119] And the decision in *X v Austria*[120] that article 6(1) does not imply a right to re-open civil litigation on the basis that fresh evidence has come to light also probably survives.

12.40 Finally, a determination or dispute for the purposes of article 6(1) must be justiciable. In *Van Marle v Netherlands*[121] the European Court

---

110 (1998) 26 EHRR 527.
111 See ibid at p534 where the Commission expressly relies on *Alsterland v Sweden* n107.
112 Note 110 at para 28; see also: *Silva Pontes v Portugal* (1996) 18 EHRR 156; *Di Pede v Italy* (Court) 26 September 1996; *Zappia v Italy* (Court) 26 September 1996; and *Hornsby v Greece* (1997) 24 EHRR 250.
113 Note 110 at para 29.
114 Note 112.
115 (1991) 71 DR 94.
116 (1991) 68 DR 177.
117 See paras 13.74 to 13.75.
118 (1987) 54 DR 207.
119 See *Comninos & National Compania Naviera S.A v UK* (1997) 23 EHRR CD 165.
120 (1978) 14 DR 171.
121 (1986) 8 EHRR 483.

declined to apply article 6(1) in proceedings to register the applicant as an accountant because the proceedings were an assessment of knowledge and experience akin to a school or university exam. The position would have been different had the applicant complained that proceedings to challenge the registration on the grounds of procedural irregularity or ultra vires did not comply with article 6(1).[122]

The application of article 6(1) where civil rights and obligations are determined by bodies other than courts or tribunals

12.41   Numerous decisions affecting civil rights and obligations are taken by bodies other than courts or tribunals; examples include professional disciplinary hearings, welfare benefit assessment boards and local authority child care decisions. The procedures followed by these bodies will not necessarily comply with article 6(1), but, recognising the inconvenience of holding all such bodies to the strict application of article 6(1), the European Court has adopted a flexible two-pronged approach:

1) either the body taking a decision which affects civil rights and obligations must itself comply with article 6(1); or

2) there must be a right of appeal or review from that body to a court or tribunal which fully complies with the requirements of article 6(1).[123]

The scope of any appeal or review where the body taking the primary decision about civil rights and obligations does not comply with article 6(1) is therefore important.

12.42   In many cases a review on the merits will be required. In *Albert and Le Compte v Belgium*[124] the European Court found that a review by the Court of Cassation of the decision of a medical disciplinary body was insufficient for article 6(1) purposes because it was confined to matters of law and could not review the merits of the decision challenged. A similar result followed in *W v UK*[125] where the European Court accepted that judicial review proceedings to

---

122 Ibid at para 35.
123 See *Albert and Le Compte v Belgium* (1983) 5 EHRR 533 at para 29.
124 Note 123.
125 (1988) 10 EHRR 29.

challenge a local authority's decision restricting the applicant's access to his child did not fully comply with article 6(1) because:

> ... on an application for judicial review, the courts will not review the merits of the decision but will confine themselves to ensuring, in brief, that the authority did not act illegally, unreasonably or unfairly.[126]

A review of the merits was required.

12.43 Against this background, the decision in *Bryan v UK*[127] requires careful examination. In that case, the applicant appealed against a planning enforcement notice, first to an inspector appointed under the Town and County Planning Act 1990 and then, by way of judicial review, to the High Court. The inspector, who had quasi-judicial functions, conducted an inquiry and the European Court found that, save in one respect, the proceedings before him were fair. It took the view that since the inspector was appointed by the Secretary of State and could be removed by him at any time, and since he was obliged to follow rules, guidance and directions of the Secretary of State, he lacked the independence required under article 6(1). Therefore, the crucial question was whether the judicial review proceedings were sufficient to save the procedure as a whole.

12.44 Following *W v UK*[128] the applicant pointed to the limited jurisdiction of the High Court in judicial review proceedings and, in particular, its inability to review the factual findings of the inspector. However, the European Court took the view that this factor alone was not conclusive. In assessing the sufficiency of the review available it was necessary to have regard to matters such as:

1) the subject matter of the decision appealed against;

2) the manner in which that decision was arrived at; and

3) the content of the dispute, including the desired and actual grounds of appeal.[129]

Noting that it was undisputed that the procedure before the Inspector had been quasi-judicial, that the applicant did not appeal to the High Court against any of the inspector's findings of fact, and that the High Court not only had jurisdiction to deal with the issues raised by the applicant – policy questions – but also did so 'point by point', the

---

126 Ibid at para 82.
127 (1996) 21 EHRR 342.
128 Note 125.
129 Note 127 at para 45.

European Court concluded that there had been no breach of article 6(1).

12.45   The decision in *Bryan v UK*[130] is therefore of limited application.[131] In non-specialist areas of the law and/or where there are challenges to the factual findings of a body taking decisions about civil rights and obligations that do not comply with article 6(1), the approach taken in *Albert and Le Compte v Belgium* and *W v UK* should prevail.

12.46   It is important to note that the flexible two-pronged approach[132] applies only where the initial decisions are taken by bodies other than courts or tribunals. It does not apply where a decision is made by 'courts of the classic kind', ie, courts and tribunals that are 'integrated within the standard judicial machinery of the country'.[133] In the case of such courts and tribunals, article 6(1) must be complied with at the trial stage and on any appeal. In addition, the flexible, two-pronged approach does not apply where procedural safeguards arise under article 8: see chapter 19.

Official investigations

12.47   Article 6(1) does not necessarily apply to official investigations and/or inquiries. In *Fayed v UK*[134] an inspector had been appointed to investigate the affairs of a public company on suspicion of fraud. The inspector's report contained findings that were detrimental to the applicant's reputation. However, the European Court found that article 6(1) did not apply to the inspector's investigations, on the basis that there was an important distinction between adjudication (covered) and investigation (not covered). Although the investigation resulted in a finding that the applicant was dishonest, this was not 'dispositive of anything' in terms of legal rights and duties in the way that a 'determination' in the article 6(1) sense needed to be.[135]

130 Note 127.
131 It was applied by the Commission in *X v UK* (1998) 25 EHRR CD 88 which concerned detailed provisions relating to the appointment of a chief executive under the Insurance Companies Act 1982.
132 See para 12.41.
133 *De Cubber v Belgium* (1984) 7 EHRR 236.
134 (1994) 18 EHRR 393.
135 For the aspect of this case concerning immunity, see para 13.18.

CHAPTER 13

The right to a fair trial in civil proceedings: the content of article 6(1) of the Convention

13.1   Introduction

13.6   The 'right of access' to a court

13.8   Restrictions on instituting proceedings

13.12   Arbitration clauses

13.14   Immunities and privileges

13.24   Limitation periods

13.28   Security for costs orders

13.32   Requirements of notice and clarity

13.33   Legal aid in civil proceedings

13.41   The right to a 'tribunal'

13.44   Independence and impartiality

13.45   Public hearings

13.51   The right to participate effectively in civil proceedings

13.52   The right to be present

13.54   Equality of arms

continued

13.55   The right to an adversarial hearing

13.59   Disclosure

13.62   Evidence and witnesses

13.63   Burden and standard of proof

13.64   Expert evidence

13.68   Reasons

13.70   Costs

13.72   The enforcement of judgments

13.74   Civil appeals

13.78   Trial within a reasonable period

Introduction

13.1   Article 6(1) of the Convention guarantees that:

> In the determination of his civil rights and obligations ... everyone is entitled to a fair and public hearing within a reasonable time by an independent and impartial tribunal established by law.

Its object and purpose is to enshrine the fundamental principle of the rule of law.[1] Accordingly it is to be construed broadly.[2]

13.2   This general requirement of fairness is common to both criminal and civil proceedings, but the more specific provisions of article 6(2) and 6(3) relate only to the former. The European Court has concluded from this that:

> The requirements inherent in the concept of 'fair hearing' are not necessarily the same in cases concerning the determination of civil rights and obligations as they are in cases concerning the determination of a criminal charge.[3]

However, this is not a basis for applying article 6(1) restrictively in civil proceedings for two reasons. First, because many of the more detailed provisions of articles 6(2) and 6(3) are treated as aspects of, rather than supplementary to, the overall requirement of fairness enshrined in article 6(1). Second, because the Court has emphasised that, certainly so far as the adversarial principle is concerned, the rights under article 6(1) are 'the same in both civil and criminal cases'.[4]

13.3   The overriding requirement of a fair hearing is:

> ... to place the 'tribunal' under a duty to conduct a proper examination of the submissions, arguments and evidence adduced by the parties, without prejudice to its assessment of whether they are relevant to its decision.[5]

The European Court's task is to determine whether this duty has been fulfilled and, in carrying out that task, it looks to the overall fairness of the proceedings, rather than technical breaches of the requirements of article 6(1). However, certain defects may be so

---

1   *Salabiaku v France* (1991) 13 EHRR 379.
2   *Delcourt v Belgium* (1979–80) 1 EHRR 355.
3   *Dombo Beheer BV v Netherlands* (1994) 18 EHRR 213 at para 32.
4   *Lobo Machado v Portugal* (1997) 23 EHRR 79; *Vermeulen v Belgium* (Court) 20 February 1996; *Niderost-Huber v Switzerland* (1998) 25 EHRR 709.
5   *Kraska v Switzerland* (1994) 18 EHRR 188 at para 30.

fundamental that compliance with other fair trial requirements cannot render the proceedings fair.[6]

13.4   Under the Human Rights Act 1998 (HRA), domestic courts may have to take a stricter approach to article 6(1). The approach of the Strasbourg bodies has been adopted because they assume that domestic courts have scrutinised the proceedings in question for fairness. And, unlike those bodies, domestic courts, at least those of first instance, do not review the proceedings as a whole retrospectively.

13.5   Fair trial presupposes effective access to the courts and therefore this aspect of article 6(1) is examined first.

The 'right of access' to a court

13.6   Unless individuals have access to a court, their right to a fair trial is meaningless. On that basis, the European Court has developed a 'right of access' out of the provisions of article 6(1). This right was first recognised in *Golder v UK*[7] where the applicant, a prisoner, was prevented, under the Prison Rules then in force, from consulting a solicitor in relation to defamation proceedings that he wanted to bring against a prison officer. Drawing on the objects and purpose of the Convention, including the rule of law referred to in the preamble, the European Court observed that:

> In civil matters one can scarcely conceive of the rule of law without there being a possibility of access to the courts ... The principle whereby a civil claim must be capable of being submitted to a judge ranks as one of the universally recognised fundamental principles of law; the same is true of the principle of international law which forbids the denial of justice. Article 6(1) must be read in light of these principles.[8]

On that basis, the Court found a breach of article 6(1): the right of access to a court must not only exist, but must also be 'effective'.

13.7   However, there are limits on the right of access to a court. The following principles emerge from the European Court's case-law and were summarised in *Lithgow v UK:*[9]

1) The right of access to the courts secured by article 6(1) is not

---

6   *Crociani v Italy* (1980) 22 DR 147 at p216.
7   (1979–80) 1 EHRR 524.
8   Ibid at paras 45–35.
9   (1986) 8 EHRR 329.

absolute but is subject to limitations; these are permitted by implication since the right of access 'by its very nature calls for regulation by the State, regulation which may vary in time and in place according to the needs and resources of the community and of individuals'.

2) In laying down such regulation, the contracting states enjoy a certain margin of appreciation,[10] but the final decision as to observance of the Convention's requirements rests with the European Court. It must be satisfied that the limitations applied do not restrict or reduce the access left to the individual in such a way or to such an extent that the very essence of the right is impaired.

3) Furthermore, a limitation will not be compatible with article 6(1) if it does not pursue a legitimate aim and if there is not a reasonable relationship of proportionality between the means employed and the aim sought to be achieved.[11]

Restrictions on instituting proceedings

13.8   The right to institute civil proceedings is one aspect of the right of access to a court.[12] It too can be restricted, but again only where the restriction in question pursues a legitimate aim and is proportionate. Restrictions on access by minors,[13] bankrupts,[14] those suffering from mental illness[15] and vexatious litigants[16] are legitimate in principle, so long as they do not restrict or reduce the access left to the individual in such a way or to such an extent that the very essence of the right is impaired.

13.9   In *Winterwerp v Netherlands*[17] the applicant complained that, as a mental patient, he was neither able to administer his own property nor be represented in proceedings which had a bearing on his property. The European Court observed that:

> Whatever the justification for depriving a person of unsound mind of the capacity to administer his property, the guarantees laid down

10 See paras 4.88 to 4.96.
11 Note 9 at para 194.
12 *Golder v UK* n7; *Philis v Greece* (1991) 13 EHRR 741.
13 See the reference at p270 in *M v UK* (1987) 52 DR 266.
14 *M v UK* n13.
15 *Ashingdane v UK* (1985) 7 EHRR 528.
16 *H v UK* (1985) 45 DR 281.
17 (1979–80) 2 EHRR 387.

in article 6(1) must nevertheless be respected. Whilst ... mental illness may render legitimate certain limitations upon the exercise of the 'right to a court', it cannot warrant the total absence of that right ...[18]

On the facts there was a breach of article 6(1).

13.10   In *Philis v Greece*[19] a rule preventing the applicant from suing for his own fees and forcing him instead to proceed through his professional body was also found to be a breach of article 6(1). So too in *Canea Catholic Church v Greece*[20] where the applicant was denied legal standing in Greece.[21]

13.11   However, a reasonable collective compensation scheme set up to avoid multiple claims may be compatible with article 6(1) even where it excludes the possibility of private litigation.[22] Similarly, where a scheme is set up to deal with multi-party litigation, article 6(1) is not breached when one party has to withdraw from the litigation because s/he fails to meet the agreed criteria for participation in the scheme, so long as:

1) s/he agreed to the establishment of the criteria in the first place;

2) the criteria are reasonable; and

3) s/he retains the ability to bring proceedings outside the scheme (albeit with a considerable added financial burden).[23]

Arbitration clauses

13.12   In general terms, an individual may waive his/her right of access to a court by, for example, entering a contract in which s/he agrees to submit disputes to arbitration.[24] In *Deweer v Belgium*,[25] which involved a settlement of criminal proceedings, the European Court observed that:

In the Contracting States' domestic legal systems a waiver of this

18 Ibid at para 75.
19 (1991) 13 EHRR 741.
20 (1999) 27 EHRR 521.
21 See also: *Holy Monastries v Greece* (1995) 20 EHRR 1.
22 *Lithgow v UK* n9. In relation to international organisations see *Lenzing AG v UK* [1999] EHRLR 132: European patent office.
23 *Taylor v UK* (1997) 23 EHRR CD 132.
24 *Deweer v Belgium* (1979–80) 2 EHRR 439; *R v Switzerland* (1987) 51 DR 83.
25 Note 24.
26 Ibid at para 49.

kind is frequently encountered ... in civil matters, notably in the shape of arbitration clauses in contracts ... the waiver, which has undeniable advantages for the individual concerned as well as for the administration of justice, does not in principle offend against the Convention.[26]

13.13   However, as the Commission emphasised in *Malmstrom v Sweden*:[27]

... a distinction must be drawn between voluntary arbitration and compulsory arbitration. Normally article 6 poses no problem where arbitration is entered into voluntarily ... If, on the other hand, arbitration is compulsory in the sense of being required by law, as in this case, the parties have no option but to refer their dispute to an arbitration Board, and the Board must offer the guarantees set forth in article 6(1).[28]

In other words, arbitration must either be truly voluntary, or the arbitration tribunal must fully comply with article 6(1) if access to the courts is denied.

Immunities and privileges

13.14   Immunities and privileges in domestic law are a serious impediment to the determination of civil rights and obligations by the courts. Sometimes the European Court has acceded to the argument that where immunities or privileges are broad-based and strictly applied their effect is to extinguish civil rights and obligations in domestic law and thus exclude the applicability of article 6(1) altogether.[29] However, where immunities and privileges apply to what is otherwise a recognised civil right, such as the right to sue for negligence, different considerations apply.

13.15   In *Ashingdane v UK*[30] the applicant, who was detained at Broadmoor hospital, had been prevented from bringing an action against the Secretary of State for breach of statutory duty because the Mental Health Act 1959[31] provided immunity from liability for any person purporting to act in pursuance of its provisions unless the act in question was done in bad faith or without reasonable care. Drawing

27   (1983) 38 DR 18.
28   Ibid at para 30.
29   See *Powell and Rayner v UK* (1990) 12 EHRR 355.
30   (1984) 6 EHRR 69.
31   Now Mental Health Act 1983.

on the right of access to a court recognised in *Golder v UK*[32] the Commission found that it had jurisdiction to review whether the immunity conferred by the mental health legislation 'unduly restricted the applicant's right of access to court, contrary to article 6(1), by an arbitrary limitation on his civil claims'.[33]

13.16   The review then undertaken by the Commission amounted to the adoption of a two-stage test, borrowed from the case-law of the European Court concerning restriction on the exercise of Convention rights under articles 8–11;[34] namely:

1) Does the immunity or privilege in question pursue a legitimate aim?

2) If so, is it a proportionate measure, bearing in mind that aim?

Applying that test, the Commission found that the restrictions imposed on the applicant's rights by the mental health legislation had a legitimate aim – to protect hospital staff from ill-founded or vexatious litigation – and were proportionate. Patients were protected from acts of bad faith and negligence and criminal safeguards existed to protect patients from ill-treatment. Therefore, 'the applicant had reasonable access to court in respect of the claims he was entitled to make'.[35]

13.17   A similar approach was adopted in a series of cases which challenged the immunity conferred by the Crown Proceedings Act 1947 on the Crown from tort actions by members of the armed forces who suffered injuries in the course of their service.[36] In each case, the Commission examined the scope of the immunity and concluded that it was legitimate for the authorities to have taken the view that members of the armed forces, as a group, were exposed to an increased risk of death or injury and that the creation of no-fault pension entitlements was an adequate alternative to the right to sue in negligence.

13.18   In *Fayed v UK*[37] the European Court effectively endorsed the Commission's approach. There, the applicant wanted to bring defamation proceedings in relation to a government inspector's

32 Note 7.
33 Note 30 at para 92.
34 See paras 4.56 to 4.66.
35 Note 30 at para 95.
36 *Ketterick v UK* (1983) 5 EHRR 465; *Pinder v UK* (1984) 7 EHRR 464; *Dyer v UK* (1984) 39 DR 246; 7 EHRR 469.
37 (1994) 18 EHRR 393.

report prepared in accordance with the provisions of the Companies Act 1985 but would inevitably have been met with a defence of qualified privilege. The European Court observed that:

> Whether a person has an actionable domestic claim may depend not only on the substantive content, properly speaking, of the relevant civil right as defined under national law but also on the existence of procedural bars preventing or limiting the possibilities of bringing potential claims to court. In the latter kind of case article 6(1) may have a degree of applicability. Certainly the Convention enforcement bodies may not create by way of interpretation of article 6(1) a substantive civil right which has no legal basis in the State concerned. However, it would not be consistent with the rule of law in a democratic society or with the basic principle underlying article 6(1) – namely that civil claims must be capable of being submitted to a judge for adjudication – if, for example, a State could, without restraint or control by the Convention enforcement bodies, remove from the jurisdiction of the courts a whole range of civil claims or confer immunities from civil liability on large groups or categories of persons.[38]

The 'restraint or control' consisted of the two-stage test outlined above.[39]

13.19   The same approach was adopted in *Osman v UK*,[40] a case which challenged the extent of police immunity in negligence proceedings.[41] The European Court held that while the rules governing police immunity pursued a legitimate aim – the avoidance of defensive policing and diversion of resources – they were disproportionate because they provided blanket immunity without regard to the merits of the case.[42]

13.20   The matter arose in a different way in *Tinnelly v UK*,[43] where the applicants issued proceedings in the Fair Employment Tribunal alleging that a decision not to grant them a government contract amounted to discrimination on religious grounds contrary to the Fair Employment Acts of 1976 and 1989. During the course of the proceedings the Secretary of State for Northern Ireland issued a certificate claiming that the decision not to grant the contract was 'an

---

38 Ibid at para 65.
39 See note 37 at paras 69–82.
40 [1999] 1 FLR 193; noted at [1999] EHRLR 228.
41 See paras 15.96 to 15.99.
42 Ibid. See also *TP and KM v UK* and *Z v UK* [1998] 624 on local authority immunity following *X v Bedfordshire CC* [1995] 3 All ER 353.
43 (1999) 27 EHRR 249.

act done for the purpose of safeguarding national security or the protection of public safety or order'. Under the legislation this certificate was conclusive evidence to that effect. The applicants complained that the issue of the certificate blocked their access to a court or tribunal for a determination of their claims that they had been discriminated against.

13.21   The applicants accepted that the protection of national security was a legitimate aim which could be invoked to justify limitations being placed on the right of access to a court, but argued that the conclusive nature of the certificate was a disproportionate measure in pursuit of that aim. For the European Court, the lack of independent scrutiny of the certificate was crucial. In particular, it noted that:

1) the Fair Employment Tribunal could not question the certificate; and

2) although judicial review proceedings were launched challenging the certificate, the High Court was restricted from full scrutiny because of an order that certain key documents not be disclosed as a result of the Secretary of State's claim to public interest immunity.

Drawing on its reasoning in *Chahal v UK*[44] the Court maintained that:

> The right guaranteed to an applicant under article 6(1) of the Convention to submit a dispute to a court or tribunal in order to have a determination on questions of both fact and law cannot be displaced by the ipse dixit of the executive.[45]

The government's assertion that the access enjoyed by the applicants was 'as effective as it could be in the circumstances' could not be sustained. The issue of a certificate in such circumstances was disproportionate and a breach of article 6(1).

13.22   One of the factors that influenced the European Court in *Tinnelly v UK*[46] was that:

> ... in other contexts it has been found possible to modify judicial procedures in such a way as to safeguard national information and yet accord the individual a substantial degree of procedural justice.[47]

And it was not persuaded by the government's argument that the introduction of special procedures under the fair employment legis-

44 (1997) 23 EHRR 413; see further chapter 18.
45 Note 44 at para 77.
46 Note 43.
47 Note 43 at para 78.

lation would undermine the independence of the judiciary in Northern Ireland. On the contrary, the Court took the view that:

> The introduction of a procedure, regardless of the framework used, which would allow an adjudicator or tribunal fully satisfying the article 6(1) requirements of independence and impartiality to examine all relevant evidence, documentary or other, and the merits of the submissions of both sides, may indeed serve to enhance public confidence.[48]

13.23 The question of international immunity from suit was raised before the Commission in *Waite and Kennedy v Germany*,[49] which concerned the European Space Agency established by an international treaty. Such immunity was found to be legitimate in its aim – to facilitate the proper functioning of international organisations – and proportionate on the facts because alternative remedies were available to the applicants to determine their rights as employees of the agency.

Limitation periods

13.24 Over-short limitation periods can breach the right of access to a court inherent in article 6(1) of the Convention. In *Stubbings v UK*[50] the applicants, who all claimed to have suffered sexual abuse when they were children, complained that the effect of the House of Lords decision in *Stubbings v Webb*[51] imposing an inflexible six-year limitation period in civil proceedings for assault (in place of a flexible three-year period) impaired their rights of access to a court under article 6(1). They argued that one of the effects of the sexual abuse they suffered was to prevent them from appreciating that it was the cause of their psychological problems until after the expiry of the limitation period. Thus, their claims for damages were time-barred before they realised they had a cause of action.

13.25 Although the European Court accepted that limitation periods, like all other restrictions on rights of access to a court, must pursue a legitimate aim and be proportionate, it rejected the applicants' argument. It reasoned that:

> ... limitation periods in personal injury cases are a common feature

48 Note 43 at para 78.
49 2 December 1997. See also *Beer and Regan v Germany* [1998] EHRLR 478.
50 (1996) 23 EHRR 213.
51 [1993] AC 498.

of the domestic legal systems of the Contracting States. They serve important purposes, namely to ensure legal certainty and finality, to protect potential defendants from stale claims which might be difficult to counter, and to prevent the injustice which might arise if courts were required to decide upon events which took place in the distant past on the basis of evidence which might have become unreliable and incomplete because of the passage of time.[52]

In the Court's view, since domestic law allowed the applicants six years from the age of 18 to bring civil proceedings and since there was no limitation period in respect of criminal proceedings, the imposition of an inflexible limitation period did not impair the very essence of the applicants' rights of access to a court.[53]

13.26   A similar decision was reached by the Commission in *Dobbie v UK*,[54] where the applicant argued that she did not realise that she had a claim for medical negligence until 15 years after she was operated upon. And in *Stedman v UK*[55] the Commission held that the two-year qualifying period in unfair dismissal and redundancy claims before industrial tribunals did not breach article 6(1) because it served a legitimate aim – protecting employers from undue burdens – and was not disproportionate. However, in *Perez de Rada Cavanilles v Spain*[56] the European Court found a breach of article 6(1) where a time limit had been subjected to a 'particularly rigorous application'.

13.27   Finally, it should be noted that in *Stubbings v UK*[57] the European Court recognised that there was a developing awareness of the problems caused by child sex abuse and its psychological effects on victims. It therefore left open the possibility of reversing its decision on the basis that:

> ... it is possible that the rules on limitation of actions applying in Member States of the Council of Europe may have to be amended to make special provision for this group of claimants in the near future.[58]

See chapter 4 for the principle that the Convention must be interpreted as a 'living instrument'.

---

52 Note 50 at para 49.
53 Note 50 at para 50.
54 Appl 28477/95 [1997] EHRLR 166.
55 (1997) 23 EHRR CD 168.
56 A/1019 (Court) 28 October 1998; noted at [1999] EHRLR 208.
57 Note 50.
58 Note 50 at para 54.

Security for costs orders

13.28 An order that one party to civil litigation pay a sum into court as security for the other party's costs has an obvious impact on the right of access to a court. So far, the European Court has only considered one case concerning the consequences of such an order at first instance.[59] In *Tolstoy Miloslavsky v UK*[60] it considered a security for costs order made at the appeal stage.[61]

13.29 In that case, the applicant had lost a libel case in the High Court and been ordered to pay the plaintiff a large sum in damages.[62] He wanted to appeal, but was prevented from doing so by an order of the Court of Appeal that he pay into court a sum of nearly £125,000 within 14 days as security for his opponent's costs. The applicant failed to pay the sum and his appeal was dismissed. He complained that the order for security for costs amounted to a total bar on his access to the Court of Appeal.

13.30 The European Court took the view that, as a measure designed to protect a successful party to the appeal from unrecoverable costs, the order was legitimate in principle. It therefore scrutinised the order to determine whether it was proportionate. It concluded that it was, having regard to the following matters:

1) the applicant had enjoyed full access to the court of first instance in a trial that had lasted 40 days and in which the applicant was able to fully adduce his evidence;

2) the sum of £125,000 was a reasonable estimate of his opponent's likely costs of the appeal;

3) there was no evidence that the applicant could not have raised the sum of £125,000, given time;

4) in making its decision the Court of Appeal had satisfied itself:

   a) that making the security for costs order would not amount to a denial of justice, and

   b) that the applicant's appeal had no reasonable prospect of success;

5) if there had been a reasonable prospect of success, it was unlikely that an order would have been made.

---

59 *Ait-Mouhoub v France* [1999] EHRLR 215. The issue also arose in *X v Sweden* (1997) 17 DR 74 but was not resolved by the Commission on the merits.

60 (1995) 20 EHRR 442.

61 See also *Grepne v UK* (1990) 66 DR 268.

62 This raised an article 10 issue, which is examined in chapter 4.

By implication, an order for security of costs against a party who cannot raise the sum in question or who has a reasonable prospect of success might breach article 6(1).[63]

13.31　　In addition, the European Court in *Tolstoy Miloslavsky v UK*[64] emphasised that it was concerned with the appeal stage. Article 6(1) does not necessarily apply to appeal hearings in the same manner that it applies to first-instance hearings.[65] As the European Court observed:

> ... the manner of application of article 6 to proceedings before such courts depends on the special features of the proceedings involved; account must be taken of the entirety of the proceedings in the domestic legal order and the role of the appellate court therein.[66]

An order for security for costs at first instance, before any of the evidence is tested, may therefore be more difficult to reconcile with article 6(1).

Requirements of notice and clarity

13.32　In a number of cases, the European Court has recognised that effective access to a court can be impaired if an individual is not given proper notice of administrative decisions affecting his/her civil rights and obligations, or the rules of procedure are so complex and unclear that they cannot properly be understood. In *De Geouffre de la Pradelle v France*[67] the Court found an issue arose under article 6(1) where the applicant was unable to challenge an order declaring that his land was environmentally protected because he did not find out about the order until the time period for challenge had elapsed. And in *Bellet v France*[68] a breach was found where the applicant was misled by confusing rules of procedure concerning his claim for damages for HIV infection.

63　See the Commission's decision in *X v Sweden* (1979) 17 DR 74, which raises the same implication.

64　Note 60.

65　See paras 13.74 to 13.77.

66　Note 60 at para 59; see also *Monnell and Morris v UK* (1988) 10 EHRR 205 and *Helmers v Sweden* (1993) 15 EHRR 285.

67　A/253-B (1992), (unreported).

68　A/333-B (1995), (unreported).

Legal aid in civil proceedings

13.33   Closely allied to the right of access to a court is the question of legal aid in civil proceedings. In *X and Y v Netherlands*[69] the Commission accepted that:

> ... in certain circumstances, high costs of proceedings may raise an issue under article 6 para 1 of the Convention ...'[70]

And this theme was developed by the European Court in *Airey v Ireland*[71] where the applicant complained that she could not enforce her civil right to divorce her alcoholic and violent husband because she could not afford legal representation and no legal aid was available to her.

13.34   In response to the Irish government's assertion that the applicant could have represented herself in the divorce proceedings the European Court observed that:

> The Convention is intended to guarantee not rights that are theoretical or illusory but rights that are practical and effective. This is particularly so of the right of access to the courts in view of the prominent place held in a democratic society by the right to a fair trial. It must therefore be ascertained whether [the applicant's] appearance before the High Court without the assistance of a lawyer would be effective, in the sense of whether she would be able to present her case properly and satisfactorily.[72]

Having regard to the complexity of the factual and legal issues and the emotional involvement of the applicant, the court concluded that it was 'most improbable' that the applicant could effectively present her own case.

13.35   In *Airey v Ireland*[73] the European Court emphasised that the consequence of its ruling was not that legal aid must be provided in all civil proceedings. Article 6(1) requires the provision of legal aid only where the assistance of a lawyer is 'indispensable for effective access to court' either because legal representation is compulsory or because of the 'complexity of the procedure or of the case'.[74]

---

69   (1975) 1 DR 66.
70   Ibid at p71.
71   (1979–80) 2 EHRR 305.
72   Ibid at para 24.
73   Note 71.
74   Note 71 at para 26.

13.36   In a series of cases since *Airey v Ireland*,[75] the Commission has rejected claims under article 6(1) based on the unavailability of legal aid in civil proceedings. In *Winer v UK*[76] it noted that:

> ... unlike article 6(3)(c) which expressly provides for legal aid in criminal cases where necessary, the Convention does not guarantee such a right of assistance in civil cases.[77]

Since domestic rules precluding the grant of legal aid in defamation proceedings were not arbitrary, there was no breach of article 6(1).

13.37   In *Munro v UK*[78] which also concerned the unavailability of legal aid in defamation proceedings the Commission sought to distinguish between the European Court's decision in *Airey v Ireland*[79] and its own decision in *Winer v UK*.[80] In doing so it contrasted the 'general nature' of defamation proceedings with the intimate nature of judicial separation proceedings which regulate the legal relationship between two people and 'may have serious consequences for children of the family'.[81] By implication, some form of legal assistance is more likely to be required in cases involving intimate personal issues than in those of a broader nature.

13.38   The European Court reconsidered the issue of legal aid in *Andronicou and Constantinou v Cyprus*.[82] It emphasised that while article 6(1) of the Convention guarantees an effective right of access to the courts for the determination of civil rights and obligations, it leaves states with a free choice of the means to be used towards that end. The provision of legal aid constituted one of those means, but there are others. On the facts of the case, the Attorney-General's ex gratia offer to provide funds to help overcome the applicants' lack of resources was sufficient.

13.39   Another means of ensuring an effective right of access to the courts is to simplify the procedures. In one case, the Commission held that legal representation was not indispensible in industrial tribunal proceedings because such proceedings are set up to be con-

---

75   Note 71.
76   (1986) 48 DR 154.
77   Ibid at p171.
78   (1987) 52 DR 158.
79   Note 71.
80   Note 78.
81   Ibid at p165. But see *Aerts v Belgium* [1998] EHRLR 777 where important issues are at stake.
82   (1998) 25 EHRR 491.

ducted in a practical and straightforward manner, without over-emphasis on formalities.[83]

13.40   Where legal aid is available in principle, questions can arise under article 6(1) about the circumstances in which it will actually be granted. In *X v UK*[84] the Commission held that the refusal of legal aid for civil proceedings which have no prospect of success does not constitute a denial of access to a court, provided the refusal is not arbitrary and where the person concerned is able to institute court proceedings by other means. In its view, it was self-evident that a legal aid scheme can operate effectively, given the limited resources available, only if rules are put in place to select which cases should be funded. In addition, requirements that there be a reasonable prospect of success and that an applicant make a financial contribution were not uncommon throughout Europe.[85]

The right to a 'tribunal'

13.41   The hearing required under article 6(1) must be by a tribunal established by law, which means a body with judicial functions and fair procedures, capable of taking binding decisions.[86] The capacity to make a recommendation or give advice is not enough. In *Van de Hurk v Netherlands*[87] the European Court found a breach of article 6(1) because the Dutch government had power not to implement the decisions of the Industrial Appeals Tribunal, albeit a power which had never been exercised.

13.42   So long as a tribunal is set up and given jurisdiction by law (ie, legislation), the fact that detailed provisions about its workings are dealt with in delegated legislation will not prevent it being 'established by law', so long as those provisions can be challenged by way of judicial review.[88] 'Established by law' also means 'established in accordance with law', so that the requirement is infringed if a

---

83 (1983), unreported. See also the Court's comment in *Airey v UK* n71 at para 26.

84 (1980) 21 DR 95.

85 Ibid at para 16. But see *Aerts v Belgium* n81 on need in some cases for courts to determine the prospects of a success.

86 *Benthem v Netherlands* (1986) 8 EHRR 1.

87 (1994) 18 EHRR 481.

88 *Crociani v Italy* (1980) 22 DR 147.

tribunal does not function in accordance with the rules that govern it.[89]

13.43   A body which carries out some administrative functions is capable of being a tribunal within the meaning of article 6(1) when it carries out other functions: see *Campbell and Fell v UK*,[90] which concerned the disciplinary function of a prison Board of Visitors. And so long as they satisfy the requirements of independence and impartiality, members of a tribunal need not be professional judges.[91]

Independence and impartiality

13.44   Article 6(1) requires that civil rights and obligations be determined by an 'independent and impartial' tribunal. The principles governing this requirement are the same in civil proceedings as in criminal and are dealt with in detail in chapter 8 above, Fair trial guarantees in criminal proceedings.[92] Their application in civil proceedings was summarised by the European Court in *Langborger v Sweden*.[93] In short, independence means independence from the executive and from the parties. Regard must be had, inter alia, to:

1) the manner of appointment of a tribunal's members and their term of office;

2) the existence of guarantees against outside pressure; and

3) whether the body in question presents an appearance of independence.

And impartiality means subjective impartiality, the lack of actual bias, and objective impartiality, the lack of the appearance of bias.

---

89 *Law of the European Convention on Human Rights*, Harris et al, Butterworths 1995 p239 referring to *Zand v Italy* (1980) 15 DR 70 at p80 and *Rossi v France* (1989) 63 DR 105.

90 (1985) 7 EHRR 165.

91 *Ettl v Austria* (1988) 10 EHRR 255; *Engel v Netherlands* (1979–80) 1 EHRR 647.

92 Paras 8.4 to 8.12.

93 (1990) 12 EHRR 416 at para 32. See *McGonnell v UK* [1999] EHRLR 335, on the bailiff in court proceedings in Guernsey.

94 *Schuler-Zgraggen v Switzerland* (1993) 16 EHRR 405.

95 (1985) 7 EHRR 165.

96 See also *Le Compte v Belgium* (1981) 4 EHRR 1 at para 59.

97 *X v Austria* (1965) 2 Digest 438.

98 *X v UK* (1977) 2 Digest 452.

Public hearings

13.45   Article 6(1) requires both a 'public hearing' and that 'judgment shall be pronounced publicly'. However, these requirements are not absolute. Article 6(1) lists a number of grounds upon which the press and public may be excluded from all or part of a trial, namely:

1) the interests of morals;

2) public order;

3) national security;

4) where the interests of juveniles or respect for the private life of the parties so require; or

5) to the extent strictly necessary where the court considers that publicity would prejudice the interests of justice.

Although this list is broad, the European Court has repeatedly emphasised that the right to a public hearing is 'of fundamental importance'.[94] And the approach it adopted in *Campbell and Fell v UK*[95] suggests not only that 'sufficient reasons' must be adduced for not sitting in public,[96] but also that a proportionality test is to be applied.

13.46   The Commission has approved private hearings in cases involving sexual offences against children,[97] divorce proceedings[98] and in medical disciplinary hearings to protect the private life of patients.[99] However, some limits were set in *Diennet v France*[100] where the European Court refused to accept that as a general rule proceedings before a medical disciplinary tribunal should be in private. It reasoned that the proper approach was to sit in public unless and until a private or confidential matter came up. And private hearings cannot be justified merely because they ease the court's caseload[101] (except possibly on appeal).[102]

13.47   The right to a public hearing can be waived,[103] but:

> ... any waiver must be made in an unequivocal manner and must not run counter to any important public interest.[104]

99 *Guenoun v France* (1990) 66 DR 181; *Imbrechts v Belgium* (1991) 69 DR 312.

100 (1996) 21 EHRR 554.

101 *Axen v Germany* (1981) Com Rep para 78.

102 See below paras 13.74, 13.77 and 13.49.

103 *Hakansson v Sweden* (1991) 13 EHRR 1; *Schuler-Zgraggen v Switzerland* n94; *Zumtobel v Austria* (1994) 17 EHRR 116.

104 *Schuler-Zgraggen v Switzerland* n94 at para 58.

Where a tribunal usually sits in private, a failure to request a public hearing can[105] amount to waiver, particularly if the parties are legally represented.[106]

13.48   The case of *X v UK*[107] gives some support to the suggestion that, in civil cases, interlocutory proceedings need not be in public. There the Commission rejected, without reasons, a complaint that Masters in the High Court sit in private. In so far as this decision was based on the notion that civil rights and obligations are not 'determined' at the interlocutory stage, it may require re-examination in light of the court's subsequent case-law.[108]

13.49   Appeals are different. So long as there has been a public hearing at first instance, a private appeal hearing may be justified by the 'special features' of appeal proceedings.[109] In *Axen v Germany*[110] the European Court approved a private appeal hearing in a personal injuries case on the basis that it helped reduce the court's case load where the first-instance hearing had been in public, the appeal was confined to matters of law and, perhaps most importantly, the appeal court would have been required to sit in public if it was contemplating reversing, rather than approving, the decision of the court of first instance.[111]

13.50   The requirement that 'judgment shall be pronounced publicly' in article 6(1) has not been interpreted literally. In *Pretto and Others v Italy*[112] the European Court held that depositing a judgment in the domestic court's registry, with written notification of its operative provisions to the parties, without a reading in open court was enough to comply with article 6(1). However, if no measures at all were taken to publish a judgment, article 6(1) would undoubtedly be violated.[113]

---

105   But does not necessarily: see *H v Belgium* (1988) 10 EHRR 339.

106   *Zumtobel v Austria*, n103.

107   (1970) 30 CD 70.

108   See paras 12.34 to 12.40. See *Scarth v UK* [1999] EHRLR 332 on need for arbitration hearings in county court to be public.

109   *Ekbatani v Sweden* (1991) 13 EHRR 504.

110   (1984) 6 EHRR 195.

111   Ibid at para 28.

112   (1984) 6 EHRR 182.

113   *Campbell and Fell v UK* (1985) 7 EHRR 165.

The right to participate effectively in civil proceedings

13.51 The right to participate effectively in legal proceedings has been specifically recognised in the criminal context.[114] It also underpins many of the fair trial guarantees in civil proceedings, for example, the right to be present, equality of arms, the right to an adversarial hearing and disclosure.

The right to be present

13.52 In the criminal context, the European Court has read a right to be present into article 6(1).[115] Although the right has not been recognised to the same extent in civil proceedings, fairness may require presence, particularly where proceedings are personal in character, involve a determination about the conduct of one of the parties[116] or where presence is indispensable to a fair disposal of the case.[117] See, for example, *X v Sweden*[118] which concerned a child-access hearing; and, perhaps less obviously, *X v Germany*,[119] a commercial case.

13.53 Like the right to a public hearing, the right to be present in civil proceedings may be restricted on appeal: see below.[120]

Equality of arms

13.54 The European Court and Commission have long recognised that 'equality of arms is an inherent element of a fair trial'.[121] In civil proceedings, equality of arms implies:

> ... that each party must be afforded a reasonable opportunity to present his case – including his evidence – under conditions that do not place him at a substantial disadvantage vis-à-vis his opponent.[122]

114 See paras 8.19 to 8.22.
115 See paras 8.19 to 8.21.
116 *X v Sweden* (1959) 2 Yearbook 354; *Muyldermans v Belgium* A/214-A (1991) Com Rep, unreported.
117 By implication from *X v Austria* (1983) 31 DR 66.
118 (1959) 2 Yearbook 354.
119 (1963) 6 Yearbook 520.
120 Paras 13.74 to 13.77.
121 *X v Germany* (1963) 6 Yearbook 520.
122 *Dombo Beheer B.V. v Netherlands* (1994) 18 EHRR 213 at para 33.

This has provided a springboard for reading some of the criminal-specific guarantees in articles 6(2) and 6(3) of the Convention into article 6(1) in the civil context, including the right to an adversarial hearing, disclosure, the calling of witnesses and the right to a reasoned decision.

The right to an adversarial hearing

13.55   One essential aspect of the equality of arms principle is that proceedings which determine civil rights and obligations should be adversarial.[123] This means that every party to a hearing must be allowed to know and to comment upon all the evidence adduced and all legal submissions made by others[124] 'with a view to influencing the court's decision'.[125]

13.56   Where a non-party makes submissions to the court, the same principle applies. In *Van Orshoven v Belgium*[126] the applicant, who had been struck off the register of the Medical Association in disciplinary proceedings, appealed to the Court of Cassation. Before that court the advocat-general appeared and made submissions to 'assist' the court and to ensure that its case-law was consistent. The applicant complained that he had been given no prior notice of the advocat-general's submissions and had not been given an opportunity to reply to them in court. The European Court found this to be a breach of article 6(1). Although the advocat-general acted with the 'strictest objectivity', the submissions he advanced were 'intended to advise and accordingly influence the Court of Cassation'.[127] Clearly this has implications for amicus lawyers, intervening parties and clerks in magistrates' courts.

13.57   The same principle applies where a court of first instance transmits documents to an appeal court. In *Niderost-Huber v Switzerland*,[128] having rejected the applicant's claim for wrongful dismissal, the Swiss Cantonal Court sent a one-page document containing its observations to the appeal court. The European Court held that these

---

123   *Brandstetter v Austria* (1993) 15 EHRR 378 at para 66; *Ruiz-Mateos v Spain* (1993) 16 EHRR 505 at para 63.

124   *Ruiz-Mateos v Spain* note 123 at para 63.

125   *Lombo Machado v Portugal* (1997) 23 EHRR 79 at para 31; *Niderost-Huber v Switzerland* (1998) 25 EHRR 709 at para 24.

126   (1998) 26 EHRR 55.

127   Ibid at para 39.

128   (1998) 25 EHRR 709.

observations were manifestly aimed at influencing the appeal court's decision and dismissed as of 'little consequence' the fact that:

1) the observations did not contain any matters not ventilated in the first-instance court;

2) the observations were unlikely to have any real impact on the appeal court; or

3) the proceedings were civil not criminal.

In its view:

> What is at stake here is litigants' confidence in the workings of justice, which is based on, inter alia, the knowledge that they have had the opportunity to express their views on every document in the [court] file.[129]

What was required was for the applicant to be given a copy of the observations and afforded an opportunity to comment upon them.

13.58   In *McMichael v UK*[130] the European Court read into the adversarial principle a general requirement for full disclosure. It reasoned that without full disclosure it would be impossible for each of the interested parties to know and comment upon all the evidence adduced. In the context of that case, which involved care proceedings in Scotland, the Court held that:

> ... the lack of disclosure of such vital documents as social reports is capable of affecting the ability of participating parents not only to influence the outcome of the children's hearing in question but also to assess their prospects of making an appeal to the Sheriff Court.[131]

As a result article 6(1) was breached.

Disclosure

13.59   Disclosure of relevant documents to all the parties in civil proceedings is a requirement of article 6(1) of the Convention. In *Feldbrugge v Netherlands*[132] the European Court held that the failure of a welfare benefits tribunal to allow the applicant access to and com-

---

129 Ibid at para 29.
130 (1995) 20 EHRR 205.
131 Ibid at para 80.
132 (1986) 8 EHRR.

ment upon expert reports on her file deprived her of the ability to participate effectively in the proceedings. Accordingly article 6(1) was breached.

13.60   The issue of non-disclosure arose again in *Kerojavi v Finland*[133] where, during the course of the applicant's claim for a war injuries pension, the Finland Insurance Court obtained his war-time medical records but did not disclose them. For the European Court this was a clear breach of article 6(1). The notion of a fair hearing required disclosure to the applicant himself so that he could assess the relevance and weight of the documents and formulate any comments he deemed appropriate.

13.61   This approach was endorsed in *McGinley and Egan v UK*[134] where the applicants, who had been stationed near Christmas Island at the time of nuclear tests in 1958, complained that the government had not disclosed documents which would have assisted them in proceedings before the Pensions Appeal Tribunal (PAT). In a strong statement of principle, the European Court held that:

> ... if it were the case that the respondent State had, without good cause, prevented the applicants from gaining access to, or falsely denied the existence of, documents in its possession which would have assisted them in establishing before the PAT that they had been exposed to dangerous levels of radiation, this would have been to deny them a fair hearing in violation of article 6(1).[135]

On the facts, however, it rejected the applicants' complaint on the basis that some of the documents in question had in fact been destroyed and that the applicants had failed to seek disclosure of the rest in the domestic proceedings.

Evidence and witnesses

13.62   Article 6(1) does not prescribe any specific rules of evidence in civil proceedings. However, it does require overall fairness and this has implications for the way in which evidence is adduced and the weight given to it. As noted above,[136] in general terms each party in civil proceedings must be given a proper opportunity to present his/her case,

---

133 A/328 (Court) 19 July 1995 [1996] EHRLR 66.
134 (1998) 27 EHRR 1.
135 Ibid at para 86.
136 See para 13.3.

including the evidence.[137] This includes the right to cross-examine witnesses.[138]

Burden and standard of proof

13.63 Article 6(1) does not govern the burden and standard of proof in civil proceedings, subject again to the requirement of overall fairness. Hence a statutory presumption that a company director is responsible for company debts does not, of itself, offend the right to a fair trial.[139] However, the burden and standard of proof in civil proceedings must not be such as to create an imbalance between the parties.[140]

Expert evidence

13.64 The role of expert witnesses in criminal proceedings has raised difficulties under the Convention.[141] The Strasbourg case-law in that context has established that all expert witnesses must be treated equally, irrespective of the party calling them and there is no reason why the same principle should not apply in civil proceedings.

13.65 Although the issue has not been specifically addressed by the European Court or Commission, it is implicit in the Court's judgment in *H v France*[142] and *Mantovanelli v France*[143] that, where expert evidence is indispensable to a fair trial, either the court should call such evidence or legal aid should be provided to enable the parties to do so. Consistent with this approach, in *Martins Moreira v Portugal*,[144] where a court-appointed medical expert had taken over two years to examine the applicant, the European Court held that, having set up an Institute for Forensic Medicine, the state was 'under a duty to provide [experts] with appropriate means ... so as to enable them to comply with the requirements of article 6(1).'[145]

137 *Dombo Beheer B.V. v Netherlands* at para 33.
138 *X v Austria* (1972) 42 CD 145.
139 *G v France* (1988) 57 DR 100.
140 Ibid at p106.
141 See chapter 9.
142 (1990) 12 EHRR 74.
143 (1997) 24 EHRR 370.
144 (1991) 13 EHRR 517.
145 Ibid at para 60.

13.66   Conversely, there is no obligation on the court to obtain an expert's report merely because one party seeks it. In *H v France* the European Court found no breach of article 6(1) where the domestic court had refused to commission an expert report because the party calling for it had failed to establish a prima facie link between his injuries and the medical treatment he complained about.

13.67   However, where the court does appoint an expert, care must be taken to ensure compliance with the adversarial principle. In *Mantovanelli v France*[146] the court appointed a medical expert in the course of proceedings brought by the applicants in relation to the death of their daughter in hospital. The applicants complained that they had not been given an opportunity to give instructions to the expert and had not been shown documents referred to in his report. Although they had been given an opportunity to cross-examine the expert when he gave his evidence at trial, the European Court took the view that article 6(1) had been breached; particularly since the issue for the domestic court turned almost entirely on the medical evidence.

Reasons

13.68   Article 6(1) obliges domestic courts to give reasons for their judgments.[147] The extent of the reasons that must be given will vary according to the nature of the decision in question. There is no need for courts to give detailed answers to every argument raised during the course of a hearing, but failure to address an important aspect of the case will breach article 6(1). A decision which on its face shows that it was made on a basis not open to the judge cannot be said to be a reasoned decision.[148]

13.69   Without reasons at first instance, parties to legal proceedings cannot properly exercise their rights of appeal.[149] However, at the leave stage itself, if the only issue is whether a question of fundamental importance is raised and/or whether the case has any prospect of success, a decision refusing leave need not be fully reasoned.[150]

---

146 (1997) 24 EHRR 370.
147 *Van de Hurk v Netherlands* (1994) 18 EHRR 481 at para 61; *Hiro Balani v Spain* (1995) 19 EHRR 566 at para 27. See also *Ruiz v Spain* [1999] EHRLR 334.
148 *De Moor v Belgium* (1994) 18 EHRR 372.
149 *Hadjianastassiou v Greece* (1993) 16 EHRR 219 (in the criminal context).
150 *X v Germany* (1981) 25 DR 240.

Costs

13.70 Article 6(1) does not guarantee a successful litigant a right to costs, but since the European Court recognised costs as an integral part of the determination of civil rights and obligations in *Robins v UK*,[151] the rules for allocating costs and the procedure by which costs are awarded must be fair. In *Grepne v UK* the Commission held, as a matter of principle, that:

> ... it is not an unreasonable requirement of civil litigation that the unsuccessful party may have to pay the adversary's costs.[152]

And it is a breach of article 6(1) if recovery of costs takes too long.[153]

13.71 Wasted costs orders do not determine civil rights and obligations.[154] Nor do they raise an issue under article 1 of Protocol 1 (the right to property).[155]

The enforcement of judgments

13.72 The fair trial guarantees of article 6(1) do not end on the pronouncement of judgment. In a number of cases the European Court has recognised that the determination of civil rights and obligations includes the enforcement of judgments. Hence, long delays in enforcement may violate the guarantee of trial within a reasonable period.[156]

13.73 The European Court expanded on this notion in *Hornsby v Greece*[157] where the Greek Ministry of Education wrongly refused to allow the applicants to set up a school. The Supreme Administrative Court quashed the ministry's decision, but the ministry refused to act on that decision. The European Court upheld the applicants' complaint that this infringed their right to effective judicial protection of their civil rights inherent in article 6(1) because:

> ... the [right to a court] would be 'illusory', if a Contracting State's domestic legal system allowed a final, binding judicial decision to

151 (1998) 26 EHRR 527.
152 Note 61 at p270; see also *Dublin Well Woman Centre Ltd v Ireland* (1997) 23 EHRR CD 125.
153 *Robins v UK* note 151.
154 *B v UK* (1984) 38 DR 213.
155 *X v Germany* (1978) 14 DR 60.
156 See *Silva Pontes v Portugal* (1994) 18 EHRR 156; *Di Pede v Italy* (Court) 26 September 1996; *Zappia v Italy* (Court) 26 September 1996.
157 (1997) 24 EHRR 250.

remain inoperative to the detriment of one party. It would be inconceivable that article 6 should describe in detail procedural guarantees afforded to litigants – proceedings that are fair, public and expeditious – without protecting the implementation of judicial decisions.[158]

Enforcement of judgments must therefore be regarded as an integral part of the 'trial' for the purposes of article 6.

Civil appeals

13.74   There is no right to appeal under the Convention itself. However, where a right of appeal is provided in domestic law, article 6(1) applies.

13.75   The manner of application of article 6(1) to civil appeal proceedings depends on the special features of the proceedings involved. Account has to be taken of the entirety of the proceedings and the role of the appellate courts in the overall process.[159] In practice, this means that some of the article 6(1) guarantees, such as the right to an oral hearing and the right of the accused to be present, are less strictly applied in appeal proceedings; particularly where the only issues raised are points of law.

13.76   If, however, an appeal court is competent to decide questions of fact as well as of law, an oral hearing in public may be required.[160] In *Helmers v Sweden*[161] the European Court held that the applicant should have been heard in person in a defamation appeal where the facts were in dispute and the outcome was important for his professional reputation.

13.77   Finally, the extent to which an appeal court can cure defects in the proceedings below is limited. So, for example, a public appeal hearing will not rectify a non-public trial.

Trial within a reasonable period

13.78   Article 6(1) specifically guarantees that civil proceedings be heard and determined within a reasonable period. The purpose of this provision is to protect 'all parties to court proceedings ... against

158 Ibid at para 40.
159 *Monnell and Morris v UK* (1988) 10 EHRR 205 (in the criminal context).
160 *Ekbatani v Sweden* (1991) 13 EHRR 504.
161 (1993) 15 EHRR 285.

excessive procedural delays'[162] and to underline 'the importance of rendering justice without delays which might jeopardise its effectiveness and credibility'.[163]

13.79   In the civil context, time usually begins to run from the initiation of court proceedings[164] and ends when the rights and obligations in question are finally determined, including any relevant appeal or judicial review proceedings. Final determination includes the determination of costs[165] and enforcement proceedings.[166]

13.80   The Strasbourg bodies have been reluctant to apply fixed criteria for assessing the reasonableness of time in civil cases and no minimum periods have been laid down.[167] Relevant factors in any overall assessment are:

1) the complexity of the case;

2) what is at stake for the applicant;

3) the conduct of the domestic authorities, including the courts themselves; and

4) the conduct of the applicant.[168]

No one factor is conclusive. The court's approach has been to examine each factor separately and then to consider the cumulative effect of delay.

13.81   What is at stake for the applicant has, however, been decisive in a number of cases, particularly where the proceedings are critical to the applicant and/or have a 'particular quality of irreversibility'.[169] These include:

1) Child care cases. In *H v UK*[170] the European Court found that pro-

---

162 *Stogmuller v Austria* (1979–80) 12 EHRR 155.

163 *H v France* (1990) 12 EHRR 74.

164 *Guincho v Portugal* (1985) 7 EHRR 223; but possibly from an earlier stage where there are difficulties obtaining legal aid, see *Golder v UK* (1979–80) 1 EHRR 524.

165 See *Robins v UK* n151, where the resolution of a costs dispute took over four years.

166 *Silva Pontes v Portugal*; *Di Pede v Italy*; *Zappia v Italy* n156.

167 However, delays during which a case does not progress for over three years and six months can be justified only by 'very exceptional circumstances' *Union Alimentaria SA v Spain* (1990) 12 EHRR 24 at para 36.

168 See *Konig v Germany* (1979–80) 2 EHRR 170 at paras 99, 102–105 and 107–111; *Buchholz v Germany* (1981) 3 EHRR 597 at para 49.

169 *H v UK* (1988) 10 EHRR 95.

170 Note 169.

ceedings lasting two years and seven months breached article 6(1) and observed that:

> In cases of this kind the authorities are under a duty to exercise exceptional diligence since, as the Commission rightly pointed out, there is always the danger that any procedural delay will result in the de facto determination of the issue submitted to the court before it had held its hearing.[171]

See also, *Hokkanen v Finland:*[172] '... it is essential that custody cases be dealt with speedily'.[173]

2) Personal injury cases. In *Silva Pontes v Portugal*[174] the European Court spoke of a need for 'special diligence' where the applicant was claiming compensation for serious injuries cause in a road traffic accident.

3) Employment disputes;[175] particularly where reinstatement is claimed in unfair dismissal cases.[176] In *Obermeier v Germany*[177] the European Court observed that:

> ... an employee who considers that he has been wrongly suspended by his employer has an important personal interest in securing the judicial decision on the lawfulness of that measure promptly.[178]

4) Cases where speed is obviously of the essence. In a series of cases against France,[179] the European Court has found that periods in excess of two years breached article 6(1) in civil claims by AIDS victims alleging negligence in blood transfusions. And in a similar case against Denmark,[180] the Court observed that:

> ... the competent administrative and judicial authorities were under a positive obligation under article 6(1) to act with the exceptional diligence required by the court's case law in disputes of this nature.[181]

171 Note 169 at para 85.
172 (1995) 19 EHRR 139.
173 Ibid at para 72.
174 (1994) 18 EHRR 156.
175 See *Obermeier v Germany* (1991) 13 EHRR 290; *Nibbio v Italy* A/228-A (1992).
176 *Buchholz v Germany* n168.
177 Note 175.
178 Note 175 at para 72.
179 *X v France* (1992) 14 EHRR 483; *Vallée v France* (1994) 18 EHRR 549; *Karakay v France* A/289-B (1994); *Demai v France* A/289-C (1994).
180 *A and Others v Denmark* (1996) 22 EHRR 458.
181 Ibid at para 78.

Speed has also been recognised as important where proceedings may have an effect on the mental health of one of the parties.[182]

13.82 Although the conduct of the applicant is relevant, the fact that in some legal systems the parties are responsible for the progress of a case does not 'absolve the courts from ensuring compliance with the requirements of article 6 concerning reasonable time'.[183] The applicant's duty is only to:

> ... show diligence in carrying out the procedural steps relevant to him, to refrain from using delaying tactics and to avail himself of the scope afforded by domestic law for shortening the proceedings.[184]

13.83 States, on the other hand, have an obligation 'to organise their legal systems so as to allow the courts to comply with the requirements of article 6(1)'.[185] Thus a failure to allocate adequate resources may engage state responsibility,[186] unless particular difficulties were unforeseeable and the state has subsequently taken remedial action reasonably promptly.[187] However, so long as they have taken the appropriate organisational steps, the domestic authorities will not be responsible for delays caused by lawyers[188] or other parties to the litigation.[189]

---

182 *Bock v Germany* (1990) 12 EHRR 247; but see also *Mahamoud v UK* [1996] EHRLR 219.
183 *Union Alimentaria Sanders SA v Spain* n167.
184 Ibid at para 35.
185 *Zimmerman and Steiner v Switzerland* (1983) 6 EHRR 17 at para 29.
186 *Guincho v Portugal* n164.
187 *Buccholz v Germany* n168 at para 51.
188 *H v France* (1990) 12 EHRR 74.
189 *Bock v Germany* n182.

PART IV

The European Convention on Human Rights: specific issues

CHAPTER 14

The right to life and physical integrity

14.1   Introduction

14.2   The right to life

14.5   The duty to protect the right to life by law

14.10   The obligation to take appropriate measures to protect life

14.14   Investigation and prosecution

14.19   Criminal investigations

14.22   The use of force and the exceptions provided for in article 2(2)

14.27   The test of absolute necessity

14.32   Abortion

14.37   Euthanasia

14.39   The death penalty

14.41   The prohibition on torture, inhuman and/or degrading treatment/punishment

14.45   Torture

14.48   Inhuman treatment/punishment

continued

14.52   **Degrading treatment/punishment**

14.56   **Procedural aspects of article 3**

14.57   **State responsibility under article 3**

14.61   **The protection of physical integrity under article 8**

14.64   **Medical care: overview**

14.66   **Medical treatment, the right to life and the prohibition on inhuman and degrading treatment.**

14.70   **Health advice**

14.72   **Access to health information**

14.74   **Medical records**

14.75   **Negligence**

Introduction

14.1 This chapter deals with the right to life and physical integrity. The absolute nature of these rights under articles 2 and 3 of the convention dictates a particularly strict approach to their interpretation. In particular, under articles 2 and 3 of the Convention, an individual's right to life and physical integrity is not to be balanced against the public interest: it cannot be argued that a breach of these provisions is justified for the common good.

The right to life

14.2 Article 2 provides that:

1) Everyone's right to life shall be protected by law. No one shall be deprived of his life intentionally save in the execution of a sentence of a court following his conviction of a crime for which this penalty is provided by law.

2) Deprivation of life shall not be regarded as inflicted in contravention of this Article when it results from the use of force which is no more than absolutely necessary:

   a) in defence of any person from unlawful violence;

   b) in order to effect a lawful arrest or to prevent the escape of a person lawfully detained;

   c) in action lawfully taken for the purpose of quelling a riot or insurrection.

The fundamental nature of the right to life is obvious and in peace time derogation from article 2 is not possible.

14.3 In the first case it ever considered under article 2, the European Court of Human Rights made the following statement on general principle:

... Article 2 ranks as one of the most fundamental provisions in the Convention ... Together with Article 3 ... it ... enshrines one of the basic values of democratic societies making up the Council of Europe. As such its provisions must be strictly construed.[1]

It added that the interpretation of article 2 must be guided by the fact that the object and purpose of the Convention, as an instrument for the protection of human beings, requires that its provisions be

1   *McCann v UK* (1996) 21 EHRR 97 at para 147.

interpreted and applied so as to make its safeguards practical and effective.[2]

14.4   Article 2 imposes two duties on the state (and its officials):

1) a duty to protect the right to life by law;

2) a duty not to deprive anyone of his/her life save in the limited circumstances prescribed by article 2(2).

These will be analysed separately.

The duty to protect the right to life by law

14.5   Article 2(1) of the Convention imposes a positive obligation on states to protect the right to life by law. There are both substantive and procedural aspects to this duty.

14.6   Substantively, the state must enact legislation to protect life. How a state fulfils this obligation lies within its discretion, but, at the very least, there must be criminal sanctions for the taking of life in breach of article 2.

14.7   Whether a law which permits the use of lethal force where it is considered to be 'reasonably justifiable' rather than 'absolutely necessary' is compatible with article 2 was considered by the European Court in *McCann v UK*.[3] In light of the government's assertion that, as interpreted by the domestic courts, there was no significant difference between the 'reasonably justifiable' and 'absolutely necessary' tests, the Court found no issue arose under article 2(1).

14.8   In the same case, the Court found it unnecessary to decide whether a right to bring civil proceedings in connection with deprivation of life can be inferred from article 2(1).[4] However, such a right can be derived from articles 6(1) and 13 of the Convention.[5] And any restrictions on that right must be legitimate and proportionate.[6]

14.9   Procedurally, the obligation on states to protect the right to life by law requires effective enforcement of the law. This means taking appropriate measures to protect life, investigating all suspicious deaths efficiently and prosecuting alleged offenders where appropriate to do so.

---

2   Ibid at para 146.
3   Note 1.
4   Ibid at para 160.
5   See paras 3.87 to 3.99 and 3.173 to 3.181.
6   *Osman v UK* Court (28 October 1998); noted at [1999] EHRLR 228.

The obligation to take appropriate measures to protect life

14.10   The obligation to take appropriate measures to protect life has been recognised for some time. Its scope was examined by the European Court in *Osman v UK*,[7] where the applicants complained that the police had failed to take reasonable preventative measures against one of the second applicant's teachers who ultimately killed the first applicant's husband (the second applicant's father) and wounded the second applicant.[8] Although the Court found no breach of article 2 on the facts, it adopted the following important principles:

1) the state's obligation under article 2 extends beyond a duty to put in place effective criminal law provisions to deter the commission of offences against the person backed up by law-enforcement machinery for the prevention, suppression and sanctioning of breaches of such provisions;

2) it also implies, in certain well-defined circumstances, a positive obligation on the authorities to take preventative operational measures to protect an individual whose life is at risk from the criminal acts of another individual;

3) bearing in mind the difficulties involved in policing modern societies, the unpredictability of human conduct and the operational choices which must be made in terms of priorities and resources, such an obligation must be interpreted in a way which does not impose an impossible or disproportionate burden on the authorities;

4) it must also be interpreted in a way which fully respects the due process and other guarantees which legitimately place restraints on the scope of their action to investigate crime and bring offenders to justice, including the guarantees contained in articles 5 and 8 of the Convention;

5) what must be shown, therefore, is that the authorities failed to do all that could reasonably be expected of them to avoid a 'real and immediate' risk to life which they knew about or ought to have known about.[9]

14.11   On that basis the European Court rejected the government's

---

7   Note 6.
8   See further chapter 15 paras 15.96 to 15.99.
9   Note 6 at para 116.

assertion that to breach article 2, the failure to perceive the risk to life or take preventative measures must be tantamount to gross negligence or wilful disregard of the duty to protect life.

14.12   In a number of previous cases, the Commission had examined the scope of the obligation to take appropriate measures to protect life in the context of paramilitary attacks in Northern Ireland. It accepted that police/security force protection may be needed in some cases – up to a point – but emphasised that 'a positive obligation to exclude any possible violence' could not be read into article 2.[10] In particular, continuous police/security forces protection could not be expected. And, on that basis, the Commission rejected a complaint where police protection, which had been in place for several years after an attempt on the applicant's life by the IRA, was discontinued.[11]

14.13   The duty to take appropriate measures to protect life is of general application and clearly extends beyond the sphere of criminal activities. A forced eviction which endangered life might raise article 2 issues.[12] And in *Barrett v UK*,[13] where the applicant complained that lack of control of alcohol consumption on a naval base coupled with inadequate medical attention contributed to the death of her husband who died after heavy drinking, the Commission observed as a general principle that:

> Where a State provides facilities for drinking in circumstances where there is an obvious and substantial risk of excessive consumption the absence of any measures designed to discourage drinking to excess and, in the event, to secure adequate care and treatment, is likely to raise issues under Article 2 of the Convention.'[14]

On the facts, however, the Commission found no breach of the Convention.

---

10   *W v UK* (1983) 32 DR 190 at p200.
11   *X v Ireland* (1973) 16 Yearbook 388.
12   See Appl 5207/71, 14 Yearbook 698; the case was not subsequently pursued; see also *WM v Germany* (1997) 24 EHRR CD 79. See also *Keenan v UK* [1998] EHRLR 648 concering death in custody.
13   (1997) 23 EHRR CD 185.
14   Ibid at p187.

Investigation and prosecution

14.14 A general legal prohibition of arbitrary killing by the state's servants or agents is a necessary requirement of article 2, but not, in itself, enough for compliance. Where an individual dies in circumstances which might amount to a breach of article 2, what is needed is 'some form of effective official investigation'.[15] This is particularly so, where state officials have, or might have, been involved in the death.

14.15 In *McCann v UK*[16] the applicants, relatives of three suspected members of the IRA killed by the SAS in Gibraltar, argued that such an investigation should take the form of an independent judicial process to which relatives had full access. In their view, the ordinary inquest procedure failed to meet this criteria.

14.16 On the facts the European Court rejected this argument. In particular, it noted that:

1) the applicants were legally represented at the inquest hearing;

2) the inquest involved a detailed review of the events surrounding the killing; and

3) the lawyers acting for the applicants were able to examine and cross-examine key witnesses including the military and police personnel involved.

Inquests where there are long delays or where the scope of any inquiry is limited (for example, because of the extensive use of public interest immunity certificates) may not so easily survive challenge.[17]

14.17 The minimum content of any investigation into suspicious deaths was considered by the Commission in *Taylor, Crampton, Gibson and King v UK*.[18] In that case, the applicants were the relatives of children killed by a former nurse at Grantham Hospital, Beverley Allitt. They complained that an inquiry set up by the regional health authority was not an adequate investigation into the circumstances giving rise to the deaths of their children. Drawing on its own decision in *McCann v UK*, the Commission observed that the 'procedural aspect' required under article 2:

... includes the minimum requirement of a mechanism whereby the

15 *McCann v UK* (1995) 21 EHRR 97 at para 161.
16 Note 15.
17 There are a number of cases currently before the Court from Northern Ireland raising these issues: see Reid *A Practitioner's Guide to the European Convention on Human Rights* (1998, Sweet & Maxwell) p363 n8.
18 (1994) 79-A DR 127.

circumstances of a deprivation of life by the agents of a state may receive public and independent scrutiny. The nature and degree of scrutiny which satisfies this minimum threshold must, in the Commission's view, depend on the circumstances of the particular case. There may be cases where the facts surrounding a deprivation of life are clear and undisputed and the subsequent inquisitorial examination may legitimately be reduced to a minimum formality. But equally, there may be other cases, where a victim dies in circumstances which are unclear, in which event the lack of an effective procedure to investigate the cause of the deprivation of life could by itself raise an issue under Article 2 of the Convention.[19]

14.18   On the facts it found the minimum requirement satisfied because there had been criminal proceedings against Allitt and, although the regional health authority's inquiry conducted its proceedings in private, it was independent, had scrutinised all the evidence and had published its report. The Commission was also influenced by the fact that it was open to the applicants to bring civil proceedings against the health authority for negligence.

Criminal investigations

14.19   The procedural aspect of article 2 extends to criminal investigations into suspicious deaths. In a series of cases from Turkey involving both article 2 and article 3, the European Court has found that wherever an individual dies in suspicious circumstances, disappears or an allegation of torture is 'arguable', article 13 (the right to an effective remedy) requires, without prejudice to the availability of any other remedy, a 'thorough and effective investigation capable of leading to the identification and punishment of those responsible and including effective access for the relatives to the investigatory procedure'.[20]

14.20   Examples where the European Court has found that there has been a failure to conduct a 'thorough and effective investigation' include;

1) failing to ascertain possible eye-witnesses;

2) failing to question suspects at an early stage;

---

19   Ibid p136.
20   See *Aksoy v Turkey* (1997) 23 EHRR 553; *Aydin v Turkey* (1998) 25 EHRR 251; *Kaya v Turkey* Court (19 February 1998); and *Kurt v Turkey* (1999) 27 EHRR 373.

3) failing to search for corroborating evidence;[21]

4) the adoption of an over-deferential attitude to those in authority;[22]

5) failing to follow up proper complaints;[23]

6) ignoring obvious evidence;[24]

7) failing to carry out a proper autopsy;[25] and

8) failing to test for gunpowder traces.[26]

14.21 An amnesty for persons convicted or suspected of homicide is not necessarily inconsistent with article 2; provided that it reflects a proper balance between the interests of the state in the particular circumstances in which the amnesty is declared and the general need to enforce the law to protect the right to life.[27]

The use of force and the exceptions provided for in article 2(2)

14.22 Article 2(2) provides that causing death does not breach article 2(1) when it results from the use of force which is no more than 'absolutely necessary' for any of the following purposes:

1) in self-defence or defence of others[28] – but not of property;[29]

2) to carry out an arrest or prevent escape;[30] or

3) to quash a riot or insurrection.[31]

Where the use of lethal force contravenes domestic law, for example

---

21 *Aydin v Turkey* n20.

22 Ibid.

23 *Kurt v Turkey* n20.

24 *Aksoy v Turkey* n20.

25 *Kaya v Turkey* n20; the autopsy in that case was vague and failed to identify the number of bullet holes.

26 Ibid.

27 *Dujardin v France* Appl 16734/90 (1991) unreported: see Harris, O'Boyle and Warbrick, *Law of the European Convention on Human Rights* (1995, Butterworths) p40.

28 See *Wolfgram v Germany* (1986) 49 DR 213; *Diaz Ruano v Spain* A/285-B (1994) unreported.

29 *The Law of the European Convention on Human Rights* n27, p48.

30 See *Farrell v UK* (1982) 30 DR 96 and (1984) 38 DR 44; and *Kelly v UK* Appl 17579/90 (1993) unreported.

31 See *Stewart v UK* (1984) 39 DR 162; and *X v Belgium* (1969) 12 Yearbook 174.

when proper authorisation has not been given for the use of firearms, article 2 will automatically be breached.[32]

14.23   Article 2(2) covers both intentional and accidental killing. So far as the former is concerned, article 2(2) does not define instances where intentional killing is permitted; it describes situations where the 'use of force' which may result – as an unintended outcome – in the deprivation of life, is permitted.[33]

14.24   The circumstances in which lethal force can be used to carry out an arrest or prevent escape are very limited. In *Kelly v UK*[34] the Commission found that the use of lethal force by soldiers in Northern Ireland to stop a car which had driven through a checkpoint was justified because the soldiers thought the car contained terrorists, no other means existed for stopping the car and 'although the risk of harm to the occupants was high, the kind of harm to be averted ... by preventing their escape was even greater, namely the freedom of terrorists to resume their dealings in death and destruction'.

14.25   This decision has been criticised on the basis that lethal force can never be 'absolutely necessary' to prevent future, undefined criminal acts.[35] At the very least, it is difficult to see how the use of lethal force to effect an arrest in a non-terrorist context can ever be justified where self-defence or the defence of others under article 2(2)(a) is not also relied upon. And in *Aytekin v Turkey*,[36] where a soldier shot dead the driver of a car which passed through a check point without stopping, the Commission distinguished *Kelly v UK*[37] on the basis that the driver had not behaved suspiciously.

14.26   Subject to the requirement that reasonable measures be taken to protect life, that suspicious deaths be investigated properly and prosecutions brought where appropriate (see above), state responsibility is not necessarily engaged where one private individual kills another private individual.

32   *X v Belgium* n31.
33   *McCann v UK* n15.
34   Note 30.
35   *The Law of the European Convention on Human Rights* n27, p53.
36   (Commission) 18 September 1997.
37   Note 30.

The test of absolute necessity

14.27   The use of the term 'absolutely necessary' in article 2(2) indicates a stricter and more compelling test of necessity than that used when determining whether state action is 'necessary in a democratic society' under articles 8–11 of the Convention. Where lethal force is used by servants or agents of the state it involves the determination of two questions:

1) whether the use of lethal force was 'strictly proportionate' to the achievement of one of the aims set out article 2(2)(a),(b) or (c)[38] – regard being had to the nature of the aim pursued, the dangers to life and limb inherent in the situation and the degree of risk that the force employed might result in the loss of life;[39] and

2) whether the operation under scrutiny was 'planned and controlled by the authorities so as to minimise, to the greatest extent possible, recourse to lethal force'.[40]

14.28   As to the first limb, the European Court has accepted that the use of lethal force by state agents or servants can be justified under article 2(2) where it is based on an honest belief that the use of such force is absolutely necessary, even if that belief subsequently turns out to be mistaken. To hold otherwise would be to impose 'an unrealistic burden' on the state and its law enforcement personnel in the execution of their duty 'perhaps to the detriment of others'.[41]

14.29   In relation to the second limb, very careful consideration must be given to all the facts before assumptions are made; particularly where those assumptions inevitably mean that lethal force will have to be used. In the context of the killing of three IRA suspects by the SAS in *McCann v UK*[42] the Court held that:

> ... the authorities were bound by their obligation to respect the right to life of the suspects to exercise the greatest of care in evaluating the information at their disposal before transmitting it to soldiers whose use of firearms automatically involved shooting to kill.[43]

---

38   *McCann v UK* n15 at para 194; *Andronicou and Constantinou v Cyprus* (1997) 25 EHRR 491 at para 171.
39   *Stewart v UK* (1984) 39 DR 162.
40   *McCann v UK* n15 para 194.
41   Ibid para 200.
42   Note 15.
43   Ibid para 211.

And in *Aytekin v Turkey*[44] the Commission found a breach of article 2 where a soldier shot an unarmed man who drove through a security check point on the basis that:

1) an insufficient number of soldiers had been posted at the checkpoint so as to ensure that such incidents could be dealt with without recourse to lethal force; and

2) those at the check point had been given inadequate information.

14.30   The obligation to show that any operation in which lethal force is used was planned and controlled by the authorities so as to minimise, to the greatest extent possible, recourse to lethal force also has training implications. In *McCann v UK*[45] the Court questioned whether the SAS members responsible for the killing had been trained or instructed to assess whether the use of firearms to wound rather than to kill the suspects might have been appropriate. In its view;

> Their reflex action in this vital respect lacks the degree of caution in the use of firearms to be expected from law enforcement personnel in a democratic society, even when dealing with dangerous terrorist suspects ...[46]

For the Court this demonstrated a lack of appropriate care in the control and organisation of the arrest operation and hence a breach of article 2.[47]

14.31   By contrast, there was no breach of article 2 in *Andronicou and Constantinou v Cyprus*.[48] Although in that case special firearms officers, trained to shoot to kill, were deployed to rescue a woman from a house where she was being held at gun point by her former partner, they had been given specific instructions to use only proportionate force and to fire only if the woman's life or their own lives were in danger.[49]

---

44   Note 36.
45   Note 15.
46   Note 15 para 212.
47   Ibid.
48   Note 38.
49   Ibid at para 185.

Abortion

14.32   Abortion raises issues under article 2 and article 8 (privacy and family life) of the Convention. So far as the former is concerned, although the European Court has yet to determine the issue, the Commission has adopted the firm view that article 2 does not require states to prohibit abortion, because a foetus has no 'absolute right' to life. In *Paton v UK*[50] the Commission reasoned that:

> The 'life' of the foetus is intimately connected with, and cannot be regarded in isolation of, the pregnant woman. If Article 2 were held to cover the foetus and its protection under the Article were, in the absence of any express limitation, seen as absolute, an abortion would have to be considered as prohibited even where the continuance of the pregnancy would involve a serious risk to the life of the pregnant woman. This would mean that the 'unborn life' of the foetus would be regarded as being of a higher value than the life of the pregnant woman. The 'right to life' of a person already born would thus be considered as subject not only to the express limitations [set out in article 2(2)] but also to a further, implied limitation.[51]

In the Commission's view such an interpretation would be contrary to the object and purpose of the Convention.

14.33   Having rejected the proposition that a foetus has an 'absolute' right to life, the Commission in *Paton v UK*[52] recognised that there were two other possible interpretations of article 2; namely (a) that a foetus has no right to life under article 2; or (b) that a foetus has *some* right to life under article 2 but that any such right is subject to certain implied restrictions. Since the abortion complained of was carried out after 10 weeks in accordance with legislation permitting abortions up to a certain stage in the pregnancy to avert the risk of injury to the physical or mental health of the pregnant woman, the Commission concluded that, even if the second stricter interpretation were adopted, there would be no breach of article 2. On that basis it declined to decide which interpretation was right.

14.34   The Commission's position was clarified in *H v Norway*[53] where it held that a lawful abortion after 14 weeks on the statutory grounds

---

50   (1980) 19 DR 244.
51   Ibid at para 19.
52   Note 50.
53   Appl 17004/90 (1992) unreported.

that the 'pregnancy, birth or care for the child may place the woman in a difficult situation in life' did not breach article 2. This goes beyond *Paton v UK*[54] in that the abortion was later in time and for social, rather than health, reasons. The Commission did not exclude the possibility that 'in certain circumstances' article 2 does offer some protection to the foetus, but did not indicate what those circumstances were.[55]

14.35   On the other hand, laws regulating abortion will not necessarily breach the Convention rights of mothers. In *Bruggemann and Scheuten v Germany*[56] two women complained that legislation restricting abortion breached their rights under article 8 because it forced them to renounce sexual intercourse or apply methods of contraception against their will. The Commission recognised that article 8 was engaged because it protects the right to establish relationships with others, including sexual relationships, but found no breach because article 8(1) could not be interpreted so as to mean that pregnancy and abortion are solely within the private sphere of the mother.[57] Legal rules which restricted abortions after a certain point could, therefore, be justified.

14.36   The father of an unborn child has a right to raise issues on his or the unborn child's behalf under both article 2 and article 8, but an ordinary member of the public has no standing to do so.[58] However, an abortion will not breach the article 8 rights of the father of an unborn child even where it conflicts with his sincerely held views because it is a measure intended to protect the rights of the mother.[59] Nor can article 8 be read so widely as to embrace a right on the part of the father to be consulted about an abortion which the mother intends to have carried out.[60]

Euthanasia

14.37   There are two forms of euthanasia: passive euthanasia, or euthanasia by omission; and active euthanasia, whereby steps are

---

54   Note 50.
55   See *The Law of the European Convention on Human Rights* n27, p42.
56   (1977) 10 DR 100.
57   Ibid at para 61.
58   *X v Austria* (1976) 7 DR 87; *Knudsen v Norway* (1985) 42 DR 247.
59   *Paton v UK* n50 at p253.
60   Ibid at p254.

actively taken to hasten death. The Commission has considered only the first and the Court has not considered either.

14.38   In *Widmer v Switzerland*[61] the Commission held that the duty to protect life by law in article 2 did not require states to make passive euthanasia a crime.

The death penalty

14.39   The death penalty is not prohibited under article 2, but in this respect article 2 has been supplemented by Optional Protocol 6 which provides that:

1) The death penalty shall be abolished. No one shall be condemned to such penalty or executed.

2) A State may make provision in its law for the death penalty in respect of acts committed in time of war or of imminent war; such penalty shall be applied only in the instances laid down in the law and in accordance with its provisions. The State shall communicate to the Secretary General of the Council of Europe the relevant provisions of that law.

3) No derogation from the provisions of this Protocol shall be made under Article 15 of the Convention.

4) No reservation may be made under [article 57] of the Convention in respect of the provisions of this Protocol.

The UK ratified Optional Protocol 6 on 27 January 1999 and the HRA gives it effect in domestic law.

14.40   The Convention implications of extraditing or deporting an individual to a country where the death penalty is maintained are considered in chapter 18.[62]

The prohibition on torture, inhuman and/or degrading treatment/punishment

14.41   Article 3 provides that:

No one shall be subjected to torture or to inhuman or degrading treatment or punishment.

---

61 Appl 20527/92 (1993), unreported.
62 Paras 18.13 to 18.18.

It is expressed in unqualified terms and in peace time derogation is not possible. Hence conduct prohibited under article 3 cannot be justified as being in the public interest, for example, to suppress terrorism.[63]

14.42   Article 3 covers three separate categories of prohibited treatment or punishment: torture; inhuman treatment/punishment; and degrading treatment/punishment. In each case conduct must 'attain a minimum level of severity' before article 3 is breached. The assessment of this minimum is relative; it depends on all the circumstances of the case, such as:

1) the duration of the treatment;

2) its physical or mental effects; and

3) in some cases, the sex, age and state of health of the victim.[64]

14.43   Consistent with its approach to the Convention as a living instrument,[65] recent case-law from the European Court demonstrates an increased sensitivity to the protection of vulnerable individuals and some of the early case-law of both the Court and Commission must now be treated with caution. Moreover, conduct not reaching the threshold of severity required under article 3 may nonetheless breach article 8, which protects physical and moral integrity as part of an individual, sphere of privacy.

14.44   When considering allegations of ill-treatment under article 3 of the Convention, the European Court has refused to place a burden of proof on either party. It will examine all the material before it, whether originating from the Commission, the parties or other sources and, if necessary, obtain material of its own motion.[66] The standard of proof adopted for article 3 is 'beyond reasonable doubt', but this can be satisfied by 'the coexistence of sufficiently strong, clear and concordant inferences' or 'similar unrebutted presumptions of fact'.[67] These issues are examined in detail in chapter 16, Police powers.[68]

---

63 *Ireland v UK* (1979–80) 2 EHRR 25; *Tomasi v France* (1993) 15 EHRR 1.

64 *Ireland v UK* n63 at para 162. Only individuals can invoke article 3, not other legal entities: *Kontakt-Information-Therapie and Hagen v Austria* (1988) 57 DR 81.

65 See paras 4.16 to 4.18.

66 *Ireland v UK* n63 at para 160.

67 Ibid at para 161.

68 Paras 15.91 to 15.95.

Torture

14.45 Torture has been defined as:

> ... deliberate inhuman treatment causing very serious and cruel suffering.[69]

'Deliberate' means that suffering must be inflicted intentionally. In the *Greek* case,[70] the Commission held that torture was an aggravated form of inhuman treatment 'which has a purpose, such as the obtaining of information or confession, or the infliction of punishment.'[71] And one of the factors that led the European Court to conclude that the serious ill-treatment inflicted on the applicant in *Aksoy v Turkey*[72] amounted to torture (rather than inhuman or degrading treatment) was that is was administered with the aim of obtaining admissions or information from the applicant.[73]

14.46 The European Court's decision in *Ireland v UK*[74] demonstrates the high threshold that must be reached before inhuman treatment/punishment becomes torture. At issue in that case were five interrogation techniques applied to suspects in Northern Ireland. These techniques were to:

1) force suspects to stand against a wall for hours in extremely uncomfortable positions;

2) force suspects to wear a dark hood during interrogation;

3) deprive suspects of sleep;

4) subject suspects to noise; and

5) deprive suspects of adequate food and drink.

The Commission found that these techniques constituted torture within the meaning of article 3. The Court disagreed. It its view they amounted to inhuman and degrading treatment, but not torture.

14.47 The Court found the threshold for torture established in *Aksoy v Turkey*[75], where the applicant was stripped naked, with his arms tied behind his back, and suspended by his arms.

---

69 *Ireland v UK* n63.
70 (1969) 12 Yearbook 1.
71 Ibid at p186.
72 (1997) 23 EHRR 553.
73 Ibid at para 64.
74 Note 63.
75 Note 72.

Inhuman treatment/punishment

14.48   Treatment/punishment will be inhuman within the meaning of article 3 if it 'causes intense physical or mental suffering'.[76] The degree of suffering caused is the distinction between torture and inhuman treatment/punishment. But a threat of torture, provided that it is 'sufficiently real and imminent' can amount to inhuman treatment/punishment.[77]

14.49   Physical assaults are likely to breach article 3, if sufficiently serious. Severe beatings, the use of weapons and/or the use of implements such as electric shock equipment clearly reach this threshold,[78] as do sexual assault and rape.[79] It is also clear from the Court's findings in *Ireland v UK*[80] that the infliction of psychological harm can breach article 3. And in *X and Y v Netherlands*[81] the Commissison found that 'mental suffering leading to acute psychiatric disturbances falls into the category of treatment prohibited by article 3 of the Convention.'[82]

14.50   Old case-law of the Commission suggesting that slaps or blows of the hand to the head and face might not breach article 3[83] has now been overruled by subsequent case-law from the European Court. In particular, in *Tomasi v France*[84] the Court held that the slapping, kicking and punching of a suspect in police custody breached article 3. See further: chapter 15, Police powers.[85]

14.51   Conditions of detention – whether police custody, prison or elsewhere – can also raise issues under article 3. These are examined in chapter 16.[86]

76   *Ireland v UK* n63.
77   *Campbell and Cosans v UK* (1982) 4 EHRR 293.
78   The *Greek* case n70.
79   *Cyprus v Turkey* (1982) 4 EHRR 482; *Aydin v Turkey* (1998) 25 EHRR 251.
80   Note 63.
81   (1986) 8 EHRR 235.
82   Commission Report p22.
83   The *Greek* case n70.
84   (1993) 15 EHRR 1.
85   Paras 15.81 to 15.87.
86   Paras 16.12 to 16.30.

Degrading treatment/punishment

14.52   Treatment/punishment is degrading if it arouses in the victim a feeling of fear, anguish and inferiority capable of humiliating and debasing the victim and possibly breaking his/her physical or moral resistance. In order for punishment to be degrading and in breach of article 3, the humiliation or debasement involved must attain a particular level of severity and must in any event be other than that usual element of humiliation inherent in any punishment.[87]

14.53   Most cases concerning degrading treatment/punishment turn on their facts and it is difficult to extract principles of general application. By way of example, racial harassment,[88] refusing to allow a suspect to change clothing soiled by his own defecation,[89] grossly defamatory remarks[90] and extreme and continuous police surveillance[91] have been found to be *capable* of being degrading contrary to article 3. Whereas discrimination against illegitimate children[92] and the wearing of uniforms by prisoners[93] have been found not to be. Social hardship, if extreme, might be degrading, but so far no case has progressed past the admissibility stage in Strasbourg.[94]

14.54   The vulnerability of the victim will often be important. In *Ribitsch v Austria*[95] the European Court held that:

> ... in respect of a person deprived of his liberty, any recourse to physical force which has not been made strictly necessary by his own conduct diminishes human dignity and is, in principle, an infringement of the right set forth in Article 3 of the Convention[96]

'Physical force' in that context meant deliberate assaults. The compatibility of corporal punishment with article 3 is examined in chapter 20.[97]

14.55   Both the European Court and Commission have recognised that the institutionalisation of certain practices can amount to degrading

---

87   *Costello-Roberts v UK* (1995) 19 EHRR 112 at para 30.
88   *Hilton v UK* (1976) 4 DR 177.
89   *Hurtado v Switzerland* A/280-A (1994) (unreported).
90   *East African Asians* case (1981) 3 EHRR 76.
91   *D'Haeses, Le Compte v Belgium* (1984) 6 EHRR 114; no breach on the facts.
92   *Marckx v Belgium* (1979–80) 2 EHRR 330.
93   *X v Austria* (1967) 24 CD 20; *Campbell v UK* (1988) 57 DR 148.   94   See *Van Volsem v Belgium* Appl 14641/89 (unreported).
95   (1996) 21 EHRR 573.
96   Ibid at para 38.
97   See paras 20.6 to 20.12.

treatment contrary to article 3. So, for example, in the *East African Asians* cases[98] the Commission found a violation of article 3 on the basis that the practice of refusing to allow British passport holders who had been expelled from Uganda, Tanzania and Kenya to take up residence in the UK amounted to institutionalised racism. This is possibly subject to the qualification introduced by the European Court in *Abdulaziz, Cabales and Balkandali v UK*[99] that degradation must be intentional to violate article 3.

Procedural aspects of article 3

14.56   The prohibition on torture, inhuman or degrading treatment/ punishment imposes clear positive obligations on the state. It requires an appropriate legal framework capable of protecting individuals from such conduct. It also requires effective enforcement of the law. As with article 2, this means taking appropriate measures to protect individuals from torture, inhuman or degrading treatment/punishment, investigating allegations of such conduct efficiently and prosecuting alleged offenders where appropriate and the same principles apply.[100]

State responsibility under article 3

14.57   States are responsible when their servants or agents engage in conduct prohibited under article 3; even when those servants or agents are acting ultra vires and/or in breach of instructions given to them.

14.58   In *Cyprus v Turkey*,[101] where the European Commission accepted allegations that a number of detainees had been raped, it held the Turkish government responsible on the basis that:

> The evidence shows that rapes were committed by Turkish soldiers and at least in two cases even by Turkish officers ... It has not been shown that the Turkish authorities took adequate measures to prevent this happening or that they generally took any disciplinary measures following such incidents. The Commission therefore

---

98 Note 90.

99 (1985) 7 EHRR 471.

100 These are set out at paras 14.5 to 14.21. See also *Assenov v Bulgaria* [1999] EHRLR 225 on need for investigation in cases of police ill-treatment.

101 (1982) 4 EHRR 482.

considers that the non-prevention of the said acts is imputable to Turkey under the Convention.[102]

14.59　The European Court adopted an even more robust approach in *Ireland v UK*,[103] in the context of a practice of ill-treatment including five interrogation techniques found to breach article 3, where it held that:

> It is inconceivable that the higher authorities of a state should be, or at least should be entitled to be, unaware of the existence of such a practice. Furthermore, under the Convention those authorities are strictly liable for the conduct of their subordinates; they are under a duty to impose their will on subordinates and cannot shelter behind their inability to ensure that it is respected.[104]

Responsibility can also arise where the state takes steps which may expose an individual to torture, inhuman or degrading treatment/ punishment by others. The source of the threat is irrelevant See, in particular, chapter 18, in relation to expulsion and deportation.

14.60　　Following *A v UK*,[105] it is also clear that state responsibility can be engaged where torture, inhuman or degrading treatment/ punishment is carried out by private individuals.[106] The nature of the responsibility in such cases is different; it derives from the positive duty on the state to take adequate and effective steps to prevent the prohibited conduct (see generally, chapter 5).

The protection of physical integrity under article 8

14.61　Physical integrity is also protected under article 8 of the Convention as an aspect of private life. The scheme of protection under article 8 is, however, different from that under article 3 in two important respects:

1) The threshold for a breach of article 8 is lower than that under article 3. Hence, article 8 may apply where the minimum level of severity required under article 3 is not attained.[107]

2) Rights under article 8 can be restricted, unlike those under article 3.

102 Ibid at para 373.
103 Note 63.
104 Ibid at para 159.
105 (1998) 2 FLR 959; (1999) 27 EHRR 611.
106 See also *Costello-Roberts v UK* n87.
107 See, eg, *Raninen v Finland* (1998) 26 EHRR 563.

14.62   Some of the European Court's most dynamic case-law on positive obligations has been developed in the context of protecting physical integrity under article 8 of the Convention: see, in particular, the protection of children from sexual abuse[108] and excessive corporal punishment.[109] In addition to their claim under article 2,[110] the applicants in *Osman v UK*[111] advanced an argument under article 8 on that basis that the failure of the police to bring to an end the campaign of harassment, vandalism and victimisation, which the second applicant's teacher waged against their property constituted a breach of this provision. The European Court rejected this. In its view the police had done all they could reasonably have been expected to do: initially there was no real evidence that the teacher was responsible for the acts complained of, and when further evidence became available, the police had attempted to arrest him. The applicants also argued that the failure to avert the wounding of the second applicant breached article 8, but in this respect, because of the close relationship between the right to life under article 2 and the right to bodily integrity under article 8, the Court felt bound by its finding under article 2.

14.66   Significantly, the European Court in *Osman v UK*[112] did not question the general proposition that article 8 can give rise to an obligation on the part of the police to take reasonable steps to protect privacy, the home and family. What steps should be taken will depend on the facts of any given case. Presumably the test for preventative action under article 8 will be similar to the test under article 2. The implication of the European Court's judgment in *Osman v UK* is that, if there had been evidence that the teacher was responsible for the campaign of harassment, vandalism and victimisation waged against the applicants' property and, having been alerted to this evidence, the police had done nothing, a breach of article 8 might have been found.

---

108 Chapter 20 paras 20.13 and 20.14.
109 Chapter 20 paras 20.6 to 20.12.
110 See paras 14.10 and 14.11.
111 Court (28 October 1998); noted at [1999] EHRLR 228.
112 Ibid.

Medical care: overview

14.64 The Convention does not expressly include a right to medical treatment. However, there may be circumstances where withholding or withdrawing medical treatment raises issues under article 2 (the right to life) and/or article 3 (the prohibition on inhuman and degrading treatment); or where an obligation is imposed on the state to give advice or provide information about health risks to identifiable individuals or groups of individuals.

14.65 Equally there may be circumstances where, if provided, medical treatment raises other Convention issues. For example, if it administered against an individual's will, or negligently.

Medical treatment, the right to life and the prohibition on inhuman and degrading treatment

14.66 The relationship between medical treatment, the right to life and the prohibition on inhuman and degrading treatment has been explored in a number of cases before the European Court and Commission, but no clear principles have yet emerged. The Commission explicitly refused to exclude the possibility that:

> ... a lack of proper medical care in a case where someone is suffering from a serious illness could in certain circumstances amount to treatment contrary to Article 3.[113]

And in *Association X v UK*,[114] concerning a complaint about a voluntary vaccination scheme, the Commission recognised that article 2 requires states to take appropriate measures to preserve life. Such an approach is consistent with the requirement that article 2 and article 3 of the Convention be interpreted and applied so as to make their safeguards 'practical and effective'.[115]

14.67 The more general question of whether article 2 imposes a duty on state authorities to provide free medical care for those whose lives are at risk was left open by the Commission in *X v Ireland*.[116] Assuming that such a duty existed, it found no breach of article 2 on the facts.

---

113 *Tanko v Finland* Appl 23634/94 (1994) unreported.
114 (1978) 14 DR 31.
115 *McCann v UK* (1996) 21 EHRR 97 at para 146; see, generally, paras 4.12 to 4.15.
116 (1976) 7 DR 78.

And, in *Hughes v UK*,[117] the Commission contemplated, but did not resolve, the question of whether article 2 required states to enact legislation imposing a general obligation on individuals to take prompt medical action in emergencies.

14.68   The more recent decision of the European Court in *D v UK*[118] establishes that, even if no general 'right' to medical treatment can be derived from the Convention, the termination or withdrawal of existing treatment in serious cases might violate article 2 or article 3. In that case, the applicant, who was in an advanced stage of a terminal and incurable illness, challenged his removal from the UK to a country where adequate medical facilities were not available.[119] Although, as a general rule, those facing deportation cannot claim any entitlement to remain in a Convention country in order to continue to benefit from medical, social or other forms of assistance provided in that country, taking into account the fact that the withdrawal of medical treatment in the UK would entail the most dramatic consequences for the applicant and undoubtedly hasten his death, the European Court held that:

> In view of these exceptional circumstances and bearing in mind the critical stage now reached in the applicant's fatal illness, the implementation of the decision to remove him to St. Kitts would amount to inhuman treatment by the respondent State in violation of article 3.[120]

Although the Court did not find it necessary to examine the complaint under article 2, there is no reason, in principle, why the same approach should not apply to the proper interpretation of that provision. Furthermore, the Court's reasoning may well apply in cases which have nothing to do with deportation; for example, a simple decision to withdraw vital medical treatment. A right to such medical treatment may then be developed, but it is difficult to see how it could be absolute in nature.

14.69   Special considerations apply in relation to the provision of medical treatment to those in custody – whether police custody, prison or elsewhere. In such circumstances, there is a duty to provide adequate medical treatment (including psychiatric care).[121] For

---

117 (1986) 48 DR 258.
118 (1997) 24 EHRR 423.
119 Para 54.
120 Para 53. See also the Commission's decision in *BB v France* [1998] EHRLR 620.
121 The *Greek* case n70; *Cyprus v Turkey* (1982) 4 EHRR 482 (first and second applications). See also *Keenan v UK* n12 which concerned death in custody.

example, in *Hurtado v Switzerland*[122] the Commission found a beach of article 3 where a suspect, with a fractured rib, was not x-rayed for six days.

Health advice

14.70   In some circumstances, a right to health advice can be read into the Convention. In *LCB v UK*[123] the applicant was the daughter of a man who had been present during nuclear testing at Christmas Island in the late 1950s when he was serving in the RAF. She complained that, contrary to the obligation to take appropriate measures to protect her life, the authorities had failed to advise her parents to monitor her health prior to her diagnosis with leukaemia. The European Court observed that:

> It has not been suggested that the respondent State intentionally sought to deprive the applicant of her life. The Court's task is, therefore, to determine whether, given the circumstances of the case, the State did all that could have been required of it to prevent the applicant's life from being avoidably put at risk.[124]

It then proceeded on the basis that the state could only reasonably have been expected to have provided advice to the applicant's parents and monitored her health if it 'appeared likely' at the time that her father's exposure to radiation 'might have engendered a real risk to her health'.

14.71   Upon analysis, the Court concluded that no such link could be made. Therefore, the state was not under a duty to give any advice to the applicant's parents or 'take any other special action in relation to her'.[125] However, the inference to be drawn from the Court's approach is that, where the state is aware (or ought to be aware) that an individual is being or has been exposed to a risk of serious injury, it may, within reason, be under a duty, derived from article 2 of the Convention, to provide medical advice and care to that individual. The significance of the fact that in *LCB v UK* it was the state that exposed the applicant to such a risk, rather than a private individual, has yet to be explored. However, in the environmental context, the European Court has been prepared to extend the duties of state

122 A/280-A (1994) (unreported).
123 (1999) 27 EHRR 212.
124 Para 36.
125 Para 41.

authorities to provide information about the health risks of pollution even where they are not directly responsible.[126]

Access to health information

14.72   Although the right of access to information in article 10 is weak, in that it depends upon voluntary disclosure,[127] a stronger right of access to health information can be read into article 8. In *McGinley and Egan v UK*[128] the applicants had themselves been exposed to radiation in the same nuclear tests as the applicant's father in *LCB v UK*. They claimed, under article 8, that they should have been provided with information sufficient to enable them to assess the possible consequences of the tests for their health.

14.73   The European Court found article 8 applicable because:

> ... given the fact that exposure to high levels of radiation is known to have hidden, but serious and long-lasting, effects on health, it is not unnatural that the applicants' uncertainty as to whether or not they had been put at risk in this way caused them substantial anxiety and distress ...
>
> ... since the [radiation level records] contained information which might have assisted the applicants in assessing radiation levels in the areas in which they were stationed during the tests, and might indeed have served to reassure them in this respect, they had an interest under article 8 in obtaining access to them.[129]

In the circumstances the Court found that a positive obligation under article 8 arose. As a matter of principle:

> Where a Government engages in hazardous activities, such as those in issue in the present case, which might have hidden adverse consequences on the health of those involved in such activities, respect for private and family life under article 8 requires that an effective and accessible procedure be established which enables persons to seek all relevant and appropriate information.[130]

On the facts, however, the Court found no breach of this positive obligation because the applicants could have sought access to the relevant documents in proceedings before the Pension Appeal Tribunal but had failed to do so.

126 See paras 22.30 to 22.36.
127 See paras 24.7 to 24.9.
128 (1998) 27 EHRR 1.
129 Para 99.
130 Para 101.

Medical records

14.74   In *Chare née Jullien v France*[131] the European Commission found that the collection of medical data and the maintenance of medical records fell within the sphere of private life protected by article 8. This notion was endorsed by the Court in *Z v Finland*,[132] where a medical adviser was ordered to disclose details from the applicant's medical file during the trial of the applicant's husband for attempted manslaughter. The European Court recognised that respecting medical confidentiality is a 'vital principle' crucial to privacy and also to confidence in the medical profession and in the health services in general.[133] As a result:

> ... any state measures compelling communication or disclosure of such information without the consent of the patient call for the most careful scrutiny ...[134]

The ability of individuals to have access to their medical records can also raise article 8 issues. The leading case is *Gaskin v UK*[135] where the court fell short of finding a general right of access, but did emphasise the need for specific justification for preventing individuals from having access to information which forms part of their private and family life. And where an individual's access to personal information held by social services is made subject to certain conditions, these must be assessed to see whether they are reasonable.[136]

Negligence

14.75   Negligent medical treatment raises issues under articles 2 (the right to life), 3 (the prohibition on inhuman and degrading treatment) and 6(1) (fair trial in civil proceedings).

14.76   In *Association X v UK*[137] the applicant association comprised parents whose children had suffered severe and lasting damage or death as a result of state vaccination schemes. One of their complaints was that the scheme was poorly administered and that

---

131   (1991) 71 DR 141.
132   (1998) 25 EHRR 371.
133   Para 95.
134   Para 96.
135   (1999) 12 EHRR 36.
136   *Martin v Switzerland* (1995) 81-A DR 136.
137   (1978) 14 DR 31.

appropriate steps were not taken to avoid the risk of serious injury or death. On the facts the Commission accepted that the state had established a proper system of control and supervision over the vaccination schemes which was 'sufficient to comply with its obligation to protect life under article 2 of the Convention'.[138] The implication is that, absent such a system of control and supervision, there might have been a breach of article 2.

14.77   The implication in *Tavares v France*[139] is the same. There the Commission rejected the applicant's complaint that his wife had died as a result of medical negligence because it found that the hospital in question had procedures in place which it had followed.[140]

14.78   So far as article 6(1) is concerned, in *H v France*[141] the European Court had no doubt that the requirements of a fair trial applied in medical negligence proceedings against a Strasbourg hospital. See, more generally, chapters 12 and 13.

138 Page 34.
139 Appl 16593/90 (1991) unreported: see *Law of the European Convention on Human Rights* n27, p41.
140 See also *X v Germany* (1985) 7 EHRR 152.
141 (1989) 12 EHRR 74.

CHAPTER 15

Police powers

15.1   Introduction

15.4   Positive obligations and policing

15.6   Police surveillance

15.9   The obligation that police surveillance be 'prescribed by law'

15.26   The obligation that police surveillance be necessary and proportionate.

15.30   Fingerprints, photographs and other personal data

15.34   Retention

15.36   Search and seizure

15.41   Agents provocateurs and entrapment

15.43   Arrest and related issues

15.46   The application of article 5 to police powers: the threshold issue

15.56   The pre-conditions of lawful arrest and detention under article 5

15.57   Grounds for arrest under the Convention

15.60   The meaning of 'reasonable suspicion'

continued

15.64   Preventative detention

15.65   Reasons for arrest

15.69   Other grounds for arrest under the Convention

15.70   Arrest and detention outside the UK

15.72   The exercise of stop and search and similar powers

15.80   Remedies for police misconduct: overview

15.81   Ill-treatment and the use of force

15.86   Handcuffs

15.88   Racism and other forms of discrimination

15.91   The burden and standard of proof in misconduct cases

15.94   Vicarious liability

15.96   Police immunity in negligence actions

15.100 Damages in civil actions against the police

15.101 Fair trial generally

Introduction

15.1 Police powers raise a number of issues under the European Convention on Human Rights. Although articles 5 (the right to liberty) and 8 (the right to privacy) provide the basic framework within which police powers must be exercised, other rights are important. The absolute rights[1] set out in articles 2, 3, 4(1) and 7 must be respected; interference with the qualified rights set out in articles 8, 9, 10, 11, 12 and protocol 1 must be justified; and, in some circumstances, the article 6 rights to a fair trial apply at an early stage of police investigation.

15.2 Provisions designed to tackle organised crime or the threat of terrorism pose particularly delicate issues. As a general principle, the European Court of Human Rights recognises the need 'for a proper balance between the defence of the institutions of democracy in the common interest and the protection of individual rights'.[2] However, even where organised crime or terrorism is involved, the balancing process cannot be stretched to the point where the very essence of individual rights is impaired[3] and the public or common interest can never justify a breach of absolute rights under the Convention such as the right to life (article 2) or the prohibition on torture, inhuman and/or degrading treatment (article 3).

15.3 This chapter examines the investigation of crime first. It then deals with arrest and other forms of detention before considering remedies for police misconduct.

Positive obligations and policing

15.4 Under the Convention, the police are not only under a duty to refrain from breaching Convention rights themselves, they are also under an obligation, in certain circumstances, to protect individuals from the actions of others. The basis and scope of this obligation is examined in chapter 5. In brief, it can take three forms:

1) A duty to safeguard the life and physical integrity of individuals known to be at risk.

---

1 For the meaning of absolute rights see para 4.2.
2 *Brogan and Others v UK* (1989) 11 EHRR 117 para 48.
3 See Murdoch JL, *Article 5 of the European Convention on Human Rights: The protection of liberty and security of person*, Human Rights Files No 12, Council of Europe Press, 1994, p11.

2) A duty to investigate crime efficiently.

3) A duty to ensure that individuals can enjoy their Convention rights, such as the right of peaceful assembly.

15.5   None of these duties is absolute. The first two derive from the special protection afforded to life and physical integrity under the Convention and are examined in chapter 14.[4] The third is of much wider application and accordingly calls for a much more balanced approach. It is examined in detail in chapter 5.[5]

Police surveillance

15.6   Police surveillance covers a wide range of activities, including telephone tapping, interception of communications, the use of covert listening devices and visual surveillance equipment. Most of these activities interfere with the right to privacy protected by article 8. That does not mean that they are prohibited under the Convention: the prevention of crime and the protection of the rights of others are legitimate grounds for interfering with article 8 rights.[6] However, it does mean that all forms of police surveillance must be justified in accordance with article 8(2) of the Convention.

15.7   To justify police surveillance under article 8(2) it is necessary to show that: (a) the activity in question is 'prescribed by law' and (b) it is necessary and proportionate.[7]

15.8   Police surveillance also raises fair trial issues under article 6 of the Convention. These are dealt with in chapter 9.[8]

---

4   Paras 14.5 to 14.21.
5   Paras 5.13 to 5.22.
6   The European Court and Commission have rarely questioned the legitimacy of police surveillance; instead they have concentrated on the 'lawfulness' and procedural aspects of such activity.
7   These concepts are examined in detail in paras 4.37 to 4.66.
8   See paras 9.30 to 9.35.

The obligation that police surveillance be 'prescribed by law'

15.9   The requirement that police surveillance be prescribed by law has three aspects. First, any power vested in the police to carry out secret surveillance must have a proper basis in law. Second, that law must be accessible to the citizen: unpublished internal guidelines are not sufficient.[9] Third, the rules governing police surveillance must be clear enough to enable citizens to understand them and regulate their conduct accordingly.

15.10   The first of these principles was established in *Klass v Germany*.[10] In that case, the European Court began by recognising that police surveillance was a necessary evil in modern society:

> Democratic societies nowadays find themselves threatened by highly sophisticated forms of espionage and by terrorism, with the result that the state must be able, in order to effectively counter such threats, to undertake secret surveillance of subversive elements operating within its jurisdiction. The Court has therefore to accept that the existence of some legislation granting powers of secret surveillance over ... post and telecommunications is, under exceptional conditions, necessary in a democratic society.[11]

But, the Court continued:

> ... this does not mean that the Contracting States enjoy unlimited discretion to subject persons within their jurisdiction to secret surveillance. The Court, being aware of the danger such a law poses of undermining or even destroying democracy on the ground of defending it, affirms that the Contracting States may not ... adopt whatever measures they deem appropriate ...

15.11   In the later case of *Malone v UK*,[12] the Court added, in the context of telephone tapping, that:

> It would be contrary to the rule of law for the legal discretion granted to the executive to be expressed in terms of an unfettered power. Consequently, the law must indicate the scope of any such discretion conferred on the competent authorities and the manner of its exercise with sufficient clarity, having regard to the legitimate aim of the measure in question, to give the individual adequate protection against arbitrary interference.[13]

9 For an overview of the principle of legality, see paras 4.29 to 4.36.
10 (1979–80) 2 EHRR 214.
11 Para 48.
12 (1985) 7 EHRR 14.
13 Para 68.

15.12   The Court's emphasis in *Klass v Germany*[14] on countering serious threats, such as espionage and terrorism, is important; as is the observation that legislation granting powers of secret surveillance should be restricted to 'exceptional cases'. Resort to telephone tapping and/or intercepting post in the course of investigating non-serious crime would be hard to justify under the convention.

15.13   The second and third principles referred to above – that the law on police surveillance must be accessible to the citizen and clear – were developed in *Malone v UK*.[15] There, a police investigation into the activities of the applicant involved intercepting his telephone calls and his post. At the time there was no comprehensive statutory code governing these activities, which were largely carried out according to administrative practice. That proved fatal to the government's case.

15.14   According to the European Court's well-established case-law, the expression 'prescribed by law' necessitates not only compliance with domestic law, but also relates to the quality of that law, requiring it to be compatible with the rule of law. In the context of secret measures of surveillance or interception of communications by public authorities, because of the lack of public scrutiny and risk of misuse of power, the domestic law must provide some protection to the individual against arbitrary interference with article 8 rights. Thus, the domestic law must be sufficiently clear in its terms to give citizens an adequate indication as to the circumstances in and conditions on which, public authorities are empowered to resort to any such secret measures.[16]

15.15   In *Malone v UK* the European Court recognised that the requirement that the law be foreseeable had to be applied sensibly, so as to avoid a suspect being put on notice before police surveillance was carried out. Nonetheless, it held that:

> ... the law must be sufficiently clear in its terms to give citizens an adequate indication as to the circumstances in which and the conditions on which public authorities are empowered to resort to this secret and potentially dangerous interference with the right to respect for private life and correspondence.[17]

UK law at the time on telephone tapping was too vague to satisfy that test.

15.16   The principles underpinning the Court's approach in *Malone v*

14 Note 10.
15 Note 12.
16 See *Halford v UK* (1997) 24 EHRR 523 at para 49.
17 Note 12 at para 67.

UK were developed in *Huvig v France*[18] where the applicant was suspected of tax evasion. In the course of investigations, a judge authorised a senior police officer to have the applicant's business and private telephone lines tapped. The resultant information was then used against the applicant in criminal proceedings for attempted armed robbery and abetting a murder.

15.17　Reiterating the point it made in *Malone v UK* that the phrase 'prescribed by law' involves an assessment of the quality of law, the European Court found a breach of article 8 for a combination of the following reasons:

1) The categories of people liable to have their telephones tapped was not defined.

2) The categories of offence for which telephone tapping could be authorised was not defined.

3) There were no limits on the duration of telephone tapping.

4) No rules existed about disclosure of records created in the course of telephone tapping, in particular, disclosure to the defence.

5) No rules existed to govern the destruction of information obtained by telephone tapping, in particular where proceedings against a suspect were not pursued and/or s/he was acquitted of criminal charges.

Although the European Court was concerned with telephone tapping in *Huvig v France*, the issues it identified as relevant to the question of whether a given measure was 'prescribed by law' apply equally to other forms of police surveillance.

15.18　The European Court recognises that as technology advances it is increasingly easy for the police and other public authorities to abuse their powers of surveillance. Therefore, it has recently insisted that having clear rules covering the issues outlined in *Huvig v France* is only the starting point. The rules must also establish how, in practice, they are to be carried into effect.

15.19　In *Kopp v Switzerland*[19] the applicant was a lawyer, whose telephone communications were intercepted even though he himself was not a suspect, because he was a 'third party' with whom it was believed those suspected would be in contact. The Swiss court ordered that 13 telephone lines be monitored, including the applicant's private and professional lines. Although the order expressly

18　(1990) 12 EHRR 528.
19　(1999) 27 EHRR 91.

mentioned, in accordance with Swiss law on legal professional privilege, that 'the lawyer's conversations [were] not to be taken into account', the European Court found a breach of article 8 because the law did not make it clear how legal professional privilege was to be protected in practice.

15.20   The Court's view was that, since telephone tapping (and other forms of communication interception) constitutes a 'serious interference' with private life, particularly in light of increasingly sophisticated technology, it must be based on 'law' that is particularly precise. It is essential to have clear, detailed rules on the subject.[20] Although Swiss law provided a number of safeguards, including the provision intended to protect legal professional privilege, the Court discerned:

> ... a contradiction between the clear text of legislation which protects legal professional privilege when a lawyer is being monitored as a third party and the practice followed in the present case. Even though the case law has established the principle ... that legal professional privilege covers only the relationship between a lawyer and his clients, the law does not clearly state how, under what conditions and by whom the distinction is to be drawn between matters specifically connected with a lawyer's work under instructions from a party to proceedings and those relating to activity other than that of counsel.[21]

In this regard, the Court found it 'astonishing' that the task of distinguishing between privileged and non-privileged matters should be left, to an official of the post office's legal department, without supervision by an independent judge. On that basis it found that Swiss law did not indicate with sufficient clarity the scope and manner of exercise of the power to intercept telephone conversations.

15.21   The Interception of Communications Act 1985 now governs telephone tapping and the interception of post in the UK. This legislation was tested in *Christie v UK*,[22] where the Commission found that an independent tribunal with limited review powers and an independent commissioner of high judicial rank and with reporting duties were acceptable for article 8 purposes. However, the legislation has only limited scope and does not cover telephone tapping on private telecommunication systems.

15.22   In *Halford v UK*[23] the interception of calls made by the former

20 Ibid at para 72.
21 Ibid at para 73.
22 (1994) 78-A DR 119.

assistant chief constable of Merseyside from her office was found by the European Court to violate article 8 of the Convention because internal communications systems operated by public authorities do not come within the ambit of the Interception of Communications Act 1985. Nor does the Act cover the use of other surveillance devices by the police, which have continued to cause difficulties in Strasbourg.

15.23 In *Govell v UK*[24] the applicant was subjected to police surveillance consisting of a hole drilled into his living room wall from an adjoining house enabling police officers to listen from next door and/or insert a listening device in the wall. At the time, the only regulation of the covert use of listening devices and visual surveillance devices by the police was contained in secret Home Office guidelines.[25] The Commission found a violation of article 8 on the basis that the use of covert surveillance devices was not 'prescribed by law' because the guidelines were neither legally binding nor publicly accessible. It also found that the Police Complaints Authority was not sufficiently independent to provide an effective remedy against abuse of the guidelines by the police.[26]

15.24 The practice of 'metering' (maintaining a register of numbers dialled from a particular telephone) also came under scrutiny in *Malone v UK*.[27] The European Court's position was that, unlike telephone tapping, metering was a legitimate and normal business activity. However, if and when records were passed to the police, article 8 issues were engaged. And the fact that the post office had an unlimited discretion whether to comply with police requests for telephone records was too loose an arrangement to satisfy the requirement that such an invasion of privacy be 'prescribed by law'.

15.25 Where police officers circumvent the law in the course of surveillance it will be impossible to show that their activities are 'prescribed by law'. In *A v France*[28] a telephone conversation between the applicant and a third party was recorded by a police officer at the instigation of the third party. During the telephone conversation,

23 (1997) 24 EHRR 523.

24 Commission (14 January 1998) noted at [1999] EHRLR 121.

25 The Police Act 1997 now governs the use of some covert surveillance devices. But, like the Interception of Communications Act 1985, it too has only limited scope; for example, it does not extend to visual surveillance, particularly surveillance using telescopic lenses and similar equipment.

26 The right to an effective remedy is dealt with at paras 3.173 to 3.182.

27 Note 12.

28 (1994) 17 EHRR 462.

plans were discussed for the commission of a crime for which the applicant was later charged. Since the police officer concerned had not obtained official authority to record the telephone call either from his superiors or from an investigating judge (as required under French law), the French government conceded, and the Court found, a breach of article 8.

The obligation that police surveillance be necessary and proportionate

15.26　In common with articles 9, 10 and 11, a breach of article 8 can be justified only if it is necessary and proportionate. A general examination of these concepts can be found in chapter 4.[29] In the present context the European Court has repeatedly emphasised that only a high degree of necessity will justify police surveillance on the basis that:

> Powers of secret surveillance of citizens, characterising as they do the police state, are tolerable under the Convention only in so far as strictly necessary for safeguarding the democratic institution.[30]

What is strictly necessary will obviously depend on a number of factors, but the following guidance can be derived from the European Court's case-law:

1) police surveillance should be limited to serious and properly defined offences;

2) it should not be exploratory or general;

3) it should be limited to cases where conventional means of enquiry are ineffective or have been unsuccessful.[31]

15.27　In addition, police surveillance is likely to satisfy the requirements of necessity and proportionality only if effective safeguards exist to prevent and detect abuse. At the very least, that means that police surveillance should be reviewed when first authorised, while it is being carried out and after it has terminated. Whether these reviews should be judicial and whether the subject of surveillance should know about them are obviously difficult issues.

29 See paras 4.37 to 4.66.

30 *Klass v Germany* n10.

31 See generally, MacDonald et al *The European System for the Protection of Human Rights* (1993, Martinus Nojhoff Publishers) p422.

15.28 In *Klass v Germany*[32] the European Court accepted that:

> As regards the first two stages, the very nature and logic of secret surveillance dictate that not only the surveillance itself but also the accompanying review should be effected without the individual's knowledge.[33]

As a consequence:

> ... it is essential that the procedures established should themselves provide adequate and equivalent guarantees safeguarding the individual's rights.[34]

This will usually mean that there should be some form of judicial control, even if only in the last resort.[35] However, schemes for reviewing the authorisation and implementation of police surveillance which do not involve the judiciary can be sufficient. In *Klass v Germany* itself the involvement of a parliamentary board and an independent commission was deemed sufficient.[36]

15.29 The question of notifying the subject when police surveillance has been terminated was also addressed in *Klass v Germany*. The applicant in that case argued that there is, in principle, little scope for recourse to the courts by the individuals concerned unless they are advised of the measures taken without their knowledge and thus are able retrospectively to challenge their legality.[37] The Court recognised the force of this argument but ultimately concluded that:

> The activity or danger against which a particular series of surveillance measures is directed may continue for years, even decades, after the suspension of these measures. Subsequent notification to each individual affected by a suspended measure might well jeopardise the long-term purpose that originally prompted the surveillance.[38]

That this conclusion amounted to a compromise between the requirements of defending a democratic society and individual rights was accepted.[39] Ultimately, it was probably the fact that under German

---

32 Note 10.
33 Para 55.
34 Ibid.
35 Ibid.
36 See also *Christie v UK* note 22 and also *Lambert v France* [1999] EHRLR 123 on third party's rights where lines are tapped.
37 Note 10 at para 57.
38 Ibid at para 58.
39 Ibid at para 59.

law the subject of surveillance had to be informed that surveillance had taken place, as soon as this could be done without jeopardising the purpose of the surveillance, which influenced the Court in finding no breach of article 8.

Fingerprints, photographs and other personal data

15.30   The taking and retention of personal data, such as fingerprints, photographs and DNA samples, raise a number of issues under article 8 (privacy). The case-law of the European Court and Commission in this area is developing and there are no landmark judgments. Some guidelines are available from the Commission, but it has not adopted a clear and consistent approach to these issues.

15.31   In a number of early cases, the Commission recognised that measures such as the search of a person's car[40] or the temporary confiscation of personal papers[41] engage article 8. And it is now beyond doubt that searches,[42] taking personal details and/or photographs of suspects interferes with their privacy and must be justified under article 8(2).[43]

15.32   The context in which photographs are taken may, however, be important. In *Friedl v Austria*[44] the Commission rejected as inadmissible a complaint that photographs taken by the police of those participating in a public demonstration breached article 8. In so far as this decision conflicts with the Court's decision in *Murray and Others v UK*,[45] where the applicant was photographed without her consent at a police station, the latter is to be preferred. But it may be that a distinction is to be drawn between photographing identifiable suspects, particularly if this is done during the course of a search or arrest, for the purposes of a criminal investigation and photographing those who are participating in a public event for much more general purposes. In *Friedl v Austria* there was no identification of the persons on the photographs and the photographs were kept in a

---

40 *X v Belgium* 45 Collection of Decisions 20.
41 *X v Germany* (1976) 3 DR 104.
42 Searches are dealt with at paras 15.36 to 15.40.
43 *Murray and Others v UK* (1995) 19 EHRR 193 at para 86.
44 A/305-B Comm Rep (1995); unreported.
45 (1995) 19 EHRR 193; the breach of article 8 was found to be justified on the facts.

general administrative file rather than being entered into the data processing system.[46]

15.33   In *McVeigh, O'Neill and Evans v UK*[47] the applicants were detained upon their arrival at Liverpool from Ireland under prevention of terrorism legislation then in force.[48] While detained they were searched, questioned and their fingerprints and photographs were taken. The Commission accepted that this interfered with their privacy under article 8, but concluded that it could be justified under article 8(2) as being necessary for the prevention of crime.[49] In its view the measures were 'prescribed by law'[50] and taken to establish the applicants' identities and to ascertain whether or not they were involved in terrorism. Since the Commission had already found that the applicants' detention for this purpose was lawful under the Convention,[51] the result was hardly surprising. However, it is clear from the Commission's decision that, had the measures gone beyond this purpose or been improper in any way, they would not have been justified.[52]

Retention

15.34   Retention of photographs, fingerprints and other personal data has to be considered separately under the Convention. Collection may be justified on the basis of preventing or detecting crime, but retention may not be. In a very early case, the Commission accepted in broad terms that:

> ... the keeping of records including documents, photographs and fingerprints, relating to criminal cases of the past is necessary in a modern democratic society for the prevention of crime and is, therefore, in the interests of public safety.[53]

However, this has not been considered by the court. And the applicant in that case had been tried on a criminal charge in

---

46 See, generally, Reid *A Practitioner's Guide to the European Convention on Human Rights* (1998, Sweet & Maxwell) p327.
47 (1981) 5 EHRR 71 and 25 DR 15.
48 The Prevention of Terrorism (Temporary Provisions) Act 1976 and the Prevention of Terrorism (Supplementary Temporary Provisions) Order 1976.
49 Note 47 at para 224.
50 See paras 4.29 to 4.36.
51 This aspect of the case is dealt with at paras 15.76 to 15.79.
52 Note 47 at para 224.
53 *X v Germany* 9 Collection of Decisions 53.

connection with which the relevant records had been compiled, although ultimately his conviction was quashed on appeal.

15.35   In *McVeigh, O'Neill and Evans v UK*[54] the Commission had to consider the issue of retention of personal data where no criminal proceedings were brought. On the facts of that case it accepted that the purpose of retention – the prevention of terrorism – was legitimate. It also accepted that retention was 'prescribed by law'. The question, therefore, was whether retention could be justified as 'necessary in a democratic society'. In this regard the Commission, influenced by the fact that the information retained was used for identification purposes only and was kept separate from criminal records, concluded that:

> Bearing in mind ... the serious threat to public safety posed by organised terrorism in the United Kingdom, the Commission considers that the retention for the time being of records such as those at issue in the present case can properly be considered necessary in the interests of public safety and for the prevention of crime.[55]

It is implicit in this conclusion that the information could only be kept for as long as it served the legitimate purpose of the prevention of terrorism.[56]

Search and seizure

15.36   Police searches invariably raise issues under article 8 of the Convention (privacy), even where they involve business or professional, rather than residential, premises.[57] Therefore, they must be justified under article 8(2).

15.37   Since the European Commission and Court have readily accepted that the purpose of most searches is to prevent crime and/or to protect the rights of others – both legitimate aims under article 8(2) – the key questions are usually whether a search is 'in accordance with

---

54 Note 47.
55 Para 230.
56 See also *Friedl v Austria* n44 at para 66 and *Williams v UK* (1992) Appl 19404/92 (unreported).
57 On the basis that most people develop relationships worthy of protection in their working lives, the Court has been unwilling to interpret article 8 so as to exclude activities of a business or professional nature. See: *Niemietz v Germany* (1993) 16 EHRR 97 at para 29.

law' and 'necessary in a democratic society'. The meaning of these phrases has been examined elsewhere.[58] In the present context, the two concepts often overlap because the Court has insisted that one of the aspects of the requirement that any search be 'necessary in a democratic society' is that the law governing searches be clear and accessible. In addition, the means employed to carry out a search must be proportionate to its aim and there must be adequate and effective safeguards against abuse. Unless it can be shown that evidence sought in a search could not realistically be obtained by other less intrusive means, these requirements are unlikely to be satisfied.

15.38   Judicial authorisation is a highly relevant factor, but not determinative. However, where there has been no judicial authorisation for a search, the Court will be 'particularly vigilant' to ensure that other safeguards exist to protect the person concerned from unnecessary intrusions into his/her privacy.[59] At the very least a proper legal framework and very strict limits on search powers will be required.

15.39   In *Funke v France*[60] the European Court found the powers vested in the customs authorities were too wide to be compatible with article 8. In particular:

> ... they had exclusive competence to assess the expediency, number, length and scale of inspections. Above all, in the absence of any requirement for a judicial warrant the restrictions and conditions provided for in law ... appear too lax and full of loopholes for the interferences in the applicant's rights to have been strictly proportionate to the legitimate aim pursued.[61]

A different result followed in *Camenzind v Switzerland*[62] where the Court was influenced by a number of factors including: (a) the fact that the search in question could only be carried out by specially trained officials; (b) that the search could not be executed on Sundays, public holidays or at night (except in exceptional circumstances); (c) that before the search commenced the investigating officer had to produce evidence of his/her identity and explain the purpose of the search; and (d) the fact that a search record had to be produced. In addition, the officials carrying out the search did not go beyond what was strictly required for the purpose of the search.[63]

---

58 See paras 4.56 to 4.66.
59 *Camenzind v Switzerland* (Court) 16 December 1997 at para 45.
60 (1993) 16 EHRR 297.
61 Ibid at para 57.
62 Note 59.
63 Ibid at para 46.

15.40   Even where a search has been judicially authorised, it will breach article 8 if the warrant is drawn in too broad terms. In *Niemietz v Germany*,[64] the Munich District Court issued a warrant to search the applicant's office (a lawyer) in an attempt to identify a third party responsible for writing an insulting letter to a judge. The European Court took the view that article 8 had been violated because:

> ... the warrant was drawn in broad terms, in that it ordered a search for and seizure of 'documents', without any limitation, revealing the identity of the author of the offensive letter ...[65]

This was particularly significant since there were no procedural safeguards, such as the presence of an independent observer. An additional factor was that, in executing the search warrant, the German police clearly went beyond what was necessary for the purpose of identifying the party responsible for the letter.[66] By way of contrast, in *Chappell v UK*[67] the European Court found that the issue and execution of an 'Anton Piller' order issued by the High Court in copyright proceedings offered sufficient safeguards for compliance with article 8.

Agents provocateurs and entrapment

15.41   The use of undercover agents in police investigations raises two issues under the Convention: fair trial (article 6) and privacy (article 8). So far as the first is concerned, the Court's case-law has established that, subject to two qualifications, the use of undercover agents in the investigation of crime is not incompatible with article 6. The first qualification is that the use of undercover agents must be restricted and adequate safeguards must be observed to prevent abuse. The second is that the actions of undercover agents must not exceed passive surveillance: prosecution for an offence incited by an undercover agent will breach article 6. These principles are examined in detail in chapter 9.[68]

15.42   The European Court considered the article 8 implications of using undercover agents in *Ludi v Switzerland*.[69] There, the applicant argued

64 Note 57.
65 Ibid at para 37.
66 Ibid.
67 (1990) 12 EHRR 1. But see also *McLeod v UK* [1999] EHRLR 125: police entry under breach of peace powers.
68 See paras 9.30 to 9.35.
69 (1993) 15 EHRR 173.

that the undercover agent in question had abused his relationship of trust to gain access to the applicant's home and private life. Although the Commission thought this an interference with the applicant's article 8 rights,[70] the Court disagreed. In its view, by engaging in criminal activities such as drug dealing, the applicant must have known that he might encounter undercover agents. In other words, he voluntarily assumed the risk of interference with his private life. Whether article 8 is violated where undercover agents exceed their role of passive surveillance and incite criminal offences was raised but not resolved in *Teixeira de Castro v Portugal*.[71]

Arrest and related issues

15.43 Arrest and detention are governed by article 5 of the convention. It has two limbs. First, it guarantees liberty and security of person: para 5(1). Second, it provides a set of procedural rights for detainees: paras 5(2)–5(5). In this context, liberty and security of person are very closely linked, the European Court and Commission rarely distinguishing between the two. At most, the reference to security of person underlines the prohibition on arbitrary detention in article 5.[72] It does not refer to physical or bodily integrity independent of liberty.[73]

15.44 The scheme of article 5(1) is to set up a positive right to liberty with limited exceptions and an overriding requirement that any deprivation of liberty must be 'in accordance with a procedure prescribed by law' and 'lawful'. It provides that:

Everyone has the right to liberty and security of person. No one shall be deprived of his liberty save in the following cases and in accordance with the procedure prescribed by law:

(a) the lawful detention of a person after conviction by a competent court;

(b) the lawful arrest or detention of a person for non-compliance with the lawful order of a court or in order to secure fulfilment of any obligation prescribed by law;

---

70 Albeit a justifiable interference.

71 (1999) 28 EHRR 101..

72 See, for example, *Bozano v France* (1987) 9 EHRR 297, which concerned 'disguised extradition' designed to circumvent proper court procedures.

73 Issues of physical or bodily integrity therefore fall to be considered by reference to other provisions such as article 3 (the prohibition on ill-treatment etc) or article 8 (privacy).

(c) the lawful arrest or detention of a person effected for the purpose of bringing him before the competent legal authority on reasonable suspicion of having committed an offence, or when it is reasonably considered necessary to prevent his committing an offence or fleeing after having done so;

(d) the detention of a minor by lawful order for the purpose of educational supervision or his lawful detention for the purpose of bringing him before the competent legal authority;

(e) the lawful detention of persons for the prevention of the spreading of infectious diseases, of persons of unsound mind, alcoholics or drug addicts or vagrants;

(f) the lawful arrest or detention of a person to prevent his effecting an unauthorised entry into the country or of a person against whom action is being taken with a view to deportation or extradition.

The exceptions provided for in paragraphs 5(1)(a)–5(1)(f) are to be narrowly construed and represent an exhaustive definition of the circumstances in which a person may lawfully be deprived of his/her liberty.[74]

15.45   The procedural safeguards for detainees, set out in paragraphs 5(2)–5(5), provide that:

(2) Everyone who is arrested shall be informed promptly, in a language which he understands, of the reasons for his arrest and of any charge against him.

(3) Everyone arrested or detained in accordance with the provisions of paragraph 1(c) of this article shall be brought promptly before a judge or other officer authorised by law to exercise judicial power and shall be entitled to trial within a reasonable period or to release pending trial. Release may be conditioned by guarantees to appear for trial.

(4) Everyone who is deprived of his liberty by arrest or detention shall be entitled to take proceedings by which the lawfulness of his detention shall be decided speedily by a court and his release ordered if the detention is not lawful.

(5) Everyone who has been the victim of arrest or detention in contravention of the provisions of this Article shall have an enforceable right to compensation.

These are examined in detail in chapters 3[75] and 7.[76]

---

74 *Winterwerp v Netherlands* (1979–80) 2 EHRR 387 at para 37.
75 See paras 3.69 to 3.86.
76 See paras 7.5 to 7.47.

The application of article 5 to police powers: the threshold issue

15.46 Before examining the issues arising under article 5 by the exercise of police powers, a threshold issue has to be determined; namely whether the exercise of police powers amounts to a deprivation of liberty within the meaning of article 5. If not, neither the substantive provisions of paragraph 5(1) nor the procedural aspects of paragraphs 5(2)–5(5) will apply.[77]

15.47 In domestic law any confinement of an individual, however short, amounts to a deprivation of liberty and, if unlawful, is actionable. Under the Convention, the position is different. An arrest clearly triggers article 5 protection, but where the exercise of police powers falls short of arrest but nonetheless prevents an individual from doing as s/he likes, the position is less clear cut. The meaning of deprivation of liberty can therefore be crucial in cases involving the exercise of stop and search and similar powers.

15.48 The starting point under the Convention is the 'concrete situation' of the person concerned. Relevant to this assessment will be a whole range of criteria such as the type of interference with liberty concerned, its duration, effect and manner of implementation.[78] Article 5 is not, in principle, concerned with mere restrictions on liberty of movement; such restrictions are governed by article 2 of the Fourth Protocol to the Convention.[79] However, the difference between deprivation of and restriction upon liberty is 'merely one of degree or intensity, and not one of nature or substance'.[80]

15.49 The period of detention is relevant, but not definitive. Where the police (or any other public officials) take action which has the effect of depriving individuals of their liberty, their objective will usually be the crucial factor. If the objective is to detain, article 5 applies. If there is some other objective, the action of the police will have to be carefully examined to see whether, in effect, it amounts to a deprivation

77 Nonetheless, article 3 and/or article 8 might still be relevant.
78 *Guzzardi v Italy* (1981) 3 EHRR 333 at para 92. See also: Murdoch, JL *Article 5 of the European Convention on Human Rights: The protection of liberty and security of person*, Human Rights Files No 12, Council of Europe Press, 1994, p11.
79 Article 2 of the Fourth Protocol provides: 'Everyone lawfully within the territory of a state shall, within that territory, have the right to freedom of movement and freedom to choose his residence.' This provision has not (yet) been ratified by the UK.
80 *Guzzardi v Italy* n78 at para 93.

of liberty within the meaning of article 5. The following cases provide some guidance.

15.50   The case of *X and Y v Sweden*[81] involved two Japanese citizens who were, for the purposes of their expulsion, arrested and detained for about an hour in Sweden before being put on a chartered aircraft taking them to Japan. The Commission found that this amounted to a deprivation of liberty within the meaning of article 5. The same result followed in *X v Austria*[82] where the applicant was taken against his will by police officers to a medical institution for a blood test pursuant to a court order in affiliation proceedings. In each of these cases the Commission was influenced by the fact that the clear object of the police was to deprive the persons concerned of their liberty. On the other hand, in *Hojemeister v Germany*,[83] the Commission held that detention incidental to a lawful search was not sufficient to trigger article 5 protection.

15.51   In *X v Germany*[84] the Commission distinguished *X and Y v Sweden* and *X v Austria*. In that case the applicant was a 10-year-old school child, who had been found in possession of fountain pens belonging to fellow pupils. She admitted to her teacher that she occasionally searched coats in the school and, since numerous thefts had occurred in the school, the headmaster informed the police. Thereafter two police officers took the applicant and two of her friends to a police station where they were questioned for about an hour. When they were not being questioned they were kept in an unlocked cell. The Commission accepted the government's argument that since the applicant was under the age of criminal responsibility, the object of the police in taking her to the police station could not have been to provisionally arrest her or to initiate criminal proceedings. In its view, unlike the cases of *X and Y v Sweden* and *X v Austria* where the 'object of the police action was clearly to deprive persons concerned of their liberty', the police action was:

> ... not aimed at depriving the children of their liberty but simply to obtain information from them about how they obtained possession of the objects found on them and about thefts which had occurred in the school previously.[85]

81   (1976) 7 DR 123.
82   (1979) 18 DR 154.
83   6 July 1981; unreported.
84   (1981) 24 DR 158.
85   At 161.

The Commission's distinction is clearly a fine one, and it is not apparent from the report of its decision whether the applicant consented to a request to attend the police station or whether she was made to believe that she was obliged to go.[86]

15.52 However, what is clear from the decision in *X v Germany* is that, because of her age, the police could not lawfully detain the applicant. In those circumstances, the decision is of very limited application; for example, it would not apply to routine post-arrest questioning. It must also be read alongside *Walverens v Belgium*[87] where the Commission found the applicant's detention at a police station violated article 5 even though he was technically a volunteer and free to leave and/or resist any search of his person. Significantly, the Commission was influenced by the fact that the applicant's ignorance of his legal standing coupled with the practical realities of the situation deterred him from leaving.

15.53 The mere fact that a person has voluntarily surrendered to detention will not automatically exclude article 5 protection. In *De Wilde, Ooms and Versyp v Belgium*[88] where the applicants had given themselves up to the police under Belgian vagrancy laws, the European Court held that:

> The right to liberty is too important in a 'democratic society' within the meaning of the Convention for a person to lose the benefit of the protection of the Convention for the single reason that he gives himself up to be taken into detention.[89]

Similarly, as noted above in *Walverens v Belgium*[90] the Commission was prepared to overlook the fact that the applicant's attendance at a police station was technically voluntary where, in reality, he felt constrained from leaving.[91]

15.54 Against this background, the case of *Guenat v Switzerland*[92] should be treated with some caution. There, the police took the applicant into custody because he was suffering from a nervous disorder and was acting bizarrely. Influenced by the fact that the applicant had consented to the police action, that he was free to move about the police

---

86 See Harris et al, *Law of the European Convention on Human Rights* (Butterworths, 1995) p100.
87 5 March 1980; unreported.
88 (1979–80) 1 EHRR 373.
89 Para 65.
90 Note 87.
91 Ibid.
92 (1995) 81-A DR 130.

station and that the police acted on humanitarian grounds, the Commission held that this did not amount to a deprivation of liberty within the meaning of article 5.

15.55　　As a general rule, an ability to leave the area of confinement will usually exclude the application of article 5. So, for example, in *SM and MT v Austria*,[93] the Commission found no deprivation of liberty where the applicants, who were Lebanese, were confined to the transit area of Vienna airport but were free to leave at any time. However, there are exceptions. In *Amwr v France*[94] the applicants, fleeing from the regime in Somalia via Syria, argued that their article 5 rights had been infringed when, having arrived at Paris-Orly airport, they were held for 20 days in the transit area and a nearby hotel (part of which had been converted as a holding area). The French government argued that although the transit area was 'closed on the French side' it was 'open to the outside', so that the applicants could have returned of their own accord to Syria. The European Court disagreed. In its view the mere fact that it was possible for the applicants to leave voluntarily did not automatically exclude the application of article 5. Since Syria could not offer protection comparable to that of France, the possibility of returning there was 'theoretical' and thus irrelevant for article 5 purposes.

The pre-conditions of lawful arrest and detention under article 5

15.56　There are three pre-conditions to a lawful arrest under article 5 of the Convention. They are:

1) That the arrest and/or detention is 'lawful'. This requirement flows from the use of the word 'lawful' in each of the paragraphs 5(1)(a)–5(1)(f).

2) That the arrest and/or detention is 'in accordance with the procedure prescribed by law'. This requirement is found in the second sentence of para 5(1) and means that domestic law must set out the procedure to be followed by those authorised to arrest and/or detain others and that the procedure must be observed in practice.

93　(1993) 74 DR 179.
94　(1996) 22 EHRR 533.

3) That the grounds for the arrest and/or detention must fall within at least one of the paragraphs 5(1)(a)–(f) of article 5. Para 5(1)(c) which provides for arrest and/or detention on reasonable suspicion that the person concerned has committed an offence will usually be relevant in this respect. However, paras 5(1)(a)–(f) of article 5 are not mutually exclusive and it is quite conceivable that a person may, at a given time, be deprived of his/her liberty in accordance with more than one of the sub-paragraphs, or that the purpose or character of detention may change so that what was initially justified under one sub-paragraph ceases to be so, but comes to be justified under another one.[95]

These pre-conditions are examined in chapter 3.[96]

Grounds for arrest under the Convention

15.57 Three grounds for arrest are included in article 5(1)(c) of the Convention. They are:

1) the existence of a reasonable suspicion that the person arrested has committed an offence;

2) when it is reasonably considered necessary to prevent the person arrested committing an offence;

3) when it is reasonably considered necessary to prevent the person arrested fleeing after having committing an offence.

The third ground justifies arrest only where there are reasonable grounds for believing that an offence has been committed.[97] It therefore overlaps with the first ground to such an extent that it is widely considered to be redundant.

15.58 In each case, the purpose must be to bring the person arrested before a competent legal authority. Therefore article 5(1)(c) has to be read in conjunction with article 5(3).[98] However, so long as an initial intention to bring a person before a competent legal authority existed at the time of arrest, the mere fact that s/he is not charged or brought before a court (eg, is released without charge) will not involve

---

95 See the Commission's comments in *McVeigh and Others v UK* (1983) 5 EHRR 71 and 25 DR 15 at para 162.

96 See paras 3.33 to 3.40.

97 *Lukanov v Bulgaria* (1997) 24 EHRR 121 at para 80 of Commission Report.

98 See para 15.45.

a breach of article 5(1)(c) because 'the existence of such a purpose is to be considered independently of its achievement'.[99]

15.59   The term 'offence' in article 5 has been widely defined by the Commission and Court and does not necessarily correspond to its domestic meaning.[100] *Brogan and Others v UK*.[101] concerned the exercise of a statutory power of arrest of any person 'concerned in the commission, preparation or instigation of acts of terrorism', where the definition of 'terrorism' was the 'use of violence for political ends'. Although no criminal offence with the same definition existed, the Court held that the prohibited conduct was 'well in keeping with the idea of an offence'.[102]

The meaning of 'reasonable suspicion'

15.60   Article 5(1)(c) authorises arrest on 'reasonable suspicion' of having committed a criminal offence. In its judgment in the case of *Fox, Campbell and Hartley v UK*[103] the European Court held that:

> The 'reasonableness' of the suspicion on which an arrest must be based forms an essential part of the safeguard against arbitrary arrest and detention which is laid down in Article 5(1)(c) ... [H]aving a 'reasonable suspicion' presupposes the existence of facts or information which would satisfy an objective observer that the person concerned may have committed the offence in question.[104]

What may be regarded as 'reasonable' will depend on all the circumstances and is to be judged on the facts known at the time of arrest, not afterwards.[105] It is not necessary to show that an offence has been committed. Nor is it necessary to show that, if an offence has been committed, the arrested person is responsible.[106] The honesty and bona fides of a suspicion constitute one indispensable element of its reasonableness,[107] but 'honest belief' alone is not enough; there must be an objective basis justifying arrest and/or detention.[108]

99 *Brogan and Others v UK* (1989) 11 EHRR 117 at para 53. See also *K-F v Germany* [1998] EHRLR 228.
100 For a discussion of autonomous meanings, see para 4.19.
101 Note 99.
102 Relying on *Ireland v UK* (1979–80) 2 EHRR 25.
103 (1991) 13 EHRR 157.
104 Para 36.
105 *Stogmuller v Austria* (1979–80) 1 EHRR 155.
106 *X v Austria* (1989) 11 EHRR 112.
107 *Murray and Others v UK* n43 at para 61.
108 *Fox, Campbell and Hartley v UK* (1991) 13 EHRR 157.

15.61 In *Brogan and Others v UK*,[109] the European Court held that detaining the applicants to further police investigations 'by way of confirming or dispelling the concrete suspicions' of involvement in unspecified acts of terrorism did not breach the Convention because article 5(1)(c):

> does not presuppose that the police should have obtained sufficient evidence to bring charges either at the point of arrest or when the applicants were in custody.[110]

15.62 Similarly in *Murray and Others v UK*,[111] which again involved anti-terrorist legislation, the European Court held that the level of suspicion required need not be sufficient to charge because:

> The object of the questioning during detention under sub-paragraph (c) of Article 5(1) is to further the criminal investigation by way of confirming or dispelling the concrete suspicion grounding the arrest. Thus, facts which raise a suspicion need not be of the same level as those necessary to justify a conviction or even the bringing of a charge, which comes at the next stage of the process of criminal investigation.[112]

However, the Court in *Murray and Others v UK* did note that 'the length of the deprivation of liberty at risk may ... be material to the level of suspicion required'.[113] In that case, the maximum period of detention was four hours. Longer periods may require more by way of reasonable suspicion.

15.62 It is important to note that the cases of *Brogan and Others v UK*,[114] *Fox, Campbell and Hartley v UK*[115] and *Murray and Others v UK*[116] all involved arrests under anti-terrorism legislation. In each case, the European Court recognised that in respect of the requirement of 'reasonable suspicion':

> ... terrorist crime falls into a special category. Because of the attendant risk of loss of life and human suffering, the police are obliged to act with utmost urgency in following up all information, including information from secret sources. Further, the police may

---

109 Note 99.
110 Para 53.
111 Note 45.
112 Ibid para 55.
113 Ibid para 56.
114 Note 99.
115 Note 108.
116 Note 45.

frequently have to arrest a suspected terrorist on the basis of information which is reliable but which cannot, without putting in jeopardy the source of the information, be revealed to the suspect or produced in court to support a charge.[117]

And, even in such cases, those responsible for an arrest must furnish 'at least some facts or information capable of satisfying the Court that the arrested person was reasonably suspected of having committed the alleged offence'.[118]

15.63   The extent to which confidential information and anonymous sources can be used to justify an arrest in more conventional cases has yet to be resolved. It is inherent in the Court's reasoning in *Murray and Others v UK*[119] that the test of 'reasonable suspicion' accepted in that case would not necessarily be enough in 'conventional' cases. On a number of occasions, the Court has been concerned about the use of evidence from anonymous informants at the trial stage,[120] but it has consistently maintained that the Convention does not preclude reliance 'at the investigation stage' on such sources.[121] How much reliance and at what stage is unclear.

Preventative detention

15.64   Although the second limb of article 5(1)(c) authorises detention to prevent the commission of offences, any such detention will always be subject to very close scrutiny. It does not authorise a policy of general prevention directed against an individual or category of individuals simply on the basis that s/he or they have a propensity to commit crime: it does no more than to afford a means of preventing a 'concrete and specific offence'.[122] In *Ireland v UK*[123] the European Court held that internment authorised by domestic law simply 'for the preservation of the peace and maintenance of order' without any need for suspicion of having committed an offence (or belief that it was necessary to prevent a crime being committed) could not be brought within the terms of article 5(1)(c).

---

117 *Fox, Campbell and Hartley* n108.
118 Ibid at para 34.
119 Note 45.
120 See chapter 9.
121 See, for example, *Doorson v Netherlands* (1996) 22 EHRR 330 at para 69.
122 *Guzzardi v Italy* n78 at para 101.
123 Note 102.

Reasons for arrest

15.65   Article 5(2) of the Convention requires that anyone arrested be informed promptly 'in a language he understands' of 'the reasons for his arrest and of any charge against him'.[124] What this means is that anyone arrested must be told 'in simple, non-technical language' that s/he can understand 'the essential legal and factual grounds for his arrest'.[125]

15.66   The purpose of this provision is to enable anyone who has been arrested to challenge the lawfulness of his/her detention.[126] No special form is required[127] and the reasons for arrest need not be in writing.[128] However, since an arrest is lawful under article 5(1)(c) only where there is a 'reasonable suspicion' that the person arrested has committed an offence, the Commission has reasoned that:

> The arrested person should ... be informed sufficiently about the facts and the evidence which are proposed to be the foundation of a decision to detain him. In particular, he should be enabled to state whether he admits or denies the alleged offence.[129]

Merely informing a person that s/he has been detained pursuant to the provisions of emergency legislation is insufficient.[130]

15.67   The question of timing was raised in *Fox, Campbell and Hartley v UK*[131] where the European Court found no breach of article 5(2) where the reasons for the applicants' arrest had been brought to their attention during their interrogation a few hours after their arrest. A similar result followed in *Murray and Others v UK*.[132] However, the Court has repeatedly emphasised that the question of promptness has to be determined on the facts of each case and it cannot be assumed that what is sufficient in 'terrorist' cases will suffice in 'conventional' cases.[133]

---

124 See para 15.45.
125 *Fox, Campbell and Hartley* n108 at para 40.
126 Ibid and *X v FRG* (1978) 16 DR 111.
127 *X v Netherlands* (1966) 9 Yearbook 474 at 480; and *X v UK* (1974) 14 Yearbook 250 at 276.
128 *X v Netherlands* (1962) 5 YB 224 at 228; and *X v FRG* n126 at 113.
129 *X v FRG* n126 at 114.
130 *Ireland v UK* n102 at para 198.
131 Note 108.
132 Note 45.
133 For the Court's remarks on the distinction between these two categories, see para 15.62.

15.68   The requirement that reasons be given for arrest and/or detention applies not only to criminal cases, but also to those deprived of their liberty by other processes of law.[134] In *Van der Leer v Netherlands*[135] the European Court found a breach of article 5(2) where the applicant became aware of a court order confining her to a psychiatric hospital only by accident ten days after it was made.

Other grounds for arrest under the Convention

15.69 While most police arrests will fall to be considered under article 5(1)(c), the other grounds provided for in article 5(1) can justify arrest in certain circumstances. Those circumstances are examined in chapter 3.

Arrest and detention outside the UK

15.70 As a general proposition,[136] states who have ratified the Convention guarantee Convention rights to those within their jurisdiction.[137] It follows that an individual usually resident in the UK who is arrested and/or detained in another state which has ratified the Convention may have a remedy against that state. There are plenty of examples of this.[138]

15.71   However, in some circumstances, the protection of article 5 may also extend to the arrest and/or detention of an individual by a state's agents outside its territory.[139] In *Reinette v France*[140] the Commission held that article 5 applied where the applicant was handed over to French officials in St Vincent because, from that point on, 'the applicant was effectively subject to French authority and consequently to French jurisdiction'.[141]

---

134 See Jacobs FG and White RA *The European Convention on Human Rights* (Clarendon Press, 1996) p88.
135 (1990) 12 EHRR 567.
136 With exceptions: see *Loizidou v Turkey* (1997) 23 EHRR 513.
137 See chapter 2.
138 See *Scott v Spain* (1997) 24 EHRR 391.
139 See Harris et al *The Law of the European Convention on Human Rights* (Butterworths, 1995) p102.
140 (1989) 63 DR 189.
141 Ibid at 193.

The exercise of stop and search and similar powers

15.72 Detention in the course of exercising stop and search and similar powers does not sit comfortably with the Convention. In many cases, no doubt, the Strasbourg bodies would take the view that cursory roadside searches are sufficiently speedy not to raise article 5 issues.[142] However, where the exercise of stop and search and similar powers does involve subjecting the person concerned to a significant period of detention, that period of detention will have to be justified under article 5.

15.73 Article 5(1)(c) of the Convention provides for arrest and/or detention on reasonable suspicion that the person concerned has committed an offence.[143] However, the overriding requirement that there be an intention to bring that person before a court would seem to rule out its applicability to the exercise of stop and search and similar powers.[144]

15.74 The only other provision capable of justifying detention during the exercise of stop and search and similar powers is article 5(1)(b) which provides for the detention of a person 'in order to secure the fulfilment of any obligation prescribed by law'. Since both the European Court and the Commission have consistently rejected a wide interpretation of this provision, it will apply only where the police can show that detention was necessary for the fulfilment of a 'specific and concrete obligation'.[145] A general obligation to obey the criminal law will not suffice.[146]

15.75 So far there is no jurisprudence from the Court at all in this area. The Commission has considered police powers in the context of legislation to prevent terrorism, but has not considered the more routine exercise of stop and search powers under the Police and Criminal Evidence Act 1984 (or other similar provisions).

15.76 In *McVeigh, O'Neill and Evans v UK*[147] the Commission had to consider the exercise of a power to order the applicants' detention pending their 'examination' under prevention of terrorism legis-

---

142 See paras 15.46 to 15.55.
143 See paras 15.60 to 15.63.
144 See para 15.58.
145 *Engel v Netherlands* (1979–80) 1 EHRR 647 at para 69.
146 *Guzzardi v Italy* n78 at para 101.
147 (1981) 5 EHRR 71 and 25 DR 15.

lation then in force.[148] The power was exercisable in relation to anyone entering or leaving Britain and the purpose of the examination was to determine: (a) whether the person stopped appeared to be concerned in terrorism, (b) whether s/he was subject to an exclusion order, or (c) whether there were grounds for suspecting that s/he had committed an offence under the prevention of terrorism legislation. Reasonable suspicion was not a pre-condition to the exercise of the power to detain or the power to examine.

15.77   The applicants, who had arrived at Liverpool by ferry from Dublin, were held for 45 hours before being released without charge. In that time they were searched, questioned and their fingerprints and photographs were taken.[149] They argued that their detention could not be justified under article 5(1)(b) because they had not failed to fulfil any pre-existing obligation imposed upon them before being stopped. The Commission found this argument powerful but, ultimately, unpersuasive. In its view:

> ... the person concerned must normally have had a prior opportunity to fulfil the 'specific and concrete' obligation incumbent on him and have failed, without proper excuse, to do so before it can be said in good faith that his detention is 'in order to secure the fulfilment' of the obligation. However, there may, in the Commission's opinion, be other limited circumstances of a pressing nature which could warrant detention in order to secure the fulfilment of an obligation.[150]

The Commission came to this view by reasoning that:

> The wording of Article 5(1)(b) does not expressly require that there should have been ... deliberate or negligent failure on the part of the detainee [to fulfil a pre-existing obligation]. It requires only that the purpose of the detention should be to secure the fulfilment of the obligation.[151]

15.78   In order to determine whether circumstances of a 'pressing nature' warrant detention to secure the fulfilment of an obligation, it is necessary to examine the nature of the obligation. In particular:

> It is necessary to consider whether its fulfilment is a matter of immediate necessity and whether the circumstances are such that

---

148 The Prevention of Terrorism (Temporary Provisions) Act 1976 and the Prevention of Terrorism (Supplementary Temporary Provisions) Order 1976.
149 As regards the taking of fingerprints and photographs, see paras 15.30 to 15.35.
150 Para 175.
151 Para 174.

no other means of securing fulfilment is reasonably practicable. A balance must be drawn between the importance in a democratic society of securing the immediate fulfilment of the obligation in question, and the importance of the right to liberty. The duration of the period of detention is also a relevant factor in drawing such a balance.[152]

Carrying out this balance in *McVeigh, O'Neill and Evans v UK*[153] the Commission concluded that circumstances of a 'pressing nature' did warrant the applicants' detention.

15.79   The following factors underpinned the Commission's decision in *McVeigh, O'Neill and Evans v UK*:[154]

1) The obligation in question was, in essence, an obligation to submit to a security check on entering Britain, the scope of the check being (broadly speaking) the prevention of terrorism.[155]

2) There was a need to control the international movement of terrorists, particularly in light of the problems experienced in the UK by the movement of terrorists between the UK and Eire and between Britain and Northern Ireland.

3) In most cases (but not the applicants') any 'examination' was carried out without the need for detention and, even where there was detention, its duration was very short.

4) In practice, the examining officer did not exercise the power of detention pending examination unless s/he had 'some suspicion' about the person concerned.

5) Since a terrorist may give false information or refuse to answer questions, it may be necessary to resort to detention.

Clearly these factors were very specific and would not, on the face of it, justify detention for routine searches.

Remedies for police misconduct: overview

15.80   Police misconduct can cover a wide range of activities. Where it involves a breach of Convention rights, individuals will be able to bring proceedings under the HRA against the police for damages.[156]

152 Para 191.
153 Note 147.
154 Ibid.
155 Ibid at para 192.
156 See chapter 2.

The rules governing investigation into and prosecution of those who violate the right to life and physical integrity are dealt with in chapter 14.[157] They apply to the police. The circumstances in which conditions of detention in themselves breach the Convention are dealt with in chapter 16.[158] This part of this chapter deals with a wider range of misconduct, including assault, battery and discrimination.

Ill-treatment and the use of force

15.81   Ill-treatment in police custody can raise issues under article 3 (the prohibition on torture, inhuman and degrading treatment) if it reaches the 'minimum level of severity' required by the Court's case-law.[159] The vulnerability of a person held in police custody has an impact on this threshold criteria.[160]

15.82   In *Tomasi v France*,[161] the applicant claimed that he had been slapped, kicked and punched by police officers during a prolonged period of police detention. Although the medical evidence was not wholly consistent with the applicant's allegations, it disclosed that he had been subjected to a number of blows of some intensity. In the European Court's view, evidence of such injuries was sufficiently serious to render the applicant's treatment in custody inhuman and degrading within the meaning of article 3. The requirements of the investigation and the undeniable difficulties inherent in the fight against crime, particularly with regard to terrorism, cannot limit the protection afforded under article 3 in respect of the physical integrity of individuals.[162]

15.83   An even more robust approach was taken in *Ribitsch v Austria*[163] where, again in the context of allegations that the applicant had been punched and kicked in police custody, causing several areas of bruising, the European Court held that:

> ... in respect of a person deprived of his liberty, any recourse to physical force which has not been made strictly necessary by his own conduct diminishes human dignity and is in principle an

157 Paras 14.5 to 14.21.
158 Paras 16.12 to 16.30.
159 See *Ireland v UK* n102.
160 *Tomasi v France* (1993) 15 EHRR 1 at paras 113 and 115.
161 Note 160.
162 Ibid at para 115; see also P *Hippen v Austria* (1994) 18 EHRR CD 93.
163 (1996) 21 EHRR 573.
164 Ibid at para 38.

infringement of the right set forth in Article 3 of the Convention.[164]

Physical force in this context relates to deliberate assaults; resort to other kinds of force, for example, the unnecessary use of handcuffs, may require more detailed examination.[165]

15.84 Where ill-treatment in police custody is proven, its purpose will be relevant. One of the factors that led the Court to conclude that the serious ill-treatment inflicted on the applicant in *Aksoy v Turkey*[166] amounted to torture (rather than inhuman or degrading treatment) was that is was administered with the aim of obtaining admissions or information from the applicant.[167]

15.85 Similarly the fact that ill-treatment consists of a number of separate acts will not prevent the Commission and Court considering their cumulative effect. At issue in the case of *Ireland v UK*[168] were five interrogation techniques applied to suspects in Northern Ireland. These techniques were:

1) to force suspects to stand against a wall for hours in extremely uncomfortable positions;

2) to force suspects to wear a dark hood during interrogation;

3) to deprive suspects of sleep;

4) to subject suspects to noise; and

5) to deprive suspects of adequate food and drink.

In its decision the Commission came to the conclusion that these five techniques constituted torture and inhuman treatment within the meaning of article 3. The Court, however, in its judgment in the same case, held them to be inhuman and degrading treatment, but not torture.

Handcuffs

15.86 Handcuffing does not normally give rise to an issue under article 3 of the Convention. However, it may do so where (a) handcuffs are used in connection with an unlawful arrest or unlawful detention or (b) their use goes beyond what can reasonably considered to be

---

165 See paras 15.86 and 15.87.
166 (1997) 23 EHRR 553.
167 Ibid at para 64.
168 Note 102.

necessary in the circumstances.[169] And in most cases it will be diffi-cult to justify the use of handcuffs as necessary where there is no evidence that the person concerned would resist arrest, abscond, cause injury, or damage or suppress evidence.[170]

15.87   Even where it is established that handcuffs were used in connec-tion with an unlawful arrest, unlawful detention or unnecessarily, a finding that article 3 has been breached will not automatically follow. In *Raninen v Finland*[171] the applicant was handcuffed for two hours during an unlawful period of detention. For some of this time he could be seen by the public, including his own support group. For the Commission, this diminished his human dignity and amounted to 'degrading treatment' in violation of article 3.[172] The Court dis-agreed. In its view, in addition to the factors taken into account by the Commission, there had to be some evidence of physical or men-tal injury to the applicant or a clear indication that the authorities' purpose in handcuffing him was to humiliate him. Since there was no such evidence or indication, the Court found no breach of article 3 and, for similar reasons, found no breach of article 8 of the Convention.

Racism and other forms of discrimination

15.88   Article 14 of the Convention prohibits discrimination on a number of grounds including sex, race colour and religion. It has a dependent nature: ie, the prohibition on discrimination operates only in conjunction with other Convention rights and is not free-standing. However, there is no need for another Convention right actually to be breached before the prohibition on discrimination is triggered. It is enough if the conduct or activity in question falls 'within the ambit' of another Convention right: see chapter 29.[173]

15.89   In the policing context, article 14 is likely to be in issue most of the time because most police investigations will be 'within the ambit' of article 8[174] and every arrest and detention will be 'within the ambit' of article 5. Whether or not stop and search powers amount to the

169 *Raninen v Finland* (1998) 26 EHRR 563.
170 Ibid at para 56.
171 Note 169.
172 Ibid at para 53.
173 Paras 29.3 to 29.9.
174 See above paras 15.6 to 15.7.

deprivation of liberty under article 5, they certainly come within its ambit. It is also important to note that institutional racism is capable of breaching article 3 of the Convention (the prohibition on inhuman treatment and/or punishment).[175]

15.90   Not all differences in treatment amount to a breach of article 14. The meaning of discrimination under the Convention is a difference in treatment which has no reasonable and objective justification.[176] However, any difference in treatment between the sexes or between different races will be particularly difficult to justify.[177]

The burden and standard of proof in misconduct cases

15.91   When considering allegations of ill-treatment under article 3 of the Convention, the European Court has refused to place a burden of proof on either party. It will examine all the material before it, whether originating from the Commission, the parties or other sources and, if necessary, obtain material of its own motion.[178] The standard of proof adopted for article 3 is 'beyond reasonable doubt', but this can be satisfied by 'the coexistence of sufficiently strong, clear and concordant inferences' or 'similar unrebutted presumptions of fact'.[179]

15.92   Presumptions of fact requiring rebuttal will arise where there is clear evidence that an individual has been injured while in police custody. So, for example, in *Ribitsch v Austria*[180] where there was medical evidence to support the applicant's contention that he had been punched and kicked in police custody (albeit not entirely consistent with his account), the Commission approached the case on the basis that:

> In the event of injuries being sustained during police custody, it was for the Government to produce evidence establishing facts which cast doubt on the account of events given by the victim, particularly if this account was supported by medical certificates.[181]

---

175 *East African Asians v UK* (1981) 3 EHRR 76.
176 See paras 29.10 to 29.17.
177 Ibid paras 29.15 to 29.17.
178 *Ireland v UK* n102 at para 160.
179 Ibid at para 161.
180 Note 163.
181 Ibid at para 31.

The European Court adopted the same approach:

> It is not disputed that Mr Ribitsch's injuries were sustained during his detention in police custody ... while he was entirely under the control of police officers ... The Government were accordingly under an obligation to provide a plausible explanation of how the applicant's injuries were caused.[182]

In the absence of any such explanation, both the Commission and the Court found a breach of article 3.

15.93   The Court reiterated this approach in strong terms in *Aksoy v Turkey*[183] where it held that:

> ... where an individual is taken into police custody in good health but is found to be injured at the time of release, it is incumbent on the State to provide a plausible explanation as to the causing of the injury, failing which a clear issue arises under Article 3 of the Convention.[184]

Vicarious liability

15.94   In a number of cases before the European Court and Commission, states have sought to escape liability by claiming that the (wrongful) actions of their servants or agents were ultra vires. Invariably this argument has been rejected. So, for example, in *Cyprus v Turkey*[185] where the Commission accepted allegations that a number of detainees had been raped, it held the Turkish government responsible on the basis that:

> The evidence shows that rapes were committed by Turkish soldiers and at least in two cases even by Turkish officers ... It has not been shown that the Turkish authorities took adequate measures to prevent this happening or that they generally took any disciplinary measures following such incidents. The Commission therefore considers that the non-prevention of the said acts is imputable to Turkey under the Convention.[186]

---

182 Ibid at para 34.
183 Note 166. See also *Assenov v Bulgaria* [1999] EHRLR 225 on need for investigation in cases of police ill-treatment.
184 Ibid at para 61; see also the Commission decision in *Selmouni v France* (1998) EHRLR 510.
185 (1982) 4 EHRR 482.
186 Ibid at para 373.

The Court adopted an even more robust approach in *Ireland v UK*[187] in the context of a practice of ill-treatment including five interrogation techniques found to breach article 3:

> It is inconceivable that the higher authorities of a state should be, or at least should be entitled to be, unaware of the existence of such a practice. Furthermore, under the Convention those authorities are strictly liable for the conduct of their subordinates; they are under a duty to impose their will on subordinates and cannot shelter behind their inability to ensure that it is respected.[188]

It is unclear how far this concept of strict liability extends, but it appears to stretch beyond article 3.

15.95   In *A v France*[189] state liability under article 8 was triggered where a police officer recorded a telephone conversation without authority and in breach of French law. And in the context of a complaint under article 10 of the Convention, the Commission in *Wille v Liechtenstein*[190] adopted the following position of principle;

> ... the responsibility of a state under the Convention may arise for acts of all its organs and servants. As in connection with international law generally, the acts of persons acting in an official capacity are imputed to the state. In particular, the obligations of a Contracting Party under the Convention can be violated by a person exercising an official function vested in him, even where his acts are performed without express authorisation and even outside or against instructions.[191]

Police imunity in negligence actions

15.96   Article 6 of the Convention is likely to have a profound impact on the scope of police immunity in negligence actions. In *Osman v UK*[192] the applicants complained that, despite a number of clear warning signals, the police had failed to take reasonable steps to prevent the second applicant's teacher attacking their family and home and, ultimately, killing the first applicant's husband (the second applicant's father) and wounding the second applicant.[193] Their claim for negli-

---

187   Note 102.
188   Ibid at para 159.
189   Note 28.
190   (1997) 24 EHRR CD 45.
191   Ibid at 48.
192   (Court) 28 October 1998; noted in [1999] EHRLR 228.
193   For facts and examination of issues under articles 3 and 8 see chapter 14.

gence in the domestic courts was struck out on the basis that, following the House of Lords' decision in *Hill v Chief Constable of West Yorkshire*,[194] no action could lie against the police in negligence in the investigation and suppression of crime on the ground that public policy required immunity from suit.[195] Before the Euro-pean Court, the applicants complained that this restricted their access to a court in breach of article 6(1) of the Convention.

15.97   Article 6(1) secures to everyone the right to have any claim relating to his/her civil rights and obligations brought before a court or tribunal. In this way, article 6 embodies the 'right to a court', of which the right of access, that is the right to institute proceedings before courts in civil matters constitutes one aspect.[196]

15.98   The applicants argued that the public interest considerations invoked by the House of Lords in *Hill v Chief Constable of West Yorkshire* as justification for the police immunity rule could not be sustained; alternatively, that, even if some immunity could be justi-fied, its operation offended the principle of proportionality because it did not distinguish between cases where the merits were strong and those where they were weak. The European Court rejected the first argument but accepted the second.

15.99   In the Court's view the purpose of the rule giving the police immunity – to avoid defensive policing and diversion of resources – was legitimate under the Convention because it was directed at main-taining the effectiveness of the police force and hence the prevention of disorder or crime. The question was therefore whether its operation in practice was proportionate to achieving that legitimate purpose. In this regard the Court observed that:

> ... the application of the rule ... without further enquiry into the existence of competing public interest considerations ... serves to confer a blanket immunity on the police for their acts and omissions during the investigation and suppression of crime ...

This amounted to:

> ... an unjustifiable restriction on an applicant's right to have a determination on the merits of his or her claim against the police in deserving cases.[197]

In the Court's judgment it must be open to a domestic court to have

---

194 [1989] AC 53.
195 See *Osman and another v Ferguson and Another* [1993] 4 All ER 344.
196 See *Golder v UK* (1979–80) 1 EHRR 524; see also chapter 13.
197 Note 192 at para 151.

regard to the presence of other public interest considerations which pull in the opposite direction to the application of the rule. Failing this, there would be no distinction made between degrees of negligence or of harm suffered or any consideration of the justice of a particular case. Accordingly there had been a breach of article 6(1).

Damages in civil actions against the police

15.100 Two types of damages are available under the Convention for violation of a Convention right. Article 41[198] provides that where the European Court finds that there has been a violation of the Convention, it can, if necessary, afford just satisfaction to the injured party. Article 5(5) is more specific. It provides that:

> Everyone who has been the victim of arrest or detention in contravention of the provisions of [article 5] shall have an enforceable right to compensation.

Where there has been wrongful imprisonment and/or police misconduct damages have been comparatively high. Examples are set out in chapter 2.[199]

Fair trial generally

15.101 Civil actions against the police amount to the determination of civil rights and obligations and the fair trial obligations of article 6(1) therefore apply.[200] These are examined in detail in chapter 13 and include:
(1) the right to an independent and impartial tribunal;
(2) the right to disclosure;
(3) the right to an adversarial hearing;
(4) the right to a reasoned decision; and
(5) the right to trial within a reasonable period.

However, police disciplinary proceedings do not appear to come within the ambit of article 6(1).[201]

---

198 Formerly article 50.
199 See paras 2.56 and 2.57.
200 *Osman v UK* note 192; *Baraona v Portugal* (1987) 13 EHRR 329.
201 See para 12.14.

CHAPTER 16

Prisoners

Phillippa Kaufmann

16.1   Introduction

16.3   Article 2

16.8   Article 3
16.12   Conditions generally
16.16   Solitary confinement
16.21   Conditions which result from the prisoner's own behaviour
16.24   Invasions of bodily integrity
16.26   Ill health
16.28   Distance between family and prisoner
16.29   Assaults by staff
16.30   Handcuffing
16.31   Length of sentence and duration of detention
16.35   Failure to secure the purpose of detention

16.37   Article 4

16.38   Article 5
16.40   Article 5(4) and preventative detention
16.43   Procedural aspects of an article 5(4) review
16.47   Right to have lawfulness of detention determined speedily
16.48   Right to compensation under article 5(5)

continued

16.49   Article 6

16.53   Articles 8(2) to 11(2) – general considerations

16.56   Article 8

16.57   Private and family life
16.60   Correspondence
16.69   Legal correspondence

16.72   Article 9

16.74   Article 10

16.79   Article 11

16.80   Article 12

16.81   Article 14

16.82   Article 1 of the First Protocol

16.84   Article 2 of the First Protocol

Introduction

16.1 Issues concerning the detention of prisoners have given rise to numerous applications under the Convention. Many of them have concerned conditions of detention, issues which engage article 3.[1]

16.2 However, the restrictive principles established under article 3 have proved to be of little benefit to prisoners, with the result that the flow of article 3 prisoner cases in the 1970s and early 1980s has been stemmed to little more than a trickle in more recent years. Another area of great significance for prisoners is their ability to establish and maintain contact with the outside world, issues which have engaged articles 8 and 10. In stark contrast with article 3, Convention jurisprudence has made a fundamental difference to prisoners' rights in this area, leading on a number of occasions to significant amendment of the Prison Rules 1964 as well as Prison Service Standing Orders.[2]

Article 2

16.3 The death of a prisoner, whether by suicide or at the hands of another inmate, is capable of giving rise to a violation of article 2 as the obligation to secure the right to life can in certain circumstances call for positive action on the part of the state, 'in particular an active measure to save lives when the authorities have taken the person in question into their custody'.[3]

16.4 The extent of this obligation will inevitably vary having regard to the source of the danger and the means available to combat it. Where there is a real and imminent risk to an identified person or group of persons, a failure by the state authorities to take appropriate steps may result in a violation.[4]

16.5 It would appear that the positive obligation incorporated in article 2 can require the authorities to force-feed a prisoner who is on hunger

---

1 *X v Switzerland* 18 DR 238 where an application relating to conditions of detention was brought under article 5 and rejected on the ground that article 3 is the lex specialis.

2 *R v Secretary of State for the Home Department ex p Leech (No 2)* [1994] QB 198.

3 *X v FRG* (1985) 7 EHRR 152 at 153 and *Rebai v France* 88-B DR 72.

4 *Osman v United Kingdom* [1999] EHRLR 228. The Commission has recently admitted the application in the case of *Keenan v United Kingdom* Appl 27229/95, which concerns the suicide of a prisoner.

strike. Where the authorities do so, it appears that a prisoner cannot claim that the force-feeding violated his rights under article 3.[5]

16.6   An issue under article 2 may also arise where the imprisonment of an individual creates a danger that a close relative will take his or her life as a result, though where other suitable measures, short of release, can be taken to prevent suicide, a violation is unlikely to be found.[6]

16.7   The necessity of ensuring the effective protection of the rights guaranteed under the Convention, which takes on added importance in the context of the right to life, has led the Convention organs to imply a procedural aspect into article 2 requiring the institution of an effective procedure to investigate the cause of death where it is uncertain.[7] The mandatory requirement that an inquest be held into the death which occurs in custody probably satisfies this requirement under article 2.

Article 3

16.8   As indicated it is under article 3 of the Convention that the largest volume of applications have been made by prisoners. Almost none of these applications have reached the Court. Most have failed because the conditions have been found to be justified by reference to the object pursued by their imposition.

16.9   The Court has defined torture as 'deliberate inhuman treatment causing very serious and cruel suffering'.[8] It is an aggravated form of inhuman treatment. The qualification that the treatment is deliberate requires that the suffering is intentionally inflicted. Mental suffering alone can be sufficient.[9]

16.10   Inhuman treatment has been defined by the Commission as

... such treatment as deliberately causes severe suffering, mental or physical, which, in the particular situation, is unjustifiable.[10]

---

5   *X v FRG* n2. The Commission's approach here is in conflict with a recognition of the autonomy of the individual and manifests a somewhat surprising degree of paternalism.

6   *Naddaf v Germany* (1987) 9 EHRR 561.

7   *McCann and Others v UK* (1996) 21 EHRR 97. See also chapter 14.

8   *Ireland v United Kingdom* (1979–80) 2 EHRR 25 para 167.

9   *Ireland v UK* note 8.

10   *Greek Case* 12 YB 1.

Treatment or punishment may be said to be degrading if it grossly humiliates the individual before others, or drives him to act against his will or conscience.[11] In *Ireland v UK* the Commission added that degrading treatment might also be:

> ... ill treatment designed to arouse in victims feelings of fear, anguish, and inferiority capable of humiliating and debasing them and possibly breaking their physical or moral resistance.

16.11   It further held that:

> ... ill treatment must attain a minimum level of severity if it is to fall within the scope of article 3. The assessment of this minimum is, in the nature of things relative; it depends on all the circumstances of the case, such as the duration of the treatment, its physical or mental effects and, in some cases, the age, sex and state of health of the victim, etc.[12]

This list of relevant circumstances has been expanded, most significantly in the context of prisoners, to include the object pursued as well as the stringency of the measure.[13] In the context of punishment, ill treatment must in any event be other than the usual element of humiliation associated with imprisonment after a criminal conviction.[14] The result is that where measures complained of are imposed for security, disciplinary or protective purposes, the Commission has shown a remarkable tolerance, irrespective of the effects of their stringency and the effects on the health of the victim.

Conditions generally

16.12   As article 3 is not engaged in connection with a prisoner's detention in normal prison conditions, the question whether the conditions of confinement violate article 3 is one which is particularly dependent on the evolving standards which flow from the Convention's status as a living instrument. What were considered to be 'normal conditions of confinement' in the mid-1970s may well be unacceptable now. Care must be taken in placing too much reliance on early

---

11   Ibid.

12   Note 8 para 162.

13   For example, *Ensslin, Baader and Raspe v FRG* (1979) 14 DR 64 and *X v UK* 21 DR 95.

14   *Tyrer v United Kingdom* (1979–80) 2 EHRR 1.

Commission decisions in this area.[15] In assessing the compatibility of general conditions with the Convention, assistance can be gained from the reports of the *European Committee for the Prevention of Torture and Inhuman or Degrading Treatment or Punishment*,[16] though it has been argued that the Committee applies a more favourable test than the Convention organs.[17]

16.13   There have been a few successful applications relating to general conditions. For example, the *Greek Case* where political detainees were held in conditions which, in varying degrees and combinations, were overcrowded and inadequate in respect of the provision of toilet, heating and sleeping facilities, food, recreation or contact with the outside world. Again, in *Cyprus v Turkey*[18] the applicants established inhuman treatment where they were deprived of food, water and medical treatment.

16.14   Failure to comply with the *Minimum Rules for the Treatment of Prisoners* adopted by the committee of ministers of the Council of Europe will not automatically lead to a finding that article 3 has been violated. In *Eggs v Switzerland*[19] a case concerning a short period of detention following a military disciplinary award, the Commission stated that it was not established that the Minimum Rules should be considered as a yardstick to be followed by member states for the treatment of those imprisoned for a short period on disciplinary grounds.

16.15   The rules were further considered in *X v FRG*[20] where a period of seven days' solitary confinement with minimum diet and hard bed was imposed as a result of disciplinary adjudication. In declaring the application manifestly ill-founded the Commission did look to Standard Minimum Conditions for the Treatment of Prisoners, which disclosed that the aggravating features such as hard bed and

---

15 For example, Appl 8295/78 *v UK* 15 DR 242 failed in respect of being held overnight in a cell containing the stale smell of urine and faeces of an earlier occupant; nor was there a violation when a prisoner was required to spend three weeks in a cockroach infested cell (*Reed v UK* (1983) 5 EHRR 114).

16 The Committee is established under article 1 of the 1987 *Convention for the Prevention of Torture and Inhuman and Degrading Treatment or Punishment*. It does not have an adjudicative function, but is responsible for investigating and reporting on compliance with the Convention by signatory states. A 1990 report found that conditions prevailing in prisons in Wandsworth, Brixton and Leeds amounted to inhuman and degrading treatment.

17 See *Murdoch*, 5 EJIL 200 (1994).

18 (1982) 4 EHRR 482 at 541.

19 6 DR 170.

20 10 DR 221.

minimum diet did not correspond with modern standards. Nonetheless, the Commission found that these conditions did not amount to inhuman and degrading treatment.

Solitary confinement

16.16 The Commission has repeatedly stated that the segregation of a prisoner from the prison community does not in itself constitute a form of inhuman treatment, though prolonged solitary confinement is undesirable particularly where the prisoner is detained on remand. The Commission's case-law has consistently tolerated extreme forms of social isolation imposed on grounds of security, order, discipline or the prevention of crime. However, even these objects will not justify some forms of treatment. Hence, complete sensory isolation coupled with complete social isolation are unjustifiable on any grounds as these can ultimately destroy the personality.[21] But it will be very rare indeed for such extreme conditions to obtain and where only one of these dual forms of isolation is present, the Commission has declined to find a violation.[22]

16.17 The most restrictive and impoverished conditions of detention usually arise with respect to terrorist detainees. The detention of members of the Red Army Faction in the late 1970s gave rise to two applications under article 3 against the Federal Republic of Germany[23] and later Switzerland[24] both of which failed despite extreme levels of social isolation. *Kröcher and Möller*[25] involved the more extreme conditions and invited substantial criticism from the Commission. Following their arrest the applicants were placed on their own in cells which were 8.4 square meters in area, on a floor

---

21 *Ensslin, Baader and Raspe v FRG*, 14 DR 64.

22 See eg *X v Denmark* 27 DR 50; *R v Denmark* 41 DR 149, 8 EHRR 60 (17 months' solitary confinement); *M v UK* 30 DR 130 (a convicted murderer who had killed two prisoners was segregated in Wakefield's special cell (the cage) for six years); *Dhoest v Belgium* DR 5 (years of solitary, but the Commission took account of fact that the applicant was dangerous and an escape risk who repeatedly abused efforts to reduce the severity of his conditions. The Commission emphasised the need for states constantly to keep under review the possibility of reducing restrictive conditions); *Treholdt v Norway* 71 D R 168; *Bonzi v Switzerland* 12 DR 185 (remand prisoner in solitary for one month to avoid the risk of collusion); and *Krause v Switzerland* 13 DR 73 (two years in solitary).

23 *Ensslin, Baader and Raspe v FRG* n21.

24 *Kröcher and Möller v Switzerland* 34 DR 24.

25 Ibid.

with no other prisoners. The cells above and below theirs were evacuated. They were placed under constant surveillance by closed circuit television. A 60-watt lamp was at all times lit in their cells. The windows to their cells were blocked to stop them seeing out. They were permitted 20 minutes' light exercise on Monday to Friday. From mid-March 1978 this was increased to 40 minutes. The exercise room was 9.5m by 5m and the window in it was open. During the weekend they could not leave their cells. They had no newspapers, magazines, radio or TV. Their watches and diaries had been confiscated. They had no contact with each other or other prisoners and could not be visited by their lawyers. As a result of various appeals these conditions were relaxed over time and in varying respects. From mid-January 1978 their lawyers were permitted to make two one-hour visits each week. Night lighting was discontinued from mid-February 1978 and their watches were returned to them. From June 1978 they were permitted to listen to the radio, watch TV and read one or two newspapers specially redacted. At the end of June the CCTV surveillance was discontinued and they were transferred to a floor with other prisoners though contacts between the applicants themselves was still prohibited. Measures continued in this way until the beginning of November 1978. The Commission found that the potential danger that the applicants presented justified stringent security measures. The Commission did not find that the degree of sensory isolation was unjustifiable by reference to the security requirements. For example, the cells were not equipped with any form of sound proofing, so even though there were no prisoners on their floor or in the cells above and below theirs they were not isolated from sound.

16.18   On the question of social isolation, total isolation lasted only for the first month after which contact with lawyers and family was established. The Commission further noted that the conditions were gradually relaxed. The Commission found that the periods of their detention on remand and under security conditions were fairly brief, given the circumstances of their case. The object was at all times one of security. As to the effects of the conditions, the Commission concluded that on the medical evidence available, it could not conclude that the conditions destroyed the personality or caused severe mental and physical suffering. They were provided with the medical care that their state of health demanded. On the use of CCTV surveillance, which was implemented between 18th February and 30th June 1978 the Commission found that the measure was 'only just within the limits of what is acceptable' and expressed its concern with the need for such measures, their usefulness and their compatibility with article 3, but recalled that the form of treatment must attain a minimum level of severity before a breach can be established. In rejecting, by a narrow margin of eight votes to five, a breach of article 3 the Commission had regard in particular to the gradual relaxation of the arrangements for the applicants' detention and the applicants' own behaviour in refusing opportunities for contact.

16.19 In *Ensslin and Others*, the Commission was influenced by its finding that the applicants could not be deemed to have been deliberately subjected to a range of physical and mental suffering designed to punish them, to destroy their personality or to break down their resistance. This approach indicates that the conditions must have been deliberately chosen with the object of debasing or humiliating so that the victims' will might be broken. This will be extremely difficult to establish in cases where the conditions are imposed on grounds of security. It is only if the measures are wholly disproportionate to the aim that an article 3 challenge is likely to succeed.

16.20 In the light of such an approach it is unsurprising that applications by prisoners held in category A conditions in the interest of security[26] or on rule 43 to preserve order or discipline,[27] have failed to establish a violation of article 3.

Conditions which result from the prisoner's own behaviour

16.21 The Commission has been presented with a number of cases in which prisoners have undoubtedly been subjected to inhuman and degrading conditions, but such conditions have been self-inflicted.[28] In these cases the Commission has not absolved the state of all responsibility towards prisoners under article 3, though no violations

---

26 *X v United Kingdom* 21 DR 95 (760 days on rule 43, in a cell which was constantly lit). The Commission found that the harshness of the regime was mitigated by intermittent periods spent back on normal location. Also, while on rule 43, he was able to mix with other category A inmates. The Commission did note that the period of segregation was unusual and undesirable; *X v United Kingdom* Appl 3 DR 5.

27 *Reed v United Kingdom* 19 DR 113; *X v United Kingdom* (1985) 7 EHRR 140.

28 For example, *X v United Kingdom* 28 DR 5 where the applicant spent 23 months clothed only in a towel or blanket because he refused to wear prison clothes and spent, as a result, long periods on rule 43.

have in fact been found. In *McFeely v UK*[29] the Commission was concerned with the appalling conditions prevailing at the Maze prison as a result of protests arising from the revocation of the special category status previously accorded to members of para-military organisations. The protest began with a refusal by the applicants to wear prison clothes or to work. This led the prison authorities to impose certain conditions on their use of washing and toilet facilities, conditions with which the applicants refused to comply and so stopped washing or leaving their cells to use the toilet. Though facilities such as the library and the exercise yard were open to them, they were conditional upon the applicants wearing prison clothing. Eventually they remained in their cells at all times and engaged in a dirty protest. The applicants brought about what the Commission described as 'self-inflicted debasement and humiliation to an almost sub-human degree'.[30] The Commission found that their object of achieving political prisoner status was not supported by international law. Accordingly the conditions which resulted from their protest were self-imposed and could not engage the responsibility of the government.[31] However, the fact that the prisoners were engaged in an unlawful challenge to the authority of the prison administration did not absolve the state from its obliga-tion under article 3. This required the prison authorities, with due regard to the ordinary and reasonable requirements of imprison-ment, to exercise their custodial authority to safeguard the health and well-being of prisoners including those engaged in protest in so far as may be possible in the circumstances. Such a requirement made it necessary for the prison authorities to keep under constant review their reaction to recalcitrant prisoners engaged in a developing and protracted protest. The Commission expressed concern that the authorities had taken an inflexible approach to the applicants, being more concerned to punish offenders against prison discipline than to explore ways of resolving such a serious deadlock. However, given the magnitude of the institutional problem posed by the protest and the supervisory sanitary precautions adopted by the

---

29   (1981) 3 EHRR 161.

30   Ibid para 45.

31   This implies that where a protest is in respect of the violation of Convention rights, the state will be engaged and responsible for any self-inflicted inhuman conditions.

authorities, the Commission concluded that there was no breach of article 3.[32]

16.22   The case of *Hilton v UK*,[33] though also rejected by the Commission, shows that where the self-inflicted conditions are brought about by characteristics of the prisoner over which he has little control, the responsibility of the state authorities under article 3 will be relatively greater. The applicant was found to have a stressful personality which resulted in his being incapable of accepting the realities of imprisonment. He was totally isolated as a result of his distrust of other inmates and staff. During the course of his imprisonment he deteriorated from an apparently normal prisoner to a man so depressed and isolated that he was reduced to an animal-like state whereby he would roll around in his own excrement. His personality difficulties resulted in many disciplinary infractions which, however petty, were met by, what the Commission found to be, the unnecessarily rigorous application of disciplinary measures. The Commission was highly critical of the measures deployed to cope with his odd personality, finding his general treatment highly unsatisfactory. However, it was persuaded that the authorities had taken some positive measures to help him – sufficient in its eyes to raise his treatment above the levels prohibited by article 3.

16.23   In a strong dissenting opinion four Commissioners found it unacceptable that a prison system should reduce a prisoner to such a state whatever his difficulties. In their view, the extremely repressive application of disciplinary measures, his isolation from other prisoners and contact with outside help, the lack of facilities, under-staffing and overcrowding, all had a destructive effect on the applicant such that he was reduced to a state of self-degradation for which the state's responsibility was engaged.[34]

---

32 See also *R, S, A and C v Portugal* 36 DR 200 where the complaint related to a delay of almost a month between the commencement by the applicants of a hunger strike and their being seen by a doctor. The applications were found to be manifestly ill-founded as the delay had largely been due to matters for which they were responsible.

33 (1981) 3 EHRR 104.

34 The increasingly humanitarian treatment of prisoners by member states may well lead the Commission to find a violation were a case raising similar facts brought today.

Invasions of bodily integrity

16.24 In *McFeely* the applicants were subjected to close body searches which involved the prisoner squatting naked while a mirror was put up close to his anus. The Commission emphasised the need that the government had established for searches of this kind. Apparently prisoners had been found with razor blades, flints, matches, cigarette lighters concealed in the recta and had used such objects for disruptive purposes. It noted that efforts had been made to reduce the degree of humiliation and to provide safeguards against abuse. It found that the degree of humiliation and debasement involved, particularly in respect of prisoners who must have been aware by reason of their campaign of the substantial security threat posed, did not reach the level of severity required for it to amount to degrading treatment. This decision leaves room for argument that where prisoners are required to squat, in the absence of any substantial evidence that a security threat is posed, the requisite level of debasement and humiliation will be reached.

16.25   Requiring a prisoner to provide a urine sample for drug testing purposes does not attain the minimum level of severity necessary to bring the treatment within article 3.[35]

Ill health

16.26 No cases have succeeded under article 3 based upon a failure to provide adequate medical treatment to a prisoner or a refusal to release a prisoner on the ground of age or ill health.[36] The Commission has held that imprisoning a person with a severe disability for purely punitive purposes may contravene article 3.[37] In deciding

35 *A B v Switzerland* 80-B DR 66. See also *Galloway v UK* [1999] EHRLR 119.

36 See, however, *Jastrzebski v Poland* 20 EHRR CD 126 (complaint that the applicant did not receive proper medical care and in particular was refused surgical intervention in a specialised civil hospital as recommended by four medical panels declared admissible); *Ayala v Portugal* DR 87B (failure properly to treat an HIV+ prisoner. Following an admissibility finding by the Commission there was a friendly settlement); and *Jeznach v Poland* Appl 27850/95 (concerning detention of an 80-year-old disabled man (recently admitted)). Cf *Remer v Germany* 82-A DR 117 (complaint in respect of a 20-month sentence imposed on an 80-year-old man for inciting racial hatred rejected. The applicant did not allege that he was unfit, for health reasons, to serve the term, nor that there would be insufficient health care, nor that he could not, if necessary, apply for a stay in accordance with German law). But see *Kudla v Poland* [1998] EHRLR 630.

37 Appls 6181/73, 5/10/74 Coll Dec 46, 188 and *Chartier v Italy* Appl 9044/80 33 DR 41. See also, *Lukanov v Bulgaria* Appl 21915/93 80A DR 108.

cases based on a prisoner's state of health the Commission pays particular attention to the conduct of the state in obtaining medical reports and acting upon the recommendations made by medical experts. Where the authorities have been able to show that they have taken reasonable and necessary measures to treat a prisoner by, for example, temporarily transferring him/her to hospital or providing for provisional release on compassionate grounds,[38] a violation is unlikely to be found.[39] If the detention itself causes ill health, inhuman treatment may be found to exist, but the Commission will first examine the medical treatment at the person's disposal as well as his or her willingness to make use of available services.[40]

16.27 In *Lockwood v UK*[41] the Commission found no violation where a medical officer delayed for four months in seeking a second opinion which ultimately resulted in a diagnosis of a malignant tumour.

Distance between family and prisoner

16.28 It has been held as recently as 1990 that there is no violation of article 3 arising from a refusal to transfer a prisoner from a prison in England to one in Scotland to facilitate visits by a fiancée.[42]

Assaults by staff

16.29 Gratuitous assaults by staff within prisons, if they can be proven, can constitute inhuman and degrading treatment.[43]

---

38 Ss 10 and 30 of the Crime (Sentences) Act 1997 empower the Secretary of State to release on compassionate grounds (which includes the ground of ill health), determinate and life sentence prisoners.

39 For example *Chartier v Italy* 27 DR 200 (applicant suffering from congenital obesity, weighing 170Kg together with respiratory disorders. The Commission recognised his detention was a particularly painful ordeal.) See also *Bonnechaux v Switzerland* 18 DR 100; *De Varga-Hirsch v France* 33 DR 158.

40 *B v FRG* Appl 55 DR 271 where the applicant claimed that depression experienced during his detention on remand for offences of tax evasion resulted from his conditions of detention causing him to re-experience his detention in a Nazi concentration camp.

41 15 EHRR CD 48.

42 *Wakefield v UK* 66 DR 251. See *Togher v UK* [1998] EHRLR 637 about mother and baby separation.

43 *Tomasi v France* (1993) 15 EHRR 1 where medical evidence attested to a large number of blows to the applicant's body, consistent with the applicant having been slapped, kicked and punched. The treatment was found to be inhuman and degrading. See also, *Hippin v Austria* 79-A DR 23.

Handcuffing

16.30   In a merits decision in the case of *Raninen v Finland*[44] the European Court found no violation of article 3 where, following a court hearing, the applicant, who had been convicted of evading military service, was transported in handcuffs back to the county prison in order to be released. See chapter 15.

Length of sentence and duration of detention

16.31   In *Singh and Hussain v UK*,[45] the Court indicated that a lifelong punitive sentence imposed on children aged between ten and 18 may well violate article 3, though the Commission found no violation where such a sentence is imposed on young adult murderers aged 18 to 21.[46]

16.32   The life sentence has given rise to special issues under article 3. The case of *Kotalla v The Netherlands*[47] concerned the question whether it was inhuman or degrading not to provide a mechanism to limit the duration of a life sentence. The Commission found that there was no provision within the Convention, including article 3, which could be read as requiring a life sentence prisoner to have the sentence reconsidered whether by a judicial or administrative authority with a view to its remission or termination.[48] The applicant also argued that his hopes had been repeatedly raised that he would be released imminently. The Commission accepted that on the evidence this might well be true, but did not consider that such expectation would constitute a special circumstance rendering his continued detention inhuman.

16.33   The Commission took a consistent approach when considering the compatibility with article 3 of Leon Brittan's 1983 policy change

---

44 [1998] EHRLR 344.

45 (1996) 22 EHRR 1.

46 *Ryan v United Kingdom* Appl 32875/96, Comm Dec, 1 July 1998. There may be cases where the imposition of a mandatory life sentence imposed for a second violent or sexual offence under s2 of the Crime (Sentences) Act 1997 could be said to be so arbitrary as to contravene article 3. Such a sentence would also be likely to contravene article 5(1). Arbitrary sentences might also be imposed under ss3 and 4 of the 1997 Act (minimum sentences for third class A drug trafficking or domestic burglary).

47 14 DR 238.

48 In its later decision in the case of *Dhoest v Belgium* 55 DR 5, at p23 the Commission appeared to leave open the question whether this issue was capable of engaging article 3.

whereby lifers who had committed certain categories of murders would be required to serve a minimum period of 20 years to satisfy the requirements of retribution and deterrence. For the applicant this meant that he would serve substantially longer than he had been led to expect. No violation of article 3 arose by reason of the policy change.[49] However, the theory of the mandatory life sentence has substantially changed in domestic law. The House of Lords has equated the Secretary of State's tariff with a sentence.[50] Arguably there would be a violation following an increase in a tariff where no new circumstances relating to the commission of the offence have been disclosed to justify a more serious view being taken of it.

16.34   In a similar vein article 3 is not violated when a prisoner is punished for the commission of a disciplinary offence with loss of remission (or additional days). In *McFeely v United Kingdom*[51] the applicants were disciplined in respect of their persistent breaches of the Prison Rules arising from their refusal to wear prison clothes or work. Punishments of lost remission were awarded. The Commission disposed very briefly of their arguments that this amounted to inhuman or degrading treatment and noted that lost remission can be restored following a period of good conduct.[52]

Failure to secure the purpose of detention

16.35   During the 1970s the Commission considered and found admissible a number of applications from patients at Broadmoor.[53] At the time the hospital was in a pitiful state and subject to major overcrowding with dangerous patients sharing dormitory accommodation. As a consequence of inadequate resources many patients were not gainfully employed. In some of these cases issues were also raised about the adequacy of the medical treatment being administered to patients. In the case of *X v United Kingdom*[54] the applicant com-

---

49 *Hogben v United Kingdom* 46 DR 231. The applicant had served 13 years and was being held in open conditions when the policy change was announced. He was immediately transferred to closed conditions.

50 *R v Secretary of State for the Home Department ex p Pierson* [1997] 3 WLR 492; [1997] 3 All ER 577.

51 (1981) 3 EHRR 161 at para 47.

52 Under Rule 50(1)(f), loss of remission has been replaced with the award of additional days. As with the previous system, additional days can be remitted under Rule 56.

53 *X v United Kingdom* (1981) 3 EHRR 131, 10 DR 5, 20 DR 5; *Y v United Kingdom* 10 DR 37; *X v United Kingdom* 28 DR 5.

plained, inter alia, about the failure to provide him with adequate medical treatment for the condition which had led to his detention under the Mental Health Act 1959. During the period of his detention he had received no suitable medication for his illness. He refused medication because he maintained that he was not in need of it because he was not ill. He was at all times under the charge of the same consultant psychiatrist. Their relationship had been most unhappy from the beginning. The Commission held by a majority that there had been no violation of article 3. However, in three powerful dissenting opinions Commissioners took an opposing position. They considered that the applicant spent four years in extremely unsatisfactory conditions subject to overcrowding etc without the treatment which it had been intended he should receive, in circumstances characterised by a most unsatisfactory relationship with the responsible doctor. It was also noted that there were considerable doubts about placing the applicant there in the first place.

16.36   These opinions may prove to be of great significance in the prison context in connection with post-tariff discretionary life sentence prisoners and HMP detainees. It is strongly arguable that once such prisoners are being held solely on preventative grounds the state is obliged to provide treatment to help reduce their dangerousness. Where such prisoners spend years in prison with no programmes being offered to them this may violate their article 3 rights.

Article 4

16.37   Article 4(3)(a) expressly excludes from the prohibition against forced labour any work to be done in the ordinary course of detention imposed in accordance with the provisions of article 5. Thus forced labour is permissible not only in relation to convicted offenders but also those held on remand.[55] Article 4 is silent on remuneration and the Commission has refused to read in any implied obligations as to the level of any payments.[56] It has been held that work done in the ordinary course of detention includes work done for private companies who contract with the prison service.[57]

---

54   28 DR 5.
55   *X v Switzerland* 18 DR 28.
56   Appl 3134/67 and Appl 3188-3206/67 Coll Dec 27 Dec, p97.
57   *Twenty one detained persons v FRG* Appls 3134/67, 3172/67 and 3188-206/67 6 April 1968, 11 Yearbook 528.

Article 5

16.38 Article 5(1) expressly allows for detention in certain enumerated circumstances including detention following conviction for a criminal offence. Article 5 is generally concerned with whether the detention in question has been imposed in accordance with a lawful procedure and for one of the expressly defined objects. It does not encompass questions relating to the nature or conditions of detention. Hence, a prisoner properly sentenced by a court cannot invoke article 5 if he is placed in solitary confinement as a result of a governor's adjudication.[58] Similarly article 5 is not engaged where the complaint relates to the security category in which a prisoner is held, or the inadequacy of the treatment which he is receiving in relation to his offending behaviour.[59] Moreover, the Court will look to the dominant purpose of detention. Hence, where an applicant was sentenced to an eight-year term of imprisonment for drug related offences, and the sentencing court directed that he be detained in an appropriate centre to receive treatment, but no such centres existed so that he served his term in prison, the Commission found no violation of article 5(1)(a). The main ground for his detention was punitive. The directions relating to treatment were merely arrangements for implementing the sentence. Failure to follow those arrangements did not engage article 5, though it may violate article 3.[60]

16.39 It is not contrary to article 5(1)(a) to enforce a sentence passed by the courts of another state. But the enforcing state should refrain from lending assistance by enforcing a sentence in respect of a conviction which has resulted from a flagrant denial of justice.[61]

---

58 *X v Switzerland* 11 DR 216.
59 See *Ashingdane v United Kingdom* (1985) 7 EHRR 529. The applicant was detained under the Mental Health Act, at first in a special hospital. He complained of the continuation of his detention in special secure conditions for a period of about two years following authorisation by the Secretary of State for his transfer to a local psychiatric hospital. The Court held that article 5(1)(e) was not concerned with restrictions on liberty of movement but with detention. The conditions in which the applicant was held in both hospitals amounted to detention. The decision that he be removed to the local hospital was not a decision that he could be restored his liberty. Nor did the differences between the two hospitals change the character of his detention. In both cases it was detention for the purposes of para (1)(e).
60 *Bizzotto v Greece* Appl 76/1995/582/668 [1997] EHRLR 178.
61 *Drozd and Janousek v France and Spain* (1992) 14 EHRR 745 para 110.

Article 5(4) and preventative detention

16.40   Article 5(4) entitles detained persons to a judicial determination of the lawfulness of their detention. Where detention follows conviction and sentence for a criminal offence, it is generally the case that article 5(4) rights are incorporated in the sentencing process, including any appellate proceedings that might be taken. This is so whenever the sentence is imposed for the purposes of retribution and deterrence. The sentence itself constitutes the lawful authority for the prisoner's detention throughout its duration.

16.41   Where detention has a preventative component, then as soon as the protection of the public becomes the sole basis for detention, the punitive element having been served, article 5(4) is engaged. This is because detention in the preventative phase is justified by reference to the prisoner's dangerousness, a characteristic which is susceptible to change over time. In passing the sentence the Court does no more than authorise a prisoner's detention so long as he remains dangerous. Article 5(4) requires that the issue of ongoing dangerousness, and hence the lawfulness of continued detention, be determined by a judicial body as soon as other grounds of detention have been extinguished, and importantly, in recognition of its mutable nature, at regular intervals thereafter. In English law, sentences which currently attract article 5(4) reviews are the discretionary life sentence and the sentence of detention at Her Majesty's Pleasure imposed on child murderers.[62] The mandatory life sentence imposed on adult murderers was held by the Court in

---

62 Convention jurisprudence on this issue has a long history, starting with *X v United Kingdom* (1982) 4 EHRR 188 and *Van Droogenbroeck v Belgium* (1982) 4 EHRR 443. The cases of *Weeks v United Kingdom* (1989) 10 EHRR 293 and *Thynne, Wilson and Gunnell v United Kingdom* (1991) 13 EHRR 666 concerned the nature of the discretionary life sentence and the right to an article 5(4) review. It was as a result of the *Thynne* case that s34 of the CJA 1991 (now s28 of the 1997 Act) was introduced, giving rise to oral hearings before discretionary lifer panels which have the power to direct a prisoner's release when s/he is no longer dangerous. In *Singh and Hussain v United Kingdom* (1996) 22 EHRR 1 the Court assimilated the position of children sentenced to mandatory detention at Her Majesty's Pleasure in cases of murder with that of discretionary lifers. The government responded by passing s28 of the 1997 Act which provides oral hearings once every two years for all post-tariff HMP detainees and discretionary lifers. In theory article 5(4) guarantees should attach to the extended part of a sentence imposed on preventative grounds by s2(2)(b) of the 1991 CJA. However, in the case of *Mansell v United Kingdom* [1997] EHRLR 666, the Commission rejected an application where half of a five-year term was imposed on preventative grounds, wrongly concluding that the sentence was wholly punitive.

Wynne v United Kingdom to be wholly punitive, attracting no article 5(4) rights once the sentencing process is complete.[63] The same view has been taken by the Commission of the sentence of custody for life imposed on young adult murderers between the ages of 18 to 21.[64]

16.42   Since the introduction of the 1991 Act, when a discretionary life sentence is passed the sentencing court will specify the period to be served to mark the requirements of retribution and deterrence.[65] Such a procedure complies with article 5(4) (and article 6). However, HMP detainees all have the punitive period or tariff fixed by the Home Secretary. In *Thompson and Venables v United Kingdom*[66] the Commission considered that such a procedure violated articles 5(4) and 6(1).

Procedural aspects of an article 5(4) review

16.43   Article 5(4) requires that the body whose task it is to determine the lawfulness of detention is independent of the executive and the parties. The procedure which it follows must be one which has 'a judicial character and gives to the individual concerned guarantees appropriate to the kind of deprivation of liberty in question, of [a] judicial procedure the forms of which may vary from one domain to another'.[67] The Parole Board has the necessary judicial character.[68] The body must have the power to take a legally binding decision to release the prisoner.[69] Other powers ancillary to the exercise of the power to direct release are not required by article 5(4). Hence, there

---

63 (1995) 19 EHRR 333. However, recent developments in domestic law, and in particular the House of Lords case of *R v Secretary of State ex p Pierson* [1997] 3 WLR 492, have largely jettisoned the theory that the mandatory life sentence is wholly punitive. The Court may soon be invited to revisit *Wynne* in the face of a strengthened case that its rationale is no different from the discretionary life sentence.

64 *John Ryan v United Kingdom* Appl 32875/96, Comm Dec, 1st July 1998.

65 S34 of the CJA 1991, now contained in s28(1) and (2) of the Crime (Sentences) Act 1997. For those discretionary lifers sentenced before the CJA 1991 came into force the Home Secretary sets the tariff. The Commission has admitted the case of *Watson v United Kingdom* Appl 21387/93, [1997] EHRLR 181, where it is argued that the tariff-fixing exercise attracts article 5(4) and/or article 6(1) safeguards, being a sentencing exercise.

66 Appl 1998.

67 *De Wilde, Ooms and Versyp v Belgium* (1979–80) 1 EHRR 373 paras 76–78; *X v United Kingdom* (1982) 4 EHRR 188, para 53.

68 *Weeks v UK* n62 para 61.

69 Both s34 of the CJA 1991 and s28 of the 1997 Act empower the Parole Board to direct release.

is no violation where the judicial authority lacks the power to direct temporary release,[70] or the transfer of a prisoner to open conditions,[71] for the purpose of testing dangerousness.

16.44   Where the assistance of other public authorities is required to secure a suitable release plan, eg obtaining a hostel placement, then, although article 5(4) does not require the Parole Board to have power to direct the authorities to find such a hostel, it does oblige the state to take measures to ensure that this step is taken or to provide for a judicial review to ensure that there is no unreasonable delay.[72]

16.45   The nature of the proceedings adopted under an article 5(4) review depends on the particular circumstances in which the proceedings take place.[73] Where questions arise involving the assessment of character or personal attitudes – as they invariably do with respect to discretionary lifers and HMP detainees – it may be essential for the proper and fair examination of the issues that the detained person be given an opportunity to participate in an oral hearing. In *Singh and Hussain v United Kingdom*[74] the Court considered that where disputed issues of fact arose, the possibility should exist of having witnesses examined and cross-examined and their credibility established in person. This is an extremely important procedural safeguard, particularly in recall cases, where the re-detention very often arises as a result of disputed allegations of misconduct on the part of a prisoner, which may or may not amount to a criminal offence. A prisoner is entitled to full disclosure of adverse material presented to the Board.[75] Article 5(4) appears to require the provision

---

70   *Roux v United Kingdom* Appl 12039/86 46 DR 263, where the Mental Health Review Tribunal adjourned its proceedings in order that the patient could have a period of unescorted leave. The Tribunal lacked the power to direct leave and the Home Office refused to grant leave on the ground that there would be an unacceptable risk to the public. See also *Ashingdane v United Kingdom* (1985) 7 EHRR 529, where the Court held that an article 5(4) review was not concerned to identify whether the applicant was receiving the treatment appropriate to detention in accordance with article 5(1)(e). The issue of appropriate treatment may arise under article 3.

71   *KM v United Kingdom* Appl 28376/95, [1997] EHRLR 299.

72   *Johnson v United Kingdom* [1999] 27 EHRR 296. This case concerned a patient detained under the Mental Health Act 1983 whose conditional discharge to a hostel was directed in June 1989. No hostel was found and in January 1993 he was finally granted an absolute discharge. The applicant was awarded £10,000 compensation. See also admissibility decision in *Tomsett v United Kingdom* Appl 25985/94 [1997] EHRLR 104.

73   *De Wilde, Ooms and Versyp v Belgium* n67.

74   (1996) 22 EHRR 1 at para 60.

75   *Weeks v United Kingdom* and *Thynne, Wilson and Gunnell v United Kingdom* n62.

of legal assistance and legal aid in cases of indigence.[76] Article 5(4) does not generally require a public hearing.[77]

16.46   Discretionary life sentence prisoners and HMP detainees who, following their conviction, are transferred to hospital by reason of mental disorder, are not currently permitted to apply to the Parole Board while they remain in hospital. Though they are entitled to apply to the MHRT, this body only has advisory powers. There appears to be a violation of article 5(4) in respect of these categories of detainees.[78]

Right to have lawfulness of detention determined speedily

16.47   This right has two aspects to it. First, it requires that a person must have access to a remedy speedily upon detention.[79] Second, once the remedy has been triggered, it must be processed speedily. Whether the condition of a speedy determination has been met is a question which depends on the circumstances of the particular case.[80] Relevant factors are the diligence shown by the national authorities or whether delay is attributable to matters for which state responsibility is engaged or for which the detainee is to blame.[81] It is for the state to justify any delay which, without more, appears to violate the need for

76 *Woukam Moudefo v France* A 141-B (1988) Com Rep paras 86–91; *Megyeri v Germany* (1993) 15 EHRR 584.

77 *Dhoest v Belgium* 55 DR 5 at 26. Hence, oral hearings before the Parole Board which are usually held in private are in conformity.

78 See the admissibility decision in the case of *Benjamin and Wilson v United Kingdom* [1998] EHRLR 226.

79 *X v United Kingdom* B 41 para 138 (Commission decision) where a delay of six months before a patient recalled under the Mental Health Act was entitled to apply to the MHRT was found to violate article 5(4). Under s32 of the 1997 Act a discretionary lifer and HMP detainee must be told of the reasons for recall on return to prison. He may then make representations against recall which will trigger an oral hearing before the Parole Board. Provided reasons are given speedily there is unlikely to be a violation.

80 *Sanchez-Reisse v Switzerland* (1987) 9 EHRR 71 para 55. See also admissibility decision in *Roux v United Kingdom* [1997] EHRLR 102.

81 See *Koendjbiharie v The Netherlands* (1991) 13 EHRR 820, where it took four months before the Court of Appeal directed release, during which time there was an adjournment without good reason and a further month before the decision was delivered. Legislation permitted three months in exceptional cases. And in *E v Norway* (1994) 17 EHRR 30 a 12-month period was also too long. Part of the delay arose from the judge's absence on vacation. The state was required to make arrangements, even during vacation, to ensure that urgent matters were dealt with speedily, given that the right to liberty was at stake.

speediness.[82] Where the review under article 5(4) is not completed until appellate or judicial review proceedings have been completed, the period ends with that final determination.[83] Hence, where proceedings for judicial review are brought in relation to a Parole Board decision suitable measures to expedite the leave application and full hearing will be required.

Right to compensation under article 5(5)

16.48 A person who has been detained in contravention of articles 5(1) to (4) is entitled to compensation. Where the initial decision to detain is one which is in accordance with article 5(1)(a) to (f) but is overturned on appeal or review, a right to compensation under article 5(5) does not arise. Hence, where a decision to recall a prisoner subject to a preventative sentence is taken and later overturned in proceedings for judicial review, the decision on review does not retrospectively affect the lawfulness of detention for the purposes of article 5(5).[84] Compensation would be payable, however, for any period of detention which violated the requirement of speediness in article 5(4).[85]

Article 6

16.49 Prisoners are subject to numerous decisions which affect the quality of their life while detained. Most of these decisions however are of an administrative kind and fall outwith the ambit of article 6 which is engaged only in relation to the determination of civil rights and obligations. So, for example, article 6 has no role to play in connection with security categorisation decisions.[86] Moreover, a dispute concerning the existence or extent of an amnesty following a criminal conviction falls outside the scope of article 6 since the dispute has ceased to involve a criminal charge against the applicant.[87]

---

82 *Koendjbiharie v The Netherlands* n81 paras 28–30.
83 *Luberti v Italy* (1984) 6 EHRR 441.
84 *Krzycki v FRG* 13 DR 57.
85 The point does not appear to have been taken in *Krzycki* despite considerable delay. Compensation was paid in *Johnson* n72.
86 *Brady v United Kingdom* Appl 8575/297 where the applicant was complaining in connection with the deliberations of the Category A Committee.
87 *Associacion De Aviadores De La Republica, Mata et al v Spain* Appl 10733/84 41 DR 211.

16.50   This does not mean that article 6 is irrelevant to prisoners.[88] Though imprisonment places some very real practical barriers in the way of the exercise of certain rights, the rights are not extinguished. Irrespective of such obstacles, a prisoner retains his/her right of access to the courts guaranteed in article 6(1).[89] The meaningful exercise of this right, therefore calls for the authorities to provide facilities to overcome the practical obstacles. So, for example, a prisoner must be afforded the facility to communicate with his/her lawyer with a view to taking legal proceedings. In the case of *Campbell and Fell v United Kingdom*[90] the Court held that ancillary to the right of access to the court is the right to have privileged communication with legal advisers.

16.51   However, the Convention organs have also recognised that in the context of imprisonment the right of access may be subject to a degree of justified restriction, for example, in the interests of security.[91] Where it is sought to restrict the right by, for instance, imposing restrictions on the conduct of visits by lawyers, the restriction must not impair the very essence of the right. It must serve a legitimate aim and comply with the principle of proportionality.[92] A general rule prohibiting privileged communication between lawyers would be impermissible, but such a restriction may be justifiable in the special circumstances of a particular case.[93] The approach of the domestic courts at common law has reflected Convention jurisprudence and prisoners are generally entitled to privileged communications with their lawyers both by correspon-

---

88   Eg see article 5(4) above, for the relevance of article 6 in the determination of the tariff for HMP detainees and discretionary lifers sentenced before the 1991 Act came into effect.

89   *Golder v UK* (1979–80) 1 EHRR 524.

90   (1985) 7 EHRR 165.

91   Ibid para 113.

92   *Ashingdane v United Kingdom* (1985) 7 EHRR 529, para 57.

93   Eg *Campbell v United Kingdom* 57 DR 148 where the matter of complaint was a visit by a lawyer which was received by the applicant, a category A lifer while he was detained in a hospital. The Commission accepted that security problems were acute in hospital and it was necessary for officers to stand by the door, which brought them within hearing distance. It also emphasised the fact that the applicant's stay in hospital was short and his lawyer was not prevented from having private communications following the applicant's return to prison.

dence and through visits.[94] However, the right of access to the court is only apt to protect communications which concern actual or contemplated civil or criminal litigation.[95] The stopping of letters to lawyers in relation to other legal matters will not violate article 6(1) but may engage article 8.[96]

16.52   The case of *Campbell and Fell* gave rise to another issue under article 6 – whether prison disciplinary proceedings involve the determination of a criminal charge calling for the guarantee of a fair trial under article 6(1). At the time, disciplinary proceedings were determined by the Board of Visitors which had far greater powers of punishment than governors do currently.[97] The applicants were charged with offences of mutiny, incitement to mutiny and gross personal violence to a prison officer.[98] The Board of Visitors was empowered to impose a penalty of up to three years, loss of remission. In fact it imposed 18 months. It held that the forfeiture of remission which the applicant, Campbell, risked incurring and the actual forfeiture awarded involved such serious consequences as regards the length of his detention that they had to be regarded, for Convention purposes, as criminal. The Court took a purposive approach to the construction of article 6. It did not matter that an award of loss of remission did not technically constitute detention, because the object and purpose of the Convention require that the imposition of a measure of such gravity should be accompanied by the guarantees of article 6. In concluding that the proceedings involved the determination of a criminal charge, the Court also took

---

94   Domestic law has closely mirrored Convention jurisprudence in this area. In *Raymond v Honey* [1983] AC 1 the House of Lords held that a prisoner retains all his civil rights that are not taken away expressly or by necessary implication and that the right of access to the Court was preserved despite imprisonment. In *R v Secretary of State for the Home Department ex p Anderson* [1984] QB 778 it was further held that the right of access to a solicitor was ancillary to that of access to the court. Finally in *R v Secretary of State for the Home Department ex p Leech* (No 2) [1994] QB 198, the Court of Appeal adopted the Convention concepts of legitimate aim and proportionality in establishing the test for determining whether a right has been infringed by necessary implication of a statute. These decisions have led to the currently worded rule 37A of the Prison Rules 1964.

95   *Grace v United Kingdom* 62 DR 22.

96   See chapter 3.

97   Governors are empowered to award a total of 42 additional days under rules 50(1)(f) and (2) of the Prison Rules 1964.

98   Since 1989 these no longer constitute offences against prison discipline. Serious offences of this kind are now dealt with under the criminal justice system.

account of the 'especially grave' character of the offences with which he was charged.[99]

Articles 8(2) to 11(2) – general considerations

16.53 Articles 8(2) to 11(2) permit limitations on the rights which are guaranteed which are in accordance with law, pursue one of the enumerated objects, and necessary in a democratic society. In its early jurisprudence the Commission fashioned a doctrine which substantially disadvantaged prisoners as compared with the general population. According to the implied limitation doctrine, as the lawful state of imprisonment necessarily creates practical barriers and hence limitations on the exercise of a right, states were absolved from justifying such limitations in accordance with the principles contained in sub-paragraphs (2) of articles 8–11. The doctrine was rejected by the Court in *Golder v United Kingdom*,[100] which held that restrictions were permissible only in accordance with the express wording of the Convention. It also noted that the right of access to a court, which was found in that case to be inherent in article 6(1) was not immune from the implied limitations doctrine, as article 6 had no similar provisions to article 8(2). The effect of this decision is that compliance with articles 8–11 imposes on a state positive obligations to facilitate the exercise of those rights in the case of prisoners.

16.54 Any restrictions on the rights of prisoners are provided for by the Prison Act 1952, the Prison Rules 1964 and internal guidance and directives such as standing orders and circular instructions. The question whether a measure is in accordance with law will turn, therefore, in each of the three articles on the same considerations. The first requirement is that the measure is in conformity with English law. This will be met where the restriction is authorised by the Rules and the relevant rule is not itself ultra vires the Prison Act

---

99 *Campbell* paras 67–72. Cf *Kiss v United Kingdom* 7 DR 55 where the Commission placed considerable reliance on the fact that loss of remission was not a deprivation of liberty in finding that the severity of the penalty was not within the criminal sphere. The penalty carried a potential of 180 days and the actual penalty imposed was 80 days' lost remission. See also, *Pelle v France* 50 DR 263 where the disciplinary offence could have been charged as a criminal offence. Here the penalty actually imposed of 18 days was found to be insufficient to bring it within the criminal sphere whether characterised as loss of liberty or not. The Commission did not find it of significance that the disciplinary offence was also criminal.

100 (1979–80) 1 EHRR 524 at para 44.

1952. Second, the law must be adequately accessible. Standing orders are now published and available to prisoners in prison libraries.[101] Circular instructions are less easily available. They are generally sent only to governors who then decide, at their discretion, how best to convey the information which they contain. The third principle is that the norm in question be formulated with sufficient precision to enable a citizen to regulate his conduct. S/he must be able to foresee to a degree that is reasonable in the circumstances, the consequences which a given action may entail. Where the norm confers a discretion, the scope of that discretion should be indicated. The greater the number of eventualities which must be covered by a norm, the broader will be the discretion which can legitimately be conferred.[102]

16.55   As well as the usual principles underlying the concepts of necessity, proportionality and the margin of appreciation applicable when determining whether the restriction of a right falls within para (2) of articles 8–11, the Convention organs have recognised that the need for an interference in the context of prisons must be evaluated having regard to 'the ordinary and reasonable requirements of imprisonment'. The 'prevention of disorder and crime', for example, may justify wider measures of interference in the case of a prisoner than in that of a person at liberty.[103]

Article 8

16.56   Imprisonment has the most drastic impact upon a prisoner's private and family life. S/he may find him/herself detained in a prison hundreds, if not thousands, of miles from his/her home community and the family and friends who live there. His location and opportunities to receive visits and correspond with the outside world are all matters which have a central bearing upon the quality of his/her life while

---

101 In *Grace v United Kingdom* 62 DR 22, the Commission was of the opinion that the censorship practices contained in standing order 5, being both public and grounded in the legal authority of the Prison Rules, were measures taken in accordance with law.
102 *Silver v United Kingdom* (1983) 5 EHRR 347.
103 *Golder v United Kingdom* n100 and 77-A DR 75.

s/he serves his/her sentence. Article 8 rights are, therefore, all impor-tant for the prisoner.[104]

Private and family life

16.57 The right to private life comprises to a certain extent the right to establish and develop relationships with other human beings, particularly in the emotional field, for the development and fulfil-ment of one's personality.[105] Prisoners are, therefore, entitled to asso-ciate with one another[106] though segregation on disciplinary grounds can be justified as a measure taken in accordance with law and necessary in a democratic society for the prevention of disorder.[107] It is an essential part of both private life and the rehabilitation of pris-oners that their contact with the outside world be maintained as far as practicable, in order to facilitate their reintegration into society on release, for example, by providing visiting facilities for the prisoners' family and friends and by allowing correspondence with them and others.[108] Meeting this obligation will only exceptionally require the transfer of a prisoner from one prison to another.[109] The refusal to transfer a prisoner from one country in which he has been sentenced

---

104 In England and Wales the relevant rules and administrative guidance concerning prisoners' opportunities for contact with the outside world are contained in rules 33, 34, 37 and 37A of the Prison Rules 1964 and standing order 5. These have been much amended both in the light of European and domestic jurisprudence and, in large measure conform with the requirements of article 8.

105 *X v Iceland* 5 DR 86.

106 *McFeely v United Kingdom* (1981) 3 EHRR 161.

107 Ibid para 82.

108 *X v United Kingdom* 30 DR 113, (1983) 5 EHRR 260, and *McCotter v United Kingdom* (1993) 15 EHRR CD 98. In *Lant v United Kingdom* 45 DR 236 the Commission found that a refusal to amend the applicant's prison records to show his new name, did not relate to his right to respect for his private life, to the public administration of prisons.

109 *Campbell v United Kingdom* Appl 7819/77, Decision, 6 May 1978 paras 30–32 unreported, and *Ouinas v France* Appl 13756/88, 65 D R 265, where the visits in question were from the applicant's daughter, in respect of whom the applicant had a court order for access. Even so the applicant's placement in a distant prison was justified on security grounds and in view of the resources the state could provide to facilitate visits. See also, *Wakefield v United Kingdom* 66 DR 251 and *S v United Kingdom* (1993) 15 EHRR CD 106 – transfer of an Irish prisoner from England to Northern Ireland.

to his country of origin under the *European Convention on the Transfer of Sentenced Prisoners* does not infringe article 8.[110]

16.58   Commission jurisprudence shows a consistent pattern: interferences with private and family life are readily found, but applications founder in the face of justifications put forward by states under article 8(2). The lawful objects pursued in this area tend to be administrative and security requirements, the prevention of disorder and crime and the protection of the rights and freedoms of others. So, for example, the state is justified in restricting family visits to once in every two months;[111] one visit of one hour every month[112]; refusing an application for temporary release to attend a family funeral on security grounds;[113] subjecting a family to closed visits within the hearing of prison officers;[114] imposing a policy restricting applications for compassionate leave to cases where a family member is dangerously ill;[115] keeping prisoners under surveillance while they use the toilet and searching them before and after visits;[116] requiring prisoners to wear prison clothing;[117] incarcerating a Bahamian prisoner in the United Kingdom;[118] transferring a prisoner from one facility to another without informing his family before they attempted to visit him;[119] disclosing to staff that a prisoner is HIV positive;[120] or requiring a prisoner under threat of penalty to provide a urine sample for drug testing purposes.[121]

110 *Hacisuleymanoglu v Italy* Appl 23241/94 79-B DR 121, where the Commission rejected the application on the ground that the Convention does not confer a right to transfer, such a transfer being subject to the prior agreement of the sentencing country.

111 Appl 7455/76, 13.12.76 unpublished.

112 *Boyle and Rice v United Kingdom* (1988) 10 EHRR 425 para 74. A claim that exceptional facilities should have been available was rejected by the Court which found that in general it is justifiable to apply to prisoners a uniform regime avoiding the appearance of arbitrariness or discrimination.

113 Appl 3603/68 4.2.70 Collection 31, p 48 para 50.

114 *X v United Kingdom* 14 DR 246.

115 *Boyle and Rice v United Kingdom* n112 paras 79–81.

116 *McFeely* n106 paras 80 and 81.

117 *McFeely* n106 para 83. See also *X v UK* 28 DR 530, (1983) 5 EHRR 162 and *T V v Finland* 76-A DR 140; (1994) 18 EHRR CD 179, where the requirement was justified when an HIV positive prisoner was required to wear prison clothing when attending outside medical appointments.

118 Appl 5712/72 Dec 18.7.74 Collection 46 p112 para 116.

119 Appl 7647/76 Dec 28.2.77 unpublished.

120 *T V v Finland* 76A DR 140, 18 EHRR CD 179.

121 *A B v Switzerland* 80-B DR 66. See also *Galloway v UK* [1999] EHRLR 119.

Moreover, the Convention organs have allowed states a wide margin of appreciation in balancing 'legitimate interests of public order and security and that of the rehabilitation of prisoners'.[122]

16.59 The issue of a right to conjugal visits has come before the Commission on a number of occasions over the years and been consistently dismissed.[123] Though a recent application received a sympathetic hearing, the time is not yet ripe for this right to be extended to prisoners.[124]

Correspondence

16.60 Prison authorities are under a duty to provide prisoners with the necessary facilities for the effective flow of authorised correspondence. Prisoners should be informed of defects in the postal service.[125]

16.61 The right to respect for correspondence does not prohibit some measure of control over prisoners' correspondence, regard being paid to the ordinary and reasonable requirements of imprisonment.[126] That being said, the Convention organs have afforded the right to respect for correspondence a special status among article 8 rights. This is explained by their recognition of the huge importance that correspondence assumes in the closed prison world, where visits are infrequent and of short duration and association within the prison is not necessarily with persons of one's choice. It is sometimes a prisoner's only link with the outside world.[127]

---

122 *Silver and Others v United Kingdom* (1981) 3 EHRR 475 (Comm Dec) para 290.

123 *X v United Kingdom* 2 DR 105 and Appl 3603/68, C D, Vol 31 p48. Some ten years later in *X and Y v Switzerland* 13 DR 241 the Commission recognised the dynamic nature of the Convention by referring expressly and with approval to 'the reformative movement in several European countries as regards an improvement of the conditions of imprisonment with the possibility for detained persons of continuing their conjugal life to a limited extent.'

124 *ELH and PBH v United Kingdom* [1998] EHRLR 231. The applicants here argued that they were practising Catholics and so could not avail themselves of facilities for artificial insemination.

125 *Grace v United Kingdom* 62 DR 22.

126 *Silver v United Kingdom* (1984) 5 EHRR 347 (Court judgment) para 98.

127 *Campbell v United Kingdom* (1993) 15 EHRR 137 at para 45. So for example, placing quotas on the number of letters which a prisoner can write has been justified for the prevention of disorder – *Chester v UK* 68 DR 65.

16.62   In the test case of *Silver and Others v United Kingdom*[128] both the Commission and Court considered the compatibility with article 8 of a substantial number of provisions prohibiting correspondence contained in rules 33 and 34 of the Prison Rules 1964 and standing orders, as they were framed until 1981. Correspondence prohibited included the following categories of material: complaints about prison treatment, even if addressed to MPs and legal advisers, which had not first been ventilated through prison channels; material intended for publication; grossly improper language or threats of violence; material deliberately calculated to hold the prison authorities up to contempt; representations about trial, conviction or sentence addressed to anyone other than the Home Secretary; discussions of crime in general or the crime of others; material attempting to stimulate public agitation or petition; and allegations against prison officers. Prisoners were also prevented from corresponding altogether with persons other than their family or friends who were already known to the prisoner before s/he commenced his/ her sentence.

16.63   The Commission rejected as disproportionate the prior ventilation rule, though it accepted that it was a legitimate aim of prison administration to ensure that complaints were internally ventilated. This aim could be met by a simultaneous ventilation rule. It found no sufficient justification for stopping letters to other persons containing 'complaints'. It emphasised the importance to a prisoner of having a channel to ventilate frustrations. Similarly, with respect to the limitation on persons with whom prisoners might correspond, the Commission found that the general prohibition had no regard to the status or otherwise of the addressee, the security risk posed by the prisoner, the contents of the correspondence or its likely effect.[129] In relation to material intended for publication, the Commission recognised legitimate but conflicting interests. On the one hand, access to the media is an important element in a democratic society. On the other, the difficult task of prison administration may be affected by the exploitation of scurrilous material in the press. It could conceive that prison staff morale might be undermined though

128 (1981) 3 EHRR 475 (Comm Dec) and (1984) 5 EHRR 347 (Court). The judgment of the Commission is of greater relevance than the Court's. Following the Commission decision the government amended standing order 5 to take account of most of the Commission's findings.

129 Similarly in *Domenichini v Italy* Appl 101/1995/607/695, [1997] EHRLR 192 the Court found judicial powers to censor a prisoner's mail framed in terms of an uncertain and unstructured discretion to be over broad.

it noted that the normal protection of the civil law of defamation and disciplinary proceedings were available. Such considerations did not justify the blanket prohibition where no account was taken of the kind of material involved, the security risk of the prisoner, the status of the addressee, the contents of the letter or its likely effect on legitimate interests of prison administration. The same approach was taken to correspondence containing allegations against prison officers.[130]

16.64   On the issue of correspondence containing material which is supposedly deliberately calculated to hold the prison authorities up to contempt, the Commission again recognised the conflicting interests at play. Prison staff morale was pitted against the need to protect a prisoner's right to express him/herself freely in correspondence which may involve the expression of his/her grievances or frustrations in emotional or vehement terms, this often being an essential outlet in closed community existence. Once again the measure was held to be over broad. With respect to correspondence containing representations about trial, conviction and sentence, the Commission could find no legitimate interest which might be threatened by a prisoner addressing such matters to persons other than the Home Secretary. The Commission found that petition-raising constituted a normal activity in a democratic society and in the prison context it might be appropriate to bring to public attention injustices, such as prison conditions. At the same time it recognised that it might be unreasonable to oblige prison authorities to offer adequate facilities to enable prisoners to organise such campaigns personally, as to do so might pose a threat to prison order. Once again a blanket prohibition was over broad. Prohibition of correspondence seeking to stimulate public agitation, on the other hand, was found to be justified for the purpose of preventing disorder and crime.

16.65   Finally, as a further mark of the central importance of correspondence to the quality of prison life, the Commission found that the prohibition on letters containing grossly improper language was not proportionate to the aims of preventing disorder or protecting morals. It was observed that it is an essential feature of freedom of expression in a democratic society that the individual may correspond freely in whatever terms he or she desires, even though such terms may be vulgar, controversial, shocking or offensive. It added

---

130 See also *Pfeifer and Plankl v Austria* (1992) 14 EHRR 692, where the communication concerned derogatory remarks about the prison authorities.

that this freedom may be particularly important for prisoners who are subject to the daily frustrations of closed community life.

16.66   The measure prohibiting letters containing threats of violence was, unsurprisingly, found to be justified under article 8(2) for the prevention of disorder and crime. The Commission also found that the rule prohibiting letters discussing crime in general or the crimes of others was justified for the prevention of disorder and crime.[131]

16.67   In a later case a restriction prohibiting prisoners from corresponding in connection with a private criminal prosecution was found to be unjustified, as was a general prohibition on prisoners' letters to unofficial or independent organisations.[132]

16.68   Restrictions which have been held to be justified are: the stopping of letters which constitute an abuse of extra letter facilities for legal matters; stopping letters to other prisoners, where in the circumstances this is justified in the interests of rehabilitation, security, good order or discipline; a prohibition against correspondence containing obscure or coded messages.[133]

Legal correspondence

16.69   In the case of *Silver* the Commission confirmed that prisoners' correspondence with lawyers is of a privileged nature and, in principle, should be unhindered. However, it also suggested that a requirement that complaints to lawyers concerning issues arising in connection with imprisonment should be simultaneously ventilated might be a justifiable restriction. As a result the government introduced a simultaneous ventilation rule. In *Grace v United Kingdom* the Commission found that the stopping of letters sent without simul-

---

131   Where the discussion consists of approving the crimes of others, or advocating crime, the Commission's approach is understandable. However, where the purpose of the letter is to raise another person's crime as a miscarriage case, there would not appear to be any legitimate aim justifying a restriction.

132   *Farrant v United Kingdom* 50 DR 5. Following the decision of the House of Lords in *Raymond v Honey* [1983] AC 1, the government removed the prohibition against letters concerning private prosecutions. See also *McCallum v UK* (1991) 13 EHRR 597.

133   *Grace v United Kingdom* 62 DR 22.

taneous ventilation was unjustified as a photocopy could have been taken by the authorities and the letter then sent out.[134]

16.70   Unlike general correspondence, correspondence between lawyers and prisoners concern matters of a private and confidential character, irrespective of whether they concern actual or contemplated litigation. In principle they are privileged under article 8. This means that the prison authorities may open a letter from a lawyer to a prisoner when they have reasonable cause to believe that it contains an illicit enclosure which the normal means of detection have failed to disclose. The letter should, however, only be opened and should not be read. Suitable guarantees for preventing the reading of a letter should be provided, eg opening the letter in the presence of the prisoner. The reading of a prisoner's mail to and from a lawyer, on the other hand, should be permitted only in exceptional circumstances when the authorities have reasonable cause to believe that the privilege is being abused in that the contents of the letter endanger prison security or the safety of others or are otherwise of a criminal nature. What may be regarded as a 'reasonable cause' will depend on all the circumstances but it presupposes the existence of facts or information which would satisfy the objective observer that the privileged channel of communication is being abused.[135] The mere possibility of abuse is outweighed by the need to respect the confidentiality attaching to the lawyer-client relationship.[136]

16.71   Standing order 5 has been amended in order to bring it in line with these Convention cases. Not all the regulations have been tested for compliance. Moreover, decisions in individual cases still fall to be justified in accordance with article 8.

134 In fact the simultaneous ventilation rule did not survive long. It was held to be ultra vires the Prison Act 1952 by the Divisional Court in *R v Secretary of State for the Home Department ex p Anderson* [1984] 1 QB 778 on the ground that it constituted an unlawful impediment to a prisoner's right of access to the courts. This presents an interesting example of the common law providing more stringent safeguards of a fundamental right than the Convention.

135 *Campbell v United Kingdom* (1993) 15 EHRR 137 at paras 45–8. The Court also held that the opening of mail from the Commission was not justified. The government's argument that prisoners may seek to forge Commission stationery to smuggle articles in, was found to be so negligible that it must be discounted.

136 Once legal correspondence is in a prisoner's possession, it is the practice in a number of prisons for it to be searched without the inmate being present. This practice was held to be intra vires and reasonable by the Court of Appeal in *R v SS for the Home Department ex p Simms* [1998] 2 All ER 491. However, it is doubtful that it complies with article 8.

Article 9

16.72   There has been very little success in applications brought by prisoners under this article. For example, though a Sikh applicant, of high caste, established that it was contrary to his religion that he should be required to sweep the floor of his cell, the Commission found that the requirement that he do so was justifiable in the interests of the protection of the applicant's and other prisoners' health.[137] There was no violation when a book containing religious and philosophical writings was withheld on the ground that it also contained an illustrated section on martial arts and techniques of self-defence which could be dangerous if used against others.[138]

16.73   Article 9 is not engaged in connection with the activities of an organisation whose aims are of an idealistic nature, such as the provision of legal advice to prisoners and the promotion of their interests on a non-commercial basis. Its concern is with the sphere of personal beliefs and religious creeds.[139] Nor does article 9 guarantee the right to special category status as a political prisoner. Moreover, freedom to manifest religion or belief 'in practice' does not include the right of a prisoner to wear his/her own clothes in prison.[140]

Article 10

16.74   Where a complaint relates to expression through correspondence then article 8 is the lex specialis. However, if expression is in the form of private writings or academic or artistic material, even if it is to be sent out of the prison, it falls within the terms of 'freedom to impart information' in article 10.[141]

16.75   The right to receive information does not entitle a prisoner to

---

137   *X v United Kingdom* 22 DR 5. See also *X v United Kingdom* Appl 1753/63, Coll Dec 16 p20.

138   *X v United Kingdom* 5 DR 100. See also *H v United Kingdom* (1993) 16 EHRR CD 44; and *Islam v UK* (1996) 22 EHRR CD 215 where the applicant complained of the prison authorities' refusal to amend its records to his new name which was changed by deed poll to reflect his religious convictions. Application admitted and withdrawn when government agreed to alter its records.

139   *Vereniging Rechtswinkels Utrecht v The Netherlands* 46 DR 200.

140   *McFeely and Others v United Kingdom* 20 DR 44, paras 27–30.

141   *T v United Kingdom* 49 DR 5.

know the identity of the members of the Category A Committee responsible for reviewing a prisoner's security category.[142] A restriction on the right to receive information in the form of access to a radio or periodicals may be justified as a disciplinary penalty. However, it is not enough that the penalty is lawfully imposed and the disciplinary measures were taken in pursuit of a permissible purpose within article 10(2); the restriction itself must directly serve such a purpose. Hence, a penalty depriving a prisoner of writing materials may be justified where those materials were the tools of acts of indiscipline, but not where the penalty is imposed for no other reason than that it is an available punishment.[143]

16.76   The case of *T v United Kingdom*[144] raised a number of issues under article 10. The applicant protested against wearing prison clothes with the result that he spent long periods of time in segregation and was subjected to a number of disciplinary measures. He complained, inter alia, of a blanket ban upon sending private writings out of the prison. The writings in issue were apparently bona fide academic articles. Consistent with its approach in *Silver* the Commission found the blanket ban unduly wide. The applicant also complained that he was refused access to books kept in the library because his attendance there was prohibited while he remained naked or dressed only in a blanket. Though the Commission was satisfied that adequate access was available by other means, its analysis demonstrates that article 10 imposes quite stringent obligations on the authorities to make information available to prisoners in the form of books, newspapers and periodicals which requires a relatively greater degree of flexibility to disciplinary problems from prisoners with an intransigent resolve against the disciplinary system. Even though the applicant was subject to disciplinary measures, the authorities' duty to secure him access to information continued, as such access had no bearing on the disciplinary problems which his case presented. Finally, the Commission concluded that the risk of the applicant's private papers being scrutinised by the authorities was justified in the interests of

142 *X v United Kingdom* 20 DR 202, where the Commission held that the concept of 'information' contained in article 10(1) was sufficiently extensive to cover the material sought.

143 See *McFeely* 20 DR 44, paras 105–111, where the materials which were removed as a disciplinary penalty had been used for improper purposes such as the sending of clandestine messages and starting fires. Cf *T v United Kingdom* 49 DR 5 where the applicant was deprived of writing materials which he had used for private writings.

144 Note 143.

public safety and the prevention of disorder and crime, for the protection of health and morals and for the protection of the rights of others.[145]

16.77   A distinction must be drawn between the absolute prohibition on the receipt of newspapers or periodicals or their prohibition over a sustained period and prohibition of individual publications on specific grounds.[146]

16.78   Article 10 does not normally include a general and unfettered right for any private citizen or organisation to have access to broadcasting time on radio or television in order to forward his/her opinion.[147] However, where a restriction is imposed by prison authorities on access which would otherwise be available, article 10 may be infringed. The issue has arisen in one case brought against the United Kingdom,[148] where the applicant, a mandatory lifer protesting his innocence, complained of a ban on telephone communications with the media contained in paragraph 2B of standing order 5 part G. This prohibits inmates, save in exceptional circumstances, telephoning the media if it is intended or likely that the call itself or the information communicated in it will be used for publication or broadcast. The Commission rejected the application, though it accepted that the applicant's article 10 rights were infringed, on the ground that it was legitimate for effective controls to be exercised on communications with the media in the interest of order and the morals or rights or freedoms of others. Effective control could not be exercised over this medium of communication by less restrictive means and the applicant had other means of communicating, namely by correspondence and to a limited extent through visits with the media.[149] In rejecting the complaint the Commission nonetheless

---

145 Following the Commission's decision amendments were made to prison service standing orders with a view to the relaxation of the regulations concerning prisoners' access to writing materials and the despatch of writings and artistic materials out of prison.

146 *Lowes v United Kingdom* 59 DR 244 where the Commission rejected an application relating to the withholding of a single issue of a magazine, which contained anti-Semitic material. As the infringement was particular rather than general the Commission afforded the authorities a wide margin of appreciation.

147 *Haider v Austria* 83-A DR 66.

148 *Bamber v United Kingdom* [1998] EHRLR 110.

149 The Commission here relied on paras 37 and 37A of standing order 5(B), which entitles journalists to visit prisoners only if they undertake not to publish anything said, or only on terms permitted by the governor (whatever they may be).

emphasised that freedom of expression is one of the essential foundations of a democratic society and that any restriction on the means available to an individual for communicating the relevant information may be such as to inhibit its effective communication. It also did not underestimate the role that the media may play in cases where there has been a miscarriage of justice. Importantly the Commission rejected one of the government's purported justifications, namely preventing distress which might be caused to victims or their families, if the applicant communicated issues relating to his conviction. Such a ground could not justify a restriction of such broad scope as to prevent the applicant from making even serious representations to the media about his conviction and irrespective of whether the call might be transmitted.[150]

Article 11

16.79   As the language of article 11 suggests, the concept of freedom of association, of which the right to form and join trade unions is a special aspect, is concerned with the right to form or be affiliated with a group organisation pursuing particular aims. It does not concern the right of prisoners to 'associate' with other persons in the sense of enjoying the personal company of others.[151] Prisoners should be free to join trade unions, though the prison authorities are under no positive obligation to protect a prisoner's rights as a trade unionist.[152]

Article 12

16.80   Under s1 of the Marriage Act 1983 prisoners are entitled to marry with the ceremony being conducted in the prison.[153] Neither articles

150   For a case challenging the restriction on visits from the media in the domestic field, see *R v Secretary of State for the Home Department ex p Simms and O'Brien* n136.

151   *X v United Kingdom* (1993) 5 EHRR 260, where the applicant's complaint that he had been prevented from receiving a visit from an acquaintance to discuss his medical history was held by the Commission to be manifestly ill-founded. And *McFeely* n143 paras 112–115.

152   *X v United Kingdom* 24 DR 57.

153   The legislation was passed following the successful case of *Hamer v UK* (1982) 4 EHRR 139. The case of *Draper v United Kingdom* 24 DR 72 raised identical issues. See also *Szrabjer and Clarke v UK* [1998] EHRLR 230 on suspension of state pensions for prisoners.

12 nor 8 have yet successfully been invoked in relation to the absence of conjugal visits.[154]

Article 14

16.81   Cases under article 14 have rarely succeeded in relation to prisoners. For example, in the case of *X v Switzerland*[155] the applicant, a 15-year-old boy held on remand was required in law to work. His complaint that this amounted to a violation of article 14 taken together with article 4 because adults detained on remand were not so required was rejected by the Commission, which did not consider that the differentiation was one between comparable groups, as a minor's position in law is fundamentally different both before and after an offence has been proved. The Swiss system, as well as a large number of Council of Europe states, provided a much wider choice of measures to deal with minors and placed more emphasis on the need for an understanding of the personality and for education and training. Article 5(1)(d) of the Convention is itself a reflection of this fundamental difference.

Article 1 of the First Protocol

16.82   The power under the Prison Rules to deduct from a prisoner's gross weekly earnings a sum to be used to provide entertainment and other facilities for prisoners, does not violate this article.[156]

16.83   Though the state pension does fall within article 1 of protocol 1, the law requiring its suspension while a pensioner is serving a term of imprisonment has been held by the Commission to be in the public interest. Prisoners have no outgoings, being kept at the expense of the state. Unsurprisingly the Commission did not find

154 *X v United Kingdom* 2 DR 105, where the Commission held that the right to found a family, though absolute, does not mean that a person must at all times be given the actual possibility to procreate his descendants. A convicted person serving a sentence of imprisonment is responsible himself for that predicament. The implied limitations doctrine is clearly relevant to article 12.

155 18 DR 28.

156 *Davis v United Kingdom* Appl 27042/95, [1997] EHRLR 298 (Comm Dec).

attractive an argument that would result in prisoners being better off than pensioners in the community.[157]

Article 2 of the First Protocol

16.84 This article confers only the right in principle for prisoners to avail themselves of the means of instruction existing at a given time. The Convention lays down no specific obligations concerning the extent of these means and the manner of their organisation or subsidisation. It is concerned primarily with elementary education and not necessarily advanced studies such as technology.[158] However, this article is of importance for young persons in custody of compulsory school age.

157 *Szrabjer and Clarke v United Kingdom* [1998] EHRLR 230.
158 2 DR 50.

CHAPTER 17

Mental health

17.1   Introduction

17.3   Detention under article 5 of the Convention

17.5   Meaning of 'unsound mind'

17.6   Lawfulness

17.7   Procedure prescribed by law

17.9   Emergency admissions

17.11   Voluntary surrender

17.12   The meaning of 'detention' under article 5

17.13   Periodic review

17.15   The reviewing body

17.17   The nature of the review

17.18   Procedural safeguards at review hearings

17.20   The timing of reviews

17.23   Release

17.28   Detention after or as a result of criminal
        proceedings

17.32   Conditions of detention: article 3

Introduction

17.1   The Convention is relevant to a number of mental health issues, in particular the circumstances in which those with mental health problems can be detained. Therefore, the starting point is usually article 5 (the right to liberty).[1] However, other provisions of the Convention are also relevant, including article 3 (the prohibition on inhuman and degrading treatment), article 6(1) (the right to a fair trial), article 8 (the protection of private life) and article 12 (the right to marry).

17.2   Mental health issues also overlap with matters covered elsewhere. Preventative detention is dealt with in chapters 15[2] and 16;[3] access to court is dealt with in chapter 13.[4]

Detention under article 5 of the Convention

17.3   The detention of 'persons of unsound mind' is permitted under the Convention. Article 5(1) provides that:

> Everyone has the right to liberty and security of person. No one shall be deprived of his liberty save in the following cases and in accordance with the procedure prescribed by law:
> ...
> (e) the lawful detention of persons for the prevention of the spreading of infectious diseases, of persons of unsound mind, alcoholics or drug addicts or vagrants.

Like all the exceptions provided for in article 5(1), paragraph (e) is to be narrowly construed.[5]

17.4   The pre-conditions of detention are, therefore, three-fold:

1) the individual in question must be of 'unsound mind';

2) the basis upon which s/he is detained must be 'lawful'; and

3) any procedure prescribed in domestic law must be strictly followed.

Each of these requires analysis.

---

1   See paras 3.21 to 3.86.
2   Para 15.64.
3   Paras 16.40 to 16.42.
4   Paras 13.6 to 13.11.
5   *Winterwerp v Netherlands* (1979–80) 2 EHRR 387 at para 37.

Meaning of 'unsound mind'

17.5   In *Winterwerp v Netherlands*[6] the European Court took the view that the term 'persons of unsound mind' was not susceptible to a definitive interpretation because its meaning was continually being evolved by advances in medical understanding and treatment, and by changes in societal attitudes. The domestic authorities are, therefore, afforded some discretion in the interpretation they adopt. To date there have been no cases in Strasbourg where the medical view about the existence of a mental illness has been challenged.[7] However, as a bare minimum, the European Court has emphasised that article 5(1)(e) cannot permit detention of an individual merely because his/her 'views or behaviour deviate from norms prevailing in a particular society'.[8]

Lawfulness

17.6   Detention is permitted under article 5(1)(e) only for self-protection and/or the protection of the public.[9] And on that basis, in the landmark case of *Winterwerp v Netherlands*, the European Court laid down three basic requirements of detention under article 5(1)(e):

1) the medical disorder relied upon to justify detention must be established by objective medical expertise;

2) the nature or degree of the disorder must be sufficiently extreme to justify detention; and

3) the detention should last only as long as the medical disorder (and its required severity) persist.[10]

In *Ashingdane v UK*[11] the Court added the requirement that the detention of a person of unsound mind is lawful only if it is in a hospital, clinic or other appropriate institution.[12]

---

6 Note 5.

7 Reid, *A Practitioner's Guide to the European Convention on Human Rights* (Sweet & Maxwell, 1998) p293.

8 Note 5 at para 37.

9 *Guzzardi v Italy* (1981) 3 EHRR 333.

10 Implicit in this requirement is the right to periodic review: see paras 17.13 to 17.22.

11 (1985) 7 EHRR 528.

12 But that does not require the state to provide any particular level of treatment so as to ensure that an individual is detained no longer than absolutely necessary.

Procedure prescribed by law

17.7   The requirement in article 5(1) that any detention be 'in accordance with the procedure prescribed by law' means that any procedures set out in domestic law for the detention of the mentally ill must be strictly followed. The principle underlying this requirement is one of 'fair and proper procedure, namely that any measure depriving a person of his liberty should issue from and be executed by an appropriate authority and should not be arbitrary'.[13]

17.8   In *Van der Leer v Netherlands*[14] the European Court emphasised that the phrase 'a procedure prescribed by law' required not only conformity with both substantive and procedural law at the domestic level but also a lack of arbitrariness. That case concerned a Dutch law which required that any court determining detention should hear from the individual concerned, unless an objection were raised and supported by a psychiatric report. Since the court ordering the applicant's detention had neither heard from the applicant nor obtained a psychiatric report, the European Court found a breach of article 5(1)(e).

Emergency admissions

17.9   The Convention requirements for emergency admissions to hospital of individuals considered to be mentally ill are not strict. In *Winterwerp v Netherlands* (above) the European Court expressly identified 'emergency cases' as constituting an exception to the principle that individuals should not be deprived of their liberty unless 'reliably' shown to be of 'unsound mind'.

17.10   The European Court endorsed this position in *X v UK*[15] and added that it could not be inferred from its judgment in *Winterwerp v Netherlands* that the 'objective medical evidence' referred to in that case must in all conceivable cases be obtained before, rather than after confinement of a person on the ground of mental health. In the Court's view, 'where a provision of domestic law is designed amongst other things, to authorise emergency confinement of persons capable of presenting a danger to others, it would be impracticable

13   *Winterwerp v Netherlands* n5 at para 45.
14   (1990) 12 EHRR 567.
15   (1982) 4 EHRR 188.

to require thorough medical examination prior to any arrest or detention.'[16] And in *Wassink v Netherlands*[17] the European Court found no breach of article 5(4) where the President of the court consulted experts and witnesses by telephone.

Voluntary surrender

17.11   The mere fact that an individual voluntarily surrendered to detention does not exclude the application of article 5 of the Convention. In *De Wilde, Ooms and Versyp v Belgium*,[18] where the applicants had given themselves up to the police under Belgian vagrancy laws, the European Court held that:

> The right to liberty is too important in a 'democratic society' within the meaning of the Convention for a person to lose the benefit of the protection of the Convention for the single reason that he gives himself up to be taken into detention.[19]

Accordingly, all the article 5 safeguards against the arbitrary deprivation of liberty are relevant.

The meaning of 'detention' under article 5

17.12   The expression 'detention' in article 5(1)(e) refers to deprivation of, and not mere restrictions upon, liberty. In *Ashingdane v UK*[20] the applicant had been committed to a mental hospital after conviction for a number of offences. He was placed in a secure special hospital but, when his condition improved, the Home Secretary authorised his return to his local psychiatric hospital. When the hospital refused to accept him and the Secretary of State refused to order the transfer to proceed, the applicant complained that his rights under article 5(1)(e) had been violated. The European Court unanimously dismissed his complaint on the basis that both the special and local hospital regimes involve a form of detention. Failure to move him was, therefore, not a wrongful continuation of his detention.

16   Ibid at para 41.
17   A/185-A Court (27 September 1990) (unreported).
18   (1979–80) 1 EHRR 373.
19   Ibid at para 65.
20   Note 11.

Periodic review

17.13   Article 5(4) provides that:

> Everyone who is deprived of his liberty by arrest or detention shall
> be entitled to take proceedings by which the lawfulness of his
> detention shall be decided speedily by a court and his release
> ordered if the detention is not lawful.

It has special relevance in mental health cases because, as noted
above, the lawfulness of detention under article 5(1)(e) depends on
the persistence of a mental disorder severe enough to justify
detention.[21] This implies not only review, but periodic review.

17.14   In *Megyeri v Germany*[22] the European Court identified as one of
the key principles to have emerged from its case-law on mental health
the following:

> A person of unsound mind who is compulsorily confined in a
> psychiatric institution for an indefinite or lengthy period is in
> principle entitled, at any rate where there is no automatic periodic
> review of a judicial character, to take proceedings 'at reasonable
> intervals' before a court to put in issue the 'lawfulness' – within the
> meaning of the Convention – of his detention.[23]

The nature of the reviewing body, the character of the decisions it
makes and the existence of procedural safeguards are, therefore, all
important Convention issues.

The reviewing body

17.15   Article 5(4) requires that any review be undertaken by a 'court': that
is, a judicial body independent of the executive with 'court-like'
attributes.[24] A specialised body such as a Mental Health Review
Tribunal may be a 'court' so long as it enjoys the necessary independence, offers sufficient procedural safeguards and can make binding
decisions.

17.16   In *X v UK*[25] the European Court found a breach of article 5(1)(e)
because the Mental Health Review Tribunal determining the appli-

---

21 See para 17.6.
22 (1993) 15 EHRR 584.
23 Ibid at para 22; see also *X v UK* n15 at para 52.
24 *Winterwerp v Netherlands* n5; *X v UK* n15.
25 Note 15.

cant's case, while otherwise satisfying the requirements of article 5(4), could only advise about, not order, release.[26] And in October 1997, the Commission declared admissible a complaint about the limited powers of mental health review tribunals in relation to those given discretionary life sentences and then transferred from prison to special hospitals.[27] In such cases, the tribunal has only advisory powers in relation to their release.

The nature of the review

17.17 Since, as noted above, the validity of detention under article 5(1)(e) depends on the persistence of a mental disorder severe enough to justify detention, it is essential that the body reviewing detention in mental health cases has power to investigate the applicant's mental state. In *X v UK* the European Court found that habeas corpus proceedings were inadequate for this purpose.

Procedural safeguards at review hearings

17.18 Article 5(4) requires that the procedure followed at review hearings has a judicial character and affords the individual concerned a number of safeguards. The nature and extent of such safeguards will depend on the circumstances in which the review takes place,[28] and the full requirements of a fair trial enshrined in article 6(1) do not necessarily apply.[29]

17.19 Nonetheless, it is essential that the person concerned should have effective access to a court and the opportunity to be heard either in person or, where necessary, through some form of representation. Additional procedural safeguards may also be needed to protect the interests of those who, on account of their mental state, are not fully able to act for themselves.[30] In particular, article 5(4) does not require individuals detained under article 5(1)(e) to take the initiative in obtaining legal advice and representation.[31]

---

26 The position was changed under the Mental Health Act 1983.
27 *Benjamin and Wilson v UK* Appl 28212/95; noted in [1998] EHRLR 226.
28 *Wassink v Netherlands* n17 at para 30.
29 *Megyeri v Germany* n22 at para 22.
30 *Winterwerp v Netherlands* n5 at para 60; *Megyeri v Germany* n22 at para 22.
31 *Winterwerp v Netherlands* n5 at para 60; *Megyeri v Germany* n22 at para 22.

The timing of reviews

17.20   The Convention requirements in relation to the timing of the initial review of detention under article 5(1)(e) and the timing of subsequent reviews are different. Note that, when an individual is recalled after having been released, the first review after recall is treated as the 'initial' review.

17.21   The initial review should take place very rapidly. Although the European Court in *Winterwerp v Netherlands* appeared ready to allow six weeks of detention before review as an 'emergency' measure, it is unlikely that such a period would survive challenge now. Implicit in the Court's judgment in *Wassink v Netherlands*[32] was a finding that three weeks is too long; in *E v Norway*[33] the Court found that a period of just under eight weeks was too long; and in *Kay v UK*,[34] the Commission found a breach of the Convention where the applicant's first review was not listed for five months.[35] Note, however, that the applicant's conduct will be a relevant factor in assessing whether a review has been conducted sufficiently speedily.[36]

17.22   The frequency of subsequent reviews will depend to some extent on the facts. However, review periods in excess of 12 months are unlikely to survive challenge under the Convention. And where conditional release has been ordered, but deferred, much shorter periods will be called for.[37]

Release

17.23   The European Court has approved the adoption of a cautious approach to release. In *Luberti v Italy*[38] it observed that:

> ... the termination of the confinement of an individual who has previously been found by a court to be of unsound mind and to present a danger to society is a matter that concerns, as well as that individual, the community in which he will live if released.[39]

32   Note 17.
33   (1994) 17 EHRR 30.
34   Commission (1 March 1994) (unreported).
35   See also *Koendjiharie v Netherlands* (1991) 13 EHRR 820.
36   See *Boucheras v France* (1991) 69 DR 236; *Keus v Netherlands* (1991) 13 EHRR 700; and *Luberti v Italy* (1984) 6 EHRR 440. On responsibility for setting up speedy reviews, see *Erkalo v Netherlands* [1999] EHRLR 117.
37   See *Johnson v UK* (1999) 27 EHRR 196 at para 62 and paras 17.25 to 17.27.
38   Note 36.
39   Ibid at para 29.

This passage was approved in *Johnson v UK*.[40]

17.24 Release which is conditional on taking medication is unlikely to breach the Convention. In *W v Sweden*[41] the Commission held that attaching conditions to release did not amount to a deprivation of liberty under article 5. And in *L v Sweden*,[42] it found that a condition that medication be taken did not violate article 8 (private life) because it could be justified under article 8(2) for the protection of the applicant's health.

17.25 The matter arose in a different way in *Johnson v UK*.[43] There a Mental Health Review Tribunal had repeatedly found that the applicant was no longer suffering from a mental illness. However, rather than ordering his immediate release, the tribunal ordered release conditional upon the applicant living in a supervised hostel environment. Since no suitable hostel could be found the applicant's release was repeatedly deferred.

17.26 The applicant argued that – since the lawfulness of detention under article 5(1)(e) depends on the persistence of a mental disorder severe enough to justify detention[44] – once the tribunal had found that he was no longer suffering from a mental illness he should have been released immediately and without conditions. The European Court rejected this analysis. In its view:

> ... it does not automatically follow from a finding by an expert authority that the mental disorder which justified a patient's compulsory confinement no longer persists, that the latter must be immediately and unconditionally released.
>
> Such a rigid approach to the interpretation of that condition would place an unacceptable degree of constraint on the responsible authority's exercise of judgment to determine in particular cases and on the basis of all the relevant circumstances whether the interests of the patient and the community into which he is to be released would in fact be best served by this course of action.[45]

The European Court was also influenced by the fact that assessment of mental illness was not 'an exact science' and that '[W]hether or not recovery from an episode of mental illness which justifies a patient's confinement is complete and definitive or merely apparent cannot in

---

40 Note 37 at para 62.
41 (1988) 59 DR 158.
42 (1986) 8 EHRR 269.
43 Note 37.
44 See para 17.6.
45 Note 37 at para 61.

all cases be measured with absolute certainty.'[46] On that basis the authority charged with making a decision about release 'should be able to retain some measure of supervision over the progress of the person once he is released into the community and to that end make his discharge subject to conditions'.[47]

17.27   However, where release is conditional, it is of paramount importance that safeguards are put in place to ensure that any deferral of release is consonant with article 5(1) and, in particular, that absolute release is not unreasonably delayed. Such safeguards were missing in *Johnson v UK*[48] because the tribunal had no power to order that suitable hostel accommodation be made available for the applicant. In the European Court's view, 'the onus was on the authorities to secure a hostel willing to admit the applicant' and to do so with all reasonable expedition.'[49] In addition, the 12-month period between reviews was unacceptable where conditional release had been ordered, but the conditions not complied with through no fault of the applicant.[50] And, on that basis, the European Court found a breach of article 5(1)(e).

Detention after or as a result of criminal proceedings

17.28   Article 5(1)(a) of the Convention provides for 'the lawful detention of a person after conviction by a competent court'; a category capable of including those with mental health problems.

17.29   In a number of early cases, neither the European Court nor the Commission clearly distinguished between detention under article 5(1)(a) and detention under article 5(1)(e). However, this issue was addressed in *X v UK*[51] where the European Court distinguished between those who had been acquitted because they were mentally ill and those who had actually been convicted of a crime despite their mental illness.

17.30   For those acquitted but nonetheless committed to an institution for treatment, only article 5(1)(e) applies. For those convicted, article

---

46 Ibid.
47 Note 37 at para 63.
48 Note 37 at para 62.
49 Note 37 at para 66.
50 Note 37 at para 67.
51 Note 15.

5(1)(a) automatically applies, but, where a court orders treatment in place of punishment, article 5(1)(e) also applies.

17.31   No initial review is required where detention is ordered by a court at the end of criminal proceedings because any assessment of the lawfulness of detention is deemed to have been incorporated in the court's decision. However, where detention has a preventative component, then as soon as the protection of the public becomes the sole basis for detention, the punitive element having been served, article 5(4) is engaged. See chapter 16.[52]

Conditions of detention: article 3

17.32   Conditions of detention are generally controlled by article 3 of the Convention which provides that:

> No one shall be subjected to torture or to inhuman or degrading treatment or punishment.

However, before article 3 is engaged a fairly high 'threshold' must be reached[53] and this has caused difficulties in mental health cases.

17.33   In *Grare v France*,[54] the Commission rejected an argument that unpleasant side effects of psychiatric treatment in the form of medication violated article 3 because they were not serious enough. In the same year, the European Court found no violation of article 3 in the case of *Herczegfalvy v Austria*[55] where handcuffs had been used to fasten a patient to a security bed. For the Court, the criterion was whether the conditions or measures conformed to 'psychiatric principles generally accepted at the time'. However, it added:

> The position of inferiority and powerlessness which is typical of patients confined in psychiatric hospitals calls for increased vigilance in reviewing whether the Convention has been complied with. While it was for the medical authorities to decide, on the basis of the recognised rules of medical science, on the therapeutic methods to be used, if necessary by force, to preserve the physical and mental health of patients who are entirely incapable of deciding for themselves, such patients nevertheless remain under the

---

52 Paras 16.40 to 16.47.
53 *Ireland v UK* (1979–80) 2 EHRR 25.
54 (1993) 15 EHRR CD 100.
55 (1993) 15 EHRR 437.

protection of article 3, whose requirements permit of no derogation.[56]

On that basis, treatment will rarely be considered inhuman or degrading where it is considered a therapeutic necessity according to contemporary psychiatric opinion.[57]

17.34   In the earlier case of *A v UK*[58] a friendly settlement was achieved following a visit by the European Commission to Broadmoor. The applicant in that case complained that during his detention in seclusion for five weeks he had had inadequate opportunities for exercise or association, inadequate furnishing, lighting and ventilation, that sanitary arrangements were humiliating and that he did not have proper clothing.

---

56   Ibid at para 82.
57   See also *Buckley v UK* (1997) 23 EHRR CD 129.
58   Appl 6840/74 Commission (16 July 1980).

CHAPTER 18

Immigration, asylum, extradition and deportation

18.1   Introduction

18.4   Inhuman and degrading treatment: the basic framework

18.8   The application of article 3 to admission cases

18.11   The application of article 3 to expulsion cases

18.13   The feared consequence

18.15   Assessing the risk

18.19   Source of the threat

18.21   The absolute nature of the prohibition

18.23   Removal to a 'safe' third country

18.24   Expulsion and the right to life

18.25   Expulsion and fair trial

18.26   Detention under article 5

18.31   Private and family life under article 8

18.35   The application of article 8 to admission cases

18.39   The application of article 8 to expulsion cases

18.44   Discrimination

18.48   Procedural safeguards in admission and expulsion cases

Introduction

18.1   The settled case-law of the European Court and Commission is to the effect that the Convention does not guarantee a right to enter, reside or remain in a particular country.[1] Nonetheless, decisions about admission to or expulsion from a state party to the Convention must be carried out within the framework of Convention rights. Such decisions will, therefore, be vulnerable to challenge where they expose individuals to the risk of conduct prohibited under article 3 (the prohibition on torture, inhuman and/or degrading treatment) or unduly interfere with family rights under article 8. Where life is at stake, article 2 may also be engaged.

18.2   Detention pending admission or expulsion is specifically pro-vided for in article 5 – but only where it is 'lawful' and follows such procedures as are prescribed in domestic law. Moreover, once a decision on admission or expulsion comes 'within the ambit' of a Convention right (without necessarily breaching it)[2] the prohibition on discrimination in article 14 applies. Measures which, in them-selves, are not incompatible with the Convention can become so where they are discriminatory.

18.3   Articles 2–4 of Protocol 4 make specific provision for freedom of movement and protection from arbitrary expulsion. The UK has not ratified this Protocol and, in any event, it does not detract from or limit such protection as is provided by other Convention rights.[3]

Inhuman and degrading treatment: the basic framework

18.4   Article 3 provides that:

> No one shall be subjected to torture or to inhuman or degrading treatment or punishment.

It is expressed in unqualified terms and in peace time derogation is not possible. It follows that conduct prohibited under article 3

---

1   *X and Y v Germany* (1977) 9 DR 219; *X v UK* (1981) 24 DR 98; *Lalljee v UK* (1986) 8 EHRR 45; *Soering v UK* (1989) 11 EHRR 439; *Crus Varas v Sweden* (1992) 14 EHRR 1; *Vilvarajah v UK* (1992) 14 EHRR 248; *Chahal v UK* (1997) 23 EHRR 413.
2   See paras 29.7 to 29.9.
3   *Abdulaziz, Cabales and Balkandali v UK* (1985) 7 EHRR 471 at para 60.

cannot be justified as being in the public interest and the European Court has therefore rejected attempts to justify particular measures on the basis that they were necessary for national security[4] or to suppress terrorism.[5]

18.5   Article 3 covers three separate categories of prohibited treatment or punishment: (a) torture; (b) inhuman treatment/punishment; and (c) degrading treatment/punishment. In each case conduct must 'attain a minimum level of severity' before article 3 is breached.[6] The assessment of this minimum is relative; it depends on all the circumstances of the case, such as the duration of the treatment, its physical or mental effects and, in some cases, the sex, age and state of health of the victim.

18.6   The guidelines given by the Court in *Ireland v UK*[7] provide a useful starting point:

1) *Torture*

   Deliberate inhuman treatment causing very serious and cruel suffering.

2) *Inhuman treatment/punishment*

   Treatment/punishment that causes intense physical and mental suffering.

3) *Degrading treatment/punishment*

   Treatment/punishment that arouses in the victim a feeling of fear, anguish and inferiority capable of humiliating and debasing the victim and possibly breaking his or her physical or moral resistance.

It is the degree of suffering caused, coupled with the question of intention, that marks the distinction between torture and inhuman treatment/punishment. See further chapter 14.

18.7   Refusal of entry and/or expulsion can raise article 3 issues. In entry cases, discrimination is usually the key factor. In expulsion cases, the issue is usually the risk of exposure to inhuman or degrading treatment/punishment.

---

4   *Chahal v UK* n1.
5   *Ireland v UK* (1979–80) 2 EHRR 25; *Tomasi v France* (1993) 15 EHRR 1.
6   *Ireland v UK* n5 at para 162.
7   Note 5.

The application of article 3 to admission cases

18.8   Once an individual is physically within the jurisdiction of a state, s/he is entitled to the full protection of his/her Convention rights, even if s/he has not technically 'entered' the country.[8] However, admission cases raising article 3 issues are rare: the most common issue being discrimination.

18.9   In *East African Asians v UK*,[9] the Commission held that discrimination based on race can, in certain circumstances, amount to degrading treatment within the meaning of article 3 of the Convention.[10] In observed that:

> ... a special importance should be attached to discrimination based on race; that publicly to single out a group of persons for differential treatment on the basis of race might, in certain circumstances, constitute a special form of affront to human dignity; and that differential treatment of a group of persons on the basis of race might therefore be capable of constituting degrading treatment when differential treatment on some other ground would raise no such question.[11]

The 'special circumstances' which, together, gave rise to a breach of article 3 were:

1) the legislation itself;[12]

2) the pledge of free entry to East African Asians/UK citizens;

3) the destitution faced by those applicants in East Africa; and

4) the manner in which immigration control was effected in the UK, in particular the practice of shuttlecocking people around.[13]

In *Lalljee v UK*[14] the Commission held that, in the absence of any aggravating features, a quota system for immigration was not, of itself, degrading.

18.10   The need for special or aggravating circumstances before discrimination can be regarded as degrading under article 3 was emphasised by the European Court in *Abdulaziz, Cabales and*

---

8   *D v UK* (1997) 24 EHRR 423 at para 48.

9   (1981) 3 EHRR 76.

10   Ibid at para 207.

11   Ibid.

12   Commonwealth Immigrants Act 1968.

13   Cf *X and Y v UK* Appl 5302/71, 44 Collected Decisions 29 and *Lalljee v UK* n1.

14   Note 1.

Balkandali v UK.[15] There the applicants, who were lawfully and permanently settled in the UK, complained that their husbands were refused permission to join them in the UK. Although the European Court found a breach of article 14 in conjunction with article 8[16] on the basis of sex discrimination, it found no breach of article 3. In its view: 'the difference in treatment ... did not denote any contempt or lack of respect for the personality of the applicants' and 'it was not designed to, and did not, humiliate or debase' them.[17]

The application of article 3 to expulsion cases

18.11   There is no right under the Convention not to be expelled or extradited from a Convention state. On many occasions, the European Court has emphasised the right of states 'to control the entry, residence and expulsion of aliens'.[18] And state parties to the Convention are free to conclude and carry out extradition agreements.[19]

18.12   However, there are very clear limits. These were set by the European Court in its landmark judgment in *Soering v UK.*[20] In particular:

> ... the decision by a Contracting State to extradite a fugitive may give rise to an issue under Article 3, and hence, engage the responsibility of that State under the Convention, where substantial grounds have been shown for believing that the person concerned, if extradited, faces a real risk of being subjected to torture or to inhuman or degrading treatment or punishment in the requesting country.[21]

The establishment of such responsibility inevitably involves an assessment of conditions in the requesting country against the standards of article 3 of the Convention. Nonetheless, there is no question of adjudicating on or establishing the responsibility of the receiving country, whether under general international law, under the Convention or otherwise. In so far as any liability under the Convention is or may be incurred, it is liability incurred by the extraditing state for taking action which has as a direct consequence the exposure of an individual to proscribed ill-treatment.

---

15   Note 3.
16   Ibid paras 81 to 83.
17   Note 3 at para 91.
18   *Chahal v UK* n1 at para 73.
19   *Altun v Germany* (1983) 36 DR 209.
20   Note 1.
21   Ibid at para 91.

The feared consequence

18.13   The ill-treatment feared as a consequence of expulsion must be severe to come within the ambit of article 3. See chapter 14. It is not enough that a conscientious objector will be forced to do military service,[22] nor that an individual faces criminal proceedings and/or a long prison sentence[23] – even for desertion.[24] Prosecution for a political offence may be enough, but only where the threat of prosecution is real and a substantial sentence is likely.[25]

18.14   In *Soering v UK*[26] the applicant faced extradition to Virginia on a charge of capital murder and the feared inhuman and/or degrading treatment/punishment was prolonged exposure to the 'death row phenomenon': ie, years on death row under sentence of death, in poor prison conditions, awaiting final execution. The European Court found that this was sufficient to engage article 3, bearing in mind the following features:

1) the length of detention pending execution (an average of six to eight years);

2) the strict and harsh conditions on death row; and

3) the applicant's age and mental state (18 with some evidence of abnormality of mind).

The form the death penalty takes[27] and its mandatory nature[28] – although not relevant in *Soering* – may in other cases render expulsion inhuman.

Assessing the risk

18.15   The mere possibility of ill-treatment is not enough to engage state responsibility under article 3. But the absolute nature of the prohibition on inhuman and/or degrading treatment/punishment under article 3 dictates a rigorous approach to the assessment of risk.

---

22   *X v Germany* (1969) 32 Collected Decisions 96; *X v Sweden* (1972) 43 Collected Decisions 111.

23   *C v Germany* (1986) 46 DR 176. See also *Barar v Sweden* [1999] EHRLR 332 concerning slavery.

24   *Popescu and Cucu v France* Commission (11 September 1995), unreported.

25   *A v Switzerland* (1986) 46 DR 257. See also *X v Germany* (1969) 32 Collected Decisions 87; *X v Germany* (1976) 5 Collected Decisions 154; *Altun v Germany* (1983) 36 DR 209.

26   Note 1.

27   See, for example, *Ng v Canada* (1993) 1 IHRR 161.

Assurances and safeguards are important, but only where it is clear that they will be effective.

18.16   In *Soering v UK* (above) the risk of exposure to the death row phenomenon depended on the likelihood of conviction for capital murder. Although there were some grounds for believing that the applicant might be acquitted and although an 'assurance' of sorts had been given that the death penalty would not be implemented, the European Court found that there was a 'significant risk' of conviction, which was not diminished by the existence of an assurance, the effectiveness of which had yet to be tested. It was thus impossible to conclude that there were 'no substantial grounds' for concluding that the applicant did not risk exposure to ill-treatment in breach of article 3.

18.17   Although the principles of risk assessment are the same in expulsion cases as they are in extradition cases, carrying out the assessment is usually much more difficult because it involves an uncertain prediction of future events. The fear is often that inhuman and/or degrading treatment will be carried out clandestinely either by the authorities in the receiving state or by third parties.[29] Although the existence of the risk must be assessed primarily by reference to the facts which were, or ought to have been, known to the authorities when the expulsion decision was taken, the approach of the European Court is to consider all relevant material, including material obtained of its own motion and that which has come to light after the expulsion decision was made. What is called for is a 'rigorous' examination focusing on the foreseeable consequences of removal, in light of the general situation in the receiving country and the individuals' personal circumstances,[30] bearing in mind that many individuals who have been subjected to ill-treatment are apprehensive toward authority and may be afraid to provide information about their case.[31]

18.18   In *Cruz Varas v Sweden*[32] the European Court was influenced by political developments in Chile since the applicant left, in rejecting his complaint that his expulsion there breached article 3. And in *Vilvarajah v UK*,[33] which concerned the expulsion of Tamils to Sri

---

28 See *Woodson v North Carolina* (1976) 428 US 280; *Furman v Georgia* (1972) 408 US 238.

29 See, for example, *Ahmed v Austria* (1997) 24 EHRR 278.

30 *Vilvarajah v UK* n1 at para 108.

31 *Cruz Varas v Sweden* n1. See also *Hatami v Sweden* [1998] EHRLR 618.

32 Note 1.

33 Note 1 at para 108.

Lanka, in the absence of any specific threat, the European Court did not consider it enough that there was a generally unsettled political situation and that some Tamils might be detained or ill-treated.

Source of the threat

18.19   The prohibition on expulsion where an individual faces the threat of exposure to treatment/punishment prohibited by article 3 applies whatever the source of the threat. In *HLR v France*,[34] where the applicant argued that if returned to Columbia he would be exposed to the risk of reprisals from drug traffickers, the European Court observed:

> ... owing to the absolute character of the right guaranteed, the Court does not rule out the possibility that Article 3 of the Convention may also apply where the danger emanates from persons or groups of persons who are not public officials. However, it must be shown that the risk is real and that the authorities in the receiving state are not able to obviate the risk by providing appropriate protection.[35]

A general situation of violence is not enough; there must be a specific threat.[36]

18.20   The European Court developed this principle one stage further in *D v UK*,[37] which concerned the deportation of a man who was in an advanced stage of a terminal and incurable illness to a country where adequate medical facilities were not available. As a general principle, the Court observed that:

> It is true that [the principle of non-expulsion] has so far been applied ... in contexts in which the risk to the individual of being subjected to any of the proscribed forms of treatment emanates from intentionally inflicted acts of the public authorities in the receiving country or from those of non-State bodies in that country when the authorities there are unable to afford him protection.
>   Aside from these situations and given the fundamental importance of Article 3 in the Convention system, the Court must reserve to itself sufficient flexibility to address the application of that Article in other contexts which might arise. It is therefore not prevented from scrutinising an applicant's claim under Article 3 where the source of the risk of proscribed treatment in the

34   (1998) 26 EHRR 29.
35   Ibid at para 40.
36   Note 34 at para 41.
37   Note 8.

receiving country stems from factors which cannot engage either directly or indirectly the responsibility of the public authorities in that country, or which, taken alone, do not in themselves infringe the standards of that Article. To limit the application of Article 3 in this manner would undermine the absolute character of its protection.[38]

In view of the exceptional circumstances in that case, and bearing in mind the critical stage reached in the applicant's fatal illness, the European Court held that implementation of the decision to remove him would amount to inhuman treatment in violation of article 3.[39]

The absolute nature of the prohibition

18.21   In a number of cases, it has been suggested that the principle of non-expulsion where there is a risk of treatment/punishment prohibited by article 3 should be applied differently where expulsion is on the ground of national security. In *Chahal v UK*,[40] where the applicant faced deportation to India on the ground that his presence in the UK was unconducive to the public good for reasons of national security, the government argued that there was an implied limitation to article 3 entitling states to expel an individual even where a real risk of ill-treatment existed, if such removal were required on national security grounds. In the alternative, it argued that the risk to the individual was one factor to be taken into account in such cases but not the determining factor.

18.22   The European Court rejected both arguments. It was 'well aware of the immense difficulties faced by States in modern times in protecting their communities from terrorist violence' but:

> ... even in these circumstances, the Convention prohibits in absolute terms torture or inhuman or degrading treatment or punishment, irrespective of the victim's conduct ...'[41]

Even in national security cases, therefore, the activities of the individual in question, however undesirable or dangerous, cannot be a material consideration. There is no room for balancing the risk of ill-

38 Ibid at para 49.
39 Note 8 at para 53; see also *Poku v UK Commission* (15 May 1996) (unreported) and *Choudry v UK Commission* (13 May 1996) (unreported). See also *BB v France* [1998] EHRLR 620 concerning treatment to inhibit development of HIV and slow infections for AIDS sufferers.
40 Note 1.
41 Note 1 at para 79.

treatment against the reasons for expulsion in determining whether a state's responsibility under article 3 is engaged.[42]

Removal to a 'safe' third country

18.23   Removal of an individual to a third country where there is no risk of ill-treatment is not prohibited by the Convention, so long as there is no chance that the third country will remove the individual in question to a country where s/he might be exposed to conduct prohibited by article 3.[43] Furthermore, the Commission has held that the repeated expulsion of an individual to a country where his/her admission is not guaranteed may in itself give rise to an issue under article 3.[44]

Expulsion and the right to life

18.24   The applicant in *D v UK* (above) raised the right to life under article 2 of the Convention, but, in light of its findings under article 3, the European Court did not find it necessary to examine the complaint under that provision. Given the fundamental character of the right to life, in principle there is no reason why state responsibility should not be engaged where expulsion puts an individual's life at risk. However, the case-law of the Commission suggests that the threshold will be very high. In *Bahaddar v Netherlands*[45] the Commission suggested that the loss of life would have to be a 'near certainty' before article 2 was relevant in expulsion cases. In the light of the European Court's subsequent case-law on article 2, this may be putting it a bit high: see chapter 14.

Expulsion and fair trial

18.25   The implications of expelling an individual to a country where s/he faces an unfair trial have yet to be fully explored by the Strasbourg bodies. In *Soering v UK*[46] the European Court observed that:

---

42   Note 1 at para 81.
43   *Giama v Belgium* (1980) 21 DR 73.
44   Ibid.
45   Commission (22 May 1995) (unreported). See also *Launder v UK* [1998] EHRLR 337.
46   Note 1.

Article 1 cannot be read as justifying a general principle to the effect that, notwithstanding its extradition obligations, a Contracting State may not surrender an individual unless satisfied that the conditions awaiting him in the country of destination are in full accord with each of the safeguards of the Convention.[47]

However, it continued:

The right to a fair trial in criminal proceedings, as embodied in Article 6, holds a prominent place in a democratic society. The Court does not exclude that an issue might exceptionally be raised under Article 6 by an extradition decision in circumstances where the fugitive has suffered or risks suffering a flagrant denial of a fair trial in the requesting country.[48]

This approach has also been adopted in the context of receiving prisoners from abroad.[49]

Detention under article 5

18.26   Article 5(1)(f) of the Convention provides that:

Everyone has the right to liberty and security of person. No one shall be deprived of his liberty save in the following cases and in accordance with the procedure prescribed by law:

...

(f) the lawful arrest or detention of a person to prevent his effecting an unauthorised entry into the country or of a person against whom action is being taken with a view to deportation or extradition.

Like all exceptions to article 5(1), paragraph (f) is to be narrowly construed.[50]

18.27   The pre-conditions of detention are therefore three-fold:

1) the individual in question must come within the category defined in paragraph (f);

2) the basis upon which s/he is detained must be 'lawful'; and

3) any procedure prescribed in domestic law must be strictly followed.

---

47 Note 1 at para 86.
48 Note 1 at para 113.
49 *Drozd and Janousek v France* (1992) 14 EHRR 745.
50 *Winterwerp v Netherlands* (1979) 2 EHRR 387 at para 37.

Moreover, inherent in the notion of lawfulness, is a prohibition on arbitrary action. In *Bozano v France*[51] the Court found a violation of article 5(1)(f) where the applicant's arrest and detention was, in reality, 'a disguised form of extradition' designed to get round an adverse court decision.[52]

18.28   A deprivation of liberty will be justified only for as long as deportation or extradition proceedings are in progress. Where deportation or extradition is impossible, article 5(1)(f) will not apply.[53] Equally, if the proceedings are not prosecuted with due diligence, detention will cease to be justified under article 5(1)(f). The Strasbourg bodies will, therefore, examine whether the duration of deportation or extradition proceedings has been excessive.[54]

18.29   Individuals deprived of their liberty under article 5(1)(f) are entitled to a review of the legality of that detention under article 5(4).[55] Delay can be a ground for challenge[56] and legal aid should usually be made available.[57]

18.30   Nonetheless, the terms of article 5(1)(f) are wide. In *Chahal v UK*[58] the European Court observed that:

> Article 5(1)(f) does not demand that the detention of a person against whom action is being taken with a view to deportation be reasonably considered necessary, for example to prevent his committing an offence or fleeing; in this respect Article 5(1)(f) provides a different level of protection from Article 5(1)(c).
>
> Indeed, all that is required under this provision is that 'action is being taken with a view to deportation'. It is therefore immaterial, for the purposes of Article 5(1)(f), whether the underlying decision to expel can be justified under national or Convention law.[59]

It follows that a subsequent finding that a deportation or extradition decision was unlawful is unlikely to affect the legality of detention under article 5(1)(f), unless it can be shown that the entire proceedings were arbitrary.

---

51   (1987) 9 EHRR 297.
52   For a fuller analysis of this case, see para 3.37.
53   *Ali v Switzerland* (Commission) Appl 24881/94, 26 February 1997; pending before the Court.
54   *Chahal v UK* n1.
55   *Bozano v France* n51; *Caprino v UK* (1980) 22 DR 5.
56   *Kolompar v Belgium* (1993) 16 EHRR 197.
57   *Zamir v UK* (1983) 40 DR 42.
58   Note 1.
59   Note 1 at para 112; see also *Zamir v UK* n57.

Private and family life under article 8

18.31   Article 8(1) provides that 'Everybody has the right to respect for his ... family life ...'. Article 8(2) prohibits public authorities from interfering with this right except where:

1) the grounds for interference are 'in accordance with law';

2) they pursue a legitimate aim (ie, one of the aims listed in article 8(2)); and

3) they are necessary and proportionate.[60]

The meaning of each of these requirements is examined in detail in chapter 4.

18.32   The European Court has construed 'family life' under article 8 fairly broadly. Marriage, almost inevitably, gives rise to family life[61] but family life also encompasses many other de facto relationships. As the Commission has observed:

> The question of the existence or non-existence of 'family life' is essentially a question of fact depending upon the real existence in practice of close personal ties.[62]

Relevant factors are:

1) whether a couple live together;

2) the length of their relationship; and

3) whether they have demonstrated their commitment to one another by having children together or by any other means.[63]

18.33   As a general rule, family life will always embrace the tie between a parent and child, even where the parents are not married and do not live together. And even though family life can be terminated, for example, by divorce, not all family relationships are severed by that act; for example, the relationship between a parent and his/her child can survive.[64]

18.34   So far, however, the Strasbourg bodies have maintained that lesbian and gay relationships raise private life issues, not family life

---

60 See paras 4.56 to 4.66.
61 See *Abdulaziz, Cabales and Balkandali v UK* n3.
62 *K v UK* [1986] 50 DR 199 at 207.
63 *Kroon v Netherlands* (1995) 19 EHRR 263 at para 30; *X, Y and Z v UK* (1997) 24 EHRR 143 at para 36.
64 *Berrehab v Netherlands* (1989) 11 EHRR 322.

issues. The consequence is that much more leeway is given to the domestic authorities on questions of admission and expulsion.[65]

The application of article 8 to admission cases

18.35   Article 8 clearly applies in immigration cases:[66] an argument to the contrary was firmly rejected by the European Court in *Abdulaziz, Cabales and Balkandali.*[67] But the exclusion of family members from a state party to the Convention is not necessarily a breach of its provisions.

18.36   The applicable principles were set out in *Abdulaziz, Cabales and Balkandali* and have been subsequently refined. In summary, (a) there is no general obligation under the Convention on state parties to admit the family members of those who are within their jurisdiction; however, (b) article 8 might be engaged if it can be shown that there are real obstacles to establishing family life elsewhere or there are special reasons why the individuals in question should not be expected to do so.

18.37   Relevant to the question of whether there are real obstacles to establishing family life elsewhere will be:

1) past residence;

2) the ability of the parties to adapt to living overseas;

3) language difficulties;

4) cultural, religious and social practices; and

5) compelling health, employment or family issues.[68]

And in marriage cases, the extent to which the individuals in question were aware of problems of admission and settlement will be relevant.[69]

18.38   The fact that one spouse will have to give up work, leave a business[70] or might be ill[71] is insufficient. But a real obstacle might be

---

65 In the immigration context, see *X and U v UK* (1983) 5 EHRR 601; and *X v UK* (1989) 11 EHRR 49.

66 *East African Asians v UK* (1981) 3 EHRR 76; *X and Y v Germany* (1977) 9 DR 219; *Lukka v UK* (1987) 9 EHRR 552.

67 Note 3.

68 *Adegbie v Austria* Commission (9 April 1996) unreported, subsequently settled (1997) 90-A DR 31.

69 *Abdulaziz, Cabales and Balkandali* n3.

70 *X v UK* Commission (28 February 1996); unreported.

71 *Akhtar v UK* Commission (12 February 1992); unreported.

established where neither spouse has any prior or family connection elsewhere.[72]

The application of article 8 to expulsion cases

18.39　Expulsion by its very nature frequently gives rise to article 8 issues, particularly where an individual has been lawfully resident in a Convention state for a considerable period. In principle, there is no prohibition on expulsion merely because family life will be disrupted. However, like other measures that disrupt family life, an expulsion decision will be compatible with article 8 only if it is lawful domestically, it pursues one of the aims set out in article 8(2) and, most importantly, the act of expulsion is strictly proportionate to the reason for it.

18.40　Relevant to the assessment of proportionality will be:

1) the reason for expulsion;

2) the applicant's ties with the deporting state;

3) the extent of the disruption of his/her family life;

4) whether there are real obstacles to establishing family life elsewhere; and

5) in criminal cases, the gravity of the offence in respect of which deportation was ordered and the applicant's criminal record.

There is a strong body of opinion in Strasbourg that those with long residence in a Convention state should be deported only in exceptional circumstances where they have committed very serious offences.[73]

18.41　In *Moustaquim v Belgium*[74] the European Court held that deportation of a Moroccan who had lived in Belgium since the age of one was not justified. The fact that the applicant's parents and siblings lived in Belgium was sufficient to establish 'family life'.[75] Although the Court recognised the state's concerns about the effect of non-deportation where there was serious criminal offending, that did

---

72　*Adegbie v Austria* Commission n68.

73　See Martens J, dissenting in *Boughanemi v France* (1996) 22 EHRR 228 and Schermers and Thune, concurring in the Commission decision in *Beldjoudi v France* (1992) 14 EHRR 801; and Schermers concurring in the Commission decision in *Lamguindaz v UK* (1994) 17 EHRR 213.

74　(1991) 13 EHRR 802.

75　Ibid at para 35.

not justify the adoption of a looser test under article 8(2) than would normally be required where family life was disrupted.[76] Having regard to the fact that the applicant was a juvenile when he committed many of his offences, that most of them had been committed over a short 11-month period, that he had left Morocco when he was two years old and that all his family was effectively in Belgium, the decision to deport him was disproportionate.[77]

18.42   In *Nasri v France*[78] the European Court found that the deportation of a deaf and dumb Algerian man, who was dependent on his family members in France and who had no close ties with Algeria, was not compatible with article 8, despite his serious criminal convictions. But a different result followed in *Boughanemi v France*[79] where the distinguishing features were that the applicant, a Tunisian, did not claim that he could not speak Arabic, had returned to Tunisia after his deportation and had retained links there which went beyond his nationality.

18.43   Particular difficulties can arise where children are concerned. Two admissibility decisions of the Commission suggest that it is inhuman to expel children to a country where there is no one to care for them on arrival.[80] And where a non-national is being expelled and his/her children are in the custody of the other parent, the disruption to family life may make the expulsion disproportionate.[81] On the other hand, the expulsion of a parent with custody of young children will not necessarily breach article 8, if they are of an 'adaptable age', even where the children have British citizenship.[82]

Discrimination

18.44   The prohibition on discrimination in article 14 of the Convention applies to immigration, asylum, extradition and deportation legislation, rules, regulations and decisions. It does not provide a *general* right to freedom from discrimination and can be invoked only in

---

76 Note 74 para 43.
77 See also *Beldjoudi v France* n73 and *Lamguindaz v UK* n73.
78 (1995) 21 EHRR 458.
79 Note 73.
80 *Taspinar v Netherlands* (1985) 44 DR 262 and *Bulus v Sweden* (1984) 35 DR 57 and 39 DR 75.
81 *Berrehab v Netherlands* (1989) 11 EHRR 322.
82 See the Commission's admissibility decisions in *Jaramillo v UK* and *Sorabjee v UK* Commission (23 October 1995); unreported.

relation to one of the other Convention rights set out in articles 2–12 and the First Protocol. However, no breach of another Convention right need be established; the test for the application of article 14 is whether the facts in issue 'fall within the ambit' of one or more of the other Convention provisions.[83]

18.45   According to the European Court's case-law, a difference in treatment is discriminatory for the purposes of article 14 if it 'has no objective and reasonable justification', that is, it does not pursue a 'legitimate aim', or if there is not a 'reasonable relationship of proportionality between the means employed and the aim sought to be realised'.[84]

18.46   Generally speaking there is a presumption under the Convention that discrimination based on nationality[85] breaches article 14, but that presumption does not apply in admission and expulsion cases. As the European Court observed in *Abdulaziz, Cabales and Balkandali:*[86]

> Most immigration policies – restricting as they do free entry – differentiate on the basis of people's nationality, and indirectly their race, ethnic origin and possibly their colour.[87]

While a state cannot implement 'policies of a purely racist nature', to give preferential treatment to its nationals or to persons from countries with which it had the closest links did not constitute 'racial discrimination'.[88]

18.47   The presumption that discrimination based on sex[89] breaches article 14, however, does apply. The European Court found no breach of article 8 taken alone in *Abdulaziz, Cabales and Balkandali* (see above), but it did find a breach of article 14 in conjunction with article 8. Although, in principle, it was legitimate to restrict the admission of non-national spouses to the UK, it was not legitimate to distinguish between the non-national spouses of males (permitted entry) and the non-national spouses of females (not permitted entry).

---

83 *Rasmussen v Denmark* (1985) 7 EHRR 371.
84 *Gaygusuz v Austria* (1996) 23 EHRR 364.
85 Ibid.
86 Note 3.
87 Ibid at para 84.
88 Note 3 at para 84; see also *Moustaquim v Belgium* n74 in relation to differential treatment between EU and non-EU nationals.
89 *Van Raalte v Netherlands* (1997) 24 EHRR 503.

Procedural safeguards in admission and expulsion cases

18.48   The fair trial requirements of article 6(1) have very little impact in admission and expulsion cases: see chapter 12. Similarly, although extradition proceedings are criminal, deportation orders are deemed not to be criminal sanctions, but security measures, thus excluding the application of articles 6 and 7.

CHAPTER 19

Family life

19.1   Introduction

19.3   The right to 'family life'
19.4   In accordance with law
19.8   Legitimate aim
19.9   Necessity and proportionality

19.11   The meaning of 'family life' under article 8

19.17   Adoptive relationships and fostering

19.21   Embryology and surrogacy

19.23   Lesbian and gay couples

19.25   Transsexuals

19.26   Wider family relationships

19.29   What does the right to family life cover?

19.32   Marriage

19.38   Founding a family

19.39   Children born out of wedlock

19.42   Divorce and separation

19.44   Custody and access

continued

19.47   The enforcement of court orders

19.48   Maintenance payments

19.50   Domestic violence

19.53   Adoption

19.55   Placing children in care

19.58   Names

19.60   Sexual identity: the position of transsexuals

19.64   Procedural fairness in proceedings concerning family life

Introduction

19.1 Family life is a broad concept which engages a number of Convention rights. It is expressly protected by article 8(1) and clearly overlaps with the right to marry and found a family under article 12.

19.2 This chapter deals with most aspects of family life, including the relationship between families and public authorities, particularly in relation to children, and the rights of family members as against each other. Other aspects of family life which fall exclusively within other chapters are dealt with elsewhere; for example, chapters 18, 20 and 21.

The right to 'family life'

19.3 Article 8(1) provides that 'Everybody has the right to respect for his ... family life ...'. And article 8(2) prohibits public authorities from interfering with this right except where:

1) the grounds for interference are 'in accordance with law';

2) they pursue a legitimate aim (ie, one of the aims listed in article 8(2)); and

3) they are necessary and proportionate.[1]

In accordance with law

19.4 The phrase 'in accordance with law' means that any interference by a public authority with family life must have a basis in domestic law. This was found to be lacking in *Eriksson v Sweden*[2] where social workers had applied restrictions on the applicants' access to their children in care which, on analysis, had no legal basis.

19.5 The requirement that any interference with family life be 'in accordance with law' also has another aspect, concerning the 'quality' of the law in question. The European Court has established that laws or rules which restrict Convention rights must be 'accessible' and clear, such that individuals whose rights are likely to be affected can find out what laws or rules apply to them and regulate their conduct accordingly.[3] A rule or law that confers a discretion is

---

1   See chapter 4.
2   (1990) 12 EHRR 183.
3   See paras 4.29 to 4.36.

not in itself inconsistent with these requirements, provided the scope of the discretion and the manner in which it is to be exercised are clear.[4]

19.6   Absolute certainty in the law is not required[5] and in the context of child protection, the European Court has recognised that some laws and rules will inevitably have to be couched in fairly general terms. For example, in *Olsson v Sweden (No 1)*[6] the Court approved legislation which permitted local authorities to intervene and take children into care where their 'health and development is jeopardised or in danger'. The Court reasoned that:

> ... the circumstances in which it may be necessary to take a child into public care and in which a care decision may fall to be implemented are so variable that it would scarcely be possible to formulate a law to cover every eventuality.[7]

19.7   Alive to the dangers inherent in any relaxation of the requirement that laws or rules restricting Convention rights be clear and predictable, the European Court has emphasised that where powers of a fairly general nature are vested in public authorities, the need for procedural safeguards is intensified. In many situations this will mean that there must be provision for effective recourse to the courts to ensure a degree of judicial supervision over the exercise of powers which interfere with family life. One of the factors that influenced the Court in the case of *Olsson v Sweden (No 1)* referred to above was that the exercise of the power in question was subject to scrutiny by the court in judicial review proceedings.[8]

Legitimate aim

19.8   Among the aims deemed legitimate under article 8(2) are 'the protection of health' and 'the protection of the rights of others', and these aims will justify most measures taken by public authorities which interfere with family life, particularly measures such as taking children into care.[9]

---

4   *Andersson v Sweden* (1992) 14 EHRR 615 at para 75.
5   *Sunday Times v UK* (1979–80) 2 EHRR 245.
6   (1989) 11 EHRR 259.
7   Ibid at para 62.
8   Ibid.
9   See paras 19.55 to 19.57.

Necessity and proportionality

19.9 Even where the aim or purpose of a particular measure is legitimate, the public authority concerned will have to establish that it was also necessary and proportionate. Relevant to this question will be whether:

1) 'relevant and sufficient reasons' can be advanced for the action taken;

2) a less restricted, but equally effective, alternative existed;

3) the rights of all interested parties have been taken into account properly; and

4) safeguards exist to prevent, or at least check, any abuse of power.[10]

19.10 In the context of family life, the European Court held in *Johansen v Norway*[11] that steps which have far-reaching consequences – such as removing a child permanently from his/her parents – should be applied only in exceptional circumstances and 'could only be justified if they were motivated by an overriding requirement pertaining to the child's best interest'.[12]

The meaning of 'family life' under article 8

19.11 The European Court has construed 'family life' under article 8 fairly broadly. Marriage, almost inevitably, gives rise to family life[13] but family life also encompasses many other *de facto* relationships.

19.12 The Commission has made it clear that:

> The question of the existence or non-existence of 'family life' is essentially a question of fact depending upon the real existence in practice of close personal ties.[14]

Relevant factors are: (a) whether a couple live together; (b) the length of their relationship; and (c) whether they have demonstrated their commitment to one another by having children together or by any other means.[15]

---

10 See paras 4.37 to 4.55.
11 (1996) 23 EHRR 33.
12 Ibid at para 78: see also *Andersson v Sweden* n4.
13 See *Abdulaziz, Cabales and Balkandali v UK* (1995) 7 EHRR 471.
14 K v UK (1986) 50 DR 199 at 207.
15 *Kroon v Netherlands* (1995) 19 EHRR 263 at para 30; *X, Y and Z v UK* (1997) 24 EHRR 143 at para 36.

19.13   As a general rule, family life will always embrace the tie between a parent and child, even where the parents are not married and do not live together. In *Keegan v Ireland*[16] the European Court held that:

> ... The notion of the 'family' in [article 8] is not confined solely to marriage-based relationships and may encompass other de facto 'family' ties where the parties are living together outside marriage. A child born out of such a relationship is not *ipso jure* part of that 'family' unit from the moment of his birth and by the very fact of it. There thus exists between the child and his parents a bond amounting to family life even if at the time of his or her birth the parents are no longer cohabiting or if their relationship has then ended.[17]

19.14   Similarly in *Kroon v Netherlands*[18] the Court found that a couple who had a long-standing relationship and four children, but who had never lived together, had a 'family life' within the meaning of article 8.

19.15   The Commission came to the same conclusion in *Soderback v Sweden*[19] where the applicant was friends with the mother of his child but had never lived with her or had a steady relationship with her. Although in that case the applicant had had very little contact with the child in question, this was partly because of the mother's opposition to such contact and the applicant clearly wanted to establish better contact. In the Commission's view article 8 not only protected family life which had already been established, but also extended to a potential relationship which might develop between a natural father and a child born out of wedlock.

19.16   Family life may be terminated, for example, by divorce. But because family life may encompass a number of relationships, the severance of one of them does not necessarily end all of them. In *Berrehab v Netherlands*[20] the relationship between the applicant and his daughter was found to survive the applicant's divorce from her mother because his frequent visits to the daughter maintained the applicant's 'close ties' with her.

---

16   (1994) 18 EHRR 342.
17   Ibid at para 44.
18   (1995) 19 EHRR 263.
19   (Commission) 22 October 1997 (1998) EHRLR 342.
20   (1989) 11 EHRR 322.

Adoptive relationships and fostering

19.17 The existence of family life between adoptive parents and their adopted children is well established.[21] The position in relation to foster parents and foster children is less clear cut.

19.18 In *Gaskin v UK*[22] the European Court found that restrictions on the applicant's access to confidential records concerning the period when he was in local authority care as a child were disproportionate and therefore breached article 8.[23] For most of the period in question the applicant was with foster parents and no issue was taken about the applicability of article 8 to the applicant's relationship with his foster parents.

19.19 Similarly in *Eriksson v Sweden*[24] the European Court acknowledged the relationship between the applicant's daughter and her foster parents, but held that it did not extinguish family ties between her and the applicant, the natural mother.[25]

19.20 On balance therefore it is probably safe to assume that the relationship between foster parents and foster children gives rise to family life considerations In any event they certainly give rise to 'private life' considerations (also protected by article 8). In *X v Switzerland*[26] the Commission proceeded on the basis that a separation order undoubtedly affected the private life of the applicant, who was the foster parent of a child for whom she had cared for many years.

Embryology and surrogacy

19.21 The European Court has yet to consider the full implications of artificial methods of insemination. In *X, Y and Z v UK*[27] it found that a family relationship existed between X, a female to male transsexual, Y his female partner and Z, Y's child by artificial insemination. X and Y had been in a stable relationship for nearly 20 years and X had acted as Z's 'father' in every respect since the birth.

---

21 *X v Belgium* (1975) 7 DR 75; *X v France* (1982) 31 DR 241.
22 (1990) 12 EHRR 36.
23 See para 19.31.
24 Note 2.
25 Note 2 at para 58.
26 (1978) 13 DR 248.
27 (1997) 24 EHRR 143.

19.22   The position of the sperm donor is, however, different. In *G v Netherlands*[28] the Commission held that the fact that a man donates his sperm in order to enable a woman to become pregnant through artificial insemination does not, of itself, give the donor a right to respect for family life with the child. On the facts of that case there had been some, but very little contact between the applicant and the child and he made no contribution, financial or otherwise, to the child's upbringing.

Lesbian and gay couples

19.23   A stable relationship between lesbian couples and/or gay couples has yet to be recognised by the Commission as constituting 'family life' within the meaning of article 8. And, so far, the issue has not been raised in any case before the European Court. In *X and Y v UK*[29] the Commission held, in the context of a deportation decision affecting a gay couple, that:

> Despite the modern evolution of attitudes towards homosexuality, the Commission finds that the applicant's relationship does not fall within the scope of respect for family life ensured by Article 8.[30]

However the Commission did find that the applicant's relationship was protected as an aspect of their 'private life'.

19.24   Since the Convention is to be interpreted as a 'living instrument' in light of present day conditions, it may well be that the decision in *X and Y v UK*[31] will be overturned in the future. As noted below, in respect of the rights of transsexuals, the European Court has repeatedly emphasised the need for its case-law to keep pace with societal developments.

Transsexuals

19.25   Although the European Court has not (yet) recognised the rights of transsexuals to change their birth certificates in England[32] or, more

28 (1993) 16 EHRR CD 38.
29 (1983) 32 DR 220.
30 Page 221; see also *Kerkhoven v Netherlands* (Commission) 19 May 1992 (unreported) in relation to lesbian couples.
31 Note 29.
32 See France: *B v France* (1994) 16 EHRR 1.

generally, to marry, it has recognised that 'family life' encompasses relationships between transsexuals and their 'opposite sex' partners. In *X, Y and Z v UK*[33] (see above) the Court found de facto family ties between X, a transsexual, Y his female partner and Z, Y's child by artificial insemination.[34]

Wider family relationships

19.26 In a number of cases the European Court and Commission have accepted that the protection of 'family life' in article 8 extends beyond the parent/child relationship and beyond the immediate family. In *Boughanemi v France*[35] one of the factors which led the Court to find that article 8 was engaged when the applicant was deported from France was that his ten siblings all lived in France.[36]

19.27 So far as the wider family is concerned, in *Marckz v Belgium*[37] the European Court observed that 'family life' includes at least the ties between near relatives such as those between grandparents and grandchildren, since such relatives may play a considerable part in family life.[38] Cohabitation is not necessary; but regular contact and visits are. On that basis, in *Price v UK*[39], the Commission found that article 8 was engaged when the applicant grandparents were denied access to their fostered grandchild.

19.28 In *Boyle v UK*[40] the Commission found that the relationship between an uncle and his nephew amounted to 'family life' where the uncle had established a clear pattern of contact and acted as a 'father figure' to his nephew. However, relationships between adult children and their parents are not usually covered by article 8(1) without evidence of 'further elements of dependency involving more than the normal emotional ties'.[41]

---

33 (1997) 24 EHRR 143.
34 Ibid at para 37.
35 (1996) 22 EHRR 228.
36 Ibid at para 35; see also *Moustaquim v Belgium* (1991) 13 EHRR 802.
37 (1979) 2 EHRR 330.
38 Ibid at para 45.
39 (1988) 55 DR 224.
40 (1994) 19 EHRR 179.
41 *Pathan v UK* Appl 26292–95 (Commission) 16 January 1996; unreported.

What does the right to family life cover?

19.29   The right to family life is not one right, but a bundle of rights. The essential ingredient of the right to family life is the right to develop normal family relationships. Where all the parties consent this will mean living together, free from state interference, and enjoying each others' company.[42] Where this is not possible, either because the adult parties have separated, or because a child has been taken into care or fostered, the right to family life safeguards contact between family members, subject only to such restrictions as can be justified under article 8(2).[43]

19.30   The European Court and Commission have long recognised that rights of this nature cannot be protected merely by state abstention from interference. They have therefore imposed positive obligations on states to ensure effective 'respect' for family life.[44] At the very least this requires the adoption of a legal framework capable of protecting all aspects of family life. In *Marckz v Belgium*[45] the Court observed that:

> ... When the State determines in its domestic legal system the regime applicable to certain family ties such as those between an unmarried mother and her child it must act in a manner calculated to allow those concerned to lead a normal family life.[46]

In some circumstances, positive obligations under article 8 will go much further than merely putting in place an appropriate legislative framework. In *Airey v Ireland*[47] what was in issue was not the existence of a satisfactory legal framework for the protection of Convention rights, but the applicant's access to it. The applicant there complained that her rights under article 8 had been breached because she was unable to divorce her alcoholic and violent husband since she could not afford legal representation and no legal aid was available to her. Having recognised that protection of family life includes the right to separate, the Court held that:

> Effective respect for private or family life obliges Ireland to make this means of protection effectively accessible, where appropriate, to anyone who may wish to have recourse thereto.

42   *Olsson v Sweden* No 1 note 6 at para 59.
43   See paras 19.3 to 19.10.
44   See chapter 5.
45   (1979) 2 EHRR 330.
46   Ibid at para 31.
47   (1979) 2 EHRR 305.

'Respect' may also include providing adequate remedies for individuals in the courts[48] and the enforcement of contact orders.[49]

19.31   Positive obligations arose in a different way in *Gaskin v UK*.[50] There, the European Court held that the right to private life imposed a positive obligation on the state to make available to the applicant confidential records relating to his childhood, when he was in local authority care. The Court reasoned that:

> ... Persons in the position of the applicant have a vital interest, protected by the Convention, in securing the information necessary to know and understand their childhood and early development.[51]

Marriage

19.32   The right to marry is specifically guaranteed in article 12 of the Convention. It has been interpreted as meaning the 'right to form a legal relationship, to acquire a status' the essence of which is 'the formation of a legally binding association between a man and a woman'.[52] The only restrictions on the right to marry permitted under the Convention are that (a) individuals wanting to marry be of 'marriageable age'; and (b) that they comply with the rules of domestic law.

19.33   Marriage can therefore be regulated by domestic law, but restrictions cannot be imposed on the right to marry if they destroy the very essence of that right.[53] Loss of welfare benefits on marriage[54] and increased tax burdens on married couples,[55] within reason, do not offend this principle.

19.34   Cohabitation is not a precondition for marriage. In *Hamer v UK*[56] the Commission found that:

> It is for [the parties to a marriage] to decide whether or not they wish to enter an association in circumstances where they cannot cohabit.[57]

---

48 See, for example, paras 19.50 to 19.52.
49 See *Hokkanen v Finland* A/299-A (1994) 19 EHRR 139.
50 (1989) 12 EHRR 36.
51 Ibid.
52 *Hamer v UK* (1979) 24 DR 5.
53 *Cossey v UK* (1990) 13 EHRR 622.
54 *Staarman v Netherlands* (1985) 42 DR 162.
55 (1986) 49 DR 181.
56 Note 52.
57 Ibid at p16.

Equally the right to marry is protected where there is no intention or possibility of procreation.[58]

19.35   Polygamous marriages may establish 'family life' within the meaning of article 8[59] but there is no obligation to give legal effect to such marriages under article 12.[60]

19.36   Where divorce is permitted, article 12 gives rise to a right to remarry. In *F v Switzerland*[61] the applicant was subject to a temporary prohibition on remarrying following his third divorce. Although measures designed to stabilise marriage were legitimate, the European Court found that this was a disproportionate interference with the applicant's article 12 rights.

19.37   To date, the European Court has held that the 'right to marry' in article 12 is not applicable to same sex couples. In *Rees v UK*,[62] a trans-sexual case, the Court observed that:

> ... the right to marry guaranteed by Article 12 refers to the traditional marriage between persons of opposite biological sex. This appears also from the wording of the Article which makes it clear that Article 12 is mainly concerned to protect marriage as the basis of the family ...[63]

It adopted the same approach in the later case of *Cossey v UK*.[64]

Founding a family

19.38   The extent of the right to found a family under article 12 is unclear. In *X and Y v Switzerland*[65] the Commission took the view that since the applicants were married they had already founded a family and this approach was followed in *Abdulaziz, Cabales and Balkandali v UK*[66] where the Court held that 'family' comes into existence upon lawful marriage. In *X and Y v Switzerland* the Commission held that article 12 could not provide the basis for conjugal visits in prison, on the basis that interference with family life permitted under article

---

58   *Hamer v UK* n52 at p16.
59   *A and A v Netherlands* (1992) 72 DR 118.
60   *Adam and Khan v UK* (1967) 10 Yearbook 478.
61   (1988) 10 EHRR 411.
62   (1987) 9 EHRR 56.
63   Ibid at para 49.
64   (1991) 13 EHRR 622.
65   (1978) 13 DR 241.
66   (1985) 7 EHRR 471.

8(2) could not amount to a violation of article 12. In a non prison context, the position is different. In *Abdulaziz, Cabales and Balkandali v UK* the European Court observed that 'it is scarcely conceivable that the right to found a family ... should not encompass the right to live together'.[67] However, as a general proposition, once children are born the protection of 'family life' in article 8 is broader than any protection found in article 12.

Children born out of wedlock

19.39   The case-law of the European Court and Commission concerning children born out of wedlock is a good example of the Convention being interpreted as a 'living instrument'. Whatever conception those drafting the Convention had of 'family life', the Strasbourg bodies have repeatedly emphasised that they cannot but be influenced by societal developments. In particular the Court has paid special regard to the preamble to the 1975 *European Convention on the legal status of children born out of wedlock* which notes that:

> ... in a great number of member States [of the Counsel of Europe] efforts have been, or are being, made to improve the legal status of children born out of wedlock by reducing the differences between their legal status and that of children born in wedlock, which are to the legal and social disadvantage of the former.

On that basis the Court and Commission have repeatedly upheld the principle that children born out of wedlock should not suffer on account of their birth.

19.40   In *Marckz v Belgium*[68] the European Court recognised that to give practical effect to this principle it was necessary for states to put in place a legal regime which would enable children born out of wedlock to develop the same ties with their parents as children born within wedlock.[69] Laws requiring an unmarried mother to adopt her own child and excluding such an adopted child from full legal rights in the family therefore breached article 8. Subsequently the Court has twice condemned laws which discriminate against children born out of wedlock in relation to inheritance.[70]

---

67   Ibid.
68   (1979) 2 EHRR 330.
69   For the limitations on this see: *B R and J v Germany* (1984) 36 DR 130.
70   *Inze v Austria* (1987) 10 EHRR 394; *Vermeire v Belgium* (1991) 15 EHRR 488.

19.41   The matter arose in a different way in *Johnston v Ireland*[71] where parents of a child argued that the prohibition on divorce preventing them remarrying and legitimising their child because the first applicant had been married before. The European Court rejected the applicant's primary complaint,[72] but found that examination of the child's position revealed that legally she was treated very differently from a legitimate child. On that basis, there was a breach of article 8. In other words, the state could maintain its laws prohibiting divorce but only if it put in place a legal regime to protect the rights of children born out of wedlock.[73]

Divorce and separation

19.42   In *Johnston v Ireland* (above) the European Court held that the right to marry under article 12 does not imply a right to divorce. The wording of article 12 was taken from article 16 of the *Universal Declaration of Human Rights*, but with the deliberate omission of the words: '[men and women of marriageable age] are entitled to equal rights as to marriage, during marriage and at its dissolution'. Societal developments did not enable the European Court to read into the Convention words deliberately left out by those drafting it.[74] Nor, reading the Convention as a whole, could a right to divorce be read into article 8 where it was deliberately left out of article 12.

19.43   However, effective protection for family life requires the law to recognise a right of married couples physically to separate and to be free from any obligation to live together.[75] Lack of legal aid for court proceedings may infringe this right.[76] And where domestic law does permit divorce, article 12 secures for divorced persons the right to remarry without unreasonable restrictions.[77]

---

71   (1986) 9 EHRR 203.
72   See paras 19.42 to 19.43.
73   Where paternity is contested there may be an obligation to provide a procedure whereby the issue can be resolved: *Rasmussen v Denmark* (1984) 7 EHRR 371.
74   Note 71 at para 52.
75   *Airey v Ireland* (1979) 2 EHRR 305.
76   See para 19.30.
77   *F v Switzerland* (1988) 10 EHRR 411: see para 19.36.

Custody and access

19.44 Custody and access decisions inevitably affect family life; particularly the right of an unsuccessful party to develop a relationship with his/her children. Article 8 does not guarantee any rights to custody and access as such, but it does recognise that after divorce or separation each parent retains an interest in his/her child which must be protected. In *Hendriks v Netherlands*[78] the Commission observed that:

> The right to respect for family life within the meaning of Article 8 of the Convention includes the right of a divorced parent, who is deprived of custody following the break up of marriage, to have access to or contact with his child.[79]

As a result, custody and access decisions must be justified, necessary and proportionate.

19.45 In all cases the best interests of the child will be paramount and usually determinative of article 8 issues. So, for example, in *Whitear v UK*[80] a complaint that an order severely restricting the applicant's contact with his daughter was incompatible with the Convention, was found to be inadmissible because it was made on the basis of the child's wellbeing and mental stability. The Commission considered that the best interests of the child were of crucial importance and interference with rights of access would be justified as pursuing a legitimate aim when intended to protect the child's health, in the broadest sense.

19.46 However, custody and access decisions must not be discriminatory, in breach of article 14 of the Convention. In *Hoffman v Austria*[81] the European Court found a violation of articles 8 and 14 where the applicant mother had been refused custody of her child because she was a Jehovah's Witness.

The enforcement of court orders

19.47 As a general proposition the non-enforcement of court orders in civil proceedings raises a fair trial issue under article 6(1) of the Con-

---

78 (1983) 5 EHRR 233.
79 Ibid at para 95.
80 Appl 28625/95 (Commission) 17 January 1997 (1997) EHRLR 291.
81 (1993) 14 EHRR 319.

vention.[82] In the context of family life and children it may also raise an issue under article 8. In *Hokkanen v Finland*[83] the European Court found a violation of the right to family life in the authorities' inaction over several years in enforcing court orders for access where the grandparents refused to return a child to the applicant father.

Maintenance payments

19.48   Imposing an obligation to make maintenance payments on an absent parent does not, of itself, infringe the right to family life under article 8. In *Logan v UK*[84] the Commission rejected the applicant's claim that the level of his maintenance payments assessed by the Child Support Agency left him with insufficient money to enable him to maintain reasonable contact with his children in breach of article 8. It left open the possibility that very high maintenance payments might need justification under article 8(2).

19.49   The Commission has also rejected a number of complaints that an obligation to pay maintenance in respect of a child who is being brought up contrary to the absent parent's wishes or religious beliefs breaches article 9 (freedom of thought, conscience and religion). In *Karakuzey v Germany*[85] the Commission held that:

> ... the obligation of a parent to pay maintenance to his child who is living with the other parent applies generally and has no specific conscientious implications in itself.

On that basis it found that article 9 did not confer on the applicant a right to refuse to pay maintenance on the basis of his religious beliefs.

Domestic violence

19.50   The State is under a positive obligation arising from article 3 (the prohibition on inhuman and degrading treatment) and article 8 (the protection of physical integrity and family life) to provide effective protection against domestic violence. One of the factors under-

---

82   See chapter 13.
83   (1994) 19 EHRR 139.
84   (1996) 22 EHRR CD 178.
85   (1996) 23 EHRR CD 92.

pinning the European Court's decision in *Airey v UK*[86] that lack of legal aid in separation proceedings breached article 8 of the Convention was the recognition that the applicant needed protection from her alcoholic and violent husband.

19.51   The issue of domestic violence was addressed more directly in *Whiteside v UK*[87] where the applicant complained that the absence of a tort of harassment in domestic law meant that she was inadequately protected against the violence of her former partner. Although the Commission found that a tort of harassment was not necessary to ensure adequate protection of the applicant's article 8 rights in view of the other remedies available to her, it did make some important observations of a general nature.

19.52   The Commission began by recalling that:

> ... the obligation to secure the effective exercise of Convention rights imposed by Article 1 of the Convention may involve positive obligations on the State and that these obligations may involve the adoption of measures even in the sphere of relations between individuals.[88]

It then found that the level of harassment – verbal and physical assaults, damage to property and following and watching the applicant – engaged the responsibility of the state such that it was under a positive obligation to secure the applicant's rights by providing adequate protection against such abuse.[89] On the facts, however, it found against the applicant.

Adoption

19.53   Adoption by its very nature is hugely disruptive of family life and, as a result, the interests of both parents must be respected. In *Keegan v Ireland*[90] the European Court could find no justification for legislation which allowed the mother of a child to place that child for adoption without the father's knowledge or consent. Moreover, adoption determines 'civil rights and obligations' and therefore the fair trial requirements of article 6(1) apply to adoption proceedings.[91]

86 Note 75.
87 (1994) 76-A DR 80.
88 Ibid at page 86; drawing on *X and Y v Netherlands* (1986) 8 EHRR 235.
89 Ibid.
90 (1994) 18 EHRR 342.
91 See chapters 12 and 13.

19.54   Adoption which precludes any contact between a natural parent and his/her child will be justified only in exceptional circumstances. In *Per Soderback v Sweden*[92] the Commission held that an adoption order made without the applicant's consent and which had the effect of depriving him of any access to his daughter breached article 8 because it had not been shown that the measure corresponded to any overriding requirement in the child's best interest.

Placing children in care

19.55   A decision to remove a child from his/her parent(s) and place him/her in care inevitably engages article 8 of the Convention and is always subject to close scrutiny. Such a decision must be justified under article 8(2) – usually 'to protect the rights of others' (the child) – and shown to be necessary and proportionate. In *Johansen v Norway*[93] the European Court laid down the following principles, which should be followed in all care proceedings:

1) taking a child into care should normally be regarded as a temporary measure to be discontinued as soon as circumstances permit;

2) any measures taken to implement a decision to place a child in temporary care should be consistent with the ultimate aim of reuniting the natural parent and child;

3) therefore a fair balance must be struck between the interests of the child in remaining in public care and those of the parent in being reunited with the child;

4) when assessing whether a fair balance has been struck, particular importance attaches to the best interests of the child which, depending on their nature and seriousness, may override those of the parent;

5) in particular, a parent cannot be entitled under article 8 to have measures taken that would harm the child's health and development.

19.56   In principle therefore, a parent retains a right of access to and contact with his/her child, even where that child is placed in care.

---

92 (Commission) 22 October 1997 (1998) EHRLR 342.
93 (1996) 23 EHRR 33.

Restrictions on visits,[94] lack of consultation on the child's future,[95] or delay[96] may therefore violate article 8.

19.57   The Convention does not rule out the possibility that children should be placed in care with a view to permanent adoption and that contact between parent and child should be terminated. However, such far-reaching measures should be applied only in exceptional circumstances and can be justified only if they are based on 'an over-riding requirement pertaining to the child's best interests'.[97]

Names

19.58   Unlike a number of other international instruments,[98] the Convention makes no express provision for family names. However, in *Burghartz v Switzerland*[99] the European Court recognised that an individual's name is a matter of private and/or family life. It is a means of identification and a link to a family.[100]

19.59   As a result, any restrictions on the choice, use or change of both forenames and surnames require justification under article 8(2) of the Convention. However, where individuals are free to use their chosen name without any real hindrance, the administrative inconvenience of changing all official records to reflect that name can justify not doing so.[101]

Sexual identity: the position of transsexuals

19.60   The question of transsexual identity has arisen in a number of cases before the European Court. In *Rees v UK*[102] a female to male transsexual complained that the government's refusal to alter his birth

94 *Eriksson v Sweden* (1990) 12 EHRR 183; *Andersson (M&R) v Sweden* n4.

95 *B v UK* A/121 (1988) 10 EHRR 87.

96 *H v UK* A/120 (1988) 10 EHRR 95; see para 19.69.

97 *Johansen v Norway* (1996) 23 EHRR 33 at para 78.

98 See, the *International Covenant on Civil and Political Rights*, article 24(2); the *Convention on the Rights of the Child*, articles 7 and 8; and *The American Convention on Human Rights*, article 18.

99 (1994) 18 EHRR 101.

100 See also *Stjerna v Finland* 24 EHRR 195; *Guillot v France* (Commission) 24 October 1996 (unreported).

101 *Guillot v France* (Commission) 24 October 1996 (unreported).

102 (1987) 9 EHRR 656.

certificate to reflect his change of sex breached his article 8 rights. Since in its view the law relating to transsexuals was in a transitional stage with no consensus across Europe, the Court approached the case cautiously and was prepared to afford the UK a wide margin of appreciation. Taking into account the fact that a birth certificate is a record of historical fact, not a document reflecting current civil status, and the administrative burden of changing the system for altering birth certificates, the Court found no breach of article 8. It did, however, add that the need for appropriate legal measures in relation to transsexuals should be kept under review having particular regard to scientific and societal development.[103]

19.61   Four years later, in *Cossey v UK*[104] the Court re-examined the birth certificate issue. However, it found that there had not been sufficient societal development to enable it to depart from its decision in *Rees v UK*. Significantly however the Court's majority dropped from 12/3 in *Rees* to 10/8 in *Cossey*.

19.62   The position was, however, different in *B v France*[105] which involved a male to female transsexual who was refused permission to alter her birth certificate. Under French law birth certificates are intended to be updated throughout the life of the person concerned, to reflect current civil status and any name changes, etc. This was markedly different from the position in the UK (see above) and accordingly the European Court found a breach of article 8.

19.63   Finally in *Sheffield and Horsham v UK*[106] two male to female transsexuals again complained about the refusal to alter their birth certificates to reflect their change of sex. The Court again followed *Rees v UK* and *Cossey v UK* but observed that:

> ... Despite [the Court's] statement in the *Rees* and *Cossey* cases on the importance of keeping the appropriate legal measures in this area under review having regard in particular to scientific and societal developments ... it would appear that the respondent State has not taken any steps to do so ... even if it finds no breach of Article 8 in this case, the Court reiterates that this area needs to be kept under review by contracting States.[107]

---

103 Ibid at para 47.
104 (1991) 13 EHRR 622.
105 (1994) 16 EHRR 1.
106 (1999) 27 EHRR 163.
107 Ibid at para 60.

In his concurring opinion, Judge Sir John Freeland added that 'Continued inaction on the part of the respondent State, together with further developments elsewhere, could well tilt the balance in the other direction' in future.[108]

Procedural fairness in proceedings concerning family life

19.64 There is a strict requirement of procedural fairness in proceedings concerning family life. This requirement is derived from articles 6(1) and 8. As far as article 6(1) is concerned, proceedings concerning family life will almost always amount to the determination of civil rights and obligations and thus attract the fair trial guarantee set out in that article. These guarantees are examined in detail in chapter 13 above. They include:

1) the right to an independent and impartial tribunal;

2) the right to disclosure;

3) the right to an adversarial hearing;

4) the right to reasons; and

5) the right to have decisions made within a reasons period.

The fact that a child has been taken into care does not extinguish a parent's civil rights and obligations under article 6(1).[109]

19.65 The requirements of fairness inherent in article 8 arise as a result of the European Court's recognition that 'respect' for family life can be achieved only if the interests of family members are taken into account when family life issues are determined. In particular, parents must be properly involved in proceedings concerning the custody, care and access of their children. If they are not so involved, any interference with family life will not be capable of being regarded as 'necessary' within the meaning of article 8.[110]

19.66 In *W v UK*[111] the Court found a violation of both article 6(1) and article 8 where the applicant was not consulted about plans to place his child with foster parents and to restrict his access to that child. In

---

108 Note 106 at p199–200.
109 *W v UK* (1987) 10 EHRR 29.
110 Ibid at paras 62 and 64.
111 Note 109.

the Court's view although article 8 contained no explicit procedural requirements;

> What ... has to be determined is whether, having regard to the particular circumstances of the case and notably the serious nature of the decisions to be taken, the parents have been involved in the decision-making process, seen as a whole, to a degree sufficient to provide them with the requisite protection of their interests.[112]

In *McMichael v UK*[113] the Court translated this into a requirement that 'the decision-making process leading to measures of interference must be fair and such as to afford due respect to the interests safeguarded by article 8'.[114]

19.67   Disclosure is particularly important in family proceedings because parents cannot be properly involved in the decision-making process if they do not know the basis upon which it is proposed a decision should be made. Hence in *McMichael v UK*[115] the European Court found a breach of article 6(1) and article 8 where social reports available to members of a children's hearing and, on appeal, to the Sheriff's Court were not disclosed to the parents in care proceedings concerning their son. The Court reasoned that:

> In the context of the present case, the lack of disclosure of such vital documents as social reports is capable of affecting the ability of participating parents not only to influence the outcome of the children's hearing in question but also to assess their prospects of making an appeal to the Sheriff Court.[116]

19.68   The case of *McMichael v UK*[117] is important in another respect. Under article 6(1), where an administrative body takes a decision affecting civil rights or obligations, either it must comply with article 6(1) or there must be the possibility of an appeal or review by a court or tribunal that does.[118] The position with respect to disclosure is stricter under article 8. The underlying rationale that parents should be involved in the decision-making process dictates that disclosure take place irrespective of the nature of the person or body taking the decision in question.[119]

112 Note 109 at para 62.
113 (1995) 20 EHRR 205.
114 Ibid at para 87.
115 Note 113.
116 Note 113 at para 80.
117 Note 113.
118 See paras 12.41 to 12.46.
119 See note 113 at para 91.

19.69   The requirement that decisions be reached within a reasonable period under article 6(1) has special application in family proceedings. In *H v UK*[120] the European Court found that childcare proceedings lasting two years and seven months breached article 6(1) because:

> In cases of this kind the authorities are under a duty to exercise exceptional diligence since, as the Commission rightly pointed out, there is always the danger that any procedural delay will result in the de facto determination of the issue submitted to the Court before it has held its hearing'[121]

See also, *Hokkanen v Finland*[122] in relation to custody cases.

120 (1987) 10 EHRR 95.
121 Ibid at para 85.
122 (1994) 19 EHRR 139.

CHAPTER 20

Children

20.1   Introduction

20.2   Parental control over children

20.6   Corporal punishment

20.13   Protection against abuse

20.15   The detention of children under article 5(1)(d) of the Convention

20.18   Children in criminal proceedings

20.22   The emergence of child-specific rights in the criminal context

20.29   The Strasbourg approach

Introduction

20.1   The Convention makes no express provision for the rights of children. However, as a general proposition, Convention rights apply to all individuals irrespective of age. And recently the European Court has been willing to attach considerable weight to the UN *Convention on the Rights of the Child.*[1] In due course, the influence of this instrument on the interpretation of the Convention may give rise to a more fully developed concept of children's rights in Strasbourg.

Parental control over children

20.2   While, as noted above, Convention rights apply to all individuals irrespective of age, the scope of protection afforded to children in respect of their dealings with adults, such as their parents or teachers, is slim. In *X v Netherlands*[2] a 14 year-old girl complained that, by returning her to her parents after she had run away, the authorities had given more weight to her parents' right to family life than to her own. The Commission agreed, but found no breach of article 8. In its view:

> As a general proposition, and in the absence of any special circumstances, the obligation of children to reside with their parents and to be otherwise subjected to particular control is necessary for the protection of childrens' health and morals, although it might constitute, from a particular child's point of view, an interference with his or her own private life.[3]

20.3   This proposition was subsequently developed by the European Court in *Nielsen v Denmark*[4] where it observed that:

> It should be observed at the outset that family life in the contracting States encompasses a broad range of parental rights and responsibilities in regard to care and custody of minor children. The care and upbringing of children normally and necessarily require that the parents or an only parent decide where the child must reside and also impose, or authorise others to impose, various restrictions on the child's liberty. Thus the children in a school or

---

1   *Olsson v Sweden* (No 2) (1994) 17 EHRR 134; *Costello-Roberts v UK* (1995) 19 EHRR 112; and *A v UK* (1998) 2 FLR 959; (1999) 27 EHRR 611.
2   (1974) 2 DR 118.
3   Ibid at p119. See also: *R v UK* (1988) 10 EHRR 74 at para 64.
4   (1988) 11 EHRR 175.

other educational or recreational institution must abide by certain rules which limit their freedom of movement and their liberty in other respects. Likewise a child may have to be hospitalised for medical treatment. Family life in this sense, and especially the rights of parents to exercise parental authority over their children, having due regard to their corresponding parental responsibilities, is recognised and protected by the Convention in particular by Article 8. Indeed the exercise of parental rights constitutes a fundamental element of family life.[5]

20.4 In that case the mother of a 12-year-old boy had placed him in a closed psychiatric ward because, on medical advice, she considered it appropriate to do so. By a narrow majority (9/7) the European Court found that this did not raise an issue under article 5 of the Convention because it amounted to the lawful exercise of parental rights under article 8.

20.5 However, there are limits to parental control over children. The Court's judgment in *Nielsen v Denmark* has been widely criticised and doubt has been expressed as to whether it will be followed in the future.[6] And, in *Nielsen* itself, the Court accepted that 'the rights of the holder of parental authority cannot be unlimited and ... it is incumbent on the State to provide safeguards against abuse'.[7]

Corporal punishment

20.6 The issue of corporal punishment has been a controversial one in Europe. In the early case of *Tyrer v UK*[8] a 15 year-old applicant complained that he had been subjected to punishment in breach of article 3 of the Convention in that he was sentenced in criminal proceedings to three strokes of a birch. The circumstances were that the punishment was administered three weeks after the court decision by police officers at a police station and involved two police officers holding the applicant while a third administered the birch to his bare buttocks.

20.7 The European Court took the view that such punishment was not sufficiently severe to amount to torture or inhuman punishment. The question was therefore whether it was degrading. Influenced by

---

5 Ibid at para 61; see also *R v UK* n3 para 64.
6 See Geraldine Van Bueren, *Protecting Children's Rights in Europe – a test case strategy* [1996] EHRLR 172 at p178.
7 Note 4 at para 72.
8 (1979) 2 EHRR 1.

developments in penal policy across Europe since the Convention was drafted, the Court found that it was. Significant factors were that the punishment involved the infliction of violence by one human being on another, that it was institutionalised and that it constituted an assault which in normal circumstances would be protected under article 3. The Court also considered that, even where punishment is carried out in the privacy of a police station, it may humiliate the applicant in his/her own eyes and therefore qualify as degrading treatment or punishment under article 3.

20.8   The question of corporal punishment in schools was first raised in *Campbell and Cosans v UK*.[9] In that case the applicant's children attended a state school. They had not actually been subjected to corporal punishment, but the Court accepted that the threat of conduct prohibited by article 3 might conflict with its provisions. On analysis, however, the European Court came to the conclusion that, in the absence of any real threat of immediate corporal punishment, the mere fact that it was a possible sanction did not cause sufficient apprehension in the applicant's children to bring their case within article 3. There was, however, a breach of article 2 of Protocol 1 (right to education) when the school refused to re-admit the applicant's children unless she agreed to subject them to the regime which included corporal punishment.

20.9   The situation was different in *Warwick v UK*[10] which again involved punishment in a state school. Having been caught smoking, a 16-year-old girl was caned on her hand causing bruising which was still visible eight days later. Although the applicant's mother complained to the police, no prosecution was brought and a civil action for damages was dismissed on the ground that the punishment was not 'improper, inappropriate or disproportionate'. Nonetheless the Commission found the punishment degrading bearing in mind that:

1) it was inflicted by a man on a 16-year-old girl;

2) the punishment caused physical injury;

3) psychological injury could not be ruled out;

4) no formal rules had been drawn up by the local education authority regulating the use of corporal punishment, which was accordingly left to the discretion of head teachers.

9   (1982) 4 EHRR 293.
10   (1986) 60 DR 5.

20.10   The issue arose again in *Costello-Roberts v UK*.[11] The distinguishing features of that case being that the punishment was administered in a private school and the child in question was only seven. As a preliminary issue the European Court had little doubt that state responsibility was engaged on the basis that the state could not absolve itself of its Convention obligations by delegating tasks such as the provision of education to private bodies or individuals.[12] However the Court went on to find that there was no breach of either article 3 or article 8 (physical integrity). The Court distinguished the case from *Tyrer v UK*[13] on the basis that the punishment was administered in private, amounted to only three strokes with a rubber-soled slipper on the buttocks through shorts. Furthermore, beyond the consequences to be expected from measures taken on a purely disciplinary plain, the applicant had adduced no evidence of any severe or long-term effect. While the Court had certain misgivings about the automatic nature of the punishment and the three-day delay before it was administered, it concluded that the minimum level of severity required by article 3 had not been reached. Although this did not automatically mean that the punishment did not breach article 8 either, having regard to the purpose and aim of the Convention as a whole, and bearing in mind that school life inevitably involved a degree of interference with private life, the Court found that article 8 was not engaged.

20.11   Finally, the question of parental punishment was raised in *A v UK*.[14] In that case the applicant, a boy of nine, had been regularly beaten by his stepfather with a cane causing severe bruising. For some time he had been placed on the local Child Protection Register and the stepfather had received a caution from the police after he admitted hitting A with a cane. When the punishment continued, A's stepfather was prosecuted for assault occasioning actual bodily harm. However, he successfully raised the defence of lawful punishment – the burden of proof being on the prosecution to prove beyond reasonable doubt that the assault was not lawful. Having reviewed the evidence, which included multiple bruising inflicted over several days, the European Court had no doubt that the conduct was prohibited by article 3. The question was therefore what responsi-

11   (1993) 19 EHRR 112.
12   Ibid at paras 26–28.
13   Note 8.
14   Note 1.

bility, if any, the state bore for the infliction of such punishment by one private individual on another private individual.

20.12   Recalling that states have a positive obligation to protect vulnerable individuals from serious breaches of their personal integrity[15] the Court found a breach of article 3. The defence of lawful chastisement was too wide and failed to protect the applicant effectively against ill treatment. In effect, the Court signalled (and the government accepted) that the defence of lawful chastisement was too wide and needed to be amended.

Protection against abuse

20.13   The case of *A v UK*,[16] referred to above, emphasizes the state's duty to protect vulnerable individuals, such as children, from serious breaches of their personal integrity. In the context of child abuse, this duty was most clearly recognised in *X and Y v Netherlands*.[17] In that case the perpetrator of a sexual assault on the second applicant had not been prosecuted because under Dutch law the fact that the victim was a 16 year-old woman with a mental disorder prevented her from initiating a criminal 'complaint'. The government argued that since it was possible to bring civil proceedings for compensation, its obligations under article 8 of the Convention had been fulfilled. The Court disagreed. In its view:

> ... the protection afforded by the civil law in the case of wrongdoing of the kind inflicted on Miss Y is insufficient. This is a case where fundamental values and essential aspects of private life are at stake. Effective deterrence is indispensable in this area and it can be achieved only by criminal law provision; indeed, it is by such provisions that the matter is normally regulated.[18]

Since Dutch law was defective in this respect, state responsibility was engaged.

20.14   The general duty to protect children from abuse was also emphasised in *Stubbings v UK*[19] which involved an argument about limitation periods. Although ultimately the applicants lost their case, the European Court began its analysis by reiterating that 'sexual

---

15   See *X and Y v Netherlands* (1985) 8 EHRR 235. See generally chapter 5.
16   Note 1.
17   Note 15.
18   Note 15 at para 27.
19   (1996) 23 EHRR 213.

abuse is unquestionably an abhorrent type of wrongdoing, with debilitating effects on its victim. Children and other vulnerable individuals are entitled to State protection, in the form of effective deterrents, from such grave types of interference with essential aspects of their private lives.'[20]

The detention of children under article 5(1)(d) of the Convention

20.15 Article 5 protects the liberty and security of children as well as adults. However, article 5(1)(d) provides two grounds of detention applicable only to children.

20.16   The first permits the detention of a child for the purpose of education supervision pursuant to a 'lawful order'. In this context the word 'lawful' connotes compliance with domestic law[21] and the reference to 'order' means an order of the court or an administrative authority. It is intended to underpin a general obligation that children attend school. Since it is the *purpose* of detention under article 5(1)(d) that is crucial, temporary detention at a police station or even at a prison can be justified if as a preliminary to a regime of supervised education.[22] However, in *Bouamar v Belgium*[23] the European Court held that the Belgian authorities could not invoke the 'educational supervision' provision in article 5(1)(d) to justify the isolated confinement of a 16 year-old child in a remand prison on nine different occasions for periods of seven to 14 days, totalling 119 days in all because:

> ... the detention of a young man in a remand prison in conditions of virtual isolation and without the assistance of staff with educational training cannot be regarded as furthering any educational aim.[24]

20.17 The second limb of article 5(1)(d) provides for the detention of a child for the purpose of bringing him/her before a 'competent legal authority'. This does not authorise detention pending criminal proceedings, which are governed by article 5(1)(c).[25] It is intended to

20 Ibid at para 64.
21 Both substantive and procedural; see paras 3.33 to 3.40.
22 *Bouamar v Belgium* (1987) 11 EHRR 1 at para 50.
23 Note 22.
24 Note 22 at para 52.
25 See paras 3.51 to 3.54.

provide for situations in which it is necessary to detain a child to 'secure his removal from harmful surroundings';[26] for example, detention pending a court order placing a child in care.[27]

Children in criminal proceedings

20.18   It has long been recognised that the fair trial rights enshrined in the Convention attach to children as well as to adults.[28] However, the idea that children might benefit from more extensive (and more generous) protection than adults – a relatively recent development in international human rights law – is not expressly provided. However, as a result of the increasing willingness of the European Court to draw on other international human rights instruments when developing its case-law, this idea is beginning to find reflection in Convention jurisprudence

20.19   The case-law of the European Court and Commission makes it clear that both articles 5 and 6 of the Convention apply to children.[29] In *Nortier v Netherlands*[30] the Commission took the view that any suggestion that children who are tried for criminal offences should not benefit fully from the fair trial guarantees of article 6 was unacceptable.[31]

20.20   The Court, although not called upon to decide the point, did not dissent from this view. However, Judge Walsh, in a concurring judgment, emphasised that:

> Juveniles facing criminal charges are as fully entitled as adults to benefit from all the Convention requirements for a fair trial. Great care must always be taken to ensure that this entitlement is not diluted by considerations of rehabilitation or of reform. These are considerations which should be in addition to all the procedural predictions available. Fair trial and proper proof of guilt are absolute conditions precedent.[32]

---

26   See the *travaux préparatoires*: 3 TP 724.
27   *Law of the European Convention on Human Rights* Harris et al, Butterworths, 1995, p121.
28   See para 20.19.
29   See, for example: *Nielsen v Denmark* (1989) 11 EHRR 175; *Singh v UK* and *Hussain v UK* (1996) 22 EHRR 1.
30   (1993) 17 EHRR 273.
31   Ibid para 60.
32   Ibid at 290.

20.21 Judge Morenilla, again in a concurring judgment, agreed. In his view:

> ... minors are as entitled to the same protection of their fundamental rights as adults but ... the developing state of their personality – and consequently their limited social responsibility – should be taken into account in applying Article 6 of the Convention.[33]

Drawing explicitly on the *UN Convention on the Rights of the Child*,[34] Judge Morenilla concluded that member states should afford children:

> ... the 'necessary protection and assistance so that they can fully assume their responsibilities within the community' and prepare them 'to live an individual life in society', by promoting 'the establishment of laws, procedures, authorities and institutions applicable to children alleged as, accused of, or recognised as having infringed the criminal law'[35]

The emergence of child-specific rights in the criminal context

20.22 The emergence of child-specific rights began with the *International Covenant on Civil and Political Rights*[36] (ICCPR), which entered into force in 1976. It provides that:

> Accused juvenile persons shall be separated from adults and brought as speedily as possible for adjudication.[37]

And, in the context of fair trial guarantees, that:

> In the case of juveniles, the procedure [for determining any criminal charge] shall be such as will take account of their age and the desirability of promoting their rehabilitation.[38]

20.23 Nine years later, these broad principles were refined in the UN Standard Minimum Rules for the Administration of Juvenile Justice

---

33 Ibid at 291.
34 See appendix G.
35 Note 11 at 291.
36 See appendix D.
37 Article 10(2)(b).
38 Article 14(4).

('the *Beijing Rules*'), adopted in 1985. One of the 'fundamental perspectives' of the *Beijing Rules* is that:

> ... juvenile justice shall be conceived as an integral part of the national development process of each country, within a comprehensive framework of social justice for all juveniles ... contributing to the protection of the young and the maintenance of a peaceful order in society ...[39]

This is supplemented by a requirement that juvenile justice be constantly improved.[40]

20.24   More specifically, rule 5.1 provides that juvenile justice systems should emphasise 'the well-being of the juvenile' and ensure 'that any reaction to juvenile offenders shall always be in proportion to the circumstances of both the offenders and the offence'. To encourage this, rule 6.1 provides that:

> In view of the varying special needs of juveniles as well as the variety of measures available, appropriate scope for discretion shall be allowed at all stages of proceedings and at the different levels of juvenile justice administration, including investigation, prosecution, adjudication and the follow-up of disposals.

This is subject to appropriate checks and balances, including proper accountability.[41]

20.25   In a similar vein, rule 18.1 deals with 'disposition measures'. It requires that:

> A large variety of disposition measures shall be made available to the competent authority, allowing for flexibility so as to avoid institutionalisation to the greatest extent possible. Such measures, some of which may be combined, include:
> (a) Care, guidance and supervision orders;
> (b) Probation;
> (c) Community service orders;
> (d) Financial penalties, compensation and restitution;
> (e) Intermediate treatment and other treatment orders;
> (f) Orders to participate on group counselling and similar activities;
> (g) Orders concerning foster care, living communities or other educational settings;
> (h) Other relevant orders.

---

39   Rule 1.4.
40   Rule 1.6.
41   Rule 6.2.

The placement of a juvenile in an institution should always be a disposition of last resort and for the minimum period necessary.[42]

20.26 In 1987 the Committee of Ministers of the Council of Europe adopted Recommendation No R(87)20 on 'Social reactions to Juvenile Delinquency'[43] which specifically recognised that 'the penal system for minors should continue to be characterised by its objective of education and social integration'. Through the Recommendation, the Committee of Ministers urged member states to review their legislation and practice with a view, inter alia, 'to avoiding committing minors to adult courts, where juvenile courts exist'.[44]

20.27 The strongest recognition in international human rights law that children accused of criminal offences should be treated differently from adults is found in the UN *Convention on the Rights of the Child*,[45] which came into force in 1990. Article 40(1) provides that:

> States Parties recognise the right of every child alleged as, accused of, or recognised as having infringed the penal law to be treated in a manner consistent with the promotion of the child's sense of dignity and worth, which reinforces the child's respect for the human rights and fundamental freedoms of others and which takes into account the child's age and the desirability of promoting the child's reintegration and the child's assuming a constructive role in society.

Article 40(3) supplements this by requiring that:

> States Parties shall seek to promote the establishment of laws, procedures, authorities and institutions specifically applicable to children alleged as, accused of, or recognised as having infringed the penal law, and, in particular:
> (a) The establishment of a minimum age below which children shall be presumed not to have the capacity to infringe the penal law;
> (b) Whenever appropriate and desirable, measures for dealing with such children without resorting to judicial proceedings, providing that human rights and legal safeguards are fully respected.

And, in accordance with article 40(4):

> A variety of dispositions, such as care, guidance and supervision orders; counselling; probation; foster care; educational and

---

42 Rule 19.1.
43 Adopted at the 410th meeting of Ministers' deputies on 17 September 1987.
44 Para 5.
45 See appendix G.

vocational training programmes and other alternatives to institutional care shall be available to ensure that children are dealt with in a manner appropriate to their well-being and proportionate both to their circumstances and the offence.

20.28   Still more specific requirements are set out in the UN Guidelines for the Prevention of Juvenile Delinquency ('the *Riyadh Guidelines*'), adopted in 1990. Among the fundamental principles of these guidelines is the recognition that 'the prevention of juvenile delinquency is an essential part of crime prevention in society'[46] such that delinquency prevention policies should:

> ... avoid criminalising and penalising a child for behaviour that does not cause serious damage to the development of the child or harm to others.

In addition, the UN *Rules for the Protection of Juveniles Deprived of their Liberty*,[47] adopted at the same time at the *Riyadh Guidelines*, insist that 'the juvenile justice system should uphold the rights and safety and promote the physical and mental well-being of juveniles ...'.[48]

The Strasbourg approach

20.29   The proper approach to the rights of children in criminal proceedings under the European Convention on Human Rights has yet to be fully developed by the European Court. In *V v UK*[49] the applicant, an 11-year old boy who had been convicted of murder, argued that his public trial in an adult court (the Crown Court) breached his right to a fair trial under article 6(1) of the Convention because he had been unable to participate effectively in the proceedings. It was argued before the Commission that, while the applicant may have had the intellectual capacity to understand some elements of the trial process, he lacked the emotional strength to follow the trial or to take decisions in his own best interests. And he did not give evidence.

20.30   As a matter of general principle, the Commission held that:

> ... where a child is faced with a criminal charge and the domestic system requires a fact-finding procedure, with a view to establishing guilt, it is essential that his age, level of maturity and intellectual

---

46 Para 1.1.
47 A/RES/45/113.
48 Rule 1.
49 Commission Report (4 December 1998); noted at [1998] EHRLR 484.

and emotional capacities be taken into account in the procedures followed.[50]

20.31   Although in *V v UK* the applicant had been provided with a social worker and court sitting periods had been shortened, these safeguards were not enough. Although article 6 generally requires a public hearing, the Commission considered that:

> ... the public trial process in an adult court with attendant publicity must be regarded in the case of an eleven year old child as a severely intimidating procedure. The way in which the trial placed the applicant in a raised dock, as the focus of intense public attention over a period of three weeks, must have seriously impinged on his ability to participate in the proceedings in any meaningful manner.[51]

The Commission therefore concluded that

> ... where the alleged offender is a child, the procedures adopted must be conducive to an active participation, as opposed to passive presence. Otherwise the trial risks presenting the appearance of an exercise in the vindication of public outrage.[52]

In the circumstances, there was a breach of article 6(1) of the European Convention, but not of article 3.

50   Para 104.
51   Ibid.
52   Para 105.

CHAPTER 21

Education

21.1   Introduction

21.5   The scope of the right to education

21.10   Regulation of the right to education

21.12   The right to respect for religious and philosophical convictions

21.15   The meaning of 'religious' and 'philosophical' convictions

21.17   The meaning of 'respect'

21.22   Whose convictions count?

21.24   The distinction between basic elementary and higher education

21.26   Private schools

21.29   Funding

21.31   Special needs

21.34   Setting the curriculum

21.38   Disciplinary matters

21.40   Corporal punishment

21.42   Suspension/expulsion

21.46   Challenging disciplinary measures

21.48   School uniform requirements

Introduction

21.1   Article 2 of the Protocol 1 of the Convention provides that:

> No person shall be denied the right to education. In the exercise of any functions which it assumes in relation to education and to teaching, the State shall respect the right of parents to ensure such education and teaching in conformity with their own religious and philosophical aims.

21.2   The UK has entered a reservation in respect of this right in the following terms:

> ... in view of certain provisions of the Education Acts in the United Kingdom, the principle affirmed in the second sentence of Article 2 is accepted by the United Kingdom only in so far as it is compatible with the provision of efficient instruction and training, and the avoidance of unreasonable public expenditure.

Under the Human Rights Act 1998 this reservation has effect in domestic law.[1]

21.3   Whether this reservation will withstand challenge in Strasbourg is not clear. In *SP v UK*,[2] the Commission expressed the view that, in light of developments in the European Court's case-law on reservations,[3] 'questions may arise' about the validity of the UK reservation. And, even if valid, it may not apply to statutory provisions which came into force after it was made.[4]

21.4   A number of other Convention rights are relevant to questions of education: for example, article 3 (the prohibition on inhuman and degrading treatment/punishment), article 8 (the right to privacy and family life), article 9 (freedom of religion), article 13 (the right to an effective remedy) and article 14 (the prohibition on discrimination). However, none of these provisions can set up a right to education where none exists under article 2 of Protocol 1.[5]

---

1   See paras 1.62 to 1.65.
2   (1997) 23 EHRR CD 139.
3   See, in particular, *Belilos v Switzerland* (1988) 10 EHRR 466 paras 52–59.
4   Note 2 at 142; see also the Court's comments in *Campbell and Cosans v UK* (1982) 4 EHRR 293 at para 37.
5   *Belgian Linguistics Case (No 2)* (1968) 1 EHRR 252.

The scope of the right to education

21.5 The wording of article 2 of Protocol 1 was a controversial issue at the drafting stage. The first draft provided that 'every person has the right to education'. Fear that this might give rise to onerous positive obligations led to the present form which merely provides that 'no person shall be denied the right to education'.[6] The significance of this change was examined by the European Court in the *Belgian Linguistics Case (No 2)*.[7]

21.6 In that case the Court held that, despite its negative formulation, there is no doubt that article 2 of Protocol 1 enshrines a 'right'. However, the drafting history of the Convention dictated that a narrow view be taken of its content. Consequently the Court found that the 'right to education' in article 2 of Protocol 1 did not bestow on individuals a right to require state authorities to set up a particular type or level of education. Rather it bestowed on them a 'right of access' to education facilities that already exist.[8] Since all member states of the Council of Europe had a system of elementary state education in place when Protocol 1 was opened for signature, the Court has taken the view that any debate about whether the Convention requires that such a system be set up is otiose.[9]

21.7 Since, like other Convention rights, the right to education is to be construed so that it is 'practical and effective',[10] a 'right of access' to education facilities is not, in itself, enough. Individuals must have the opportunity to draw benefit from the education they receive.[11] According to the Court in the *Belgian Linguistics Case (No 2)*[12] this means at the very least that:

1) there is a right to be taught in the national language, or one of the national languages, as the case may be; and

2) there should be official recognition of any qualifications obtained on the completion of studies.[13]

6 See Harris, O'Boyle and Warbrick, *Law of the European Convention on Human Rights* (Butterworths, 1995) p541.

7 Note 5.

8 Note 5 at para 3.

9 Ibid.

10 See paras 4.12 to 4.15.

11 Note 5 at para 4.

12 Note 5.

13 This does not mean that states must recognise as valid in their own jurisdiction, qualifications obtained in foreign jurisdictions, see: *X v Belgium* (1979) 16 DR 82 and *Glazewska v Sweden* (1985) 45 DR 300.

21.8   However, there is no right for individuals to be taught in the language of their, or their parents', choice.[14] Nor is there a right of access to a particular school of choice. Parents who complained of the closure of a local school had their complaint to the Commission rejected on the basis that the children were able to attend another school a mile further away.[15]

21.9   Education has been defined widely by the Court. In *Campbell and Cosans v UK*[16] it observed that:

> ... the education of children is the whole process whereby, in any society, adults endeavour to transmit their beliefs, culture and other values to the young, whereas teaching or instruction refers in particular to the transmission of knowledge and to intellectual development.[17]

Consequently, where private bodies or individuals undertake education in this broad sense, the state should refrain from interfering save to the extent that it can legitimately regulate education in accordance with article 2 of Protocol 1.

Regulation of the right to education

21.10   According to the European Court in *Belgian Linguistics Case (No 2)*:[18]

> ... the right to education guaranteed by the first sentence of Article 2 of the [First] Protocol by its very nature calls for regulation by the State.[19]

Such restriction 'may vary in time and place according to the needs and resources of the community and of individuals' but 'must never injure the substance of the right to education nor conflict with other rights enshrined in the Convention'.[20]

21.11   Pursuant to this principle, states can regulate both public and private schools. This will often take the form of quality control. States

---

14 Note 5 at para 6.
15 *X v UK* (Commission) 1 December 1986 (unreported): see Reid, *A Practitioner's Guide to the European Convention on Human Rights* (Sweet & Maxwell, 1998) p202.
16 (1982) 4 EHRR 293.
17 Ibid at para 33.
18 Note 5.
19 Note 5 at para 5.
20 Ibid.

can refuse private bodies permission to run schools where they do not provide education to the required standard.[21] In addition, states may make schooling compulsory and punish parents who refuse to comply with any attendant obligations.[22] They can also require all parents to co-operate in assessing the educational attainments of their children.[23]

The right to respect for religious and philosophical convictions

21.12   The second sentence of article 2 of Protocol 1 enjoins the state to respect parents' religious and philosophical convictions. This duty is broad in its extent because it applies not only to the content of education and the manner of its provision but also to the performance of all the 'functions' assumed by the state.

21.13   In *Campbell and Cosans v UK*[24] the government argued that functions relating to the internal administration of a school, such as discipline, were ancillary to education and therefore that the convictions of parents were not relevant to their enforcement. The European Court rejected this on the basis that 'the use of corporal punishment may, in a sense, be said to belong to the internal administration of a school, but at the same time it is, when used, an integral part of the process whereby a school seeks to achieve the object for which it was established'.[25]

21.14   Whether article 2 of Protocol 1 gives parents a right not to send their children to school, but rather to educate them at home, remains unclear. However, where education at home is permitted, the state does not breach the requirement to respect parents' convictions by requiring them to co-operate in the assessment of their children's educational attainments.[26]

21 *Jordebo v Sweden* (1987) 51 DR 125.
22 *Family H v UK* (1984) 37 DR 105.
23 Ibid.
24 Note 16.
25 Note 16 at para 33; see also, *Kjeldsen, Busk Madsen and Pedersen v Denmark* (1976) 1 EHRR 711 at para 50.
26 *Family H v UK* n22.

The meaning of 'religious' and 'philosophical' convictions

21.15   Religious convictions are relatively easy to identify. Philosophical convictions less so. The adjective 'philosophical' is not capable of exhaustive definition and the European Court has declined attempts to do so. However, it has consistently maintained that philosophical convictions will not be relevant under article 2 of Protocol 1 unless;

1) such convictions are worthy of respect in a 'democratic society';

2) they are not incompatible with human dignity; and

3) they do not conflict with the fundamental right of the child to education.[27]

The propriety or otherwise of corporal punishment satisfies each of these criteria.[28]

21.16   The word 'convictions' is not synonymous with the word 'opinions' or 'ideas' used in article 10 of the Convention (freedom of expression). It is more akin to the word 'beliefs' in article 9 (freedom of thought, conscience and religion). As such, it denotes views that attain a certain level of cogency, seriousness, cohesion and importance.[29]

The meaning of 'respect'

21.17   The word 'respect' means more than 'acknowledge' or 'take into account'. And in addition to a primarily negative undertaking, it implies some positive obligations on the part of the state.[30]

21.18   However, the duty to 'respect' parents' convictions does not put state authorities under a duty to comply with such convictions. There is, in effect, no absolute right for parents to have their children educated in accordance with their religious or philosophical convictions; only a right to have such convictions 'respected'.[31]

21.19   In *W and Others v UK*[32] the applicants complained that, according to their convictions, their children should have been given places in

---

27   *Campbell and Cosans v UK* n16 at para 36.

28   Ibid.

29   Ibid.

30   *Campbell and Cosans v UK* n16 at para 37; *Valsamis v Greece* (1996) 24 EHRR 294 at para 27.

31   *Family H v UK* n22.

32   (1984) 37 DR 96.

a local single-sex grammar school, not a mixed-sex comprehensive school. The Commission disagreed. In its view, there was no evidence that the way in which children are taught in comprehensive schools conflicted with article 2 of Protocol 1 and the local education authority's reasons for placing the applicants' children in the comprehensive school – lack of grammar school places and efficient use of resources – did not conflict with the Convention.

21.20 This is consistent with the reasoning in the Court's analysis of the obligations arising under article 2 of Protocol 1 in the *Belgian Linguistics Case (No 2)*[33] and follows *X v UK*[34] where the applicant claimed that the state's failure to provide funding for a non-denominational school in Northern Ireland conflicted with his religious and philosophical beliefs. The Commission rejected the complaint on the basis that, interpreting article 2 of Protocol 1 as a whole, there is no positive obligation on the state to fund or subsidise any particular form of education in order to respect the religious and philosophical convictions of parents. It is enough if the relevant authorities respect such convictions within the existing system of education.[35] See also *W and KL v Sweden*[36] on the funding of private schools.[37]

21.21 Moreover, 'respect' is to be interpreted objectively. In *Valsamis v Greece*[38] the applicants complained that their daughter had been required, on pain of suspension, to take part in a school parade contrary to their convictions as Jehovah's Witnesses. The European Court rejected this on the basis that, whatever the parents thought, it could discern nothing in the purpose of the parade or in the arrangements for it which could offend the applicants' pacifist convictions to the extent prohibited by article 2 of Protocol 1.[39]

Whose convictions count?

21.22 Although article 2 of Protocol 1 refers to the philosophical and religious convictions of 'parents', in reality legal custody is the defining factor. So, for example, in *X v Sweden*[40] the Commission

33 Note 5.
34 (1978) 14 DR 179.
35 Ibid at 180.
36 (1985) 45 DR 143.
37 Paras 21.29 to 21.30.
38 (1996) 24 EHRR 294.
39 Ibid at para 31.
40 (1977) 12 DR 192.

refused to admit a complaint from the applicant father that his child was not being educated in accordance with his philosophical and religious convictions where, by a court order, legal custody vested in the child's mother. For the Commission:

> ... the right to determine the mode of a child's education is an integral part of the right of custody ...[41]

21.23   Similarly, where custody has been transferred to adoptive parents, their convictions prevail over those of the natural parents.[42] In *X v UK*,[43] the Commission left open the question of whether there is any duty not to transfer parental authority of a child to someone who does not share the convictions of the natural parents.[44] And where a child is simply taken into care, the convictions of the natural parents are still relevant.[45]

The distinction between basic elementary and higher education

21.24   In its decision in the *Belgian Linguistics* case, the Commission stated that the right to education 'includes entry to nursery, primary, secondary and higher education'.[46] However, it has subsequently distinguished between elementary and higher education and maintained that 'the right to education envisaged in [article 2 of Protocol 1] is concerned primarily with elementary education and not necessarily advanced studies'.[47] Individual rights in respect of one level of education may not be the same for another.

21.25   In particular, it seems that while article 2 of Protocol 1 requires universal access to elementary education,[48] selective access to

---

41   Ibid at 194.
42   *X v UK* (1977) 11 DR 160.
43   Ibid.
44   Ibid at 168.
45   *Aminoff v Sweden* (1985) 43 DR 120.
46   (Commission) 23 July 1968 (merits) p22.
47   See: *X v UK* (1975) 2 DR 50; 15 *Foreign Students v UK* (1977) 9 DR 185; *Yanasik v Turkey* (1993) 74 DR 14; and *Sulak v Turkey* (1996) 84-A DR 98.
48   See Harris, O'Boyle and Warbrick, *Law of the European Convention on Human Rights* (Butterworths, 1995) p541; Wildhaber in Macdonald et al, *The European System for the Protection of Human Rights* (Martinus Nijhoff Publishers, 1993) p533.

higher education is permitted.[49] In *X v UK*[50] the Commission held that:

> ... where certain, limited, higher education facilities are provided by a State, in principle it is not incompatible with Article 2 of Protocol 1, to restrict access thereto to those students who have attained the academic level required to most benefit from the courses offered.[51]

The distinction may also have an impact where a student has exceeded the maximum permitted period for certain studies[52] or is expelled.[53]

Private schools

21.26 Private schools are not incompatible with the Convention. In *Kjeldsen, Busk Madsen and Pedersen v Denmark*[54] the European Court noted that the travaux preparatoires indicated an intention on the part of those drafting the Convention to guarantee 'freedom' to set up and maintain private schools. And, although the text of article 2 of Protocol 1 makes no reference to this freedom, in *Jordebo v Sweden*[55] the Commission spoke in terms of a 'right' to set up and run private schools;[56] a view it subsequently affirmed in *Verein Gemeinsam Lernen v Austria*.[57]

21.27 However, this right is not unlimited. In *Jordebo v Sweden*[58] the Commission observed that:

> It must be subject to regulation by the State in order to ensure a proper educational system as a whole.[59]

There was no breach therefore when the state refused a private school permission to engage in teaching above a certain level when it failed to meet the required standards of quality.

49 See further, *Law of the European Convention on Human Rights* n48, p541.
50 (1980) 23 DR 228.
51 Ibid at 229; see also *Glazewska v Sweden* (1985) 45 DR 300 at 302.
52 Appl 5492/72 (Commission) 16 July 1973, 44 Coll 63.
53 See paras 21.42 to 21.45.
54 (1976) 1 EHRR 711.
55 (1987) 51 DR 125.
56 Ibid at 128.
57 (1995) 82-A DR 41.
58 Note 55.
59 Ibid at 128.

21.28   Moreover, the state remains responsible for ensuring that Convention rights are respected in private schools. For example, in the administration of corporal punishment and in the requirement that the religious and philosophical convictions of parents be respected.[60]

Funding

21.29   Numerous cases before the Commission have raised the question of state funding for particular schools. On the basis of the European Court's analysis of the obligations imposed on the state by article 2 of Protocol 1 in *Belgian Linguistics Case (No 2)*[61] – essentially that there is no obligation to provide or subsidise any particular type of education – the Commission has rejected them all. The list includes cases in which applicants have claimed that their religious or philosophical convictions require the funding of non-denominational schools,[62] single-sex grammar schools,[63] private schools[64] and schools for children with special educational needs.[65]

21.30   However, there is an important qualification. Even though there is no duty to fund particular schools, where the state funds some schools and not others, it must not infringe the prohibition on discrimination set out in article 14.[66]

Special needs

21.31   The education of children with special needs has been raised in a number of cases before the Commission, but not (as yet) before the European Court. Essentially, two complaints have been made, reflecting the different stand-points of the applicants:

1)   Some applicants have argued that by not providing special edu-

---

60   *Kjeldsen, Busk Madsen and Pedersen v Denmark* n54; *Campbell and Cosans v UK* n16.

61   Note 5.

62   *X v UK* n34.

63   *W and Others v UK* n32.

64   See *X v Sweden* (Commission) 7 May 1984; *Y v Sweden* (Commission) 7 May 1984; *W and KL v Sweden* (1985) 45 DR 143; *Verein Gemeinsam Lernen v Austria* n57.

65   *Simpson v UK* (1989) 64 DR 188.

66   See *Verein Gemeinsam Lernen v Austria* n57.

cational facilities for children with special needs, the state has denied them the right to education contrary to the meaning of the first sentence of article 1 of Protocol 1.

2) Alternatively, other applicants have argued that by insisting that children with special needs should be educated in special schools, the state has failed to respect their philosophical conviction that their children should be educated in mainstream schools alongside other children.

21.32 The first argument was raised in *Simpson v UK*[67] where a local education authority refused to provide funding for the applicant, a dyslexic child, to attend a special school because it took the view that he could be adequately educated in the local comprehensive school, which had a specialist department. On the basis that the right to education is not an absolute right, but one that can be regulated according to the needs and resources of the community, the Commission found no breach of article 1 of Protocol 1. In its view:

> ... there must be a wide measure of discretion left to the appropriate authorities as to how to make the best use possible of the resources available to them in the interests of disabled children generally.[68]

While the authorities were under an obligation to give weight to the views of the applicant and his parents, article 1 of Protocol 1 did not require them to place the applicant in a special school when a place was available for him in an ordinary school with facilities for teaching him.

21.33 The second argument was raised in *PD and LD v UK*[69] and *Graeme v UK*.[70] In both cases, the applicants complained that the authorities' insistence that their children be educated in special schools conflicted with their deeply held views regarding integrated schooling for disabled children. The Commission accepted that the second sentence of article 2 of Protocol 1 required education authorities to exercise their powers so as to conform with the applicants' philosophical views as far as possible. It also accepted that 'there is an increasing body of opinion which holds that, whenever possible, disabled children should be brought up with normal children of their own age.'[71] However, drawing on the Court's judgment in *Kjeldsen*,

67 Note 65.
68 Ibid at 195.
69 (1989) 62 DR 292.
70 (1990) 64 DR 158.
71 Ibid at 166.

Busk Madsen and Pedersen v Denmark,[72] it held that article 2 of Protocol 1 could not, for practical reasons, require that educational facilities be provided to cater for all parental philosophical and religious convictions.[73]

Setting the curriculum

21.34   Setting and planning of the curriculum are matters which fall in principle within the state's competence. Indoctrination is forbidden. But, so long as 'information or knowledge included in the curriculum' is conveyed in an 'objective, critical and pluralistic manner',[74] parents cannot expect teaching simply to reflect their own religious or philosophical convictions.

21.35   Schools – state or private – are not forbidden from imparting information or knowledge of a directly or indirectly religious or philosophical kind. Nor can parents object to the integration of such teaching into the school curriculum; otherwise all institutionalised teaching would become impracticable. In *X, Y and Z v Germany*[75] the Commission rejected as inadmissible a complaint that a seven-year-old child should have been given the opportunity to take a course in elementary school arithmetic instead of modern mathematics.

21.36   In *Kjeldsen, Busk Madsen and Pedersen v Denmark*[76] the parents of school-age children objected to compulsory sex education integrated into the curriculum of state primary schools on the basis that it offended their religious convictions. The European Court took the view that there was no question of indoctrination; the teaching was not aimed at instilling in children knowledge they did not have or could not acquire by other means, but was aimed at giving them such knowledge correctly, precisely, objectively and scientifically.

21.37   The Court recognised that the curriculum inevitably involved teachers in making assessments capable of encroaching on the religious or philosophical convictions of parents, but found that the instruction in question did not overstep the bounds of what a democratic state may regard as the public interest. The instruction given to the children did not advocate any specific kind of sexual

72 Note 54.
73 Note 70 at 166.
74 *Kjeldsen, Busk Madsen and Pedersen v Denmark* n54.
75 (1982) 29 DR 224.
76 Note 54.

behaviour, nor did it affect the right of parents to teach their children in accordance with their own convictions. Moreover, if parents objected vehemently to compulsory sex education, they had the option under Dutch law to send their children to private schools or teach them at home.

Disciplinary matters

21.38 In principle the imposition of disciplinary measures in schools and colleges is not incompatible with the Convention. On the contrary, in *Valsamis v Greece*[77] the European Court held that:

> The imposition of disciplinary penalties is an integral part of the process whereby a school seeks to achieve the object for which it was established, including the development and moulding of the character and mental powers of its pupils.[78]

There are, however, limits.

21.39 A disciplinary measure should not be imposed if:

1) it conflicts with a parent's religious or philosophical convictions;

2) it breaches another Convention right; in particular the prohibition on inhuman and degrading treatment/punishment under article 3 and the right to protection for physical integrity under article 8; or

3) it violates the principle of non-discrimination enshrined in article 14.

The scope of these restrictions has been analysed by the European Court in a number of cases concerning corporal punishment and suspension/expulsion.

Corporal punishment

21.40 The infliction of corporal punishment will engage the responsibility of the state whether it is carried out in state or private schools.[79] And any punishment which is inhuman or degrading within the meaning of article 3 of the Convention is absolutely prohibited. Relevant factors are whether:

77 Note 38.
78 Ibid at para 29.
79 *Costello-Roberts v UK* (1993) 19 EHRR 105.

1) physical injury is caused, or there is the possibility of psychological harm;

2) punishment is carried out in public or private;

3) it is carried out by a male on a female;

4) the circumstances in which punishment can be carried out are clear and accessible.[80]

This aspect of corporal punishment is analysed in chapter 20.[81]

21.41   So far as the philosophical convictions of parents are concerned, in *Campbell and Cosans v UK*[82] the Court found a breach of article 2 of Protocol 1 where no possibility existed for exempting their children from the regime of corporal punishment at their school.[83] In the subsequent case of *Warwick v UK*,[84] the Commission was less rigorous, finding no lack of respect where the local education authority refused to give the applicant an assurance that her daughter would not be subjected to corporal punishment.

Suspension/expulsion

21.42   The suspension or expulsion of a pupil from a school or college is not the determination of a 'criminal' charge,[85] even when that term is interpreted autonomously.[86] Neither is suspension or expulsion, in principle, a breach of the right of access to education under article 2 of Protocol 1,[87] subject to two qualifications:

1) Suspension or expulsion which prevents enrolment at another school or college is subject to close scrutiny.[88]

2) Suspension or expulsion must not breach other Convention rights.

---

80 See paras 20.6 to 20.12.
81 Ibid.
82 Note 16.
83 Ibid para 4.
84 (1986) 60 DR 5.
85 *Yanasik v Turkey* n47 at 25.
86 For the meaning of a criminal charge, see chapter 6.
87 Suspension of a 16-year-old child for bad behaviour was not found to be a denial of education where his return was conditional on his undertaking to be of good behaviour: *X v UK* Appl 13477/87 (Commission) 4 October 1989; unreported.
88 *Yanasik v Turkey* n47 at 27.

21.43 The first qualification is derived from *Yanasik v Turkey*[89] where, in the context of a complaint that the applicant had been expelled from military college because of his participation in a Muslim fundamentalist movement, the Commission observed that:

> It would not be contrary to Article 2 of Protocol 1 for pupils to be suspended or expelled, provided that the national regulations did not prevent them from enrolling in another establishment to pursue their studies.[90]

The subsequent case of *Sulak v Turkey*[91] narrowed this qualification somewhat where the Commission found no issue arose under article 2 of Protocol 1 where the applicant was expelled from a university for cheating and thus prevented from enrolling at other higher education institutions.

21.44 Reading the two cases together, and taking into account the principle of proportionality, it appears that two conclusions can be drawn. First, that expulsion from higher education institutions may be less strictly controlled than expulsion from primary education institutions: the state's obligations being more flexible in relation to the former. Second, that where an individual is prevented from enrolling elsewhere because of his/her expulsion from a higher education institution, the reason for expulsion will be relevant to any assessment under article 2 of Protocol 1.

21.45 The scope of the second qualification set out above – that suspension or expulsion must not breach other Convention rights – was explored by the European Court in *Campbell and Cosans v UK*[92] where the second applicant's son had been suspended from school and refused re-admission because the applicant refused to accept the right of the headmaster to administer corporal punishment. The Court observed that:

> The right to education guaranteed by the first sentence of Article 2 by its very nature calls for regulation by the State, but such regulation must never injure the substance of the right nor conflict with other rights enshrined in the Convention or its Protocols.
>
> The suspension of Jeffrey Cosans – which remained in force for nearly a whole school year – was motivated by his and his parents' refusal to accept that he receive or be liable to corporal chastisement ... His return to school could have been secured only if his parents had acted contrary to their convictions ... A condition of access to an

89 Note 47.
90 Ibid at 27.
91 Note 47.
92 Note 16.

educational establishment that conflicts in this way with another right enshrined in Protocol 1 cannot be described as reasonable and in any event falls outside the State's power of regulation under Article 2.[93]

On that basis there was a breach of article 2 of Protocol 1.

Challenging disciplinary measures

21.46   Where it is 'arguable' that a disciplinary measure violates a Convention right, article 13 (the right to an effective remedy)[94] of the Convention dictates that an opportunity must be provided in domestic law to challenge it. In *Valsamis v Greece*[95] the applicants complained that they had no opportunity to challenge a one-day suspension imposed on their daughter because they would not let her take part in a school parade which they considered incompatible with their convictions as Jehovah's Witnesses. Although the European Court found no breach of article 2 of Protocol 1, the applicants' complaint was 'arguable' and 'the applicants were therefore entitled to have a remedy in order to raise their allegations'.[96] There is no requirement for a judicial remedy, but to be effective there must be a remedy capable of quashing the measure in question.

21.47   In *Warwick v UK*[97] it was the lack of any remedy in English law for degrading treatment that was in issue. There the Commission found a violation of article 3 where a 16-year-old girl was caned on her hand[98] and a violation of article 13 because neither the civil nor the criminal law prohibited degrading treatment, not constituting assault.

School uniform requirements

21.48   In *Stevens v UK*[99] the Commission rejected a complaint about school uniforms as manifestly ill-founded. To enforce rules about school uniform did not violate article 8 (private and family life) or the right to education under article 2 of Protocol 1.

---

93 Ibid at para 41.
94 See paras 3.173 to 3.182.
95 Note 38.
96 Ibid at para 47.
97 (1986) 60 DR 5.
98 See paras 20.6 to 20.12.
99 (Commission) 3 March 1986; unreported.

CHAPTER 22

Housing, planning and the environment

22.1 Introduction

22.5 Housing rights under article 8(1)

22.6 The meaning of 'home' under article 8(1)

22.12 Restrictions on article 8(1) rights

22.14 Housing rights under article 1 of Protocol 1

22.15 The meaning of property/possessions

22.19 The test for deprivation and control of property/possessions

22.24 The overlap with article 8

22.25 Access and occupation of a 'home'

22.27 Eviction

22.30 Peaceful enjoyment and the environment

22.37 Planning

22.39 Procedural fairness in housing matters

22.40 Article 6(1)

22.42 Article 8

22.44 Does the Convention provide a 'right' to housing?

22.48 Discrimination

Introduction

22.1   Article 8 protects the right of individuals to 'respect' for their private life, family life and 'home' and article 1 of Protocol 1 protects the right of property, which can include any interest in property, including a tenancy or licence. Together, these rights provide protection such as the right of individuals to access to, occupation and peaceful enjoyment of their homes. In extreme circumstances, the Convention may also impose a duty on the state, through its public authorities, to house vulnerable individuals.[1]

22.2   While the essential object of article 8 of the Convention is to protect individuals against arbitrary interference with their private life, family life and 'home', it does not merely compel the state to abstain from such interference: in addition to this negative undertaking, 'positive obligations' can arise to ensure that article 8 rights are protected effectively.[2] These obligations can put the state under a duty to take measures designed to protect article 8 rights, even where the threat to such rights does not come from the state, but comes from private individuals.[3] So, for example, in *Lopez Ostra v Spain*[4] and *Guerra v Italy*,[5] which both concerned pollution,[6] the question for the European Court was not whether the state caused the pollution – in both cases it did not – but whether the appropriate authorities took adequate steps to prevent pollution by others.

22.3   In housing cases, under the HRA, where one party to a dispute is a public authority (eg, a local housing authority), article 8 automatically applies. Where, on the other hand, both parties are private individuals (eg, a straight-forward landlord and tenant dispute), article 8 will still be relevant if it can be argued that the state, which in this context includes any public authority, has failed to take adequate steps to give effective 'respect' to the private life, family life and 'home' of an individual. The inclusion of courts and tribunals within the definition of 'public authorities' under the HRA adds a dynamic dimension to this aspect of civil litigation because, under the Act, it

1   See paras 22.44 to 22.47.
2   See chapter 5.
3   See *X and Y v Netherlands* (1986) 8 EHRR 235; *Lopez-Ostra v Spain* (1995) 20 EHRR 277; *Stjerna v Finland* (1997) 24 EHRR 195; *Boti v Italy* (1998) 26 EHRR 241 at para 33; and *Guerra v Italy* (1998) 26 EHRR 357.
4   Note 3.
5   Note 3.
6   See paras 22.30 to 22.36.

is unlawful for any public authority to act in a way which is incompatible with Convention rights.[7]

22.4 In addition, many housing disputes – particularly landlord and tenant disputes – will involve the determination of 'civil rights and obligations'. As a result, the procedural guarantees of a fair trial in article 6(1) of the Convention will apply to them.

Housing rights under article 8(1)

22.5 Article 8(1) provides that:

> Everybody has the right to respect for his private and family life, his home and his correspondence.

All four interests are relevant to housing issues because measures such as pollution, eviction and compulsory purchase orders touch on individuals' private and family lives just as much as they touch on the right to respect for their 'home'.

The meaning of 'home' under article 8(1)

22.6 The word 'home' in article 8(1) includes any premises or shelter used by an individual as his/her home and in which s/he has a legal interest. It can also extend to premises or shelter which an individual is occupying unlawfully, so long as s/he has a legal interest either in the premises or shelter, or in the land on which they stand. So, for example, in *Wiggins v UK*,[8] where the applicant owned a house but had no legal permission to occupy it, the European Commission held that it qualified as 'home within the meaning of Article 8(1)'.

22.7 A more restrictive approach was taken in *S v UK*,[9] which concerned rights of succession. There the Commission took the view that since, under domestic law, the applicant's entitlement to occupy the house in question came to an end when her partner died, the house could no longer be regarded as her 'home' within the meaning of article 8(1). Had the Commission found that a family relationship between the applicant and her partner – a lesbian couple – existed, the result might have been different.

---

7   See paras 1.39 to 1.41.
8   (1978) 13 DR 40.
9   (1986) 47 DR 274.

22.8   The European Court has endorsed the wider approach to the definition of 'home' taken by the Commission in *Wiggins v UK*.[10] In *Buckley v UK*,[11] where the applicant was living in a caravan on her own property, but without planning permission, and where the local authority had issued an enforcement order requiring the caravan to be moved, the government argued that only a 'home' legally established could attract the protection of article 8(1). The Court rejected this. In its view, since the applicant had bought the land in question to live on and since she had been living on it for nearly five years, it was her 'home' within the meaning of article 8(1), whether she had permission to be there or not.[12]

22.9   In the earlier case of *Gillow v UK*[13] the European Court found that the applicants' house was their 'home' within the meaning of article 8(1) where they had been refused permission to live there and prosecuted for unlawful occupancy.[14] And in *Mabey v UK*[15] the Commission observed that:

> ... whether or not a particular habitation constitutes a 'home' for the purposes of Article 8(1) will depend on the factual circumstances of the particular case, namely the existence of sufficient and continuous links. It is not limited necessarily to those homes which have been lawfully occupied or lawfully established.[16]

Residence by the applicant for 20 years in a caravan on a plot of land he owned was sufficient.

22.10   Following *Buckley v UK*[17] it is clear that a caravan may be a 'home' and, by analogy, the protection of article 8(1) of the Convention extends to other forms of shelter used by individuals as their place of abode. In *Turner v UK*[18] the Commission treated an enforcement notice issued against the applicant who lived in a caravan on a plot of land as interference with the right to respect for her home, without reaching a conclusion about whether she owned the land in question or not. However, whether article 8(1) extends to a camping

---

10 Note 8.
11 (1996) 23 EHRR 101.
12 Note 11 at para 54.
13 (1989) 11 EHRR 335.
14 Note 13 at para 46.
15 (1996) 22 EHRR CD 123.
16 Note 15 at 124.
17 Note 11.
18 (1997) 23 EHRR CD 181. See also *Smith v UK* [1998] EHRLR 499.

van parked on a public road was left open by the Commission in
Kanthak v Germany.[19]

22.11   Although, in the context of article 8(1), the word 'home' implies
a sanctuary against intrusion by public authorities,[20] the European
Court and Commission have interpreted it broadly so as to give effect
to more specific housing rights such as the right of individuals to
access to, occupation and peaceful enjoyment of their homes.[21] And
in *G and E v Norway*[22] the Commission accepted as a matter of
principle, that 'a minority group is, in principle, entitled to claim the
right to respect for the particular lifestyle it may lead as being private
life, family life or home'.[23]

Restrictions on article 8(1) rights

22.12   The right of individuals to 'respect' for their private life, family life
and 'home' under article 8(1) is not absolute. Article 8(2) permits
public authorities to restrict article 8(1) rights but only where:

1) the grounds for interference are 'in accordance with law';

2) they pursue a legitimate aim (ie, one of the aims listed in article
8(2)); and

3) they are necessary and proportionate.

The meaning of these requirements is examined in detail in chapter
4.

22.13   In brief: (a) the phrase 'in accordance with law' means that any
interference with private or family life and/or the right of an individual to 'respect' for his/her home must have a basis in domestic
law; (b) the aims deemed legitimate under article 8(2) that are most
relevant in the housing context are 'the protection of health' and 'the
protection of the rights of others'; and (c) relevant to any assessment
of necessity and proportionality will be:

1) whether 'relevant and sufficient reasons' can be advanced for the
action taken;

---

19 (1988) 58 DR 94.
20 *The Law of the European Convention on Human Rights*, Harris, O'Boyle and
Warbrick, Butterworths, 1995, p319.
21 See paras 22.25 to 22.36.
22 (1983) 35 DR 30.
23 Note 22 at p35.

2) whether the rights of all interested parties have been taken into account properly; and

3) whether safeguards exist to prevent, or at least check, any abuse of power.[24]

In the housing context, the European Court has repeatedly emphasised the importance of an individual's right to respect for his/her home in view of its impact on personal security and well-being.[25] For that reason, procedural fairness will often be an integral part of necessity and proportionality.[26]

Housing rights under article 1 of Protocol 1

22.14　Article 1 of the First Protocol provides that:

> Every natural or legal person is entitled to the peaceful enjoyment of his possessions. No one shall be deprived of his possessions except in the public interest and subject to the conditions provided for by law and by the general principles of international law.
>
> The preceding provision shall not, however, in any way impair the right of a state to enforce such laws as it deems necessary to control the use of property in accordance with the general interest or to secure the payment of taxes or other contributions or penalties.

In effect, therefore, article 1 of Protocol 1 guarantees the right to peaceful enjoyment of possessions/property, but reserves to the state power to deprive individuals of their possessions and to control the use of property, subject to certain qualifications.

The meaning of property/possessions

22.15　The term 'possessions' in this context includes all property, chattels and acquired rights with economic interest. Hence it covers landlords' interests in their property, including their leasehold interests,[27]

24　For a more detailed analysis, see paras 4.37 to 4.55.
25　*Gillow v UK* n13 para 55; *Buckley v UK* n11 at 130.
26　See paras 22.39 to 22.43.
27　*James v UK* (1986) 8 EHRR 123.

and the interests of tenants[28] or licensees, contractual rights being regarded as acquired rights with economic interest.[29]

22.16 The scope of article 1 of Protocol 1 in housing cases is clear from the Commission's decision in *S v UK*[30] where it held that a decision by the Lands Tribunal in Northern Ireland to deprive the applicant of the benefit of two restrictive covenants – a repairing covenant and a restricted use covenant – amounted to an interference with her 'possessions' within the meaning of article 1 of Protocol 1.[31] Note, however, a repossession clause is not, in itself, a 'possession' capable of protection under article 1 of Protocol 1.[32]

22.17 In *Panikian v Bulgaria*,[33] where the applicants bought property from the state, which it had seized from a third party as part of a state nationalisation scheme, the Commission took the view that their occupancy for 35 years was sufficient to engage article 1 of Protocol 1 even if, strictly speaking, their title was null and void. However, in the absence of some other legal interest, once a right to occupy under a tenancy or licence comes to an end, no article 1 of Protocol 1 issue arises.[34]

22.18 Article 1 of Protocol 1 is primarily concerned with protecting individuals against the actions of public authorities. Consequently, unless state responsibility – through a public authority – is engaged in some way, it may be of limited relevance in straight-forward litigation between two private individuals, such as ordinary landlord and tenant disputes.[35] Where, however, it is argued that the law itself contravenes the Convention, state responsibility is engaged.[36] And, under the HRA, courts and tribunals are themselves public authorities.[37]

---

28 See *DP v UK* (1986) 51 DR 195.
29 See, for example, *Association of General Practitioners v Denmark* (1989) 62 DR 226; *Gasus Dosier- und Fordertechnik GmbH v Netherlands* (1995) 20 EHRR 403.
30 (1984) 41 DR 226.
31 Ibid at p232.
32 *Antoniades v UK* (1990) 64 DR 232.
33 (1997) 24 EHRR CD 63.
34 Note 9.
35 See *DP v UK* n28.
36 See *James v UK* n27.
37 See paras 1.39 to 1.43.

The test for deprivation and control of property/ possessions

22.19   So far as the 'deprivation' of property is concerned, the public interest requires:

1) that any deprivation be for a legitimate purpose; and

2) that the achievement of that purpose strikes a 'fair balance' between the demands of the general interest of the community and the need to protect individual rights – ie, that it does not impose an excessive burden on the individual.[38]

Although article 1 of Protocol 1 does not expressly guarantee a right to compensation, deprivation of property without some (but not necessarily full[39]) compensation is likely to be justifiable only in exceptional circumstances.

22.20   The principles to be applied when assessing whether 'control' of property complies with the Convention are similar but less strict. In particular:

1) the measure in question must have a legitimate aim, in the sense of not being 'manifestly without reasonable foundation'; and

2) there must be a reasonable relationship of proportionality between the means employed and the achievement of that aim.[40]

Again there must be a 'fair balance' between the demands of the general interest of the community and the need to protect individual rights.

22.21   The public interest can include the pursuit of legitimate 'social, economic or other policies', even where it is not the community at large that benefits from the measures taken. On that basis, the applicants in *James v UK*,[41] who were trustees of a substantial estate, were not deprived of their property in breach of article 1 of Protocol 1 when a number of their tenants exercised their legislative right to buy the properties they were renting. For the European Court, the elimination of social injustice by leasehold reform legislation was a legitimate aim and could not be characterised as manifestly unreason-

---

38   *James v UK* n27.
39   Ibid.
40   *Wasa Liv Omsesidigt, Forsakringbolaget valands Pensionsstiftelse v Sweden* (1988) 58 DR 163.
41   Note 27.

able.[42] Nor was full compensation at market rates a requirement of article 1 of Protocol 1.[43]

22.22 Similarly, in *Spadea and Scalabrino v Italy*[44] the Court found no breach of article 1 of Protocol 1 where eviction orders were suspended as part of a government programme to ease a housing crisis. The aim of the programme, which included freezing rents[45] and extending leases as well as suspending eviction orders, was to prevent a large number of people potentially becoming homeless at the same time; and that aim was legitimate.[46] The fact that the state may have contributed to the housing crisis was irrelevant. The only loss to the applicants was their inability to relet the same premises at higher rents – a control, rather than a deprivation, of property[47] – and therefore the programme was not disproportionate to the legitimate aim pursued.[48]

22.23 In *Antoniades v UK*,[49] the Commission held that legal clarification of the status of the applicant's tenant (tenant not licensee) did not amount to a deprivation of property, even where it had an impact on the level of rent that could be charged. In any event, UK rent legislation pursued the legitimate aim of protecting the interests of tenants in a situation where there was a shortage of cheap housing.[50]

The overlap with article 8

22.24 Many housing cases raise issues under both article 8 and article 1 of Protocol 1. However, it will be only in very rare circumstances that a case which fails under article 8 succeeds under article 1 of Protocol 1. As the Commission explained in *Howard v UK*:[51]

> ... where administrative action impinges on two separate but partially overlapping provisions of the Convention, the application of the relevant provisions must be reconciled.[52]

42 Note 27 at paras 46–47.
43 Note 27 at paras 55–57.
44 (1995) 21 EHRR 482.
45 See also *X v Austria* (1979) 3 EHRR 285 concerning rent control.
46 Note 44 at paras 31–32.
47 Note 44 at para 28.
48 Note 44 at para 40; see also *Scollo v Italy* (1996) 22 EHRR 514.
49 Note 32.
50 See also *Kilbourn v UK*, Commission (16 May 1985) (unreported).
51 (1985) 52 DR 198.
52 Ibid at 206.

Moreover, as noted above, article 1 of Protocol 1 has only limited relevance in the resolution of property disputes between individuals, where no public authority is involved.[53]

Access and occupation of a 'home'

22.25   An individual's right to respect for his/her home implies a right of access to and occupation of it. So, for example, rules regulating occupancy,[54] compulsory purchase orders[55] and eviction orders[56] are all breaches of article 8(1) of the Convention, which require justification under article 8(2).

22.26   The right of an individual to 'access to' his/her home means that article 8(1) can be invoked even before occupancy is taken up. In *Gillow v UK*[57] the applicants bought a house in Guernsey, but then left for 17 years. When they returned, they were refused permission to live in their house and ultimately prosecuted for unlawful occupancy. Since the applicants had sold the only other property they owned and had clearly returned to Guernsey to set up home, the Court found that article 8(1) was engaged.

Eviction

22.27   An eviction interferes with an individual's right to occupy his/her home and, on the face of it, is a breach of article 8(1). However, where any legal rights of occupancy have elapsed, for example where a tenancy or licence agreement has come to an end, it may be that the premises in question no longer qualify as a 'home' and hence no article 8 issue arises.[58]

22.28   Where any rights of occupation have not elapsed, any eviction by a public authority will have to be justified under article 8(2); and state responsibility for the actions of private landlords might arise where domestic law provides no, or no adequate, protection against

---

53 See *DP v UK* n28.
54 See *Wiggins v UK* n8; *Gillow v UK* n13; *Buckley v UK* n11.
55 See *X v UK* (1982) 28 DR 177; *Howard v UK* n51.
56 *S v UK* (1986) n9; *Buckley v UK* n11.
57 Note 13.
58 *S v UK* n9.

arbitrary eviction.[59] However, subject to any argument under articles 2 or 3,[60] so long as evictions are carried out according to domestic law, they are capable of being justified under article 8(2) as a measure to protect the rights of others; in particular, the right of a landlord to have property back at the end of a tenancy or licence agreement.[61] In *Wood v UK*,[62] the Commission applied the same reasoning to the rights of money-lenders to secure their loan in a repossession case.

22.29   The suspension of an eviction order will not necessarily breach a landlord's rights under article 1 of Protocol 1. As noted above,[63] in *Spadea and Scalabrino v Italy*,[64] the European Court found no breach of article 1 of Protocol 1 where eviction orders were suspended as part of a government programme to ease a housing crisis and prevent homelessness. Similarly restrictions on a landlord's rights of repossession can be justified as being in the public interest where they are designed to protect the well-being of tenants.[65]

Peaceful enjoyment and the environment

22.30   Article 8 guarantees individuals the right to peaceful enjoyment of their homes. The state is therefore under a positive obligation to ensure that this right is protected effectively: see chapter 5.

22.31   Ensuring that individuals are protected from harassment is one aspect of that obligation. In *Whiteside v UK*[66] the applicant complained that she was inadequately protected from the violent actions of her former partner. Although the Commission found against the applicant, it did recognise that the level of harassment – verbal and physical assaults, damage to property and following and watching the applicant – engaged the responsibility of the state such that it was under a positive obligation to secure the applicant's rights by providing adequate protection against such abuse.[67] Similarly in *Osman*

---

59 See, by analogy, the cases in which a private employer dismisses a private employee – *Stedman v UK* (1997) 23 EHRR CD 168 – and paras 5.11 to 5.12.
60 See paras 22.44 to 22.47.
61 *S v UK* n9 at p278. But protection from eviction legislation must not be discriminatory: *Larkos v Cyprus* [1998] EHRLR 653.
62 (1997) 24 EHRR CD 69.
63 Paras 22.21 to 22.22.
64 Note 44.
65 *Velosa Bareto v Portugal* A/334 [1996] EHRLR 212.
66 (1994) 76-A DR 80.
67 Ibid at p86.

v UK[68] the European Court accepted, in principle, that article 8 gave rise to an obligation on the part of the police to take reasonable steps to protect privacy, the home and family. What steps should be taken will depend on the facts of each case.[69]

22.32   So far as the wider issue of protecting the environment is concerned, in a number of early cases, the Commission was fairly sceptical about using the Convention to protect the environment at all.[70] It subsequently admitted several cases involving excessive noise from Gatwick airport,[71] but only on the basis that in those cases there was 'an intolerable and exceptional noise nuisance'.[72] The European Court, however, has been much more robust and has now overruled most, if not all, of these early decisions.[73]

22.33   In *Fredin v Sweden*[74] the European Court recognised that 'in today's society the protection of the environment is an increasingly important consideration'. On that basis, revocation of the applicant's licence to extract gravel was neither an 'inappropriate' nor a 'dispro-portionate' interference with his property rights under article 1 of Protocol 1. In the subsequent case of *Pine Valley Development v Ireland*[75] the Court confirmed this approach, holding that interfer-ence with the applicant's right to peaceful enjoyment of its property was 'designed to protect the environment' – a legitimate aim – and 'in accordance with the general interest'.

22.34   In *Lopez-Ostra v Spain*[76] the European Court considered environ-mental issues from the article 8 perspective of protecting the right of the individual to respect for his/her family life and home. In that case the applicant complained about heavy pollution emitted from a waste-treatment plant near her home. Although the Spanish authorities did not operate the plant, which was in the hands of a private company, the Court held them responsible on the basis that

---

68   (Court) 28 October 1998; noted at [1999] EHRLR 228.
69   See chapters 5 and 14.
70   See *X and Y v Germany* (1976) 15 DR 161; *X v Germany* (1981) 26 DR 270.
71   *Arrondelle v UK* (1980) 19 DR 186 and 26 DR 5; and *Baggs v UK* (1985) 44 DR 13 and 52 DR 29 – both were subsequently settled by the government.
72   See the reasoning in *Vearncombe v UK* (1987) 59 DR 186 and also *S v France* (1988) 65 DR 250.
73   See Sands P, *Human Rights, Environment and the Lopez Ostra Case: context and consequences* [1996] EHRLR 597.
74   (1990) 13 EHRR 784.
75   (1991) 14 EHRR 319.

they had granted permission for the plant to be built and had subsidised its construction.[77]

22.35 So far as the threshold for article 8 was concerned, the Court held that:

> ... severe environmental pollution may affect individuals' well-being and prevent them from enjoying their homes in such a way as to affect their private and family life adversely, without, however, seriously endangering their health.[78]

The only relevant question, therefore, was whether the authorities had taken 'the measures necessary for protecting the applicant's right to respect for her home and her private and family life under Article 8'.[79] In the Court's judgment they had not done so; on the contrary by opposing the applicant's legal action to close the waste-treatment plant, the authorities had prolonged her exposure to pollution.

22.36 In *Guerra v Italy*[80] the European Court developed these principles. The facts in that case were similar: the applicants lived near a chemical factory which was classified as 'high risk'. The Court found a breach of article 8 on the basis that, once the authorities became aware of essential information about the dangers inherent in the running of the factory, they delayed for several years before passing that information to the applicants and therefore prevented them from assessing the risks they and their families ran by continuing to live in the vicinity of the factory.[81]

Planning

22.37 Planning restrictions amount to control on the use of property and, therefore, must be justified under article 1 of Protocol 1: ie, they must have a legitimate aim – in the sense of not being 'manifestly without reasonable foundation' – and proportionate. Protection of the environment is a legitimate aim[82] and factors relevant to proportionality are whether the applicant knew or was subject to the

76 Note 3.
77 Note 3 at para 52.
78 Note 3 at para 51.
79 Note 3 at para 55.
80 (1998) 26 EHRR 357.
81 See also the cases on access to health information in paras 14.70 to 14.72.
82 See: *Fredin v Sweden* (1990) 13 EHRR 784; *Pine Valley Development v Ireland* note 75.

restriction when s/he took over the property,[83] the existence of legitimate expectations or acceptance of risk on purchase,[84] the extent to which restrictions prevent use of the land[85] and the availability of procedures importing flexibility and fairness.[86]

22.38   Since planning restrictions amount to control on the use of property, the fair trial requirements of article 6(1) apply to planning disputes. These are examined in chapter 13. Of particular importance is the case of *Bryan v UK.*[87]

Procedural fairness in housing matters

22.39   A requirement of procedural fairness in housing matters can arise under article 6(1), article 8 or both.

Article 6(1)

22.40   Article 6(1) of the Convention guarantees a fair trial in the 'determination' of 'civil rights and obligations'. Broadly speaking, this covers any proceedings which are decisive for private rights and obligations.[88] As a result, all landlord and tenant disputes are subject to the fair trial guarantees of article 6(1). In addition, some, but not all, disputes between an individual and a public authority come within its terms.[89]

22.41   The requirements of article 6(1)are detailed and specific (see chapter 13). They include:

1) the right to an independent and impartial tribunal;

2) the right to disclosure;

3) the right to an adversarial hearing;

4) the right to reasons; and

5) the right to have decisions made within a reasonable period.

---

83 *Allan Jacobsson v UK* (1987) 52 DR 250.

84 *Fredin v Sweden* note 82; *Pine Valley Development v Ireland* note 75.

85 *Allan Jacobsson v UK* note 83.

86 See Reid, *A Practitioner's Guide to the European Convention on Human Rights* (Sweet & Maxwell, 1998) p302.

87 (1995) 21 EHRR 342: see paras 12.41 to 12.46.

88 See paras 12.2 to 12.8.

89 Ibid.

Where housing decisions are taken by an administrative body, special considerations apply: see chapter 12.

Article 8

22.42 Requirements of procedural fairness can also arise under article 8 in two ways. First, the condition under article 8(2) that any restriction on article 8(1) rights be 'in accordance with law'[90] means that where domestic law provides a procedure to be followed when public authorities take housing decisions, it must be followed. Second, whether or not a procedure is laid down in domestic law, procedural fairness is a factor under the Convention when determining whether any interference with an individual's right to respect for his/her home under article 8 is 'necessary' and 'proportionate'.[91]

22.43   In many cases, both articles 6(1) and 8 will apply and their requirements for procedural protection will overlap. However, where article 6(1) does not apply, the requirements of procedural fairness under article 8 assume considerable importance. In *Buckley v UK*[92] the Court emphasised the following general principle;

> Whenever discretion capable of interfering with the enjoyment of a Convention right such as [an individual's right to respect for his/her home] is conferred on national authorities, the procedural safeguards available to the individual will be especially material in determining whether the respondent State has, when fixing the regulatory framework, remained within its margin of appreciation. Indeed, it is settled case law that, whilst Article 8 contains no explicit procedural requirements, the decision-making process leading to measures of interference must be fair and such as to afford due respect to the interests safeguarded to the individual by Article 8.[93]

The requirements of fairness will vary according to the facts, but in many cases, particularly where a housing issue has a family law dimension, it will be necessary to show that the applicant was properly involved in the decision-making process.

---

90 See paras 12.12 to 12.13.
91 See paras 4.37 to 4.55.
92 Note 11.
93 Note 11 at para 76; see also *McMichael v UK* (1995) 20 EHRR 205.

Does the Convention provide a 'right' to housing?

22.44 Most of the case-law of the European Court and Commission suggests that article 8(1) of the Convention protects only a home in which the individual actually has an identifiable claim. So, for example, in one of its very early cases,[94] the Commission rejected an argument that article 8(1) imposed a duty on the state to provide the applicant with a decent home. However, that does not mean that there are no circumstances in which the state might come under a duty to provide accommodation to vulnerable individuals.

22.45   In *Burton v UK*[95] the applicant, who was suffering from cancer, complained that, in failing to provide her with a place where she could live out her days in a caravan according to her Romany gypsy background, her local authority had failed in its obligations under article 8(1). The Commission rejected this, but nonetheless made the following observations:

> In so far as the applicant complains that she has not been able to return to living in a caravan due to a failure of the local authority to provide a site or an alternative mobile home, the Commission recalls that although the essential object of Article 8 is to protect against arbitrary interference by public authorities, there may in addition be positive obligations inherent in an effective 'respect' for family life ... However, the Commission does not consider that Article 8 can be interpreted in such a way as to extend a positive obligation to provide alternative accommodation of an applicant's choosing.[96]

By implication, in some circumstances, a limited obligation to provide housing to identifiable individuals may arise.

22.46   Such an obligation is most likely to arise where article 2 (the right to life) or article 3 (the prohibition on inhuman or degrading treatment) is also engaged. In *D v UK*,[97] the European Court held that the removal of the applicant, who was in an advanced stage of a terminal and incurable illness, from the UK to St Kitts would amount to a breach of article 3 (the prohibition on inhuman and degrading treatment): since there were inadequate medical facilities in St Kitts, removal would entail 'the most dramatic consequences for the

---

94 *X v Germany* (1956) 1 Yearbook 202.
95 (1996) 22 EHRR CD 135.
96 Ibid at p135.
97 (1997) 24 EHRR 423.

applicant and undoubtedly hasten his death'.[98] By analogy, a decision to evict an individual, in similarly stark circumstances, might be open to challenge under article 2 and/or article 3.

22.47   In *Burton v UK*,[99] (see above) the applicant also raised an argument under article 3. This too was rejected by the Commission, but again it recognised that an obligation to provide housing to identifiable individuals may arise in certain circumstances. In particular, it observed that:

> Whereas it is not excluded that a failure to take steps by a public authority may engage responsibility under [Article 3], the Commission finds that the local authority cannot be said in the circumstances of this case to have subjected the applicant to ill-treatment contrary to Article 3 of the Convention.[100]

That was primarily because, on the facts, the applicant's suffering did not reach the threshold of severity required under article 3.[101]

Discrimination

22.48   The prohibition on discrimination in article 14 of the Convention applies in the field of housing. It does not provide a general right to freedom from discrimination and can be invoked only in relation to one of the other Convention rights set out in articles 2 to 12 and the First Protocol. However, no breach of another Convention right need be established: the test for the application of article 14 is whether the facts in issue 'fall within the ambit' of one or more of the other Convention provisions.[102] See chapter 29.

98 Ibid at para 53.
99 Note 95.
100 Note 95 at p135.
101 See paras 14.41 to 14.60.
102 *Rasmussen v Denmark* A/87 (1984) 7 EHRR 371.

CHAPTER 23

Welfare benefits and entitlements

23.1   Introduction

23.3   Welfare benefits and entitlements as property rights

23.4   The meaning of property/possessions

23.9   The test for deprivation and control of property/ possessions

23.11   Welfare benefits and entitlements and article 8

23.12   Procedural fairness in the determination of welfare benefits and entitlements

23.13   The applicability of article 6(1)

23.22   The specific guarantees of article 6(1)

23.23   Discrimination

Introduction

23.1   The Convention does not expressly provide a right to welfare benefits and entitlements, such as social security payments, sickness benefits, industrial accident payments or pension entitlements.[1] However, some of these benefits and entitlements are treated as 'property' under article 1 of Protocol 1 (the right to property);[2] and most qualify as 'civil' rights, such that the fair trial requirements of article 6(1) of the Convention[3] apply to their 'determination'.

23.2   In addition, although the prohibition on discrimination in article 14 of the Convention is not free-standing, it is engaged when the facts in issue 'fall within the ambit' of one or more of the other Convention provisions.[4] It follows that where article 1 of Protocol 1 or article 6(1) apply to welfare benefits and entitlements, the prohibition on discrimination in article 14 is also applicable.

Welfare benefits and entitlements as property rights

23.3   Article 1 of the First Protocol provides that:

> Every natural or legal person is entitled to the peaceful enjoyment of his possessions. No one shall be deprived of his possessions except in the public interest and subject to the conditions provided for by law and by the general principles of international law.
>
> The preceding provision shall not, however, in any way impair the right of a state to enforce such laws as it deems necessary to control the use of property in accordance with the general interest or to secure the payment of taxes or other contributions or penalties.

In effect, therefore, article 1 of Protocol 1 guarantees the right to peaceful enjoyment of possessions/property, but reserves to the state power to (a) deprive individuals of their possessions; and (b) to control the use of property; subject to certain qualifications.[5]

---

1   See *Muller v Austria* (1975) 3 DR 25 at 31; *X v Sweden* (1986) 8 EHRR 252.
2   See chapter 26.
3   See chapters 12 and 13.
4   *Rasmussen v Denmark* (1984) 7 EHRR 371.
5   See chapter 26.

The meaning of property/possessions

23.4 The extent to which welfare benefits and entitlements constitute 'property' or 'possessions' within the meaning of article 1 of Protocol 1 has been considered in a number of cases before the European Court and Commission. In *X v Sweden*,[6] the Commission held that, although there is no right to a pension as such under the Convention:

> ... the payment of contributions to a pension fund may in certain circumstances create a property right in a portion of such a fund and a modification of the pension rights under such a system could therefore in principle raise an issue under [article 1 of Protocol 1].[7]

This general principle applies to compulsory pension schemes[8] and pension schemes based on employment. In *X v Sweden*,[9] the Commission continued:

> ... the right to a pension which is based on employment can in certain circumstances be assimilated to a property right, and this can be the case, whether special contributions have been paid or the employer has given a more general undertaking to pay a pension on conditions which can be considered to be part of the employment contract.[10]

23.5 However, the right in question is a right to 'derive benefit' from the system, not a right to a pension of a particular amount. As the Commission explained in *Muller v Austria*:[11]

> The operation of a social security system is essentially different from the management of a private life insurance company. Because of its public importance, the social security system must take account of political considerations, in particular those of financial policy. It is conceivable, for instance, that a deflationary trend may oblige a State to reduce the nominal amount of pensions. Fluctuations of this kind have nothing to do with the guarantee of ownership as a human right.[12]

That said, as the Commission accepted, a substantial reduction in the amount of a pension might be regarded as destroying the very

---

6 Note 1.
7 See also: Appl 2116/64 (1996) 23 Yearbook 9; and *Muller v Austria* (1975) 3 DR 25.
8 *Muller v Austria* n7.
9 Note 1.
10 Ibid at 270.
11 Note 7.
12 Ibid at 32.

substance of the right to retain benefit from the scheme.[13] A three per cent modification, however, did not have such an effect.[14]

23.6   The European Court has endorsed this general approach. In *Gaygusuz v Austria*[15] the applicant was refused an 'emergency assistance' payment in the form of an advance on his pension because he was not an Austrian national. Since entitlement to the payment in question was linked to the payment of contributions to an unemployment insurance fund, the Court found that:

> ... the right to emergency assistance – in so far as provided for in the applicable legislation – is a pecuniary right for the purposes of Article 1 of Protocol 1.[16]

Discrimination between Austrian nationals and others as regards entitlement to such emergency assistance could not be justified and accordingly the Court found a violation of article 14 taken in conjunction with article 1 of Protocol 1.

23.7   The same reasoning was applied by the Commission to UK earnings-related pensions in *Szrabjer and Clarke v UK*.[17] Although the earnings-related pension scheme was set up out of a sense of social solidarity, as opposed to being a purely earnings-related pension, the right to such a pension was dependent on some contribution and therefore did constitute a pecuniary right for the purposes of article 1 of Protocol 1. Suspension of the applicants' pension was therefore a deprivation of their property under article 1 of Protocol 1, but since they were prisoners who were being kept at the state's expense, such deprivation was justified as being in the public interest.

23.8   In relation to the UK, a series of cases were lodged with the Commission in 1997 challenging legislation which provides for various benefits and allowances available to widows but not widowers.[18] And in *Carlin v UK*[19] the Commission found it unnecessary to decide whether Industrial Injuries Invalidity Benefit, an index-linked benefit set by law, constituted property within the meaning of article 1 of Protocol 1.

---

13 Ibid.
14 See also *X v Sweden* n1.
15 (1996) 23 EHRR 364.
16 Ibid at para 41.
17 [1998] EHRLR 230.
18 See [1997] EHRLR 452. See *Coke and others v UK* [1999] EHRLR 130 about the armed forces pension scheme.
19 [1998] EHRLR 351. See *Stevens and Knight v UK* [1999] EHRLR 126 on the CRU scheme in personal injury cases.

The test for deprivation and control of property/ possessions

23.9   So far as the 'deprivation' of property is concerned, the public interest requires:

1) that any deprivation be for a legitimate purpose; and

2) that the achievement of that purpose strikes a 'fair balance' between the demands of the general interest of the community and the need to protect individual rights – ie, that it does not impose an excessive burden on the individual.[20]

Although article 1 of the First Protocol does not expressly guarantee a right to compensation, deprivation of property without some (but not necessarily full[21]) compensation is likely to be justifiable only in exceptional circumstances.

23.10   The principles to be applied when assessing whether 'control' of property complies with the Convention are similar but less strict. In particular:

1) the measure in question must have a legitimate aim, in the sense of not being 'manifestly without reasonable foundation'; and

2) there must be a reasonable relationship of proportionality between the means employed and the achievement of that aim.[22]

Again there must be a 'fair balance' between the demands of the general interest of the community and the need to protect individual rights: see, generally, chapter 26.

Welfare benefits and entitlements and article 8

23.11   In two cases involving the payment of emergency assistance in Austria to the unemployed, the applicants have raised an argument that non-payment breached article 8, which protects an individual's right to respect for his/her family life and home. In *CG v Austria*[23] the Commission declared the complaint under article 8 admissible, but the case was subsequently settled. And in *Gaygusuz v Austria*,[24]

20 *James v UK* (1986) 8 EHRR 123.
21 Ibid.
22 *Wasa Liv Omsesidigt, Forsakringbolaget valands Pensionsstiftelse v Sweden* (1988) 58 DR 163.
23 (1994) 18 EHRR CD 51.
24 Note 15.

having found a violation of article 14 taken in conjunction with article 1 of Protocol 1, neither the Court not the Commission found it necessary to adjudicate on article 8.

Procedural fairness in the determination of welfare benefits and entitlements

23.12   Article 6(1) provides that:

> In the determination of his civil rights and obligations ... everyone is entitled to a fair and public hearing within a reasonable time by an independent and impartial tribunal established by law.

There are three pre-conditions to its application in civil proceedings:

1) the rights or obligations in question must be 'civil' in nature;

2) those rights must have a basis in domestic law; and

3) there must be a 'determination' of rights or obligations.

It follows that its applicability in civil proceedings has to be examined in three stages. The first two pre-conditions are examined in chapter 12 and the third in chapter 13.

The applicability of article 6(1)

23.13   The meaning of 'civil' rights and obligations in article 6(1) has given rise to a great deal of case-law, particularly in the field of welfare benefits and entitlements. For the Court, the important question is whether the proceedings in question are 'decisive for private rights and obligations'.[25] It is not necessary that both parties should be private persons[26] and, therefore, the mere fact that one party to a dispute is the state will not exclude the application of article 6(1). Neither will the fact that a particular right is classified in domestic law as a 'public law' right;[27] the phrase 'civil rights and obligations' has an autonomous Convention meaning.

23.14   The application of article 6(1) to welfare benefits and entitlements first arose for consideration by the European Court in *Feldbrugge v Netherlands*[28] where the applicant, whose statutory sickness benefit

---

25   *Ringeisen v Austria* (1971) (1979–80) 1 EHRR 455 at para 94.
26   Ibid.
27   *Konig v Germany* (1978) 2 EHRR 170.
28   (1986) 8 EHRR 425.

was stopped on the basis that she was fit for work, complained that the appeal procedures open to her did not comply with article 6(1). Having rejected the suggestion that classification of statutory sickness benefit as a public law right in Dutch law was conclusive, the Court proceeded to examine the characteristics of the Dutch scheme to determine whether the public law features outweighed the private law features.

23.15   Among the public law features were: (a) the fact that the relevant legislation imposed responsibility on the state to set up and regulate sickness benefit payments and (b) the fact that contributions to the sickness benefit scheme were compulsory. However, in the Court's opinion, these were outweighed by the private law features which included:

1) The personal and economic nature of the right in issue. The benefits claimed affected the applicant's means of subsistence rather than her relationship with the state. In this respect, the Court observed that:

> For the individual asserting it, such a right is often of crucial importance; this is especially so in the case of health insurance benefits when the employee who is unable to work by reason of illness enjoys no other source of income. In short, the right in question was a personal, economic and individual right, a factor that brought it close to the civil sphere.[29]

2) The fact that the availability of sickness benefits was determined by reference to the applicant's contract of employment.

3) The similarities between the statutory sickness benefits scheme in the Netherlands and private health insurance schemes, including the collection of contributions, the calculation of risks and the verification of claims.

Article 6(1) therefore applied.

23.16   A similar result followed in *Deumeland v Germany*,[30] which involved a statutory scheme for widows' pensions. In that case, the benefits paid were derived directly from statute, but in the European Court's view they were grafted onto the applicant's husband's contract of employment and 'formed one of the constituents of the relationship between employer and employee'.[31] Article 6(1) has subsequently been applied to:

29 Ibid at para 37.
30 (1986) 8 EHRR 448.
31 Ibid at para 72.

1) Industrial accident benefits derived from legislation rather than the employment contract: see *Minniti v Italy*.[32]

2) Disability pensions arising from industrial accidents or occupational diseases: see *Schuler-Zgraggen v Switzerland*[33] and *Lo Giacco v Italy*;[34] even where the applicant was a public servant.[35]

3) An annuity payable in respect of war injuries: see *Kerojavi v Finland*.[36]

In *Schuler-Zgraggen v Switzerland*[37] the Court held that its development of the law in the cases of *Feldbrugge v Netherlands* and *Deumeland v Germany* and the principle of equality meant that 'as a general rule' article 6(1) applied in the field of social insurance, despite the involvement of the state in the administration of the various schemes and the payment of benefits.[38]

23.17   The cases of *Feldbrugge* and *Deumeland* both involved welfare benefit schemes which in one sense or another were based on contributions. In *Salesi v Italy*[39] the applicant, who was claiming a monthly disability payment, argued that the same principles as to the applicability of article 6(1) should apply, even though the scheme in question was based purely on need, not contributions.

23.18   The European Court agreed. It began by observing that :

> ... the development in the law that was initiated by [the] judgments [in *Feldbrugge* and *Deumeland*] and the principle of equality of treatment warrant taking the view that today the general rule is that Article 6(1) does apply in the field of social insurance ...

It then continued:

> ... In the present case ... the question arises in connection with welfare assistance and not ... social insurance. Certainly there are differences between the two, but they cannot be regarded as fundamental at the present stage of development of social security law. This justifies following, in relation to the entitlement to welfare allowances, the opinion which emerges from [the judgments in *Feldbrugge* and *Deumeland*] as regards the classification of the right

---

32 (1987) 59 DR 5.
33 (1993) 16 EHRR 405.
34 (1989) 69 DR 7.
35 *Lombardo v Italy* (1992) 21 EHRR 188.
36 [1996] EHRLR 66.
37 Note 33.
38 Ibid at para 46. See also *Pauger v Austria* (1997) 25 EHRR 105.
39 A/257-E (1993); unreported.

to social insurance benefits, namely that State intervention is not sufficient to establish that Article 6(1) is inapplicable.'[40]

On the facts, the Court found no distinction between welfare benefits and rights to social insurance benefits.

23.19   However, the 'general rule' expounded in *Schuler-Zgraggen v Switzerland*[41] and *Salesi v Italy*[42] applies automatically only to the *receipt* of benefits and not to the *payment* of contributions. In *Schouten and Meldrum v Netherlands*,[43] the European Court recognised that the link between the receipt of benefits and the means of subsistence of the individual in question did not exist in cases involving the payment of contributions and that the application of article 6(1) therefore had to be assessed on a case by case basis.

23.20   The appropriate course to adopt in such cases is therefore to follow the method of analysis adopted in *Feldbrugge v Netherlands*: ie, to identify and balance the public law characteristics of the scheme in question against the private law features. On the facts of *Schouten and Meldrum v Netherlands*,[44] the European Court concluded that, notwithstanding the absence of any real link between the payment of contributions and the means of subsistence of the individual, the private law features of the Dutch health insurance contributions scheme outweighed its public law features and that accordingly article 6(1) applied.

23.21   Where the payment of benefits is discretionary, however, different considerations apply. Consistent with its approach to discretionary and ex gratia payments generally,[45] in *Machatova v Slovak Republic*,[46] where the applicant was claiming a discretionary hardship payment, the Commission held that article 6(1) did not apply.

The specific guarantees of article 6(1)

23.22   The requirements of article 6(1) are detailed and specific. They include:

1) the right to an independent and impartial tribunal;

---

40 Ibid at para 19.
41 Note 33.
42 Note 39.
43 (1994) 19 EHRR 432.
44 Ibid.
45 See chapter 12.
46 (1997) 24 EHRR CD 44.

2) the right to disclosure;

3) the right to an adversarial hearing;

4) the right to reasons; and

5) the right to have decisions made within a reasonable period.

See chapter 13. Special considerations apply where welfare benefits and entitlements are determined, at least in the first instance, by administrative bodies: see chapter 12.

Discrimination

23.23   The prohibition on discrimination in article 14 of the Convention applies to welfare benefits and entitlements.[47] It does not provide a *general* right to freedom from discrimination and can be invoked only in relation to one of the other Convention rights set out in articles 2–12 and the First Protocol. However, no breach of another Convention right need be established: the test for the application of article 14 is whether the facts in issue 'fall within the ambit' of one or more of the other Convention provisions.[48] See chapter 29.

---

47   See *Gaygusuz v Austria* n15; and *Van Raalte v Netherlands* (1997) 24 EHRR 503.

48   *Rasmussen v Denmark* (1984) 7 EHRR 371.

CHAPTER 24

Freedom of expression

24.1   Introduction

24.4   The scope of article 10

24.6   The medium of expression

24.7   Access to information

24.10   Licensing of broadcasting, television and cinema enterprises

24.14   Restrictions on freedom of expression

24.19   Restrictions imposed by other private individuals

24.24   Prior restraint

24.25   Defamation proceedings

24.27   Public interest defences

24.34   Fair comment

24.36   Protection of the judiciary

24.39   Court reporting and contempt of court

24.42   Disclosure of journalists' sources and other journalistic
        materials

24.44   Commercial speech

24.46   Artistic expression

24.48   Race hatred

Introduction

24.1   Article 10 of the Convention provides:

1) Everyone has the right to freedom of expression. This right shall include freedom to hold opinion and to receive and impart information and ideas without interference by public authority and regardless of frontiers. This article shall not prevent states from requiring the licensing of broadcasting, television or cinema enterprises.

2) The exercise of these freedoms, since it carries with it duties and responsibilities, may be subject to such formalities, conditions, restrictions or penalties as are prescribed by law and are necessary in a democratic society, in the interests of national security, territorial integrity or public safety, for the prevention of disorder or crime, for the protection of health or morals, for the protection of the rights of others, for preventing the disclosure of information received in confidence, or for maintaining the authority and impartiality of the judiciary.

Freedom of expression enjoys a special status under the Convention. The European Court frequently refers to it as 'one of the essential foundations of a democratic society'[1] and recognises that the protection of free speech is a prerequisite for the enjoyment of many of the other rights and freedoms protected under the Convention.

24.2   As a consequence of its special status, restrictions on freedom of expression are subjected to very close scrutiny under the Convention. According to the Court 'as a matter of general principle' the 'necessity' for any restriction of freedom of expression must be 'convincingly established'.[2] This is all the more so when restrictions are placed on the press because of its public watchdog role.

24.3   Article 10 overlaps with a number of other articles, most notably articles 8, 9 and 11. The right to hold opinions in article 10 is virtually indistinguishable from freedom of thought and conscience in article 9.[3]

---

1   See for example *Handyside v UK* (1979)1 EHRR 737; *Jersild v Denmark* (1994) 19 EHRR 1; and *Goodwin v UK* (1996) 22 EHRR 123.

2   *Sunday Times v UK* (No 2) (1992) 14 EHRR 123.

3   See chapter 27.

The scope of article 10

24.4   Freedom of expression is a very broad concept under article 10. It covers both political and commercial speech as well as artistic expression.[4] In *Muller v Switzerland*[5] the European Court held that article 10 does not distinguish between the various forms of expression. In particular, freedom to receive or impart information and ideas 'affords the opportunity to take part in the public exchange of cultural, political and social information and ideas of all kinds'.

24.5   Freedom of expression also includes valueless and/or offensive speech. According to the European Court in the landmark case of *Handyside v UK*:[6]

> [Freedom of expression] is applicable not only to 'information' or 'ideas' that are favourably received or regarded as inoffensive or as a matter of indifference, but also to those that offend, shock or disturb the State or any sector of the population. Such are the demands of ... pluralism, tolerance and broadmindedness, without which there is no democratic society.[7]

The medium of expression

24.6   Article 10 applies not only to the content of expression or ideas but also the means of transmission or reception, since any restriction imposed on the means necessarily interferes with the right to receive and impart information.[8] On that basis it covers words,[9] pictures,[10] video,[11] cinema,[12] electronic transmission and even conduct which is intended to convey an idea or information.[13]

---

4 See below.
5 (1988) 13 EHRR 212.
6 Note 1.
7 Note 1 at para 49.
8 *Autronic AG v Switzerland* (1990) 12 EHRR 485 at para 47.
9 *Barthold v Germany* (1985) 7 EHRR 383.
10 *Muller v Switzerland* (1991) 13 EHRR 212.
11 *Otto-Preminger Institute v Austria* (1995) 19 EHRR 34.
12 Ibid.
13 *Stevens v UK* (1986) 46 DR 245.

Access to information

24.7   Freedom of expression under article 10(1) specifically includes freedom to 'receive and impart information and ideas' without interference and regardless of frontiers. However, this does not confer a right of access to information as such. In *Gaskin v UK*[14] the applicant sought disclosure of local authority records about the time he spent as a child in care and with foster parents. The European Court found that this raised an article 8 issue, not an article 10 issue. The right to receive information under article 10(1) prohibits restrictions on the receipt of information, but does not oblige public authorities to disclose information against their will.[15] Although this approach was endorsed in *Guerra v Italy*,[16] in that case the Court considerably expanded the scope of article 8 in relation to access to information.[17]

24.8   Nonetheless, freedom to receive and impart information and ideas will protect those who are prevented from receiving information that others are willing to impart. For example, it was successfully invoked by the applicant company in *Autronic AG v Switzerland*[18] where the European Court held that the reception of television programmes by means of a dish or other aerial comes within the scope of article 10 without reference to the purpose for which the right is exercised.[19] See also *Open Door Dublin Well Women v Ireland*.[20]

24.9   Furthermore, the rights to receive and impart information and ideas are not simply the corollary of one another. Under article 10, there is a right to impart information and ideas and a right to receive information and ideas imparted by others.[21]

---

14   (1990) 12 EHRR 36.
15   See also: *Leander v Sweden* (1987) 9 EHRR 433; *Z v Austria* (1988) 56 DR 13; and *Bader v Austria* (1996) 22 EHRR CD 213.
16   (1998) 26 EHRR 357.
17   See paras 5.23 to 5.27.
18   Note 8.
19   Note 8 at para 47.
20   (1992) 15 EHRR 244.
21   *Sunday Times v UK* (1980) 2 EHRR 245.

Licensing of broadcasting, television and cinema enterprises

24.10   The licensing of broadcasting, television and cinema enterprises is specifically permitted under article 10(1). Consequently action can be taken against unlicensed broadcasters.[22] However, licensing arrangements are very closely monitored by the European bodies.

24.11   It is now clear that article 10(1) authorises licensing only in respect of the technical means of broadcasting, not the information imparted through broadcasts.[23] Older Commission case-law to the contrary is therefore overruled.[24] Consequently, while it is not automatically a breach of the Convention to impose non-technical licence conditions on broadcasting – such as conditions relating to the nature and objectives of the broadcasting company – such conditions have to be justified under article 10(2).

24.12   In *Informationsverein Lentia v Austria*[25] the Austrian government sought to uphold a state monopoly for radio and for broadcasting on the basis that such monopolies were the only way to guarantee the objectivity and impartiality of reporting, diversity of opinion, balanced programming and the independence of the persons and bodies responsible for programmes. The European Court found this unconvincing:

> Of all the means of ensuring that these values are respected, a public monopoly is one which imposes the greatest restrictions on freedom of expression...[26]

As a result of technical progress – particularly in the number of frequencies and channels available – such a restrictive approach could no longer be justified.

24.13   In the subsequent case of *Radio ABC v Austria*[27] a breach of article 10 was found where only two frequencies were reserved for private radio stations transmitting in the Vienna region. However, licence conditions restricting coverage of individuals whose statements the authorities thought might further the cause of terrorism were found

---

22   *X v UK* (1978) 16 DR 190; *Radio X, S, W and A v Switzerland* (1984) 37 DR 236; and *Bellis v UK* (1997) 24 EHRR CD 71.

23   *Groppera Radio AG v Switzerland* (1990) 12 EHRR 321.

24   See *X and Association Z v UK* 38 CD 86.

25   (1993) 17 EHRR 93.

26   Ibid at para 39.

27   (1997) 25 EHRR 185.

to be legitimate and proportionate in *Purcell v Ireland*[28] and *Brind v UK*.[29]

Restrictions on freedom of expression

24.14   A restriction on freedom of expression will not be compatible with the Convention unless:

1) it is 'prescribed by law'; and

2) it pursues a legitimate aim; and

3) it is necessary in a democratic society.

The meaning of these requirements is examined in detail in chapter 4.

24.15   In outline, a restriction will not be prescribed by law unless there is a clear basis for it in domestic law and the applicable rules or regulations are both accessible to those likely to be affected and clear to understand. A restriction will pursue a legitimate aim only if it is genuinely designed to protect one of the interests set out in article 10(2). And a restriction will not be necessary in a democratic society unless it has convincingly been established that there was both a 'pressing social need' to take some action to restrict freedom of expression and the action taken was a proportionate response to that need. As the European Court made clear in *Sunday Times v UK*,[30] what is at stake is not a 'choice between two conflicting principles' but 'a freedom of expression that is subject to a number of exceptions which must be narrowly construed'.[31]

24.16   These requirements are strictly applied by the European Court in article 10 cases. It will examine whether the government has advanced relevant and sufficient reasons for the restriction and whether less restrictive measures existed. For example, in *Informationsverein Lentia v Austria*[32] the Court did not question the legitimacy of quality control in broadcasting but was heavily influenced by the fact that such quality control could be achieved by imposing conditions on the licences of private broadcasters; a significantly less restrictive measure than banning them.[33]

28   (1989) 70 DR 262.
29   (1994) 77-A DR 42.
30   Note 21.
31   Note 21 at para 65.
32   Note 25.
33   Note 25 at para 39.

24.17   Also relevant will be the duration of any restriction on freedom of expression and the public interest for and against the exercise of the right. In *Steel v UK*,[34] the European Court considered the removal of three peace activists from the scene of their protest a disproportionate interference with their article 10 right to free speech.

24.18   The meaning of restrictions has been interpreted broadly. It covers criminal[35] and civil[36] measures, including injunctions,[37] forfeiture,[38] the refusal of a licence[39] or classification certificate,[40] dismissal for the expression of views[41] and the imposition of an exclusion order.[42]

Restrictions imposed by other private individuals

24.19   Article 10(1) refers only to the rights of individuals to receive and impart information and ideas without interference 'by public authority'. However, it does not leave relations between private individuals unregulated.

24.20   One of the fundamental principles underpinning the whole of the Convention is that the rights conferred should be practical and effective, not theoretical and illusory.[43] As a result the Court has developed a theory of positive obligations whereby states are required to take steps to ensure that individuals can enjoy their Convention rights even when the state itself does not threaten them.[44]

24.21   So far as freedom of expression is concerned it is clear that the state is under an obligation to put in place laws which maintain the right balance between the interests of private individuals.[45] It is also under a duty to take practical measures such as protecting one set of

34 Court (28 September 1998); noted at [1999] EHRLR 109.
35 *Barfod v Denmark* (1991) 13 EHRR 493.
36 *Tolstoy Miloslavsky v UK* (1995) 20 EHRR 442.
37 *Observer and Guardian v UK* (1992) 14 EHRR 153.
38 *Muller v Switzerland* n5.
39 *Autronic AG v Switzerland* n8.
40 *Wingrove v UK* (1997) 24 EHRR 1.
41 *Vogt v Germany* (1995) 21 EHRR 205.
42 *Adams and Benn v UK* (1996) 23 EHRR CD 160.
43 See chapter 4.
44 See chapter 5.
45 See paras 5.13 to 5.22.

protesters from the activities of anti-protestors.[46] In *Rommelfanger v Germany*[47] the Commission rejected the applicant's assertion that the Catholic church that had dismissed him was a public authority, but nonetheless examined his complaint on the basis that the German courts had failed to protect his freedom of expression against the sanction of dismissal by his employer.[48] A similar approach was adopted by the European Court in the context of trade union rights under article 11.[49]

Prior restraint

24.22   Article 10 does not in terms prohibit prior restraint[50] but the European Court has made it clear that:

> ... the dangers inherent in prior restraint are such that they call for the most careful scrutiny.[51]

This is especially so as far as the press is concerned because 'news is a perishable commodity and to delay its publication, even for a short period, may well deprive it of all its value and interest'.[52]

24.23   Once confidential information has entered the public domain, prior restraint will rarely, if ever, be justified. In *The Observer and The Guardian v UK*[53] the European Court accepted the government's argument that there was a legitimate aim for restricting publication of the *Spycatcher* book, but found that once the book was published elsewhere in the world, the injunction in question was no longer necessary.

24.24   Consistent with this approach, the HRA has placed special restrictions on the imposition of pre-trial injunctions in article 10 cases; and ex parte injunctions are permitted only in exceptional circumstances.[54]

---

46   *Plattform Ärtze für Das Leben v Austria* (1991) 13 EHRR 304: see further para 5.22.
47   (1989) 62 DR 15.
48   Ibid at p160.
49   *Young, James and Webster v UK* (1982) 4 EHRR 38.
50   *Markt Intern Verlag & Beermann v Germany* (1990) 12 EHRR 161.
51   *Observer and Guardian v UK* n37 at para 60.
52   Ibid.
53   Note 37.
54   See paras 1.49 to 1.53.

Defamation proceedings

24.25   The right to reputation is expressly protected in article 10(2). However, defamation proceedings inevitably interfere with freedom of expression and so must be justified as necessary and proportionate on a case by case basis.

24.26   In *Tolstoy Miloslavsky v UK*[55] the European Court found an award of £1.5 million excessive even allowing for the exceptionally serious nature of the libel. More generally, the Court has repeatedly found violations of article 10 where in criminal defamation proceedings, domestic law requires the defendant to establish the truth of his/her publication[56] or opinion.[57] However, a legal right of reply does not infringe the article 10 rights of those who publish and broadcast.[58]

Public interest defences

24.27   The European Court has not explicitly recognised a public interest defence under the Convention, but its case-law discloses the need for very effective protection in domestic law for freedom of expression where the publication concerns a public official or the subject-matter is in the public interest.

24.28   In *Lingens v Austria*,[59] where the applicant published an article critical of the Austrian Chancellor, the European Court observed that:

> Whilst the press must not overstep the bounds set, inter alia, for the protection of the reputation of others, it is nevertheless incumbent on it to impart information and ideas on political issues just as on those in other areas of public interest.[60]

It then continued:

> The limits of acceptable criticism are accordingly wider as regards a politician as such than as regards a private individual. Unlike the latter, the former inevitably and knowingly lays himself open to close scrutiny of every word and deed by both journalists and the public at large, and he must consequently display a greater degree

55 (1995) 20 EHRR 442.
56 *Lingens v Austria* (1986) 8 EHRR 407.
57 *Thorgiersen v Iceland* (1992) 14 EHRR 843.
58 *Ediciones Tiempo SA v Spain* (1989) 62 DR 247.
59 Note 56.
60 Ibid at para 41.

of tolerance. No doubt Article 10(2) enables the reputation of others – that is to say, of all individuals – to be protected, and this protection extends to politicians too, even when they are not acting in their private capacity; but in such cases the requirements of such protection have to be weighed in relation to the interest of open discussion of political issues.[61]

See also *Oberschlick v Austria*[62] where the European Court held that the applicant's actions in publishing draft criminal charges against the Secretary General of the Austrian Liberal Party contributed to a public debate on a matter of public importance. His prosecution therefore violated article 10.

24.29   Freedom to criticise the government is wider still. In *Castells v Spain*,[63] the applicant, an elected representative of one of the opposition parties in Spain, had complained about the lack of police accountability in relation to their operations in the Basque country. In an article in a weekly magazine critical of the government, the applicant accused the police of having murdered Basque activists and suggested that they were being protected by the authorities from prosecution. He was convicted of insulting the government in criminal proceedings and disqualified from political office. During his trial, the Spanish courts ruled that evidence of the truth of the applicant's statements was inadmissible.

24.30   Expanding on the notion of a 'public figure'[64] which it had developed in *Oberschlick v Austria* above, the European Court spoke in terms of the applicant's 'right to criticise the government'[65] and held that 'the limits of permissible criticism are wider with regard to the government than in relation to a private citizen, or even a politician'. In the Court's view:

> In a democratic system the actions or omissions of the government must be subject to the close scrutiny not only of the legislative and judicial authorities but also of the press and public opinion.[66]

Conceding that some measures may be necessary if public order was in issue to protect a government from defamatory, false or malicious accusations, the Court nonetheless suggested that the dominant

---

61 Note 56 at para 42.
62 (1991) 19 EHRR 389 at paras 57–59.
63 (1992) 14 EHRR 445.
64 For the US version of the public figure defence, see *New York Times v Sullivan* (1964) 376 US 254.
65 Note 63 at para 43.
66 Note 63 at para 46.

position occupied by the government required it to display restraint before resorting to the criminal law particularly where other means were available for replying to unjustified attacks and criticisms.

24.31 The question of imposing a burden on the defendant to establish the truth of his/her publication as a defence to criminal defamation proceedings was raised again in *Thorgierson v Iceland*.[67] There the applicant was an Icelandic citizen and a writer, resident in Reykjavik. He published two articles in a daily newspaper in Iceland in which he made allegations of brutality against the Reykjavik police force. He was charged with and convicted of criminal defamation on the basis that he was unable to justify his allegations, namely that unspecified members of the Reykjavik police force had committed a number of acts of serious assault resulting in disablement of their victims, as well as forgery and other criminal offences.

24.32 The European Court recognised that the applicant's allegations consisted essentially of references to 'stories', 'rumours' and 'public opinion' emanating from elsewhere; the applicant was essentially reporting what was being said by others about police brutality. However, in the Court's view – and accepting the good faith of the applicant – to require him to prove the truth of these allegations was an 'unreasonable' if not 'impossible' task.[68] The circumstances of the case showed that the applicant's aim was to encourage a public investigation into complaints of police brutality, not to defame the Reykjavik police force and his publications bore on an undisputed matter of serious public concern. Although he used strong language, it was not excessive and his conviction was capable of discouraging open discussion on matters of public interest. In the Court's view, the interference with his article 10 rights was therefore not proportionate to the legitimate aim of protecting the reputation of the police force.[69]

24.33 The European Court's ruling in *Thorgierson v Iceland*[70] on a preliminary point of general principle is also important. It emphatically rejected the suggestion advanced by the Icelandic government that a distinction could be drawn between political discussion and discussion of other matters of public concern. This is in line with

---

67 (1992) 14 EHRR 843.
68 Ibid at para 65.
69 Note 67 at paras 63–68. See also *Bladet Tromso As and Others v Norway* (1997) 23 EHRR CD 40. See also on public interest defences *Dalban v Romania* [1998] EHRLR 641.
70 Note 67.

previous case-law to the effect that the special protection afforded to political speech under the Convention is not restricted to 'high politics'.[71]

Fair comment

24.34   While emphatically rejecting the notion that value judgments, opinions and/or comments must be shown to be true,[72] the European Court has not yet determined what basis, if any, is needed for such expression. In *Schwabe v Austria*,[73] the European Commission, confirming that politicians must be prepared to accept criticism even if far fetched, thought that such criticism must be founded on correct factual statements; but it then continued by suggesting that 'not every word can be weighed to exclude any possibility of misunderstanding'.[74] The European Court in the same case conflated the facts and opinion and held that they amounted to 'a value judgement for which no proof is possible'.[75]

24.35   In *Thorgierson v Iceland*[76] the European Court noted the legitimate intention of the applicant in publishing his allegations of police brutality and that it had not been established that the 'stories' upon which the applicant based his publication were untrue or invented. It then concluded that to require him to prove the truth of these allegations was an 'unreasonable' if not 'impossible' task. This arguably suggests that from a Strasbourg standpoint good faith, sincerity and proportionality are the proper basis for value judgments, opinions and/or comments.

Protection of the judiciary

24.36   Although it recognises 'the great importance of not discouraging members of the public, for fear of criminal or other sanctions, from voicing their opinions on issues of public concern',[77] the European

---

71   *Barfod v Denmark* n35; *Barthold v Germany* (1985) 7 EHRR 383. See also *Hertel v Switzerland* [1999] EHRLR 116 on public interest speech.

72   See above.

73   A/242-B (28 August 1992); unreported.

74   Ibid at para 55.

75   Note 73 at para 34.

76   Note 67.

77   *Barfod v Denmark* n35.

Court has accepted 'the special role of the judiciary'[78] in a democratic society. On that basis it has been prepared to extend to judges protection from criticism which would be unacceptable in relation to other public officials, politicians and/or governments. There is, however, a fine line between legitimate criticism and contempt.

24.37 In *Barfod v Denmark*[79] the applicant's comments fell on the wrong side of the line; while it was legitimate to question the nomination of judges, such criticism could have been made without resort to personal attacks on the character of two lay judges. A similar result followed in *Prager and Obserschlick v Austria*[80] where the applicant was prosecuted for criminal libel after a scathing attack on the judges of the Vienna Regional Criminal Court. The European Court found no breach of article 10 on the basis that the applicant was unable to establish that his factual allegations were true or that his comments were fair.

24.38 However, in *De Haes and Gijsels v Belgium*[81] the European Court found that proceedings against the applicants in relation to a 'well-researched' yet virulent publication attacking four Belgian judges were disproportionate. Although expressed in strong and aggressive language, the applicants' comments were proportionate to the stir and indignation caused by the case itself.

Court reporting and contempt of court

24.39 Court reporting is an important aspect of the right to a fair trial guaranteed under article 6(1) of the Convention. In *Axen v Germany*[82] the European Court held that:

> By rendering the administration of justice visible, publicity contributed to the achievement of the aims of Article 6(1), namely a fair trial.[83]

However, restrictions on publication which might prejudice pending proceedings are legitimate.

---

78 *Prager and Obserschlick v Austria* (1995) 21 EHRR 1 at para 35.
79 Note 35.
80 Note 78 at para 35.
81 (1997) 25 EHRR 1.
82 (1984) 6 EHRR 195.
83 Ibid at para 25. See also *Atkinson, Crook and The Independent v UK* (1990) 67 DR 244.

24.40   In *Sunday Times v UK*[84] the Court observed that:

> ... in so far as the law of contempt may serve to protect the rights of litigants, this purpose is already included in the phrase 'maintaining the authority and impartiality of the judiciary': the rights so protected are the rights of individuals in their capacity as litigants, that is as persons involved in the machinery of justice, and the authority of that machinery will not be maintained unless protection is afforded to all those involved in or having recourse to it.[85]

Nonetheless the restriction imposed – an injunction – was not proportionate to the aim of protecting the litigants in the civil proceedings in question because the publication complained about was couched in moderate language, and was unlikely to have added significant pressure to the parties involved and would not have had an adverse effect on the authority of the judiciary.

24.41   Different results followed in *Hodgson and Others v UK*[86] and *C Ltd v UK*[87] both of which concerned criminal proceedings. However, in *Worm v Austria*[88] the European Court observed that, as a matter of general principle

> There is general recognition of the fact that courts cannot operate in a vacuum. Whilst the courts are the forum for the determination of a person's guilt or innocence on a criminal charge, this does not mean that there can be no prior or contemporaneous discussion of the subject-matter of criminal trials elsewhere, be it in specialised journals, in the general press or amongst the public at large.
>   Provided it does not overstep the bounds imposed in the interests of the proper administration of justice, reporting, including comment, on court proceedings contributes to their publicity and is thus perfectly consonant with the requirement under Article 6(1) of the Convention that hearings be in public.[89]

The bounds imposed in the interests of the proper administration of justice are that 'comment may not extend to statements which are likely to prejudice, whether intentionally or not, the chances of a person receiving a fair trial or to undermine the confidence of the public in the role of the courts in the administration of criminal justice'.[90]

---

84 Note 21.
85 Note 21 at para 56.
86 (1987) 51 DR 136.
87 (1989) 61 DR 285.
88 (1997) 25 EHRR 454.
89 Ibid at para 50.
90 Ibid.

Disclosure of journalists' sources and other journalistic materials

24.42 Disclosure of journalists' sources is very well protected under the Convention. In *Goodwin v UK*[91] where a journalist was fined £5,000 for refusing to disclose the source of his information about a private company's confidential financial report, the European Court observed:

> Protection of journalistic sources is one of the basic conditions for press freedom, as is reflected by the laws and professional codes of conduct in a number of Contracting States and is affirmed in several international instruments on journalistic freedoms. Without such protection, sources may be deterred from assisting the press in informing the public on matters of public interest. As a result the vital public watchdog role of the press may be undermined and the ability of the press to provide accurate and reliable information may be adversely affected. Having regard to the importance of the protection of journalistic sources and press freedom in a democratic society and the potentially chilling effect an order of source disclosure has on the exercise of that freedom, such a measure cannot be compatible with Article 10 of the Convention unless it is justified by an overriding requirement in the public interest.[92]

Since an injunction already in place adequately protected the company's legitimate interests in the confidentiality of its financial affairs, the order that the applicant reveal his source was unnecessary and disproportionate.[93]

24.43 Where disclosure is ordered in the course of criminal proceedings, the protection afforded to journalists in this sphere may be less extensive. In *BBC v UK*[94] – decided before *Goodwin v UK* – the Commission found no breach of article 10 where the BBC was ordered to produce video footage in criminal proceedings brought against two police officers. For the Commission the duty to give evidence was a normal 'civic duty' which necessitated testimony and the production of materials on the ground that 'it is necessary for the maintenance of the authority and impartiality of the judiciary'.[95]

91 (1996) 22 EHRR 123.
92 Ibid at para 39.
93 See also *K v Austria* A/255-B (1993) Com Rep; unreported and see *Fressoz and Roire v France* [1999] EHRLR 339 on publication in breach of professional confidence.
94 (1996) 84-A DR 129.
95 Ibid at p133.

Commercial speech

24.44   Receiving ideas and imparting commercial ideas is clearly protected under article 10. In *Markt Intern and Beermann v Germany*[96] the German government sought to argue that article 10 was inapplicable because the wording and aim of the information bulletin in question demonstrated that it was not intended to influence or mobilise public opinion, but to promote economic interests of a small group of individuals. The European Court rejected this. In its view commercial information cannot be excluded from article 10.[97]

24.45   However, respect for confidentiality and the protection of business interests is likely to legitimise fairly wide-ranging restrictions on the disclosure of commercial information. In *Markt Intern and Beermann v Germany* the European Court upheld an injunction on the publication of an information bulletin criticising a mail order company that had failed to deal promptly with a complaint about its products. And in *Jacubowski v Germany*[98] the applicant was prevented from distributing a circular which criticised his former employer and sought to persuade its customers to switch to the applicant's enterprise.

Artistic expression

24.46   Artistic expression is protected by article 10. Although not expressly referred to, it is inherent in the exchange of ideas and information guaranteed. In *Muller v Switzerland*[99] the European Court confirmed its view that freedom of expression extended to the field of art by reference to article 19(2) of the *International Covenant on Civil and Political Rights* which specifically includes within the right to freedom of expression, information and ideas 'in the form of art'.

24.47   Restrictions are permissible on pornography for the protection of crime or the protection of morals.[100] However, the protection of morals cannot extend to those who wish to make use of such material.[101]

---

96 (1989) 12 EHRR 161.
97 See also *Casado Coca v Spain* (1994) 18 EHRR 1 and *Jacubowski v Germany* (1994) 19 EHRR 64. See also *Hertel v Switzerland* [1999] EHRLR 116.
98 Note 97.
99 (1988) 13 EHRR 212.
100 See *Hoare v UK* [1997] EHRLR 678.
101 *Scherer v Switzerland* (1994) 18 EHRR 276.

Race hatred

24.48 Restrictions on the expression of racist ideas are legitimate under article 10(2) as being for the protection of the rights of others. They are also specifically provided for in article 17 of the Convention, which reads:

> Nothing in this Convention may be interpreted as implying for any State, group or person any right to engage in any activity or perform any act aimed at the destruction of any of the rights and freedoms set forth herein or at their limitation to a greater extent than is provided for in the Convention.

Its purpose, in so far as it refers to groups or to individuals, is to make it impossible for extremists to take advantage of the provisions of the Convention to perform acts aimed at destroying the Convention rights of others.[102]

24.49 In *Glimmerveen and Hagenbeek v Netherlands*[103] article 17 was successfully invoked to justify the prosecution of the applicants for possessing leaflets likely to incite racial hatred and their exclusion from local elections. The same result followed in *Kuhnen v Germany*[104] where the applicant was convicted for publishing pamphlets advocating fascism and racism.

24.50 On the other hand the European Court found a violation of article 10 in *Jersild v Denmark*[105] where a journalist was prosecuted for aiding and abetting race hatred when he broadcast the views of three self-avowed racists in a television documentary. The Court emphasised 'the vital importance of combating racial discrimination in all its forms and manifestations' and indicated that the object and purpose pursued by the *International Covenant on the Elimination of All Forms of Racism* (1996) were of 'great importance' in determining whether the applicant's conviction 'was necessary within the meaning of article 10(2)'.[106]

24.51 Nonetheless the applicant had not made racist comments himself and had attempted to produce a balanced programme. In addition:

---

102 *Lawless v Ireland* (No 2) (1961) 1 EHRR 15; see also *KDP v Germany* (1957) 1 Yearbook 222 and *Glimmerveen and Hagenbeek v Netherlands* (1979) 18 DR 187 at p195.
103 Note 102.
104 (1988) 56 DR 205.
105 (1994) 19 EHRR 1.
106 Ibid at para 30.

News reporting based on interviews, whether edited or not, constitutes one of the most important means whereby the press is able to play its vital role as a public watchdog.[107]

In the circumstances, the prosecution and conviction of the applicant was disproportionate to the legitimate aim of protecting the rights of others.

CHAPTER 25

Protest and public order

25.1   Introduction

25.7   Positive obligations under article 11

25.10   Using the highway as a forum for protest

25.14   Types of conduct protected by article 11

25.17   Balancing freedom of assembly and the prevention of disorder

25.24   Orders banning meetings and marches

Introduction

25.1   Activities such as protests, demonstrations and marches raise issues under article 10 (freedom of expression) and article 11 (freedom of assembly) of the Convention. The scheme of each article is first to set out the positive right protected and then to circumscribe the grounds upon which it can legitimately be restricted. The relevant parts are as follows:

> *Article 10*
>
> 1) Everyone has the right to freedom of expression. This right shall include freedom to hold opinion and to receive and impart information and ideas without interference by public authority and regardless of frontiers ...
>
> 2) The exercise of these freedoms, since it carries with it duties and responsibilities, may be subject to such formalities, conditions, restrictions or penalties as are prescribed by law and are necessary in a democratic society, in the interests of national security, territorial integrity or public safety, for the prevention of disorder or crime, for the protection of health or morals, for the protection of the rights of others, for preventing the disclosure of information received in confidence, or for maintaining the authority and impartiality of the judiciary.
>
> *Article 11*
>
> 1) Everyone has the right to freedom of assembly ...
>
> 2) No restriction shall be placed on the exercise of these rights other than such as are prescribed by law and are necessary in a democratic society in the interests of national security or public safety, for the prevention of disorder or crime, for the protection of health or morals or for the protection of the rights of others. This Article shall not prevent the imposition of lawful restrictions on the exercise of these rights by members of the armed forces, of the police or of the administration of the State.

25.2   Although articles 10(2) and 11(2) appear to provide wide grounds for restricting both freedom of expression and freedom of assembly, the European Court has adopted a fairly strict approach to restrictions. It is for the state authority seeking to impose a restriction to justify its action and all restrictions are to be narrowly construed.[1] In addition, all restrictions must also:

---

1   See chapter 4.

1) be 'prescribed by law',

2) have a legitimate aim, and

3) be 'necessary in a democratic society'.

These principles, which essentially define the appropriate balance between the exercise of individual rights and the public interest (if any) in restricting such exercise, are fundamental to the operation of articles 10 and 11 and are dealt with in detail in chapter 4.[2]

25.3   Freedom of assembly under article 11 of the Convention does not just cover static meetings such as demonstrations and sit-ins.[3] It includes marches and processions.[4] And also includes both public and private events.[5] The inter-relationship between articles 10 and 11 is very close. In many cases freedom of assembly amounts to the collective expression of an opinion.[6] So, for example, in *Steel and Others v UK*,[7] the European Court found a breach of article 10 when three protestors were removed from outside an arms fair in London.[8]

25.4   In keeping with this broad interpretation of freedom of assembly, the Court has extended the protection of article 11 beyond the actual participants in marches and demonstrations. In *Christians Against Racism and Fascism v UK*,[9] the organisation which arranged a march through London – a corporate body – was considered a 'victim' of article 11 enabling it to pursue a case in Strasbourg.

25.5   As a general rule, the purpose of an assembly is irrelevant under article 11.[10] The only limitation under the Convention is that an assembly must be 'peaceful'. However, the mere fact that an assembly may not be peaceful does not automatically preclude the application of article 11. Peaceful intent is sufficient, even if disorder results. In *Christians Against Racism and Fascism v UK*[11] the Commission held that:

2   See paras 4.56 to 4.66.

3   See paras 25.14 to 25.16.

4   *Christians Against Racism and Fascism v UK* (1980) 21 DR 138.

5   *Rassemblement Jurassien and Unite Jurassienne v Switzerland* (1979) 17 DR 93.

6   The European Commission on Human Rights has left open the question whether article 10 protects symbolic speech: *X v UK* (1978) 3 EHRR 63.

7   (24 September 1998) Court; noted at [1999] EHRLR 109.

8   Ibid pp 109–110.

9   Note 4.

10   But see *Anderson v UK* (27 October 1997) where the Commission held that article 11 does not include a right to assemble for purely social purposes: see para 25.12.

11   Note 4.

Under Article 11(1) of the Convention, the right to freedom of peaceful assembly is secured to everyone who has the intention of organising a peaceful demonstration. In the Commission's opinion the possibility of violent counter-demontrations, or the possibility of extremists with violent intentions, not members of the organising association, joining the demonstration cannot as such take away that right. Even if there is a real risk of a public procession resulting in disorder by developments outside the control of those organising it, such procession does not for this reason alone fall outside the scope of Article 11(1) of the Convention ...[12]

Hence the possibility that the National Front or other extremists might hijack or disrupt a march did not oust article 11 protection for the organisers.

25.6   Article 11 applies even where an assembly is illegal. So, for example, in *G v Germany*,[13] where the applicant was convicted for participation in a sit-in, the Commission found that although the event was illegal in domestic law it was not violent and the interference with the applicant's rights therefore required justification under article 11(2).

Positive obligations under article 11

25.7   The public nature of most marches and demonstrations and the potential for conflict between groups with different interests has led the European Court and Commission to recognise that the guarantee of freedom of assembly will often require state action to safeguard the rights of those seeking to exercise their article 11 rights. Two distinct obligations have been identified. The first is for state authorities[14] to abstain from interfering with freedom of assembly. The second is for state authorities to ensure that those who wish to exercise their article 11 rights are able to do so.

25.8   The second obligation is clearly much broader than the first and can require state authorities to take positive steps to safeguard freedom of assembly.[15] It was most clearly articulated in *Plattform*

12 Note 4 at para 4.
13 (1989) 60 DR 256.
14 Which includes 'public authorities' under the HRA: see paras 1.39 to 1.41.
15 The theoretical basis for imposing positive obligations on state authorities and the development of the doctrine are dealt with in chapter 5.

Ärzte für das Leben v Austria[16] where pro-abortion and anti-abortion groups clashed in Salzburg. The applicant organisation complained that, in breach of article 11, the state had failed to take adequate measures to protect its demonstration, which had been notified to the authorities in advance.

25.9   The Austrian government argued that article 11 did not create any positive obligation to protect demonstrators from others who opposed their views. In an important passage, the European Court established the following principles:

> ... a demonstration may annoy or give offence to persons opposed to the ideas or claims that it is seeking to promote. The participants must however be able to hold the demonstration without having to fear that they will be subjected to physical violence by their opponents; such a fear would be liable to deter associations or other groups supporting common ideas or interests from openly expressing their opinions on highly controversial issues affecting the community. In a democracy the right to counter-demonstrate cannot extend to inhibiting the exercise of the right to demonstrate.
>
> Genuine, effective freedom of peaceful assembly cannot, therefore, be reduced to a mere duty on the part of the state not to interfere; a purely negative conception would not be compatible with the object and purpose of Article 11. Like Article 8, Article 11 sometimes requires positive measures to be taken, even in the sphere of relations between individuals, if need be.'[17]

Although it declined to develop a 'general theory of positive obligations' this passage from the Court's judgment is obviously of general application and has been relied upon in numerous subsequent cases.[18] Moreover this approach is consistent with the 'principle of effectiveness'[19] according to which the European Court and Commission have maintained that the Convention is intended to guarantee rights that are 'practical and effective' not rights that are 'theoretical or illusory'.[20]

---

16 (1988) 13 EHRR 204.
17 Note 16 at para 32.
18 See chapter 5.
19 See paras 4.12 to 4.15.
20 See, for example, *Artico v Italy* (1981) 3 EHRR 1 and *Soering v UK* (1989) 11 EHRR 439.

Using the highway as a forum for protest

25.10   Article 11 confers a right to hold meetings, marches and demonstrations on the public highway. This was established in the early case of *Rassemblement Jurassien and Unite Jurassienne v Switzerland*,[21] where the Commission began its analysis of article 11 with the following statement of principle:

> The Commission wishes to state at the outset that the right of peaceful assembly stated in this Article is a fundamental right in a democratic society and, like the right to freedom of expression, is one of the foundations of such society ... as such this right covers both private meetings and meetings in public thoroughfares ...[22]

25.11   This approach has subsequently been endorsed by the European Court, which has never questioned the applicability of article 11 to activities in public places such as the highway. For example, in *Plattform Ärtze für das Leben v Austria*,[23] the activity – a demonstration – took place in a public street. Similarly in *Ezelin v France*[24] the Court held that in joining a public demonstration in the street, the applicant availed himself of his freedom of peaceful assembly.[25] And in *Chorherr v Austria*,[26] the European Court held that the applicant's arrest for engaging in a peaceful demonstration in a public square violated his freedom of expression under article 10(1) of the Convention albeit justified on the facts under article 10(2).

25.12   *Anderson and Others v UK*[27] confirmed that the right to freedom of assembly should not be interpreted restrictively. However, in its view, the right does not include a right to gather for purely social purposes, such as hanging out in a shopping centre. Had there been any organised assembly, the result would have been different.

25.13   Maintaining an appropriate balance between those who wish to use the highway for assemblies and other activities and those who want to use the highway for travel can, however, be a delicate exercise. In *MG v Germany*[28] the applicant had participated in a demon-

---

21   Note 5.
22   Note 5 at 119.
23   (1988) 13 EHRR 204.
24   (1992) 14 EHRR 362.
25   Para 41.
26   (1993) 17 EHRR 358.
27   [1998] EHRLR 218.
28   Appl 13079/87 (1989) unreported.

stration in front of a military barracks blocking the road for 12 minutes every hour. The Commission accepted that a non-violent 'sit-in' on a public highway came within the scope of article 11, but took the view that the applicant's arrest and conviction for obstruction was justified because 'the blocking of the road' caused 'more obstruction than would normally arise from the exercise of the right of peaceful assembly'.[29] It appears therefore that some obstruction caused by the exercise of article 11 rights is legitimate and must therefore be tolerated, so long as it does not extend beyond what, in the circumstances, can be considered reasonable.

Types of conduct protected by article 11

25.14 The European Court and Commission have made it clear that freedom of assembly under article 11, like freedom of speech under article 10, is intended to cover a wide range of speech and conduct. As noted above, in *Plattform Ärtze für das Leben v Austria*[30] the Court held that: '... a demonstration may annoy or give offence to persons opposed to the ideas or claims that it is seeking to promote' but must nonetheless be protected.[31] A similar position was taken in *Piermont v France*.[32] There the applicant, a German MEP, visited French Polynesia at the invitation of a local politician and took part in a pro-independence and anti-nuclear demonstration. As she was about to leave, she was served with an order for her expulsion and exclusion, and she was subsequently excluded from New Caledonia. She complained that the measures infringed her freedom of movement (contrary to article 2 of the Fourth Protocol[33]) and her freedom of expression (contrary to article 10 of the Convention).

25.15 On the question of article 10, the European Court took the view that, having regard to the particular circumstances of the case, the order expelling the applicant from Polynesia pursued two legitimate aims, namely the prevention of disorder and upholding territorial integrity. However, in keeping with its pluralistic approach, the Court insisted that, even if there were a legitimate reason for some restriction on freedom of expression, those opposed to official ideas and

---

29 Ibid at p7.
30 Note 23.
31 Note 23 at para 32.
32 (1995) 20 EHRR 301.
33 Not ratified by the UK.

policy must be able to find a place in the political arena to air their views.

25.16   Although the political atmosphere prevailing in Polynesia and the prospective elections were matters of some weight, as was the fact that the applicant had been requested to exercise discretion when speaking in public, her utterances were made during a peaceful authorised demonstration. She had not called for violence or disorder and she had been speaking in support of the anti-nuclear and independence demands made by several local parties. In the circumstances, the Court found a breach of article 10 on the basis that a fair balance had not been struck between, on the one hand, the public interest in preventing disorder and, on the other, the applicant's freedom of expression.[34]

Balancing freedom of assembly and the prevention of disorder

25.17   The grounds upon which freedom of assembly may legitimately be restricted have been set out above.[35] The prevention of disorder is invoked most frequently and analysis of the European Court's case-law discloses the following principles:

1) although the prevention of disorder is a legitimate aim under article 11, the balance struck between freedom of assembly and the prevention of disorder should not result in individuals being discouraged from making clear their beliefs;

2) the imposition of penalties after an event – for example by instituting criminal proceedings or imposing disciplinary sanctions – is just as much an interference with article 11 as the physical removal of the participants at the time;

3) while it can be legitimate to take action against individuals for their own reprehensible behaviour it can rarely, if ever, be legitimate to take action against individuals merely because they failed to disassociate themselves from the conduct of others.

25.18   In *Ezelin v France*[36] the applicant was a lawyer who took part in a public demonstration, in his capacity as a lawyer, to protest against

---

34 Note 32 at paras 77–78.
35 See para 25.1
36 (1991) 14 EHRR 362.

court decisions whereby prison sentences and fines were imposed on three members of an independence movement for criminal damage to public buildings. During the demonstration, some of the participants shouted anti-police slogans and daubed graffiti on the walls of public buildings. The applicant, who had not himself broken the law in any way, was reprimanded under professional rules of conduct by the French Bar Council on the basis that he had not disassociated himself from the demonstration once the graffiti-writing and abuse began. The European Court found this to be a breach of article 11. The penalty imposed on the applicant was at the lower end of the scale of disciplinary penalties, but it had moral force and therefore amounted to a restriction on freedom of assembly. And although the prevention of disorder was a legitimate aim under article 11, the Court held that the balance struck between freedom of assembly and the prevention of disorder should not result in individuals being discouraged, under threat of criminal or disciplinary sanctions, from making clear their beliefs. The imposition of disciplinary sanctions for not disassociating from others who had engaged in reprehensible conduct went too far because the applicant himself had done nothing more than peacefully demonstrate.

25.19   The same principles were applied with a different result in *Chorherr v Austria*.[37] There the applicant had demonstrated his disapproval of the purchase of fighter aircraft by holding up banners and handing out leaflets at a military ceremony. When it became clear that members of the public were becoming increasingly agitated by the applicant's conduct he was asked by the police to desist. In particular, the banner displayed by the applicant, strapped to his back, prevented some of the crowd from seeing the ceremony. When the applicant refused to comply with the police request, he was arrested for breach of the peace and subsequently fined.

25.20   The European Court found no breach of article 11. It took the view that the police were justified in arresting the applicant to preserve public order. The applicant had intentionally caused agitation in the crowd, the threat to public order was clear (some of the crowd had threatened the applicant with physical violence) and, given the nature and scale of the ceremony, other means of preserving public order were not realistic. The applicant was detained for only a short period (three hours), which in the Court's view was not excessive. And the Austrian constitutional court had scrutinised the applicant's deten-

37 Note 26.

tion to ensure that it was genuinely to prevent violence and not to frustrate his freedom of expression.

25.21   The issue of balancing between freedom of expression and preventing public disorder arose again in the case of *Steel and Others v UK*.[38] There the European Court had to consider whether an arrest for breach of the peace and periods of subsequent detention in a police station were proportionate to the otherwise legitimate aim of preventing disorder and crime. In relation to the first applicant, who had walked in front of a grouse shooter physically preventing him from shooting, the Court[39] found no violation of the Convention because it considered that the applicant's conduct created 'a danger of serious physical injury to herself and others' and formed part of a protest which 'risked culminating in disorder and crime'.[40]

25.22   The Court came to the same conclusion in relation to the second applicant who had placed herself in front of machinery in order to impede engineering works at the site of a motorway extension.[41] However, in relation to the third, fourth and fifth applicants, who had in effect been picketing an arms fair in London (with banners and leaflets), the Court found a breach of article 10 because the applicants' arrest for breach of the peace was a disproportionate response to an otherwise legitimate fear of disorder.[42]

25.23   In this context it is important to recall that the test of 'necessity' under the Convention is fairly strict. In *Arrowsmith v UK*[43] the Commission held that the concept of 'necessity' in article 10(2) as a justification for restrictions, penalties, etc, on freedom of expression implies a pressing social need which must include the 'clear and present danger' test and must be assessed in the light of the particular circumstances of the case.[44]

Orders banning meetings and marches

25.24   Under the Convention, orders banning meetings and marches can be justified only in extreme circumstances. In *Christians against*

---

38 Note 7.
39 By a very narrow majority of one vote.
40 Note 38 at para 105.
41 The Court described this conduct as 'arguably less serious': n38 at para 109.
42 Note 38 at para 110.
43 (1978) 3 EHRR 218.
44 Ibid at para 95.

Racism and Fascism v UK[45] the applicant association had planned to hold a procession to promote its aims: unity in the love of God and opposition to racism and fascism. It was prevented from doing so because of an order made under the (then) Public Order Act 1936[46] prohibiting all processions other than those of a religious, educational, festive or ceremonial character for a period of four weeks. It complained that its rights under articles 10 and 11 of the Convention had been violated.

25.25   The Commission began by observing that:

> Under Article 11(1) of the Convention, the right to freedom of peaceful assembly is secured to everyone who has the intention of organising a peaceful demonstration. In the Commission's opinion the possibility of violent counter-demonstrations, or the possibility of extremists with violent intentions, not members of the organising association, joining the demonstration cannot as such take away that right. Even if there is a real risk of a public procession resulting in disorder by developments outside the control of those organising it, such procession does not for this reason alone fall outside the scope of Article 11(1) of the Convention, but any restriction placed on such an assembly must be in conformity with the terms of paragraph 2 of that provision.[47]

On the question of necessity, the Commission held:

> A general ban on demonstrations can only be justified if there is a real danger of their resulting in disorder which cannot be prevented by other less stringent measures. In this connection, the authority must also take into account the effect of a ban on processions which do not by themselves constitute a danger for public order. Only if the disadvantage of such processions being caught by the ban is clearly outweighed by the security considerations justifying the issue of the ban, and if there is no possibility of avoiding such undesirable side effects of the ban by a narrow circumspection of its scope in terms of its territorial application and duration, can the ban be regarded as being necessary within the meaning of Article 11(2) of the Convention.[48]

On the facts the Commission found that the situation existing in London at the time (and not contested by the applicant) was

---

45   (1980) 21 DR 138.
46   Now Public Order Act 1986.
47   Note 45 at para 4.
48   Note 45 at para 5.

characterised by a tense atmosphere resulting in a series of riots and disturbances caused by public processions of the National Front and counter-demonstrators, particulary in the run up to a by-election in Lambeth. In view of this prevailing atmosphere of violence and the impending by-election and the fact that the applicant's procession could have taken place two days later (when the ban ran out), the Commission found no violation of article 11.

25.26   In *Rai and Others v UK*[49] the Commission had to consider government policy not to allow meetings in Trafalgar Square on issues related to Northern Ireland. Having reviewed the origin and scope of the policy, the Commission concluded that:

> Having regard to the fact that the refusal of permission did not amount to a blanket prohibition on the holding of the applicant's rally but only prevented the use of a high profile location (other venues being available in Central London) the Commission concludes that that restriction in the present case may be regarded as proportionate and justified as necessary in a democratic society ...

Had the policy been more broadly drawn, or alternative venues not available, the decision might have been different.

---

49   (1995) 82-A DR 134. See also *Pendragon v UK* [1999] EHRLR 223.

CHAPTER 26

Property rights

26.1	**Introduction**
26.3	**The 'fair balance' test**
26.5	**Compensation**
26.8	**Meaning of 'possessions'**
26.11	**Deprivation of property**
26.13	The public interest
26.14	Conditions provided for by law
26.15	International law
26.16	Fair balance
26.17	**Control on the use of property/possessions**
26.19	**Peaceful enjoyment of possessions**
26.21	**Taxes, other contributions and penalties**
26.22	**Procedural rights**

Introduction

26.1   Article 1 of the First Protocol provides that:

> Every natural or legal person is entitled to the peaceful enjoyment of his possessions. No one shall be deprived of his possessions except in the public interest and subject to the conditions provided for by law and by the general principles of international law.
>
>   The preceding provision shall not, however, in any way impair the right of a state to enforce such laws as it deems necessary to control the use of property in accordance with the general interest or to secure the payment of taxes or other contributions or penalties.

In effect it guarantees a right to property.[1] And in this context, the words 'possessions' and 'property' are interchangeable.

26.2   On analysis, article 1 of Protocol 1 essentially comprises three rules:

1) Individuals are entitled to the peaceful enjoyment of their property/possessions.

2) The state can deprive individuals of their property/possessions but only in the circumstances set out in article 1 of Protocol 1.

3) The state can control the use of the property/possessions of individuals, but again only in the circumstances set out in article 1 of Protocol 1.

In practice, the Strasbourg bodies consider the second and third rules before the first.

The 'fair balance' test

26.3   Despite the language of article 1 of Protocol 1, running through all three rules is a 'fair balance' test, ie, an assessment of whether the right balance has been achieved between 'the demands of the general interest of the community and the requirements of the protection of the individual's fundamental rights'.[2]

26.4   The application of this test will vary according to the measure in issue. Clearly the deprivation of property is harder to justify than mere control – and a 'public interest' in deprivation must be

---

1   *Marckx v Belgium* (1979) 2 EHRR 330.
2   *Sporrong and Lonnroth v Sweden* (1983) 5 EHRR 35.

identified. Equally control is harder to justify than mere interference. However, there are no elements of the test that are strictly applied in all circumstances and no irreducible minimum.

Compensation

26.5 The payment of compensation is not required under article 1 of Protocol 1, but it will be a highly relevant factor in determining whether a 'fair balance' has been struck between the community at large and the rights of the individual in question.

26.6 In *Lithgow v UK*[3] the European Court observed that the deprivation of property/possessions without compensation was justified only in exceptional circumstances throughout the member states of the Council of Europe and that:

> As far as Article 1 [of Protocol 1] is concerned, the protection of the right of property it affords would be largely illusory and ineffective in the absence of any equivalent principle.[4]

Where no compensation at all is payable, a breach of article 1 of Protocol 1 is therefore likely.[5]

26.7 Compensation should be 'reasonably related' to the value of any property taken. However, article 1 of Protocol 1 does not require full compensation or the same level of compensation for every type of interference with property/possessions.[6] In *James v UK*[7] the European Court found it legitimate for the state to pay less than the market value where it was pursuing economic reform or social justice.[8]

Meaning of 'possessions'

26.8 The term 'possessions' in the first paragraph of article 1 of the First Protocol has an autonomous Convention meaning and has been interpreted broadly. It includes all property and chattels and also

---

3 (1986) 8 EHRR 329.
4 Ibid at para 120.
5 See, for example, *Erkner and Hofauer v Austria* (1987) 9 EHRR 464.
6 *Lithgow v UK* n3 para 121.
7 (1986) 8 EHRR 123.
8 Ibid at para 54.

acquired rights with economic interests, such as shares,[9] patents,[10] fishing rights,[11] alcohol licences,[12] planning consents,[13] the ownership of a debt[14] and, in some circumstances, even 'goodwill'.[15]

26.9   However, article 1 of Protocol 1 applies only to existing property/ possessions and does not confer a right to acquire property.[16] On that basis, income is a 'possession' only where it has already been earned or there is an enforceable claim to it.[17]

26.10   In *Pressos Compania Naviera SA v Belgium*[18] the European Court construed possessions so as to include a claim for negligence, which had been removed by retrospective legislation. Welfare benefits and other similar benefits can also constitute possessions; see chapter 22.

Deprivation of property

26.11 The meaning of 'deprivation' in article 1 of Protocol 1 has been considered in a number of cases. In *Sporrong and Lonroth v Sweden*[19] where there was no formal expropriation of property, the European Court nonetheless held that:

> ... it must look behind the appearances and investigate the realities of the situation complained of. Since the Convention is intended to guarantee rights that are 'practical and effective', it has to be ascertained whether [the] situations amounted to a de facto expropriation ...[20]

On analysis, it took the view that measures which severely restricted the applicants' ability to dispose of their properties did not amount to de facto deprivation because they could still use them and, with difficulty, sell them.

26.12   Under the terms of the second sentence of the first paragraph of

9   *Bramelid and Malmstrom v Sweden* (1982) 29 DR 64.
10 *Smith Kline and French Laboratories Ltd v Netherlands* (1990) 66 DR 70.
11 *Baner v Sweden* (1989) 60 DR 128.
12 *The Traktorer Aktiebolag v Sweden* (1991) 13 EHRR 309.
13 *Pine Valley Developments Ltd v Ireland* (1992) 14 EHRR 319.
14 *Agneessens v Belgium* (1988) 58 DR 63.
15 *Van Marle v Netherlands* (1986) 8 EHRR 483.
16 *Marckx v Belgium* n1.
17 *X v Germany* (1980) 18 DR 216.
18 (1996) 21 EHRR 301.
19 Note 2.
20 Note 2 at para 63.

article 1 of Protocol 1, three conditions must be satisfied before individuals can be deprived of their property/possessions:

1) the taking must be in the public interest;
2) it must be subject to conditions provided by law; and
3) it must be subject to the conditions provided for by the general principles of international law.

Each requires brief analysis.

The public interest

26.13 When it deprives individuals of their property/possessions, it is for the state to identify what interest is actually being pursued. However, there are few limitations and the grounds are wide. For example, in *James v UK*[21] the European Court held that the 'taking of property in pursuance of a policy calculated to enhance social justice within the community can properly be described as being in the public interest.'[22]

Conditions provided for by law

26.14 The requirement that any deprivation of property/possessions be 'provided for by law' has much the same meaning as the requirement that interference with Convention rights under article 8 be 'in accordance with law' or under articles 9 to 11 be 'prescribed by law'. This imports into article 1 of Protocol 1 the principle that domestic law permitting the deprivation of property/possessions must be both accessible and clear.[23]

International law

26.15 The requirement that any deprivation of property/possessions should be in accordance with 'the general principles of international law' adds very little in most cases. International law has no application where a state deprives its own nationals of property.[24]

---

21 Note 7.
22 Note 7 at para 41.
23 *Lithgow v UK* n3 at para 110, referring to *Malone v UK* (1985) 7 EHRR 14.
24 *James v UK* (1986) n7 at paras 58–66; *Lithgow v UK* n3 at para 112.

Fair balance

26.16   So far as the 'fair balance' test is concerned, the European Court established in *James v UK*[25] that in deprivation cases, achieving a fair balance precludes the imposition of an excessive burden on the individual in question. Overall, there must be 'a reasonable relationship of proportionality between the means employed and the aim sought to be realised.'[26] And, in making this assessment, the question of compensation will be relevant, as will the risks taken by the individual when s/he acquired the property/possessions in question.[27] For example, in *Pine Valley Development Ltd v Ireland*[28] the European Court was influenced by the speculative nature of the applicant's activities in purchasing a plot of land with outline planning permission for industrial and office development.

Control on the use of property/possessions

26.17   Control on the use of property/possessions is a wide concept covering positive requirements to use property in a certain way and negative restrictions on the use of property, for example, rent restrictions[29] or planning controls.[30]

26.18   There is no concept of the 'public interest' as such, but the European Court has established that the measure in question must nonetheless have a legitimate aim, in the sense of not being 'manifestly without reasonable foundation'. And, the 'fair balance test' again requires that there be a reasonable relationship of proportionality between the means employed and the achievement of that aim.[31]

25   Note 7.
26   *Hakansson and Sturesson v Sweden* (1991) 13 EHRR 1 at para 51.
27   *Hakansson and Sturesson v Sweden* n26.
28   Note 13.
29   *Mellacher v Austria* (1990) 12 EHRR 391.
30   *Pine Valley Developments Ltd v Ireland* n13.
31   *Wasa Liv Omsesidigt, Forsakringsbolaget valands Pensionsstiftelse v Sweden* (1988) 58 DR 163.

Peaceful enjoyment of possessions

26.19   Although expressed in wide terms, the principle that individuals have the right to peaceful enjoyment of their possessions is subject to a number of qualifications. Most importantly, the European Court has implied restrictions on the right to peaceful enjoyment of property/possession by reference to the 'fair balance' test.[32] This ties the three 'rules' under article 1 of Protocol 1 together and ensures that interference with the peaceful enjoyment of property is considered under this head only where it is neither deprivation of, nor control over, the use of property/possessions.

26.20   In addition, only interferences which touch on the financial value of property/possessions engage the right to peaceful enjoyment of them. Hence in *S v France*[33] and *Rayner v UK*[34] the Commission considered noise nuisance only from the perspective of diminution in the value of property.[35] And, private law restrictions are deemed to be defining of, rather than interferences with, property/possessions.[36]

Taxes, other contributions and penalties

26.21   Article 1 of Protocol 1 specifically leaves states with wide powers to control property/possessions to secure the payment of taxes or other contributions or penalties. The 'fair balance' test applies, and will require procedural guarantees to establish the applicant's liability to make payments. However, the state is largely unconstrained about levels of taxation, the means of assessment and the manner it chooses to exact taxes. In *Gasus Dosier-und Fordertechnik GmbH v Netherlands*[37] even the operation of the fair balance did not preclude the European Court concluding that recovering tax debts against a third party's assets was not arbitrary.[38]

---

32 See para 26.16.
33 (1990) 65 DR 250.
34 (1986) 47 DR 5.
35 For the article 8 perspective on environmental issues see chapter 22.
36 See *X v UK* (1978) 14 DR 234.
37 (1995) 20 EHRR 403.
38 Ibid at para 59; see, however, *Hentrich v France* (1994) A/296-A.

Procedural rights

26.22   Interference with property will often involve the determination of civil rights and obligations within the meaning of article 6(1). Where it does so, the fair trial guarantees of that provision will apply; see chapters 12 and 13.

26.23   In addition, a 'fair balance' under article 1 of Protocol 1 may require additional or separate procedural safeguards, such as the opportunity for individuals to challenge particular measures affecting their property.[39]

---

39   See, for example, *Sporrong and Lonnroth v Sweden* n2.

CHAPTER 27

Thought, conscience and religion

27.1   Introduction

27.5   The scope of freedom of thought, conscience and religion

27.10   Manifesting a religion or belief

27.13   Obeying the law

27.19   Proselytism

27.21   Positive obligations under article 9

27.23   Restricting article 9(1) rights

27.27   Blasphemy and freedom of expression

27.34   Religious discrimination

27.36   Who can raise an article 9 claim?

27.37   Conscientious objectors

27.38   The special provision made for freedom of religion in the HRA

Introduction

27.1   Questions of thought, conscience and religion can arise under any article in the Convention, particularly in light of the general prohibition on discrimination contained in article 14.[1] However, article 9 (freedom of thought, conscience and religion), article 10 (freedom of expression) and article 4(3)(b) (the limited recognition of the right of conscientious objectors in relation to military service) are the most relevant. And, of those provisions, article 9 has special importance.

27.2   Article 9 provides that:

1) Everyone has the right to freedom of thought, conscience and religion; this right includes freedom to change his religion or belief and freedom, either alone or in community with others and in public or private, to manifest his religion or belief, in worship, teaching, practice and observance.

2) Freedom to manifest one's religion or beliefs shall be subject only to such limitations as are prescribed by law and are necessary in a democratic society in the interests of public safety, for the protection of public order, health or morals, or for the protection of the rights and freedoms of others.

It therefore has two aspects. First, it protects freedom of thought, conscience and religion. Second, it protects the manifestation of religion or belief.

27.3   The distinction between these two aspects is of crucial importance. The right to hold, or adhere to, a religion or belief is unqualified; whereas the right to manifest that religion or belief is subject to restriction under article 9(1).

27.4   Moreover, the Strasbourg bodies have interpreted the right to hold, or adhere to, a religion or belief broadly, but have interpreted manifestation – or, more accurately, the word 'practice' in article 9(1) – narrowly. In other words, the observance of freedom of thought, conscience and religion in the personal sphere is afforded much greater protection than outward conduct motivated, or influenced, by religious or other beliefs. On that basis, although the European Court and Commission have been prepared to accept that article 9 covers many and varied religions and beliefs, they have repeatedly emphasised that it does not protect 'each and every act which is motivated or influenced by religion or belief'.[2]

---

1   See chapter 29.
2   *Arrowsmith v UK* (1978) 19 DR 5.

The scope of freedom of thought, conscience and religion

27.5   The approach of the European Court and Commission to the inter-
pretation of article 9 has enabled them to accept, in principle, that its
protection extends to Druidism,[3] pacifism,[4] and veganism;[5] and to the
Muslim religion,[6] the Krishna consciousness movement,[7] Jehovah's
Witnesses,[8] the Divine Light Zentrum[9] and the Church of
Scientology.[10]

27.6   It clearly covers non-religious beliefs. In *Kokkinakis v Greece*[11] the
European Court observed that:

> [Article 9] is, in its religious dimension, one of the most vital
> elements that go to make up the identity of believers and of their
> conception of life, but it is also a precious asset for atheists,
> agnostics, sceptics and the unconcerned.[12]

For the Court, therefore, the pluralism of a democratic society
depends on freedom of thought, conscience and religion.[13]

27.7   However, article 9 protection does not extend beyond 'the sphere
of private, personal beliefs' to cover the espousal of purely idealistic
or political views or goals, such as those of a prisoners' support
group[14] or IRA prisoners claiming 'special category status'.[15] The
espousal of such views or goals may nonetheless be protected under
article 10 (freedom of expression).[16]

27.8   Any indoctrination or action by the state to coerce or compel
people's thinking, or to make them reveal their beliefs, is contrary to
article 9 and cannot be justified as being in the public interest,[17] and

3 *Chappell v UK* (1987) 53 DR 241.
4 *Arrowsmith v UK* n2.
5 *X v UK* (Commission) Appl 18187/91 (10 February 1993).
6 *Ahmad v UK* (1982) 4 EHRR 126.
7 *Iskcon v UK* (1994) 76A DR 90.
8 *Kokkinakis v Greece* (1994) 17 EHRR 397.
9 *Omkarananda and the Divine Light Zentrum v Switzerland* (1981) 25 DR 105.
10 *X and Church of Scientology v Sweden* (1979) 16 DR 68.
11 Note 8.
12 Note 8 at para 31.
13 Ibid.
14 *Vereniging Rechtswinkels Utrecht v Netherlands* (1986) 46 DR 200.
15 *McFeeley v UK* (1980) 20 DR 44.
16 See chapter 24.
17 *Human Rights in Europe*, Robertson A H, Manchester University Press, 1993
p145.

freedom of religion includes freedom to change one's religion.[18] In this context, however, indoctrination implies some positive action directed against the individual. As long as s/he is free to hold his/her own religion or belief, article 9(1) will not be breached.

27.9   The maintenance of an established church is not, of itself, a violation of article 9.[19] Nor, within limits, is the promulgation of policies based on religious beliefs.[20] The limits to the promulgation of such policies were explored in *Dudgeon v UK*,[21] where the government argued that there was a strong body of opposition to the decriminalisation of consensual adult homosexual activity.[22] The Court acknowledged the existence of such a body of opinion but held that:

> ... this cannot of itself be decisive as to the necessity for the interference with the applicant's private life resulting from the measures being challenged.[23]

In other words, while the promulgation of policies based on religious, or other, beliefs may not, of itself, breach article 9(1), where those policies infringe other Convention rights, they will have to be justified in the usual way.[24]

Manifesting a religion or belief

27.10   Article 9(1) protects the right of individuals 'to manifest' their religion or belief in public or in private, alone or with others. It specifically refers to the acts of 'worship, teaching, practice and observance'.

27.11   In *Arrowsmith v UK*[25] the Commission held that the word 'practice' does not cover every act 'which is motivated or influenced by a religion or belief'. In *C v UK*[26] it elaborated on this a little when it observed that:

---

18 *Angelini v Sweden* (1986) 51 DR 41.
19 *Darby v Sweden* (1991) Comm Rep (unreported).
20 See, for example, the rules on divorce in Ireland examined in *Johnston v Ireland* (1987) 9 EHRR 203, which were clearly influenced by the Roman Catholic religion.
21 (1982) 4 EHRR 149.
22 Ibid at para 57.
23 Note 21 at para 59; see also *Norris v Ireland* (1991) 13 EHRR 186.
24 See generally, chapter 4.
25 Note 2.
26 (1983) 37 DR 142.

Article 9 primarily protects the sphere of personal beliefs and religious creeds, ie, the area which is sometimes called the forum internum. In addition it protects acts which are intimately linked to these attitudes, such as acts of worship or devotion which are aspects of the practice of a religion or belief in a generally recognised form.

However, in protecting this personal sphere, Article 9 of the Convention does not always guarantee the right to behave in the public sphere in a way which is dictated by belief: – for instance by refusing to pay certain taxes because part of the revenue so raised may be applied for military expenditure.[27]

In practice the distinction between manifestation in the personal (protected) and public (not necessarily unprotected) sphere may be difficult to discern.

27.12   In *Arrowsmith v UK* itself, the distribution of leaflets to soldiers advising them to go absent or to refuse to serve in Northern Ireland was held not to be a 'manifestation' of pacifist belief within the meaning of article 9(1). It gave as an example of the activity which it considered would fall within article 9(1):

> ... public declarations proclaiming generally the idea of pacifism and urging the acceptance of a commitment to non-violence ...[28]

This is hardly a convincing distinction and the better course would have been for the Commission to have accepted the applicant's conduct as a manifestation of her pacifist beliefs under article 9(1) and then to have gone on to consider the application of article 9(2).

Obeying the law

27.13   The European Court and Commission have been very reluctant to find that the manifestation of a religious or other belief can justify a refusal to comply with domestic law of general application. In most cases, they have found that laws of general application have no article 9 implications because they do not interfere with the private sphere it protects. However, some laws of general application clearly do enter that sphere and they will need to be justified under article 9(2).

27.14   In *C v UK*[29] the Commission rejected the application of a Quaker,

---

27 Ibid at p147.
28 Note 2 at p20.
29 Note 26.

who objected on religious grounds to state expenditure on defence and wished to have the relevant portion of his taxes directed to other purposes, on the basis that:

> The obligation to pay taxes is a general one which has no specific conscientious implications in itself. Its neutrality in this sense is also illustrated by the fact that no tax payer can influence or determine the purpose for which his or her contributions are applied, once they are collected. Furthermore, the power of taxation is expressly recognised by the Convention system and is ascribed to the State by Article 1, First Protocol.
>
> It follows that Article 9 does not confer on the applicant the right to refuse, on the basis of his convictions to abide by legislation, the operation of which is provided for by the Convention, and which applies neutrally and generally in the public sphere, without impinging on the freedoms guaranteed by Article 9.[30]

The same result followed in *Bouessel du Bourg v France*.[31]

27.15   A claim for exemption from a compulsory pension scheme failed on the same basis in *V v Netherlands*;[32] as did an argument in *Karakuzey v Germany*[33] that a court-imposed maintenance order breached the applicant's rights under article 9 because his daughter was being brought up contrary to his religious convictions.

27.16   A similar approach was adopted in *Iskcon v UK*,[34] where the Krishna consciousness movement complained about the rejection of a planning application which prevented the use of an estate owned by it for the purposes of public religious worship. The Commission held that sufficient weight had been given to religious freedom in the planning process and that article 9 could not be used to circumvent planning laws of general application.

27.17   As noted above, where legislation, although of general application, does clearly impinge on the sphere of personal beliefs and religious creeds recognised in *C v UK*,[35] different considerations will apply and such legislation will have to be justified under article 9(2).

27.18   A requirement that Sikhs wear crash-helmets on motorbikes might be justifiable on the grounds of public health;[36] and closing

---

30 Ibid at p147.
31 (1993) 16 EHRR CD 49.
32 (1984) 39 DR 267.
33 (1997) 23 EHRR CD 92.
34 Note 7.
35 Note 26.
36 See *X v UK* (1978) 14 DR. See further *X v UK* (1976) 5 DR 100 and *X v UK* (1982) 28 DR 5.

Stonehenge to Druids during the solstice might be justified on grounds of public safety.[37] But legislation of general application prohibiting all proselytism could not be justified in *Kokkinakis v Greece*.[38]

Proselytism

27.19 Where proselytism is an essential aspect of religious belief, states must carefully balance the rights of those who want to convert others and the rights of those who do not want to be subjected to their attempts to do so. In *Kokkinakis v Greece* (above), which involved the conviction of a Jehovah's Witness for proselytism, the European Court sought to distinguish between bearing Christian witness and improper proselytism in the context of Greek laws prohibiting proselytism. It observed that:

> The former corresponds to true evangelism, which a report drawn up in 1956 under the auspices of the World Council of Churches describes as an essential mission and a responsibility of every Christian and every Church. The latter represents a corruption or deformation of it. It may, according to the same report, take the form of activities offering material or social advantages with a view to gaining new members for a Church or exerting improper pressure on people in distress or in need; it may even entail the use of violence or brainwashing; more generally, it is not compatible with respect for the freedom of thought, conscience and religion of others.[39]

On that basis, a law which simply criminalised all proselytism was disproportionate and not 'necessary in a democratic society'.

27.20 The question of espousing religious beliefs arose in a different way in *X and Church of Scientology v Sweden*,[40] where the Commission had to determine whether placing an advert for an E-meter – an electronic instrument for measuring the mental state of an individual – amounted to the manifestation of religion. It observed that:

> ... the manifestation of a belief in practice does not confer protection on statements of purported religious belief which appear as selling 'arguments' in advertisements of a purely commercial nature by a religious group ... the Commission would draw a

37 *Chappell v UK* n3.
38 Note 8.
39 Note 8 at para 48. See also *Larissis v Greece* [1998] EHRLR 505.
40 Note 10.

distinction ... between advertisements which are merely 'informational' or 'descriptive' in character and commercial advertisements, offering objects for sale. Once an advertisement enters into the latter sphere ... [it represents] more the manifestation of a desire to market goods for profit than the manifestation of a belief in practice.[41]

On that basis the advert was not protected under article 9(1).

Positive obligations under article 9

27.21 The state has responsibility under the Convention for ensuring the peaceful enjoyment of article 9 rights to those who hold religious or other beliefs.[42] This will often involve a delicate balance between competing Convention rights: the tension between blasphemy laws and freedom of expression is an obvious example.[43] In *Dubowska and Skup v Poland*[44] the Commission observed that;

> ... there may be certain positive obligations on the part of a State inherent in an effective respect for rights guaranteed under Article 9 of the Convention, which may involve the adoption of measures designed to secure respect for freedom of religion even in the sphere of the relations of individuals between themselves ... Such measures may, in certain circumstances, constitute a legal means of ensuring that an individual will not be disturbed in his worship by the activities of others.[45]

27.22 In *Lemon v UK*[46] the Commission found the law of blasphemy an acceptable means of protecting the article 9 rights of Christians;[47] but in *Choudhury v UK*[48] it rejected a complaint based on the failure of English blasphemy law to protect Muslims.

---

41 Note 10 at p72.
42 *Otto-Preminger Institute v Austria* (1995) 19 EHRR 34 at para 47.
43 See paras 27.27 to 27.33.
44 (1997) 24 EHRR CD 75.
45 Ibid at p78.
46 (1982) 28 DR 77.
47 See below.
48 Appl 17439/90 Commission (5 March 1991).

Restricting article 9(1) rights

27.23 As noted above, only the right to hold, or adhere to, a religion or belief is unqualified. The manifestation of a religion or belief can be restricted but only where:

1) the grounds for interference are 'in accordance with law';

2) they pursue a legitimate aim (ie, one of the aims set out in article 9(2)); and

3) they are necessary and proportionate.

These requirements are examined in detail in chapter 4.[49]

27.24　　In *Kokkinakis v Greece*[50] the European Court interpreted article 9(2) as a recognition that in a democratic society, in which several religions coexist, it may be necessary to place restrictions on the manifestation of religion or belief, to reconcile the interests of the various groups and ensure that everyone's beliefs are respected.[51] However, any such restrictions will be subject to very close scrutiny. As noted above, in that case, laws which failed to distinguish between bearing Christian witness and proselytism were found by the Court to be disproportionate.

27.25　　In *Manoussakis v Greece*[52] the applicant Jehovah's Witnesses were convicted under a Greek law prohibiting the operation of a place of worship without prior ministerial approval. They had first applied for approval in 1984 and by the time of the European Court's decision in 1996 they had still not received a definitive reply. The Court found that the law had been used by the authorities to restrict the activities of non-Orthodox faiths and, accordingly, that article 9 had been breached.

27.26　　The Commission has determined a series of cases from the UK concerning the extent to which prison rules make provision for prisoners to manifest their religion or beliefs. These are examined in chapter 16.[53]

49　Paras 4.41 to 4.77.
50　Note 8.
51　Note 8 at para 33.
52　(1997) 23 EHRR 387
53　Paras 16.72 to 16.73.

Blasphemy and freedom of expression

27.27   The relationship between freedom of expression under article 10 of the Convention and protection of religion under article 9 has been explored by the European Court on a number of occasions. As a general principle, the Court has recognised that:

> Those who choose to exercise the freedom to manifest their religion, irrespective of whether they do so as members of a religious majority or a minority, cannot reasonably expect to be exempt from all criticism. They must tolerate and accept the denial by others of ... doctrines hostile to their faith.[54]

However, the manner in which religious beliefs and doctrines are opposed may raise an issue under article 9.

27.28   In *Otto-Preminger Institute v Austria*,[55] criminal proceedings were brought to prevent the showing of a satirical film on a charge of 'disparaging religious doctrines'. In the course of those proceedings, which were ultimately discontinued, the film itself was seized. The applicant, a non-profit-making organisation, claimed that the proceedings and seizure breached article 10 of the Convention.

27.29   Dealing first with the question of legitimate aim, the European Court, drawing on the case of *Kokkinakis v Greece*,[56] observed that, in the context of article 9, a state may repress certain forms of conduct, including the imparting of information and ideas, judged incompatible with the respect for the freedom of thought, conscience and religion of others. It continued:

> The respect for the religious feelings of believers as guaranteed in Article 9 can legitimately be thought to have been violated by provocative portrayals of objects of religious veneration; and such portrayals can be regarded as malicious violation of the spirit of tolerance, which must also be a feature of democratic society. The Convention is to be read as a whole and therefore the interpretation and application of Article 10 in the present case must be in harmony with the logic of the Convention.[57]

The aim of the measures taken could therefore be justified as legitimate.

---

54   *Otto-Preminger Institute v Austria* A/295-A (1995) 19 EHRR 1 at para 47.
55   Note 42.
56   Note 8.
57   Note 8 at para 47.

27.30   However, to be 'necessary in a democratic society', the measures in question also had to be proportionate. Legislation prohibiting the publication of *all* provocative portrayals of objects of religious veneration might fail to satisfy this requirement; only prohibiting that which was 'gratuitously offensive' and did not contribute to any form of public debate capable of furthering progress in human affairs could be justified under article 10(2).[58] Since, however, the question whether the film was 'gratuitously offensive' involved moral questions, the European Court was prepared to afford the national authorities a wide margin of appreciation in making their assessment. Since they did not appear to have overstepped the mark, no violation of article 10 was found.

27.31   The European Court applied a stricter test in *Wingrove v UK*,[59] where the applicant's video work, *Visions of Ecstasy*, was refused a classification certificate on the ground that it infringed the criminal law of blasphemy. The Court observed that:

> ... the English law of blasphemy does not prohibit the expression, in any form, of views hostile to the Christian religion. Nor can it be said that opinions which are offensive to Christians necessarily fall within its ambit ... it is the manner in which views are advocated rather than the views themselves which the law seeks to control.[60]

Since the manner in which views are advocated is controlled only where they reached a high degree of profanity, the Court found no breach of article 10; again affording the state a wide margin of appreciation.

27.32   Restriction on freedom of expression under article 10 to protect freedom of religion under article 9 is therefore legitimate; but only if:

1) the restrictions apply only to the *manner* in which information or ideas are conveyed;

2) a high profanity threshold is applied; and

3) there are effective safeguards against the over-broad application of any such restrictions.

27.33   Notably, in *Wingrove v UK*[61] the European Court examined the extent to which blasphemy was retained as a criminal offence throughout

---

58   Note 8 at para 49.
59   (1997) 24 EHRR 1.
60   Ibid at para 60.
61   Note 59.

Europe. It noted that while it remained in place in various European countries, it was rarely used and that some states had repealed blasphemy legislation altogether. However, it felt that at that stage,[62] there was not yet sufficient common ground in the legal and social orders of the member states of the Council of Europe to conclude that the imposition of restrictions on the propagation of material on the basis that it is blasphemous is, in itself, unnecessary in a democratic society. On the basis that the Convention is to be interpreted as a 'living instrument'[63] the issue may well have to be reconsidered in the future.

Religious discrimination

27.34   Article 14 prohibits discrimination in the exercise of Convention rights on a number of grounds, including religion and political or other opinion. The principles underpinning article 14 are examined in chapter 29.

27.35   Broadly speaking, any difference in treatment based solely on religious grounds will be very difficult to justify. In *Hoffman v Austria*[64] the European Court had very little doubt that a court order depriving the applicant of custody of her children, as against her husband, because she was a Jehovah's Witness breached articles 8 and 14. In the circumstances, it did not consider article 9 separately.[65]

Who can raise an article 9 claim?

27.36   The rights conferred under article 9 may be exercised by an individual, by a church body or by an association with religious and philosophical objects.[66] However, it may be more difficult for a church body or association than for an individual to establish that its activities amount to a manifestation of religion or belief.[67]

---

62 1996.
63 See chapter 4.
64 (1994) 17 EHRR 293.
65 See also *M v Bulgaria* (1996) 22 EHRR CD 101.
66 *Chappell v UK*, n3 at para 1.
67 *Church of X v UK* (1969) 12 Yearbook 306.

Conscientious objectors

27.37   A series of complaints before the Commission have concerned the question of conscientious objection to military service. So far, all such complaints have been rejected on the basis that article 4[68] specifically envisages compulsory military service.[69] Thus, in countries where compulsory military service exists, article 9 does not require substituted civilian service[70] and where such substituted service does exist, a person cannot resist it by invoking article 9.[71]

The special provision made for freedom of religion in the HRA

27.38   Section 13 of the HRA makes special provision for freedom of religion. It requires that any court or tribunal determining any question arising under the HRA which *might* affect the exercise by a religious organisation (itself or its members collectively) of the Convention right of freedom of thought, conscience and religion must have 'particular regard to the importance of that right'. It is intended to 'reassure' churches and other religious organisations that the Act will not be used to 'intrude upon genuinely held religious beliefs or practices'.[72]

---

68   See chapter 3.
69   See, Clements L, *European Human Rights*, Sweet & Maxwell 1994, p168.
70   *A v Switzerland* (1984) 38 DR 219.
71   *N v Sweden* (1984) 40 DR 203.
72   Home Secretary, HC Debs, cols 1020–1021, 20 May 1998.

CHAPTER 28

Workplace rights

28.1   Introduction

28.2   The applicability of article 6(1) in the employment context

28.6   The special position of public officials

28.15   Specific workplace rights

28.16   Slavery, servitude and forced labour

28.25   The right to form and join a trade union

28.29   The right not to join a trade union

28.31   Trade union activities

28.34   Industrial action

28.36   Excluded groups

28.38   The protection of other Convention rights in the workplace

28.39   Privacy at work

28.42   Security vetting

28.44   Freedom of thought, conscience and religion

28.49   Freedom of expression

28.55   The prohibition on discrimination

continued

28.56   Contracting out of Convention rights

28.57   The applicability of the Convention between private individuals

Introduction

28.1 Although there is no right to work as such under the ECHR,[1] its provisions do protect a number of workplace activities and the European Court has attached considerable weight to the right to earn a livelihood.[2] Recourse to the Convention is possible in three ways:

1) Private law relations between employers and employees are governed by the fair trial requirements of article 6(1).

2) Specific workplace rights are guaranteed under article 4, which prohibits (among other things) 'forced labour' and under article 11, which protects the right to form and join trade unions.

3) Other Convention rights, such as the right to privacy (article 8), freedom of thought, conscience and religion (article 9), freedom of expression (article 10) and the prohibition on discrimination (article 14), extend into the workplace.

In addition, under the Human Rights Act 1998, it will be unlawful for any public authority to act in a way which is incompatible with Convention rights.[3]

The applicability of article 6(1) in the employment context

28.2 Article 6(1) of the Convention guarantees the right to a fair trial in the determination of 'civil rights and obligations'. Specific aspects include:

1) the right to an independent and impartial tribunal;

2) the right to disclosure;

3) the right to an adversarial hearing;

4) the right to reasons; and

5) the right to have decisions made within a reasonable period.

See chapters 12 and 13.

28.4 In the employment context, it is settled case-law of the European Court that disputes relating to private law relations between employers and employees are 'civil' disputes within the meaning of

1 See *X v Denmark* (1975) 3 DR 153 and the cases referred to therein.
2 See *Young, James and Webster v UK* (1982) 4 EHRR 38.
3 See chapter 1.

article 6(1).[4] However, article 6(1) does not apply to all employer/ employee disputes. It clearly applies to those disputes which have a decisive impact on the ability of an individual to continue his/her job or profession, such as suspension,[5] dismissal[6] or disbarment.[7] It may also apply where significant economic interests are at stake, such as the payment of a salary or pension entitlements.[8] However, in *X v UK*[9] the Commission held that disciplinary proceedings resulting in a reprimand did not fall within the scope of article 6(1). Unless the maximum penalty is fixed before such proceedings are commenced, this decision may cause considerable practical difficulties; the safest course is, therefore, to assume that article 6(1) applies where dismissal is an option.

28.4   Individuals may be subject to disciplinary proceedings affecting their job or profession in a number of different ways, for example, (a) internal disciplinary proceedings conducted by or on behalf of an employer; (b) external disciplinary proceedings conducted by a professional body; and/or (c) external disciplinary proceedings conducted by a statutory body or other executive regulation. The principle in each case is the same: either the disciplinary proceedings themselves must comply with article 6(1) (which is unlikely in respect of internal disciplinary proceedings) or there must be a right of appeal or review to a court or tribunal which does.[10] Where, as in the UK, there is a right to challenge the lawfulness of dismissal in an industrial tribunal, that body must comply with article 6(1). This requirement is reinforced by the Human Rights Act 1998, which makes all courts and tribunals public authorities, with the consequence that it is unlawful for an industrial tribunal to act in a way which is incompatible with Convention rights.[11]

28.5   The application of article 6(1) to professional disciplinary tribunals is dealt with in chapter 12, where a number of specific examples are set out.

---

4   *Obermeier v Austria* (1991) 13 EHRR 290.
5   Ibid.
6   Ibid. Also see *X v UK* (1984) 6 EHRR 583.
7   *Albert and Le Compte v Belgium* (1983) 5 EHRR 533.
8   *Lombardo v Italy* (1996) 21 EHRR 188 and *Massa v Italy* (1994) 18 EHRR 266.
9   (1984) 6 EHRR 583.
10 *Albert and Le Compte v Belgium* n7 at para 29. See also chapter 12.
11 See s6(1) and chapter 1.

The special position of public officials

28.6   The application of article 6(1) in cases concerning public officials is complicated. In a series of cases, the European Commission held that, as a general rule, disputes relating to the recruitment, employment and dismissal of public officials are outside the scope of article 6(1).[12] The European Court endorsed this general approach in *Lombardo v Italy*[13] and applied it in *Neigel v France*.[14] The basis for the distinction between private individuals and public officials has never been satisfactorily addressed. However, it probably stems from the fact that, when the Convention was drafted, a clause providing that 'everyone has the right of equal access to public service in his country'[15] was initially included in Protocol 7 and then deliberately omitted.[16]

28.7   In *Neigel v France* the applicant, a shorthand typist in the French civil service, claimed that her rights under article 6(1) had not been respected in relation to a dispute about her reinstatement after a one-year leave of absence. The European Court found that article 6(1) did not apply because the applicant's request for reinstatement clearly related to her 'recruitment', 'career' and the 'termination of [her] service' as a civil servant.

28.8   Judge Palm, dissenting, criticised the 'thin reasoning' of the majority which effectively deprived 'all public servants governed by public law who are involved in a dispute with their public employer of the basic procedural safeguards in article 6(1)'. While the Convention may not provide a right of access to public service, Judge Palm contended that, as the applicant already had a job as a shorthand typist and there was no evaluation of her qualifications, there was no question of access to public service. She had a clearly defined right to a post within a certain time period and had the right to take a case to the national courts, bringing her case within the ambit of article 6(1).[17]

28.9   The European Court's decision in *Neigel v France* was followed by

---

12   These cases are listed in chronological order in *Lombardo v Italy* n8 at 196.
13   Note 8 at para 17. See also *Massa v Italy* n8.
14   17 March 1997 (unreported) [1997] EHRLR 424.
15   Guaranteed under article 25 of the International Covenant on Civil and Political Rights.
16   See *Glasenapp v Germany* (1986) 9 EHRR 25.
17   See note in [1997] EHRLR 425.

the Commission in *Balfour v UK*,[18] where the applicant was dismissed from his post in the Foreign and Commonwealth Office.[19] However, its application is limited in two important respects:

1) It does not apply to disputes relating to 'purely economic' issues, such as the payment of a salary[20] or pension,[21] or 'essentially' economic issues.[22]

2) The European Commission has found that article 6(1) applies where an individual is employed by a public authority, so long as s/he is not technically a civil servant, particularly where such employment is based on a written contract and/or where the terms and conditions of employment provide the individual with access to the ordinary courts for the determination of any dispute, including dismissal.

28.10   So far as the first qualification set out above is concerned, in *Lombardo v Italy*,[23] the applicant was a former member of the Italian Carabinieri, who claimed to be entitled to an enhanced pension from his former employer because he had been invalided out of service by work-related illnesses. The Italian government argued that article 6(1) did not apply because the applicant had been a public official whose employment was governed by public law. The European Court found this unconvincing. It observed that:

> Notwithstanding the public aspects pointed out by the Government, what is concerned here is essentially an obligation on the State to pay a pension to a public servant in accordance with the legislation in force. In performing this obligation the State is not using discretionary powers and may be compared, in this respect, with an employer who is a party to a contract of employment governed by private law. Consequently, the right of a carabinierie to receive an 'enhanced ordinary pension' if he fulfils the necessary conditions of injury and disability is to be regarded as a 'civil right' within the meaning of Article 6(1) ...[24]

18 Commission (Admissibility Decision) 2 July 1997. Noted in [1997] EHRLR 665.
19 See chapter 12.
20 *De Santa v Italy, Lapalorcia v Italy* and *Abenavoli v Italy* European Court (2 September 1997); *Couez v France* and *Benkessiouer v France* European Court (24 August 1998).
21 *Lombardo v Italy* n8, see below.
22 *Nicodemo v Italy* European Court (2 September 1997) (unreported); *Couez v France* n20 and *Benkessiouer v France* n20.
23 Note 8.
24 Ibid at para 17.

Similar reasoning led to the same result in *Massa v Italy*,[25] which concerned the right of the husband of a headmistress to a reversionary pension when she died.

28.11 The limits of the European Court's approach in *Lombardo v Italy* have been explored in a series of cases against France. In *Huber v France*[26] the applicant was a civil servant in the state education service who complained about the length of proceedings to quash a decision to send him on leave and suspend the payment of his salary. The government argued that the proceedings raised issues concerning the applicant's career, not his pecuniary interests. The European Commission rejected this on the basis that the suspension of the applicant's salary had clear pecuniary consequences. The European Court agreed with the approach adopted by the Commission but disagreed with its analysis. On the question of the proper approach to be adopted the Court noted that:

> ... disputes relating to the recruitment, careers and termination of service of civil servants are as a general rule outside the scope of Article 6(1). Matters are nonetheless different where the claims in issue relate to a 'purely economic right' – such as payment of a salary or pension or at least an 'essentially economic' one.[27]

However, on the facts, the Court took the view that the applicant's complaint stemmed from and was essentially related to the decision to send him on leave. This primarily concerned his career. And the mere fact that the consequences were also partly pecuniary did not suffice to make the proceedings in issue 'civil' within the meaning of article 6(1).[28]

28.12 The result was the same in *Maillard v France*[29] where the applicant, a French naval officer, complained about an assessment made of his abilities, which affected his promotion, pay and pension. Having made it clear that the approach adopted in *Huber v France* applied notwithstanding the fact that the applicant was employed under general regulations rather than a contract of employment, the European Court found the pecuniary implications of his assessment secondary to the primary issue of his career.

28.13 The thin line between disputes that affect pecuniary interests sufficiently to trigger article 6(1) protection and those which do not

25 Note 8.
26 (1998) 26 EHRR 457.
27 Ibid at para 36.
28 Ibid at para 37.
29 (1999) 27 EHRR 232.

was exposed in *Couez v France*[30] and *Benkessiouer v France.*[31] In both cases, the applicants' claims concerned their entitlement to sick leave on the basis that they had been injured in work-related accidents. In *Couez v France* the applicant was a police officer and in *Benkessiouer v France* he was a post office worker. In *Couez v France* the Court found that:

> Unlike the position in [*Neigel v France*] and [*Huber v France*], where what was in issue was essentially the applicant's re-instatement in the public service, Mr Couez's claims at first sight concerned his 'career' and the 'termination of [his] service' ...; however, their outcome – whether in his favour or not – was bound to have a decisive effect on his economic rights, since if the [administrative court] had quashed the authorities' refusal to regard his sick-leave as having been due to a work-related accident, the rules on civil servants injured in the execution of their duty would have applied to him and also he would not have been sent on compulsory unpaid leave of absence.
>
> More specifically, recognition by a competent authority that his accident had occurred in the performance of his duties would have enabled him to be paid his full salary until he was fit to return to work or until he was retired and to be reimbursed the medical fees and expenses directly entailed by the accident. In the event of disablement due to such an accident, he could have claimed a temporary disablement allowance payable in addition to his salary. Lastly, being granted extended sick-leave would have entitled him to payment of his full salary for one year and half his salary for a further two years.[32]

Article 6(1) was therefore applicable. The same result followed in *Benkessiouer v France*, making it clear that article 6(1) applies to employment disputes involving public officials not only where the dispute is purely or primarily pecuniary in nature, but also where it is bound to have a decisive effect on the applicant's economic rights.

28.14   So far as the second qualification set out above in para 28.9 is concerned, in *C v UK*,[33] which concerned the dismissal of a school caretaker, the European Commission observed that:

> ... whilst internal professional disciplinary proceedings against persons employed in public service may not attract the guarantees of Article 6 para 1 of the Convention, when a contract of

---

30 Note 20.
31 Ibid.
32 Ibid at para 25.
33 (1987) 54 DR 162.

employment, albeit in the public service, permits access to the civil courts to determine the respective civil liabilities of the parties, the proceedings before the normal courts may usually be said to determine civil rights and obligations within the meaning of Article 6 para 1 of the Convention and, therefore, enjoy the guarantees laid down in this provision ...[34]

A similar statement of principle was made in *Darnell v UK*,[35] which concerned an employee of Trent Regional Health Authority.

Specific workplace rights

28.15 Specific workplace rights are guaranteed under article 4, which prohibits (among other things) 'forced labour', and under article 11, which protects the right to form and join trade unions.

Slavery, servitude and forced labour

28.16 Article 4 of the Convention provides that:

1) No one shall be held in slavery or servitude.

2) No one shall be required to perform forced or compulsory labour.

But forced or compulsory labour does not include:

1) Any work required to be done in the ordinary course of detention imposed according to the provisions of article 5 of the Convention or during conditional release from such detention.

2) Any service of a military character or, in case of conscientious objectors in countries where they are recognised, service exacted instead of compulsory military service.

3) Any service exacted in case of an emergency or calamity threatening the life or well-being of the community.

4) Any work or service which forms part of normal civic obligations.[36]

28.17 Slavery has not been defined by the European Court or Commission, but is likely to be interpreted in accordance with the 1926 *Slavery Convention*.[37] There, slavery is defined as 'the status or condition of a

34 Ibid at 167.
35 (1991) 69 DR 306.
36 Article 4(3).
37 Cmnd 2910. See Harris D, O'Boyle M and Warbrick C *Law of the European Convention on Human Rights* (Butterworths, 1995) p91.

person over whom any or all of the powers attaching to the right of ownership are exercised'. The difference between slavery and servitude is one of degree: slavery connotes ownership, servitude does not. This distinction was made clear by the European Commission in *Van Droogenbroeck v Belgium*[38] where it held that:

> ... in addition to the obligation to provide another with certain services, the concept of servitude includes the obligation on the part of the 'serf' to live on another's property and the impossibility of changing his condition.[39]

In that case, both the Commission and the Court rejected a complaint that work performed by a prisoner after his release from prison amounted to servitude because it was part of the order made by a court following a criminal trial, was limited in time and was subject to review by the court.

28.18   Military service is unlikely to amount to servitude, even where individuals enlist for long periods with no prospect of early discharge. In *W, X, Y and Z v UK*,[40] the Commission found that no issue of servitude arose where the applicants' parents had consented to their enlistment in the army and navy when they were 15 and 16 years old. Nor did any issue of forced or compulsory labour arise because article 4(3)(b) excluded military service from such definition.

28.19   Article 4 does not define what is meant by 'forced or compulsory labour' and no guidance on this point is to be found in the preparatory documents relating to the drafting of the Convention. However, article 4 was based on the *International Labour Organisation Convention No 29 concerning Forced and Compulsory Labour* and its provisions are therefore highly relevant.[41] Also relevant is *ILO Convention No 105* which refers to five categories of forced labour. These are set out in chapter 3.[42] In this context, labour is not restricted to manual work but includes professional work.[43]

28.20   The starting point for the interpretation of 'forced or compulsory labour' is article 2 of *ILO Convention No 29*, which defines such labour as:

> ... all work or service which is exacted from any person under the

38   (1982) 4 EHRR 443.
39   B/44 (1980) Comm Rep 79.
40   Appl 3435-38/67 (1968) 11 Yearbook 562
41   See *Van der Mussele v Belgium* (1984) 6 EHRR 163 at para 32.
42   Paras 3.21 to 3.27.
43   See *Van der Mussele v Belgium* n41 at para 33.

menace of any penalty and for which the said person has not offered himself voluntarily ...'[44]

However, the European Court has emphasised that the notion of forced or compulsory labour is likely to change over time and that article 4 must be interpreted 'in the light of the notions currently prevailing in democratic States'.[45]

28.21   The adjective 'forced' connotes physical or mental constraint.[46] The adjective 'compulsory' is more complex. It does not refer to any form of legal compulsion or obligation because most work is undertaken on such a basis. What there has to be is work 'exacted ... under the menace of any penalty' and also performed against the will of the person concerned – that is work which '... he has not offered himself voluntarily.'[47] Paid work is capable of fulfilling this criterion.[48]

28.22   In *Van der Mussele v Belgium*[49] the European Court found that the obligation on pupil barristers to provide their services free to those without legal aid did not amount to forced or compulsory labour. Although the prospect of disciplinary action by their professional body was sufficiently daunting to constitute 'the menace of a penalty', the work lacked the degree of compulsion required under article 4. In particular:

1) The services rendered did not fall outside the ambit of the normal activities of an advocate and constituted one means by which the state could fulfil its obligation to provide legal representation in criminal cases under article 6(3)(c) of the Convention.

2) There were considerable advantages attached to the profession, including exclusive rights of audience in the courts.

3) The services in question contributed to the applicant's general training.

4) The burden on the applicant was not disproportionate: it only accounted for a small proportion of his time and allowed sufficient time for the applicant to perform paid work.[50]

The fact that the applicant voluntarily entered the profession know-

---

44 Set out in *Van der Mussele v Belgium* n41 at para 32.
45 Ibid.
46 Ibid at para 34.
47 Ibid at para 34.
48 Ibid para 40.
49 Ibid at para 40. See also *X v Germany* (1974) 46 Coll Dec 22.
50 Ibid at para 39.

ing that he would have to undertake unpaid work was relevant, but not determinative.[51]

28.23   An obligation on practising lawyers to undertake legal aid work for which they receive reasonable remuneration does not constitute forced or compulsory labour. Nor does the refusal of an advance on their fees in respect of preliminary work already completed. It is for the state to decide how the remuneration of legal aid counsel is to be fixed and paid.[52] Similarly a cap on the fees which a notary can claim in respect of work done for non-profit making organisations raises no issue under article 4(2).[53] Nor does an obligation on employers to administer tax schemes by calculating and deducting tax from their employees.[54]

28.24   In *X v Netherlands*,[55] the Commission rejected an argument that to require an unemployed person to accept a job offer on pain of losing his or her unemployment benefit amounted to forced or compulsory labour. A similar result followed in *Talmon v Netherlands*,[56] where unemployment benefit was conditional upon the applicant looking for suitable work. He considered that the only suitable employment for him was that of 'independent scientist and social critic' and refused to look for other work. As a result, his benefits were reduced. The European Commission took the view that no issue arose under article 4(2) because the applicant had not been forced to perform any kind of labour. This leaves open the position of a similarly placed applicant who has been forced to take up alternative employment to which s/he objects.

The right to form and join a trade union

28.25   Article 11 of the Convention provides that:

> [E]veryone has the right ... to freedom of association with others, including the right to form and join trade unions for the protection of his interests.

51   Ibid at para 36. This represents a somewhat broader definition of forced labour than that adopted in *Iversen v Norway* (1963) 6 Yearbook 278, which concerned an obligation imposed on dentists to work in the public sector for one year after qualification.

52   *X and Y v Germany* (1978) 10 DR 224. See also *X v Germany* (1982) 26 DR 97.

53   *X v Germany* (1980) 18 DR 216.

54   *W, X, Y and Z v Austria* (1977) 7 DR 148.

55   (1976) 7 DR 161.

56   [1997] EHRLR 448.

Any restriction on this right must comply with the strict requirements of article 11(2), which are:

1) that the restriction in question be 'prescribed by law';

2) that the reason for the restriction be listed in article 11(2); and

3) that the restriction be 'necessary in a democratic society'.

The meaning of these requirements is considered in detail in chapter 2.

28.26   The right to join a trade union does not override (reasonable) union rules about membership. In *Cheall v UK*[57] the applicant was expelled from his trade union (APEX) pursuant to a decision of the disputes committee of the TUC. He complained that the rules were unreasonable and an unjustified restriction on his right to join a trade union under article 11 of the Convention. The Commission rejected this. In its view:

> The right to join a union 'for the protection of his interests' cannot be interpreted as conferring a general right to join the union of one's choice irrespective of the rules of the union. In the exercise of their rights under Article 11 para 1, unions must remain free to decide, in accordance with union rules, questions concerning admission to and expulsion from the union.'[58]

Nonetheless, for the right to join a trade union to be effective[59] the state must protect the individual against any abuse of a dominant position by trade unions. Such abuse might occur, for example, where exclusion or expulsion was not in accordance with union rules or where the rules were wholly unreasonable or arbitrary or where the consequences of exclusion or expulsion resulted in exceptional hardship such as job loss because of a closed shop agreement.[60]

28.27   The terms of ILO Convention 87 are relevant to the question of trade union autonomy. In *Cheall v UK*,[61] the Commission held, by reference to articles 3 and 5 of Convention 87, that the right to form trade unions involves (at least) 'the right of trade unions to draw up their own rules, to administer their own affairs and to establish and join trade union federation'.[62]

---

57 (1985) 42 DR 178.

58 Ibid at 185.

59 For the principle of effectiveness, see chapter 4.

60 *Cheall v UK* n57 at 186.

61 Note 57.

62 Ibid at 185.

The right not to join a trade union

28.29   A right not to join a trade union was recognised in *Young, James and Webster v UK*,[63] where all employees of British Rail were required to belong to a particular trade union under a 'closed shop' agreement. The applicants, who had joined British Rail before the closed shop agreement was made, refused to join the designated trade union and were dismissed without compensation. Although the European Court recognised that 'compulsion to join a particular trade union may not always be contrary to the Convention', it found a breach of article 11 on the basis that:

> ... a threat of dismissal involving loss of livelihood is a most serious form of compulsion and, in the present instance, it was directed against persons engaged by British Rail before the introduction of any obligation to join a particular trade union.
>
> In the Court's opinion, such a form of compulsion, in the circumstances of the case, strikes at the very substance of the freedom guaranteed by Article 11.[64]

The Court has since confirmed the negative right of association in broader terms in *Sigurjonsson v Iceland*.[65]

28.30   The position was different in *Sibson v UK*[66] where the applicant was expelled from his trade union following allegations of dishonesty. He then joined another trade union. His colleagues threatened to strike if the applicant continued to work at their depot and his employer requested that he either rejoin the first union or move to another depot owned and operated by the same employer. The applicant refused to do so and, having been told that he would (in effect) be suspended without pay, he treated himself as constructively dismissed. The European Court found no violation of article 11. Unlike the position in *Young, James and Webster v UK*, the applicant was not threatened with dismissal and his employer had been contractually entitled to require him to move to another depot.[67]

---

63   (1982) 4 EHRR 38.
64   Ibid at para 55.
65   (1993) 16 EHRR 462.
66   (1994) 17 EHRR 193.
67   Ibid at para 29. See also *Englund v Sweden* (1994) 77-A DR 10.

Trade union activities

28.31 Article 11 protects the right of an individual to join a trade union 'for the protection of his interests'. These words are important and the European Court has construed them to mean that:

> ... the Convention safeguards freedom to protect the occupational interests of trade union members by trade union action, the conduct and development of which the Contracting States must both permit and make possible.[68]

According to the Court in *National Union of Belgian Police v Belgium*[69] it follows from this that 'the members of a trade union have a right, in order to protect their interests, that the trade union should be heard.'[70]

28.32 Consultation is one means by which a trade union's views can be heard. But since it is not the only means, no right to consultation can be read into the Convention. So long as the right to be heard is respected, states have a discretion as to how precisely it is to be guaranteed in domestic law.[71]

28.33 A similar approach is adopted to collective bargaining. It is one means by which a trade union can protect the rights of its members. In *Swedish Engine Drivers' Union v Sweden*[72] the European Commission held that the right to engage in collective bargaining should be read into article 11. The Court found it unnecessary to decide that issue and confined itself to the question of whether article 11 requires the state as employer to enter into collective agreements with trade unions. On that question it noted that:

> ... while Article 11(1) presents trade union freedom as one form or a special aspect of freedom of association, the Article does not secure any particular treatment of trade unions, or their members, by the State, such as the right that the State should conclude any given collective agreement with them. Not only is this latter right not mentioned in Article 11(1), but neither can it be said that all the Contracting States incorporate it in their national law or practice, or that it is indispensable for the effective enjoyment of trade union freedom.[73]

---

68 *National Union of Belgian Police v Belgium* (1979–80) 1 EHRR 578 at para 39.
69 Ibid.
70 Ibid at para 39.
71 *National Union of Belgian Police v Belgium* n68 at para 39.
72 (1979–80) 1 EHRR 617. See also *Gustafsson v Sweden* (1996) 22 EHRR 409.
73 *Swedish Engine Drivers' Union v Sweden* n72 at para 39.

By implication, activity which is indispensable for the effective enjoyment of trade union freedom is expressly protected under article 11.

Industrial action

28.34   The right to take industrial action is inherent in article 11, but not absolute. In *Schmidt and Dahlström v Sweden*,[74] which concerned the compatibility with article 11 of clauses in a collective agreement restricting the benefit of retrospective salary increases to members of unions which did not take part in previous strike action, the Court observed that:

> The grant of a right to strike represents without any doubt one of the most important means [by which a trade union can protect its members interests], but there are others. Such a right, which is not expressly enshrined in article 11, may be subject under national law to regulation ... that limits its exercise in certain instances.[75]

By implication, an absolute ban on strike action would violate article 11: an implication supported by the Court's references to the European Social Charter, which guarantees a right to strike (subject to regulation).[76]

28.35   In *NATFHE v UK*[77] the Commission found that an obligation under the balloting provisions of the Trade Union and Labour Relations (Consolidation) Act 1992[78] to disclose the names of trade union members to an employer before strike action was taken, was not a 'significant limitation on the right to take collective action'. In its view:

> ... even in the often tense context of industrial disputes, a requirement to disseminate information with a view to furthering debate and discussions between the parties cannot be seen as inherently incompatible with Article 11 of the Convention.[79]

It acknowledged, however, that the position might be different where there is evidence to show that an 'anti-union' employer might use the information provided to put undue pressure on employees not to participate in a ballot, or to vote in a particular way.

74 (1979–80) 1 EHRR 632.
75 Ibid at para 36.
76 Ibid.
77 (1998) 25 EHRR CD 122.
78 Section 22A.
79 Note 77 at 126.

Excluded groups

28.36   Article 11(2) provides that:

> This Article shall not prevent the imposition of lawful restrictions on the exercise of these rights by members of the armed forces, of the police or of the administration of the State.

The extent of this limitation was considered by the European Commission in *CCSU v UK*[80] where the applicant trade union complained about the then prime minister's decision to remove the right of individual employees at the national security communications centre at GCHQ. So far as the definition of the phrase 'members ... of the administration of the State' is concerned, the Commission recognised its uncertainty. Since the phrase appeared in the same sentence as members of the armed forces and police, it was safe to assume that it covered at least those state employees whose functions are similar to or resemble those of individuals falling into those two categories. That included all the staff at GCHQ because they were concerned with official and military communications, a vital function in protecting national security. By implication, the phrase 'members ... of the administration of the State' cannot be read too broadly and does not include all public officials.

28.37   The need for restrictions on members of the armed forces, police or the administration of the state to be 'lawful' has two aspects. First, the restriction in question must be in accordance with domestic law. Second, it must not be arbitrary.[81] The strict requirements of proportionality[82] probably do not apply but, nonetheless, proportionality is obviously relevant to the question of arbitrariness. Judged against these criteria, the ban on trade union membership at GCHQ did not exceed the limits of the special restriction on the article 11 rights of members of the administration of the state.

The protection of other Convention rights in the workplace

28.38   Individuals do not lose their Convention rights when they are at work. However, the terms under which they are employed are

80   (1987) 50 DR 228.
81   Ibid at 242.
82   See chapter 4.

relevant to the extent to which they can freely exercise those rights, in particular, rights arising under articles 8, 9 and 10.

Privacy at work

28.39   Article 8 of the Convention guarantees individuals the right to respect for their private life.[83] Like article 11 (trade union rights: see above) it is not absolute. However, any interference with an individual's private life must:

1) be 'in accordance with law';

2) imposed for a reason listed in article 8(2); and

3) be 'necessary in a democratic society'.

The meaning of these requirements is considered in detail in chapter 4.

28.40   It is clear that privacy extends to the workplace. In *Halford v UK*[84] the applicant, the former assistant chief constable of Merseyside police, complained that her private calls from work, made on an internal police telecommunications system, were intercepted. The government argued that, since the calls were made from the applicant's workplace, they fell outside the scope of article 8. The European Court rejected this. It held that:

> ... it is clear from [the Court's] case-law that telephone calls made from business premises as well as from the home may be covered by the notions of 'private life' and 'correspondence' within the meaning of Article 8(1).[85]

Since the applicant had not been warned that calls on the internal telecommunications system might be intercepted, the applicant had a 'reasonable expectation' of privacy.

28.41   The European Court also found that the applicant's expectation of privacy was reinforced by the fact that she had been provided with two phones in her office, one of which was specifically designated for her private use. Furthermore she had been given an assurance that she could use her office telephones in relation to a sex discrimina-

---

83   See chapter 3. On dress codes at work, see *Kara v UK* [1999] EHRLR 232.

84   (1997) 24 EHRR 523.

85   Ibid at para 44. See also *Klass v Germany* (1979–80) 2 EHRR 214; *Malone v UK* (1985) 7 EHRR 14; *Huvig v France* (1990) 12 EHRR 528; and *Niemietz v Germany* (1993) 16 EHRR 97.

tion claim she was pursuing against the Merseyside police.[86] Since internal telecommunications systems fell outside the ambit of the Interception of Communications Act 1985 and were therefore unregulated, the interception of the applicant's calls was not 'in accordance with law' and, accordingly, article 8 had been breached.

Security vetting

28.42 Security vetting and the retention of information also raise issues under article 8 of the Convention. In *Leander v Sweden*,[87] the European Court was in no doubt that storing information about the applicant in a secret police register and releasing it to his prospective employers during the course of security vetting amounted to an interference with the applicant's article 8 rights.[88] However, on analysis, it found that the interference could be justified as 'necessary in a democratic society'. In its view:

> There can be no doubt as to the necessity, for the purposes of protecting national security, for the Contracting States to have laws granting the competent domestic authorities power, firstly, to collect and store in registers not accessible to the public, information on persons and, secondly, to use this information when assessing the suitability of candidates for employment in posts of importance for national security.[89]

The use of such information for vetting candidates for posts which are not of importance for national security would be harder to justify.

28.43 In security vetting cases, special rules about the meaning of a 'victim' and the requirement of legal certainty apply. These are dealt with in chapters 2,[90] 4[91] and 15.[92]

---

86 Note 84 at para 45.
87 (1987) 9 EHRR 433.
88 Ibid at para 48. See also *Hilton v UK* (1988) 57 DR 108.
89 Note 87 at para 59.
90 Paras 2.22 onwards.
91 Paras 4.31 onwards.
92 Paras 15.6 onwards.

Freedom of thought, conscience and religion

28.44   As with article 8, freedom of thought, conscience and religion under article 9 of the Convention extend to the workplace. To date, the European Court has not considered the inter-relationship of article 9 with contractual rights and obligations in the employment context. The Commission's approach has been to focus, rather narrowly, on the question of whether contractual rights and obligations extinguish (or at least severely restrict) the manifestation of religious beliefs. If not, there will be no breach of article 9.

28.45   In *X v Denmark*[93] the applicant, a Danish clergyman, complained that he was required by his church to abandon a particular practice of christening contrary to his religious beliefs. The Commission rejected this on the basis that;

> ... in a State church system its servants are employed for the purpose of applying and teaching a specific religion. Their individual freedom of thought, conscience or religion is exercised at the moment they accept or refuse employment as clergymen, and their right to leave the church guarantees their freedom of religion in case they oppose its teaching.[94]

In other words, since the applicant was not obliged to take the job as clergyman and was free to leave, requiring him to perform tasks contrary to his religious beliefs was no breach of article 9.[95]

28.46   A similar approach has been adopted in cases which do not concern religious manifestations in the course of the performance of professional functions, but concern absence from work for the performance of such manifestations. In *Ahmad v UK*,[96] where the applicant schoolteacher complained that he was forced to resign because he was refused permission to attend a mosque during working hours, the Commission found no breach of article 9. In coming to this conclusion, the Commission was clearly influenced by the fact that the applicant had not raised any issue of worship when he was interviewed for the job and when he knew the working hours and the fact that he was free to resign if and when he found that his teaching obligations conflicted with his religious duties.

---

93   (1976) 5 DR 157.
94   Ibid at 158.
95   See also *Knudsen v Norway* (1985) 42 DR 247 to the same effect.
96   (1982) 4 EHRR 126.

28.47 The Commission's narrow approach has even been applied where an individual is dismissed for refusing to work certain hours in conflict with his/her religious beliefs. In *Stedman v UK*[97] the applicant was dismissed for refusing to work on Sundays in accordance with her Christian beliefs. Without any real analysis, the Commission rejected her claim on the basis that the applicant was not dismissed because of her religious convictions but because she refused to respect her working hours.[98] In those circumstances, although the applicant's refusal to work Sundays was motivated by her religious convictions, no article 9 issue arose.[99]

28.48 However, in *Knudsen v Norway*[100] the Commission suggested that article 9 might apply where an individual is already employed and faces dismissal unless s/he changes his/her beliefs. This is consistent with the high priority attached to freedom of belief when compared with the priority attached to the manifestation of a belief.[101]

Freedom of expression

28.49 Freedom of expression extends to the workplace, but can be restricted in accordance with article 10(2). In *Glasenapp v Germany*[102] the European Court found no breach of article 10 where the applicant's appointment as a teacher was revoked because she was a member of the communist party. Although the full guarantees of the Convention extend to all public sector workers, including civil servants, a condition that applicants for jobs in the civil service undertake to uphold the free democratic constitutional system in Germany was not incompatible with the Convention.[103] And a similar result followed in *Kosiek v Germany*.[104]

28.50 The limits of the European Court's approach in *Glasenapp* and *Kosiek* were explored in the subsequent case of *Vogt v Germany*[105] where the applicant was dismissed from her post as a teacher because

97 (1997) 23 EHRR CD 168.
98 See also Appl 24949/94 Commission (3 December 1996).
99 See further chapter 27.
100 Note 95.
101 See chapter 27.
102 (1987) 9 EHRR 25.
103 Ibid at para 52.
104 (1986) 9 EHRR 328.
105 (1996) 21 EHRR 205.

she was an active member of the communist party. The Court began by reiterating that, since the right of recruitment to the civil service was deliberately omitted from the Convention, the refusal to appoint a person as a civil servant could not as such provide the basis for a complaint under it. However:

> This does not mean ... that a person who has been appointed as a civil servant cannot complain on being dismissed if that dismissal violates one of his or her rights under the Convention.[106]

The cases of *Glasenapp* and *Kosiek* could be distinguished because in those cases the Court analysed the authorities' action as a refusal to grant the applicants access to the civil service on the ground that they did not possess one of the qualifications. Access to the civil service was therefore the heart of the issue submitted to the Court. By contrast, the applicant in *Vogt* had been a teacher for seven years before she was dismissed. Article 10 was therefore engaged.

28.51   On the question of whether the applicant's dismissal could be justified as 'necessary in a democratic society', the Court proceeded on the basis that a democratic state is entitled to require civil servants to be loyal to the constitutional principles on which it is founded.[107] Even so, the absolute nature of the duty owed in Germany was striking. It was owed equally by every civil servant without distinction as to function or rank and made no distinction between work-related activities and private life. Bearing in mind the fact that the applicant's job had no security risks and that she had not been criticised for attempting to exert improper influence on her pupils, the applicant's dismissal for active membership of the communist party was a disproportionate measure and thus breached article 10.[108]

28.52   More generally, the European Commission has taken the view that some employment by its very nature involves a degree of restriction on free speech. In *Morissens v Belgium*[109] it held that:

> ... by entering the civil service [as a teacher], the applicant accepted certain restrictions on the exercise of her freedom of expression, as being inherent in her duties.[110]

---

106 Ibid at para 43.
107 Ibid at para 58.
108 A different result followed in *Van der Heijden v Netherlands* (1985) 41 DR 264 where the applicant who worked at an immigration foundation belonged to a political party which was hostile to immigrant workers.
109 (1988) 56 DR 127.
110 Ibid at 136.

In this respect, the Commission drew on its own case-law in *Kosiek v Germany*[111] where it held that 'a duty of moderation, which is a widespread feature of the regulations of the civil services of member states of the Council of Europe, arises from the duties and responsibilities which civil servants have as the agents through which the State operates'.

28.53   The manner and mode in which an employee speaks out against his/her employer is also highly relevant under article 10. By attacking the reputation of her superiors in a television broadcast, the applicant in *Morissens v Belgium* had breached her duty of moderation. As a result, the authorities were justified in disciplining her. A similar result followed in *Tucht v Germany*[112] where the applicant, a specialist in mental and lung diseases in the German regional health service, was dismissed after writing to his superiors criticising aspects of the organisation of the service. The letters were copied to the regional parliament, trade unions, professional associations, colleagues and political parties. The letters had been written in intemperate and abusive language just after the applicant failed to obtain a promotion. Consequently, the Commission took the view that the applicant had been dismissed not because of the content of his letters, but because of the manner in which he had chosen to express himself. Accordingly, his dismissal could be justified under article 10(2) on the basis of preventing disclosure of confidential information and protecting the reputation of others.[113]

28.54   The issue of freedom of expression arose in a different way in *Ahmed v UK*[114] which concerned a restriction imposed by statute on senior local government officers limiting their ability to participate in certain types of political activity, such as standing for election as a local councillor. The European Court found no violation of article 10 on the basis that the restrictions in question were not disproportionate to the applicant's freedom of expression, having regard to the legitimacy of the need addressed by the regulations and the margin of appreciation enjoyed by the state.[115]

---

111 Commission Decision (11 May 1984) para 85.

112 Appl 9336/81 (1982) (unreported).

113 See also *Haseldine v UK* (1992) 73 DR 225. But see also *Grigoriades v Greece* [1998] EHRLR 222.

114 (1998) *Times* 2 October.

115 As to the application of the margin of appreciation in domestic law, see chapter 4.

The prohibition on discrimination

28.55   The prohibition on discrimination in article 14 of the Convention applies in the employment context. It does not provide a general right to freedom from discrimination and can only be invoked in relation to one of the other Convention rights set out in articles 2 to 12 and the First Protocol. However, no breach of another Convention right need be established: the test for the application of article 14 is whether the facts in issue 'fall within the ambit' of one or more of the other Convention provisions. See chapter 29.

Contracting out of Convention rights

28.56   It is possible to restrict Convention rights by contract, but this is subject to strict limits which are dealt with elsewhere.[116] As noted above, in the employment context, the Commission has recognised that implied restrictions can be read into a contract of employment in relation to the exercise of article 10 rights.[117] However, in *Rommelfanger v Germany*[118] the Commission recognised that, in certain circumstances, domestic courts are under a duty to protect individuals from unreasonable restrictions on their Convention rights, even when such restrictions have been agreed in a contract of employment.

The applicability of the Convention between private individuals

28.57   The extent to which individuals can have recourse to the Convention in disputes between purely private parties, including many employer/employee situations, has been considered in chapters 2[119] and 5.[120] In the employment context, it is well established that the domestic authorities are not free to ignore the Convention simply because the measures said to restrict Convention rights are carried

---

116   Chapter 4.
117   See paras 28.49 to 28.54.
118   (1989) 62 DR 151.
119   Paras 2.75 to 2.80.
120   Paras 5.36 to 5.39.

out by a private employer. A legal framework which adequately protects Convention rights is required[121] and, once a case is before them, the domestic courts come under a duty to protect individual Convention rights.[122] Hence, in *Stedman v UK*[123] and *Van der Heijden v Netherlands*[124] the fact that the applicants were dismissed by private companies did not preclude the Commission from examining their complaints.

121 *Young, James and Webster v UK* (1982) 4 EHRR 38.
122 See, for example, *Van der Heijden v Netherlands* (1985) 41 DR 264 and *Rommelfanger v Germany* (1989) 62 DR 151.
123 Note 97.
124 (1985) 41 DR 264.

CHAPTER 29

Discrimination

29.1   Introduction

29.3   The dependent nature of article 14

29.7   The ambit test

29.10   The meaning of discrimination

29.11   Differential treatment

29.15   Legitimate aim

29.16   Proportionality

29.17   Suspect groups

29.18   Indirect discrimination

29.19   Positive discrimination

29.21   Discrimination as degrading treatment

29.22   Developing article 14 principles

Introduction

29.1 The prohibition of discrimination is central to the protection of human rights. It runs through all international human rights instruments and has inspired specialist treaties such as the *International Convention on the Elimination of All Forms of Racial Discrimination* 1966[1] and the *Convention on the Elimination of All Forms of Discrimination against Women* 1979.[2]

29.2 Under the European Convention of Human Rights, the prohibition of discrimination is framed in wide terms and no question of compliance with the Convention can be divorced from it. Article 14 provides that:

> The enjoyment of the rights and freedoms set forth in this Convention shall be secured without discrimination on any ground such as sex, race, colour, language, religion, political or other opinion, national or social origin, association with a national minority, property, birth or other status.

It is clear from this wording – in particular the use of the words 'such as' and 'other status' – that the categories of prohibited discrimination under the Convention are not closed. This is a significant departure from the protection afforded in domestic law before the implementation of the HRA.

The dependent nature of article 14

29.3 Unlike article 26 of the *International Covenant on Civil and Political Rights*[3] – the UN equivalent of the European Convention – which sets out a free-standing right to equality, the reach of the prohibition of discrimination under article 14 of the European Convention is limited to those rights embodied in the Convention and its Protocols. It can be invoked only in conjunction with one of the other Convention rights. And, in that sense, it is dependent upon those other Convention rights.

29.4 However, the dependent character of article 14 is qualified in two respects. First, a breach of article 14 can be found even where there is no violation of a substantive right. According to the European Court:

1   Ratified by the UK in 1994.
2   Ratified by the UK in 1986.
3   Ratified by the UK in 1976.

While it is true that this guarantee has no independent existence in the sense that under the terms of Article 14 it relates solely to 'rights and freedoms set forth in the Convention', a measure which in itself is in conformity with the requirements of the Article enshrining the right or freedom in question may however infringe this Article when read in conjunction with Article 14 for the reason that it is of a discriminatory nature.[4]

In other words, while there can never be a breach of article 14 considered in isolation, there may be a breach of article 14 considered in conjunction with another article of the Convention in cases where there would be no violation of that other article taken alone.[5]

29.5   An example of this principle in operation is the case of *Abdulaziz, Cabales and Balkandali*,[6] where the applicants, who were lawfully and permanently settled in the UK, complained that their husbands were refused permission to join them in the UK. The European Court found no breach of article 8 taken alone, but did find a breach of article 14 in conjunction with article 8. Although it was legitimate to restrict the admission of non-national spouses to the UK, it was not legitimate to distinguish between the non-national spouses of males (permitted entry) and the non-national spouses of females (not permitted entry).

29.6   The second respect in which the dependent character of article 14 is qualified is that issues of discrimination may arise even in areas where states are not obliged to provide specific protection. Where a state chooses to do more than is strictly required to 'secure' a Convention right in its domestic law, article 14 applies to all aspects of the right provided. The classic example was given by the European Court in the *Belgian Linguistics Case*:[7]

... Article 6 of the Convention does not compel States to institute a system of appeal courts. A State which does set up such courts consequently goes beyond its obligations under Article 6. However, it would violate that Article, read in conjunction with Article 14, were it to debar certain persons from these remedies without legitimate reason while making them available to others in respect of the same type of actions.[8]

4   *Belgian Linguistics Case (No 2)* (1979–80) 1 EHRR 252 at para 9.
5   Jacobs and White, *The European Convention on Human Rights* Clarendon Press, 1996 pp285–286.
6   (1985) 7 EHRR 471.
7   Note 4.
8   Note 4 at para 9.

In other words a claim may fail on the basis that the state had no duty to provide the right sought by the applicant, but succeed under article 14 if the right has, in fact, been provided, but on a discriminatory basis.

The ambit test

29.7   As noted above, a breach of article 14 can be found even where there is no violation of a substantive right. The test for the application of article 14 is whether the facts in issue 'fall within the ambit' of one or more of the other Convention provisions.[9] The relationship that this phrase implies between article 14 and another Convention rights is not easy to identify from the case-law of the European Court and Commission.

29.8   In *X v Germany*,[10] a case involving alleged discrimination against male homosexuals, the Commission examined the case under article 14 on the basis that 'it is sufficient that the 'subject matter' falls within the scope of the Article in question.'[11] And in numerous welfare benefit cases, the Commission has examined article 14 at the same time as rejecting the notion that the benefit in question is a 'possession' within the meaning of article 1 of Protocol 1.[12]

29.9   In *Schmidt and Dahlström v Sweden*[13] the European Court found that only a very loose relationship between article 14 and another Convention right is necessary to trigger the article 14 non-discrimination provisions. That case concerned a number of detrimental measures aimed at members of a trade union which had sanctioned strike action. Despite the fact that the measures in question – retroactive salary increases – did not in themselves violate any Convention rights, the European Court found that they were 'linked' to the article 11 right of trade unions to protect their members interests[14] and therefore that it was legitimate to examine the question of discrimination.

---

9   *Rasmussen v Denmark* (1985) 7 EHRR 371.
10   (1976) 19 Yearbook 276.
11   Ibid at p286.
12   For example: *X v Netherlands* (1971) 38 Coll Dec 9; and *X v Netherlands* (1973) 16 Yearbook 274. See further, chapter 23.
13   (1979–80) 1 EHRR 632.
14   See chapter 28.

The meaning of discrimination

29.10 Article 14 does not prohibit all kinds of distinction or differential treatment. The meaning of discrimination under article 14 is a difference in treatment which has 'no reasonable and objective justification'. And such justification depends upon:

1) the aim and effect of the measure; and

2) whether there is a reasonable relationship of proportionality between the means employed and the aim sought to be realised.[15]

The burden is on the applicant to establish a difference in treatment; it then shifts to the state authority in question to justify that difference.

Differential treatment

29.11 To establish differential treatment, an applicant must show that s/he has been treated less favourably than others who are in a similar or analogous situation.[16]

29.12 The list of characteristics which might render differential treatment discriminatory under article 14 – sex, race, colour, language, religion, political or other opinion, national or social origin, association with a national minority, property, birth or other status – is the starting point. 'Other status' has been interpreted to include sexual orientation, marital status, illegitimacy, status as a trade union, military status, conscientious objection, professional status and imprisonment.[17] It also includes disability.[18] But it is important to show that any difference in treatment is based on the characteristic identified.

29.13 In *Van der Mussele v Belgium*[19] a trainee barrister claimed that he had been treated less favourably than apprentices in other professions because, unlike them, he was obliged to work for free by providing unpaid legal representation. The European Court rejected his claim on the basis that there were fundamental differences

---

15 *Belgian Linguistics Case*, n4.

16 *Marckx v Belgium* (1979–80) 2 EHRR 330; *Van der Mussele v Belgium* (1984) 6 EHRR 163.

17 Harris, O'Boyle and Warbrick, *Law of the European Convention on Human Rights*, Butterworths, 1995 p470,

18 *Malone v UK* [1996] EHRLR 440.

19 Note 16.

between the various professions and, accordingly, like was not being compared to like. Similarly, married couples are not in an analogous position to unmarried couples.[20]

29.14   There is no requirement in article 14 that differential treatment cause detriment to the complainant. But it is important to make an overall assessment of the 'treatment' in issue. A juvenile prisoner is not in an analogous position to an adult prisoner;[21] nor is an IRA category A prisoner in an analogous position to prisoners of no security risk.[22]

Legitimate aim

29.15   Few cases in Strasbourg turn on the question of legitimate aim because most states recognise that once a difference in treatment is established it requires rational justification. Where no real justification is advanced, a breach of article 14 will be found; the classic example being *Darby v Sweden*[23] where the Swedish government did not seek to justify a discriminatory tax policy because, in reality, it was based on no more than administrative convenience.

Proportionality

29.16   The principle of proportionality runs throughout the Convention and is examined in detail in chapter 4.[24] According to the European Court, what has to be ascertained is whether the '... disadvantage suffered by the applicant is excessive in relation to the legitimate aim pursued.'[25] Such an assessment inevitably involves a detailed analysis of a number of factors including:

1) whether 'relevant and sufficient' reasons have been advanced in support of the measure in question;

2) whether there was a less restrictive alternative; and

3) what the actual effects are on the individuals in question.[26]

---

20 *Lindsay v UK* (1986) 49 DR 181.
21 *Nelson v UK* (1986) 49 DR 170.
22 *X v UK* Commission (9 December 1992) (unreported).
23 (1991) 13 EHRR 774.
24 Paras 4.37 to 4.55.
25 *National Union of Belgian Police v Belgium* (1979–80) 1 EHRR 578.
26 See paras 4.37 to 4.55.

Where there is a common standard concerning the prohibition of discrimination in Europe it will be difficult to justify a measure that falls short of that standard.[27] And the European Court has, in effect, now developed a number of 'suspect groups' where very weighty reasons will have to be advanced by a state seeking to establish that a discriminatory measure was proportionate.

Suspect groups

29.17 The basis for 'suspect groups' can be discerned from the European Court's remarks in *Abdulaziz, Cabales and Balkandali v UK*[28] concerning sex discrimination:

> ... the advancement of the equality of the sexes is today a major goal in the Member States of the Council of Europe ... very weighty reasons would have to be advanced before a difference in treatment on the grounds of sex could be considered compatible with the Convention.[29]

Similar remarks have been expressed in relation to discrimination based on race,[30] nationality,[31] illegitimacy[32] and religion.[33] However, nationality is not a suspect category in the immigration field.[34]

Indirect discrimination

29.18 Indirect discrimination may fall within article 14. In the *Belgian Linguistics Case*[35] the European Court held that the existence of 'reasonable and objective justification' had to be assessed in relation to the 'aim and effects' of the measure in question. However, the burden of proving indirect discrimination is not easy: see *Abdulaziz, Cabales and Balkandali v UK*.[36]

27 *Rasmussen v Denmark* (1985) 7 EHRR 371.
28 Note 6.
29 Note 6 at para 78; see also *Karlheinz Schmidt v Germany* (1994) 18 EHRR 513; and *Van Raalte v Netherlands* (1997) 24 EHRR 503.
30 *East African Asians v UK* (1981) 3 EHRR 76.
31 *Gaygusuz v Austria* (1996) 23 EHRR 364.
32 *Inze v Austria* (1988) 10 EHRR 394.
33 *Hoffmann v Austria* (1994) 17 EHRR 293.
34 See para 18.46.
35 Note 4.
36 Note 6.

Positive discrimination

29.19   The aim of redressing a pre-existing situation of inequality has been accepted as a legitimate objective of differential treatment. In the *Belgian Linguistics Case* (above) the European Court observed that not all instances of differential treatment breached article 14 and that 'certain legal inequalities tend only to correct factual inequalities.'[37]

29.20   In *Lindsay v UK*[38] the government sought to justify tax legislation under which women who were sole breadwinners paid less tax than men in the same position, on the basis that it was designed to encourage more married women to work and thereby overcome male prejudice toward them and advance the equality of the sexes. The Commission found that this objective was reasonable and objective 'in the aim of providing positive discrimination in favour of married woman who work'.[39]

Discrimination as degrading treatment

29.21   Discriminatory treatment is capable of amounting to degrading treatment under article 3. In *East African Asians v UK*,[40] the Commission observed that 'publicly to single out a group of persons for differential treatment on the basis of race might, in certain circumstances, constitute a special form of affront to human dignity'.[41] The threshold, however, is high and is unlikely to be reached in the absence of special or aggravating circumstances.[42]

Developing article 14 principles

29.22   There has been a marked reluctance on the part of the European Court to develop its jurisprudence under article 14. Typical was its approach in *Dudgeon v UK*[43] where the applicant complained that the criminalisation of consensual adult homosexual activity in Northern

---

37   *Belgian Linguistics' Case (No 2)* (1979–80) 1 EHRR 252 at para 10.
38   Note 20; see also *Marckx v Belgium* (1979–80) 2 EHRR 330.
39   Note 20 at p191; but see also *Van Raalte v Netherlands*, n29.
40   Note 30.
41   Note 30 at para 207.
42   *Abdulaziz, Cabales and Balkandali v UK*, n6.
43   (1982) 4 EHRR 149.

Ireland breached his privacy rights and was discriminatory. Having found a breach of article 8, the Court restricted its further consideration of the case on the basis that:

> Where a substantive Article of the Convention has been invoked both on its own and in conjunction with Article 14 and a separate breach has been found of the substantive Article, it is not generally necessary for the Court to examine the case under Article 14, though the position is otherwise if a clear inequality of treatment in the enjoyment of the right in question is a fundamental aspect of the case.[44]

In that case, the Court found that the complaint under article 14 was 'in effect, the same complaint, albeit seen from a different angle' to the complaint under article 8 and therefore that it did not require separate consideration.

29.23   In addition, both the Court and Commission have not infrequently invoked the margin of appreciation in article 14 cases, leaving it to the domestic authorities to assess whether and to what extent differences in otherwise similar situations may justify different treatment in law[45] – albeit with supervision at the Strasbourg level.[46]

29.24   This has meant that the scope and extent of many of the principles underpinning article 14 have remained unexplored. Nonetheless, as the finding in *Dudgeon v UK* (above) makes clear, where article 14 shares common principles with the protection of other Convention rights – such as the principles of legitimacy and proportionality[47] – the interpretation and development of those principles elsewhere is instructive to the proper interpretation and development of article 14. And, as noted in chapter 4, the margin of appreciation is inapplicable under the HRA.

---

44 Ibid at para 67.
45 *Rasmussen v Denmark*, n27.
46 *Abdulaziz, Cabales and Balkandali v UK*, n6 at para 72.
47 These concepts are examined in detail in chapter 4 at paras 4.37 to 4.55 and 4.57 to 4.59.

Pursuing a case to the European Court of Human Rights

CHAPTER 30

The practice and procedure of the European Court of Human Rights

Mitchell Woolf

30.1   Introduction

30.6   Locus standi

30.7   Victim status

30.9   Making a complaint

30.11   Admissibility

30.15   Friendly settlement

30.16   Merits

30.18   Costs

30.19   Referral to the Grand Chamber

30.20   Admissibility: special considerations
30.21   The six-month rule
30.25   Exhaustion of domestic remedies
30.31   Manifestly ill-founded
30.32   Anonymity
30.33   Substantially the same
30.34   Incompatible with the Convention
30.35   Abuse of the right of petition

continued

30.36   Striking out of the list

30.37   Interim relief and urgent applications

30.40   Legal aid

30.44   Advisory opinions

30.45   Binding force and the execution of judgments

Introduction

30.1 While incorporation of the HRA will now give domestic courts and tribunals the ability to consider Convention issues, the Strasbourg system will not be rendered otiose. This is clear from the case-law involving those states which have already incorporated the Convention into their domestic law. Cases will continue to be brought before the European Court where an applicant believes that the domestic authorities have violated his/her rights and no effective remedy is provided in domestic law. Additionally, cases from the UK may also be taken where the common law or legislation is incompatible with the Convention, particularly where the government does not use the fast-track procedure available to remedy 'declarations of incompatibility'.

30.2 The increasing popularity of the petitioning mechanism over the last 20 years[1] together with the growing number of contracting state parties, particularly from Eastern Europe, has resulted in an overload of work for the Strasbourg institutions. The response of the Council of Ministers to the unsatisfactory amount of time taken to determine a case,[2] the increasing backlog of applications[3] as well as other procedural problems came with the adoption of Protocol 11, which came into force on 1 November 1998. This Protocol has seen the Commission and Court replaced by a single full-time Court,[4] with the right of individual petition becoming automatic. Other significant changes include the abolition of the decision-making function of the Committee of Ministers, whose role is now limited to supervising the execution of judgments.[5] In addition, provision for the possibility of a third party intervention by a state or other interested persons either at the request, or with leave, of the President of the Chamber.[6]

1 The number of applications registered increased from 404 in 1981 to 2,037 in 1993.

2 On average it took 4–5 years from the initial application to the decision by the Court.

3 By 1 December 1996, there was a backlog of 5,472 cases of which 3,999 were still awaiting first examination by the Commission.

4 The Commission will continue to function until 31 October 1999 to deal with those cases that had been declared admissible prior to the Protocol's coming into force. The transitional rules for this year are set out in Rules 97–102.

5 Article 46(2).

6 Article 36 and Rule 61. Amicus curiae briefs had previously been submitted on rare occasions. Eg, *McCann v UK* (1996) 21 EHRR 97; *Chahal v UK* (1997) 23 EHRR 413.

30.3   Rather than being a continuation of the Commission or the old Court, the new Court is sui generis. However, it is largely intended to be an amalgamation of the strongest aspects of both of its predecessors. Although it is not bound by the previous case-law of the Commission and Court, those opinions and decisions will continue to be of great relevance. While the opinions of the Commission were not binding (unlike the decisions of the old Court), their jurisprudence should not be overlooked. However, the fact that the new Court has the ability to adopt different approaches means that areas where the views of the Commission and the old Court conflicted may receive renewed consideration.

30.4   The new Court will be composed of four parts. The Plenary Court will be responsible for such matters as appointing the President of the Chambers, constituting chambers and adopting rules of procedure. However, it will not hear cases.[7] When hearing cases, article 27 has established that the Court will sit in committees of three judges, chambers of seven judges, and a Grand Chamber of seventeen judges. The judge of the respondent state will always sit ex officio as part of the chamber or the Grand Chamber. If the judge is unable to sit, the Court will choose someone from that state to sit in the capacity of judge.[8]

30.5   There are two ways in which a state party may be the subject of a complaint before the European Court. Inter-state complaints can be made by one country to the Convention against another.[9] Such cases are rare, mainly because states are reluctant to criticise others for fear of having their own practices scrutinised.[10] In the vast majority of cases, individual complaints will be made under article 34. Therefore, the following analysis concentrates on the individual petitioning mechanism.

Locus standi

30.6   Any person, non-governmental organisation or group of individuals whose rights have been violated may bring an application to Strasbourg. Additionally, a person may be given authority to act by a

---

7 Article 26.
8 Article 27(2).
9 Article 33.
10 The only inter-state complaint to have been determined before the old Court was *Ireland v UK* (1979–80) 2 EHRR 25.

person whose rights have been violated. There is no requirement in the Convention that a person must have 'legal capacity' in order to bring an action. Therefore, complainants may include children and the mentally ill. Parents may act on behalf of their children unless there is a conflict of interests, or they do not have the necessary legal standing to represent the child.[11] The Convention does not preclude applications from 'legal persons', such as companies. In addition, a claim may be taken by a group of individuals so long as they independently qualify as victims. However, non-governmental organisations must be private rather than public organisations.

Victim status

30.7 Article 34 provides that:

> The Court may receive applications from any person, non-governmental organisation or group of individuals claiming to be the victim of a violation by one of the High Contracting Parties of the rights set forth in the Convention or protocols thereto. The High Contracting Parties undertake not to hinder in any way the effective exercise of this right.

The meaning of 'victim' in this context is examined in detail in chapter 2.

30.8 Usually the applicant must be specifically and directly affected, but the Court and Commission have declined to apply this requirement too strictly. In *Klass v Germany*[12] the applicants complained of a violation of their right to privacy and correspondence because legislation authorised secret surveillance of persons without notification. Although they could not prove that their telephones had been tapped, the Court held that they might be affected and so could bring a claim. Otherwise there was a risk that article 8 rights would be nullified.

Making a complaint

30.9 It is possible to introduce a complaint to the Court without utilising the application form provided by the Court.[13] For example, it can be

11 *Hokkanen v Finland* (1995) 19 EHRR 139.
12 (1979–80) 2 EHRR 214.
13 See appendix K.

done by letter. The Registry will open a provisional file.[14] However, it will almost always be necessary to complete the form later. The details to be contained in the application are set out in Rule 47 of the Rules of Court.[15] Complaints should be directed to:

Secretary of the Court of Human Rights
Council of Europe
F-67075 Strasbourg Cedex
France
Tel: 00 33 88 41 2000

30.10   The following information will be required:

1) The applicant's name, age, address and occupation.

2) The name, address and occupation of anyone acting as the representative.

3) The respondent country.

4) A clear and concise statement of the facts including the exact dates.

5) The relevant domestic law.

6) The provisions of the Convention on which it is relied together with any relevant case-law.

7) The object of the application (for example, the repeal or amendment of certain legislation or the reversal of a decision and compensation).

8) The details of all remedies (including any appeal) which have been pursued within the country concerned and, where appropriate, an explanation of why any available remedies have not been pursued.

9) The judgments, decisions and any other documents relating to the complaint.

Failure to include the content requested may result in the case not being registered with the effect that the case will not be examined.[16]

Admissibility

30.11   Once a case is registered, the first objective of the Court is to decide whether the application is admissible.[17] The chamber will assign a

---

14 The functions of the Registry are set out in Rule 17.
15 See appendix I.
16 Rule 47(3).

judge to act as rapporteur.[18] The rapporteur may request factual or other material from the parties and decide whether to report to the chamber or to refer the case to a committee.[19]

30.12   The committee may, by unanimous vote only, decide that a case is inadmissible.[20] Its decision cannot be appealed. Otherwise, all cases will go to the chamber which will decide on the admissibility and merits of the application.[21] The decision on admissibility and merits will be taken separately unless the Court, exceptionally, decides otherwise. The likelihood is that, in keeping with practice developed by the Commission, the Court will need not take a specific decision on admissibility where a state does not raise any issue of inadmissibility.

30.13   The establishment of facts is primarily a task for the chamber. It may, either at the request of a third party or of its own motion, ask for or hear any evidence that it considers will assist in the carrying out of its functions.[22] In *Cruz Varas v Sweden*[23] medical evidence was taken to find out if the applicant had previously been subjected to inhuman and degrading treatment, while in *Young, James and Webster v UK* a TUC representative gave evidence on questions of fact during the hearing.[24] The Court may also send a delegation to carry out fact-finding missions at locations, such as in *A v UK* where the conditions of detention at Broadmoor were of particular relevance,[25] and in *Akdivar v Turkey*[26] where they investigated allegations of the destruction of a village.

30.14   The chamber will first decide whether the application is admissible or not. Unless it is clear that the case is inadmissible, the chamber will give notice of the application to the respondent state and invite it to submit observations in writing.[27] Written observations or documents may not be filed after the time limit unless the

---

17 The question of admissibility is extremely important and will be expanded upon below.
18 Rule 49.
19 The common practice will be for the application to be passed to a committee in the first place.
20 Article 28.
21 Article 29.
22 Rule 42.
23 (1992) 14 EHRR 1.
24 (1982) 4 EHRR 38.
25 (1980) 20 DR 5.
26 (1997) 23 EHRR 143.
27 Rule 38 is concerned with the process of written proceedings.

President of the Chamber decides otherwise.[28] The parties may then be invited to submit further written observations. The chamber will then subsequently hold a hearing.[29] The practice of the Commission was to impose strict limits on the time provided for oral hearings, with each party being given 30 minutes to state their case, followed by a further period (usually 15 minutes) to respond to any questions. Even complex cases, or cases with a large number of parties were rarely given more than an extra 90 minutes. The parties will almost always be invited to address the merits of the application.[30] The rules of the new Court have established that, unlike the previous procedure, the pleadings and hearings before the Court will, save in exceptional circumstances, be public.[31] As with the committee, there is no right of appeal against any decision on admissibility by the chamber.[32]

Friendly settlement

30.15   Having declared an application admissible, two avenues will be simultaneously pursued; friendly settlement and the merits of the case.[33] On the instructions of the chamber, the Registrar of the Court will contact the parties to see whether there is a possibility of securing a friendly settlement.[34] The Secretary of the Commission used to pass on any written proposals by the parties. If there were a possibility of a settlement being achieved, separate or joint meetings were arranged. It was the practice of the Commission to communicate to both sides, in confidence, its provisional view on the merits of the complaint. However, there is (as yet) no indication whether the new Court will follow this procedure. The explanatory report to Protocol 11 indicates that the judge rapporteur may take steps with a view to a friendly settlement. The rules state that the chamber will take any steps to facilitate such a settlement.[35] It is

28 Rule 38(1).
29 Rule 54(2).
30 The conduct of hearings is covered in Rules 63–70.
31 Article 40.
32 Protocol 8 enables cases that are clearly inadmissible to be disposed of by a one-page decision, thereby cutting down on time and resources. The intention of Article 45 is to ensure that this practice is maintained.
33 Article 38.
34 Rule 62.
35 Rule 62(1).

unclear whether the Court will become involved in the settlement negotiations. Any friendly settlement reached will need to be verified by the Court.[36]

Merits

30.16 The chamber will continue to examine the merits of the case. It may invite the parties to submit further evidence and written observations.[37] The chamber may also decide to hold a hearing of its own volition. Alternatively, one may be requested by either of the parties, provided there has been no hearing on the merits at the admissibility stage.[38] The chamber will then make a finding on the merits.

30.17 If the Court decides that there has been a violation, it may award 'just satisfaction' in the form of pecuniary and non-pecuniary damages and legal costs and expenses.[39] The concept of 'just satisfaction' is examined in chapter 2 above. A request for 'just satisfaction' must be set out when the written observations on the merits are filed, or in a special document that must be filed within two months of the admissibility decision.[40]

Costs

30.18 In order to obtain costs, an applicant must prove that s/he has or is liable to pay those costs claimed. The applicant may also receive reimbursement for expenses which are considered by the Court to be useful rather than just necessary.[41] In *The Sunday Times v UK,*[42] the Court did not distinguish between costs in relation to those violations that were successfully argued and those which were rejected on the basis that a lawyer has a duty to present his client's case as fully and ably as possible. The Court recognised when making costs awards that, in view of the high costs of litigation, it

---

36 Rule 62(3).
37 Rule 59.
38 Rule 59(2).
39 Article 41 and Rules 60 and 75.
40 Article 60(1).
41 *Konig v Germany* (1979-80) 2 EHRR 170.
42 (1979–80) 2 EHRR 245.

would be inappropriate for it 'to constitute a serious impediment to the effective protection of human rights'.[43] There are no fees payable to the Court and there is no liability to meet the costs of the government in any event.

Referral to the Grand Chamber

30.19   There are two possible occasions when an individual application will be referred to the Grand Chamber.[44] The first is where a chamber relinquishes its jurisdiction to the Grand Chamber.[45] This can occur where a case raises a serious question affecting the interpretation of the Convention, or where the resolution of an issue before a chamber might have a result inconsistent with a judgment previously delivered by the Court. However, relinquishment cannot take place if one of the parties to the case objects. Second, the Grand Chamber may act, in exceptional circumstances, as an appeal body.[46] The request must come from one of the parties within three months from the date of judgment of the chamber. It will be considered by a panel of five judges,[47] and only accepted:

> if the case raises a serious question affecting the interpretation or application of the Convention or the Protocols thereto, or a serious issue of general importance.

Those provisions relating to proceedings before the chamber apply, mutatis mutandis, to the Grand Chamber.[48] The explanatory report clarifies that the Grand Chamber will give its judgment after written, and if it so decides, oral proceedings.[49] The judgment of the Grand Chamber shall be final.[50]

---

43 *Young, James and Webster v UK* (1982) 4 EHRR 38.
44 Article 44(2) states at which point the judgment of the chamber will become final.
45 Article 30 and Rule 72.
46 Article 43 and Rule 73.
47 The composition of the panel is set out in Rule 24(6).
48 Rule 71.
49 The details to be outlined in the content of the judgment are set out in Rule 74.
50 Article 44(1).

Admissibility: special considerations

30.20 Article 35, introduced by Protocol 11, is based on the same criteria as the previous articles on admissibility. The decisions of the Commission in this area will therefore remain a major source of guidance for the new Court. The importance of meeting the admissibility requirements cannot be over-estimated; only about 5 per cent of cases proceed beyond this stage. And once admissibility in determined, the state cannot raise any further admissibility points. However, the Court may at any time re-open the issue and reject a case on the grounds of inadmissibility.[51]

The six-month rule

30.21 The rule that an application must be communicated within six months of the last domestic remedy cannot be waived by the respondent or by Strasbourg.[52] Time will start running from the day after the final decision rejecting the applicant's claim. Where the decision is not publicly pronounced, it will be the date on which the applicant or his/her lawyer is informed.[53] Where the complaint relates to an act or omission for which there is no domestic remedy, time will start running from the date of the alleged violation or the date of its knowledge.[54] Where an applicant uses a remedy which is obviously ineffective, time will run from the time when s/he became, or should reasonably have become, aware of the fact.[55]

30.22 The rule will not apply where the alleged violation is continuous or on-going in nature, such as in *Dudgeon v UK* where the applicant was complaining about the criminalisation of homosexual acts.[56] In the case of *McFeeley v UK* where the applicant was repeatedly punished for persistently refusing to obey prison rules, time will start to run when that continuous situation comes to an end.[57]

30.23 The introduction of an application to the Court will stop time

---

51 In *De Wilde, Ooms and Versyp v Belgium* (1979–80) 1 EHRR 373 the Court considered that it was competent to re-examine the admissibility decisions of the Commission.

52 *X v France* (1982) 29 DR 228 at 240.

53 *K,C and M v Netherlands* 80-A DR 87 at 88.

54 *Hilton v UK* (1988) 57 DR 108 at 113; *Christians against Racism and Fascism v UK* (1980) 21 DR 138 at 147.

55 *Lacin v Turkey* (1995) 81-A DR 76 at 81.

56 (1982) 4 EHRR 149.

57 (1980) 20 DR 44 at 76.

from running. This may be in the form of a letter which in general terms sets out the allegations rather than the application form itself. However, applications must be pursued actively and an unreasonable delay in the subsequent communication may lead the Strasbourg bodies to disregard the introductory letter.[58]

30.24   The rule is subject to a special circumstances qualification. Detention without contact might fall within this qualification. However, in *K v Ireland* the applicant's illness and depressive state were not regarded as special circumstances;[59] nor has lack of knowledge about the law.[60]

Exhaustion of domestic remedies[61]

30.25   Article 35(1) provides:

> The Court may only deal with the matter after all domestic remedies have been exhausted, according to the generally recognised rules of international law, and within a period of six months from the date on which the final decision was taken.

This reflects the fact that the primary responsibility for observing the provisions of the Convention rests with the states who are parties to it.

> ...the machinery of protection established by the Convention is subsidiary to the national systems safeguarding human rights ... The Convention leaves to each Contracting State, in the first place, the task of securing the rights and freedoms it enshrines. The institutions created by it make their own contribution to this task but they become involved only through contentious proceedings and once all domestic remedies have been exhausted.[62]

The Convention also affords member states an opportunity, in accordance with general principles of international law, to redress any violation of its terms within the domestic arena.[63]

---

58   *X and Y v Ireland* (1980) 22 DR 51 at 72; *Kelly v UK* (1985) 42 DR 205 at 207; *Mercier de Bettens v Switzerland* (1987) 54 DR 178 at 185.

59   (1984) 38 DR 158 at 160; Also see *X v Austria* (1975) 2 DR 87 at 88.

60   *Bozano v Italy* (1984) 39 DR 147.

61   For further analysis see, N Bratza and A Padfield, 'Exhaustion of Domestic Remedies under the European Convention of Human Rights' in [1998] JR 220.

62   *Handyside v UK* (1979–80) 1 EHRR 737 at para 48.

63   *De Wilde, Ooms and Versyp v Belgium* (1979–80) 1 EHRR 373 at para 50; *D v FRG* (1984) 36 DR 24 at 30; *Cardot v France* (1991) 13 EHRR 853 at para 34; *Hentrich v France* (1994) 18 EHRR 440 at para 33.

30.26   The Commission and Court have consistently held that, in accordance with international law, the rule of exhaustion of domestic remedies requires that an applicant make 'normal use' of remedies 'likely to be effective and adequate'.[64] In other words, such remedies as 'are available to the persons concerned and are sufficient, that is to say capable of providing redress for their complaints'.[65] There is thus no requirement that ineffective remedies offering no prospect of success be pursued.[66] Conversely, the requirement that domestic remedies be exhausted is not limited to applications to courts and tribunals, but extends to administrative remedies such as, in the UK, a petition to the Home Secretary or a complaint to a prison board of visitors concerning matters of prison administration such as complaints regarding conditions of detention.[67]

30.27   Remedies which, although available as a matter of legal theory, are not available as a matter of practice, are not required to be exhausted as a condition of admissibility.[68] This may be satisfied by settled legal opinion which states that no effective redress is provided for the complaint.[69] An adequate remedy is one that is sufficient to provide redress for the applicant's complaint.[70] Mere doubts about the prospect of success of national proceedings will not absolve the applicant from the obligation of exhaustion.[71] The terms of complaint before Strasbourg need not have been directly pleaded before the domestic court provided the substance of the complaint has been raised, since admissibility issues must be applied with 'some degree of flexibility and without excessive formalism'.[72] Where there is a choice of remedies open to an applicant to redress an alleged violation of the Convention, there is no obligation on an

64 *Donnelly v UK* (1972) 4 DR 4 at 72.
65 *Stogmuller v Austria* (1979–80) 1 EHRR 155 at para 11; *De Wilde, Ooms & Versyp v Belgium* n63 at para 61; *Vernillo v France* (1991) 13 EHRR 880 at para 27; *Navarra v France* (1994) 17 EHRR 594 at para 24.
66 *Campbell v UK* (1978) 14 DR 186 at 190; *J v Switzerland* (1989) 62 DR 269 at 275.
67 *McFeeley v UK* (1980) 20 DR 44 at 72.
68 *Vernillo v France* n65 at para 27; *Cremieux v France* (1989) 59 DR 67 at 80.
69 *De Wilde, Ooms & Versyp v Belgium* n63 at para 62; *McFeeley v UK* (1980) 20 DR 44 at 71–76; *K, F and P v UK* (1984) 40 DR 298 at 300.
70 *Lawless v UK* (1958) 2 YB 308 at 326; *Donnelly v UK* (1975) 4 DR 4 at 78–9.
71 *Donnelly v UK* (1975) 4 DR 4 at 72; *McDonnell v Ireland* (1990) 64 DR 203
72 *Cardot v France* (1991) 13 EHRR 853. Also see *Van Oosterwijck v Belgium* (1981) 3 EHRR 557 at paras 30–41.

applicant to make use of more than one legal remedy where the objective of each remedy is essentially the same.[73]

30.28   There are exceptional situations where it has been regarded as inappropriate to apply the exhaustion rule, such as in *Hilton v UK*[74] where a prisoner was repeatedly denied the opportunity to consult with his solicitor over a significant period of time.[75] The situations under which an applicant is not required to exhaust domestic remedies are defined very narrowly. The applicant's position as a mental patient and his lack of legal knowledge did not absolve him from the duty to exhaust domestic remedies in *X v UK*,[76] or in the case of *Van Oosterwijck v Belgium* where the applicant did not have legal aid.[77] Other grounds of exemption are where an applicant shows the existence of an administrative practice of violations of the Convention (ie, a pattern of identical or analogous breaches and official tolerance of such breaches).[78] In *Akdivar v Turkey* the Court went a step further and held that the absence of any meaningful investigation by the authorities into the applicants' allegations of destruction of their homes by the security forces, combined with the insecurity and vulnerability of the applicants' position following such destruction and the risk of reprisals against the applicants by the security forces, absolved them from the obligation to commence civil proceedings.[79]

30.29   The burden of proving the existence of available and sufficient domestic remedies is on the state seeking to rely upon non-exhaustion as a ground of inadmissibility.[80] The state must prove not only that the domestic remedies unused by an applicant are available and sufficient but that they are 'sufficiently certain not only in theory but also in practice'.[81] However, once the state has established the existence of available domestic remedies, the burden shifts to the applicant to show that these remedies are not adequate or effective

---

73   *Cremieux v France* (1989) 59 DR 67 at 80; *Yagci and Sargin v Turkey* (1995) 20 EHRR 505 at paras 41–43.

74   (1976) 4 DR 177.

75   See also *Reed v UK* (1979) 19 DR 113.

76   *X v UK* (1977) 10 DR 5.

77   (1981) 3 EHRR 557 at para 38. Although, the applicant did not apply for legal aid or provide details of his financial position to Strasbourg.

78   *Donnelly v UK* (1975) 4 DR 4.

79   Note 26 paras 73–75.

80   *De Wilde, Ooms & Versyp v Belgium* n63 at para 60; *De Weer v Belgium* (1980) A 35 para 26; *Guincho v Portugal* (1982) 29 DR 129 at 140.

81   *Vernillo v France* n65 at para 27; *Cremieux v France* (1989) 59 DR 67 at 80.

to provide redress in respect of the particular complaints or that there existed special circumstances absolving him from the requirement.[82]

30.30   Where there has been a change in domestic law, the question of exhaustion will be considered by reference to the situation at the date of the decision on admissibility rather than at the date on which the application is made to Strasbourg.[83] This may become important once the HRA comes into force.

Manifestly ill-founded

30.31   This aspect requires a consideration of the merits of the case. Cases will be manifestly ill-founded if they disclose no prima facie breach of a Convention right,[84] the complaint is unsubstantiated or the applicant has ceased to be a victim.

Anonymity

30.32   An applicant must disclose his/her identity when completing the application form. The President of the Chamber may ensure that the identity of the applicant is not disclosed to the public where exceptional reasons justify a departure from the normal course.[85]

Substantially the same

30.33   The Court will not hear a case if it is based on the same facts that have previously been rejected even if the subsequent application introduces new legal argument.[86] The case would be admissible if it were based on new factual information.

Incompatible with the Convention

30.34   It will be incompatible in time (ratione temporis) where it relates to events that occurred before the treaty came into force or was ratified, and when the right of individual petition was accepted (ie, after 1966 in the UK). Complaints which take place outside the territory and

---

82   *Donnelly v UK* n78 at para 64; *Akdivar v Turkey* n26 at para 68.
83   *Ringeisen v Austria* (1979–80) 1 EHRR 455 at paras 89–93.
84   *Logan v UK* (1996) 86-A DR 74.
85   Rule 47(3).
86   *X v UK* (1981) 25 DR 147.

have no link with any contracting party (ratione loci) will also be inadmissible. Applications may also be made alleging violations which are not covered by the substantive provisions of the Convention. For instance, in *X v UK*, the right to hold a position in public service was not guaranteed. Nor does it enshrine rights covered by other international treaties such as the right to self-determination.[87]

Abuse of the right of petition

30.35   This ground is directed against complaints which have no legal foundation. It may be that the Court is being misled, or that there are political motivations behind its introduction, or because the confidentiality or decorum of proceedings have been compromised.

Striking out of the list

30.36   Article 37 states that the Court may decide to strike an application out of the list at any stage where it concludes that the applicant does not intend to pursue the petition, or that the matter has been resolved by informal settlement (as opposed to a 'friendly settlement' where the Court intervenes) between the parties as in *Abbott v UK*.[88] The Court may also decide that it can no longer justify the examination of the application,[89] such as where new legislation is passed or other acts rectify an alleged violation. However, even where the applicant does not intend to pursue the application, as in the case of *Tyrer v UK*,[90] the Court will continue the examination if it would be in the interests of human rights to do so.

Interim relief and urgent applications

30.37   Under Protocol 11, there is still no binding obligation on states to adhere to the Court's request to provide interim or injunctive relief.[91] This maintains the narrow reversal of a decision of the Commission

---

87   6742/74 3 DR 98 at 102.
88   (1990) 67 DR 290.
89   Article 37(1)(c).
90   (1979–80) 2 EHRR 1 at para 21.
91   Article 39.

by the old Court in *Cruz Varas v Sweden*. In that case, a failure to comply with a request not to deport the applicant did not amount to a breach of the obligation not to hinder the effectiveness of the right of individual petition.[92] Interim relief has usually, but not exclusively, been used in extradition cases where there is a fear of the applicant being subject to ill-treatment in contravention of articles 2 or 3 of the Convention. It has also been applied where there are health risks, such as in *Poku v UK* where the applicant was in the latter stages of a difficult pregnancy and had a history of miscarriages.[93] In *D v UK* the applicant suffered from AIDS and stated that he would have no access to treatment on deportation.[94]

30.38   Requests for interim measures will receive urgent attention. The registrar, with the authorisation of the President of the Court, may, without prejudice to the proceedings, communicate the application to the respondent government in order to deal with the matter speedily.[95]

30.39   The normal practice of the chamber will be to deal with applications in the order in which they are ready, but it has the power to give priority if urgency is required.[96] The case of *Soering v UK* completed the whole Strasbourg procedure in under a year.[97]

Legal aid

30.40   It has not been the practice of the UK Legal Aid Board to grant legal aid for commencing complaints to the European Court, since Strasbourg has its own system for providing legal aid.[98] However, it will be available only for work carried out once a case has been communicated to the respondent government.[99] The European Court recognises the validity of contingency fee agreement. However, in *Dudgeon v UK*, it rejected that portion of the applicant's costs claim which was to be payable only once the application was

---

92 (1992) 14 EHRR 1.
93 (1996) 26985/95 unpublished.
94 (1997) 24 EHRR 423.
95 Rule 40.
96 Rule 41.
97 (1989) 11 EHRR 439.
98 Rules 91–96.
99 Rule 91.

declared admissible, on the basis that there was no legal liability on the applicant under domestic law to pay those fees.[100]

30.41   The practice has been for the Strasbourg authorities, on receipt of the applicant's means form and certificate of indigence which are provided by the Legal Aid Board,[101] to send copies to the government in case it wishes to comment.[102] It is possible for persons who are above the UK threshold to receive legal aid.[103] The income of a parent or spouse may be considered only if it is not inconsiderable and that person could be reasonably expected to contribute.

30.42   The rate of legal aid is fixed in accordance with the legal aid scales in force.[104] Traditionally, it has not compared favourably with the UK legal aid levels, and is only intended to contribute to fees and expenses.

30.43   If legal aid is granted, the applicant will not be expected to refund any amount awarded if no violation is found,[105] although, any award will be deducted from any damages received by the applicant.

Advisory opinions

30.44   The opportunity was not taken in Protocol 11 to expand on the narrow confines in which an advisory opinion may be sought from the Court.[106] It is not possible to request an opinion on any of the substantive provisions of the Convention or Protocols.[107]

Binding force and the execution of judgments

30.45   A final judgment by the Court will not be binding on states and will not have the effect of quashing national decisions or striking down legislation. However, the state parties to the Convention have undertaken to respect the final judgment of any action in which they

---

100 A 59 para 22.
101 Rule 93(1).
102 Rule 93(2).
103 This was so in *Goodwin v UK* (1996) 22 EHRR 123.
104 Rule 95.
105 Nor would any applicant, legally aided or not, be asked to pay the costs of the respondent state.
106 Article 47.
107 Articles 47 (1) & (2). The procedure is laid out in Rules 82–90.

are a party.[108] The Committee of Ministers will then supervise its execution.[109] If a state party does not meet its obligation the Committee of Ministers can decide, so long as there is a two-thirds majority of the votes cast (and it is supported by a majority of the total number of states), to take measures. In practice there is very little that may be done under the Convention to persuade a state to respect its obligations. However, the Committee of Ministers has the power to suspend or even expel any contracting party from the Council of Europe, where it have been found guilty of serious human rights abuses.[110]

108 Article 46(1).
109 Article 46(2).
110 Article 8 of the Statute of the Council of Europe.

APPENDICES

A Human Rights Act 1998

B European Convention on Human Rights

C Universal Declaration of Human Rights

D UN Covenant on Civil and Political Rights

E UN Convention on the elimination of all forms of racial discrimination

F UN Convention on the elimination of all forms of discrimination against women

G UN Convention on the rights of the child

H European Social Charter

I Rules of the European Court of Human Rights

J Rules of the Committee of Ministers

K European Court of Human Rights complaint form

L European Court of Human Rights form of authority

Human Rights Act 1998

INTRODUCTION

The Convention Rights

1 (1) In this Act 'the Convention rights' means the rights and fundamental freedoms set out in –

    (a) Articles 2 to 12 and 14 of the Convention,

    (b) Articles 1 to 3 of the First Protocol, and

    (c) Articles 1 and 2 of the Sixth Protocol,

    as read with Articles 16 to 18 of the Convention.

(2) Those Articles are to have effect for the purposes of this Act subject to any designated derogation or reservation (as to which see sections 14 and 15).

(3) The Articles are set out in Schedule 1.

(4) The Secretary of State may by order make such amendments to this Act as he considers appropriate to reflect the effect, in relation to the United Kingdom, of a protocol.

(5) In subsection (4) 'protocol' means a protocol to the Convention –

    (a) which the United Kingdom has ratified; or

    (b) which the United Kingdom has signed with a view to ratification.

(6) No amendment may be made by an order under subsection (4) so as to come into force before the protocol concerned is in force in relation to the United Kingdom.

Interpretation of Convention rights

2 (1) A court or tribunal determining a question which has arisen in connection with a Convention right must take into account any –

    (a) judgment, decision, declaration or advisory opinion of the European Court of Human Rights,

    (b) opinion of the Commission given in a report adopted under Article 31 of the Convention,

    (c) decision of the Commission in connection with Article 26 or 27(2) of the Convention, or

    (d) decision of the Committee of Ministers taken under Article 46 of the Convention,

    whenever made or given, so far as, in the opinion of the court or tribunal, it is relevant to the proceedings in which that question has arisen.

(2) Evidence of any judgment, decision, declaration or opinion of which account may have to be taken under this section is to be given in

proceedings before any court or tribunal in such manner as may be provided by rules.

(3) In this section 'rules' means rules of court or, in the case of proceedings before a tribunal, rules made for the purposes of this section –
   (a) by the Lord Chancellor or the Secretary of State, in relation to any proceedings outside Scotland;
   (b) by the Secretary of State, in relation to proceedings in Scotland; or
   (c) by a Northern Ireland department, in relation to proceedings before a tribunal in Northern Ireland –
      (i) which deals with transferred matters; and
      (ii) for which no rules made under paragraph (a) are in force.

LEGISLATION
Interpretation of legislation
3 (1) So far as it is possible to do so, primary legislation and subordinate legislation must be read and given effect in a way which is compatible with the Convention rights.

(2) This section –
   (a) applies to primary legislation and subordinate legislation whenever enacted;
   (b) does not affect the validity, continuing operation or enforcement of any incompatible primary legislation; and
   (c) does not affect the validity, continuing operation or enforcement of any incompatible subordinate legislation if (disregarding any possibility of revocation) primary legislation prevents removal of the incompatibility.

Declaration of incompatibility
4 (1) Subsection (2) applies in any proceedings in which a court determines whether a provision of primary legislation is compatible with a Convention right.

(2) If the court is satisfied that the provision is incompatible with a Convention right, it may make a declaration of that incompatibility.

(3) Subsection (4) applies in any proceedings in which a court determines whether a provision of subordinate legislation, made in the exercise of a power conferred by primary legislation, is compatible with a Convention right.

(4) If the court is satisfied –
   (a) that the provision is incompatible with a Convention right, and
   (b) that (disregarding any possibility of revocation) the primary legislation concerned prevents removal of the incompatibility,
   it may make a declaration of that incompatibility.

(5) In this section 'court' means –
   (a) the House of Lords;
   (b) the Judicial Committee of the Privy Council;
   (c) the Courts-Martial Appeal Court;
   (d) in Scotland, the High Court of Justiciary sitting otherwise than as a trial court or the Court of Session;
   (e) in England and Wales or Northern Ireland, the High Court or the Court of Appeal.

(6) A declaration under this section ('a declaration of incompatibility') –
  (a) does not affect the validity, continuing operation or enforcement of the provision in respect of which it is given; and
  (b) is not binding on the parties to the proceedings in which it is made.

Right of Crown to intervene

5 (1) Where a court is considering whether to make a declaration of incompatibility, the Crown is entitled to notice in accordance with rules of court.

(2) In any case to which subsection (1) applies –
  (a) a Minister of the Crown (or a person nominated by him),
  (b) a member of the Scottish Executive,
  (c) a Northern Ireland Minister,
  (d) a Northern Ireland department,
  is entitled, on giving notice in accordance with rules of court, to be joined as a party to the proceedings.

(3) Notice under subsection (2) may be given at any time during the proceedings.

(4) A person who has been made a party to criminal proceedings (other than in Scotland) as the result of a notice under subsection (2) may, with leave, appeal to the House of Lords against any declaration of incompatibility made in the proceedings.

(5) In subsection (4) –
  'criminal proceedings' includes all proceedings before the Courts-Martial Appeal Court; and
  'leave' means leave granted by the court making the declaration of incompatibility or by the House of Lords.

PUBLIC AUTHORITIES
Acts of public authorities

6 (1) It is unlawful for a public authority to act in a way which is incompatible with a Convention right.

(2) Subsection (1) does not apply to an act if –
  (a) as the result of one or more provisions of primary legislation, the authority could not have acted differently; or
  (b) in the case of one or more provisions of, or made under, primary legislation which cannot be read or given effect in a way which is compatible with the Convention rights, the authority was acting so as to give effect to or enforce those provisions.

(3) In this section 'public authority' includes –
  (a) a court or tribunal, and
  (b) any person certain of whose functions are functions of a public nature,
  but does not include either House of Parliament or a person exercising functions in connection with proceedings in Parliament.

(4) In subsection (3) 'Parliament' does not include the House of Lords in its judicial capacity.

(5) In relation to a particular act, a person is not a public authority by virtue only of subsection (3)(b) if the nature of the act is private.

(6) 'An act' includes a failure to act but does not include a failure to –
   (a) introduce in, or lay before, Parliament a proposal for legislation; or
   (b) make any primary legislation or remedial order.

Proceedings

7 (1) A person who claims that a public authority has acted (or proposes to act) in a way which is made unlawful by section 6(1) may –
   (a) bring proceedings against the authority under this Act in the appropriate court or tribunal, or
   (b) rely on the Convention right or rights concerned in any legal proceedings,
   but only if he is (or would be) a victim of the unlawful act.

(2) In subsection (1)(a) 'appropriate court or tribunal' means such court or tribunal as may be determined in accordance with rules; and proceedings against an authority include a counterclaim or similar proceeding.

(3) If the proceedings are brought on an application for judicial review, the applicant is to be taken to have a sufficient interest in relation to the unlawful act only if he is, or would be, a victim of that act.

(4) If the proceedings are made by way of a petition for judicial review in Scotland, the applicant shall be taken to have title and interest to sue in relation to the unlawful act only if he is, or would be, a victim of that act.

(5) Proceedings under subsection (1)(a) must be brought before the end of –
   (a) the period of one year beginning with the date on which the act complained of took place; or
   (b) such longer period as the court or tribunal considers equitable having regard to all the circumstances,
   but that is subject to any rule imposing a stricter time limit in relation to the procedure in question.

(6) In subsection (1)(b) 'legal proceedings' includes –
   (a) proceedings brought by or at the instigation of a public authority; and
   (b) an appeal against the decision of a court or tribunal.

(7) For the purposes of this section, a person is a victim of an unlawful act only if he would be a victim for the purposes of Article 34 of the Convention if proceedings were brought in the European Court of Human Rights in respect of that act.

(8) Nothing in this Act creates a criminal offence.

(9) In this section 'rules' means –
   (a) in relation to proceedings before a court or tribunal outside Scotland, rules made by the Lord Chancellor or the Secretary of State for the purposes of this section or rules of court,
   (b) in relation to proceedings before a court or tribunal in Scotland, rules made by the Secretary of State for those purposes,
   (c) in relation to proceedings before a tribunal in Northern Ireland –
      (i) which deals with transferred matters; and
      (ii) for which no rules made under paragraph (a) are in force,
      rules made by a Northern Ireland department for those purposes,

and includes provision made by order under section 1 of the Courts and Legal Services Act 1990.

(10) In making rules, regard must be had to section 9.

(11) The Minister who has power to make rules in relation to a particular tribunal may, to the extent he considers it necessary to ensure that the tribunal can provide an appropriate remedy in relation to an act (or proposed act) of a public authority which is (or would be) unlawful as a result of section 6(1), by order add to –
(a) the relief or remedies which the tribunal may grant; or
(b) the grounds on which it may grant any of them.

(12) An order made under subsection (11) may contain such incidental, supplemental, consequential or transitional provision as the Minister making it considers appropriate.

(13) 'The Minister' includes the Northern Ireland department concerned.

Judicial remedies

8 (1) In relation to any act (or proposed act) of a public authority which the court finds is (or would be) unlawful, it may grant such relief or remedy, or make such order, within its powers as it considers just and appropriate.

(2) But damages may be awarded only by a court which has power to award damages, or to order the payment of compensation, in civil proceedings.

(3) No award of damages is to be made unless, taking account of all the circumstances of the case, including –
(a) any other relief or remedy granted, or order made, in relation to the act in question (by that or any other court), and
(b) the consequences of any decision (of that or any other court) in respect of that act,
the court is satisfied that the award is necessary to afford just satisfaction to the person in whose favour it is made.

(4) In determining –
(a) whether to award damages, or
(b) the amount of an award,
the court must take into account the principles applied by the European Court of Human Rights in relation to the award of compensation under Article 41 of the Convention.

(5) A public authority against which damages are awarded is to be treated –
(a) in Scotland, for the purposes of section 3 of the Law Reform (Miscellaneous Provisions) (Scotland) Act 1940 as if the award were made in an action of damages in which the authority has been found liable in respect of loss or damage to the person to whom the award is made;
(b) for the purposes of the Civil Liability (Contribution) Act 1978 as liable in respect of damage suffered by the person to whom the award is made.

(6) In this section –
'court' includes a tribunal;
'damages' means damages for an unlawful act of a public authority; and
'unlawful' means unlawful under section 6(1).

Judicial acts

9 (1) Proceedings under section 7(1)(a) in respect of a judicial act may be brought only –
(a) by exercising a right of appeal;
(b) on an application (in Scotland a petition) for judicial review; or
(c) in such other forum as may be prescribed by rules.

(2) That does not affect any rule of law which prevents a court from being the subject of judicial review.

(3) In proceedings under this Act in respect of a judicial act done in good faith, damages may not be awarded otherwise than to compensate a person to the extent required by Article 5(5) of the Convention.

(4) An award of damages permitted by subsection (3) is to be made against the Crown; but no award may be made unless the appropriate person, if not a party to the proceedings, is joined.

(5) In this section –
'appropriate person' means the Minister responsible for the court concerned, or a person or government department nominated by him;
'court' includes a tribunal;
'judge' includes a member of a tribunal, a justice of the peace and a clerk or other officer entitled to exercise the jurisdiction of a court;
'judicial act' means a judicial act of a court and includes an act done on the instructions, or on behalf, of a judge; and
'rules' has the same meaning as in section 7(9).

REMEDIAL ACTION
Power to take remedial action

10 (1) This section applies if –
(a) a provision of legislation has been declared under section 4 to be incompatible with a Convention right and, if an appeal lies –
(i) all persons who may appeal have stated in writing that they do not intend to do so;
(ii) the time for bringing an appeal has expired and no appeal has been brought within that time; or
(iii) an appeal brought within that time has been determined or abandoned; or
(b) it appears to a Minister of the Crown or Her Majesty in Council that, having regard to a finding of the European Court of Human Rights made after the coming into force of this section in proceedings against the United Kingdom, a provision of legislation is incompatible with an obligation of the United Kingdom arising from the Convention.

(2) If a Minister of the Crown considers that there are compelling reasons for proceeding under this section, he may by order make such amendments to the legislation as he considers necessary to remove the incompatibility.

(3) If, in the case of subordinate legislation, a Minister of the Crown considers –
(a) that it is necessary to amend the primary legislation under which the subordinate legislation in question was made, in order to enable the incompatibility to be removed, and

(b) that there are compelling reasons for proceeding under this section,
he may by order make such amendments to the primary legislation as he
considers necessary.

(4) This section also applies where the provision in question is in subordinate
legislation and has been quashed, or declared invalid, by reason of
incompatibility with a Convention right and the Minister proposes to
proceed under paragraph 2(b) of Schedule 2.

(5) If the legislation is an Order in Council, the power conferred by subsection
(2) or (3) is exercisable by Her Majesty in Council.

(6) In this section 'legislation' does not include a Measure of the Church
Assembly or of the General Synod of the Church of England.

(7) Schedule 2 makes further provision about remedial orders.

OTHER RIGHTS AND PROCEEDINGS
Safeguard for existing human rights

11   A person's reliance on a Convention right does not restrict –

(a) any other right or freedom conferred on him by or under any law having
effect in any part of the United Kingdom; or

(b) his right to make any claim or bring any proceedings which he could
make or bring apart from sections 7 to 9.

Freedom of expression

12 (1) This section applies if a court is considering whether to grant any relief
which, if granted, might affect the exercise of the Convention right to
freedom of expression.

(2) If the person against whom the application for relief is made ('the
respondent') is neither present nor represented, no such relief is to be
granted unless the court is satisfied –

(a) that the applicant has taken all practicable steps to notify the
respondent; or

(b) that there are compelling reasons why the respondent should not be
notified.

(3) No such relief is to be granted so as to restrain publication before trial
unless the court is satisfied that the applicant is likely to establish that
publication should not be allowed.

(4) The court must have particular regard to the importance of the Convention
right to freedom of expression and, where the proceedings relate to material
which the respondent claims, or which appears to the court, to be
journalistic, literary or artistic material (or to conduct connected with such
material), to –

(a) the extent to which –

(i) the material has, or is about to, become available to the public; or

(ii) it is, or would be, in the public interest for the material to be
published;

(b) any relevant privacy code.

(5) In this section –
'court' includes a tribunal; and
'relief' includes any remedy or order (other than in criminal proceedings).

Freedom of thought, conscience and religion

13 (1) If a court's determination of any question arising under this Act might affect the exercise by a religious organisation (itself or its members collectively) of the Convention right to freedom of thought, conscience and religion, it must have particular regard to the importance of that right.

(2) In this section 'court' includes a tribunal.

DEROGATIONS AND RESERVATIONS
Derogations

14 (1) In this Act 'designated derogation' means –
   (a) the United Kingdom's derogation from Article 5(3) of the Convention; and
   (b) any derogation by the United Kingdom from an Article of the Convention, or of any protocol to the Convention, which is designated for the purposes of this Act in an order made by the Secretary of State.

(2) The derogation referred to in subsection (1)(a) is set out in Part I of Schedule 3.

(3) If a designated derogation is amended or replaced it ceases to be a designated derogation.

(4) But subsection (3) does not prevent the Secretary of State from exercising his power under subsection (1)(b) to make a fresh designation order in respect of the Article concerned.

(5) The Secretary of State must by order make such amendments to Schedule 3 as he considers appropriate to reflect –
   (a) any designation order; or
   (b) the effect of subsection (3).

(6) A designation order may be made in anticipation of the making by the United Kingdom of a proposed derogation.

Reservations

15 (1) In this Act 'designated reservation' means –
   (a) the United Kingdom's reservation to Article 2 of the First Protocol to the Convention; and
   (b) any other reservation by the United Kingdom to an Article of the Convention, or of any protocol to the Convention, which is designated for the purposes of this Act in an order made by the Secretary of State.

(2) The text of the reservation referred to in subsection (1)(a) is set out in Part II of Schedule 3.

(3) If a designated reservation is withdrawn wholly or in part it ceases to be a designated reservation.

(4) But subsection (3) does not prevent the Secretary of State from exercising his power under subsection (1)(b) to make a fresh designation order in respect of the Article concerned.

(5) The Secretary of State must by order make such amendments to this Act as he considers appropriate to reflect –
   (a) any designation order; or
   (b) the effect of subsection (3).

Period for which designated derogations have effect

16 (1) If it has not already been withdrawn by the United Kingdom, a designated derogation ceases to have effect for the purposes of this Act –
   (a) in the case of the derogation referred to in section 14(1)(a), at the end of the period of five years beginning with the date on which section 1(2) came into force;
   (b) in the case of any other derogation, at the end of the period of five years beginning with the date on which the order designating it was made.

(2) At any time before the period –
   (a) fixed by subsection (1)(a) or (b), or
   (b) extended by an order under this subsection,
   comes to an end, the Secretary of State may by order extend it by a further period of five years.

(3) An order under section 14(1)(b) ceases to have effect at the end of the period for consideration, unless a resolution has been passed by each House approving the order.

(4) Subsection (3) does not affect –
   (a) anything done in reliance on the order; or
   (b) the power to make a fresh order under section 14(1)(b).

(5) In subsection (3) 'period for consideration' means the period of forty days beginning with the day on which the order was made.

(6) In calculating the period for consideration, no account is to be taken of any time during which –
   (a) Parliament is dissolved or prorogued; or
   (b) both Houses are adjourned for more than four days.

(7) If a designated derogation is withdrawn by the United Kingdom, the Secretary of State must by order make such amendments to this Act as he considers are required to reflect that withdrawal.

Periodic review of designated reservations

17 (1) The appropriate Minister must review the designated reservation referred to in section 15(1)(a) –
   (a) before the end of the period of five years beginning with the date on which section 1(2) came into force; and
   (b) if that designation is still in force, before the end of the period of five years beginning with the date on which the last report relating to it was laid under subsection (3).

(2) The appropriate Minister must review each of the other designated reservations (if any) –
   (a) before the end of the period of five years beginning with the date on which the order designating the reservation first came into force; and
   (b) if the designation is still in force, before the end of the period of five years beginning with the date on which the last report relating to it was laid under subsection (3).

(3) The Minister conducting a review under this section must prepare a report on the result of the review and lay a copy of it before each House of Parliament.

JUDGES OF THE EUROPEAN COURT OF HUMAN RIGHTS
Appointment to European Court of Human Rights

18 (1) In this section 'judicial office' means the office of –
   (a) Lord Justice of Appeal, Justice of the High Court or Circuit judge, in England and Wales;
   (b) judge of the Court of Session or sheriff, in Scotland;
   (c) Lord Justice of Appeal, judge of the High Court or county court judge, in Northern Ireland.

(2) The holder of a judicial office may become a judge of the European Court of Human Rights ('the Court') without being required to relinquish his office.

(3) But he is not required to perform the duties of his judicial office while he is a judge of the Court.

(4) In respect of any period during which he is a judge of the Court –
   (a) a Lord Justice of Appeal or Justice of the High Court is not to count as a judge of the relevant court for the purposes of section 2(1) or 4(1) of the Supreme Court Act 1981 (maximum number of judges) nor as a judge of the Supreme Court for the purposes of section 12(1) to (6) of that Act (salaries etc.);
   (b) a judge of the Court of Session is not to count as a judge of that court for the purposes of section 1(1) of the Court of Session Act 1988 (maximum number of judges) or of section 9(1)(c) of the Administration of Justice Act 1973 ('the 1973 Act') (salaries etc.);
   (c) a Lord Justice of Appeal or judge of the High Court in Northern Ireland is not to count as a judge of the relevant court for the purposes of section 2(1) or 3(1) of the Judicature (Northern Ireland) Act 1978 (maximum number of judges) nor as a judge of the Supreme Court of Northern Ireland for the purposes of section 9(1)(d) of the 1973 Act (salaries etc.);
   (d) a Circuit judge is not to count as such for the purposes of section 18 of the Courts Act 1971 (salaries etc.);
   (e) a sheriff is not to count as such for the purposes of section 14 of the Sheriff Courts (Scotland) Act 1907 (salaries etc.);
   (f) a county court judge of Northern Ireland is not to count as such for the purposes of section 106 of the County Courts Act Northern Ireland) 1959 (salaries etc.).

(5) If a sheriff principal is appointed a judge of the Court, section 11(1) of the Sheriff Courts (Scotland) Act 1971 (temporary appointment of sheriff principal) applies, while he holds that appointment, as if his office is vacant.

(6) Schedule 4 makes provision about judicial pensions in relation to the holder of a judicial office who serves as a judge of the Court.

(7) The Lord Chancellor or the Secretary of State may by order make such transitional provision (including, in particular, provision for a temporary increase in the maximum number of judges) as he considers appropriate in relation to any holder of a judicial office who has completed his service as a judge of the Court.

PARLIAMENTARY PROCEDURE
Statements of compatibility

19 (1) A Minister of the Crown in charge of a Bill in either House of Parliament must, before Second Reading of the Bill –

    (a) make a statement to the effect that in his view the provisions of the Bill are compatible with the Convention rights ('a statement of compatibility'); or

    (b) make a statement to the effect that although he is unable to make a statement of compatibility the government nevertheless wishes the House to proceed with the Bill.

  (2) The statement must be in writing and be published in such manner as the Minister making it considers appropriate.

SUPPLEMENTAL
Orders etc under this Act

20 (1) Any power of a Minister of the Crown to make an order under this Act is exercisable by statutory instrument.

  (2) The power of the Lord Chancellor or the Secretary of State to make rules (other than rules of court) under section 2(3) or 7(9) is exercisable by statutory instrument.

  (3) Any statutory instrument made under section 14, 15 or 16(7) must be laid before Parliament.

  (4) No order may be made by the Lord Chancellor or the Secretary of State under section 1(4), 7(11) or 16(2) unless a draft of the order has been laid before, and approved by, each House of Parliament.

  (5) Any statutory instrument made under section 18(7) or Schedule 4, or to which subsection (2) applies, shall be subject to annulment in pursuance of a resolution of either House of Parliament.

  (6) The power of a Northern Ireland department to make –

    (a) rules under section 2(3)(c) or 7(9)(c), or

    (b) an order under section 7(11),

is exercisable by statutory rule for the purposes of the Statutory Rules (Northern Ireland) Order 1979.

  (7) Any rules made under section 2(3)(c) or 7(9)(c) shall be subject to negative resolution; and section 41(6) of the Interpretation Act Northern Ireland) 1954 (meaning of 'subject to negative resolution') shall apply as if the power to make the rules were conferred by an Act of the Northern Ireland Assembly.

  (8) No order may be made by a Northern Ireland department under section 7(11) unless a draft of the order has been laid before, and approved by, the Northern Ireland Assembly.

Interpretation, etc

21 (1) In this Act –

'amend' includes repeal and apply (with or without modifications);

'the appropriate Minister' means the Minister of the Crown having charge

of the appropriate authorised government department (within the meaning of the Crown Proceedings Act 1947);
'the Commission' means the European Commission of Human Rights;
'the Convention' means the Convention for the Protection of Human Rights and Fundamental Freedoms, agreed by the Council of Europe at Rome on 4th November 1950 as it has effect for the time being in relation to the United Kingdom;
'declaration of incompatibility' means a declaration under section 4;
'Minister of the Crown' has the same meaning as in the Ministers of the Crown Act 1975;
'Northern Ireland Minister' includes the First Minister and the deputy First Minister in Northern Ireland;
'primary legislation' means any –
   (a) public general Act;
   (b) local and personal Act;
   (c) private Act;
   (d) Measure of the Church Assembly;
   (e) Measure of the General Synod of the Church of England;
   (f) Order in Council –
      (i) made in exercise of Her Majesty's Royal Prerogative;
      (ii) made under section 38(1)(a) of the Northern Ireland Constitution Act 1973 or the corresponding provision of the Northern Ireland Act 1998; or
      (iii) amending an Act of a kind mentioned in paragraph (a), (b) or (c);
   and includes an order or other instrument made under primary legislation (otherwise than by the National Assembly for Wales, a member of the Scottish Executive, a Northern Ireland Minister or a Northern Ireland department) to the extent to which it operates to bring one or more provisions of that legislation into force or amends any primary legislation;
'the First Protocol' means the protocol to the Convention agreed at Paris on 20th March 1952;
'the Sixth Protocol' means the protocol to the Convention agreed at Strasbourg on 28th April 1983;
'the Eleventh Protocol' means the protocol to the Convention (restructuring the control machinery established by the Convention) agreed at Strasbourg on 11th May 1994;
'remedial order' means an order under section 10;
'subordinate legislation' means any –
   (a) Order in Council other than one –
      (i) made in exercise of Her Majesty's Royal Prerogative;
      (ii) made under section 38(1)(a) of the Northern Ireland Constitution Act 1973 or the corresponding provision of the Northern Ireland Act 1998; or
      (iii) amending an Act of a kind mentioned in the definition of primary legislation;
   (b) Act of the Scottish Parliament;
   (c) Act of the Parliament of Northern Ireland;

(d) Measure of the Assembly established under section 1 of the Northern Ireland Assembly Act 1973;

(e) Act of the Northern Ireland Assembly;

(f) order, rules, regulations, scheme, warrant, byelaw or other instrument made under primary legislation (except to the extent to which it operates to bring one or more provisions of that legislation into force or amends any primary legislation);

(g) order, rules, regulations, scheme, warrant, byelaw or other instrument made under legislation mentioned in paragraph (b), (c), (d) or (e) or made under an Order in Council applying only to Northern Ireland;

(h) order, rules, regulations, scheme, warrant, byelaw or other instrument made by a member of the Scottish Executive, a Northern Ireland Minister or a Northern Ireland department in exercise of prerogative or other executive functions of Her Majesty which are exercisable by such a person on behalf of Her Majesty;

'transferred matters' has the same meaning as in the Northern Ireland Act 1998; and

'tribunal' means any tribunal in which legal proceedings may be brought.

(2) The references in paragraphs (b) and (c) of section 2(1) to Articles are to Articles of the Convention as they had effect immediately before the coming into force of the Eleventh Protocol.

(3) The reference in paragraph (d) of section 2(1) to Article 46 includes a reference to Articles 32 and 54 of the Convention as they had effect immediately before the coming into force of the Eleventh Protocol.

(4) The references in section 2(1) to a report or decision of the Commission or a decision of the Committee of Ministers include references to a report or decision made as provided by paragraphs 3, 4 and 6 of Article 5 of the Eleventh Protocol (transitional provisions).

(5) Any liability under the Army Act 1955, the Air Force Act 1955 or the Naval Discipline Act 1957 to suffer death for an offence is replaced by a liability to imprisonment for life or any less punishment authorised by those Acts; and those Acts shall accordingly have effect with the necessary modifications.

Short title, commencement, application and extent

22 (1) This Act may be cited as the Human Rights Act 1998.

(2) Sections 18, 20 and 21(5) and this section come into force on the passing of this Act.

(3) The other provisions of this Act come into force on such day as the Secretary of State may by order appoint; and different days may be appointed for different purposes.

(4) Paragraph (b) of subsection (1) of section 7 applies to proceedings brought by or at the instigation of a public authority whenever the act in question took place; but otherwise that subsection does not apply to an act taking place before the coming into force of that section.

(5) This Act binds the Crown.

(6) This Act extends to Northern Ireland.

(7) Section 21(5), so far as it relates to any provision contained in the Army Act 1955, the Air Force Act 1955 or the Naval Discipline Act 1957, extends to any place to which that provision extends.

SCHEDULE 1: THE ARTICLES
PART I: THE CONVENTION: Rights and freedoms
Article 2: Right to life

(1) Everyone's right to life shall be protected by law. No one shall be deprived of his life intentionally save in the execution of a sentence of a court following his conviction of a crime for which this penalty is provided by law.

(2) Deprivation of life shall not be regarded as inflicted in contravention of this Article when it results from the use of force which is no more than absolutely necessary:

   (a) in defence of any person from unlawful violence;
   (b) in order to effect a lawful arrest or to prevent the escape of a person lawfully detained;
   (c) in action lawfully taken for the purpose of quelling a riot or insurrection.

Article 3: Prohibition of torture

No one shall be subjected to torture or to inhuman or degrading treatment or punishment.

Article 4: Prohibition of slavery and forced labour

(1) No one shall be held in slavery or servitude.

(2) No one shall be required to perform forced or compulsory labour.

(3) For the purpose of this Article the term 'forced or compulsory labour' shall not include:

   (a) any work required to be done in the ordinary course of detention imposed according to the provisions of Article 5 of this Convention or during conditional release from such detention;
   (b) any service of a military character or, in case of conscientious objectors in countries where they are recognised, service exacted instead of compulsory military service;
   (c) any service exacted in case of an emergency or calamity threatening the life or well-being of the community;
   (d) any work or service which forms part of normal civic obligations.

Article 5: Right to liberty and security

(1) Everyone has the right to liberty and security of person. No one shall be deprived of his liberty save in the following cases and in accordance with a procedure prescribed by law:

   (a) the lawful detention of a person after conviction by a competent court;
   (b) the lawful arrest or detention of a person for non-compliance with the lawful order of a court or in order to secure the fulfilment of any obligation prescribed by law;
   (c) the lawful arrest or detention of a person effected for the purpose of bringing him before the competent legal authority on reasonable

suspicion of having committed an offence or when it is reasonably considered necessary to prevent his committing an offence or fleeing after having done so;

(d) the detention of a minor by lawful order for the purpose of educational supervision or his lawful detention for the purpose of bringing him before the competent legal authority;

(e) the lawful detention of persons for the prevention of the spreading of infectious diseases, of persons of unsound mind, alcoholics or drug addicts or vagrants;

(f) the lawful arrest or detention of a person to prevent his effecting an unauthorised entry into the country or of a person against whom action is being taken with a view to deportation or extradition.

(2) Everyone who is arrested shall be informed promptly, in a language which he understands, of the reasons for his arrest and of any charge against him.

(3) Everyone arrested or detained in accordance with the provisions of paragraph 1(c) of this Article shall be brought promptly before a judge or other officer authorised by law to exercise judicial power and shall be entitled to trial within a reasonable time or to release pending trial. Release may be conditioned by guarantees to appear for trial.

(4) Everyone who is deprived of his liberty by arrest or detention shall be entitled to take proceedings by which the lawfulness of his detention shall be decided speedily by a court and his release ordered if the detention is not lawful.

(5) Everyone who has been the victim of arrest or detention in contravention of the provisions of this Article shall have an enforceable right to compensation.

Article 6: Right to a fair trial

(1) In the determination of his civil rights and obligations or of any criminal charge against him, everyone is entitled to a fair and public hearing within a reasonable time by an independent and impartial tribunal established by law. Judgment shall be pronounced publicly but the press and public may be excluded from all or part of the trial in the interest of morals, public order or national security in a democratic society, where the interests of juveniles or the protection of the private life of the parties so require, or to the extent strictly necessary in the opinion of the court in special circumstances where publicity would prejudice the interests of justice.

(2) Everyone charged with a criminal offence shall be presumed innocent until proved guilty according to law.

(3) Everyone charged with a criminal offence has the following minimum rights:

(a) to be informed promptly, in a language which he understands and in detail, of the nature and cause of the accusation against him;

(b) to have adequate time and facilities for the preparation of his defence;

(c) to defend himself in person or through legal assistance of his own choosing or, if he has not sufficient means to pay for legal assistance, to be given it free when the interests of justice so require;

(d) to examine or have examined witnesses against him and to obtain the attendance and examination of witnesses on his behalf under the same conditions as witnesses against him;

(e) to have the free assistance of an interpreter if he cannot understand or speak the language used in court.

Article 7: No punishment without law

(1) No one shall be held guilty of any criminal offence on account of any act or omission which did not constitute a criminal offence under national or international law at the time when it was committed. Nor shall a heavier penalty be imposed than the one that was applicable at the time the criminal offence was committed.

(2) This Article shall not prejudice the trial and punishment of any person for any act or omission which, at the time when it was committed, was criminal according to the general principles of law recognised by civilised nations.

Article 8: Right to respect for private and family life

(1) Everyone has the right to respect for his private and family life, his home and his correspondence.

(2) There shall be no interference by a public authority with the exercise of this right except such as is in accordance with the law and is necessary in a democratic society in the interests of national security, public safety or the economic well-being of the country, for the prevention of disorder or crime, for the protection of health or morals, or for the protection of the rights and freedoms of others.

Article 9: Freedom of thought, conscience and religion

(1) Everyone has the right to freedom of thought, conscience and religion; this right includes freedom to change his religion or belief and freedom, either alone or in community with others and in public or private, to manifest his religion or belief, in worship, teaching, practice and observance.

(2) Freedom to manifest one's religion or beliefs shall be subject only to such limitations as are prescribed by law and are necessary in a democratic society in the interests of public safety, for the protection of public order, health or morals, or for the protection of the rights and freedoms of others.

Article 10: Freedom of expression

(1) Everyone has the right to freedom of expression. This right shall include freedom to hold opinions and to receive and impart information and ideas without interference by public authority and regardless of frontiers. This Article shall not prevent States from requiring the licensing of broadcasting, television or cinema enterprises.

(2) The exercise of these freedoms, since it carries with it duties and responsibilities, may be subject to such formalities, conditions, restrictions or penalties as are prescribed by law and are necessary in a democratic society, in the interests of national security, territorial integrity or public safety, for the prevention of disorder or crime, for the protection of health or morals, for the protection of the reputation or rights of others, for preventing the disclosure of information received in confidence, or for maintaining the authority and impartiality of the judiciary.

Article 11: Freedom of assembly and association

(1) Everyone has the right to freedom of peaceful assembly and to freedom of association with others, including the right to form and to join trade unions for the protection of his interests.

(2) No restrictions shall be placed on the exercise of these rights other than such as are prescribed by law and are necessary in a democratic society in the interests of national security or public safety, for the prevention of disorder or crime, for the protection of health or morals or for the protection of the rights and freedoms of others. This Article shall not prevent the imposition of lawful restrictions on the exercise of these rights by members of the armed forces, of the police or of the administration of the State.

Article 12: Right to marry

Men and women of marriageable age have the right to marry and to found a family, according to the national laws governing the exercise of this right.

Article 14: Prohibition of discrimination

The enjoyment of the rights and freedoms set forth in this Convention shall be secured without discrimination on any ground such as sex, race, colour, language, religion, political or other opinion, national or social origin, association with a national minority, property, birth or other status.

Article 16: Restrictions on political activity of aliens

Nothing in Articles 10, 11 and 14 shall be regarded as preventing the High Contracting Parties from imposing restrictions on the political activity of aliens.

Article 17: Prohibition of abuse of rights

Nothing in this Convention may be interpreted as implying for any State, group or person any right to engage in any activity or perform any act aimed at the destruction of any of the rights and freedoms set forth herein or at their limitation to a greater extent than is provided for in the Convention.

Article 18: Limitation on use of restrictions on rights

The restrictions permitted under this Convention to the said rights and freedoms shall not be applied for any purpose other than those for which they have been prescribed.

PART II: THE FIRST PROTOCOL
Article 1: Protection of property

Every natural or legal person is entitled to the peaceful enjoyment of his possessions. No one shall be deprived of his possessions except in the public interest and subject to the conditions provided for by law and by the general principles of international law.

The preceding provisions shall not, however, in any way impair the right of a State to enforce such laws as it deems necessary to control the use of property in accordance with the general interest or to secure the payment of taxes or other contributions or penalties.

Article 2: Right to education

No person shall be denied the right to education. In the exercise of any functions which it assumes in relation to education and to teaching, the State shall respect the right of parents to ensure such education and teaching in conformity with their own religious and philosophical convictions.

Article 3: Right to free elections

The High Contracting Parties undertake to hold free elections at reasonable intervals by secret ballot, under conditions which will ensure the free expression of the opinion of the people in the choice of the legislature.

PART III: THE SIXTH PROTOCOL
Article 1: Abolition of the death penalty

The death penalty shall be abolished. No one shall be condemned to such penalty or executed.

Article 2: Death penalty in time of war

A State may make provision in its law for the death penalty in respect of acts committed in time of war or of imminent threat of war; such penalty shall be applied only in the instances laid down in the law and in accordance with its provisions. The State shall communicate to the Secretary General of the Council of Europe the relevant provisions of that law.

SCHEDULE 2: REMEDIAL ORDERS
Orders

1 (1) A remedial order may –
  (a) contain such incidental, supplemental, consequential or transitional provision as the person making it considers appropriate;
  (b) be made so as to have effect from a date earlier than that on which it is made;
  (c) make provision for the delegation of specific functions;
  (d) make different provision for different cases.

  (2) The power conferred by sub-paragraph (1)(a) includes –
  (a) power to amend primary legislation (including primary legislation other than that which contains the incompatible provision); and
  (b) power to amend or revoke subordinate legislation (including subordinate legislation other than that which contains the incompatible provision).

  (3) A remedial order may be made so as to have the same extent as the legislation which it affects.

  (4) No person is to be guilty of an offence solely as a result of the retrospective effect of a remedial order.

Procedure

2   No remedial order may be made unless –
  (a) a draft of the order has been approved by a resolution of each House of Parliament made after the end of the period of 60 days beginning with the day on which the draft was laid; or

(b) it is declared in the order that it appears to the person making it that, because of the urgency of the matter, it is necessary to make the order without a draft being so approved.

Orders laid in draft

3 (1) No draft may be laid under paragraph 2(a) unless –
  (a) the person proposing to make the order has laid before Parliament a document which contains a draft of the proposed order and the required information; and
  (b) the period of 60 days, beginning with the day on which the document required by this sub-paragraph was laid, has ended.

(2) If representations have been made during that period, the draft laid under paragraph 2(a) must be accompanied by a statement containing –
  (a) a summary of the representations; and
  (b) if, as a result of the representations, the proposed order has been changed, details of the changes.

Urgent cases

4 (1) If a remedial order ('the original order') is made without being approved in draft, the person making it must lay it before Parliament, accompanied by the required information, after it is made.

(2) If representations have been made during the period of 60 days beginning with the day on which the original order was made, the person making it must (after the end of that period) lay before Parliament a statement containing –
  (a) a summary of the representations; and
  (b) if, as a result of the representations, he considers it appropriate to make changes to the original order, details of the changes.

(3) If sub-paragraph (2)(b) applies, the person making the statement must –
  (a) make a further remedial order replacing the original order; and
  (b) lay the replacement order before Parliament.

(4) If, at the end of the period of 120 days beginning with the day on which the original order was made, a resolution has not been passed by each House approving the original or replacement order, the order ceases to have effect (but without that affecting anything previously done under either order or the power to make a fresh remedial order).

Definitions

5 In this Schedule –
'representations' means representations about a remedial order (or proposed remedial order) made to the person making (or proposing to make) it and includes any relevant Parliamentary report or resolution; and
'required information' means –
  (a) an explanation of the incompatibility which the order (or proposed order) seeks to remove, including particulars of the relevant declaration, finding or order; and
  (b) a statement of the reasons for proceeding under section 10 and for making an order in those terms.

Calculating periods

6   In calculating any period for the purposes of this Schedule, no account is to be taken of any time during which –
(a) Parliament is dissolved or prorogued; or
(b) both Houses are adjourned for more than four days.

SCHEDULE 3: DEROGATION AND RESERVATION
PART I: DEROGATION
The 1988 notification

The United Kingdom Permanent Representative to the Council of Europe presents his compliments to the Secretary General of the Council, and has the honour to convey the following information in order to ensure compliance with the obligations of Her Majesty's Government in the United Kingdom under Article 15(3) of the Convention for the Protection of Human Rights and Fundamental Freedoms signed at Rome on 4 November 1950.

There have been in the United Kingdom in recent years campaigns of organised terrorism connected with the affairs of Northern Ireland which have manifested themselves in activities which have included repeated murder, attempted murder, maiming, intimidation and violent civil disturbance and in bombing and fire raising which have resulted in death, injury and widespread destruction of property. As a result, a public emergency within the meaning of Article 15(1) of the Convention exists in the United Kingdom.

The Government found it necessary in 1974 to introduce and since then, in cases concerning persons reasonably suspected of involvement in terrorism connected with the affairs of Northern Ireland, or of certain offences under the legislation, who have been detained for 48 hours, to exercise powers enabling further detention without charge, for periods of up to five days, on the authority of the Secretary of State. These powers are at present to be found in Section 12 of the Prevention of Terrorism (Temporary Provisions) Act 1984, Article 9 of the Prevention of Terrorism (Supplemental Temporary Provisions) Order 1984 and Article 10 of the Prevention of Terrorism (Supplemental Temporary Provisions) (Northern Ireland) Order 1984.

Section 12 of the Prevention of Terrorism (Temporary Provisions) Act 1984 provides for a person whom a constable has arrested on reasonable grounds of suspecting him to be guilty of an offence under Section 1, 9 or 10 of the Act, or to be or to have been involved in terrorism connected with the affairs of Northern Ireland, to be detained in right of the arrest for up to 48 hours and thereafter, where the Secretary of State extends the detention period, for up to a further five days. Section 12 substantially re-enacted Section 12 of the Prevention of Terrorism (Temporary Provisions) Act 1976 which, in turn, substantially re-enacted Section 7 of the Prevention of Terrorism (Temporary Provisions) Act 1974.

Article 10 of the Prevention of Terrorism (Supplemental Temporary Provisions) (Northern Ireland) Order 1984 (SI 1984/417) and Article 9 of the Prevention of Terrorism (Supplemental Temporary Provisions) Order

1984 (SI 1984/418) were both made under Sections 13 and 14 of and Schedule 3 to the 1984 Act and substantially re-enacted powers of detention in Orders made under the 1974 and 1976 Acts. A person who is being examined under Article 4 of either Order on his arrival in, or on seeking to leave, Northern Ireland or Great Britain for the purpose of determining whether he is or has been involved in terrorism connected with the affairs of Northern Ireland, or whether there are grounds for suspecting that he has committed an offence under Section 9 of the 1984 Act, may be detained under Article ·9 or 10, as appropriate, pending the conclusion of his examination. The period of this examination may exceed 12 hours if an examining officer has reasonable grounds for suspecting him to be or to have been involved in acts of terrorism connected with the affairs of Northern Ireland.

Where such a person is detained under the said Article 9 or 10 he may be detained for up to 48 hours on the authority of an examining officer and thereafter, where the Secretary of State extends the detention period, for up to a further five days.

In its judgment of 29 November 1988 in the Case of Brogan and Others, the European Court of Human Rights held that there had been a violation of Article 5(3) in respect of each of the applicants, all of whom had been detained under Section 12 of the 1984 Act. The Court held that even the shortest of the four periods of detention concerned, namely four days and six hours, fell outside the constraints as to time permitted by the first part of Article 5(3). In addition, the Court held that there had been a violation of Article 5(5) in the case of each applicant.

Following this judgment, the Secretary of State for the Home Department informed Parliament on 6 December 1988 that, against the background of the terrorist campaign, and the over-riding need to bring terrorists to justice, the Government did not believe that the maximum period of detention should be reduced. He informed Parliament that the Government were examining the matter with a view to responding to the judgment. On 22 December 1988, the Secretary of State further informed Parliament that it remained the Government's wish, if it could be achieved, to find a judicial process under which extended detention might be reviewed and where appropriate authorised by a judge or other judicial officer. But a further period of reflection and consultation was necessary before the Government could bring forward a firm and final view.

Since the judgment of 29 November 1988 as well as previously, the Government have found it necessary to continue to exercise, in relation to terrorism connected with the affairs of Northern Ireland, the powers described above enabling further detention without charge for periods of up to 5 days, on the authority of the Secretary of State, to the extent strictly required by the exigencies of the situation to enable necessary enquiries and investigations properly to be completed in order to decide whether criminal proceedings should be instituted. To the extent that the exercise of these powers may be inconsistent with the obligations imposed by the Convention the Government has availed itself of the right of derogation conferred by Article 15(1) of the Convention and will continue to do so until further notice.

23 December 1988.

The 1989 notification

The United Kingdom Permanent Representative to the Council of Europe presents his compliments to the Secretary General of the Council, and has the honour to convey the following information.

In his communication to the Secretary General of 23 December 1988, reference was made to the introduction and exercise of certain powers under section 12 of the Prevention of Terrorism (Temporary Provisions) Act 1984, Article 9 of the Prevention of Terrorism (Supplemental Temporary Provisions) Order 1984 and Article 10 of the Prevention of Terrorism (Supplemental Temporary Provisions) (Northern Ireland) Order 1984.

These provisions have been replaced by section 14 of and paragraph 6 of Schedule 5 to the Prevention of Terrorism (Temporary Provisions) Act 1989, which make comparable provision. They came into force on 22 March 1989. A copy of these provisions is enclosed.

The United Kingdom Permanent Representative avails himself of this opportunity to renew to the Secretary General the assurance of his highest consideration.

23 March 1989

PART II: RESERVATION

At the time of signing the present (First) Protocol, I declare that, in view of certain provisions of the Education Acts in the United Kingdom, the principle affirmed in the second sentence of Article 2 is accepted by the United Kingdom only so far as it is compatible with the provision of efficient instruction and training, and the avoidance of unreasonable public expenditure.

20 March 1952

Made by the UK Permanent Representative to the Council of Europe.

SCHEDULE 4: JUDICIAL PENSIONS
Duty to make orders about pensions

1 (1) The appropriate Minister must by order make provision with respect to pensions payable to or in respect of any holder of a judicial office who serves as an ECHR judge.

(2) A pensions order must include such provision as the Minister making it considers is necessary to secure that –

(a) an ECHR judge who was, immediately before his appointment as an ECHR judge, a member of a judicial pension scheme is entitled to remain as a member of that scheme;

(b) the terms on which he remains a member of the scheme are those which would have been applicable had he not been appointed as an ECHR judge; and

(c) entitlement to benefits payable in accordance with the scheme continues to be determined as if, while serving as an ECHR judge, his salary was that which would (but for section 18(4)) have been payable to him in respect of his continuing service as the holder of his judicial office.

Contributions

2   A pensions order may, in particular, make provision –

(a) for any contributions which are payable by a person who remains a member of a scheme as a result of the order, and which would otherwise be payable by deduction from his salary, to be made otherwise than by deduction from his salary as an ECHR judge; and

(b) for such contributions to be collected in such manner as may be determined by the administrators of the scheme.

Amendments of other enactments

3   A pensions order may amend any provision of, or made under, a pensions Act in such manner and to such extent as the Minister making the order considers necessary or expedient to ensure the proper administration of any scheme to which it relates.

Definitions

4   In this Schedule –

'appropriate Minister' means –

(a) in relation to any judicial office whose jurisdiction is exercisable exclusively in relation to Scotland, the Secretary of State; and

(b) otherwise, the Lord Chancellor;

'ECHR judge' means the holder of a judicial office who is serving as a judge of the Court;

'judicial pension scheme' means a scheme established by and in accordance with a pensions Act;

'pensions Act' means –

(a) the County Courts Act Northern Ireland) 1959;

(b) the Sheriffs' Pensions (Scotland) Act 1961;

(c) the Judicial Pensions Act 1981; or

(d) the Judicial Pensions and Retirement Act 1993; and

'pensions order' means an order made under paragraph 1.

European Convention on Human Rights

(relevant extracts)

Article 1[1] – Obligation to respect human rights

The High Contracting Parties shall secure to everyone within their jurisdiction the rights and freedoms defined in Section I of this Convention.

SECTION I – RIGHTS AND FREEDOMS

Article 2[1] – Right to life

(1) Everyone's right to life shall be protected by law. No one shall be deprived of his life intentionally save in the execution of a sentence of a court following his conviction of a crime for which this penalty is provided by law.

(2) Deprivation of life shall not be regarded as inflicted in contravention of this article when it results from the use of force which is no more than absolutely necessary:

a in defence of any person from unlawful violence;

b in order to effect a lawful arrest or to prevent the escape of a person lawfully detained;

c in action lawfully taken for the purpose of quelling a riot or insurrection.

Article 3[1] – Prohibition of torture

No one shall be subjected to torture or to inhuman or degrading treatment or punishment.

Article 4[1] – Prohibition of slavery and forced labour

(1) No one shall be held in slavery or servitude.

(2) No one shall be required to perform forced or compulsory labour.

(3) For the purpose of this article the term 'forced or compulsory labour' shall not include:

a any work required to be done in the ordinary course of detention imposed according to the provisions of Article 5 of this Convention or during conditional release from such detention;

b any service of a military character or, in case of conscientious objectors in countries where they are recognised, service exacted instead of compulsory military service;

c any service exacted in case of an emergency or calamity threatening the life or well-being of the community;

d any work or service which forms part of normal civic obligations.

Article 5[1] – Right to liberty and security

(1) Everyone has the right to liberty and security of person. No one shall be deprived of his liberty save in the following cases and in accordance with a procedure prescribed by law:

   a   the lawful detention of a person after conviction by a competent court;
   b   the lawful arrest or detention of a person for non-compliance with the lawful order of a court or in order to secure the fulfilment of any obligation prescribed by law;
   c   the lawful arrest or detention of a person effected for the purpose of bringing him before the competent legal authority on reasonable suspicion of having committed an offence or when it is reasonably considered necessary to prevent his committing an offence or fleeing after having done so;
   d   the detention of a minor by lawful order for the purpose of educational supervision or his lawful detention for the purpose of bringing him before the competent legal authority;
   e   the lawful detention of persons for the prevention of the spreading of infectious diseases, of persons of unsound mind, alcoholics or drug addicts or vagrants;
   f   the lawful arrest or detention of a person to prevent his effecting an unauthorised entry into the country or of a person against whom action is being taken with a view to deportation or extradition.

(2) Everyone who is arrested shall be informed promptly, in a language which he understands, of the reasons for his arrest and of any charge against him.

(3) Everyone arrested or detained in accordance with the provisions of paragraph 1.c of this article shall be brought promptly before a judge or other officer authorised by law to exercise judicial power and shall be entitled to trial within a reasonable time or to release pending trial. Release may be conditioned by guarantees to appear for trial.

(4) Everyone who is deprived of his liberty by arrest or detention shall be entitled to take proceedings by which the lawfulness of his detention shall be decided speedily by a court and his release ordered if the detention is not lawful.

(5) Everyone who has been the victim of arrest or detention in contravention of the provisions of this article shall have an enforceable right to compensation.

Article 6[1] – Right to a fair trial

(1) In the determination of his civil rights and obligations or of any criminal charge against him, everyone is entitled to a fair and public hearing within a reasonable time by an independent and impartial tribunal established by law. Judgment shall be pronounced publicly but the press and public may be excluded from all or part of the trial in the interests of morals, public order or national security in a democratic society, where the interests of juveniles or the protection of the private life of the parties so require, or to the extent strictly necessary in the opinion of the court in special circumstances where publicity would prejudice the interests of justice.

(2) Everyone charged with a criminal offence shall be presumed innocent until proved guilty according to law.

(3) Everyone charged with a criminal offence has the following minimum rights:
  a to be informed promptly, in a language which he understands and in detail, of the nature and cause of the accusation against him;
  b to have adequate time and facilities for the preparation of his defence;
  c to defend himself in person or through legal assistance of his own choosing or, if he has not sufficient means to pay for legal assistance, to be given it free when the interests of justice so require;
  d to examine or have examined witnesses against him and to obtain the attendance and examination of witnesses on his behalf under the same conditions as witnesses against him;
  e to have the free assistance of an interpreter if he cannot understand or speak the language used in court.

Article 7¹ – No punishment without law

(1) No one shall be held guilty of any criminal offence on account of any act or omission which did not constitute a criminal offence under national or international law at the time when it was committed. Nor shall a heavier penalty be imposed than the one that was applicable at the time the criminal offence was committed.
(2) This article shall not prejudice the trial and punishment of any person for any act or omission which, at the time when it was committed, was criminal according to the general principles of law recognised by civilised nations.

Article 8¹ – Right to respect for private and family life

(1) Everyone has the right to respect for his private and family life, his home and his correspondence.
(2) There shall be no interference by a public authority with the exercise of this right except such as is in accordance with the law and is necessary in a democratic society in the interests of national security, public safety or the economic well-being of the country, for the prevention of disorder or crime, for the protection of health or morals, or for the protection of the rights and freedoms of others.

Article 9¹ – Freedom of thought, conscience and religion

(1) Everyone has the right to freedom of thought, conscience and religion; this right includes freedom to change his religion or belief and freedom, either alone or in community with others and in public or private, to manifest his religion or belief, in worship, teaching, practice and observance.
(2) Freedom to manifest one's religion or beliefs shall be subject only to such limitations as are prescribed by law and are necessary in a democratic society in the interests of public safety, for the protection of public order, health or morals, or for the protection of the rights and freedoms of others.

Article 10¹ – Freedom of expression

(1) Everyone has the right to freedom of expression. This right shall include freedom to hold opinions and to receive and impart information and ideas without interference by public authority and regardless of frontiers. This

article shall not prevent States from requiring the licensing of broadcasting, television or cinema enterprises.

(2) The exercise of these freedoms, since it carries with it duties and responsibilities, may be subject to such formalities, conditions, restrictions or penalties as are prescribed by law and are necessary in a democratic society, in the interests of national security, territorial integrity or public safety, for the prevention of disorder or crime, for the protection of health or morals, for the protection of the reputation or rights of others, for preventing the disclosure of information received in confidence, or for maintaining the authority and impartiality of the judiciary.

Article 11¹ – Freedom of assembly and association

(1) Everyone has the right to freedom of peaceful assembly and to freedom of association with others, including the right to form and to join trade unions for the protection of his interests.

(2) No restrictions shall be placed on the exercise of these rights other than such as are prescribed by law and are necessary in a democratic society in the interests of national security or public safety, for the prevention of disorder or crime, for the protection of health or morals or for the protection of the rights and freedoms of others. This article shall not prevent the imposition of lawful restrictions on the exercise of these rights by members of the armed forces, of the police or of the administration of the State.

Article 12¹ – Right to marry

Men and women of marriageable age have the right to marry and to found a family, according to the national laws governing the exercise of this right.

Article 13¹ – Right to an effective remedy

Everyone whose rights and freedoms as set forth in this Convention are violated shall have an effective remedy before a national authority notwithstanding that the violation has been committed by persons acting in an official capacity.

Article 14¹ – Prohibition of discrimination

The enjoyment of the rights and freedoms set forth in this Convention shall be secured without discrimination on any ground such as sex, race, colour, language, religion, political or other opinion, national or social origin, association with a national minority, property, birth or other status.

Article 15¹ – Derogation in time of emergency

(1) In time of war or other public emergency threatening the life of the nation any High Contracting Party may take measures derogating from its obligations under this Convention to the extent strictly required by the exigencies of the situation, provided that such measures are not inconsistent with its other obligations under international law.

(2) No derogation from Article 2, except in respect of deaths resulting from lawful acts of war, or from Articles 3, 4 (paragraph 1) and 7 shall be made under this provision.

(3) Any High Contracting Party availing itself of this right of derogation shall keep the Secretary General of the Council of Europe fully informed of the measures which it has taken and the reasons therefor. It shall also inform the Secretary General of the Council of Europe when such measures have ceased to operate and the provisions of the Convention are again being fully executed.

Article 16[1] – Restrictions on political activity of aliens

Nothing in Articles 10, 11 and 14 shall be regarded as preventing the High Contracting Parties from imposing restrictions on the political activity of aliens.

Article 17[1] – Prohibition of abuse of rights

Nothing in this Convention may be interpreted as implying for any State, group or person any right to engage in any activity or perform any act aimed at the destruction of any of the rights and freedoms set forth herein or at their limitation to a greater extent than is provided for in the Convention.

Article 18[1] – Limitation on use of restrictions on rights

The restrictions permitted under this Convention to the said rights and freedoms shall not be applied for any purpose other than those for which they have been prescribed.

SECTION II – EUROPEAN COURT OF HUMAN RIGHTS[2]
Article 19 – Establishment of the Court

To ensure the observance of the engagements undertaken by the High Contracting Parties in the Convention and the Protocols thereto, there shall be set up a European Court of Human Rights, hereinafter referred to as 'the Court'. It shall function on a permanent basis.

Article 20 – Number of judges

The Court shall consist of a number of judges equal to that of the High Contracting Parties.

Article 21 – Criteria for office

(1) The judges shall be of high moral character and must either possess the qualifications required for appointment to high judicial office or be jurisconsults of recognised competence.
(2) The judges shall sit on the Court in their individual capacity.
(3) During their term of office the judges shall not engage in any activity which is incompatible with their independence, impartiality or with the demands of a full-time office; all questions arising from the application of this paragraph shall be decided by the Court.

Article 22 – Election of judges

(1) The judges shall be elected by the Parliamentary Assembly with respect to each High Contracting Party by a majority of votes cast from a list of three candidates nominated by the High Contracting Party.

(2) The same procedure shall be followed to complete the Court in the event of the accession of new High Contracting Parties and in filling casual vacancies.

Article 23 – Terms of office

(1) The judges shall be elected for a period of six years. They may be re-elected. However, the terms of office of one-half of the judges elected at the first election shall expire at the end of three years.

(2) The judges whose terms of office are to expire at the end of the initial period of three years shall be chosen by lot by the Secretary General of the Council of Europe immediately after their election.

(3) In order to ensure that, as far as possible, the terms of office of one-half of the judges are renewed every three years, the Parliamentary Assembly may decide, before proceeding to any subsequent election, that the term or terms of office of one or more judges to be elected shall be for a period other than six years but not more than nine and not less than three years.

(4) In cases where more than one term of office is involved and where the Parliamentary Assembly applies the preceding paragraph, the allocation of the terms of office shall be effected by a drawing of lots by the Secretary General of the Council of Europe immediately after the election.

(5) A judge elected to replace a judge whose term of office has not expired shall hold office for the remainder of his predecessor's term.

(6) The terms of office of judges shall expire when they reach the age of 70.

(7) The judges shall hold office until replaced. They shall, however, continue to deal with such cases as they already have under consideration.

Article 24 – Dismissal

No judge may be dismissed from his office unless the other judges decide by a majority of two-thirds that he has ceased to fulfil the required conditions.

Article 25 – Registry and legal secretaries

The Court shall have a registry, the functions and organisation of which shall be laid down in the rules of the Court. The Court shall be assisted by legal secretaries.

Article 26 – Plenary Court

The plenary Court shall:

a   elect its President and one or two Vice-Presidents for a period of three years; they may be re-elected;

b   set up Chambers, constituted for a fixed period of time;

c   elect the Presidents of the Chambers of the Court; they may be re-elected;

d   adopt the rules of the Court, and

e   elect the Registrar and one or more Deputy Registrars.

Article 27 – Committees, Chambers and Grand Chamber

(1) To consider cases brought before it, the Court shall sit in committees of three judges, in Chambers of seven judges and in a Grand Chamber of

seventeen judges. The Court's Chambers shall set up committees for a fixed period of time.

(2) There shall sit as an ex officio member of the Chamber and the Grand Chamber the judge elected in respect of the State Party concerned or, if there is none or if he is unable to sit, a person of its choice who shall sit in the capacity of judge.

(3) The Grand Chamber shall also include the President of the Court, the Vice-Presidents, the Presidents of the Chambers and other judges chosen in accordance with the rules of the Court. When a case is referred to the Grand Chamber under Article 43, no judge from the Chamber which rendered the judgment shall sit in the Grand Chamber, with the exception of the President of the Chamber and the judge who sat in respect of the State Party concerned.

Article 28 – Declarations of inadmissibility by committees

A committee may, by a unanimous vote, declare inadmissible or strike out of its list of cases an application submitted under Article 34 where such a decision can be taken without further examination. The decision shall be final.

Article 29 – Decisions by Chambers on admissibility and merits

(1) If no decision is taken under Article 28, a Chamber shall decide on the admissibility and merits of individual applications submitted under Article 34.

(2) A Chamber shall decide on the admissibility and merits of inter-State applications submitted under Article 33.

(3) The decision on admissibility shall be taken separately unless the Court, in exceptional cases, decides otherwise.

Article 30 – Relinquishment of jurisdiction to the Grand Chamber

Where a case pending before a Chamber raises a serious question affecting the interpretation of the Convention or the protocols thereto, or where the resolution of a question before the Chamber might have a result inconsistent with a judgment previously delivered by the Court, the Chamber may, at any time before it has rendered its judgment, relinquish jurisdiction in favour of the Grand Chamber, unless one of the parties to the case objects.

Article 31 – Powers of the Grand Chamber

The Grand Chamber shall:

a determine applications submitted either under Article 33 or Article 34 when a Chamber has relinquished jurisdiction under Article 30 or when the case has been referred to it under Article 43; and

b consider requests for advisory opinions submitted under Article 47.

Article 32 – Jurisdiction of the Court

(1) The jurisdiction of the Court shall extend to all matters concerning the interpretation and application of the Convention and the protocols thereto which are referred to it as provided in Articles 33, 34 and 47.

(2) In the event of dispute as to whether the Court has jurisdiction, the Court shall decide.

Article 33 – Inter-State cases

Any High Contracting Party may refer to the Court any alleged breach of the provisions of the Convention and the protocols thereto by another High Contracting Party.

Article 34 – Individual applications

The Court may receive applications from any person, non-governmental organisation or group of individuals claiming to be the victim of a violation by one of the High Contracting Parties of the rights set forth in the Convention or the protocols thereto. The High Contracting Parties undertake not to hinder in any way the effective exercise of this right.

Article 35 – Admissibility criteria

(1) The Court may only deal with the matter after all domestic remedies have been exhausted, according to the generally recognised rules of international law, and within a period of six months from the date on which the final decision was taken.

(2) The Court shall not deal with any application submitted under Article 34 that:
   a   is anonymous; or
   b   is substantially the same as a matter that has already been examined by the Court or has already been submitted to another procedure of international investigation or settlement and contains no relevant new information.

(3) The Court shall declare inadmissible any individual application submitted under Article 34 which it considers incompatible with the provisions of the Convention or the protocols thereto, manifestly ill-founded, or an abuse of the right of application.

(4) The Court shall reject any application which it considers inadmissible under this Article. It may do so at any stage of the proceedings.

Article 36 – Third party intervention

(1) In all cases before a Chamber of the Grand Chamber, a High Contracting Party one of whose nationals is an applicant shall have the right to submit written comments and to take part in hearings.

(2) The President of the Court may, in the interest of the proper administration of justice, invite any High Contracting Party which is not a party to the proceedings or any person concerned who is not the applicant to submit written comments or take part in hearings.

Article 37 – Striking out applications

(1) The Court may at any stage of the proceedings decide to strike an application out of its list of cases where the circumstances lead to the conclusion that
   a   the applicant does not intend to pursue his application; or
   b   the matter has been resolved; or

c   for any other reason established by the Court, it is no longer justified to continue the examination of the application.

However, the Court shall continue the examination of the application if respect for human rights as defined in the Convention and the protocols thereto so requires.

(2) The Court may decide to restore an application to its list of cases if it considers that the circumstances justify such a course.

Article 38 – Examination of the case and friendly settlement proceedings

(1) If the Court declares the application admissible, it shall:

a   pursue the examination of the case, together with the representatives of the parties, and if need be, undertake an investigation, for the effective conduct of which the States concerned shall furnish all necessary facilities;

b   place itself at the disposal of the parties concerned with a view to securing a friendly settlement of the matter on the basis of respect for human rights as defined in the Convention and the protocols thereto.

(2) Proceedings conducted under paragraph 1.b shall be confidential.

Article 39 – Finding of a friendly settlement

If a friendly settlement is effected, the Court shall strike the case out of its list by means of a decision which shall be confined to a brief statement of the facts and of the solution reached.

Article 40 – Public hearings and access to documents

(1) Hearings shall be in public unless the Court in exceptional circumstances decides otherwise.

(2) Documents deposited with the Registrar shall be accessible to the public unless the President of the Court decides otherwise.

Article 41 – Just satisfaction

If the Court finds that there has been a violation of the Convention or the protocols thereto, and if the internal law of the High Contracting Party concerned allows only partial reparation to be made, the Court shall, if necessary, afford just satisfaction to the injured party.

Article 42 – Judgments of Chambers

Judgments of Chambers shall become final in accordance with the provisions of Article 44, paragraph 2.

Article 43 – Referral to the Grand Chamber

(1) Within a period of three months from the date of the judgment of the Chamber, any party to the case may, in exceptional cases, request that the case be referred to the Grand Chamber.

(2) A panel of five judges of the Grand Chamber shall accept the request if the case raises a serious question affecting the interpretation or application of the Convention or the protocols thereto, or a serious issue of general importance.

(3) If the panel accepts the request, the Grand Chamber shall decide the case by means of a judgment.

Article 44 – Final judgments

(1) The judgment of the Grand Chamber shall be final.
(2) The judgment of a Chamber shall become final:
   a   when the parties declare that they will not request that the case be referred to the Grand Chamber; or
   b   three months after the date of the judgment, if reference of the case to the Grand Chamber has not been requested; or
   c   when the panel of the Grand Chamber rejects the request to refer under Article 43.
(3) The final judgment shall be published.

Article 45 – Reasons for judgments and decisions

(1) Reasons shall be given for judgments as well as for decisions declaring applications admissible or inadmissible.
(2) If a judgment does not represent, in whole or in part, the unanimous opinion of the judges, any judge shall be entitled to deliver a separate opinion.

Article 46 – Binding force and execution of judgments

(1) The High Contracting Parties undertake to abide by the final judgment of the Court in any case to which they are parties.
(2) The final judgment of the Court shall be transmitted to the Committee of Ministers, which shall supervise its execution.

Article 47 – Advisory opinions

(1) The Court may, at the request of the Committee of Ministers, give advisory opinions on legal questions concerning the interpretation of the Convention and the protocols thereto.
(2) Such opinions shall not deal with any question relating to the content or scope of the rights or freedoms defined in Section I of the Convention and the protocols thereto, or with any other question which the Court or the Committee of Ministers might have to consider in consequence of any such proceedings as could be instituted in accordance with the Convention.
(3) Decisions of the Committee of Ministers to request an advisory opinion of the Court shall require a majority vote of the representatives entitled to sit on the Committee.

Article 48 – Advisory jurisdiction of the Court

The Court shall decide whether a request for an advisory opinion submitted by the Committee of Ministers is within its competence as defined in Article 47.

Article 49 – Reasons for advisory opinions

(1) Reasons shall be given for advisory opinions of the Court.
(2) If the advisory opinion does not represent, in whole or in part, the unanimous opinion of the judges, any judge shall be entitled to deliver a separate opinion.

(3) Advisory opinions of the Court shall be communicated to the Committee of Ministers.

Article 50 – Expenditure on the Court
The expenditure on the Court shall be borne by the Council of Europe.

Article 51 – Privileges and immunities of judges
The judges shall be entitled, during the exercise of their functions, to the privileges and immunities provided for in Article 40 of the Statute of the Council of Europe and in the agreements made thereunder.

SECTION III – MISCELLANEOUS PROVISIONS[3,1]

Article 52[1] – Inquiries by the Secretary General
On receipt of a request from the Secretary General of the Council of Europe any High Contracting Party shall furnish an explanation of the manner in which its internal law ensures the effective implementation of any of the provisions of the Convention.

Article 53[1] – Safeguard for existing human rights
Nothing in this Convention shall be construed as limiting or derogating from any of the human rights and fundamental freedoms which may be ensured under the laws of any High Contracting Party or under any other agreement to which it is a Party.

Article 54[1] – Powers of the Committee of Ministers
Nothing in this Convention shall prejudice the powers conferred on the Committee of Ministers by the Statute of the Council of Europe.

Article 55[1] – Exclusion of other means of dispute settlement
The High Contracting Parties agree that, except by special agreement, they will not avail themselves of treaties, conventions or declarations in force between them for the purpose of submitting, by way of petition, a dispute arising out of the interpretation or application of this Convention to a means of settlement other than those provided for in this Convention.

Article 56[1] – Territorial application
(1)[4] Any State may at the time of its ratification or at any time thereafter declare by notification addressed to the Secretary General of the Council of Europe that the present Convention shall, subject to paragraph 4 of this Article, extend to all or any of the territories for whose international relations it is responsible.

(2) The Convention shall extend to the territory or territories named in the notification as from the thirtieth day after the receipt of this notification by the Secretary General of the Council of Europe.

(3) The provisions of this Convention shall be applied in such territories with due regard, however, to local requirements.

(4)[4] Any State which has made a declaration in accordance with paragraph 1 of this article may at any time thereafter declare on behalf of one or more of the territories to which the declaration relates that it accepts the competence of the Court to receive applications from individuals, non-governmental organisations or groups of individuals as provided by Article 34 of the Convention.

Article 57¹ – Reservations

(1) Any State may, when signing this Convention or when depositing its instrument of ratification, make a reservation in respect of any particular provision of the Convention to the extent that any law then in force in its territory is not in conformity with the provision. Reservations of a general character shall not be permitted under this article.

(2) Any reservation made under this article shall contain a brief statement of the law concerned.

Article 58¹ – Denunciation

(1) A High Contracting Party may denounce the present Convention only after the expiry of five years from the date on which it became a party to it and after six months' notice contained in a notification addressed to the Secretary General of the Council of Europe, who shall inform the other High Contracting Parties.

(2) Such a denunciation shall not have the effect of releasing the High Contracting Party concerned from its obligations under this Convention in respect of any act which, being capable of constituting a violation of such obligations, may have been performed by it before the date at which the denunciation became effective.

(3) Any High Contracting Party which shall cease to be a member of the Council of Europe shall cease to be a Party to this Convention under the same conditions.

(4)⁴ The Convention may be denounced in accordance with the provisions of the preceding paragraphs in respect of any territory to which it has been declared to extend under the terms of Article 56.

Article 59¹ – Signature and ratification

(1) This Convention shall be open to the signature of the members of the Council of Europe. It shall be ratified. Ratifications shall be deposited with the Secretary General of the Council of Europe.

(2) The present Convention shall come into force after the deposit of ten instruments of ratification.

(3) As regards any signatory ratifying subsequently, the Convention shall come into force at the date of the deposit of its instrument of ratification.

(4) The Secretary General of the Council of Europe shall notify all the members of the Council of Europe of the entry into force of the Convention, the names of the High Contracting Parties who have ratified it, and the deposit of all instruments of ratification which may be effected subsequently.

1   Heading added according to the provisions of Protocol No 11 (ETS No 155).
2   New Section II according to the provisions of Protocol No 11 (ETS No 155).
3   The articles of this Section are renumbered according to the provisions of Protocol No 11 (ETS No 155).
4   Text amended according to the provisions of Protocol No 11 (ETS No 155).

PROTOCOL TO THE CONVENTION FOR THE PROTECTION OF HUMAN RIGHTS AND FUNDAMENTAL FREEDOMS, AS AMENDED BY PROTOCOL NO 11

Article 1 – Protection of property

Every natural or legal person is entitled to the peaceful enjoyment of his possessions. No one shall be deprived of his possessions except in the public interest and subject to the conditions provided for by law and by the general principles of international law.

The preceding provisions shall not, however, in any way impair the right of a State to enforce such laws as it deems necessary to control the use of property in accordance with the general interest or to secure the payment of taxes or other contributions or penalties.

Article 2 – Right to education

No person shall be denied the right to education. In the exercise of any functions which it assumes in relation to education and to teaching, the State shall respect the right of parents to ensure such education and teaching in conformity with their own religious and philosophical convictions.

Article 3 – Right to free elections

The High Contracting Parties undertake to hold free elections at reasonable intervals by secret ballot, under conditions which will ensure the free expression of the opinion of the people in the choice of the legislature.

Article 4[1] – Territorial application

Any High Contracting Party may at the time of signature or ratification or at any time thereafter communicate to the Secretary General of the Council of Europe a declaration stating the extent to which it undertakes that the provisions of the present Protocol shall apply to such of the territories for the international relations of which it is responsible as are named therein.

Any High Contracting Party which has communicated a declaration in virtue of the preceding paragraph may from time to time communicate a further declaration modifying the terms of any former declaration or terminating the application of the provisions of this Protocol in respect of any territory.

A declaration made in accordance with this article shall be deemed to have been made in accordance with paragraph 1 of Article 56 of the Convention.

Article 5 – Relationship to the Convention

As between the High Contracting Parties the provisions of Articles 1, 2, 3 and 4 of this Protocol shall be regarded as additional articles to the Convention and all the provisions of the Convention shall apply accordingly.

Article 6 – Signature and ratification

This Protocol shall be open for signature by the members of the Council of Europe, who are the signatories of the Convention; it shall be ratified at the same time as or after the ratification of the Convention. It shall enter into force after the deposit of ten instruments of ratification. As regards any signatory ratifying subsequently, the Protocol shall enter into force at the date of the deposit of its instrument of ratification.

The instruments of ratification shall be deposited with the Secretary General of the Council of Europe, who will notify all members of the names of those who have ratified.

Done at Paris on the 20th day of March 1952, in English and French, both texts being equally authentic, in a single copy which shall remain deposited in the archives of the Council of Europe. The Secretary General shall transmit certified copies to each of the signatory governments.

1   Text amended according to the provisions of Protocol No. 11 (ETS No. 155).

PROTOCOL NO 6 TO THE CONVENTION FOR THE PROTECTION OF HUMAN RIGHTS AND FUNDAMENTAL FREEDOMS CONCERNING THE ABOLITION OF THE DEATH PENALTY, AS AMENDED BY PROTOCOL NO.11

Article 1 – Abolition of the death penalty

The death penalty shall be abolished. No-one shall be condemned to such penalty or executed.

Article 2 – Death penalty in time of war

A State may make provision in its law for the death penalty in respect of acts committed in time of war or of imminent threat of war; such penalty shall be applied only in the instances laid down in the law and in accordance with its provisions. The State shall communicate to the Secretary General of the Council of Europe the relevant provisions of that law.

Article 3 – Prohibition of derogations

No derogation from the provisions of this Protocol shall be made under Article 15 of the Convention.

Article 4¹ – Prohibition of reservations

No reservation may be made under Article 57 of the Convention in respect of the provisions of this Protocol.

Article 5 – Territorial application

(1) Any State may at the time of signature or when depositing its instrument of ratification, acceptance or approval, specify the territory or territories to which this Protocol shall apply.

(2) Any State may at any later date, by a declaration addressed to the Secretary General of the Council of Europe, extend the application of this Protocol to any other territory specified in the declaration. In respect of such territory the Protocol shall enter into force on the first day of the month following

the date of receipt of such declaration by the Secretary General.

(3) Any declaration made under the two preceding paragraphs may, in respect of any territory specified in such declaration, be withdrawn by a notification addressed to the Secretary General. The withdrawal shall become effective on the first day of the month following the date of receipt of such notification by the Secretary General.

Article 6 – Relationship to the Convention

As between the States Parties the provisions of Articles 1 to 5 of this Protocol shall be regarded as additional articles to the Convention and all the provisions of the Convention shall apply accordingly.

Article 7 – Signature and ratification

The Protocol shall be open for signature by the member States of the Council of Europe, signatories to the Convention. It shall be subject to ratification, acceptance or approval. A member State of the Council of Europe may not ratify, accept or approve this Protocol unless it has, simultaneously or previously, ratified the Convention. Instruments of ratification, acceptance or approval shall be deposited with the Secretary General of the Council of Europe.

Article 8 – Entry into force

(1) This Protocol shall enter into force on the first day of the month following the date on which five member States of the Council of Europe have expressed their consent to be bound by the Protocol in accordance with the provisions of Article 7.

(2) In respect of any member State which subsequently expresses its consent to be bound by it, the Protocol shall enter into force on the first day of the month following the date of the deposit of the instrument of ratification, acceptance or approval.

Article 9 – Depositary functions

The Secretary General of the Council of Europe shall notify the member States of the Council of:

a any signature;
b the deposit of any instrument of ratification, acceptance or approval;
c any date of entry into force of this Protocol in accordance with Articles 5 and 8;
d any other act, notification or communication relating to this Protocol.

1 Text amended according to the provisions of Protocol No 11 (ETS No 155).

Universal Declaration of Human Rights
(relevant extracts)

Article 1
All human beings are born free and equal in dignity and rights. They are endowed with reason and conscience and should act towards one another in a spirit of brotherhood.

Article 2
Everyone is entitled to all the rights and freedoms set forth in this Declaration, without distinction of any kind, such as race, colour, sex, language, religion, political or other opinion, national or social origin, property, birth or other status.

Furthermore, no distinction shall be made on the basis of the political, jurisdictional or international status of the country or territory to which a person belongs, whether it be independent, trust, non-self-governing or under any other limitation of sovereignty.

Article 3
Everyone has the right to life, liberty and security of person.

Article 4
No one shall be held in slavery or servitude; slavery and the slave trade shall be prohibited in all their forms.

Article 5
No one shall be subjected to torture or to cruel, inhuman or degrading treatment or punishment.

Article 6
Everyone has the right to recognition everywhere as a person before the law.

Article 7
All are equal before the law and are entitled without any discrimination to equal protection of the law. All are entitled to equal protection against any discrimination in violation of this Declaration and against any incitement to such discrimination.

Article 8
Everyone has the right to an effective remedy by the competent national tribunals for acts violating the fundamental rights granted him by the constitution or by law.

Article 9
No one shall be subjected to arbitrary arrest, detention or exile.

Article 10
Everyone is entitled in full equality to a fair and public hearing by an independent and impartial tribunal, in the determination of his rights and obligations and of any criminal charge against him.

Article 11
Everyone charged with a penal offence has the right to be presumed innocent until proved guilty according to law in a public trial at which he has had all the guarantees necessary for his defence.

No one shall be held guilty of any penal offence on account of any act or omission which did not constitute a penal offence, under national or international law, at the time when it was committed. Nor shall a heavier penalty be imposed than the one that was applicable at the time the penal offence was committed.

Article 12
No one shall be subjected to arbitrary interference with his privacy, family, home or correspondence, nor to attacks upon his honour and reputation. Everyone has the right to the protection of the law against such interference or attacks.

Article 13
Everyone has the right to freedom of movement and residence within the borders of each State. Everyone has the right to leave any country, including his own, and to return to his country.

Article 14
Everyone has the right to seek and to enjoy in other countries asylum from persecution. This right may not be invoked in the case of prosecutions genuinely arising from non-political crimes or from acts contrary to the purposes and principles of the United Nations.

Article 15
Everyone has the right to a nationality. No one shall be arbitrarily deprived of his nationality nor denied the right to change his nationality.

Article 16
Men and women of full age, without any limitation due to race, nationality or religion, have the right to marry and to found a family. They are entitled to equal rights as to marriage, during marriage and at its dissolution.

Marriage shall be entered into only with the free and full consent of the intending spouses. The family is the natural and fundamental group unit of society and is entitled to protection by society and the State.

Article 17
Everyone has the right to own property alone as well as in association with others. No one shall be arbitrarily deprived of his property.

Article 18

Everyone has the right to freedom of thought, conscience and religion; this right includes freedom to change his religion or belief, and freedom, either alone or in community with others and in public or private, to manifest his religion or belief in teaching, practice, worship and observance.

Article 19

Everyone has the right to freedom of opinion and expression; this right includes freedom to hold opinions without interference and to seek, receive and impart information and ideas through any media and regardless of frontiers.

Article 20

Everyone has the right to freedom of peaceful assembly and association. No one may be compelled to belong to an association.

Article 21

Everyone has the right to take part in the government of his country, directly or through freely chosen representatives.

Everyone has the right to equal access to public service in his country. The will of the people shall be the basis of the authority of government; this will shall be expressed in periodic and genuine elections which shall be by universal and equal suffrage and shall be held by secret vote or by equivalent free voting procedures.

Article 22

Everyone, as a member of society, has the right to social security and is entitled to realization, through national effort and international co-operation and in accordance with the organization and resources of each State, of the economic, social and cultural rights indispensable for his dignity and the free development of his personality.

Article 23

Everyone has the right to work, to free choice of employment, to just and favourable conditions of work and to protection against unemployment. Everyone, without any discrimination, has the right to equal pay for equal work.

Everyone who works has the right to just and favourable remuneration ensuring for himself and his family an existence worthy of human dignity, and supplemented, if necessary, by other means of social protection. Everyone has the right to form and to join trade unions for the protection of his interests.

Article 24

Everyone has the right to rest and leisure, including reasonable limitation of working hours and periodic holidays with pay.

Article 25

Everyone has the right to a standard of living adequate for the health and well-being of himself and of his family, including food, clothing, housing and medical care and necessary social services, and the right to security in the event of unemployment, sickness, disability, widowhood, old age or other lack of livelihood in circumstances beyond his control. Motherhood and childhood are entitled to special care and assistance. All children, whether born in or out of wedlock, shall enjoy the same social protection.

Article 26

Everyone has the right to education. Education shall be free, at least in the elementary and fundamental stages. Elementary education shall be compulsory. Technical and professional education shall be made generally available and higher education shall be equally accessible to all on the basis of merit.

Education shall be directed to the full development of the human personality and to the strengthening of respect for human rights and fundamental freedoms. It shall promote understanding, tolerance and friendship among all nations, racial or religious groups, and shall further the activities of the United Nations for the maintenance of peace.

Parents have a prior right to choose the kind of education that shall be given to their children.

Article 27

Everyone has the right freely to participate in the cultural life of the community, to enjoy the arts and to share in scientific advancement and its benefits.

Everyone has the right to the protection of the moral and material interests resulting from any scientific, literary or artistic production of which he is the author.

Article 28

Everyone is entitled to a social and international order in which the rights and freedoms set forth in this Declaration can be fully realized.

Article 29

Everyone has duties to the community in which alone the free and full development of his personality is possible. In the exercise of his rights and freedoms, everyone shall be subject only to such limitations as are determined by law solely for the purpose of securing due recognition and respect for the rights and freedoms of others and of meeting the just requirements of morality, public order and the general welfare in a democratic society. These rights and freedoms may in no case be exercised contrary to the purposes and principles of the United Nations.

Article 30

Nothing in this Declaration may be interpreted as implying for any State, group or person any right to engage in any activity or to perform any act aimed at the destruction of any of the rights and freedoms set forth herein.

International Covenant on Civil and Political Rights
(relevant extracts)

PART I
Article 1

(1) All peoples have the right of self-determination. By virtue of that right they freely determine their political status and freely pursue their economic, social and cultural development.

(2) All peoples may, for their own ends, freely dispose of their natural wealth and resources without prejudice to any obligations arising out of international economic co-operation, based upon the principle of mutual benefit, and international law. In no case may a people be deprived of its own means of subsistence.

(3) The States Parties to the present Covenant, including those having responsibility for the administration of Non-Self-Governing and Trust Territories, shall promote the realization of the right of self-determination, and shall respect that right, in conformity with the provisions of the Charter of the United Nations.

PART II
Article 2

(1) Each State Party to the present Covenant undertakes to respect and to ensure to all individuals within its territory and subject to its jurisdiction the rights recognized in the present Covenant, without distinction of any kind, such as race, colour, sex, language, religion, political or other opinion, national or social origin, property, birth or other status.

(2) Where not already provided for by existing legislative or other measures, each State Party to the present Covenant undertakes to take the necessary steps, in accordance with its constitutional processes and with the provisions of the present Covenant, to adopt such laws or other measures as may be necessary to give effect to the rights recognized in the present Covenant.

(3) Each State Party to the present Covenant undertakes:

  (a) To ensure that any person whose rights or freedoms as herein recognized are violated shall have an effective remedy, notwithstanding that the violation has been committed by persons acting in an official capacity;

  (b) To ensure that any person claiming such a remedy shall have his right thereto determined by competent judicial, administrative or legislative authorities, or by any other competent authority provided for by the legal system of the State, and to develop the possibilities of judicial remedy;

(c) To ensure that the competent authorities shall enforce such remedies when granted.

Article 3

The States Parties to the present Covenant undertake to ensure the equal right of men and women to the enjoyment of all civil and political rights set forth in the present Covenant.

Article 4

(1) In time of public emergency which threatens the life of the nation and the existence of which is officially proclaimed, the States Parties to the present Covenant may take measures derogating from their obligations under the present Covenant to the extent strictly required by the exigencies of the situation, provided that such measures are not inconsistent with their other obligations under international law and do not involve discrimination solely on the ground of race, colour, sex, language, religion or social origin.

(2) No derogation from articles 6, 7, 8 (paragraphs 1 and 2), 11, 15, 16 and 18 may be made under this provision.

(3) Any State Party to the present Covenant availing itself of the right of derogation shall immediately inform the other States Parties to the present Covenant, through the intermediary of the Secretary-General of the United Nations, of the provisions from which it has derogated and of the reasons by which it was actuated. A further communication shall be made, through the same intermediary, on the date on which it terminates such derogation.

Article 5

(1) Nothing in the present Covenant may be interpreted as implying for any State, group or person any right to engage in any activity or perform any act aimed at the destruction of any of the rights and freedoms recognized herein or at their limitation to a greater extent than is provided for in the present Covenant.

(2) There shall be no restriction upon or derogation from any of the fundamental human rights recognized or existing in any State Party to the present Covenant pursuant to law, conventions, regulations or custom on the pretext that the present Covenant does not recognize such rights or that it recognizes them to a lesser extent.

PART III
Article 6

(1) Every human being has the inherent right to life. This right shall be protected by law. No one shall be arbitrarily deprived of his life.

(2) In countries which have not abolished the death penalty, sentence of death may be imposed only for the most serious crimes in accordance with the law in force at the time of the commission of the crime and not contrary to the provisions of the present Covenant and to the Convention on the Prevention

and Punishment of the Crime of Genocide. This penalty can only be carried out pursuant to a final judgement rendered by a competent court.

(3) When deprivation of life constitutes the crime of genocide, it is understood that nothing in this article shall authorize any State Party to the present Covenant to derogate in any way from any obligation assumed under the provisions of the Convention on the Prevention and Punishment of the Crime of Genocide.

(4) Anyone sentenced to death shall have the right to seek pardon or commutation of the sentence. Amnesty, pardon or commutation of the sentence of death may be granted in all cases.

(5) Sentence of death shall not be imposed for crimes committed by persons below eighteen years of age and shall not be carried out on pregnant women.

(6) Nothing in this article shall be invoked to delay or to prevent the abolition of capital punishment by any State Party to the present Covenant.

Article 7

No one shall be subjected to torture or to cruel, inhuman or degrading treatment or punishment. In particular, no one shall be subjected without his free consent to medical or scientific experimentation.

Article 8

(1) No one shall be held in slavery; slavery and the slave-trade in all their forms shall be prohibited.

(2) No one shall be held in servitude.

(3) (a) No one shall be required to perform forced or compulsory labour;

(b) Paragraph 3 (a) shall not be held to preclude, in countries where imprisonment with hard labour may be imposed as a punishment for a crime, the performance of hard labour in pursuance of a sentence to such punishment by a competent court;

(c) For the purpose of this paragraph the term 'forced or compulsory labour' shall not include:

(i) Any work or service, not referred to in subparagraph (b), normally required of a person who is under detention in consequence of a lawful order of a court, or of a person during conditional release from such detention;

(ii) Any service of a military character and, in countries where conscientious objection is recognized, any national service required by law of conscientious objectors;

(iii) Any service exacted in cases of emergency or calamity threatening the life or well-being of the community;

(iv) Any work or service which forms part of normal civil obligations.

Article 9

(1) Everyone has the right to liberty and security of person. No one shall be subjected to arbitrary arrest or detention. No one shall be deprived of his liberty except on such grounds and in accordance with such procedure as are established by law.

(2) Anyone who is arrested shall be informed, at the time of arrest, of the

reasons for his arrest and shall be promptly informed of any charges against him.

(3) Anyone arrested or detained on a criminal charge shall be brought promptly before a judge or other officer authorized by law to exercise judicial power and shall be entitled to trial within a reasonable time or to release. It shall not be the general rule that persons awaiting trial shall be detained in custody, but release may be subject to guarantees to appear for trial, at any other stage of the judicial proceedings, and, should occasion arise, for execution of the judgement.

(4) Anyone who is deprived of his liberty by arrest or detention shall be entitled to take proceedings before a court, in order that court may decide without delay on the lawfulness of his detention and order his release if the detention is not lawful.

(5) Anyone who has been the victim of unlawful arrest or detention shall have an enforceable right to compensation.

Article 10

(1) All persons deprived of their liberty shall be treated with humanity and with respect for the inherent dignity of the human person.

(2) (a) Accused persons shall, save in exceptional circumstances, be segregated from convicted persons and shall be subject to separate treatment appropriate to their status as unconvicted persons;
(b) Accused juvenile persons shall be separated from adults and brought as speedily as possible for adjudication. 3. The penitentiary system shall comprise treatment of prisoners the essential aim of which shall be their reformation and social rehabilitation. Juvenile offenders shall be segregated from adults and be accorded treatment appropriate to their age and legal status.

Article 11

No one shall be imprisoned merely on the ground of inability to fulfil a contractual obligation.

Article 12

(1) Everyone lawfully within the territory of a State shall, within that territory, have the right to liberty of movement and freedom to choose his residence.

(2) Everyone shall be free to leave any country, including his own.

(3) The above-mentioned rights shall not be subject to any restrictions except those which are provided by law, are necessary to protect national security, public order (ordre public), public health or morals or the rights and freedoms of others, and are consistent with the other rights recognized in the present Covenant.

(4) No one shall be arbitrarily deprived of the right to enter his own country.

Article 13

An alien lawfully in the territory of a State Party to the present Covenant may be expelled therefrom only in pursuance of a decision reached in accordance with law and shall, except where compelling reasons of national security otherwise require, be allowed to submit the reasons against his expulsion and to have his case reviewed by, and be represented for the purpose before, the competent authority or a person or persons especially designated by the competent authority.

Article 14

(1) All persons shall be equal before the courts and tribunals. In the determination of any criminal charge against him, or of his rights and obligations in a suit at law, everyone shall be entitled to a fair and public hearing by a competent, independent and impartial tribunal established by law. The press and the public may be excluded from all or part of a trial for reasons of morals, public order (ordre public) or national security in a democratic society, or when the interest of the private lives of the parties so requires, or to the extent strictly necessary in the opinion of the court in special circumstances where publicity would prejudice the interests of justice; but any judgement rendered in a criminal case or in a suit at law shall be made public except where the interest of juvenile persons otherwise requires or the proceedings concern matrimonial disputes or the guardianship of children.

(2) Everyone charged with a criminal offence shall have the right to be presumed innocent until proved guilty according to law.

(3) In the determination of any criminal charge against him, everyone shall be entitled to the following minimum guarantees, in full equality:

(a) To be informed promptly and in detail in a language which he understands of the nature and cause of the charge against him;

(b) To have adequate time and facilities for the preparation of his defence and to communicate with counsel of his own choosing;

(c) To be tried without undue delay;

(d) To be tried in his presence, and to defend himself in person or through legal assistance of his own choosing; to be informed, if he does not have legal assistance, of this right; and to have legal assistance assigned to him, in any case where the interests of justice so require, and without payment by him in any such case if he does not have sufficient means to pay for it;

(e) To examine, or have examined, the witnesses against him and to obtain the attendance and examination of witnesses on his behalf under the same conditions as witnesses against him;

(f) To have the free assistance of an interpreter if he cannot understand or speak the language used in court;

(g) Not to be compelled to testify against himself or to confess guilt.

(4) In the case of juvenile persons, the procedure shall be such as will take account of their age and the desirability of promoting their rehabilitation.

(5) Everyone convicted of a crime shall have the right to his conviction and sentence being reviewed by a higher tribunal according to law.

(6) When a person has by a final decision been convicted of a criminal offence and when subsequently his conviction has been reversed or he has been pardoned on the ground that a new or newly discovered fact shows conclusively that there has been a miscarriage of justice, the person who has suffered punishment as a result of such conviction shall be

compensated according to law, unless it is proved that the non-disclosure of the unknown fact in time is wholly or partly attributable to him.

(7) No one shall be liable to be tried or punished again for an offence for which he has already been finally convicted or acquitted in accordance with the law and penal procedure of each country.

Article 15

(1) No one shall be held guilty of any criminal offence on account of any act or omission which did not constitute a criminal offence, under national or international law, at the time when it was committed. Nor shall a heavier penalty be imposed than the one that was applicable at the time when the criminal offence was committed. If, subsequent to the commission of the offence, provision is made by law for the imposition of the lighter penalty, the offender shall benefit thereby.

(2) Nothing in this article shall prejudice the trial and punishment of any person for any act or omission which, at the time when it was committed, was criminal according to the general principles of law recognized by the community of nations.

Article 16

Everyone shall have the right to recognition everywhere as a person before the law.

Article 17

(1) No one shall be subjected to arbitrary or unlawful interference with his privacy, family, home or correspondence, nor to unlawful attacks on his honour and reputation.

(2) Everyone has the right to the protection of the law against such interference or attacks.

Article 18

(1) Everyone shall have the right to freedom of thought, conscience and religion. This right shall include freedom to have or to adopt a religion or belief of his choice, and freedom, either individually or in community with others and in public or private, to manifest his religion or belief in worship, observance, practice and teaching.

(2) No one shall be subject to coercion which would impair his freedom to have or to adopt a religion or belief of his choice.

(3) Freedom to manifest one's religion or beliefs may be subject only to such limitations as are prescribed by law and are necessary to protect public safety, order, health, or morals or the fundamental rights and freedoms of others.

(4) The States Parties to the present Covenant undertake to have respect for the liberty of parents and, when applicable, legal guardians to ensure the religious and moral education of their children in conformity with their own convictions.

Article 19

(1) Everyone shall have the right to hold opinions without interference.

(2) Everyone shall have the right to freedom of expression; this right shall include freedom to seek, receive and impart information and ideas of all kinds, regardless of frontiers, either orally, in writing or in print, in the form of art, or through any other media of his choice.

(3) The exercise of the rights provided for in paragraph 2 of this article carries with it special duties and responsibilities. It may therefore be subject to certain restrictions, but these shall only be such as are provided by law and are necessary:

    (a) For respect of the rights or reputations of others;

    (b) For the protection of national security or of public order (ordre public), or of public health or morals.

Article 20

(1) Any propaganda for war shall be prohibited by law.

(2) Any advocacy of national, racial or religious hatred that constitutes incitement to discrimination, hostility or violence shall be prohibited by law.

Article 21

The right of peaceful assembly shall be recognized. No restrictions may be placed on the exercise of this right other than those imposed in conformity with the law and which are necessary in a democratic society in the interests of national security or public safety, public order (ordre public), the protection of public health or morals or the protection of the rights and freedoms of others.

Article 22

(1) Everyone shall have the right to freedom of association with others, including the right to form and join trade unions for the protection of his interests.

(2) No restrictions may be placed on the exercise of this right other than those which are prescribed by law and which are necessary in a democratic society in the interests of national security or public safety, public order (ordre public), the protection of public health or morals or the protection of the rights and freedoms of others. This article shall not prevent the imposition of lawful restrictions on members of the armed forces and of the police in their exercise of this right.

(3) Nothing in this article shall authorize States Parties to the International Labour Organisation Convention of 1948 concerning Freedom of Association and Protection of the Right to Organize to take legislative measures which would prejudice, or to apply the law in such a manner as to prejudice, the guarantees provided for in that Convention.

Article 23

(1) The family is the natural and fundamental group unit of society and is entitled to protection by society and the State.

(2) The right of men and women of marriageable age to marry and to found a family shall be recognized.

(3) No marriage shall be entered into without the free and full consent of the intending spouses.

(4) States Parties to the present Covenant shall take appropriate steps to ensure equality of rights and responsibilities of spouses as to marriage, during marriage and at its dissolution. In the case of dissolution, provision shall be made for the necessary protection of any children.

Article 24

(1) Every child shall have, without any discrimination as to race, colour, sex, language, religion, national or social origin, property or birth, the right to such measures of protection as are required by his status as a minor, on the part of his family, society and the State.

(2) Every child shall be registered immediately after birth and shall have a name.

(3) Every child has the right to acquire a nationality.

Article 25

Every citizen shall have the right and the opportunity, without any of the distinctions mentioned in article 2 and without unreasonable restrictions:

(a) To take part in the conduct of public affairs, directly or through freely chosen representatives;

(b) To vote and to be elected at genuine periodic elections which shall be by universal and equal suffrage and shall be held by secret ballot, guaranteeing the free expression of the will of the electors;

(c) To have access, on general terms of equality, to public service in his country.

Article 26

All persons are equal before the law and are entitled without any discrimination to the equal protection of the law. In this respect, the law shall prohibit any discrimination and guarantee to all persons equal and effective protection against discrimination on any ground such as race, colour, sex, language, religion, political or other opinion, national or social origin, property, birth or other status.

Article 27

In those States in which ethnic, religious or linguistic minorities exist, persons belonging to such minorities shall not be denied the right, in community with the other members of their group, to enjoy their own culture, to profess and practise their own religion, or to use their own language.

UN Convention on the elimination of all forms of racial discrimination
(relevant extracts)

PART I
Article 1

(1) In this Convention, the term 'racial discrimination' shall mean any distinction, exclusion, restriction or preference based on race, colour, descent, or national or ethnic origin which has the purpose or effect of nullifying or impairing the recognition, enjoyment or exercise, on an equal footing, of human rights and fundamental freedoms in the political, economic, social, cultural or any other field of public life.

(2) This Convention shall not apply to distinctions, exclusions, restrictions or preferences made by a State Party to this Convention between citizens and non-citizens.

(3) Nothing in this Convention may be interpreted as affecting in any way the legal provisions of States Parties concerning nationality, citizenship or naturalization, provided that such provisions do not discriminate against any particular nationality.

(4) Special measures taken for the sole purpose of securing adequate advancement of certain racial or ethnic groups or individuals requiring such protection as may be necessary in order to ensure such groups or individuals equal enjoyment or exercise of human rights and fundamental freedoms shall not be deemed racial discrimination, provided, however, that such measures do not, as a consequence, lead to the maintenance of separate rights for different racial groups and that they shall not be continued after the objectives for which they were taken have been achieved.

Article 2

(1) States Parties condemn racial discrimination and undertake to pursue by all appropriate means and without delay a policy of eliminating racial discrimination in all its forms and promoting understanding among all races, and, to this end:

(a) Each State Party undertakes to engage in no act or practice of racial discrimination against persons, groups of persons or institutions and to ensure that all public authorities and public institutions, national and local, shall act in conformity with this obligation;

(b) Each State Party undertakes not to sponsor, defend or support racial discrimination by any persons or organizations;

(c) Each State Party shall take effective measures to review governmental, national and local policies, and to amend, rescind or nullify any laws and regulations which have the effect of creating or perpetuating racial discrimination wherever it exists;

(d) Each State Party shall prohibit and bring to an end, by all appropriate means, including legislation as required by circumstances, racial discrimination by any persons, group or organization;

(e) Each State Party undertakes to encourage, where appropriate, integrationist multiracial organizations and movements and other means of eliminating barriers between races, and to discourage anything which tends to strengthen racial division.

(2) States Parties shall, when the circumstances so warrant, take, in the social, economic, cultural and other fields, special and concrete measures to ensure the adequate development and protection of certain racial groups or individuals belonging to them, for the purpose of guaranteeing them the full and equal enjoyment of human rights and fundamental freedoms. These measures shall in no case entail as a con sequence the maintenance of unequal or separate rights for different racial groups after the objectives for which they were taken have been achieved.

Article 3

States Parties particularly condemn racial segregation and apartheid and undertake to prevent, prohibit and eradicate all practices of this nature in territories under their jurisdiction.

Article 4

States Parties condemn all propaganda and all organizations which are based on ideas or theories of superiority of one race or group of persons of one colour or ethnic origin, or which attempt to justify or promote racial hatred and discrimination in any form, and undertake to adopt immediate and positive measures designed to eradicate all incitement to, or acts of, such discrimination and, to this end, with due regard to the principles embodied in the Universal Declaration of Human Rights and the rights expressly set forth in article 5 of this Convention, inter alia:

(a) Shall declare an offence punishable by law all dissemination of ideas based on racial superiority or hatred, incitement to racial discrimination, as well as all acts of violence or incitement to such acts against any race or group of persons of another colour or ethnic origin, and also the provision of any assistance to racist activities, including the financing thereof;

(b) Shall declare illegal and prohibit organizations, and also organized and all other propaganda activities, which promote and incite racial discrimination, and shall recognize participation in such organizations or activities as an offence punishable by law;

(c) Shall not permit public authorities or public institutions, national or local, to promote or incite racial discrimination.

Article 5

In compliance with the fundamental obligations laid down in article 2 of this Convention, States Parties undertake to prohibit and to eliminate racial discrimination in all its forms and to guarantee the right of everyone, without distinction as to race, colour, or national or ethnic origin, to equality before the law, notably in the enjoyment of the following rights:

(a) The right to equal treatment before the tribunals and all other organs administering justice;

(b) The right to security of person and protection by the State against violence or bodily harm, whether inflicted by government officials or by any individual group or institution;

(c) Political rights, in particular the right to participate in elections-to vote and to stand for election-on the basis of universal and equal suffrage, to take part in the Government as well as in the conduct of public affairs at any level and to have equal access to public service;

(d) Other civil rights, in particular:
   (i) The right to freedom of movement and residence within the border of the State;
   (ii) The right to leave any country, including one's own, and to return to one's country;
   (iii) The right to nationality;
   (iv) The right to marriage and choice of spouse;
   (v) The right to own property alone as well as in association with others;
   (vi) The right to inherit;
   (vii) The right to freedom of thought, conscience and religion;
   (viii) The right to freedom of opinion and expression;
   (ix) The right to freedom of peaceful assembly and association;

(e) Economic, social and cultural rights, in particular:
   (i) The rights to work, to free choice of employment, to just and favourable conditions of work, to protection against unemployment, to equal pay for equal work, to just and favourable remuneration;
   (ii) The right to form and join trade unions;
   (iii) The right to housing;
   (iv) The right to public health, medical care, social security and social services;
   (v) The right to education and training;
   (vi) The right to equal participation in cultural activities;

(f) The right of access to any place or service intended for use by the general public, such as transport hotels, restaurants, cafes, theatres and parks.

Article 6

States Parties shall assure to everyone within their jurisdiction effective protection and remedies, through the competent national tribunals and other State institutions, against any acts of racial discrimination which violate his human rights and fundamental freedoms contrary to this Convention, as well as the right to seek from such tribunals just and adequate reparation or satisfaction for any damage suffered as a result of such discrimination.

Article 7

States Parties undertake to adopt immediate and effective measures, particularly in the fields of teaching, education, culture and information, with a view to combating prejudices which lead to racial discrimination and to promoting understanding, tolerance and friendship among nations and racial or ethnical groups, as well as to propagating the purposes and principles of the Charter of the United Nations, the Universal Declaration of Human Rights, the United Nations Declaration on the Elimination of All Forms of Racial Discrimination, and this Convention.

UN Convention on the elimination of all forms of discrimination against women

(relevant extracts)

PART I
Article 1

For the purposes of the present Convention, the term 'discrimination against women' shall mean any distinction, exclusion or restriction made on the basis of sex which has the effect or purpose of impairing or nullifying the recognition, enjoyment or exercise by women, irrespective of their marital status, on a basis of equality of men and women, of human rights and fundamental freedoms in the political, economic, social, cultural, civil or any other field.

Article 2

States Parties condemn discrimination against women in all its forms, agree to pursue by all appropriate means and without delay a policy of eliminating discrimination against women and, to this end, undertake:

To embody the principle of the equality of men and women in their national constitutions or other appropriate legislation if not yet incorporated therein and to ensure, through law and other appropriate means, the practical realization of this principle;

To adopt appropriate legislative and other measures, including sanctions where appropriate, prohibiting all discrimination against women;

To establish legal protection of the rights of women on an equal basis with men and to ensure through competent national tribunals and other public institutions the effective protection of women against any act of discrimination;

To refrain from engaging in any act or practice of discrimination against women and to ensure that public authorities and institutions shall act in conformity with this obligation;

To take all appropriate measures to eliminate discrimination against women by any person, organization or enterprise;

To take all appropriate measures, including legislation, to modify or abolish existing laws, regulations, customs and practices which constitute discrimination against women;

To repeal all national penal provisions which constitute discrimination against women.

Article 3

States Parties shall take in all fields, in particular in the political, social, economic and cultural fields, all appropriate measures, including legislation, to ensure the full development and advancement of women , for the purpose of guaranteeing them the exercise and enjoyment of human rights and fundamental freedoms on a basis of equality with men.

Article 4

Adoption by States Parties of temporary special measures aimed at accelerating de facto equality between men and women shall not be considered discrimination as defined in the present Convention, but shall in no way entail as a consequence the maintenance of unequal or separate standards; these measures shall be discontinued when the objectives of equality of opportunity and treatment have been achieved.

Adoption by States Parties of special measures, including those measures contained in the present Convention, aimed at protecting maternity shall not be considered discriminatory.

Article 5

States Parties shall take all appropriate measures:

To modify the social and cultural patterns of conduct of men and women, with a view to achieving the elimination of prejudices and customary and all other practices which are based on the idea of the inferiority or the superiority of either of the sexes or on stereotyped roles for men and women;

To ensure that family education includes a proper understanding of maternity as a social function and the recognition of the common responsibility of men and women in the upbringing and development of their children, it being understood that the interest of the children is the primordial consideration in all cases.

Article 6

States Parties shall take all appropriate measures, including legislation, to suppress all forms of traffic in women and exploitation of prostitution of women.

PART II
Article 7

States Parties shall take all appropriate measures to eliminate discrimination against women in the political and public life of the country and, in particular, shall ensure to women, on equal terms with men, the right:

To vote in all elections and public referenda and to be eligible for election to all publicly elected bodies;

To participate in the formulation of government policy and the implementation thereof and to hold public office and perform all public functions at all levels of government;

To participate in non-governmental organizations and associations concerned with the public and political life of the country.

Article 8
States Parties shall take all appropriate measures to ensure to women, on equal terms with men and without any discrimination, the opportunity to represent their Governments at the international level and to participate in the work of international organizations.

Article 9
States Parties shall grant women equal rights with men to acquire, change or retain their nationality. They shall ensure in particular that neither marriage to an alien nor change of nationality by the husband during marriage shall automatically change the nationality of the wife, render her stateless or force upon her the nationality of the husband.

States Parties shall grant women equal rights with men with respect to the nationality of their children.

PART III
Article 10
States Parties shall take all appropriate measures to eliminate discrimination against women in order to ensure to them equal rights with men in the field of education and in particular to ensure, on a basis of equality of men and women:

The same conditions for career and vocational guidance, for access to studies and for the achievement of diplomas in educational establishments of all categories in rural as well as in urban areas; this equality shall be ensured in pre-school, general, technical, professional and higher technical education, as well as in all types of vocational training;

Access to the same curricula, the same examinations, teaching staff with qualifications of the same standard and school premises and equipment of the same quality

The elimination of any stereotyped concept of the roles of men and women at all levels and in all forms of education by encouraging coeducation and other types of education which will help to achieve this aim and, in particular, by the revision of textbooks and school programmes and the adaptation of teaching methods;

The same opportunities t0 benefit from scholarships and other study grants;

The same opportunities for access to programmes of continuing education, including adult and functional literacy programmes, particularly those aimed at reducing, at the earliest possible time, any gap in education existing between men and women;

The reduction of female student drop-out rates and the organization of programmes for girls and women who have left school prematurely;

The same Opportunities to participate actively in sports and physical education;

Access to specific educational information to help to ensure the health and well-being of families, including information and advice on family planning.

Article 11
States Parties shall take all appropriate measures to eliminate discrimination against women in the field of employment in order to ensure, on a basis of equality of men and women, the same rights, in particular:

The right to work as an inalienable right of all human beings;

The right to the same employment opportunities, including the application of the same criteria for selection in matters of employment;

The right to free choice of profession and employment, the right to promotion, job security and all benefits and conditions of service and the right to receive vocational training and retraining, including apprenticeships, advanced vocational training and recurrent training;

The right to equal remuneration, including benefits, and to equal treatment in respect of work of equal value, as well as equality of treatment in the evaluation of the quality of work;

The right to social security, particularly in cases of retirement, unemployment, sickness, invalidity and old age and other incapacity to work, as well as the right to paid leave;

The right to protection of health and to safety in working conditions, including the safeguarding of the function of reproduction.

In order to prevent discrimination against women on the grounds of marriage or maternity and to ensure their effective right to work, States Parties shall take appropriate measures:

To prohibit, subject to the imposition of sanctions, dismissal on the grounds of pregnancy or of maternity leave and discrimination in dismissals on the basis of marital status;

To introduce maternity leave with pay or with comparable social benefits without loss of former employment, seniority or social allowances;

To encourage the provision of the necessary supporting social services to enable parents to combine family obligations with work responsibilities and participation in public life, in particular through promoting the establishment and development of a network of child-care facilities;

To provide special protection to women during pregnancy in types of work proved to be harmful to them.

Protective legislation relating to matters covered in this article shall be reviewed periodically in the light of scientific and technological knowledge and shall be revised, repealed or extended as necessary.

Article 12
States Parties shall take all appropriate measures to eliminate discrimination against women in the field of health care in order to ensure, on a basis of equality of men and women, access to health care services,

including those related to family planning.

Notwithstanding the provisions of paragraph I of this article, States Parties shall ensure to women appropriate services in connection with pregnancy, confinement and the post-natal period, granting free services where necessary, as well as adequate nutrition during pregnancy and lactation.

Article 13

States Parties shall take all appropriate measures to eliminate discrimination against women in other areas of economic and social life in order to ensure, on a basis of equality of men and women, the same rights, in particular:

The right to family benefits;

The right to bank loans, mortgages and other forms of financial credit;

The right to participate in recreational activities, sports and all aspects of cultural life.

Article 14

States Parties shall take into account the particular problems faced by rural women and the significant roles which rural women play in the economic survival of their families, including their work in the non-monetized sectors of the economy, and shall take all appropriate measures to ensure the application of the provisions of the present Convention to women in rural areas.

States Parties shall take all appropriate measures to eliminate discrimination against women in rural areas in order to ensure, on a basis of equality of men and women, that they participate in and benefit from rural development and, in particular, shall ensure to such women the right:

To participate in the elaboration and implementation of development planning at all levels;

To have access to adequate health care facilities, including information, counselling and services in family planning;

To benefit directly from social security programmes;

To obtain all types of training and education, formal and non-formal, including that relating to functional literacy, as well as, inter alia, the benefit of all community and extension services, in order to increase their technical proficiency;

To organize self-help groups and co-operatives in order to obtain equal access to economic opportunities through employment or self employment;

To participate in all community activities;

To have access to agricultural credit and loans, marketing facilities, appropriate technology and equal treatment in land and agrarian reform as well as in land resettlement schemes;

To enjoy adequate living conditions, particularly in relation to housing, sanitation, electricity and water supply, transport and communications.

PART IV
Article 15
States Parties shall accord to women equality with men before the law.
States Parties shall accord to women, in civil matters, a legal capacity identical to that of men and the same opportunities to exercise that capacity. In particular, they shall give women equal rights to conclude contracts and to administer property and shall treat them equally in all stages of procedure in courts and tribunals.

States Parties agree that all contracts and all other private instruments of any kind with a legal effect which is directed at restricting the legal capacity of women shall be deemed null and void.

States Parties shall accord to men and women the same rights with regard to the law relating to the movement of persons and the freedom to choose their residence and domicile.

Article 16
(1) States Parties shall take all appropriate measures to eliminate discrimination against women in all matters relating to marriage and family relations and in particular shall ensure, on a basis of equality of men and women:

The same right to enter into marriage;

The same right freely to choose a spouse and to enter into marriage only with their free and full consent;

The same rights and responsibilities during marriage and at its dissolution;

The same rights and responsibilities as parents, irrespective of their marital status, in matters relating to their children; in all cases the interests of the children shall be paramount;

The same rights to decide freely and responsibly on the number and spacing of their children and to have access to the information, education and means to enable them to exercise these rights;

The same rights and responsibilities with regard to guardianship, wardship, trusteeship and adoption of children, or similar institutions where these concepts exist in national legislation; in all cases the interests of the children shall be paramount;

The same personal rights as husband and wife, including the right to choose a family name, a profession and an occupation;

The same rights for both spouses in respect of the ownership, acquisition, management, administration, enjoyment and disposition of property, whether free of charge or for a valuable consideration.

(2) The betrothal and the marriage of a child shall have no legal effect, and all necessary action, including legislation, shall be taken to specify a minimum age for marriage and to make the registration of marriages in an official registry compulsory.

UN Convention on the rights of the child
(relevant extracts)

PART I
Article 1
For the purposes of the present Convention, a child means every human being below the age of eighteen years unless under the law applicable to the child, majority is attained earlier.

Article 2
(1) States Parties shall respect and ensure the rights set forth in the present Convention to each child within their jurisdiction without discrimination of any kind, irrespective of the child's or his or her parent's or legal guardian's race, colour, sex, language, religion, political or other opinion, national, ethnic or social origin, property, disability, birth or other status.

(2) States Parties shall take all appropriate measures to ensure that the child is protected against all forms of discrimination or punishment on the basis of the status, activities, expressed opinions, or beliefs of the child's parents, legal guardians, or family members.

Article 3
(1) In all actions concerning children, whether undertaken by public or private social welfare institutions, courts of law, administrative authorities or legislative bodies, the best interests of the child shall be a primary consideration.

(2) States Parties undertake to ensure the child such protection and care as is necessary for his or her well-being, taking into account the rights and duties of his or her parents, legal guardians, or other individuals legally responsible for him or her, and, to this end, shall take all appropriate legislative and administrative measures.

(3) States Parties shall ensure that the institutions, services and facilities responsible for the care or protection of children shall conform with the standards established by competent authorities, particularly in the areas of safety, health, in the number and suitability of their staff, as well as competent supervision.

Article 4
States Parties shall undertake all appropriate legislative, administrative, and other measures for the implementation of the rights recognized in the present Convention. With regard to economic, social and cultural rights, 779

States Parties shall undertake such measures to the maximum extent of their available resources and, where needed, within the framework of international co-operation.

Article 5

States Parties shall respect the responsibilities, rights and duties of parents or, where applicable, the members of the extended family or community as provided for by local custom, legal guardians or other persons legally responsible for the child, to provide, in a manner consistent with the evolving capacities of the child, appropriate direction and guidance in the exercise by the child of the rights recognized in the present Convention.

Article 6

(1) States Parties recognize that every child has the inherent right to life.
(2) States Parties shall ensure to the maximum extent possible the survival and development of the child.

Article 7

(1) The child shall be registered immediately after birth and shall have the right from birth to a name, the right to acquire a nationality and. as far as possible, the right to know and be cared for by his or her parents.
(2) States Parties shall ensure the implementation of these rights in accordance with their national law and their obligations under the relevant international instruments in this field, in particular where the child would otherwise be stateless.

Article 8

(1) States Parties undertake to respect the right of the child to preserve his or her identity, including nationality, name and family relations as recognized by law without unlawful interference.
(2) Where a child is illegally deprived of some or all of the elements of his or her identity, States Parties shall provide appropriate assistance and protection, with a view to re-establishing speedily his or her identity.

Article 9

(1) States Parties shall ensure that a child shall not be separated from his or her parents against their will, except when competent authorities subject to judicial review determine, in accordance with applicable law and procedures, that such separation is necessary for the best interests of the child. Such determination may be necessary in a particular case such as one involving abuse or neglect of the child by the parents, or one where the parents are living separately and a decision must be made as to the child's place of residence.
(2) In any proceedings pursuant to paragraph 1 of the present article, all interested parties shall be given an opportunity to participate in the proceedings and make their views known.
(3) States Parties shall respect the right of the child who is separated from one or both parents to maintain personal relations and direct contact with both parents on a regular basis, except if it is contrary to the child's best interests.

(4) Where such separation results from any action initiated by a State Party, such as the detention, imprisonment, exile, deportation or death (including death arising from any cause while the person is in the custody of the State) of one or both parents or of the child, that State Party shall, upon request, provide the parents, the child or, if appropriate, another member of the family with the essential information concerning the whereabouts of the absent member(s) of the family unless the provision of the information would be detrimental to the well-being of the child. States Parties shall further ensure that the submission of such a request shall of itself entail no adverse consequences for the person(s) concerned.

Article 10

(1) In accordance with the obligation of States Parties under article 9, paragraph 1, applications by a child or his or her parents to enter or leave a State Party for the purpose of family reunification shall be dealt with by States Parties in a positive, humane and expeditious manner. States Parties shall further ensure that the submission of such a request shall entail no adverse consequences for the applicants and for the members of their family.

(2) A child whose parents reside in different States shall have the right to maintain on a regular basis, save in exceptional circumstances personal relations and direct contacts with both parents. Towards that end and in accordance with the obligation of States Parties under article 9, paragraph 1, States Parties shall respect the right of the child and his or her parents to leave any country, including their own, and to enter their own country. The right to leave any country shall be subject only to such restrictions as are prescribed by law and which are necessary to protect the national security, public order (ordre public), public health or morals or the rights and freedoms of others and are consistent with the other rights recognized in the present Convention.

Article 11

(1) States Parties shall take measures to combat the illicit transfer and non-return of children abroad.

(2) To this end, States Parties shall promote the conclusion of bilateral or multilateral agreements or accession to existing agreements.

Article 12

(1) States Parties shall assure to the child who is capable of forming his or her own views the right to express those views freely in all matters affecting the child, the views of the child being given due weight in accordance with the age and maturity of the child.

(2) For this purpose, the child shall in particular be provided the opportunity to be heard in any judicial and administrative proceedings affecting the child, either directly, or through a representative or an appropriate body, in a manner consistent with the procedural rules of national law.

Article 13

(1) The child shall have the right to freedom of expression; this right shall include freedom to seek, receive and impart information and ideas of all

kinds, regardless of frontiers, either orally, in writing or in print, in the form of art, or through any other media of the child's choice.

(2) The exercise of this right may be subject to certain restrictions, but these shall only be such as are provided by law and are necessary:
  (a) For respect of the rights or reputations of others; or
  (b) For the protection of national security or of public order (ordre public), or of public health or morals.

Article 14

(1) States Parties shall respect the right of the child to freedom of thought, conscience and religion.

(2) States Parties shall respect the rights and duties of the parents and, when applicable, legal guardians, to provide direction to the child in the exercise of his or her right in a manner consistent with the evolving capacities of the child.

(3) Freedom to manifest one's religion or beliefs may be subject only to such limitations as are prescribed by law and are necessary to protect public safety, order, health or morals, or the fundamental rights and freedoms of others.

Article 15

(1) States Parties recognize the rights of the child to freedom of association and to freedom of peaceful assembly.

(2) No restrictions may be placed on the exercise of these rights other than those imposed in conformity with the law and which are necessary in a democratic society in the interests of national security or public safety, public order (ordre public), the protection of public health or morals or the protection of the rights and freedoms of others.

Article 16

(1) No child shall be subjected to arbitrary or unlawful interference with his or her privacy, family, home or correspondence, nor to unlawful attacks on his or her honour and reputation.

(2) The child has the right to the protection of the law against such interference or attacks.

Article 17

States Parties recognize the important function performed by the mass media and shall ensure that the child has access to information and material from a diversity of national and international sources, especially those aimed at the promotion of his or her social, spiritual and moral well-being and physical and mental health. To this end, States Parties shall:
  (a) Encourage the mass media to disseminate information and material of social and cultural benefit to the child and in accordance with the spirit of article 29;
  (b) Encourage international co-operation in the production, exchange and dissemination of such information and material from a diversity of cultural, national and international sources;
  (c) Encourage the production and dissemination of children's books;
  (d) Encourage the mass media to have particular regard to the linguistic

needs of the child who belongs to a minority group or who is indigenous;

(e) Encourage the development of appropriate guidelines for the protection of the child from information and material injurious to his or her well-being, bearing in mind the provisions of articles 13 and 18.

Article 18

(1) States Parties shall use their best efforts to ensure recognition of the principle that both parents have common responsibilities for the upbringing and development of the child. Parents or, as the case may be, legal guardians, have the primary responsibility for the upbringing and development of the child. The best interests of the child will be their basic concern.

(2) For the purpose of guaranteeing and promoting the rights set forth in the present Convention, States Parties shall render appropriate assistance to parents and legal guardians in the performance of their child-rearing responsibilities and shall ensure the development of institutions, facilities and services for the care of children.

(3) States Parties shall take all appropriate measures to ensure that children of working parents have the right to benefit from child-care services and facilities for which they are eligible.

Article 19

(1) States Parties shall take all appropriate legislative, administrative, social and educational measures to protect the child from all forms of physical or mental violence, injury or abuse, neglect or negligent treatment, maltreatment or exploitation, including sexual abuse, while in the care of parent(s), legal guardian(s) or any other person who has the care of the child.

(2) Such protective measures should, as appropriate, include effective procedures for the establishment of social programmes to provide necessary support for the child and for those who have the care of the child, as well as for other forms of prevention and for identification, reporting, referral, investigation, treatment and follow-up of instances of child maltreatment described heretofore, and, as appropriate, for judicial involvement.

Article 20

(1) A child temporarily or permanently deprived of his or her family environment, or in whose own best interests cannot be allowed to remain in that environment, shall be entitled to special protection and assistance provided by the State.

(2) States Parties shall in accordance with their national laws ensure alternative care for such a child.

(3) Such care could include, inter alia, foster placement, kafalah of Islamic law, adoption or if necessary placement in suitable institutions for the care of children. When considering solutions, due regard shall be paid to the desirability of continuity in a child's upbringing and to the child's ethnic, religious, cultural and linguistic background.

Article 21

States Parties that recognize and/or permit the system of adoption shall ensure that the best interests of the child shall be the paramount consideration and they shall:

(a) Ensure that the adoption of a child is authorized only by competent authorities who determine, in accordance with applicable law and procedures and on the basis of all pertinent and reliable information, that the adoption is permissible in view of the child's status concerning parents, relatives and legal guardians and that, if required, the persons concerned have given their informed consent to the adoption on the basis of such counselling as may be necessary;

(b) Recognize that inter-country adoption may be considered as an alternative means of child's care, if the child cannot be placed in a foster or an adoptive family or cannot in any suitable manner be cared for in the child's country of origin;

(c) Ensure that the child concerned by inter-country adoption enjoys safeguards and standards equivalent to those existing in the case of national adoption;

(d) Take all appropriate measures to ensure that, in inter-country adoption, the placement does not result in improper financial gain for those involved in it;

(e) Promote, where appropriate, the objectives of the present article by concluding bilateral or multilateral arrangements or agreements, and endeavour, within this framework, to ensure that the placement of the child in another country is carried out by competent authorities or organs.

Article 22

(1) States Parties shall take appropriate measures to ensure that a child who is seeking refugee status or who is considered a refugee in accordance with applicable international or domestic law and procedures shall, whether unaccompanied or accompanied by his or her parents or by any other person, receive appropriate protection and humanitarian assistance in the enjoyment of applicable rights set forth in the present Convention and in other international human rights or humanitarian instruments to which the said States are Parties.

(2) For this purpose, States Parties shall provide, as they consider appropriate, co-operation in any efforts by the United Nations and other competent intergovernmental organizations or non-governmental organizations co-operating with the United Nations to protect and assist such a child and to trace the parents or other members of the family of any refugee child in order to obtain information necessary for reunification with his or her family. In cases where no parents or other members of the family can be found, the child shall be accorded the same protection as any other child permanently or temporarily deprived of his or her family environment for any reason , as set forth in the present Convention.

Article 23

(1) States Parties recognize that a mentally or physically disabled child should enjoy a full and decent life, in conditions which ensure dignity, promote self-reliance and facilitate the child's active participation in the community.

(2) States Parties recognize the right of the disabled child to special care and shall encourage and ensure the extension, subject to available resources, to the eligible child and those responsible for his or her care, of assistance for which application is made and which is appropriate to the child's condition and to the circumstances of the parents or others caring for the child.

(3) Recognizing the special needs of a disabled child, assistance extended in accordance with paragraph 2 of the present article shall be provided free of charge, whenever possible, taking into account the financial resources of the parents or others caring for the child, and shall be designed to ensure that the disabled child has effective access to and receives education, training, health care services, rehabilitation services, preparation for employment and recreation opportunities in a manner conducive to the child's achieving the fullest possible social integration and individual development, including his or her cultural and spiritual development

(4) States Parties shall promote, in the spirit of international co-operation, the exchange of appropriate information in the field of preventive health care and of medical, psychological and functional treatment of disabled children, including dissemination of and access to information concerning methods of rehabilitation, education and vocational services, with the aim of enabling States Parties to improve their capabilities and skills and to widen their experience in these areas. In this regard, particular account shall be taken of the needs of developing countries.

Article 24

(1) States Parties recognize the right of the child to the enjoyment of the highest attainable standard of health and to facilities for the treatment of illness and rehabilitation of health. States Parties shall strive to ensure that no child is deprived of his or her right of access to such health care services.

(2) States Parties shall pursue full implementation of this right and, in particular, shall take appropriate measures:

(a) To diminish infant and child mortality;

(b) To ensure the provision of necessary medical assistance and health care to all children with emphasis on the development of primary health care;

(c) To combat disease and malnutrition, including within the framework of primary health care, through, inter alia, the application of readily available technology and through the provision of adequate nutritious foods and clean drinking-water, taking into consideration the dangers and risks of environmental pollution;

(d) To ensure appropriate pre-natal and post-natal health care for mothers;

(e) To ensure that all segments of society, in particular parents and children, are informed, have access to education and are supported in the use of basic knowledge of child health and nutrition, the advantages of breast feeding, hygiene and environmental sanitation and the prevention of accidents;

(f) To develop preventive health care, guidance for parents and family planning education and services.

(3) States Parties shall take all effective and appropriate measures with a view to abolishing traditional practices prejudicial to the health of children.

(4) States Parties undertake to promote and encourage international co-operation with a view to achieving progressively the full realization of the right recognized in the present article. In this regard, particular account shall be taken of the needs of developing countries.

Article 25

States Parties recognize the right of a child who has been placed by the competent authorities for the purposes of care, protection or treatment of his or her physical or mental health, to a periodic review of the treatment provided to the child and all other circumstances relevant to his or her placement.

Article 26

(1) States Parties shall recognize for every child the right to benefit from social security, including social insurance, and shall take the necessary measures to achieve the full realization of this right in accordance with their national law.

(2) The benefits should, where appropriate, be granted, taking into account the resources and the circumstances of the child and persons having responsibility for the maintenance of the child, as well as any other consideration relevant to an application for benefits made by or on behalf of the child.

Article 27

(1) States Parties recognize the right of every child to a standard of living adequate for the child's physical, mental, spiritual, moral and social development.

(2) The parent(s) or others responsible for the child have the primary responsibility to secure, within their abilities and financial capacities, the conditions of living necessary for the child's development.

(3) States Parties, in accordance with national conditions and within their means, shall take appropriate measures to assist parents and others responsible for the child to implement this right and shall in case of need provide material assistance and support programmes, particularly with regard to nutrition, clothing and housing.

(4) States Parties shall take all appropriate measures to secure the recovery of maintenance for the child from the parents or other persons having financial responsibility for the child, both within the State Party and from abroad. In particular, where the person having financial responsibility for the child lives in a State different from that of the child, States Parties shall promote the accession to international agreements or the conclusion of such agreements, as well as the making of other appropriate arrangements.

Article 28

(1) States Parties recognize the right of the child to education, and with a view to achieving this right progressively and on the basis of equal opportunity, they shall, in particular:

(a) Make primary education compulsory and available free to all;
(b) Encourage the development of different forms of secondary education, including general and vocational education, make them available and accessible to every child, and take appropriate measures such as the introduction of free education and offering financial assistance in case of need;
(c) Make higher education accessible to all on the basis of capacity by every appropriate means;
(d) Make educational and vocational information and guidance available and accessible to all children;
(e) Take measures to encourage regular attendance at schools and the reduction of drop-out rates.

(2) States Parties shall take all appropriate measures to ensure that school discipline is administered in a manner consistent with the child's human dignity and in conformity with the present Convention.

(3) States Parties shall promote and encourage international co-operation in matters relating to education, in particular with a view to contributing to the elimination of ignorance and illiteracy throughout the world and facilitating access to scientific and technical knowledge and modern teaching methods. In this regard, particular account shall be taken of the needs of developing countries.

Article 29

(1) States Parties agree that the education of the child shall be directed to:
(a) The development of the child's personality, talents and mental and physical abilities to their fullest potential;
(b) The development of respect for human rights and fundamental freedoms, and for the principles enshrined in the Charter of the United Nations;
(c) The development of respect for the child's parents, his or her own cultural identity, language and values, for the national values of the country in which the child is living, the country from which he or she may originate, and for civilizations different from his or her own;
(d) The preparation of the child for responsible life in a free society, in the spirit of understanding, peace, tolerance, equality of sexes, and friendship among all peoples, ethnic, national and religious groups and persons of indigenous origin;
(e) The development of respect for the natural environment.

(2) No part of the present article or article 28 shall be construed so as to interfere with the liberty of individuals and bodies to establish and direct educational institutions, subject always to the observance of the principle set forth in paragraph 1 of the present article and to the requirements that the education given in such institutions shall conform to such minimum standards as may be laid down by the State.

Article 30

In those States in which ethnic, religious or linguistic minorities or persons of indigenous origin exist, a child belonging to such a minority or who is indigenous shall not be denied the right, in community with other members of his or her group, to enjoy his or her own culture, to profess and practise his or her own religion, or to use his or her own language.

Article 31

(1) States Parties recognize the right of the child to rest and leisure, to engage in play and recreational activities appropriate to the age of the child and to participate freely in cultural life and the arts.

(2) States Parties shall respect and promote the right of the child to participate fully in cultural and artistic life and shall encourage the provision of appropriate and equal opportunities for cultural, artistic, recreational and leisure activity.

Article 32

(1) States Parties recognize the right of the child to be protected from economic exploitation and from performing any work that is likely to be hazardous or to interfere with the child's education, or to be harmful to the child's health or physical, mental, spiritual, moral or social development.

(2) States Parties shall take legislative, administrative, social and educational measures to ensure the implementation of the present article. To this end, and having regard to the relevant provisions of other international instruments, States Parties shall in particular:

(a) Provide for a minimum age or minimum ages for admission to employment;

(b) Provide for appropriate regulation of the hours and conditions of employment;

(c) Provide for appropriate penalties or other sanctions to ensure the effective enforcement of the present article.

Article 33

States Parties shall take all appropriate measures, including legislative, administrative, social and educational measures, to protect children from the illicit use of narcotic drugs and psychotropic substances as defined in the relevant international treaties, and to prevent the use of children in the illicit production and trafficking of such substances.

Article 34

States Parties undertake to protect the child from all forms of sexual exploitation and sexual abuse. For these purposes, States Parties shall in particular take all appropriate national, bilateral and multilateral measures to prevent:

(a) The inducement or coercion of a child to engage in any unlawful sexual activity;

(b) The exploitative use of children in prostitution or other unlawful sexual practices;

(c) The exploitative use of children in pornographic performances and materials.

Article 35
States Parties shall take all appropriate national, bilateral and multilateral measures to prevent the abduction of, the sale of or traffic in children for any purpose or in any form.

Article 36
States Parties shall protect the child against all other forms of exploitation prejudicial to any aspects of the child's welfare.

Article 37
States Parties shall ensure that:
(a) No child shall be subjected to torture or other cruel, inhuman or degrading treatment or punishment. Neither capital punishment nor life imprisonment without possibility of release shall be imposed for offences committed by persons below eighteen years of age;
(b) No child shall be deprived of his or her liberty unlawfully or arbitrarily. The arrest, detention or imprisonment of a child shall be in conformity with the law and shall be used only as a measure of last resort and for the shortest appropriate period of time;
(c) Every child deprived of liberty shall be treated with humanity and respect for the inherent dignity of the human person, and in a manner which takes into account the needs of persons of his or her age. In particular, every child deprived of liberty shall be separated from adults unless it is considered in the child's best interest not to do so and shall have the right to maintain contact with his or her family through correspondence and visits, save in exceptional circumstances;
(d) Every child deprived of his or her liberty shall have the right to prompt access to legal and other appropriate assistance, as well as the right to challenge the legality of the deprivation of his or her liberty before a court or other competent, independent and impartial authority, and to a prompt decision on any such action.

Article 38
(1) States Parties undertake to respect and to ensure respect for rules of international humanitarian law applicable to them in armed conflicts which are relevant to the child.
(2) States Parties shall take all feasible measures to ensure that persons who have not attained the age of fifteen years do not take a direct part in hostilities.
(3) States Parties shall refrain from recruiting any person who has not attained the age of fifteen years into their armed forces. In recruiting among those persons who have attained the age of fifteen years but who have not attained the age of eighteen years, States Parties shall endeavour to give priority to those who are oldest.
(4) In accordance with their obligations under international humanitarian law to protect the civilian population in armed conflicts, States Parties shall take all feasible measures to ensure protection and care of children who are affected by an armed conflict.

Article 39

States Parties shall take all appropriate measures to promote physical and psychological recovery and social reintegration of a child victim of: any form of neglect, exploitation, or abuse; torture or any other form of cruel, inhuman or degrading treatment or punishment; or armed conflicts. Such recovery and reintegration shall take place in an environment which fosters the health, self-respect and dignity of the child.

Article 40

(1) States Parties recognize the right of every child alleged as, accused of, or recognized as having infringed the penal law to be treated in a manner consistent with the promotion of the child's sense of dignity and worth, which reinforces the child's respect for the human rights and fundamental freedoms of others and which takes into account the child's age and the desirability of promoting the child's reintegration and the child's assuming a constructive role in society.

(2) To this end, and having regard to the relevant provisions of international instruments, States Parties shall, in particular, ensure that:

(a) No child shall be alleged as, be accused of, or recognized as having infringed the penal law by reason of acts or omissions that were not prohibited by national or international law at the time they were committed;

(b) Every child alleged as or accused of having infringed the penal law has at least the following guarantees:

(i) To be presumed innocent until proven guilty according to law;

(ii) To be informed promptly and directly of the charges against him or her, and, if appropriate, through his or her parents or legal guardians, and to have legal or other appropriate assistance in the preparation and presentation of his or her defence;

(iii) To have the matter determined without delay by a competent, independent and impartial authority or judicial body in a fair hearing according to law, in the presence of legal or other appropriate assistance and, unless it is considered not to be in the best interest of the child, in particular, taking into account his or her age or situation, his or her parents or legal guardians;

(iv) Not to be compelled to give testimony or to confess guilt; to examine or have examined adverse witnesses and to obtain the participation and examination of witnesses on his or her behalf under conditions of equality;

(v) If considered to have infringed the penal law, to have this decision and any measures imposed in consequence thereof reviewed by a higher competent, independent and impartial authority or judicial body according to law;

(vi) To have the free assistance of an interpreter if the child cannot understand or speak the language used;

(vii) To have his or her privacy fully respected at all stages of the proceedings. 3. States Parties shall seek to promote the establishment of laws, procedures, authorities and institutions specifically applicable to children alleged as, accused of, or recognized as having infringed the penal law, and, in particular:

(a) The establishment of a minimum age below which children shall be presumed not to have the capacity to infringe the penal law;

(b) Whenever appropriate and desirable, measures for dealing with such children without resorting to judicial proceedings, providing that human rights and legal safeguards are fully respected.

(4) A variety of dispositions, such as care, guidance and supervision orders; counselling; probation; foster care; education and vocational training programmes and other alternatives to institutional care shall be available to ensure that children are dealt with in a manner appropriate to their well-being and proportionate both to their circumstances and the offence.

Article 41

Nothing in the present Convention shall affect any provisions which are more conducive to the realization of the rights of the child and which may be contained in:

(a) The law of a State party; or

(b) International law in force for that State.

European Social Charter
(relevant extracts)

PART I

The Contracting Parties accept as the aim of their policy, to be pursued by all appropriate means, both national and international in character, the attainment of conditions in which the following rights and principles may be effectively realised:

(1) Everyone shall have the opportunity to earn his living in an occupation freely entered upon.

(2) All workers have the right to just conditions of work.

(3) All workers have the right to safe and healthy working conditions.

(4) All workers have the right to a fair remuneration sufficient for a decent standard of living for themselves and their families.

(5) All workers and employers have the right to freedom of association in national or international organisations for the protection of their economic and social interests.

(6) All workers and employers have the right to bargain collectively.

(7) Children and young persons have the right to a special protection against the physical and moral hazards to which they are exposed.

(8) Employed women, in case of maternity, and other employed women as appropriate, have the right to a special protection in their work.

(9) Everyone has the right to appropriate facilities for vocational guidance with a view to helping him choose an occupation suited to his personal aptitude and interests.

(10) Everyone has the right to appropriate facilities for vocational training.

(11) Everyone has the right to benefit from any measures enabling him to enjoy the highest possible standard of health attainable.

(12) All workers and their dependants have the right to social security.

(13) Anyone without adequate resources has the right to social and medical assistance.

(14) Everyone has the right to benefit from social welfare services.

(15) Disabled persons have the right to vocational training, rehabilitation and resettlement, whatever the origin and nature of their disability.

(16) The family as a fundamental unit of society has the right to appropriate social, legal and economic protection to ensure its full development.

(17) Mothers and children, irrespective of marital status and family relations, have the right to appropriate social and economic protection.

793

(18) The nationals of any one of the Contracting Parties have the right to engage in any gainful occupation in the territory of any one of the others on a footing of equality with the nationals of the latter, subject to restrictions based on cogent economic or social reasons.

(19) Migrant workers who are nationals of a Contracting Party and their families have the right to protection and assistance in the territory of any other Contracting Party.

PART II

The Contracting Parties undertake, as provided for in Part III, to consider themselves bound by the obligations laid down in the following articles and paragraphs.

Article 1 – The right to work

With a view to ensuring the effective exercise of the right to work, the Contracting Parties undertake:

(1) To accept as one of their primary aims and responsibilities the achievement and maintenance of as high and stable a level of employment as possible, with a view to the attainment of full employment;

(2) To protect effectively the right of the worker to earn his living in an occupation freely entered upon;

(3) To establish or maintain free employment services for all workers;

(4) To provide or promote appropriate vocational guidance, training and rehabilitation.

Article 2 – The right to just conditions of work

With a view to ensuring the effective exercise of the right to just conditions of work, the Contracting Parties undertake:

(1) To provide for reasonable daily and weekly working hours, the working week to be progressively reduced to the extent that the increase of productivity and other relevant factors permit;

(2) To provide for public holidays with pay;

(3) To provide for a minimum of two weeks annual holiday with pay;

(4) To provide for additional paid holidays or reduced working hours for workers engaged in dangerous or unhealthy occupations as prescribed;

(5) To ensure a weekly rest period which shall, as far as possible, coincide with the day recognised by tradition or custom in the country or region concerned as a day of rest.

Article 3 – The right to safe and healthy working conditions

With a view to ensuring the effective exercise of the right to safe and healthy working conditions, the Contracting Parties undertake:

(1) To issue safety and health regulations;

(2) To provide for the enforcement of such regulations by measures of supervision;

(3) To consult, as appropriate, employers' and workers' organisations on measures intended to improve industrial safety and health.

Article 4 – The right to a fair remuneration

With a view to ensuring the effective exercise of the right to a fair remuneration, the Contracting Parties undertake:

(1) To recognise the right of workers to a remuneration such as will give them and their families a decent standard of living;

(2) To recognise the right of workers to an increased rate of remuneration for overtime work, subject to exceptions in particular cases;

(3) To recognise the right of men and women workers to equal pay for work of equal value;

(4) To recognise the right of all workers to a reasonable period of notice for termination of employment;

(5) To permit deductions from wages only under conditions and to the extent prescribed by national laws or regulations or fixed by collective agreements or arbitration awards.

The exercise of these rights shall be achieved by freely concluded collective agreements, by statutory wage-fixing machinery, or by other means appropriate to national conditions.

Article 5 – The right to organise

With a view to ensuring or promoting the freedom of workers and employers to form local, national or international organisations for the protection of their economic and social interests and to join those organisations, the Contracting Parties undertake that national law shall not be such as to impair, nor shall it be so applied as to impair, this freedom. The extent to which the guarantees provided for in this article shall apply to the police shall be determined by national laws or regulations. The principle governing the application to the members of the armed forces of these guarantees and the extent to which they shall apply to persons in this category shall equally be determined by national laws or regulations.

Article 6 – The right to bargain collectively

With a view to ensuring the effective exercise of the right to bargain collectively, the Contracting Parties undertake:

(1) To promote joint consultation between workers and employers;

(2) To promote, where necessary and appropriate, machinery for voluntary negotiations between employers or employers' organisations and workers' organisations, with a view to the regulation of terms and conditions of employment by means of collective agreements;

(3) To promote the establishment and use of appropriate machinery for conciliation and voluntary arbitration for the settlement of labour disputes; and recognise:

(4) The right of workers and employers to collective action in cases of conflicts of interest, including the right to strike, subject to obligations that might arise out of collective agreements previously entered into.

Article 7 – The right of children and young persons to protection

With a view to ensuring the effective exercise of the right of children and young persons to protection, the Contracting Parties undertake:

(1) To provide that the minimum age of admission to employment shall be 15 years, subject to exceptions for children employed in prescribed light work without harm to their health, morals or education;

(2) To provide that a higher minimum age of admission to employment shall be fixed with respect to prescribed occupations regarded as dangerous or unhealthy;

(3) To provide that persons who are still subject to compulsory education shall not be employed in such work as would deprive them of the full benefit of their education;

(4) To provide that the working hours of persons under 16 years of age shall be limited in accordance with the needs of their development, and particularly with their need for vocational training;

(5) To recognise the right of young workers and apprentices to a fair wage or other appropriate allowances;

(6) To provide that the time spent by young persons in vocational training during the normal working hours with the consent of the employer shall be treated as forming part of the working day;

(7) To provide that employed persons of under 18 years of age shall be entitled to not less than three weeks' annual holiday with pay;

(8) To provide that persons under 18 years of age shall not be employed in night work with the exception of certain occupations provided for by national laws or regulations;

(9) To provide that persons under 18 years of age employed in occupations prescribed by national laws or regulations shall be subject to regular medical control;

(10) To ensure special protection against physical and moral dangers to which children and young persons are exposed, and particularly against those resulting directly or indirectly from their work.

Article 8 – The right of employed women to protection

With a view to ensuring the effective exercise of the right of employed women to protection, the Contracting Parties undertake:

(1) To provide either by paid leave, by adequate social security benefits or by benefits from public funds for women to take leave before and after childbirth up to a total of at least 12 weeks;

(2) To consider it as unlawful for an employer to give a woman notice of dismissal during her absence on maternity leave or to give her notice of dismissal at such a time that the notice would expire during such absence;

(3) To provide that mothers who are nursing their infants shall be entitled to sufficient time off for this purpose;

(4) (a) To regulate the employment of women workers on night work in industrial employment;

    (b) To prohibit the employment of women workers in underground mining, and, as appropriate, on all other work which is unsuitable for them by reason of its dangerous, unhealthy, or arduous nature.

Article 9 – The right to vocational guidance

With a view to ensuring the effective exercise of the right to vocational guidance, the Contracting Parties undertake to provide or promote, as necessary, a service which will assist all persons, including the handicapped, to solve problems related to occupational choice and progress, with due regard to the individual's characteristics and their relation to occupational opportunity: this assistance should be available free of charge, both to young persons, including school children, and to adults.

Article 10 – The right to vocational training

With a view to ensuring the effective exercise of the right to vocational training, the Contracting Parties undertake:

(1) To provide or promote, as necessary, the technical and vocational training of all persons, including the handicapped, in consultation with employers' and workers' organisations, and to grant facilities for access to higher technical and university education, based solely on individual aptitude;

(2) To provide or promote a system of apprenticeship and other systematic arrangements for training young boys and girls in their various employments;

(3) To provide or promote, as necessary:
   - adequate and readily available training facilities for adult workers;
   - special facilities for the re-training of adult workers needed as a result of technological development or new trends in employment;

(4) To encourage the full utilisation of the facilities provided by appropriate measures such as:
   (a) reducing or abolishing any fees or charges;
   (b) granting financial assistance in appropriate cases;
   (c) including in the normal working hours time spent on supplementary training taken by the worker, at the request of his employer, during employment;
   (d) ensuring, through adequate supervision, in consultation with the employers' and workers' organisations, the efficiency of apprenticeship and other training arrangements for young workers, and the adequate protection of young workers generally.

Article 11 – The right to protection of health

With a view to ensuring the effective exercise of the right to protection of health, the Contracting Parties undertake, either directly or in co-operation with public or private organisations, to take appropriate measures designed inter alia:

(1) To remove as far as possible the causes of ill-health;

(2) To provide advisory and educational facilities for the promotion of health and the encouragement of individual responsibility in matters of health;

(3) To prevent as far as possible epidemic, endemic and other diseases.

Article 12 – The right to social security

With a view to ensuring the effective exercise of the right to social security, the Contracting Parties undertake:

(1) To establish or maintain a system of social security;
(2) To maintain the social security system at a satisfactory level at least equal to that required for ratification of International Labour Convention (No. 102) Concerning Minimum Standards of Social Security;
(3) To endeavour to raise progressively the system of social security to a higher level;

To take steps, by the conclusion of appropriate bilateral and multilateral agreements, or by other means, and subject to the conditions laid down in such agreements, in order to ensure:

(a) equal treatment with their own nationals of the nationals of other Contracting Parties in respect of social security rights, including the retention of benefits arising out of social security legislation, whatever movements the persons protected may undertake between the territories of the Contracting Parties;

(b) the granting, maintenance and resumption of social security rights by such means as the accumulation of insurance or employment periods completed under the legislation of each of the Contracting Parties.

Article 13 – The right to social and medical assistance

With a view to ensuring the effective exercise of the right to social and medical assistance, the Contracting Parties undertake:

(1) To ensure that any person who is without adequate resources and who is unable to secure such resources either by his own efforts or from other sources, in particular by benefits under a social security scheme, be granted adequate assistance, and, in case of sickness, the care necessitated by his condition;

(2) To ensure that persons receiving such assistance shall not, for that reason, suffer from a diminution of their political or social rights;

(3) To provide that everyone may receive by appropriate public or private services such advice and personal help as may be required to prevent, to remove, or to alleviate personal or family want;

(4) To apply the provisions referred to in paragraphs 1, 2 and 3 of this article on an equal footing with their nationals to nationals of other Contracting Parties lawfully within their territories, in accordance with their obligations under the European Convention on Social and Medical Assistance, signed at Paris on 11th December 1953.

Article 14 – The right to benefit from social welfare services

With a view to ensuring the effective exercise of the right to benefit from social welfare services, the Contracting Parties undertake:

(1) To promote or provide services which, by using methods of social work, would contribute to the welfare and development of both individuals and groups in the community, and to their adjustment to the social environment;

(2) To encourage the participation of individuals and voluntary or other organisations in the establishment and maintenance of such services.

Article 15 – The right of physically or mentally disabled persons to vocational training, rehabilitation and social resettlement

With a view to ensuring the effective exercise of the right of the physically or mentally disabled to vocational training, rehabilitation and resettlement, the Contracting Parties undertake:

(1) To take adequate measures for the provision of training facilities, including, where necessary, specialised institutions, public or private;

(2) To take adequate measures for the placing of disabled persons in employment, such as specialised placing services, facilities for sheltered employment and measures to encourage employers to admit disabled persons to employment.

Article 16 – The right of the family to social, legal and economic protection

With a view to ensuring the necessary conditions for the full development of the family, which is a fundamental unit of society, the Contracting Parties undertake to promote the economic, legal and social protection of family life by such means as social and family benefits, fiscal arrangements, provision of family housing, benefits for the newly married, and other appropriate means.

Article 17 – The right of mothers and children to social and economic protection

With a view to ensuring the effective exercise of the right of mothers and children to social and economic protection, the Contracting Parties will take all appropriate and necessary measures to that end, including the establishment or maintenance of appropriate institutions or services.

Article 18 – The right to engage in a gainful occupation in the territory of other Contracting Parties

With a view to ensuring the effective exercise of the right to engage in a gainful occupation in the territory of any other Contracting Party, the Contracting Parties undertake:

(1) To apply existing regulations in a spirit of liberality;

(2) To simplify existing formalities and to reduce or abolish chancery dues and other charges payable by foreign workers or their employers;

(3) To liberalise, individually or collectively, regulations governing the employment of foreign workers; and recognise:

(4) The right of their nationals to leave the country to engage in a gainful occupation in the territories of the other Contracting Parties.

Article 19 – The right of migrant workers and their families to protection and assistance

With a view to ensuring the effective exercise of the right of migrant workers and their families to protection and assistance in the territory of any other Contracting Party, the Contracting Parties undertake:

(1) To maintain or to satisfy themselves that there are maintained adequate and free services to assist such workers, particularly in obtaining accurate

information, and to take all appropriate steps, so far as national laws and regulations permit, against misleading propaganda relating to emigration and immigration;

(2) To adopt appropriate measures within their own jurisdiction to facilitate the departure, journey and reception of such workers and their families, and to provide, within their own jurisdiction, appropriate services for health, medical attention and good hygienic conditions during the journey;

(3) To promote co-operation, as appropriate, between social services, public and private, in emigration and immigration countries;

(4) To secure for such workers lawfully within their territories, insofar as such matters are regulated by law or regulations or are subject to the control of administrative authorities, treatment not less favourable than that of their own nationals in respect of the following matters:
   (a) remuneration and other employment and working conditions;
   (b) membership of trade unions and enjoyment of the benefits of collective bargaining;
   (c) accommodation;

(5) To secure for such workers lawfully within their territories treatment not less favourable than that of their own nationals with regard to employment taxes, dues or contributions payable in respect of employed persons;

(6) To facilitate as far as possible the reunion of the family of a foreign worker permitted to establish himself in the territory;

(7) To secure for such workers lawfully within their territories treatment not less favourable than that of their own nationals in respect of legal proceedings relating to matters referred to in this article;

(8) To secure that such workers lawfully residing within their territories are not expelled unless they endanger national security or offend against public interest or morality;

(9) To permit, within legal limits, the transfer of such parts of the earnings and savings of such workers as they may desire;

(10) To extend the protection and assistance provided for in this article to self-employed migrants insofar as such measures apply.

Rules of the European Court of Human Rights
(relevant extracts)

Rule 1 – Definitions

For the purposes of these Rules unless the context otherwise requires:

(a) the term 'Convention' means the Convention for the Protection of Human Rights and Fundamental Freedoms and the Protocols thereto;

(b) the expression 'plenary Court' means the European Court of Human Rights sitting in plenary session;

(c) the term 'Grand Chamber' means the Grand Chamber of seventeen judges constituted in pursuance of Article 27 §1 of the Convention;

(d) the term 'Section' means a Chamber set up by the plenary Court for a fixed period in pursuance of Article 26 (b) of the Convention and the expression 'President of the Section' means the judge elected by the plenary Court in pursuance of Article 26 (c) of the Convention as President of such a Section;

(e) the term 'Chamber' means any Chamber of seven judges constituted in pursuance of Article 27 §1 of the Convention and the expression 'President of the Chamber' means the judge presiding over such a 'Chamber';

(f) the term 'Committee' means a Committee of three judges set up in pursuance of Article 27 §1 of the Convention;

(g) the term 'Court' means either the plenary Court, the Grand Chamber, a Section, a Chamber, a Committee or the panel of five judges referred to in Article 43 §2 of the Convention;

(h) the expression 'ad hoc judge' means any person, other than an elected judge, chosen by a Contracting Party in pursuance of Article 27 §2 of the Convention to sit as a member of the Grand Chamber or as a member of a Chamber;

(i) the terms 'judge' and 'judges' mean the judges elected by the Parliamentary Assembly of the Council of Europe or ad hoc judges;

(j) the term 'Judge Rapporteur' means a judge appointed to carry out the tasks provided for in Rules 48 and 49;

(k) the term 'Registrar' denotes the Registrar of the Court or the Registrar of a Section according to the context;

(l) the terms 'party' and 'parties' mean
   - the applicant or respondent Contracting Parties;
   - the applicant (the person, non-governmental organisation or group of individuals) that lodged a complaint under Article 34 of the Convention;

801

(m) the expression 'third party' means any Contracting State or any person concerned who, as provided for in Article 36 §§1 and 2 of the Convention, has exercised its right or been invited to submit written comments or take part in a hearing;

(n) the expression 'Committee of Ministers' means the Committee of Ministers of the Council of Europe;

(o) the terms 'former Court' and 'Commission' mean respectively the European Court and European Commission of Human Rights set up under former Article 19 of the Convention.

TITLE I – ORGANISATION AND WORKING OF THE COURT
CHAPTER I – JUDGES
Rule 2 – Calculation of term of office

(1) The duration of the term of office of an elected judge shall be calculated as from the date of election. However, when a judge is re-elected on the expiry of the term of office or is elected to replace a judge whose term of office has expired or is about to expire, the duration of the term of office shall, in either case, be calculated as from the date of such expiry.

(2) In accordance with Article 23 §5 of the Convention, a judge elected to replace a judge whose term of office has not expired shall hold office for the remainder of the predecessor's term.

(3) In accordance with Article 23 §7 of the Convention, an elected judge shall hold office until a successor has taken the oath or made the declaration provided for in Rule 3.

Rule 3 – Oath or solemn declaration

(1) Before taking up office, each elected judge shall, at the first sitting of the plenary Court at which the judge is present or, in case of need, before the President of the Court, take the following oath or make the following solemn declaration:

'I swear' – or 'I solemnly declare' – 'that I will exercise my functions as a judge honourably, independently and impartially and that I will keep secret all deliberations.'

(2) This act shall be recorded in minutes.

Rule 4 – Incompatible activities

In accordance with Article 21 §3 of the Convention, the judges shall not during their term of office engage in any political or administrative activity or any professional activity which is incompatible with their independence or impartiality or with the demands of a full-time office. Each judge shall declare to the President of the Court any additional activity. In the event of a disagreement between the President and the judge concerned, any question arising shall be decided by the plenary Court.

Rule 5 – Precedence

(1) Elected judges shall take precedence after the President and Vice-Presidents of the Court and the Presidents of the Sections, according to the

date of their election; in the event of re-election, even if it is not an immediate re-election, the length of time during which the judge concerned previously held office as a judge shall be taken into account.

(2) Vice-Presidents of the Court elected to office on the same date shall take precedence according to the length of time they have served as judges. If the length of time they have served as judges is the same, they shall take precedence according to age. The same Rule shall apply to Presidents of Sections.

(3) Judges who have served the same length of time as judges shall take precedence according to age.

(4) Ad hoc judges shall take precedence after the elected judges according to age.

Rule 6 – Resignation
Resignation of a judge shall be notified to the President of the Court, who shall transmit it to the Secretary General of the Council of Europe. Subject to the provisions of Rules 24 §3 in fine and 26 §2, resignation shall constitute vacation of office.

Rule 7 – Dismissal from office
No judge may be dismissed from his or her office unless the other judges, meeting in plenary session, decide by a majority of two-thirds of the elected judges in office that he or she has ceased to fulfil the required conditions. He or she must first be heard by the plenary Court. Any judge may set in motion the procedure for dismissal from office.

CHAPTER II –PRESIDENCY OF THE COURT
Rule 8 – Election of the President and Vice-Presidents of the Court and the Presidents and Vice-Presidents of the Sections

(1) The plenary Court shall elect its President, two Vice-Presidents and the Presidents of the Sections for a period of three years, provided that such period shall not exceed the duration of their terms of office as judges. They may be re-elected.

(2) Each Section shall likewise elect for a renewable period of three years a Vice-President, who shall replace the President of the Section if the latter is unable to carry out his or her duties.

(3) The Presidents and Vice-Presidents shall continue to hold office until the election of their successors.

(4) If a President or a Vice-President ceases to be a member of the Court or resigns from office before its normal expiry, the plenary Court or the relevant Section, as the case may be, shall elect a successor for the remainder of the term of that office.

(5) The elections referred to in this Rule shall be by secret ballot; only the elected judges who are present shall take part. If no judge receives an absolute majority of the elected judges present, a ballot shall take place between the two judges who have received most votes. In the event of a tie, preference shall be given to the judge having precedence in accordance with Rule 5.

Rule 9 – Functions of the President of the Court

(1) The President of the Court shall direct the work and administration of the Court. The President shall represent the Court and, in particular, be responsible for its relations with the authorities of the Council of Europe.

(2) The President shall preside at plenary meetings of the Court, meetings of the Grand Chamber and meetings of the panel of five judges.

(3) The President shall not take part in the consideration of cases being heard by Chambers except where he or she is the judge elected in respect of a Contracting Party concerned.

Rule 10 – Functions of the Vice-Presidents of the Court

The Vice-Presidents of the Court shall assist the President of the Court. They shall take the place of the President if the latter is unable to carry out his or her duties or the office of President is vacant, or at the request of the President. They shall also act as Presidents of Sections.

Rule 11 – Replacement of the President and the Vice-Presidents

If the President and the Vice-Presidents of the Court are at the same time unable to carry out their duties or if their offices are at the same time vacant, the office of President of the Court shall be assumed by a President of a Section or, if none is available, by another elected judge, in accordance with the order of precedence provided for in Rule 5.

Rule 12 – Presidency of Sections and Chambers

The Presidents of the Sections shall preside at the sittings of the Section and Chambers of which they are members. The Vice-Presidents of the Sections shall take their place if they are unable to carry out their duties or if the office of President of the Section concerned is vacant, or at the request of the President of the Section. Failing that, the judges of the Section and the Chambers shall take their place, in the order of precedence provided for in Rule 5.

Rule 13 – Inability to preside

Judges of the Court may not preside in cases in which the Contracting Party of which they are nationals or in respect of which they were elected is a party.

Rule 14 – Balanced representation of the sexes

In relation to the making of appointments governed by this and the following chapter of the present Rules, the Court shall pursue a policy aimed at securing a balanced representation of the sexes.

CHAPTER III – THE REGISTRY
Rule 15 – Election of the Registrar

(1) The plenary Court shall elect its Registrar. The candidates shall be of high moral character and must possess the legal, managerial and linguistic knowledge and experience necessary to carry out the functions attaching to the post.

(2) The Registrar shall be elected for a term of five years and may be re-elected.

The Registrar may not be dismissed from office, unless the judges, meeting in plenary session, decide by a majority of two-thirds of the elected judges in office that the person concerned has ceased to fulfil the required conditions. He or she must first be heard by the plenary Court. Any judge may set in motion the procedure for dismissal from office.

(3) The elections referred to in this Rule shall be by secret ballot; only the elected judges who are present shall take part. If no candidate receives an absolute majority of the elected judges present, a ballot shall take place between the two candidates who have received most votes. In the event of a tie, preference shall be given, firstly, to the female candidate, if any, and, secondly, to the older candidate.

(4) Before taking up office, the Registrar shall take the following oath or make the following solemn declaration before the plenary Court or, if need be, before the President of the Court:

'I swear' – or 'I solemnly declare' – 'that I will exercise loyally, discreetly and conscientiously the functions conferred upon me as Registrar of the European Court of Human Rights.'

This act shall be recorded in minutes.

Rule 16 – Election of the Deputy Registrars

(1) The plenary Court shall also elect two Deputy Registrars on the conditions and in the manner and for the term prescribed in the preceding Rule. The procedure for dismissal from office provided for in respect of the Registrar shall likewise apply. The Court shall first consult the Registrar in both these matters.

(2) Before taking up office, a Deputy Registrar shall take an oath or make a solemn declaration before the plenary Court or, if need be, before the President of the Court, in terms similar to those prescribed in respect of the Registrar. This act shall be recorded in minutes.

Rule 17 – Functions of the Registrar

(1) The Registrar shall assist the Court in the performance of its functions and shall be responsible for the organisation and activities of the Registry under the authority of the President of the Court.

(2) The Registrar shall have the custody of the archives of the Court and shall be the channel for all communications and notifications made by, or addressed to, the Court in connection with the cases brought or to be brought before it.

(3) The Registrar shall, subject to the duty of discretion attaching to this office, reply to requests for information concerning the work of the Court, in particular to enquiries from the press.

(4) General instructions drawn up by the Registrar, and approved by the President of the Court, shall regulate the working of the Registry.

Rule 18 – Organisation of the Registry

(1) The Registry shall consist of Section Registries equal to the number of Sections set up by the Court and of the departments necessary to provide the legal and administrative services required by the Court.

(2) The Section Registrar shall assist the Section in the performance of its functions and may be assisted by a Deputy Section Registrar.

(3) The officials of the Registry, including the legal secretaries but not the Registrar and the Deputy Registrars, shall be appointed by the Secretary General of the Council of Europe with the agreement of the President of the Court or of the Registrar acting on the President's instructions.

CHAPTER IV – THE WORKING OF THE COURT
Rule 19 – Seat of the Court

(1) The seat of the Court shall be at the seat of the Council of Europe at Strasbourg. The Court may, however, if it considers it expedient, perform its functions elsewhere in the territories of the member States of the Council of Europe.

(2) The Court may decide, at any stage of the examination of an application, that it is necessary that an investigation or any other function be carried out elsewhere by it or one or more of its members.

Rule 20 – Sessions of the plenary Court

(1) The plenary sessions of the Court shall be convened by the President of the Court whenever the performance of its functions under the Convention and under these Rules so requires. The President of the Court shall convene a plenary session if at least one-third of the members of the Court so request, and in any event once a year to consider administrative matters.

(2) The quorum of the plenary Court shall be two-thirds of the elected judges in office.

(3) If there is no quorum, the President shall adjourn the sitting.

Rule 21 – Other sessions of the Court

(1) The Grand Chamber, the Chambers and the Committees shall sit full time. On a proposal by the President, however, the Court shall fix session periods each year.

(2) Outside those periods the Grand Chamber and the Chambers shall be convened by their Presidents in cases of urgency.

Rule 22 – Deliberations

(1) The Court shall deliberate in private. Its deliberations shall remain secret.

(2) Only the judges shall take part in the deliberations. The Registrar or the designated substitute, as well as such other officials of the Registry and interpreters whose assistance is deemed necessary, shall be present. No other person may be admitted except by special decision of the Court.

(3) Before a vote is taken on any matter in the Court, the President may request the judges to state their opinions on it.

Rule 23 – Votes

(1) The decisions of the Court shall be taken by a majority of the judges present. In the event of a tie, a fresh vote shall be taken and, if there is still a tie, the President shall have a casting vote. This paragraph shall apply unless otherwise provided for in these Rules.

(2) The decisions and judgments of the Grand Chamber and the Chambers shall be adopted by a majority of the sitting judges. Abstentions shall not be allowed in final votes on the admissibility and merits of cases.

(3) As a general rule, votes shall be taken by a show of hands. The President may take a roll-call vote, in reverse order of precedence.

(4) Any matter that is to be voted upon shall be formulated in precise terms.

CHAPTER V – THE CHAMBERS
Rule 24 – Composition of the Grand Chamber

(1) The Grand Chamber shall be composed of seventeen judges and three substitute judges.

(2) The Grand Chamber shall be constituted for three years with effect from the election of the presidential office-holders referred to in Rule 8.

(3) The Grand Chamber shall include the President and Vice-Presidents of the Court and the Presidents of the Sections. In order to complete the Grand Chamber, the plenary Court shall, on a proposal by its President, divide all the other judges into two groups which shall alternate every nine months and whose membership shall be geographically as balanced as possible and reflect the different legal systems among the Contracting Parties. The judges and substitute judges who are to hear each case referred to the Grand Chamber during each nine-month period shall be designated in rotation within each group; they shall remain members of the Grand Chamber until the proceedings have been completed, even after their terms of office as judges have expired.

(4) If he or she does not sit as a member of the Grand Chamber by virtue of paragraph 3 of the present Rule, the judge elected in respect of any Contracting Party concerned shall sit as an ex officio member of the Grand Chamber in accordance with Article 27 §§2 and 3 of the Convention.

(5) (a) Where any President of a Section is unable to sit as a member of the Grand Chamber, he or she shall be replaced by the Vice-President of the Section.

   (b) If other judges are prevented from sitting, they shall be replaced by the substitute judges in the order in which the latter were selected under paragraph 3 of the present Rule.

   (c) If there are not enough substitute judges in the group concerned to complete the Grand Chamber, the substitute judges lacking shall be designated by a drawing of lots amongst the members of the other group.

6 (a) The panel of five judges of the Grand Chamber called upon to consider requests submitted under Article 43 of the Convention shall be composed of:
   – the President of the Court,
   – the Presidents or, if they are prevented from sitting, the Vice-Presidents of the Sections other than the Section from which was constituted the Chamber that dealt with the case whose referral to the Grand Chamber is being sought,
   – one further judge designated in rotation from among the judges other than those who dealt with the case in the Chamber.

(b) No judge elected in respect of, or who is a national of, a Contracting Party concerned may be a member of the panel.

(c) Any member of the panel unable to sit shall be replaced by another judge who did not deal with the case in the Chamber, who shall be designated in rotation.

Rule 25 – Setting up of Sections

(1) The Chambers provided for in Article 26 (b) of the Convention (referred to in these Rules as 'Sections') shall be set up by the plenary Court, on a proposal by its President, for a period of three years with effect from the election of the presidential office-holders of the Court under Rule 8. There shall be at least four Sections.

(2) Each judge shall be a member of a Section. The composition of the Sections shall be geographically and gender balanced and shall reflect the different legal systems among the Contracting Parties.

(3) Where a judge ceases to be a member of the Court before the expiry of the period for which the Section has been constituted, the judge's place in the Section shall be taken by his or her successor as a member of the Court.

(4) The President of the Court may exceptionally make modifications to the composition of the Sections if circumstances so require.

(5) On a proposal by the President, the plenary Court may constitute an additional Section.

Rule 26 – Constitution of Chambers

(1) The Chambers of seven judges provided for in Article 27 §1 of the Convention for the consideration of cases brought before the Court shall be constituted from the Sections as follows.

(a) The Chamber shall in each case include the President of the Section and the judge elected in respect of any Contracting Party concerned. If the latter judge is not a member of the Section to which the application has been assigned under Rule 51 or 52, he or she shall sit as an ex officio member of the Chamber in accordance with Article 27 §2 of the Convention. Rule 29 shall apply if that judge is unable to sit or withdraws.

(b) The other members of the Chamber shall be designated by the President of the Section in rotation from among the members of the relevant Section.

(c) The members of the Section who are not so designated shall sit in the case as substitute judges.

(2) Even after the end of their terms of office judges shall continue to deal with cases in which they have participated in the consideration of the merits.

Rule 27 – Committees

(1) Committees composed of three judges belonging to the same Section shall be set up under Article 27 §1 of the Convention. After consulting the Presidents of the Sections, the President of the Court shall decide on the number of Committees to be set up.

(2) The Committees shall be constituted for a period of twelve months by

rotation among the members of each Section, excepting the President of the Section.

(3) The judges of the Section who are not members of a Committee may be called upon to take the place of members who are unable to sit.

(4) Each Committee shall be chaired by the member having precedence in the Section.

Rule 28 – Inability to sit, withdrawal or exemption

(1) Any judge who is prevented from taking part in sittings shall, as soon as possible, give notice to the President of the Chamber.

(2) A judge may not take part in the consideration of any case in which he or she has a personal interest or has previously acted either as the Agent, advocate or adviser of a party or of a person having an interest in the case, or as a member of a tribunal or commission of inquiry, or in any other capacity.

(3) If a judge withdraws for one of the said reasons, or for some special reason, he or she shall inform the President of the Chamber, who shall exempt the judge from sitting.

(4) If the President of the Chamber considers that a reason exists for a judge to withdraw, he or she shall consult with the judge concerned; in the event of disagreement, the Chamber shall decide.

Rule 29 – Ad hoc judges

(1) If the judge elected in respect of a Contracting Party concerned is unable to sit in the Chamber or withdraws, the President of the Chamber shall invite that Party to indicate within thirty days whether it wishes to appoint to sit as judge either another elected judge or, as an ad hoc judge, any other person possessing the qualifications required by Article 21 §1 of the Convention and, if so, to state at the same time the name of the person appointed. The same rule shall apply if the person so appointed is unable to sit or withdraws.

(2) The Contracting Party concerned shall be presumed to have waived its right of appointment if it does not reply within thirty days.

(3) An ad hoc judge shall, at the opening of the first sitting fixed for the consideration of the case after the judge has been appointed, take the oath or make the solemn declaration provided for in Rule 3. This act shall be recorded in minutes.

Rule 30 – Common interest

(1) If several applicant or respondent Contracting Parties have a common interest, the President of the Court may invite them to agree to appoint a single elected judge or ad hoc judge in accordance with Article 27 §2 of the Convention. If the Parties are unable to agree, the President shall choose by lot, from among the persons proposed as judges by these Parties, the judge called upon to sit ex officio.

(2) In the event of a dispute as to the existence of a common interest, the plenary Court shall decide.

TITLE II – PROCEDURE

CHAPTER I – GENERAL RULES

Rule 31 – Possibility of particular derogations

The provisions of this Title shall not prevent the Court from derogating from them for the consideration of a particular case after having consulted the parties where appropriate.

Rule 32 – Practice directions

The President of the Court may issue practice directions, notably in relation to such matters as appearance at hearings and the filing of pleadings and other documents.

Rule 33 – Public character of proceedings

(1) Hearings shall be public unless, in accordance with paragraph 2 of this Rule, the Chamber in exceptional circumstances decides otherwise, either of its own motion or at the request of a party or any other person concerned.

(2) The press and the public may be excluded from all or part of a hearing in the interest of morals, public order or national security in a democratic society, where the interests of juveniles or the protection of the private life of the parties so require, or to the extent strictly necessary in the opinion of the Chamber in special circumstances where publicity would prejudice the interests of justice.

(3) Following registration of an application, all documents deposited with the Registry, with the exception of those deposited within the framework of friendly-settlement negotiations as provided for in Rule 62, shall be accessible to the public unless the President of the Chamber, for the reasons set out in paragraph 2 of this Rule, decides otherwise, either of his or her own motion or at the request of a party or any other person concerned.

(4) Any request for confidentiality made under paragraphs 1 or 3 above must give reasons and specify whether the hearing or the documents, as the case may be, should be inaccessible to the public in whole or in part.

Rule 34 – Use of languages

(1) The official languages of the Court shall be English and French.

(2) Before the decision on the admissibility of an application is taken, all communications with and pleadings by applicants under Article 34 of the Convention or their representatives, if not in one of the Court's official languages, shall be in one of the official languages of the Contracting Parties.

(3) (a) All communications with and pleadings by such applicants or their representatives in respect of a hearing, or after a case has been declared admissible, shall be in one of the Court's official languages, unless the President of the Chamber authorises the continued use of the official language of a Contracting Party.

(b) If such leave is granted, the Registrar shall make the necessary arrangements for the oral or written translation of the applicant's observations or statements.

(4) (a) All communications with and pleadings by Contracting Parties or third parties shall be in one of the Court's official languages. The President of the Chamber may authorise the use of a non-official language.

    (b) If such leave is granted, it shall be the responsibility of the requesting party to provide for and bear the costs of interpreting or translation into English or French of the oral arguments or written statements made.

(5) The President of the Chamber may invite the respondent Contracting Party to provide a translation of its written submissions in the or an official language of that Party in order to facilitate the applicant's understanding of those submissions.

(6) Any witness, expert or other person appearing before the Court may use his or her own language if he or she does not have sufficient knowledge of either of the two official languages. In that event the Registrar shall make the necessary arrangements for interpreting or translation.

Rule 35 – Representation of Contracting Parties

The Contracting Parties shall be represented by Agents, who may have the assistance of advocates or advisers.

Rule 36 – Representation of applicants

(1) Persons, non-governmental organisations or groups of individuals may initially present applications under Article 34 of the Convention themselves or through a representative appointed under paragraph 4 of this Rule.

(2) Following notification of the application to the respondent Contracting Party under Rule 54 §3(b), the President of the Chamber may direct that the applicant should be represented in accordance with paragraph 4 of this Rule.

(3) The applicant must be so represented at any hearing decided on by the Chamber or for the purposes of the proceedings following a decision to declare the application admissible, unless the President of the Chamber decides otherwise.

(4) (a) The representative of the applicant shall be an advocate authorised to practise in any of the Contracting Parties and resident in the territory of one of them, or any other person approved by the President of the Chamber.

    (b) The President of the Chamber may, where representation would otherwise be obligatory, grant leave to the applicant to present his or her own case, subject, if necessary, to being assisted by an advocate or other approved representative.

    (c) In exceptional circumstances and at any stage of the procedure, the President of the Chamber may, where he or she considers that the circumstances or the conduct of the advocate or other person appointed under the preceding sub-paragraphs so warrant, direct that the latter may no longer represent or assist the applicant and that the applicant should seek alternative representation.

(5) The advocate or other approved representative, or the applicant in person if he or she seeks leave to present his or her own case, must have an adequate knowledge of one of the Court's official languages. However, leave to use a

non-official language may be given by the President of the Chamber under Rule 34 §3.

Rule 37 – Communications, notifications and summonses

(1) Communications or notifications addressed to the Agents or advocates of the parties shall be deemed to have been addressed to the parties.

(2) If, for any communication, notification or summons addressed to persons other than the Agents or advocates of the parties, the Court considers it necessary to have the assistance of the Government of the State on whose territory such communication, notification or summons is to have effect, the President of the Court shall apply directly to that Government in order to obtain the necessary facilities.

(3) The same rule shall apply when the Court desires to make or arrange for the making of an investigation on the spot in order to establish the facts or to procure evidence or when it orders the appearance of a person who is resident in, or will have to cross, that territory.

Rule 38 – Written pleadings

(1) No written observations or other documents may be filed after the time-limit set by the President of the Chamber or the Judge Rapporteur, as the case may be, in accordance with these Rules. No written observations or other documents filed outside that time-limit or contrary to any practice direction issued under Rule 32 shall be included in the case file unless the President of the Chamber decides otherwise.

(2) For the purposes of observing the time-limit referred to in paragraph 1, the material date is the certified date of dispatch of the document or, if there is none, the actual date of receipt at the Registry.

Rule 39 – Interim measures

(1) The Chamber or, where appropriate, its President may, at the request of a party or of any other person concerned, or of its own motion, indicate to the parties any interim measure which it considers should be adopted in the interests of the parties or of the proper conduct of the proceedings before it.

(2) Notice of these measures shall be given to the Committee of Ministers.

(3) The Chamber may request information from the parties on any matter connected with the implementation of any interim measure it has indicated.

Rule 40 – Urgent notification of an application

In any case of urgency the Registrar, with the authorisation of the President of the Chamber, may, without prejudice to the taking of any other procedural steps and by any available means, inform a Contracting Party concerned in an application of the introduction of the application and of a summary of its objects.

Rule 41 – Case priority

The Chamber shall deal with applications in the order in which they become ready for examination. It may, however, decide to give priority to a particular application.

Rule 42 – Measures for taking evidence

(1) The Chamber may, at the request of a party or a third party, or of its own motion, obtain any evidence which it considers capable of providing clarification of the facts of the case. The Chamber may, inter alia, request the parties to produce documentary evidence and decide to hear as a witness or expert or in any other capacity any person whose evidence or statements seem likely to assist it in the carrying out of its tasks.

(2) The Chamber may, at any time during the proceedings, depute one or more of its members or of the other judges of the Court to conduct an inquiry, carry out an investigation on the spot or take evidence in some other manner. It may appoint independent external experts to assist such a delegation.

(3) The Chamber may ask any person or institution of its choice to obtain information, express an opinion or make a report on any specific point.

(4) The parties shall assist the Chamber, or its delegation, in implementing any measures for taking evidence.

(5) Where a report has been drawn up or some other measure taken in accordance with the preceding paragraphs at the request of an applicant or respondent Contracting Party, the costs entailed shall be borne by that Party unless the Chamber decides otherwise. In other cases the Chamber shall decide whether such costs are to be borne by the Council of Europe or awarded against the applicant or third party at whose request the report was drawn up or the other measure was taken. In all cases the costs shall be taxed by the President of the Chamber.

Rule 43 – Joinder and simultaneous examination of applications

(1) The Chamber may, either at the request of the parties or of its own motion, order the joinder of two or more applications.

(2) The President of the Chamber may, after consulting the parties, order that the proceedings in applications assigned to the same Chamber be conducted simultaneously, without prejudice to the decision of the Chamber on the joinder of the applications.

Rule 44 – Striking out and restoration to the list

(1) When an applicant Contracting Party notifies the Registrar of its intention not to proceed with the case, the Chamber may strike the application out of the Court's list under Article 37 of the Convention if the other Contracting Party or Parties concerned in the case agree to such discontinuance.

(2) The decision to strike out an application which has been declared admissible shall be given in the form of a judgment. The President of the Chamber shall forward that judgment, once it has become final, to the Committee of Ministers in order to allow the latter to supervise, in accordance with Article 46 §2 of the Convention, the execution of any undertakings which may have been attached to the discontinuance, friendly settlement or solution of the matter.

(3) When an application has been struck out, the costs shall be at the discretion of the Court. If an award of costs is made in a decision striking out an application which has not been declared admissible, the President of the Chamber shall forward the decision to the Committee of Ministers

(4) The Court may restore an application to its list if it concludes that exceptional circumstances justify such a course.

CHAPTER II – INSTITUTION OF PROCEEDINGS
Rule 45 – Signatures

(1) Any application made under Articles 33 or 34 of the Convention shall be submitted in writing and shall be signed by the applicant or by the applicant's representative.

(2) Where an application is made by a non-governmental organisation or by a group of individuals, it shall be signed by those persons competent to represent that organisation or group. The Chamber or Committee concerned shall determine any question as to whether the persons who have signed an application are competent to do so.

(3) Where applicants are represented in accordance with Rule 36, a power of attorney or written authority to act shall be supplied by their representative or representatives.

Rule 46 – Contents of an inter-State application

Any Contracting Party or Parties intending to bring a case before the Court under Article 33 of the Convention shall file with the registry an application setting out:

(a) the name of the Contracting Party against which the application is made;

(b) a statement of the facts;

(c) a statement of the alleged violation(s) of the Convention and the relevant arguments;

(d) a statement on compliance with the admissibility criteria (exhaustion of domestic remedies and the six-month rule) laid down in Article 35 §1 of the Convention;

(e) the object of the application and a general indication of any claims for just satisfaction made under Article 41 of the Convention on behalf of the alleged injured party or parties; and

(f) the name and address of the person(s) appointed as Agent; and accompanied by

(g) copies of any relevant documents and in particular the decisions, whether judicial or not, relating to the object of the application.

Rule 47 – Contents of an individual application

(1) Any application under Article 34 of the Convention shall be made on the application form provided by the registry, unless the President of the Section concerned decides otherwise. It shall set out:

(a) the name, date of birth, nationality, sex, occupation and address of the applicant;

(b) the name, occupation and address of the representative, if any;

(c) the name of the Contracting Party or Parties against which the application is made;

(d) a succinct statement of the facts;

(e) a succinct statement of the alleged violation(s) of the Convention and the relevant arguments;

(f) a succinct statement on the applicant's compliance with the admissibility criteria (exhaustion of domestic remedies and the six-month rule) laid down in Article 35 §1 of the Convention; and

(g) the object of the application as well as a general indication of any claims for just satisfaction which the applicant may wish to make under Article 41 of the Convention; and be accompanied by

(h) copies of any relevant documents and in particular the decisions, whether judicial or not, relating to the object of the application.

(2) Applicants shall furthermore:

(a) provide information, notably the documents and decisions referred to in paragraph 1(h) above, enabling it to be shown that the admissibility criteria (exhaustion of domestic remedies and the six-month rule) laid down in Article 35 §1 of the Convention have been satisfied; and

(b) indicate whether they have submitted their complaints to any other procedure of international investigation or settlement.

(3) Applicants who do not wish their identity to be disclosed to the public shall so indicate and shall submit a statement of the reasons justifying such a departure from the normal rule of public access to information in proceedings before the Court. The President of the Chamber may authorise anonymity in exceptional and duly justified cases.

(4) Failure to comply with the requirements set out in paragraphs 1 and 2 above may result in the application not being registered and examined by the Court.

(5) The date of introduction of the application shall as a general rule be considered to be the date of the first communication from the applicant setting out, even summarily, the object of the application. The Court may for good cause nevertheless decide that a different date shall be considered to be the date of introduction.

(6) Applicants shall keep the Court informed of any change of address and of all circumstances relevant to the application.

CHAPTER III – JUDGE RAPPORTEURS

Rule 48 – Inter-State applications

(1) Where an application is made under Article 33 of the Convention, the Chamber constituted to consider the case shall designate one or more of its judges as Judge Rapporteur(s), who shall submit a report on admissibility when the written observations of the Contracting Parties concerned have been received. Rule 49 §4 shall, in so far as appropriate, be applicable to this report.

(2) After an application made under Article 33 of the Convention has been declared admissible, the Judge Rapporteur(s) shall submit such reports, drafts and other documents as may assist the Chamber in the carrying out of its functions.

Rule 49 – Individual applications

(1) Where an application is made under Article 34 of the Convention, the President of the Section to which the case has been assigned shall designate a judge as Judge Rapporteur, who shall examine the application.

(2) In their examination of applications Judge Rapporteurs

(a) may request the parties to submit, within a specified time, any factual information, documents or other material which they consider to be relevant;

(b) shall, subject to the President of the Section directing that the case be considered by a Chamber, decide whether the application is to be considered by a Committee or by a Chamber.

(3) Where a case is considered by a Committee in accordance with Article 28 of the Convention, the report of the Judge Rapporteur shall contain
(a) a brief statement of the relevant facts;
(b) a brief statement of the reasons underlying the proposal to declare the application inadmissible or to strike it out of the list.

(4) Where a case is considered by a Chamber pursuant to Article 29 §1 of the Convention, the report of the Judge Rapporteur shall contain
(a) a statement of the relevant facts, including any information obtained under paragraph 2 of this Rule;
(b) an indication of the issues arising under the Convention in the application;
(c) a proposal on admissibility and on any other action to be taken, together, if need be, with a provisional opinion on the merits.

(5) After an application made under Article 34 of the Convention has been declared admissible, the Judge Rapporteur shall submit such reports, drafts and other documents as may assist the Chamber in the carrying out of its functions.

Rule 50 – Grand Chamber proceedings

Where a case has been submitted to the Grand Chamber either under Article 30 or under Article 43 of the Convention, the President of the Grand Chamber shall designate as Judge Rapporteur(s) one or, in the case of an inter-State application, one or more of its members.

CHAPTER IV – PROCEEDINGS ON ADMISSIBILITY

Inter-State applications

Rule 51

(1) When an application is made under Article 33 of the Convention, the President of the Court shall immediately give notice of the application to the respondent Contracting Party and shall assign the application to one of the Sections.

(2) In accordance with Rule 26 §1 (a), the judges elected in respect of the applicant and respondent Contracting Parties shall sit as ex officio members of the Chamber constituted to consider the case. Rule 30 shall apply if the application has been brought by several Contracting Parties or if applications with the same object brought by several Contracting Parties are being examined jointly under Rule 43 §2.

(3) On assignment of the case to a Section, the President of the Section shall constitute the Chamber in accordance with Rule 26 §1 and shall invite the respondent Contracting Party to submit its observations in writing on the admissibility of the application. The observations so obtained shall be communicated by the Registrar to the applicant Contracting Party, which may submit written observations in reply.

(4) Before ruling on the admissibility of the application, the Chamber may decide to invite the parties to submit further observations in writing.

(5) A hearing on the admissibility shall be held if one or more of the Contracting Parties concerned so requests or if the Chamber so decides of its own motion.

(6) After consulting the Parties, the President of the Chamber shall fix the written and, where appropriate, oral procedure and for that purpose shall lay down the time-limit within which any written observations are to be filed.

(7) In its deliberations the Chamber shall take into consideration the report submitted by the Judge Rapporteur(s) under Rule 48 §1.

Individual applications
Rule 52 – Assignment of applications to the Sections

(1) Any application made under Article 34 of the Convention shall be assigned to a Section by the President of the Court, who in so doing shall endeavour to ensure a fair distribution of cases between the Sections.

(2) The Chamber of seven judges provided for in Article 27 §1 of the Convention shall be constituted by the President of the Section concerned in accordance with Rule 26 §1 once it has been decided that the application is to be considered by a Chamber.

(3) Pending the constitution of a Chamber in accordance with the preceding paragraph, the President of the Section shall exercise any powers conferred on the President of the Chamber by these Rules.

Rule 53 – Procedure before a Committee

(1) In its deliberations the Committee shall take into consideration the report submitted by the Judge Rapporteur under Rule 49 §3.

(2) The Judge Rapporteur, if he or she is not a member of the Committee, may be invited to attend the deliberations of the Committee.

(3) In accordance with Article 28 of the Convention, the Committee may, by a unanimous vote, declare inadmissible or strike out of the Court's list of cases an application where such a decision can be taken without further examination. This decision shall be final.

(4) If no decision pursuant to paragraph 3 of the present Rule is taken, the application shall be forwarded to the Chamber constituted under Rule 52 §2 to examine the case.

Rule 54 – Procedure before a Chamber

(1) In its deliberations the Chamber shall take into consideration the report submitted by the Judge Rapporteur under Rule 49 §4.

(2) The Chamber may at once declare the application inadmissible or strike it out of the Court's list of cases.

(3) Alternatively, the Chamber may decide to:
   (a) request the parties to submit any factual information, documents or other material which it considers to be relevant;
   (b) give notice of the application to the respondent Contracting Party and invite that Party to submit written observations on the application;
   (c) invite the parties to submit further observations in writing.

(4) Before taking its decision on admissibility, the Chamber may decide, either at the request of the parties or of its own motion, to hold a hearing. In that event, unless the Chamber shall exceptionally decide otherwise, the parties shall be invited also to address the issues arising in relation to the merits of the application.

(5) The President of the Chamber shall fix the procedure, including time-limits, in relation to any decisions taken by the Chamber under paragraphs 3 and 4 of this Rule.

Inter-State and individual applications
Rule 55 – Pleas of inadmissibility
Any plea of inadmissibility must, in so far as its character and the circumstances permit, be raised by the respondent Contracting Party in its written or oral observations on the admissibility of the application submitted as provided in Rule 51 or 54, as the case may be.

Rule 56 – Decision of a Chamber
(1) The decision of the Chamber shall state whether it was taken unanimously or by a majority and shall be accompanied or followed by reasons.

(2) The decision of the Chamber shall be communicated by the Registrar to the applicant and to the Contracting Party or Parties concerned.

Rule 57 – Language of the decision
(1) Unless the Court decides that a decision shall be given in both official languages, all decisions shall be given either in English or in French. Decisions given shall be accessible to the public.

(2) Publication of such decisions in the official reports of the Court, as provided for in Rule 78, shall be in both official languages of the Court.

CHAPTER V – PROCEEDINGS AFTER THE ADMISSION OF AN APPLICATION
Rule 58 – Inter-State applications
(1) Once the Chamber has decided to admit an application made under Article 33 of the Convention, the President of the Chamber shall, after consulting the Contracting Parties concerned, lay down the time-limits for the filing of written observations on the merits and for the production of any further evidence. The President may however, with the agreement of the Contracting Parties concerned, direct that a written procedure is to be dispensed with.

(2) A hearing on the merits shall be held if one or more of the Contracting Parties concerned so requests or if the Chamber so decides of its own motion. The President of the Chamber shall fix the oral procedure.

(3) In its deliberations the Chamber shall take into consideration any reports, drafts and other documents submitted by the Judge Rapporteur(s) under Rule 48 §2.

Rule 59 – Individual applications
(1) Once the Chamber has decided to admit an application made under Article 34 of the Convention, it may invite the parties to submit further evidence and written observations.

(2) A hearing on the merits shall be held if the Chamber so decides of its own motion or, provided that no hearing also addressing the merits has been held at the admissibility stage under Rule 54 §4, if one of the parties so requests. However, the Chamber may exceptionally decide that the discharging of its functions under Article 38 §1 (a) of the Convention does not require a hearing to be held.

(3) The President of the Chamber shall, where appropriate, fix the written and oral procedure.

(4) In its deliberations the Chamber shall take into consideration any reports, drafts and other documents submitted by the Judge Rapporteur under Rule 49 §5.

Rule 60 – Claims for just satisfaction

(1) Any claim which the applicant Contracting Party or the applicant may wish to make for just satisfaction under Article 41 of the Convention shall, unless the President of the Chamber directs otherwise, be set out in the written observations on the merits or, if no such written observations are filed, in a special document filed no later than two months after the decision declaring the application admissible.

(2) Itemised particulars of all claims made, together with the relevant supporting documents or vouchers, shall be submitted, failing which the Chamber may reject the claim in whole or in part.

(3) The Chamber may, at any time during the proceedings, invite any party to submit comments on the claim for just satisfaction.

Rule 61 – Third-party intervention

(1) The decision declaring an application admissible shall be notified by the Registrar to any Contracting Party one of whose nationals is an applicant in the case, as well as to the respondent Contracting Party under Rule 56 §2.

(2) Where a Contracting Party seeks to exercise its right to submit written comments or to take part in an oral hearing, pursuant to Article 36 §1 of the Convention, the President of the Chamber shall fix the procedure to be followed.

(3) In accordance with Article 36 §2 of the Convention, the President of the Chamber may, in the interests of the proper administration of justice, invite or grant leave to any Contracting State which is not a party to the proceedings, or any person concerned who is not the applicant, to submit written comments or, in exceptional cases, to take part in an oral hearing. Requests for leave for this purpose must be duly reasoned and submitted in one of the official languages, within a reasonable time after the fixing of the written procedure.

(4) Any invitation or grant of leave referred to in paragraph 3 of this Rule shall be subject to any conditions, including time-limits, set by the President of the Chamber. Where such conditions are not complied with, the President may decide not to include the comments in the case file.

(5) Written comments submitted in accordance with this Rule shall be submitted in one of the official languages, save where leave to use another language has been granted under Rule 34 §4. They shall be transmitted by

the Registrar to the parties to the case, who shall be entitled, subject to any conditions, including time-limits, set by the President of the Chamber, to file written observations in reply.

Rule 62 – Friendly settlement

(1) Once an application has been declared admissible, the Registrar, acting on the instructions of the Chamber or its President, shall enter into contact with the parties with a view to securing a friendly settlement of the matter in accordance with Article 38 §1 (b) of the Convention. The Chamber shall take any steps that appear appropriate to facilitate such a settlement.

(2) In accordance with Article 38 §2 of the Convention, the friendly settlement negotiations shall be confidential and without prejudice to the parties' arguments in the contentious proceedings. No written or oral communication and no offer or concession made in the framework of the attempt to secure a friendly settlement may be referred to or relied on in the contentious proceedings.

(3) If the Chamber is informed by the Registrar that the parties have agreed to a friendly settlement, it shall, after verifying that the settlement has been reached on the basis of respect for human rights as defined in the Convention and the protocols thereto, strike the case out of the Court's list in accordance with Rule 44 §2.

CHAPTER VI – HEARINGS
Rule 63 – Conduct of hearings

(1) The President of the Chamber shall direct hearings and shall prescribe the order in which Agents and advocates or advisers of the parties shall be called upon to speak.

(2) Where a fact-finding hearing is being carried out by a delegation of the Chamber under Rule 42, the head of the delegation shall conduct the hearing and the delegation shall exercise any relevant power conferred on the Chamber by the Convention or these Rules.

Rule 64 – Failure to appear at a hearing

Where, without showing sufficient cause, a party fails to appear, the Chamber may, provided that it is satisfied that such a course is consistent with the proper administration of justice, nonetheless proceed with the hearing.

Rule 65 – Convocation of witnesses, experts and other persons; costs of their appearance

(1) Witnesses, experts and other persons whom the Chamber or the President of the Chamber decides to hear shall be summoned by the Registrar.

(2) The summons shall indicate:
   (a) the case in connection with which it has been issued;
   (b) the object of the inquiry, expert opinion or other measure ordered by the Chamber or the President of the Chamber;
   (c) any provisions for the payment of the sum due to the person summoned.

(3) If the persons concerned appear at the request or on behalf of an applicant

or respondent Contracting Party, the costs of their appearance shall be borne by that Party unless the Chamber decides otherwise. In other cases, the Chamber shall decide whether such costs are to be borne by the Council of Europe or awarded against the applicant or third party at whose request the person summoned appeared. In all cases the costs shall be taxed by the President of the Chamber.

Rule 66 – Oath or solemn declaration by witnesses and experts

(1) After the establishment of the identity of the witness and before testifying, every witness shall take the following oath or make the following solemn declaration:

'I swear' – or 'I solemnly declare upon my honour and conscience' – 'that I shall speak the truth, the whole truth and nothing but the truth.'

This act shall be recorded in minutes.

(2) After the establishment of the identity of the expert and before carrying out his or her task, every expert shall take the following oath or make the following solemn declaration:

'I swear' – or 'I solemnly declare' – 'that I will discharge my duty as an expert honourably and conscientiously.'

This act shall be recorded in minutes.

(3) This oath may be taken or this declaration made before the President of the Chamber, or before a judge or any public authority nominated by the President.

Rule 67 – Objection to a witness or expert; hearing of a person for information purposes

The Chamber shall decide in the event of any dispute arising from an objection to a witness or expert. It may hear for information purposes a person who cannot be heard as a witness.

Rule 68 – Questions put during hearings

(1) Any judge may put questions to the Agents, advocates or advisers of the parties, to the applicant, witnesses and experts, and to any other persons appearing before the Chamber.

(2) The witnesses, experts and other persons referred to in Rule 42 §1 may, subject to the control of the President of the Chamber, be examined by the Agents and advocates or advisers of the parties. In the event of an objection as to the relevance of a question put, the President of the Chamber shall decide.

Rule 69 – Failure to appear, refusal to give evidence or false evidence

If, without good reason, a witness or any other person who has been duly summoned fails to appear or refuses to give evidence, the Registrar shall, on being so required by the President of the Chamber, inform the Contracting Party to whose jurisdiction the witness or other person is subject. The same provisions shall apply if a witness or expert has, in the opinion of the Chamber, violated the oath or solemn declaration provided for in Rule 66.

Rule 70 – Verbatim record of hearings

(1) The Registrar shall, if the Chamber so directs, be responsible for the making of a verbatim record of a hearing. The verbatim record shall include

   (a) the composition of the Chamber at the hearing;

   (b) a list of those appearing before the Court, that is to say Agents, advocates and advisers of the parties and any third party taking part;

   (c) the surnames, forenames, description and address of each witness, expert or other person heard;

   (d) the text of statements made, questions put and replies given;

   (e) the text of any decision delivered during the hearing by the Chamber or the President of the Chamber.

(2) If all or part of the verbatim record is in a non-official language, the Registrar shall, if the Chamber so directs, arrange for its translation into one of the official languages.

(3) The representatives of the parties shall receive a copy of the verbatim record in order that they may, subject to the control of the Registrar or the President of the Chamber, make corrections, but in no case may such corrections affect the sense and bearing of what was said. The Registrar shall lay down, in accordance with the instructions of the President of the Chamber, the time-limits granted for this purpose.

(4) The verbatim record, once so corrected, shall be signed by the President and the Registrar and shall then constitute certified matters of record.

CHAPTER VII – PROCEEDINGS BEFORE THE GRAND CHAMBER
Rule 71 – Applicability of procedural provisions

Any provisions governing proceedings before the Chambers shall apply, mutatis mutandis, to proceedings before the Grand Chamber.

Rule 72 – Relinquishment of jurisdiction by a Chamber in favour of the Grand Chamber

(1) In accordance with Article 30 of the Convention, where a case pending before a Chamber raises a serious question affecting the interpretation of the Convention or the protocols thereto or where the resolution of a question before it might have a result inconsistent with a judgment previously delivered by the Court, the Chamber may, at any time before it has rendered its judgment, relinquish jurisdiction in favour of the Grand Chamber, unless one of the parties to the case has objected in accordance with paragraph 2 of this Rule. Reasons need not be given for the decision to relinquish.

(2) The Registrar shall notify the parties of the Chamber's intention to relinquish jurisdiction. The parties shall have one month from the date of that notification within which to file at the Registry a duly reasoned objection. An objection which does not fulfil these conditions shall be considered invalid by the Chamber.

Rule 73 – Request by a party for referral of a case to the Grand Chamber

(1) In accordance with Article 43 of the Convention, any party to a case may

exceptionally, within a period of three months from the date of delivery of the judgment of a Chamber, file in writing at the Registry a request that the case be referred to the Grand Chamber. The party shall specify in its request the serious question affecting the interpretation or application of the Convention or the protocols thereto, or the serious issue of general importance, which in its view warrants consideration by the Grand Chamber.

(2) A panel of five judges of the Grand Chamber constituted in accordance with Rule 24 §6 shall examine the request solely on the basis of the existing case file. It shall accept the request only if it considers that the case does raise such a question or issue. Reasons need not be given for a refusal of the request.

(3) If the panel accepts the request, the Grand Chamber shall decide the case by means of a judgment.

CHAPTER VIII – JUDGMENTS
Rule 74 – Contents of the judgment

(1) A judgment as referred to in Articles 42 and 44 of the Convention shall contain:
   (a) the names of the President and the other judges constituting the Chamber concerned, and the name of the Registrar or the Deputy Registrar;
   (b) the dates on which it was adopted and delivered;
   (c) a description of the parties;
   (d) the names of the Agents, advocates or advisers of the parties;
   (e) an account of the procedure followed;
   (f) the facts of the case;
   (g) a summary of the submissions of the parties;
   (h) the reasons in point of law;
   (i) the operative provisions;
   (j) the decision, if any, in respect of costs;
   (k) the number of judges constituting the majority;
   (l) where appropriate, a statement as to which text is authentic.

(2) Any judge who has taken part in the consideration of the case shall be entitled to annex to the judgment either a separate opinion, concurring with or dissenting from that judgment, or a bare statement of dissent.

Rule 75 – Ruling on just satisfaction

(1) Where the Chamber finds that there has been a violation of the Convention, it shall give in the same judgment a ruling on the application of Article 41 of the Convention if that question, after being raised in accordance with Rule 60, is ready for decision; if the question is not ready for decision, the Chamber shall reserve it in whole or in part and shall fix the further procedure.

(2) For the purposes of ruling on the application of Article 41 of the Convention, the Chamber shall, as far as possible, be composed of those judges who sat to consider the merits of the case. Where it is not possible to constitute the original Chamber, the President of the Court shall complete or compose the Chamber by drawing lots.

(3) The Chamber may, when affording just satisfaction under Article 41 of the

Convention, direct that if settlement is not made within a specified time, interest is to be payable on any sums awarded.

(4) If the Court is informed that an agreement has been reached between the injured party and the Contracting Party liable, it shall verify the equitable nature of the agreement and, where it finds the agreement to be equitable, strike the case out of the list in accordance with Rule 44 §2.

Rule 76 – Language of the judgment

(1) Unless the Court decides that a judgment shall be given in both official languages, all judgments shall be given either in English or in French. Judgments given shall be accessible to the public.

(2) Publication of such judgments in the official reports of the Court, as provided for in Rule 78, shall be in both official languages of the Court.

Rule 77 – Signature, delivery and notification of the judgment

(1) Judgments shall be signed by the President of the Chamber and the Registrar.

(2) The judgment may be read out at a public hearing by the President of the Chamber or by another judge delegated by him or her. The Agents and representatives of the parties shall be informed in due time of the date of the hearing. Otherwise the notification provided for in paragraph 3 of this Rule shall constitute delivery of the judgment.

(3) The judgment shall be transmitted to the Committee of Ministers. The Registrar shall send certified copies to the parties, to the Secretary General of the Council of Europe, to any third party and to any other person directly concerned. The original copy, duly signed and sealed, shall be placed in the archives of the Court.

Rule 78 – Publication of judgments and other documents

In accordance with Article 44 §3 of the Convention, final judgments of the Court shall be published, under the responsibility of the Registrar, in an appropriate form. The Registrar shall in addition be responsible for the publication of official reports of selected judgments and decisions and of any document which the President of the Court considers it useful to publish.

Rule 79 – Request for interpretation of a judgment

(1) A party may request the interpretation of a judgment within a period of one year following the delivery of that judgment.

(2) The request shall be filed with the Registry. It shall state precisely the point or points in the operative provisions of the judgment on which interpretation is required.

(3) The original Chamber may decide of its own motion to refuse the request on the ground that there is no reason to warrant considering it. Where it is not possible to constitute the original Chamber, the President of the Court shall complete or compose the Chamber by drawing lots.

(4) If the Chamber does not refuse the request, the Registrar shall communicate it to the other party or parties and shall invite them to submit any written comments within a time-limit laid down by the President of the Chamber. The President of the Chamber shall also fix the date of the

hearing should the Chamber decide to hold one. The Chamber shall decide by means of a judgment.

Rule 80 – Request for revision of a judgment

(1) A party may, in the event of the discovery of a fact which might by its nature have a decisive influence and which, when a judgment was delivered, was unknown to the Court and could not reasonably have been known to that party, request the Court, within a period of six months after that party acquired knowledge of the fact, to revise that judgment.

(2) The request shall mention the judgment of which revision is requested and shall contain the information necessary to show that the conditions laid down in paragraph 1 have been complied with. It shall be accompanied by a copy of all supporting documents. The request and supporting documents shall be filed with the Registry.

(3) The original Chamber may decide of its own motion to refuse the request on the ground that there is no reason to warrant considering it. Where it is not possible to constitute the original Chamber, the President of the Court shall complete or compose the Chamber by drawing lots.

(4) If the Chamber does not refuse the request, the Registrar shall communicate it to the other party or parties and shall invite them to submit any written comments within a time-limit laid down by the President of the Chamber. The President of the Chamber shall also fix the date of the hearing should the Chamber decide to hold one. The Chamber shall decide by means of a judgment.

Rule 81 – Rectification of errors in decisions and judgments

Without prejudice to the provisions on revision of judgments and on restoration to the list of applications, the Court may, of its own motion or at the request of a party made within one month of the delivery of a decision or a judgment, rectify clerical errors, errors in calculation or obvious mistakes.

CHAPTER IX – ADVISORY OPINIONS
Rule 82

In proceedings relating to advisory opinions the Court shall apply, in addition to the provisions of Articles 47, 48 and 49 of the Convention, the provisions which follow. It shall also apply the other provisions of these Rules to the extent to which it considers this to be appropriate.

Rule 83

The request for an advisory opinion shall be filed with the Registry. It shall state fully and precisely the question on which the opinion of the Court is sought, and also

(a) the date on which the Committee of Ministers adopted the decision referred to in Article 47 §3 of the Convention;

(b) the names and addresses of the person or persons appointed by the Committee of Ministers to give the Court any explanations which it may require.

The request shall be accompanied by all documents likely to elucidate the question.

Rule 84

(1) On receipt of a request, the Registrar shall transmit a copy of it to all members of the Court.

(2) The Registrar shall inform the Contracting Parties that the Court is prepared to receive their written comments.

Rule 85

(1) The President of the Court shall lay down the time-limits for filing written comments or other documents.

(2) Written comments or other documents shall be filed with the Registry. The Registrar shall transmit copies of them to all the members of the Court, to the Committee of Ministers and to each of the Contracting Parties.

Rule 86

After the close of the written procedure, the President of the Court shall decide whether the Contracting Parties which have submitted written comments are to be given an opportunity to develop them at an oral hearing held for the purpose.

Rule 87

If the Court considers that the request for an advisory opinion is not within its consultative competence as defined in Article 47 of the Convention, it shall so declare in a reasoned decision.

Rule 88

(1) Advisory opinions shall be given by a majority vote of the Grand Chamber. They shall mention the number of judges constituting the majority.

(2) Any judge may, if he or she so desires, attach to the opinion of the Court either a separate opinion, concurring with or dissenting from the advisory opinion, or a bare statement of dissent.

Rule 89

The advisory opinion shall be read out in one of the two official languages by the President of the Court, or by another judge delegated by the President, at a public hearing, prior notice having been given to the Committee of Ministers and to each of the Contracting Parties.

Rule 90

The opinion, or any decision given under Rule 87, shall be signed by the President of the Court and by the Registrar. The original copy, duly signed and sealed, shall be placed in the archives of the Court. The Registrar shall send certified copies to the Committee of Ministers, to the Contracting Parties and to the Secretary General of the Council of Europe.

CHAPTER X – LEGAL AID
Rule 91

(1) The President of the Chamber may, either at the request of an applicant lodging an application under Article 34 of the Convention or of his or her own motion, grant free legal aid to the applicant in connection with the

presentation of the case from the moment when observations in writing on the admissibility of that application are received from the respondent Contracting Party in accordance with Rule 54 §3 (b), or where the time-limit for their submission has expired.

(2) Subject to Rule 96, where the applicant has been granted legal aid in connection with the presentation of his or her case before the Chamber, that grant shall continue in force for purposes of his or her representation before the Grand Chamber.

Rule 92

Legal aid shall be granted only where the President of the Chamber is satisfied:

(a) that it is necessary for the proper conduct of the case before the Chamber;

(b) that the applicant has insufficient means to meet all or part of the costs entailed.

Rule 93

(1) In order to determine whether or not applicants have sufficient means to meet all or part of the costs entailed, they shall be required to complete a form of declaration stating their income, capital assets and any financial commitments in respect of dependants, or any other financial obligations. The declaration shall be certified by the appropriate domestic authority or authorities.

(2) The Contracting Party concerned shall be requested to submit its comments in writing.

(3) After receiving the information mentioned in paragraphs 1 and 2 above, the President of the Chamber shall decide whether or not to grant legal aid. The Registrar shall inform the parties accordingly.

Rule 94

(1) Fees shall be payable to the advocates or other persons appointed in accordance with Rule 36 §4. Fees may, where appropriate, be paid to more than one such representative.

(2) Legal aid may be granted to cover not only representatives' fees but also travelling and subsistence expenses and other necessary expenses incurred by the applicant or appointed representative.

Rule 95

On a decision to grant legal aid, the Registrar shall:

(a) fix the rate of fees to be paid in accordance with the legal-aid scales in force;

(b) the level of expenses to be paid.

Rule 96

The President of the Chamber may, if satisfied that the conditions stated in Rule 92 are no longer fulfilled, revoke or vary a grant of legal aid at any time.

TITLE III — TRANSITIONAL RULES
Rule 97 — Judges' terms of office
The duration of the terms of office of the judges who were members of the Court at the date of the entry into force of Protocol No. 11 to the Convention shall be calculated as from that date.

Rule 98 — Presidency of the Sections
For a period of three years from the entry into force of Protocol No. 11 to the Convention,
(a) the two Presidents of Sections who are not simultaneously Vice-Presidents of the Court and the Vice-Presidents of the Sections shall be elected for a term of office of eighteen months;
(b) the Vice-Presidents of the Sections may not be immediately re-elected.

Rule 99 — Relations between the Court and the Commission
(1) In cases brought before the Court under Article 5 §§4 and 5 of Protocol No. 11 to the Convention the Court may invite the Commission to delegate one or more of its members to take part in the consideration of the case before the Court.
(2) In cases referred to in the preceding paragraph the Court shall take into consideration the report of the Commission adopted pursuant to former Article 31 of the Convention.
(3) Unless the President of the Chamber decides otherwise, the said report shall be made available to the public through the Registrar as soon as possible after the case has been brought before the Court.
(4) The remainder of the case file of the Commission, including all pleadings, in cases brought before the Court under Article 5 §§2 to 5 of Protocol No. 11 shall remain confidential unless the President of the Chamber decides otherwise.
(5) In cases where the Commission has taken evidence but has been unable to adopt a report in accordance with former Article 31 of the Convention, the Court shall take into consideration the verbatim records, documentation and opinion of the Commission's delegations arising from such investigations.

Rule 100 — Chamber and Grand Chamber proceedings
(1) In cases referred to the Court under Article 5 §4 of Protocol No. 11 to the Convention, a panel of the Grand Chamber constituted in accordance with Rule 24 §6 shall determine, solely on the basis of the existing case file, whether a Chamber or the Grand Chamber is to decide the case.
(2) If the case is decided by a Chamber, the judgment of the Chamber shall, in accordance with Article 5 §4 of Protocol No. 11, be final and Rule 73 shall be inapplicable.
(3) Cases transmitted to the Court under Article 5 §5 of Protocol No. 11 shall be forwarded by the President of the Court to the Grand Chamber.
(4) For each case transmitted to the Grand Chamber under Article 5 §5 of the Protocol No 11, the Grand Chamber shall be completed by judges designated by rotation within one of the groups mentioned in Rule 24 §3,

the cases being allocated to the groups on an alternate basis.

Rule 101 – Grant of legal aid

Subject to Rule 96, in cases brought before the Court under Article 5 §§2 to 5 of Protocol No. 11 to the Convention, a grant of legal aid made to an applicant in the proceedings before the Commission or the former Court shall continue in force for the purposes of his or her representation before the Court.

Rule 102 – Request for interpretation or revision of a judgment

(1) Where a party requests interpretation or revision of a judgment delivered by the former Court, the President of the Court shall assign the request to one of the Sections in accordance with the conditions laid down in Rule 51 or 52, as the case may be.

(2) The President of the relevant Section shall, notwithstanding Rules 79 §3 and 80 §3, constitute a new Chamber to consider the request.

(3) The Chamber to be constituted shall include as ex officio members:
  (a) the President of the Section; and, whether or not they are members of the relevant Section,
  (b) the judge elected in respect of any Contracting Party concerned or, if he or she is unable to sit, any judge appointed under Rule 29;
  (c) any judge of the Court who was a member of the original Chamber that delivered the judgment in the former Court.

(4) (a) The other members of the Chamber shall be designated by the President of the Section by means of a drawing of lots from among the members of the relevant Section.
  (b) The members of the Section who are not so designated shall sit in the case as substitute judges.

TITLE IV – FINAL CLAUSES

Rule 103 – Amendment or suspension of a Rule

(1) Any Rule may be amended upon a motion made after notice where such a motion is carried at the next session of the plenary Court by a majority of all the members of the Court. Notice of such a motion shall be delivered in writing to the Registrar at least one month before the session at which it is to be discussed. On receipt of such a notice of motion, the Registrar shall inform all members of the Court at the earliest possible moment.

(2) A Rule relating to the internal working of the Court may be suspended upon a motion made without notice, provided that this decision is taken unanimously by the Chamber concerned. The suspension of a Rule shall in this case be limited in its operation to the particular purpose for which it was sought.

Rule 104 – Entry into force of the Rules

The present Rules shall enter into force on 1 November 1998.

Rules of the Committee of Ministers

(relevant extracts)

RULES ADOPTED BY THE COMMITTEE OF MINISTERS FOR THE APPLICATION OF ARTICLE 32 OF THE EUROPEAN CONVENTION ON HUMAN RIGHTS

A RULES OF SUBSTANCE

Rule 1

When exercising its functions under Article 32 of the Convention, the Committee of Ministers is entitled to discuss the substance of any case on which the Commission has submitted a report, for example by considering a written or oral statements of the parties and hearing of witnesses (see Rule 4).

Rule 2

The representative of any member state on the Committee of Ministers shall be fully qualified to take part in exercising the functions and powers set forth in Article 32 of the Convention, even if that state has not yet ratified the Convention.

Rule 3

Each representative on the Committee of Ministers has an intrinsic right to make submissions and deposit documents. Consequently, the representative on the Committee of Ministers of a government which was not a party to the proceedings before the Commission, may play a full part in the proceedings before the Committee of Ministers.[2]

Rule 4

While the Committee of Ministers must have all the necessary powers to reach a decision on a report of the Commission, nevertheless it may not itself wish to undertake the task of taking evidence, etc., should the need arise. The procedure to be followed in such a case will be decided ad hoc.[1]

Rule 5

The text approved at the 181st meeting of the Ministers' Deputies contained a restatement of the rules previously adopted at the 68th (January 1959), 94th (January 1961), 99th (May 1961), 140th (April 1965) and 164th (October 1967) meetings.

See appendix, paragraph 1.

See appendix, paragraph 2.

Rule 5 was deleted by the Ministers' Deputies on 19 December 1991.

Rule 6

The Committee of Ministers considers that the Commission is not entitled to make proposals under Article 31, paragraph 3, of the Convention in cases where it considers that there has not been a violation of the Convention.

Rule 6 bis

Prior to taking a decision under Article 32, paragraph 1, of the Convention, the Committee of Ministers may be informed of a friendly settlement, arrangement or other fact of a kind to provide a solution of the matter. In that event. it may decide to discontinue its examination of the case, after satisfying itself that the solution envisaged is based on respect for human rights as defined in the Convention.

B PROCEDURAL RULES
Rule 7

If the chairmanship of the Committee of Ministers is held by the representative of a state which is party to a dispute referred to the Committee of Ministers, that representative shall step down from the chair during the discussion of the Commission's report.

Rule 8

The Chairman of the Committee shall obtain the opinion of the representatives of the State Party or States Parties to the dispute in regard to the procedure to be followed, and the Committee shall specify, if necessary, in what order and within what time-limits any written submissions or other documents are to be deposited.'

Rule 9

(1) During the examination of the case and before taking the decision mentioned in Article 32, paragraph 1, of the Convention, the Committee of Ministers may, if it deems advisable, request the Commission for information on particular points in the report which it has transmitted to the Committee.

(2) After taking a decision under Article 32, paragraph 1, to the effect that there has been a violation of the Convention, the Committee of Ministers may request the Commission to make proposals concerning in particular the appropriateness, nature and extent of just satisfaction for the injured party.

Rule 9 bis

When a vote is taken in accordance with Article 32, paragraph 1, and the majority required to decide whether there has been a violation of the Convention has not been attained, a second and final vote shall be taken at one of the three following meetings of the Committee of Ministers.

(1) This rule applies not only to inter-state disputes but also when the Committee of Ministers is considering the report of the Commission on an individual application.

Rule 9 ter

(1) The Commission's report shall be published when the Committee of Ministers has completed consideration of the case under Article 32, paragraph 1.

(2) The Committee of Ministers may, by way of exception and without prejudice to Article 32, paragraph 3, decide not to publish a report of the Commission or a part thereof upon a reasoned request of a Contracting Party or of the Commission.

Rule 10

In the matter of voting, the rules laid down in Article 20 of the Statute should, in general, apply.' In particular:

(a) the parties to the dispute shall have the right to vote;

(b) decisions taken in pursuance of Rule 6 bis require a two-thirds majority of the representatives casting a vote and a majority of the representatives entitled to sit on the Committee;

(c) certain questions of procedure, such as in what order and within what time-limits any written submissions or other documents are to be deposited, shall be determined by a simple majority of the representatives entitled to sit on the Committee.

Rule 11

The decision taken under Article 32, paragraph 1, will be published in the form of a resolution adopted by a two-thirds majority of the representatives casting a vote and a majority of the representatives entitled to sit on the Committee.

(1) In the case of a decision by the Committee of Ministers on the question whether there has been a violation of the Convention, paragraph 1 of Article 32 of the Convention already provides that 'the Committee of Ministers shall decide by a majority of two-thirds of the members entitled to sit on the Committee whether there has been a violation of the Convention'.

APPENDIX

Other points discussed by the Committee of Ministers:

1 With reference to Rule 3 above, the Committee of Ministers reserved its position on the possibility that the representative of a government which had not been a party to the proceedings before the Commission might make a request to the Committee of Ministers which had not been made before the Commission (for example, a request for damages).

2 In connection with Rule 4, the Committee of Ministers considered that while it must have all the necessary powers to reach a decision on a case submitted to it, nevertheless it is not well-equipped to take evidence, etc. and ought not normally to undertake such tasks. If therefore it should become necessary for the Committee of Ministers to take evidence, etc. when it is considering a case under Article 32, there are the following possibilities:

(a) to conclude a protocol to the Convention conferring on the Commission the power to undertake such tasks on behalf of the Committee of Ministers;

(b) to invite the Commission to undertake these tasks on its behalf, since the Commission is in its nature better equipped to do so, if the Commission agrees to this procedure;

(c) the Committee of Ministers could take evidence, etc. in plenary sessions (possibly with alternate members) or appoint a sub-committee for the purpose;

(d) under Article 17 of the Statute, the Committee of Ministers may set up advisory and technical committees for specific purposes.

The Committee of Ministers decided not to adopt the first of these possibilities but to leave the choice open for a decision ad hoc should the need arise.

2 bis The Committee of Ministers decided that in every case in which it finds there has been a violation of the Convention, it would consider, taking into account any proposals from the Commission, whether just satisfaction should be afforded to the injured party and, if necessary, indicate measures on this subject to the state concerned.

3 (a) The Committee of Ministers decided not to establish a procedure permitting the communication to an applicant of the report of the Commission on his application, or the communication to the Committee of Ministers of the applicant's observations on the report.

(b) The communication to an individual applicant of the complete text or extracts from the report of the Commission should take place only as an exceptional measure (for example, where the Committee of Ministers wishes to obtain the observations of the applicant), only on a strictly confidential basis, and only with the consent of the state against which the application was lodged.

(c) Since the individual applicant is not a party to the proceedings before the Committee of Ministers under Article 32 of the Convention, he has no right to be heard by the Committee of Ministers or to have any written communication considered by the Committee.

This should be explained by the Secretary General to the applicant when he writes to inform him that the report of the Commission on his case has been transmitted to the Committee of Ministers in accordance with the provisions of Article 31 of the Convention.

(d) If communications from the individual applicant intended for the Committee of Ministers are nevertheless received, the Secretary General should acknowledge their receipt and explain to the applicant why they will not form part of the proceedings before the Committee of Ministers and cannot be considered as a document in the case. in appropriate cases, the Secretary General might add that it is possible for the applicant to submit a new application to the Commission if he wishes to invoke important new information.

4 The Committee of Ministers decided not to make provisions in its Rules for participation by delegates of the Commission in its proceedings, since the Commission considered that such participation would be outside its powers as defined in the Convention.

The Committee of Ministers at the 307th meeting of the Ministers' Deputies (September 1979) adopted the following additional rules:

(a) an individual applicant ought normally to be informed of the outcome of the examination of his case before the Committee of Ministers. It would be for the Committee of Ministers to decide in each particular case on the information to be communicated and on the procedure to be followed;

(b) a decision to inform an individual applicant about the outcome of his case should be taken. in accordance with Article 21(b) of the Statute, by unanimous vote;

(c) the Committee of Ministers could indicate in its communication to the applicant if any of the information conveyed to him is to be treated as confidential.

1   At the 245th meeting of the Ministers' Deputies (May 1975), the Deputies agreed, unless otherwise decided in a particular case. to transmit to the European Commission of Human Rights, at the end of their discussions on a case referred to the Committee of Ministers in accordance with Article 32 of the European Convention on Human Rights, the texts of every decision appearing in their conclusions, on the understanding that these texts are not made public; they agreed also that this decision cannot be regarded as a precedent with regard to other decisions of the Committee.

RULES ADOPTED BY THE COMMITTEE OF MINISTERS FOR THE APPLICATION OF ARTICLE 54 OF THE EUROPEAN CONVENTION ON HUMAN RIGHTS

Rule 1
When a judgment of the Court is transmitted to the Committee of Ministers in accordance with Article 54 of the Convention, the case shall be inscribed on the agenda of the Committee without delay.

Rule 2
(a) When, in the judgment transmitted to the Committee of Ministers in accordance with Article 54 of the Convention, the Court decides that there has been a violation of the Convention and/or affords just satisfaction to the injured party under Article 50 of the Convention, the Committee shall invite the state concerned to inform it of the measures which it has taken in consequence of the judgment, having regard to its obligation under Article 53 of the Convention to abide by the judgment.

(b) If the state concerned informs the Committee of Ministers that it is not yet in a position to inform it of the measures taken, the case shall be automatically inscribed on the agenda of a meeting of the Committee taking place not more than six months later, unless the Committee of Ministers decides otherwise; the same rule will be applied on expiration of this and any subsequent period.

Rule 3
The Committee of Ministers shall not regard its functions under Article 54 of the Convention as having been exercised until it has taken note of the information supplied in accordance with Rule 2 and, when just satisfaction has been afforded, until it has satisfied itself that the state concerned has awarded this just satisfaction to the injured party.

Rule 4

The decision in which the Committee of Ministers declares that its functions under Article 54 of the Convention have been exercised shall take the form of a resolution.

(1) At the 21st meeting of the Ministers' Deputies (November 1972), it was agreed that the Committee of Ministers is entitled to consider a communication from an individual who claims that he has not received damages in accordance with a decision of the Court under Article 50 of the Convention affording him just satisfaction as an injured party, as well as any further information furnished to it concerning the execution of such a judgment of the Court. and that, consequently, any such communication should be distributed to the Committee of Ministers.

European Court of Human Rights complaint form

EUROPEAN COURT OF HUMAN RIGHTS

Council of Europe

Strasbourg, France

APPLICATION

under Article 34 of the European Convention on Human Rights and
Rules 45 and 47 of the Rules of Court

IMPORTANT: This application is a formal legal document and may affect your rights and obligations.

I THE PARTIES

A The Applicant
(Fill in the following details of the applicant and the representative, if any)

1 Surname . . . .   2 First name(s) . . . .

Sex: male/female

3 Nationality . . . .   4 Occupation . . . .

5 Date and place of birth . . . .

6 Permanent address . . . .

7 Tel No . . . .

8 Present address (if different from 6) . . . .

9 Name of representative* . . . .

10 Occupation of representative . . . .

11 Address of representative . . . .

12 Tel No . . . .   Fax No . . . .

B The High Contracting Party
(Fill in the name of the State(s) against which the application is directed)

13 . . . .

---

* A form of authority signed by the applicant should be submitted if a representative is appointed.

II STATEMENT OF THE FACTS
(See Part II of the Explanatory Note)

14

Continue on a separate sheet if necessary

III STATEMENT OF ALLEGED VIOLATION(S) OF THE CONVENTION AND/OR PROTOCOLS AND OF RELEVANT ARGUMENTS
(See Part III of the Explanatory Note)

15

IV STATEMENT RELATIVE TO ARTICLE 35 §1 OF THE CONVENTION
(See Part IV of the Explanatory Note. If necessary, give the details mentioned below under points 16 to 18 on a separate sheet for each separate complaint)

16 Final decision (date, court or authority and nature of decision)

17 Other decisions (list in chronological order, giving date, court or authority and nature of decision for each of them)

18 Is there or was there any other appeal or other remedy available to you which you have not used? If so, explain why you have not used it.

Continue on a separate sheet if necessary

V STATEMENT OF THE OBJECT OF THE APPLICATION AND PROVISIONAL CLAIMS FOR JUST SATISFACTION
(See Part V of the Explanatory Note)

19

VI STATEMENT CONCERNING OTHER INTERNATIONAL PROCEEDINGS
(See Part VI of the Explanatory Note)

20 Have you submitted the above complaints to any other procedure of international investigation or settlement? If so, give full details.

VII LIST OF DOCUMENTS
(NO ORIGINAL DOCUMENTS, ONLY PHOTOCOPIES)
(See Part VII of the Explanatory Note. Include copies of all decisions referred to in Parts IV and VI above. If you do not have copies, you should obtain them. If you cannot obtain them, explain why not. No documents will be returned to you.)

21   a). . . . .

b) . . . .

c). . . . .

VIII DECLARATION AND SIGNATURE
(See Part VIII of the Explanatory Note)

22 I hereby declare that, to the best of my knowledge and belief, the information I have given in the present application form is correct.

Place . . . .

Date. . . . .

(Signature of the applicant or of the representative)

European Court of Human Rights form of authority

EUROPEAN COURT OF HUMAN RIGHTS

AUTHORITY

I, ...

(name and address of applicant)

hereby authorise

....

(name and address of representative)

to represent me in the proceedings before the European Commission of Human Rights, and in any subsequent proceedings under the European Convention on Human Rights, concerning my application introduced under Article 34 of the Convention against

....

(respondent State)

....

(place and date)

....

(applicant's signature)   (representative's signature)

Index

Ability to leave detention area 3.29,
    15.55
Abortion 14.32–14.36
Absconding detainees 3.83
Absconding witnesses 9.17–9.18
Absence of defendants from trial
    8.23–8.24
Absence of legislation, effects on
    Convention rights 1.35
Absent parents, maintenance
    payments 19.48–19.49
Absolute necessity, use of force 14.7,
    14.22, 14.27–14.31
Absolute rights 4.2
Abuse of process, applications to
    ECHR 30.35
Access to
    children 19.44–19.46
    children in care 19.56–19.57
    education 21.24–21.25
    home 22.25–22.26
    individual's own medical records
        14.74
    information 24.7–24.9
    lawyer, police questioning
        7.49–7.51, 9.70
    pre-trial proceedings 7.47–7.51
Access to documents. See Disclosure
Access to lawyer, pre-trial
    proceedings 7.47–7.51
Accessibility, restrictions on
    Convention rights 4.31
Accidental killing 14.23
Accomplices' evidence 9.49–9.51
Accused
    communication with lawyer
        7.52–7.53

pre-trial proceedings 7.11–7.12
right to information 3.87
Acoustics, fair trial 8.22
Acquitted because of mental illness
    17.28–17.31
Act, meaning 1.39
Activities aimed at destruction of
    Convention rights, permitted
    restrictions 4.85–4.87
Acts of private individuals, state
    responsibility 2.16, 2.75, 14.60
Address, European Court of Human
    Rights 30.9
Adequate remedies, exhaustion
    30.25–30.30
Administration of justice, permitted
    restrictions on court reporting
    24.39–24.41
Administration of the state. See
    Public officials
Administrative decisions, notice
    requirement 13.32
Admissibility of complaints, ECHR
    30.11–30.35
Admissibility of confessions
    9.46–9.48
Admission cases. See Immigration
    cases
Adoption
    proceedings 19.53–19.54
    relationships 19.17
Adversarial hearing
    equality of arms 13.55–13.58
    intervening parties 13.56
    non-party submissions 13.56
Adverse inferences, silence during
    police questioning 7.49–7.51,

845

Adverse inferences *continued*
9.67–9.74
Advice, state duties 5.23–5.27
Advisory opinions, ECHR 30.44
Age of marriage 3.171, 19.32
Agents provocateurs 9.30–9.35,
15.41–15.42
Aggravated damages 2.45–2.47
Agnostics 27.6
Aiding and abetting race hatred 24.50
Air force. *See* Armed forces
Alcohol licences. *See* Property
Alcoholics, lawful detention 3.22,
3.58–3.64
Aliens, political activity, permitted
restrictions 4.83–4.84
Ambiguity, interpretation of
legislation 1.24, 1.73
Ambit test, discrimination 29.7–29.9
Amendment
primary legislation 1.30–1.32
remedial orders 1.55–1.58
American Convention on Human
Rights 4.25
Amnesty, persons convicted of
homicide 14.21
Anonymous applications to ECHR
30.32
Anonymous information
fearful witnesses 9.19–9.22
reasonable suspicion 15.63
Anonymous police officers 9.6,
9.27–9.29
Anonymous witnesses 9.11,
9.23–9.29
Anti-terrorist legislation 3.50
Anti-union employers 28.47
Anxiety. *See* Non-pecuniary loss
Any legal proceedings, protection of
Convention rights 2.79–2.80
Appeal judgments, reasons
10.25–10.26
Appeal proceedings
presence at trial 13.53
public hearing 13.49
security for costs 13.28–13.31
Appeals
See also Criminal appeals

against declarations of
incompatibility 1.34
civil proceedings 13.74–13.77
to Grand Chamber 30.19
Appearance in person, pre-trial
proceedings 7.11–7.12
Applications to ECHR
incompatible with Convention
30.34
legal aid 30.40–30.43
locus standi 30.6–30.8
manifestly ill-founded 30.31
previously rejected 30.33
procedure 30.9–30.10
striking out 30.36
time limits 30.14
Arbitration clauses 13.12–13.13
Arguability, breaches of Convention
rights 1.7
Armed forces
disciplinary proceedings 6.32
restriction on freedom of assembly
and association 3.162–3.163
restriction on trade union rights
3.151, 28.48–28.50
tort actions against Crown 13.17
Arrest abroad 15.70–15.71
Arrested persons, lawful detention
3.22, 3.51–3.54
Arrests
police powers 15.43–15.45
testing legality 7.28–7.32
use of force 14.22, 14.24
Artificial insemination 19.21–19.22
Artistic expression 24.46–24.47
Assaults
in custody, breaches of article 3
3.13
in police custody 15.81–15.87
inhuman treatment/punishment
14.49–14.51
on prisoners 16.29
Assessment boards, welfare benefits
12.41
Assessment of educational
attainment 21.14
Assistance with defence 3.87
Associations

article 9 claims 27.36
registration 3.158
regulations on own activities 3.157
Asylum. *See* Immigration cases
Atheists 27.6
Authorisation
lethal force 14.22
search and seizure 15.38–15.40
Autonomous interpretation, legal
terms 4.19

Bail
conditions 7.25–7.27
criminal cases 3.72, 7.12
pre-trial proceedings 7.13–7.16
refusal 7.12–7.16
Ballots, trade unions 28.35
Banning orders
marches or meetings 25.24–25.26
proportionality 25.26
Beijing Rules. *See* United Nations
Standard Minimum Rules for
the Administration of Juvenile
Justice
Belief. *See* Freedom of thought [etc.]
Bermuda, constitution 1.28
Beyond reasonable doubt 8.48–8.49
Binding nature, ECHR judgments
30.45
Birch. *See* Corporal punishment
Birth certificates, transsexuals 19.25,
19.60–19.63
Blasphemy
conflict with freedom of expression
27.27–27.33
freedom of thought [etc.]
27.21–27.22
gratuitous offence 27.30
margin of appreciation
27.30–27.31
Blood samples 9.75
Boards of Visitors 16.52
Bodily tissues 9.75
Body samples 9.75, 16.24–16.25
Body searches 16.24–16.25
Breach of the peace 3.156, 25.19
Breaches of Convention rights
arguability 1.7

caused by national legislation
3.177–3.178
effective remedies 1.7
information and advice 5.23–5.27
judicial acts 2.69–2.72
liability 2.17
remedies 1.7, 5.28–5.29
state duties 5.13–5.17, 5.28–5.29
threats of torture 3.13
Breath samples 9.75
Broadcasting
licensing 3.146, 24.10–24.13
quality control 24.16
Broadmoor
immunity from liability 13.15
inadequate medical treatment
16.35
visit by ECHR delegation 30.13
Burden of proof
adequate and effective remedies
30.29
civil proceedings 13.63
criminal proceedings 8.42–8.47
fair trial 8.42–8.47
police misconduct 15.91–15.93
strict liability offences 8.47
Business premises
search and seizure 15.36–15.40
searches 3.120

Canada, case law, effect on UK law
1.48
Caning. *See* Corporal punishment
Caravans, whether homes 22.10
Care proceedings 19.55–19.57
Case files, disclosure 7.65
Causation, pecuniary loss 2.55
Certainty
common law 6.25
criminal law 3.105–3.106,
4.32–4.35, 6.22–6.26
family life 19.6
restrictions on Convention rights
4.32–4.35
Challenges to
disciplinary proceedings in schools
21.46–21.47
subordinate legislation 1.37–1.38

Change of sex. *See* Transsexuals
Changes in domestic law, effect on
    ECHR applications 30.30
Changing
    pleas 8.50
    religion 3.133, 27.8
Charges
    criminal cases 3.89
    meaning 6.7, 6.18–6.20
    pre-trial proceedings 7.41–7.46
Chattels. *See* Property
Chemical factories, pollution 22.36
Child abuse 20.13–20.14
Child care cases
    damages 2.66
    local authorities 12.41–12.42
    proceedings 19.55–19.57, 19.69
    trial within reasonable time 13.81
Child Poverty Action Group,
    representative actions 2.37
Child Protection Register 20.11
Child Support Agency 19.48
Children
See also Family life; Parent and child;
    Parents
    age limits 3.55
    applications to ECHR 30.6
    born out of wedlock 4.22,
        19.39–19.41
    inheritance 19.40
Convention rights 20.29–20.31
    corporal punishment 20.6–20.12
    criminal proceedings 20.18–20.21,
        20.22–20.27
    effective participation
        20.29–20.31
    custody 19.44–19.46
    disposition measures 20.25
    duration of sentences 16.31,
        16.45–16.46
    education supervision 3.56, 20.16
    expulsion from school 21.42–21.45
    expulsion to lack of care 18.43
    fair trial 20.18–20.21, 20.22–20.24
    harmful surroundings 3.57
    in detention, education 16.84
    lawful detention 3.22, 3.55–3.57,
        15.51

life sentences 10.6, 16.36, 16.41,
    16.41–16.42, 16.45–16.46
mentally handicapped, protection
    from sexual assault 3.123
obligation to live with parents 20.2
parental control 20.2–20.5
preventive detention 16.36, 16.41
protection from sexual assault 3.123
removal from harmful
    surroundings 3.57, 20.17
restrictions on liberty 20.2–20.5
sexual abuse 20.14
special needs 21.31–21.33
Child's best interest
    custody and access 19.45
    removal from parents 19.10
Child-specific rights, criminal
    proceedings 20.22–20.28
Choice of legislature 3.198–3.202
Church of Scientology 3.131, 27.5
Churches, article 9 claims 27.36
Cinema
    freedom of expression 3.143, 24.6
    licensing 3.146, 24.10–24.13
Circumstantial evidence 9.2
Civic obligations 3.18
Civil cases
    against police 12.20, 15.100
    civil rights or obligations 11.1–11.3
    determination of civil rights or
        obligations 3.90–3.91
    employment 28.2–28.5
    inhuman treatment/punishment
        11.11
    obligations 3.90–3.91
    restrictions on instituting
        proceedings 13.8–13.11
Civil proceedings
    against public authorities, HRA
        11.6
    appeals 13.74–13.77
    burden of proof 13.63
    Convention rights 11.4–11.6
    costs 13.70–13.71
    disclosure 13.59–13.61
    effective remedies 11.9–11.13
    enforcement of judgments
        13.72–13.73

evidence 13.62
expert evidence 13.64–13.67
fair trial 11.7, 11.14–11.15,
    13.1–13.5
hearings in camera 13.45–13.46
judgments 13.72–13.73
judicial review 11.8
legal aid 13.33–13.40
limitation of actions 13.24–13.27
margin of appreciation 13.7
necessary in a democratic society
    11.4
presence at trial 13.52–13.53
public hearing 13.45–13.50
public interest immunity 7.71
right of access to courts 13.6–13.7
right to effective participation
    13.51
security for costs 13.28–13.31
standard of proof 13.63
taking of life 14.8
witnesses 13.62
Civil rights and obligations 12.1–12.9
adoptive parents and children
    19.53–19.54
civil cases 3.90–3.91, 11.1–11.3
classification 12.5
determination 11.7, 12.34–12.40
distinguished from Convention
    rights 11.2
domestic law basis 12.32–12.33
employment 28.2–28.5
employment disputes 12.27
European Community law 12.8
family proceedings 12.18
housing cases 22.4, 22.40–22.41
immunities 12.33, 13.14–13.23
indirect determination 12.35
nationality cases 12.28
notice requirement 13.32
parties 12.4
private rights 12.5
privileges 12.33, 13.14–13.23
procedural rules 13.32
property cases 12.10–12.14
public officials 12.14, 28.6–28.14
qualified privilege 13.18
restrictions 12.33, 13.14–13.23

rules of procedure 13.32
tax proceedings 12.15–12.17
Civil servants. *See* Public officials
Civilian service, alternative to military
    service 3.18, 3.136, 27.37
Claims for compensation from public
    authorities 12.19–12.21
Classification of human rights
    4.1–4.4
Clear and present danger 25.23
Close personal ties, family life
    19.11–19.16
Closed shop agreements 28.26,
    28.29–28.30
Clothes, prisoners 16.58, 16.73, 16.76
Co-habitation, relation to marriage
    19.34
Co-habitees, witnesses 9.7–9.11
Collaboration with the enemy 3.107
Collective bargaining, trade unions
    28.31–28.33
Collusion between lawyer and client
    7.53
Colour discrimination 3.183–3.187,
    29.11–29.14
Commercial information 24.44–24.45
Commission for Racial Equality 1.72
Commission of further offences 7.23
Committee of Ministers
    Council of Europe 1.2, 30.2, 30.45
    function changed by Protocol 11
    30.2
Common law
    certainty 6.25
    developments, human rights 1.73,
        2.76–2.78
    effect of HRA 1.42–1.43
    foreseeability 4.35
    interpretation of legislation 1.17
Communication
    See also Correspondence; Telephones
    between lawyer and client, privacy
        7.52–7.53
    between prisoners and lawyers
        3.121, 16.50–16.51, 16.69–16.71
    interception, police powers
        15.21–15.25

Companies
  applications to ECHR 30.6
  whether victims 2.18–2.35
Compellability
  witnesses 9.7–9.11
  defendants 9.60
Compensation 2.48–2.54
  claims against public authorities
    12.19–12.21
  criminal injuries 12.25
  deprivation of property
    22.20–22.21, 26.5–26.7
  discretionary payments
    12.23–12.24
  ex gratia payments 12.23–12.25
  from public authorities
    12.19–12.21
  HRA 2.43–2.44
  statutory rights 12.22
  wrongful detention 3.84–3.86,
    3.176, 16.48
Complaints by prisoners 16.63–16.64
Complaints procedure, ECHR
  30.9–30.10
Compulsory arbitration 13.13
Compulsory education 21.11
Compulsory labour, prohibition
  3.15–3.20
Compulsory military service. See
  Military service
Compulsory pension schemes 22.5,
  27.15
Compulsory purchase orders
  22.25–22.26
Compulsory questioning
  DTI investigations 9.62–9.64
  suspected terrorists 9.71–9.74
Compulsory sex education
  21.36–21.37
Conditional release, persons of
  unsound mind 17.24–17.25
Conditions
  benefits, unemployed persons
    28.24
  peaceful assembly 3.155
Conditions in prisons 16.12–16.15,
  16.21–16.23
Conditions of bail 7.25–7.27

Conditions of detention, persons of
  unsound mind 17.32–17.34
Conduct
  conveying ideas or information
    24.6
  criminal liability 6.32–6.36
  expressing religion or belief 3.132
  protected under Convention
    6.32–6.36
Confessions 9.46–9.48
Confidential information 15.63
  reasonable suspicion 15.63
Confidentiality
  communications between lawyer
    and client 7.52–7.53
  medical records 14.74
  criminal cases 9.38–9.41
Conjugal visits. See Prison visits
Conscientious objection, military
  service 3.18, 3.136, 27.37
Consensual sado-masochistic acts
  6.36
Construction. See subheading
  interpretation
Constructive dismissal 28.30
Consultation with trade unions
  28.31–28.33
Contempt of court 24.39–24.41
Contingency fee agreements 30.40
Continuing proceedings, moral
  interest 2.44
Contracting out of Convention rights
  28.56
Contributions-based benefits
  23.17–23.21
Control of property
  fair balance 26.18
  meaning 26.17
  proportionality 3.192, 26.18
  public interest test 22.20–22.23
  whether permissible 3.190, 3.192,
    4.71–4.74
Convention on the Rights of the
  Child 1.73, 20.27
Convention rights 3.1–3.3
  children 20.29–20.31
  civil proceedings 11.4–11.6
  compatibility of legislation

1.14–1.19
contracting out 28.56
distinguished from civil rights or
   obligations 11.2
housing 22.44–22.47
implied restrictions 4.75
incorporation into domestic law
   1.25–1.26
migrants 18.8–18.10
permitted restrictions 4.2–4.4,
   4.26–4.27, 4.29–4.36, 4.56
protection under HRA 1.6–1.8,
   2.79–2.80
relation to criminal liability
   6.33–6.36
UK courts 30.1
waiver 4.97–4.98
Conversion. *See* Proselytism
Convicted persons, lawful detention
   3.22, 3.41–3.45, 10.1–10.7, 16.38
Conviction abroad, lawful detention
   3.45, 16.39
Corporal punishment
breaches of article 3 3.13
by parents 20.11–20.12
children 20.6–20.12
parents' beliefs 21.15
schools 20.8–20.10, 21.40–21.41
Correspondence
See also Communication
interception 15.20
prisoners 16.60–16.68
privacy 3.121–3.122
Costs
civil proceedings 13.70–13.71
civil rights and obligations 12.37
Convention 2.68
criminal cases 8.52–8.54
ECHR 30.18
Council of Europe
Committee of Ministers 1.2, 30.2,
   30.45
function changed by Protocol 11
   30.2
Counter-demonstrations, freedom of
   assembly 25.25
Court of Appeal
criminal cases 10.19–10.24

declaration of incompatibility 1.33
new evidence 10.27–10.28
Court of Session, declaration of
   incompatibility 1.33
Court orders, enforcement of lawful
   detention 3.22, 3.46–3.50
Court reporting, freedom of
   expression 24.39–24.41
Courts
judicial acts 2.69–2.72
pre-trial proceedings 7.11–7.12
public authorities 2.7
responsibility for developing law
   2.76–2.78
striking down legislation 1.1
subordinate legislation 1.1
Courts-Martial Appeal Court,
   declaration of incompatibility
   1.33
Courts-martial procedural cases,
   damages 2.61
Crash helmets, Sikhs 27.18
Crime prevention, grounds for arrest
   3.51–3.54, 15.57
Criminal appeals 10.8–10.11
equality of arms 10.21
legal aid 10.12–10.16
limitation of actions 10.11
new evidence 10.27–10.28
public hearing 10.17–10.18
Criminal cases
costs 8.52–8.54
damages 2.62
date of trial 3.72
determination of charges 3.89
innocent third parties 9.38–9.41
international co-operation
   8.55–8.56
leave to appeal 10.8, 10.19–10.21
pre-trial proceedings 7.1–7.4
pre-trial rights 3.71–3.72
protection of innocent third parties
   9.38–9.41
protection of the public 3.76
secret surveillance 9.30–9.35
undercover agents 9.30–9.35
Criminal charge, meaning 6.7–6.12

Criminal defamation proceedings
24.26, 24.31
Criminal injuries compensation, ex
gratia payments 12.25
Criminal investigations, suspicious
deaths 14.19–14.20
Criminal law
certainty 3.105–3.106, 6.22–6.26
foreseeability 4.32–4.35
Criminal liability, relation to
Convention rights 6.33–6.36
Criminal offences, retrospective
3.102–3.106, 6.27–6.31
Criminal proceedings
children 20.18–20.21, 20.22–20.27
child-specific rights 20.22–20.28
effective participation 8.19–8.22
expert evidence 9.52–9.54
HRA 6.21
notification of hearing 8.20
pre-trial 7.1–7.4
prohibition of self-incrimination
9.60–9.74
prohibition of torture [etc.] 6.3
protection of Convention rights
61–6.8, 6.1–6.8
quashing indictments 2.42
right to effective participation
8.19–8.22
right to silence 9.60–9.74
self-incrimination 9.60–9.74
staying 2.42
Criminal sanctions
protection of Convention rights
5.7–5.12
taking of life 14.6
Criticism
acceptable limits 24.28–24.33
judiciary 24.36–24.38
private individuals 24.28–24.33
public figures 24.28–24.35
Crown immunity 13.17
Curfews 3.27
Curriculum
education 21.34–21.37
indoctrination 21.34
philosophical convictions
21.34–21.35

religious convictions 21.34–21.35
Custody of children 19.44–19.46
Customs files, disclosure 7.61

Damages
against police, civil cases 12.20,
15.100
Convention 2.48–2.54
HRA 2.40–2.41, 2.43–2.44
police misconduct 2.58–2.59
privacy 2.65
Dangerous chemicals, pollution 22.36
Dangerousness
indeterminate sentences 10.6
preventive detention 15.57, 15.64,
16.40–16.42
Date of trial, criminal cases 3.72
Death investigations 14.14–14.18
Death of
applicant during proceedings 2.44
prisoner 16.3–16.7
witness 9.12–9.16
Death penalty 3.5–3.5, 14.39–14.40
UK 14.39–14.40
Death row phenomenon, United
States 18.14, 18.16
Deaths in custody, inquests 16.7
Debasement, degrading
treatment/punishment
14.52–14.55
Declaration of incompatibility
conflict between Parliament and
judiciary 1.29
designated courts 1.33
discretionary remedies 1.32
effects 1.30–1.32
notification to Crown 1.34
primary legislation 1.1, 1.30–1.30
reference to ECHR 30.1
remedies 30.1
Defamation proceedings, freedom of
expression 24.25–24.26
Defence case
evidence 9.55–9.59
information needed 7.43–7.46
legal representation 3.87
time and facilities for preparation
7.72–7.75

Defendants
  absence from trial 8.23–8.24
  compellability as witnesses 9.60
  legal aid 8.25–8.29
  legal representation 8.30–8.36
  presence at trial 8.21–8.22
  right to defend self 8.36
Definitions. *See subheadings*
  interpretation and meaning
Degrading treatment/punishment
  civil cases 11.11
  discrimination 29.21
  institutionalised racism 14.55
  meaning 6.3
  possible justification 3.14
  prisoners 16.8–16.15
  prohibition 3.10–3.14, 14.41–14.44,
    14.48–14.55
  schools 20.8–20.10
  vulnerable individuals 14.54
Delay in proceedings, damages 2.62
Delegation of obligations, state
  responsibility 2.16
Democracy, meaning 1.26, 4.11
Demonstrations
  freedom of assembly and
    association 25.1, 25.3, 25.10
  freedom of expression 25.1–25.6
Denial of access to courts, damages
  2.64
Department of Trade and Industry
  investigations 9.62–9.64
Deportation
See also Expulsion cases; Extradition
  international co-operation
    8.55–8.56
  lawful detention 3.22, 3.65–3.68
  long-term residents 18.40
Deprivation of liberty. *See* Arrests;
  Detention
Deprivation of property
  compensation 22.20–22.21,
    26.5–26.7
  fair balance 26.3–26.4, 26.16
  international law 26.15
  meaning 26.11
  proportionality 26.16
  public interest test 22.19–22.22,

26.4, 26.13
  welfare benefits 23.9–23.10
  whether permissible 3.190–3.191,
    4.71–4.74
Derogable rights 4.2
Derogations
  Convention 1.6, 1.59, 4.81–4.82
  by UK 1.60, 3.73, 4.82, 7.9–7.10
  prohibition of slavery [etc.] 3.15
  prohibition of torture [etc.] 3.10
  right to liberty 3.73
  right to life 3.4
Designated courts, declaration of
  incompatibility 1.33
Destruction of Convention rights,
  permitted restrictions 4.85–4.87
Detainees
  medical treatment 14.69
  procedural rights 15.43–15.45
  procedural safeguards 15.43–15.45
  solitary confinement 16.15–16.20
Detention
See also Lawful detention
  ability to leave area 3.29
  acquitted because of mental illness
    17.28–17.31
  arrest abroad 15.70–15.71
  children
    education supervision 3.56,
      20.16
    removal from harmful
      surroundings 3.57, 20.17
  criminal cases, pre-trial rights
    3.71–3.72
  duration 15.49–15.52
  expulsion cases 18.26–18.30
  extradition 18.26–18.30
  lawful searches 15.50
  lawfulness 3.22–3.37
  meaning 17.12
  pending further investigations
    15.61
  persons of unsound mind
    after conviction 17.28–17.31
    periodic reviews 17.13–17.22
  police powers, thresholds
    15.46–15.55

Detention *continued*
  pre-trial rights, criminal cases
    3.71–3.72
  preventive grounds 16.36, 16.41
  procedural safeguards 3.38–3.40,
    3.69–3.83
  protection of the public 3.76
  reasons, given to detainee
    3.69–3.70, 15.65–15.68
  stop and search 15.72–15.79
  testing legality 7.28–7.32
Detention for life
  children 16.36, 16.41
  young persons 16.36
Detention on remand 4.69
Determination of charges
  criminal cases 3.89
  appeals 10.8
Determination of civil rights and
  obligations 3.90–3.91, 11.7,
  12.34–12.40
Different treatment. *See* Prohibition
  of, discrimination
Directly affected, meaning 2.22
Dirty protest, prisoners 16.21–16.23
Disability pensions 23.16
Disability Rights Commission 1.72
Disbarment 28.3
Disciplinary proceedings
  armed forces 6.32
  employment cases 28.3–28.4
  medical cases 13.46
  police misconduct 12.14
  prisoners, loss of remission 16.34
  prisons 6.11, 8.14, 16.52
  professional regulatory bodies
    12.41–12.42
  schools 21.38–21.39, 21.46–21.47
Disclosure
  adversarial hearing 13.58
  civil proceedings 13.59–13.61
  customs files 7.61
  family proceedings 19.67–19.68
  pre-trial proceedings 7.32,
    7.54–7.67
  psychiatric reports 7.66
Discretionary life prisoners, release
  16.44–16.46

Discretionary life sentences
  preventive grounds 16.36
  tariff 10.6, 16.42
Discretionary payments,
  compensation 12.23–12.24
Discretionary remedies, declaration
  of incompatibility 1.32
Discrimination 29.1–29.2,
  29.22–29.24
See also Colour discrimination;
  Indirect discrimination;
  Nationality discrimination;
  Political discrimination; Positive
  discrimination; Racial
  discrimination; Religious
  discrimination; Sexual
  discrimination; Social
  discrimination
  ambit test 29.7–29.9
  custody and access 19.46
  degrading treatment/punishment
    14.52–14.55, 29.21
  differential treatment 29.11–29.14
  employment 28.55
  expulsion cases 18.44–18.47
  housing 22.48
  immigration cases 18.44–18.47
  legitimate aim 29.15
  margin of appreciation 29.23
  meaning 15.90, 29.10–29.16
  migrants 18.8–18.10
  personal status 3.183–3.187
  prisoners 16.81
  proportionality 29.16
  relation to other Convention rights
    29.3–29.6
  right to privacy 29.5
  same sex couples 29.7–29.9
  suspect groups 29.17
  welfare benefits 23.23
Disease prevention, lawful detention
  3.22, 3.58–3.64
Dismissal 28.3
  public officials 28.6, 28.51
Disposition measures, children 20.25
Disputes
  landlord and tenant 22.4
  private individuals 28.57

Disputes between individuals,
property 22.24
Distress. *See* Non-pecuniary loss
Divine Light Zentrum 3.131, 27.5
Divorce 3.169, 19.42
access to children 19.44–19.46
hearings in camera 13.46
right to remarry 19.36
DNA samples
evidence 9.75
police powers 15.30–15.35
Doctors, whether public authorities
2.10
Documents
See also Disclosure
translations 8.41
Domestic law
changes, effect on ECHR
applications 30.30
civil rights and obligations
12.32–12.33
detention
lawfulness 3.34–3.35
procedural safeguards 3.38–3.40
whether refusal justified by
religion or belief 27.13–27.18
Domestic remedies, exhaustion
30.25–30.30
Domestic violence 19.50–19.52
Double jeopardy 8.57–8.58
Drug addicts, lawful detention 3.22,
3.58–3.64
Drug trafficking 6.32
Druidism 3.131, 27.5, 27.18
DTI. *See* Department of Trade and
Industry
Duration
lawful detention 3.26
mandatory life sentences 10.6,
16.31–16.33
sentences 16.31–16.34
Duties imposed on states by
Convention. *See* State duties
Duty to hold free elections
3.198–3.202

E-mail. *See* Correspondence;
Electronic transmission

Earnings-related pension schemes
23.7
ECHR. *See* European Court of
Human Rights
Economic interests. *See* Property
Education
assessment of attainment 21.14
by parents at home 21.14
children and young persons in
detention 16.84
children with special needs
21.31–21.33
Convention rights 21.5–21.9
curriculum 21.34–21.37
disciplinary proceedings
21.38–21.39
Jehovah's Witnesses 21.21
language 21.7
meaning 21.9
parents' philosophical and
religious convictions
21.12–21.23
prisoners 16.84
public law right 12.29
state responsibility 20.10
supervision 3.56, 20.16
Effective participation
criminal proceedings 8.19–8.22
children 20.29–20.31
Effective remedies
breaches of Convention rights 1.7,
3.173–3.182
civil proceedings 11.9–11.13
degree of effectiveness 3.179–3.182
exhaustion 30.25–30.30
HRA 3.174
secret surveillance 3.179
surveillance 3.179
Effectiveness
Convention 4.12–4.15
right of access to courts, civil
proceedings 13.6–13.7
Elections 3.198–3.202
implied restrictions 4.79–4.80
political rights 12.30–12.31
Electronic transmission, freedom of
expression 24.6

Elementary education
  Convention rights 21.6
  distinguished from higher
    education 21.24–21.25
Emergency admissions, persons of
  unsound mind 17.9–17.10
Emergency assistance
  property rights 23.6
  welfare benefits 23.6, 23.11
Emergency medical action 14.67
Emergency work 3.18, 28.16
Employment
  See also Trade unions; Work during
    legal detention
  civil rights and obligations
    28.2–28.5
  Convention rights 28.38
  discrimination 28.55
  effects of religious convictions
    28.45–28.48
  freedom of expression 28.49–28.54
  freedom of thought [etc.]
    28.44–28.48
  public officials 28.6–28.14
  right to earn a livelihood 28.1
  right to privacy 28.39–28.41
  security vetting 28.42–28.43
  telephone tapping 28.40–28.41
Employment disputes
  civil rights and obligations 12.27
  disciplinary proceedings 28.3–28.4
  fair trial 13.81, 28.2–28.5
  public officials 28.6–28.14
Employment pension schemes 22.5
Employment prospects. *See* Non-
  pecuniary loss
Employment rights, public officials
  28.6–28.14
Enforcement
  court orders
  custody and access 19.47
  lawful detention 3.22, 3.46–3.50
  judgments
    civil proceedings 13.72–13.73
    civil rights and obligations 12.38
    lawful detention 3.22, 3.46–3.50
    protection of life 14.9
Entrapment 9.30–9.35, 15.41–15.42

Environmental cases, damages 2.67
Environmental pollution. *See*
  Pollution
Environmental problems, peaceful
  enjoyment of property
  22.30–22.36
Equal Opportunities Commission
  1.72
  representative actions 2.37
Equality of arms
  adversarial hearing 13.55–13.58
  civil proceedings 13.54
  criminal appeals 10.21
  defence evidence 9.55–9.59
  expert evidence 9.52–9.54
  fair trial 3.96, 8.2
  habeas corpus proceedings 3.79
  pre-trial proceedings 7.31
Escape
  prevention
    grounds for arrest 3.51–3.54
    use of force 14.22, 14.24
Established church 3.133, 27.9
European Agreement Relating to
  Persons Participating in
  Proceedings of the European
  Commission and Court of
  Human Rights 7.53
European Commission of Human
  rights 1.2, 30.2
European Community law, civil
  rights and obligations 12.8
European Convention on Human
  Rights 1.1–1.3
See also Convention rights;
  subheading Convention
  article 2, right to life 3.4–3.9,
    14.2–14.40
  article 3, prohibition of torture
    [etc.] 3.10–3.14, 14.41–14.47
  article 4, prohibition of slavery
    [etc.] 3.15–3.20
  article 5, right to liberty 3.21–3.86
  article 6, right to a fair trial
    3.87–3.101
  article 7, prohibition of
    retrospective criminal offences
    3.102–3.106

article 8, right to privacy
3.108–3.129
article 9, freedom of thought [etc.]
3.130–3.140
article 10, freedom of expression
3.141–3.150
article 11, freedom of assembly
and association 3.151–3.159
article 12, right to marry and found
a family 3.115, 3.168–3.172
article 13, right to an effective
remedy 3.173–3.182
article 14, prohibition of
discrimination 3.183–3.187
classification of human rights
4.1–4.4
derogations 1.6, 1.59, 4.81–4.82
effectiveness 4.12–4.15
First Protocol
article 1, right to property
3.188–3.193
article 2, right to education
3.194–3.197
article 3, right to fee elections
3.198–3.202
interpretation 1.25–1.26, 3.179,
4.1–4.4
effectiveness 4.12–4.15
objects and purpose 4.9–4.11
present day conditions 4.16–4.18
Strasbourg bodies 1.44–1.47
living instrument 4.16–4.18
objects and purpose 4.9–4.11
Protocols 3.188–3.202
relation to other human rights
instruments 4.21–4.25
Seventh Protocol, double jeopardy
8.57–8.58
Sixth Protocol, death penalty
3.198–3.202
European Convention on the Status
of Children Born out of
Wedlock 4.22, 19.39
European Convention on
Transfrontier Television 4.22
European Court of Human Rights 1.2
address 30.9
admissibility of complaints

30.11–30.35
advisory opinions 30.44
chambers, new Court 30.4
committees, new Court 30.4
complaints procedure 30.9–30.10
costs 30.18
fees 30.18
final decision of Grand Chamber
30.19
friendly settlement 30.15
Grand Chamber, new Court 30.4,
30.19
hearings 30.14
judgments, binding nature 30.45
legal aid 30.40–30.43
living instrument 4.16–4.18
merits of case 30.16–30.17
new Court
admissibility of complaints
30.11–30.14
complaints procedure
30.9–30.10
composition 30.3–30.5
petitioning mechanism 30.2
reconstitution by Protocol 11
30.2
references from UK 30.1
European Extradition Convention
4.22
European Social Charter 4.22, 28.34
Euthanasia 14.37–14.38
Evangelism. *See* Proselytism
Eviction
home 22.25–22.26
property 22.22
state responsibility 22.27–22.29
Evidence
See also Circumstantial evidence;
Confessions; Expert evidence;
Hearsay evidence; New
evidence; Unlawfully obtained
evidence; Witnesses
accomplices 9.49–9.51
civil proceedings 13.62
criminal cases 9.1–9.3
defence case 9.55–9.59
expert witnesses 9.52–9.54
fingerprints 9.75

Evidence *continued*
  intimate body searches 9.75
  non-intimate samples 9.75
  urine samples 9.75
Evidence of Parliamentary intention
  1.9–1.10
Ex gratia payments, compensation
  12.23–12.25
Ex parte procedure, public interest
  immunity 7.70
Ex parte relief, relation to freedom of
  expression 1.50–1.51
Exceptional situations, exhaustion of
  domestic remedies 30.28
Excessive delay in proceedings,
  damages 2.62
Execution of judgments, supervision
  by Committee of Ministers 30.2,
  30.45
Exemplary damages 2.45–2.47
Exhaustion of domestic remedies
  30.25–30.30
  special circumstances 30.28
Existing human rights, public interest
  litigation 1.71
Existing provisions, human rights
  1.3, 1.70–1.71
Expenses
  Convention 2.68
  ECHR 30.18
Expert evidence
  civil proceedings 13.64–13.67
  criminal proceedings 9.52–9.54
Exposure of miscarriages of justice
  16.78
Expression of race hatred, permitted
  restrictions 24.48–24.51
Expulsion cases
See also Deportation; Extradition
  children, lack of care 18.43
  detention 18.26–18.30
  discrimination 18.44–18.47
  fair trial 18.25
  family life 18.31–18.34,
    18.39–18.43
  fear of torture [etc.] 18.13–18.14
  inhuman treatment/punishment
    18.11–18.12

lack of care, children 18.43
  private life 18.31–18.34
  procedural safeguards 18.48
  proportionality 18.39–18.40
  removal to safe third country 18.23
  right to life 18.24
Expulsion from school 21.42–21.45
Extradition
See also Deportation; Expulsion
  breaches of article 3 3.13
  detention 18.26–18.30
  fear of torture [etc.] 18.13–18.14
  inhuman treatment/punishment
    18.11–18.12
  interim relief, ECHR 30.37–30.39
  international co-operation
    8.55–8.56
  lawful detention 3.22, 3.65–3.68

Facilities for preparation of defence
  case 7.72–7.75
Failure to act. *See* Act
Failure to perceive risk to life
  14.11–14.13
Fair balance
See also Proportionality
  control of property 26.18
  deprivation of property 26.3–26.4,
    26.16
    welfare benefits 23.10
  property measures 3.192–3.193,
    22.20
Fair comment 24.34–24.35
Fair trial 3.87–3.101, 8.1–8.3
See also Procedural safeguards
  acoustics 8.22
  burden of proof 8.42–8.47
  children 20.18–20.21, 20.22–20.24
  civil proceedings 11.7, 11.14–11.15,
    13.1–13.5
    public interest immunity
      13.21–13.22
  criminal appeals 10.8–10.11
  damages 2.60–2.64
  disclosure 7.32, 7.54–7.67
  double jeopardy 8.57–8.58
  employment disputes 13.81,
    28.2–28.5

equality of arms 3.96, 8.2
expulsion cases 18.25
family life 10.64–10.69
housing cases 22.40–22.41
legal aid 8.25–8.29
legal representation 8.30–8.36
meaning 13.3
permitted limitations 3.99
planning restrictions 22.38
pre-trial publicity 7.76–7.81
procedural safeguards 3.101
property cases 12.10–12.14
public hearing 8.13–8.18
public interest immunity, civil
    proceedings 13.21–13.22
remedy for breach of Convention
    3.176
security for costs 13.31
sentencing 10.3
tax proceedings 12.15–12.17
undercover agents 9.30–9.35
Family life 19.26, 19.27, 19.28
See also Children; Grandparents and
    grandchildren; Parent and child;
    Parents; Siblings; Uncles and
    nephews
certainty 19.6
close personal ties 19.11–19.16
expulsion cases 18.31–18.34,
    18.39–18.43
fair trial 10.64–10.69
immigration cases 18.33–18.38
meaning 18.33–18.34, 19.1–19.2,
    19.11–19.16
migrants 18.31–18.34
names 19.58–19.59
positive obligations 5.18–5.21
prisoners 16.57–16.59
privacy 3.113–3.116
procedural safeguards 19.7,
    19.64–19.69
relationships 3.113–3.114
Family members, witnesses 9.7–9.11
Family proceedings
civil rights and obligations 12.18
disclosure 19.67–19.68
Family relationships 3.113–3.114
Fathers of unborn children 14.36

Faxes. *See* Correspondence
Fear of absconding, refusal of bail
    7.18–7.20
Fear of reprisals, witnesses 9.19–9.22
Fear of torture [etc.], expulsion cases
    18.13–18.14
Fees, ECHR 30.18
Films
freedom of expression 3.143
licensing 3.146
Final decision, Grand Chamber 30.19
Fingerprints
evidence 9.75
police powers 15.30–15.35
Fishing rights. *See* Property
Fleeing. *See* Escape
Foetus, right to life 14.32
Forced or compulsory labour
meaning 28.19–28.24
prohibition 3.15–3.20, 28.15–28.24
Force-feeding prisoners 16.5
Foreseeability, certainty of law
    4.32–4.35
Forfeiture, whether criminal
    proceedings 6.13–6.14
Forum internum 27.11
Fostering, relationships 19.17–19.20
Founding a family. *See* Right to
    marry and found a family
Free elections
legislature 3.198–3.202
right to vote 3.200
Freedom of artistic expression
    24.46–24.47
Freedom of assembly and association
    3.151–3.159
counter-demonstrations 25.25
demonstrations 25.1, 25.3, 25.10
permitted restrictions 3.162–3.167,
    16.79, 25.14–25.26
positive obligations 25.7–25.9
prevention of disorder 25.14–25.23
streets 25.10–25.13
strikes 28.34
Freedom of belief 3.130–3.140
Freedom of conscience 3.130–3.140
Freedom of expression 3.141–3.150,
    24.1–24.9

Freedom of expression *continued*
  commercial information
    24.44–24.45
  conflict with blasphemy
    27.27–27.33
  court reporting 24.39–24.41
  defamation proceedings
    24.25–24.26
  demonstrations 25.1–25.6
  electronic transmission 24.6
  employment 28.49–28.54
  fair comment 24.34–24.35
  films 3.143
  HRA 1.49–1.54
  marches 25.1–25.6
  medium of expression 24.6
  permitted restrictions 3.147–3.150,
    16.74–16.78
    employment 28.49–28.54
  public officials 28.52–28.54
  pictures 3.143, 24.6
  political speech 3.143
  press 3.142, 24.2
  pre-trial injunctions 24.24
  prior restraint 24.22–24.24
  prisoners 16.60–16.68, 16.74–16.78
  processions 25.1–25.6
  protests [etc] 25.1–25.6
  public interest 24.27–24.33
  public officials 3.144
  relations between private
    individuals 24.19–24.21
  sit-ins 25.1–25.6
  video 3.143, 24.6
  words 3.143, 24.6
Freedom of opinions 3.141–3.150
Freedom of religion, HRA 1.54, 27.38
Freedom of religion or belief
  Convention 3.130–3.140
  manifestation 27.3–27.4,
    27.10–27.12
  permitted restrictions 3.137–3.140,
    16.72–16.73, 27.23–27.26
  proportionality 27.23–27.26
  proselytism 27.19–27.20
Freedom of the press, pre-trial
    publicity 7.76–7.81
Freedom of thought [etc.]

  3.130–3.140, 27.1–27.9
  blasphemy 27.21–27.22
  employment 28.44–28.48
  positive obligations 27.21–27.22
Frequency
  periodic reviews of mental health
    cases 17.20–17.22
  reviews of pre-trial detention 3.77
Friendly settlement, ECHR cases
    30.15
Funding, schools 21.20, 21.29–21.30
Further offences, refusal of bail 7.23
Future legislation, interpretation 1.18

Gay couples. *See* Same sex couples
Goodwill. See Property
Government costs, ECHR cases 30.18
Government departments, public
    authorities 2.8
Grandparents and grandchildren
    19.27
Gratuitous offence, blasphemy 27.30
Greenpeace, representative actions
    2.37
Grounds for arrest 3.22, 3.51–3.54,
    15.56–15.59
  crime prevention 3.51–3.54, 15.57
  prevention of crime 3.51–3.54
  prevention of escape 3.51–3.54,
    15.57
  reasonable suspicion 3.22,
    3.51–3.54, 15.57
Grounds for detention, prevention of
    crime 15.57, 15.64
Grounds for refusal of bail 7.17
Groups of individuals, applications to
    ECHR 30.6–30.8
Guardians. *See* Parent or guardian

Habeas corpus proceedings 3.74–3.83
  absconding detainees 3.83
  speedy hearing 3.80–3.82
Handcuffs
  police custody 15.83, 15.86–15.87
  prisoners 16.30
Hansard, evidence of Parliamentary
    intention 1.9–1.10

Harassment
at home 3.117, 22.31
domestic violence 19.51–19.52
Harmful surroundings, children 3.57
Health advice, state responsibility
14.70–14.71
Health information, right of access
14.72–14.73
Health or morals, legitimate aims
4.57–4.59
Health reason for abortion 14.33
Health risks
information and advice 5.23–5.27
interim relief, ECHR 30.37–30.39
Hearings
See also Adversarial hearing; Public
hearing; Speedy hearing
ECHR 30.14
Hearings in camera
civil proceedings 13.45–13.46
criminal proceedings 8.14, 8.17
Hearsay evidence 9.4–9.6
anonymous police officers 9.6,
9.27–9.29
anonymous witnesses 9.11,
9.23–9.29
death or illness of witnesses
9.12–9.16
non-compellable witnesses 9.8
police officers 9.6
High Court, declaration of
incompatibility 1.33
High Court of Justiciary, declaration
of incompatibility 1.33
Higher education, distinguished from
elementary education
21.24–21.25
HMP detainees. *See* Children, life
sentences; Young persons, life
sentences
Home
access 22.25–22.26
compulsory purchase orders
22.25–22.26
eviction 22.25–22.26
meaning 22.6–22.11
occupation 22.25–22.26
privacy 3.117–3.120, 22.12–22.13

right to property 22.1–22.4
searches 3.120
Homosexual acts 6.34–6.35
Homosexual couples. *See* Same sex
couples
Honest belief 15.60
Horizontal family relationships 3.114
Hospitals, emergency admissions,
persons of unsound mind
17.9–17.10
House of Lords, declaration of
incompatibility 1.33
Housing
Convention rights 22.44–22.47
discrimination 22.48
disputes 22.4
positive obligations 22.44–22.47
Housing cases
civil rights and obligations
22.40–22.41
fair trial 22.40–22.41
parties 22.3–22.4
procedural fairness 22.42–22.47
right to property 22.16–22.18
Housing rights 22.14–22.18
HRA. *See* Human Rights Act 1998
Human rights
breaches, before coming into force
of HRA 1.5, 2.81
classification 4.1–4.4
existing provisions 1.3, 1.70–1.71
New Zealand, interpretation
1.22–1.24
Human Rights Act 1998 1.1–1.3,
2.1–2.6
coming into force 1.4–1.5
criminal proceedings 6.21
effects on common law 1.42–1.43
freedom of expression 24.24
freedom of religion 27.38
incorporation of Convention 30.1
interpretation 1.27–1.28, 5.39
interpretation of Convention
4.1–4.4
jurisdictions affected 1.66–1.69
margin of appreciation 4.94–4.96
meaning of public authorities
4.94–4.96

Human Rights Act 1998 *continued*
  positive obligations 5.36–5.39
  pre-trial injunctions 24.24
  rights protected 1.6–1.8
  transitional relief 1.73
  UK derogation from Convention
    rights 7.10
  UK reservation from Convention
    rights 3.196, 21.2–21.3
  victims 2.18–2.35
Human Rights Commission 1.72
Humiliation, degrading
    treatment/punishment
    14.52–14.55
Hybrid bodies 2.10–2.11

Ideas
See also Freedom of expression;
    Information
  freedoms 3.141–3.150
Illegitimate children. *See* Children,
    born out of wedlock
Illegitimate criticism of judiciary
    24.36–24.38
Illness
  prisoners 16.26–16.27
  witnesses 9.12–9.16
Ill-treatment in police custody
    15.81–15.87
ILO. *See* International Labour
    Organization
Immigration cases
See also Migrants
  civil rights and obligations 12.28
  discrimination 18.44–18.47
  family life 18.33–18.38
  lawful detention 3.22, 3.65–3.68
  procedural safeguards 18.48
  quotas 18.9
Immigration officers, public
    authorities 2.8
Immunities, civil rights and
    obligations 12.33, 13.14–13.23
Immunity, supergrasses 9.50
Impartiality
  courts 8.4–8.12
  judges 8.10–8.12
  tribunals 3.92–3.93, 13.44

Implementation. *See subheading*
    coming into force
Implied restrictions
  Convention rights 4.75
  duty to hold free elections 3.200,
    3.202
  elections 4.79–4.80
  peaceful enjoyment of property
    26.19–26.20
  prohibition of torture [etc.] 18.21
  right to a fair trial 4.76–4.77
  right to education 4.78–4.78
Inadequate medical treatment,
    Broadmoor 16.35
Incitement to commit an offence
    9.30–9.35
Incitement to race hatred 24.48–24.51
Income, possessions 26.9
Incompatibility with Convention,
    applications to ECHR 30.34
Independence
  courts 8.4–8.12
  inquests 14.18
  planning inspectors 12.43–12.47
  Police Complaints Authority 3.181
  tribunals 3.92–3.93, 13.44
Indeterminate sentences 10.6
India, case law, effect on UK law 1.48
Indirect determination, civil rights
    and obligations 12.35
Indirect discrimination 29.18
Indirect victims 2.29–2.30
Individuals
  applications to ECHR 30.6–30.8
  article 9 claims 27.36
  complaints, ECHR 30.5
  rights under HRA 1.1
  status, lawful detention 3.30–3.32
Indoctrination
  curriculum 21.34
  state religion 3.133, 27.8
Industrial accidents
  benefits 23.16
  public officials 28.13
Industrial action. *See* Strikes
Industrial tribunals, unfair dismissal
    28.3–28.4
Inequality, positive discrimination

29.19–29.20
Information
  freedoms 3.141–3.150, 24.5–24.9
  needed for defence 7.43–7.46
Information and advice, state duties
  5.23–5.27
Inheritance, children born out of
  wedlock 19.40
Inhuman treatment/punishment
  civil cases 11.11
  expulsion cases 18.11–18.12
  meaning 6.3
  migrants 18.4–18.7
  physical assaults 14.49–14.51
  prisoners 16.8–16.15
  prohibition 3.10–3.14, 14.41–14.44,
    14.48–14.55
  psychological harm 14.49–14.51
Inner circle, private life 3.110
Innocent third parties, criminal cases
  9.38–9.41
Inquests 14.14–14.18, 16.7
Instituting proceedings, civil cases
  13.8–13.11
Institutionalised racism
  breaches of article 3 3.13
  degrading treatment/punishment
    14.55
  police 15.89
Insurrection, use of force 14.22
Intention of Parliament 1.1, 1.8–1.10,
  1.14–1.19
Interception of communications,
  police powers 15.21–15.25
Interest, awards under Convention
  2.50
Interests in property 22.15
Interfering with justice, refusal of
  bail 7.21–7.22
Interim relief, ECHR 30.37–30.39
Interlocutory proceedings, public
  hearing 13.48
Internal communications systems
  15.22
International co-operation, criminal
  cases 8.55–8.56
International Covenant on Civil and
  Political Rights 1.73, 9.60

child-specific rights 20.22
  discrimination 29.3
International Covenant on the
  Elimination of All Forms of
  Discrimination against Women
  1.73, 29.1
International Covenant on the
  Elimination of All Forms of
  Racial Discrimination 1.73, 29.1
International immunities 13.23
International Labour Organization
  Conventions 1.73, 3.161, 4.18, 4.25
  forced or compulsory labour 3.17,
    28.19–28.20
  trade unions 28.27
International law
  deprivation of property 26.15
  interpretation of Convention
    1.25–1.26
Interpreters for accused 3.87,
  8.37–8.41
Interrogation techniques, breaches of
  article 3 3.13
Inter-state complaints, ECHR 30.5
Intervening parties, adversarial
  hearing 13.56
Intimate body searches
  evidence 9.75
  prisoners 16.24–16.25
Investigation, deaths 14.9,
  14.14–14.18
Islam 27.5

Jehovah's Witnesses 3.131, 27.5
  education 21.21
  place of worship 27.25
  proselytism 27.19
Joint Council for the Welfare of
  Immigrants, representative
  actions 2.37
Journalists, protection of sources
  24.42–24.43
Judges, impartiality 8.10–8.12
Judgments
  civil proceedings, enforcement
    13.72–13.73
  ECHR, binding nature 30.45

Judgments *continued*
  enforcement, civil proceedings
    13.72–13.73
  reasons
    civil proceedings 13.68–13.69
    criminal proceedings 8.51
  to be public 8.18, 13.50
Judicial acts, alleged breaches of
    Convention rights 2.69–2.72
Judicial Committee of the Privy
    Council, declaration of
    incompatibility 1.33
Judicial review
  civil proceedings 11.8
    effective remedies 11.9–11.13
    fair trial 11.14–11.15
  common law and Convention
    2.38–2.39
  public interest groups 2.37
  sufficient interest 2.36
  whether effective remedy 3.182
Jurisdiction, meaning 2.20
Jury
  impartiality 8.9–8.10
  protection from prejudicial
    influences 7.76–7.81
Just satisfaction 2.48–2.54
Juveniles. *See* Children; Young
    persons

Killing, by private individuals 14.26
Krishna consciousness movement
    3.131, 27.5

Landlord and tenant
  disputes 22.4
  end of tenancy agreement 22.28
Landlords
  interests in property 22.15
  possession of property, end of
    tenancy agreement 22.28
Language 3.87, 8.37–8.41
  discrimination 3.183–3.187,
    29.11–29.14
  education 21.7
Lawful, meaning 3.36
Lawful arrest 15.56–15.59
Lawful chastisement 20.11–20.12

Lawful detention 15.56
  alcoholics 3.22, 3.58–3.64
  anti-terrorist legislation 3.50
  arrested persons 3.22, 3.51–3.54
  children 3.22, 3.55–3.57, 15.51
  convicted persons 3.22, 3.41–3.45,
    10.1–10.7, 16.38
  conviction abroad 3.45, 16.39
  disease prevention 3.22, 3.58–3.64
  drug addicts 3.22, 3.58–3.64
  duration 3.26
  extradition 3.22, 3.65–3.68
  immigration cases 3.22, 3.65–3.68
  meaning 3.22–3.37
  non-compliance with court order
    3.22, 3.46–3.50
  personal status 3.30–3.32
  persons of unsound mind 3.22,
    3.58–3.64, 17.3–17.4
  status of individuals 3.30–3.32
  vagrants 3.22, 3.58–3.64
  voluntary surrender 3.28,
    15.53–15.55
Lawful searches, detention 15.50
Lawfulness of detention
  persons of unsound mind 17.6
  speedy hearing 16.47
Lawyers
  See also Legal representation
  access by accused 7.47–7.51
  communication with
    clients 7.52–7.53
    prisoners 3.121, 16.50–16.51,
    16.69–16.71
  failure to defend effectively
    8.30–8.34
Leasehold interests 22.15
Leasehold reform 22.21
Leave to appeal
  civil rights and obligations 12.39
  criminal cases 10.8, 10.19–10.21
Leaving detention area 3.29, 15.55
Legal aid 3.96
  applications to ECHR 30.40–30.43
  civil proceedings 13.33–13.40
  criminal appeals 10.12–10.16
  expert evidence, civil proceedings
    13.65

fair trial 8.25–8.29
preventing breaches of Convention
    rights 5.30–5.32
Legal correspondence, prisoners
    16.69–16.71
Legal persons, applications to ECHR
    30.6
Legal proceedings, protection of
    Convention rights 2.79–2.80
Legal representation 3.96
See also Lawyers
    civil proceedings 13.33–13.40
    criminal appeals 10.12–10.16
    defence case 3.87
    fair trial 8.30–8.36
Legal terms, interpretation 4.19
Legality, arrest and detention
    7.28–7.32
Legality principle, permitted
    restrictions on Convention
    rights 4.29–4.36
Legislation
See also Primary legislation;
    Subordinate legislation
    causing violation of Convention
    rights 3.177–3.178
    interpretation
        EC law 1.20–1.21
        HRA 1.1, 1.14–1.19
        New Zealand 1.22–1.24
        passed after HRA. *See* New
        legislation
Legislature, free elections
    3.198–3.202
Legitimate aims
    discrimination 29.15
    immunities, civil cases 13.16
    permitted restrictions on
        Convention rights 4.57–4.59
    protection of health or morals
        4.57–4.59
    protection of others' rights
        4.57–4.59
    rights of others 4.57–4.59
Lesbian couples. *See* Same sex
    couples
Less restrictive alternatives 4.46–4.47
Lethal force

authorisation 14.22
proportionality 14.27
Letters. *See* Correspondence
Liability
    breaches of Convention rights 2.17
    HRA, effectiveness principle 4.14
Libraries, prisons 16.54, 16.76
Licensees, interests in property 22.15
Licensing
    associations 3.158
    broadcasting 3.146, 24.10–24.13
    films 3.146
    television 3.146, 24.10–24.13
Life insurance, distinguished from
    social security benefits 23.5
Life prisoners, recall 16.45
Life sentences
    children 10.6, 16.36, 16.41–16.42
    duration 16.31–16.33, 16.43–16.46
    young persons 10.6, 16.36,
        16.41–16.42
Limitation of actions
    civil proceedings 13.24–13.27
    criminal appeals 10.11
    ECHR 30.21–30.24
    HRA 2.73–2.74
    medical negligence 13.26
    redundancy 13.26
    unfair dismissal 13.26
Limits to criticism 24.28–24.33
Listening devices, police powers 15.23
Local authorities
    child care cases 12.41–12.42
    housing 22.44–22.47
    negative obligations 5.35
    positive obligations 5.32,
        22.44–22.47
    public authorities 2.8
Local government officers. *See* Public
    officials
Locus standi
    applications to ECHR 30.6–30.8
    article 9 claims 27.36
Long-term residents, deportation
    18.40
Loss of employment prospects. *See*
    Non-pecuniary loss

Loss of time pending appeal
  10.22–10.24

Magistrates, judicial acts 2.69–2.72
Maintenance payments, absent
  parents 19.48–19.49
Mandatory life sentences, duration
  10.6, 16.31–16.33
Manifestation, religion or belief
  27.3–27.4, 27.10–27.12
Manifestly ill-founded applications to
  ECHR 30.31
Marches
See also Freedom of assembly
  banning orders 25.24–25.26
  freedom of expression 25.1–25.6
Margin of appreciation 1.47,
  4.88–4.93
  blasphemy 27.30–27.31
  civil proceedings 13.7
  discrimination 29.23
  HRA 4.94–4.96
Marriage
See also Right to marry and found a
  family
  age 3.171
  prisoners 16.80
  procedural requirements 3.172
Marriageable age 3.171, 19.32
Married couples
See also Divorce
  separation 19.43
Mauritius, constitution 1.28
Media
See also Broadcasting; Press;
  Television
  exposure of miscarriages of justice
  16.78
Medical care, whether rights exist
  14.64–14.69
Medical cases, disciplinary
  proceedings 13.46
Medical confidentiality, criminal
  cases 9.38–9.41
Medical negligence 14.75–14.77
  limitation of actions 13.26
Medical records, right to privacy
  14.74

Medical treatment
  detainees 14.69
  prisoners 14.69, 16.26–16.27
Medium of expression, freedom of
  expression 24.6
Meetings
See also Freedom of assembly
  banning orders 25.24–25.26
Membership rules, trade unions
  28.26
Mental health cases
See also Persons of unsound mind
  frequency of reviews 17.20–17.22
  periodic reviews 17.13–17.17
  procedural safeguards 17.18–17.19
Mental Health Review Tribunals
  17.15–17.16
Mental illness, severity 17.26–17.27
Mental patients
  applications to ECHR 30.6
  restriction on civil proceedings
  13.8–13.9
Mentally handicapped children,
  protection from sexual assault
  3.123
Merits of case, examination by ECHR
  30.16–30.17
Metering, telephones 15.24
Migrants
See also Deportation; Immigration
  Convention rights 18.8–18.10
  discrimination 18.8–18.10
  family life 18.31–18.34
  inhuman treatment/punishment
  18.4–18.7
  private life 18.31–18.34
  racial discrimination 18.46
  sexual discrimination 18.47
Military disciplinary proceedings 6.32
Military service 3.18, 28.16, 28.18
  conscientious objection 3.18, 3.136,
  27.37
Minorities, discrimination
  3.183–3.187
Minors. *See* Children; Young persons
Miscarriages of justice, exposure by
  media 16.78
Mixed sentences 10.6

M'Naughton rules 8.46
Moral interest, continuing
    proceedings 2.35
Morals, legitimate aims 4.57–4.59
Muslim religion 27.5

Names, family life 19.58–19.59
National authorities, effective
    remedies 1.7, 3.173–3.182
National security 13.20–13.21
    legitimate aims 4.57–4.59
    restriction on trade union rights
        28.36–28.37
    security vetting 28.42–28.43
Nationality cases, civil rights and
    obligations 12.28
Nationality discrimination
    29.11–29.14
    migrants 18.46
    prohibition 3.183–3.187
Navy. *See* Armed forces
Necessary in a democratic society
    4.60–4.66
    civil proceedings 11.4
    police surveillance 15.26–15.29
    proportionality 4.61
    relation to absolute necessity 14.27
    relevant and sufficient reasons
        4.65–4.66
    restrictions on family life
        19.9–19.10
    restrictions on freedom of
        assembly and association 3.167,
        25.23
    restrictions on freedom of
        expression 3.147–3.150
    restrictions on freedom of religion
        or belief 3.137–3.140
    restrictions on privacy 3.129
    search and seizure 15.37
    security vetting 28.42–28.43
Negative obligations 5.1, 5.33–5.45
Negligence
See also Medical negligence
    police immunity 13.19,
        15.96–15.99
New evidence, criminal appeals
    10.27–10.28

New legislation 1.11–1.13
    incompatible with HRA 1.13
    statement of compatibility
        1.11–1.13
New offences, refusal of bail 7.23
New Zealand
    case law, effect on UK law 1.48
    human rights, interpretation
        1.22–1.24
    unlawfully obtained evidence 9.45
Newspapers. *See* Press
Noise nuisance 3.117, 22.32
Non-attendance of witnesses
    9.17–9.18
Non-compellable witnesses, hearsay
    evidence 9.8
Non-compliance with court order,
    lawful detention 3.22, 3.46–3.50
Non-governmental organisations,
    applications to ECHR 30.6–30.8
Non-intimate samples, evidence 9.75
Non-party submissions, adversarial
    hearing 13.56
Non-pecuniary loss 2.50, 2.57
Non-religious beliefs 27.6
Non-retrospectivity. *See* Retrospective
    criminal offences
Northern Ireland
    application of HRA 1.69
    paramilitary attacks 14.12
Notice requirement
    administrative decisions 13.32.
    peaceful assembly 3.155
Notification of hearing, criminal
    proceedings 8.20
Nursery education. *See* Elementary
    education

Obeying domestic law, whether
    refusal justified by religion or
    belief 27.13–27.18
Obligations, civil cases 3.90–3.91
Obstruction, streets 25.13
Occupation of home 22.25–22.26
Occupational pension schemes 22.5
Offence, meaning 3.52, 15.59
Opinions, freedoms 3.141–3.150

Optional Protocol No.6 3.5–3.5
Outside UK. *See* Arrest abroad;
   Conviction abroad

Pacifism 3.131, 27.5
Pain and distress. *See* Non-pecuniary
   loss
Paramilitary attacks, Northern
   Ireland 14.12
Parent and child
See also Children
   personal ties 19.13–19.16
   surrogacy 19.21–19.22
Parent or guardian, representative
   actions 2.31–2.32
Parents
See also Children
   access to children 19.44–19.46
   applications to ECHR 30.6
   control over children 20.2–20.5
   corporal punishment of children
      20.11–20.12
   meaning 21.22–21.23
   philosophical convictions, respect
      in education 21.12–21.23
   religious convictions, respect in
      education 21.12–21.23
   right to detain children for
      education 3.31
Parliament
   intention 1.1, 1.8–1.10
   whether public authority 2.7–2.8
Parliamentary Committee on Human
   Rights (proposed) 1.72
Parole Board 16.43–16.46
Parties
See also Third parties
   civil rights and obligations 12.4
   housing cases 22.3–22.4
Patents. *See* Property
Peaceful assembly 3.153–3.156,
   25.5–25.6
   breach of the peace 3.156
   notice requirement 3.155
Peaceful enjoyment of property
   3.188–3.193, 22.1–22.4,
   26.19–26.20
   environmental problems

      22.30–22.36
   implied restrictions 26.19–26.20
Pecuniary loss 2.55–2.56
Pension funds, property rights
   22.5–23.7
Pensions, public officials 28.10–28.11
Period of detention. *See* Detention,
   duration
Periodic reviews
   detention of persons of unsound
      mind 17.13–17.22
   preventive sentences 10.6
Permitted exceptions, retrospective
   criminal offences 3.107
Permitted restrictions
   activities aimed at destruction of
      Convention rights 4.85–4.87
   Convention rights 4.2–4.4,
      4.26–4.27, 4.29–4.36, 4.56
      legality principle 4.29–4.36, 4.56
      legitimate aim 4.57–4.59
      necessary in a democratic
         society 4.60–4.66
      proportionality 4.37–4.42
   court reporting 24.39–24.41
   destruction of Convention rights
      4.85–4.87
   effect on prisoners 16.53–16.55
   expression of race hatred
      24.48–24.51
   fair trial 3.99
   family life 19.3–19.10
   freedom of assembly and
      association 3.162–3.167,
      4.56–4.66, 16.79, 25.14–25.26
   freedom of expression
      3.147–3.150, 4.56–4.66,
      16.74–16.78, 24.2, 24.14–24.18,
      24.7–24.9
      employment 28.49–28.54
      public officials 28.52–28.54
   freedom of religion or belief
      3.137–3.140, 4.56–4.66,
      16.72–16.73, 27.23–27.26
   peaceful enjoyment of property
      3.188–3.193
   political activity of aliens 4.83–4.84
   privacy 3.125–3.129, 4.56–4.66,

16.56
race hatred 24.48–24.51
retrospective criminal offences
3.107
right of access to courts 13.7
right to liberty 4.67–4.69
right to marry and found a family
4.70
right to property 4.71–4.74,
26.11–26.16
trade union rights 3.151,
28.36–28.37
Person, meaning 2.21
Personal beliefs. *See* Freedom of
belief
Personal data
See also DNA samples; Fingerprints;
Photographs
police powers 15.30–15.35
Personal injury cases, trial within
reasonable time 13.81
Personal status
discrimination 3.183–3.187
lawful detention 3.30–3.32
Personal ties, family life 19.11–19.16
Persons convicted of homicide,
amnesty 14.21
Persons in custody, medical
treatment 14.69
Persons of unsound mind
acquitted because of mental illness
17.28–17.31
conditional release 17.24–17.25
conditions of detention
17.32–17.34
detention
after conviction 17.28–17.31
periodic reviews 17.13–17.22
emergency admissions 17.9–17.10
lawful detention 3.22, 3.58–3.64,
4.68, 17.3–17.4
meaning 17.5
protection from arbitrary detention
17.7–17.8
release 17.23–17.27
voluntary surrender 17.11
wrongful detention 17.12
Petitioning mechanism, ECHR 30.2

Philosophical associations, article 9
claims 27.36
Philosophical convictions
curriculum 21.34–21.35
respect 21.12–21.23
respect in education 21.12–21.23
Photographs, police powers
15.30–15.35
Physical assaults, inhuman
treatment/punishment
14.49–14.51
Pictures, freedom of expression
3.143, 24.6
Planning inspectors, independence
12.43–12.47
Planning restrictions 22.37–22.38
fair trial 22.38
proportionality 22.37
right to property 22.37–22.38
whether refusal justified by
religion or belief 27.16
Pleas, changing 8.50
Plenary Court, ECHR 30.4
Police
damages awards in civil cases
12.20, 15.100
institutionalised racism 15.89
racial discrimination 15.88–15.90
restriction on freedom of assembly
and association 3.162–3.163
restriction on trade union rights
3.151, 28.36–28.37
Police Complaints Authority, degree
of independence 3.181
Police custody, use of force
15.81–15.87
Police immunity, negligence 13.19,
15.96–15.99
Police misconduct
breaches of Convention rights 5.29
damages 2.58–2.59
disciplinary proceedings 12.14
proof 15.91–15.93
remedies 5.29, 15.80
standard of proof 15.91–15.93
Police officers
hearsay evidence 9.6
public authorities 2.8

Police powers 15.1–15.3
  anti-terrorist legislation 3.50
  arrests 15.43–15.45
  detention, thresholds 15.46–15.55
  DNA samples 15.30–15.35
  fingerprints 15.30–15.35
  interception of communications
    15.20–15.25
  listening devices 15.23
  personal data 15.30–15.35
  photographs 15.30–15.35
  positive obligations 15.4–15.5
  search and seizure 15.36–15.40
  stop and search 15.72–15.79
  surveillance 15.6–15.15
    necessary in a democratic
    society 15.26–15.29
  telephone tapping 15.16–15.19
Police questioning
  access to lawyer 7.49–7.51, 9.70
  right to a fair trial 6.20
Policies based on religious beliefs
  27.9
Political activity of aliens, permitted
  restrictions 4.83–4.84
Political discrimination 3.183–3.187,
  29.11–29.14
Political rights, elections 12.30–12.31
Political speech, freedom of
  expression 3.143
Pollution
  damages 2.67
  dangerous chemicals 22.36
  information and advice 5.23–5.27
  positive obligations 5.20
  waste treatment 22.34
Polygamous marriages 19.35
Positive discrimination 29.19–29.20
Positive obligations 2.13, 2.75, 2.80,
  5.1–5.4
  domestic violence 19.50–19.52
  existing law inadequate 5.22
  family life 5.18–5.21
  free elections 3.198–3.202
  freedom of assembly and
    association 25.7–25.9
  freedom of expression, relations
    between private individuals
    24.19–24.21
  freedom of thought [etc.]
    27.21–27.22
  housing 22.44–22.47
  HRA 5.36–5.39
  local authorities 5.32
  police powers 15.4–15.5
  pollution 5.20
  privacy 3.123–3.124
  private life 5.18–5.21
  protection from torture [etc.]
    5.14–5.17, 14.56
  protection of life 5.14–5.17, 14.5,
    14.10–14.13
  protection of physical integrity
    14.61–14.63
  protection of vulnerable
    individuals 20.12–20.14
  right of access to health
    information 14.73
  right to family life 19.29–19.31
  right to life 3.6–3.7, 14.5–14.21
    prisoners 16.3–16.7
  right to property 22.2–22.3
Possession of property, end of
  tenancy agreement 22.28
Possessions
  income 26.9
  meaning 3.189, 22.15–22.18,
    26.8–26.10
  welfare benefits 23.4–23.8
Practising religion or belief
  27.3–27.4, 27.10–27.12
Precedent
  Convention 4.17, 4.20
  ECHR judgments 30.45
Prescribed by law, meaning 15.14
Presence at trial
  civil proceedings 13.52–13.53
  defendants 8.21–8.22
  unfit defendants 8.21–8.22
  waiver 8.21
Press
  freedom of expression 3.142, 24.2
  pre-trial publicity 7.76–7.81
Pressing social need 4.60–4.64
  prevention of disorder 25.23
  restrictions on freedom of

expression 24.14–24.18
Presumption of fact 8.43, 8.45
Presumption of innocence 3.87,
    3.100, 6.5, 8.42, 9.1
  effects of costs decisions 8.52–8.54
Presumption of law 8.43, 8.45
Presumption of sanity 8.46
Pre-trial detention
  frequent reviews 3.77
  speedy hearing 7.5–7.8, 7.33–7.40
Pre-trial injunctions
  freedom of expression, HRA 24.24
  relation to freedom of expression
    1.52–1.53
Pre-trial proceedings
  access to lawyer 7.47–7.51
  charges 7.41–7.46
  criminal cases 7.1–7.4
  disclosure 7.32, 7.54–7.67
  equality of arms 7.31
  public interest immunity 7.68–7.71
Pre-trial publicity 7.76–7.81
Pre-trial rights, criminal cases
    3.71–3.72
Preventing breaches of Convention
    rights 5.13–5.17
Preventing formation of associations
    3.158
Prevention of crime
  grounds for arrest 3.51–3.54
  grounds for detention 15.57, 15.64
  legitimate aims 4.57–4.59
  use of force 14.22, 14.25
Prevention of disorder
  clear and present danger 25.23
  freedom of assembly and
    association 25.14–25.23
  legitimate aims 4.57–4.59
  pressing social need 25.23
  proportionality 25.21
Prevention of escape
  grounds for arrest 3.51–3.54, 15.57
  use of force 14.22, 14.24
Prevention of terrorism, stop and
    search 15.76–15.79
Preventive detention 15.57, 15.64,
    16.40–16.42
  acquitted because of mental illness

17.28–17.31
  children 16.36, 16.41
  dangerousness 15.57, 15.64,
    16.40–16.42
  young persons 16.36, 16.41
Preventive grounds, detention 16.36,
    16.41
Preventive sentences 10.5–10.6
Previously rejected applications to
    ECHR 30.33
Primary education. *See* Elementary
    education
Primary legislation
  amendment 1.30–1.32
  remedial orders 1.55–1.58
  declaration of incompatibility 1.1
  interpretation 1.14–1.19
Prior restraint, freedom of expression
    24.22–24.24
Prison officers
  assaults on prisoners 16.29
  public authorities 2.8
Prison visits 16.28, 16.57, 16.59,
    16.80, 19.38
Prisoners
  body samples 16.24–16.25
  body searches 16.24–16.25
  clothes 16.58, 16.73, 16.76
  communication with lawyers
    3.121, 16.50–16.51, 16.69–16.71
  complaints 16.63–16.64
  correspondence 16.60–16.68
  deduction from earnings 16.82
  degrading treatment/punishment
    16.8–16.15
  dirty protest 16.21–16.23
  disciplinary offences, loss of
    remission 16.34
  discrimination 16.81
  education 16.84
  force-feeding 16.5
  freedom of assembly and
    association 16.79
  freedom of expression 16.60–16.68
  handcuffs 16.30
  illness 16.26–16.27
  inhuman treatment/punishment
    16.8–16.15

Prisoners *continued*
  intimate body searches
    16.24–16.25
  legal correspondence 16.69–16.71
  marriage 16.80
  medical treatment 14.69
  preventive detention 16.40–16.42
  provision of body samples
    16.24–16.25
  psychiatric treatment 14.69
  quality of life 16.49
  receipt from abroad 8.55–8.56
  release on medical grounds 16.26
  right of access to courts
    16.50–16.52
  right to life 16.3–16.7
  right to receive information
    16.75–16.78
  sentences, duration 16.31–16.34
  solitary confinement 16.15–16.20
  state pension 16.83
  telephone use 16.78
  work during legal detention
    3.18–3.19, 16.37
Prisons
  Boards of Visitors 16.52
  conditions 16.12–16.15
    breaches of article 3 3.13
    result of prisoner's behaviour
      16.21–16.23
  disciplinary proceedings 6.11, 8.14,
    16.52
  libraries 16.54, 16.76
Privacy 3.108–3.129
  communications between lawyer
    and client 7.52–7.53
  damages 2.65
  home 3.117–3.120, 22.12–22.13
  permitted restrictions 3.125–3.129,
    16.56
  positive obligations 3.123–3.124
  secret surveillance 3.112
  security vetting 28.42–28.43
  state duties 3.123–3.124
  surveillance 3.112
  undercover agents 9.30–9.35
  victims 2.27–2.28
Private actions, by public authorities
    2.8
Private assemblies. *See* Freedom of
    assembly
Private beliefs. *See* Freedom of belief
Private individuals
  acts, state responsibility 2.16, 2.75,
    14.60
  criticism 24.28–24.33
  disputes 28.57
    Convention rights 28.57
Private life
  expulsion cases 18.31–18.34
  inner circle 3.110
  meaning 3.109–3.111
  migrants 18.31–18.34
  positive obligations 5.18–5.21
  prisoners 16.57–16.59
Private life insurance, distinguished
    from social security benefits
    23.5
Private rights, civil rights and
    obligations 12.5
Private schools 21.9, 21.26–21.28
  funding 21.20, 21.29–21.30
  quality control 21.11
  regulation by state 21.11
Private security companies, whether
    public authorities 2.10
Privileges, civil rights and obligations
    12.33, 13.14–13.23
Procedural fairness
  housing cases 22.42–22.47
  proportionality 4.48–4.51
  welfare benefits 23.12–23.12
Procedural requirements, marriage
    3.172
Procedural rules, civil rights and
    obligations 13.32
Procedural safeguards
See also Fair trial
  detainees 15.43–15.45
  detention 3.38–3.40, 3.69–3.83
  expulsion cases 18.48
  fair trial 3.101
  family life 19.7, 19.64–19.69
  immigration cases 18.48
  mental health cases 17.18–17.19
  property cases 26.22–26.23

proportionality 4.52–4.53
release of persons of unsound
    mind 17.27
Procedure
    meaning 3.40
    remedial orders 1.57–1.58
Proceedings against public
    authorities 1.41
Processions, freedom of expression
    25.1–25.6
Professional premises, search and
    seizure 15.36–15.40
Professional regulatory bodies 3.159
    disciplinary proceedings
        12.41–12.42
Prohibition of
    degrading treatment/punishment
        3.10–3.14, 14.41–14.44,
        14.48–14.55
    discrimination 3.183–3.187,
        29.11–29.14
    forced or compulsory labour
        3.15–3.20, 28.15–28.24
    inhuman treatment/punishment
        3.10–3.14, 14.41–14.44,
        14.48–14.55
    religious discrimination
        3.183–3.187, 27.34–27.35
    retrospective criminal offences
        3.102–3.106, 6.8
    self-incrimination in criminal
        proceedings 9.60–9.74
    sexual discrimination 3.183–3.187
    slavery [etc.] 3.15–3.20,
        28.15–28.24
    social discrimination 3.183–3.187
    torture [etc.] 3.10–3.14,
        14.41–14.47, 18.21–18.22
        criminal proceedings 6.3
        implied restrictions 18.21
Prompt hearing. *See* Speedy hearing
Proof
See also Burden of proof; Standard of
    proof
    police misconduct 15.91–15.93
Property
See also Control of property;
    Deprivation of property; Right to

property
    disputes between individuals 22.24
    eviction orders 22.22
    meaning 22.15–22.18
    prohibition of discrimination
        3.183–3.187
    right to peaceful enjoyment
        3.188–3.193
    welfare benefits 23.4–23.8
Property cases
    civil rights and obligations
        12.10–12.14
    pecuniary loss 2.56
    procedural safeguards 26.22–26.23
Property developers, whether public
    authorities 2.10
Property measures, fair balance
    3.192–3.193, 22.20
Property rights
    emergency assistance 23.6
    pension funds 22.5–23.7
Proportional representation 3.201
Proportionality
    ban on meetings 25.26
    between individuals and the
        community 5.6
    control of property 3.192, 26.18
    deprivation of property 26.16
    discrimination 29.16
    expulsion cases 18.39–18.40
    freedom of religion or belief
        27.23–27.26
    immunities, civil cases 13.16
    less restrictive alternatives
        4.46–4.47
    lethal force 14.27
    necessary in a democratic society
        4.61
    planning restrictions 22.37
    police immunity, negligence 15.99
    police surveillance 15.26–15.29
    prevention of disorder 25.21
    procedural fairness 4.48–4.51
    procedural safeguards 4.52–4.53
    prohibition of discrimination
        3.187, 4.41
    relevant and sufficient reasons
        4.43–4.45

Proportionality *continued*
  restriction on trade union rights
    28.36–28.37
  restrictions on Convention rights
    4.37–4.42
  restrictions on family life
    19.9–19.10
  restrictions on freedom of
    expression 24.14–24.18
  right to liberty 4.67–4.69
  right to property 4.71–4.74, 22.33
  search and seizure 15.37
  security for costs 13.30
  sentences 10.5–10.6
  'very essence' test 4.54–4.55
Proselytism, freedom of religion
    27.19–27.20
Protection from
  arbitrary detention
    persons of unsound mind
      17.7–17.8
    state responsibility 3.32, 3.37
  blasphemy 27.21–27.22
  domestic violence 19.50–19.52
  sexual assault, mentally
    handicapped children 3.123
  torture [etc.]
    positive obligations 5.14–5.17,
      14.56
    state responsibility 14.57–14.60
Protection of
  children born out of wedlock
    19.39–19.41
  health or morals, legitimate aims
    4.57–4.59
  innocent third parties, criminal
    cases 9.38–9.41
  judiciary from illegitimate
    criticism 24.36–24.38
  jury from prejudicial influences
    7.76–7.81
  life
    enforcement 14.9
    interpretation 14.10
    positive obligations 5.14–5.17,
      14.5, 14.10–14.13
    national security 13.20–13.21
    others' rights, legitimate aims

    4.57–4.59
  physical integrity, positive
    obligations 14.61–14.63
  victims 9.36–9.41
    sexual offences cases 9.37, 13.46
  vulnerable individuals
    positive obligations 20.12–20.14
    state obligations 20.12–20.14
  witnesses 9.36–9.41
    sexual offences cases 9.37, 13.46
Protection of Convention rights
  criminal proceedings 61–6.8
  HRA 5.36–5.39
  legal proceedings 2.79–2.80
  state duties 4.88–4.93, 5.7–5.12
Protection of sources
  journalists 24.42–24.43
  video news films 24.43
Protests, freedom of expression
    25.1–25.6
Protocols to Convention 3.188–3.202
Provision of body samples, prisoners
    16.24–16.25
Psychiatric reports, disclosure 7.66
Psychiatric treatment, prisoners 14.69
Psychological harm, inhuman
    treatment/punishment
    14.49–14.51
Psychological interrogation
    techniques, breaches of article 3
    3.13
Public assemblies. *See* Freedom of
    assembly
Public authorities
  civil proceedings by individuals,
    HRA 11.6
  compensation claims 12.19–12.21
  meaning 1.1, 1.40, 2.7–2.11
    Convention case law 2.12–2.17
    HRA 4.94–4.96
  positive obligations, HRA
    5.36–5.39
  private actions 2.8
  unlawful acts 1.1, 1.39–1.41
Public employees. *See* Public officials
Public figures, criticism 24.28–24.35
Public health rules, whether refusal
    justified by religion or belief

27.18
Public hearing 3.87–3.101
  appeals, civil proceedings 13.76
  civil proceedings 13.45–13.50
  criminal appeals 10.17–10.18
  fair trial 8.13–8.18
Public highways. *See* Streets
Public interest, freedom of expression
  24.27–24.33
Public interest groups
  judicial review 2.37
  sufficient interest 2.37
Public interest immunity
  civil proceedings 13.21–13.22
  pre-trial proceedings 7.68–7.71
Public interest litigation 2.38–2.39
  existing human rights 1.71
Public interest test
  control of property 22.20–22.23
  deprivation of property
    22.19–22.22, 26.4, 26.13
Public judgment 3.92–3.93
Public law, employment of public
  officials 28.6–28.14
Public officials
  breaches of Convention rights 5.29
  civil rights and obligations 12.14,
    28.6–28.14
  dismissal 28.6, 28.51
  employment rights 28.6–28.14
  freedom of expression 3.144
  industrial accidents 28.13
  pensions 28.10–28.11
  recruitment 28.50
  restriction on freedom of assembly
    and association 3.162–3.163
  restriction on trade union rights
    3.151, 28.36–28.37
  strict liability of states 14.57–14.60,
    15.94–15.95
  ultra vires 14.57–14.60,
    15.94–15.95
Public order, refusal of bail 7.24
Public safety, legitimate aims
  4.57–4.59
Public safety rules, whether refusal
  justified by religion or belief
  27.18

Public schools, regulation by state
  21.11
Punitive sentences 10.5–10.6

Qualified privilege, civil rights and
  obligations 13.18
Qualified rights 4.2
Quality control
  broadcasting 24.16
  private schools 21.11
Quality of life, prisoners 16.49
Quashing indictments, criminal
  proceedings 2.42
Quotas, immigration 18.9

Race hatred, permitted restrictions
  24.48–24.51
Racial discrimination 1.73, 29.1,
  29.11–29.14
  by police 15.88–15.90
  migrants 18.46
  police 15.88–15.90
  prohibition 3.183–3.187
Radio. *See* Broadcasting
Railtrack, whether public authority
  2.10
Rape, breaches of article 3 3.13
Reasonable justification, use of force
  14.7
Reasonable suspicion
  confidential information 15.63
  grounds for arrest 3.22, 3.51–3.54,
    15.57
  meaning 3.53, 15.60–15.63
Reasonable time, trial 7.34–7.35,
  13.78–13.83
Reasons
  appeal judgments 10.25–10.26
  detention, given to detainee
    3.69–3.70, 15.65–15.68
  judgments
    civil proceedings 13.68–13.69
    criminal proceedings 8.51
Recall of life prisoners 16.45
Recruitment of public officials 28.50
Redundancy, limitation of actions
  13.26
References from UK, ECHR 30.1

Referenda 3.201
Refunding legal aid, ECHR 30.43
Refusal of bail 7.16–7.16
  commission of further offences
    7.23
  fear of absconding 7.18–7.20
  further offences 7.23
  interfering with justice 7.21–7.22
  new offences 7.23
  public order 7.24
  relevant and sufficient reasons
    7.16
  serious offences 7.12
Refusal to obey domestic law,
    whether justified by religion or
    belief 27.13–27.18
Registration of associations 3.158
Regulation of abortion 14.35
Regulation of schools 21.11
Reimbursement of expenses, ECHR
    30.18
Relations between individuals, state
    responsibility 5.11–5.12
Relationships, family life 3.113–3.114
Release
  discretionary life prisoners
    16.44–16.46
  persons of unsound mind
    17.23–17.27
  prisoners, medical grounds 16.26
Relevant and sufficient reasons
  necessary in a democratic society
    4.65–4.66
  proportionality 4.43–4.45
  refusal of bail 7.16
Religion
  changing 3.133, 27.8
  manifestation 27.3–27.4,
    27.10–27.12
Religious associations, article 9
    claims 27.36
Religious conversion. See Proselytism
Religious convictions
  curriculum 21.34–21.35
  effects on employment
    28.45–28.48
  respect in education 21.19–21.23
Religious discrimination 29.11–29.14

prohibition 3.183–3.187,
    27.34–27.35
Religious groups, representative
    actions 2.31–2.32
Remedial orders, HRA 1.55,
    1.57–1.58
Remedies
  See also Compensation; Damages;
    Discretionary remedies
  breaches of Convention rights 1.7,
    5.28–5.29
  for police misconduct 15.80
  HRA 1.55–1.58, 2.40–2.44
  inequality, positive discrimination
    29.19–29.20
Removal from harmful surroundings,
    children 3.57, 20.17
Removal from parents, child's best
    interest 19.10
Removal to safe third country,
    expulsion cases 18.23
Rent control 22.23
Representative actions
  Convention 2.38–2.39
  HRA 2.31–2.32
Reservations
  Convention 1.6, 1.62–1.65
  UK, right to education 3.196,
    21.2–21.3
Residential premises. See Home
Respect
  meaning 21.17–21.21
  philosophical convictions
    21.12–21.23
Restrictions
  children's liberty 20.2–20.5
  civil rights and obligations 12.33,
    13.14–13.23
  Convention rights, proportionality
    4.37–4.42
  freedom of assembly and
    association, police 3.162–3.163
  freedom of expression
    pressing social need
      24.14–24.18
    proportionality 24.14–24.18
  instituting proceedings, civil cases
    13.8–13.11

right of property
tax burdens 26.21
tax payments 26.21
trade union rights
armed forces 3.151, 28.36–28.37
police 3.151, 28.36–28.37
proportionality 28.36–28.37
public officials 3.151,
28.36–28.37
Retention, personal data, police
powers 15.34–15.35
Retrospective claims, HRA 2.81
Retrospective criminal offences
3.102–3.106, 6.27–6.31
permitted exceptions 3.107
prohibition 3.102–3.106, 6.8
Retrospective effect, remedial orders
1.57
Retrospective penalties 6.29–6.31,
10.4
Reviews
pre-trial detention 3.77
preventive sentences 10.6
Right not to join associations 3.157,
28.29–28.30
Right of access to courts 3.95
civil proceedings 13.6–13.7
prisoners 16.50–16.52
waiver 13.12–13.13
Right of access to health information
14.72–14.73
positive obligations 14.73
Right of access to individual's own
medical records 14.74
Right of petition, abuse of process
30.35
Right to a fair trial 3.87–3.101
criminal proceedings 6.5–6.6
implied restrictions 4.76–4.77
police questioning 6.20
public hearing 8.13–8.18
Right to a tribunal 13.41–13.43
Right to an effective remedy
3.173–3.182
Right to be brought promptly before a
court 7.5–7.8
Right to defend self 8.36
Right to detain children for

education, schools 3.31
Right to earn a livelihood 28.1
Right to education 3.194–3.197,
21.5–21.9
implied restrictions 4.78–4.78
UK reservation 3.196
Right to effective participation
civil proceedings 13.51
criminal proceedings 8.19–8.22
Right to enter, reside or remain in a
particular country 18.1
Right to family life 19.29–19.31
positive obligations 19.29–19.31
Right to free elections 3.198–3.202
Right to information, accused 3.87
Right to join trade unions
3.151–3.167, 28.25–28.27
Right to legal assistance 7.47–7.51
Right to liberty 3.21–3.86
See also Arrests; Detention
criminal proceedings 6.4
permitted restrictions 4.67–4.69
proportionality 4.67–4.69
relation to arrest 15.43–15.45
speedy hearing 7.5–7.8
Right to life 3.4–3.9, 14.2–14.40
expulsion cases 18.24
foetus 14.32
positive obligations 3.6–3.7,
14.5–14.21
prisoners 16.3–16.7
relation to medical care 14.67
state duties 3.6–3.7
Right to marry and found a family
3.115, 3.168–3.172, 19.32–19.38,
19.38
permitted restrictions 4.70
Right to peaceful enjoyment of
property 3.188–3.193
Right to privacy 3.108–3.129
employment 28.39–28.41
medical records 14.74
Right to property 3.188–3.193,
26.1–26.2
housing cases 22.16–22.18
permitted restrictions 4.71–4.74,
26.11–26.16
planning restrictions 22.37–22.38

Right to property *continued*
  positive obligations 22.2–22.3
  proportionality 4.71–4.74, 22.33
  relation to environmental
    protection 22.32–22.36
Right to public hearing, waiver 13.47
Right to receive information,
  prisoners 16.75–16.78
Right to remarry, after divorce 19.36
Right to separate
  families 5.19
  family life 19.30
Right to silence, criminal proceedings
  9.60–9.74
Right to stand for election 3.200
Right to strike, European Social
  Charter 28.34
Right to vote, free elections 3.200
Rights of others, legitimate aims
  4.57–4.59
Rights of succession 22.7
Rights protected, HRA 1.6–1.8,
  3.1–3.3
Riot control, use of force 14.22
Risk of torture [etc.]
  expulsion cases 18.15–18.18
  non-official sources 18.19–18.20
Risk to life, failure to perceive
  14.11–14.13
Riyadh Guidelines. *See* United
  Nations Guidelines for the
  Prevention of Juvenile
  Delinquency
Rules of procedure, civil rights and
  obligations 13.32
Running of time. *See* Time running

Sado-masochistic acts 6.36
Same sex couples 19.23–19.24, 19.27
  discrimination 29.7–29.9
Samples
  evidence 9.75
  prisoners 16.24–16.25
Sanity, presumption 8.46
Sceptics 27.6
Schools
  corporal punishment 20.8–20.10,
    21.40–21.41

disciplinary proceedings
  21.38–21.39
  challenges 21.46–21.47
expulsion or suspension
  21.42–21.45
funding 21.20
right to detain children for
  education 3.31
uniforms 21.48
Scientology 3.131, 27.5
Scotland
  application of HRA 1.66–1.67
  Court of Session, declaration of
    incompatibility 1.33
  High Court, declaration of
    incompatibility 1.33
Search and seizure
  business premises 3.120
  home 3.120
  necessary in a democratic society
    15.37
  police powers 15.36–15.40
  professional premises 15.36–15.40
  proportionality 15.37
Secondary legislation. *See*
  Subordinate legislation
Secret ballots 3.198–3.202
Secret surveillance
  criminal cases 9.30–9.35
  effective remedies 3.179
  privacy 3.112
Security companies, whether public
  authorities 2.10
Security for costs, civil proceedings
  13.28–13.31
Security of the person 3.21–3.86
Security services
  surveillance
    effective remedies 3.179
    privacy 3.112
Security vetting
  employment 28.42–28.43
  necessary in a democratic society
    28.42–28.43
  privacy 28.42–28.43
Seizure. *See* Search and seizure
Self-defence, use of force 14.22
Self-incrimination

body samples 9.75
criminal proceedings 9.60–9.74
Sentences
classification 10.5–10.6
duration 16.31–16.34
loss of time pending appeal
10.22–10.24
proportionality 10.5–10.6
severity 10.5–10.6
Sentencing
fair trial 10.3
in camera 8.17
involvement of victims 10.7
Separation
access to children 19.44–19.46
married couples 19.43
Serious offences, refusal of bail 7.12
Servitude. *See* Slavery
Severance, subordinate legislation
1.38
Severity
corporal punishment, children 20.7
mental illness 17.26–17.27
sentences 10.5–10.6, 16.31–16.34
Sex education 21.36–21.37
Sexual abuse of children 20.14
Sexual discrimination 1.73, 29.1,
29.11–29.14
migrants 18.47
prohibition 3.183–3.187
suspect groups 29.17
welfare benefits 23.8
Sexual identity. *See* Transsexuals
Sexual offences cases, protection of
victims and witnesses 9.37,
13.46
Shares. *See* Property
Shelters, whether homes 22.10
Siblings, family life 19.26
Sikhs 27.18
Silence during police questioning,
adverse inferences 7.49–7.51,
9.67–9.74
Sit-ins, freedom of expression
25.1–25.6
Six-month rule, admissibility of
complaints, ECHR 30.21–30.24
Slavery

distinguished from servitude 28.17
prohibition 3.15–3.20
Slavery Convention 1926 28.17
Social discrimination 29.11–29.14
prohibition 3.183–3.187
Social insurance, distinguished from
welfare assistance 23.17–23.21
Social reasons for abortion 14.34
Social security benefits, distinguished
from private life insurance 23.5
Solitary confinement 16.15–16.20
Special circumstances
exhaustion of domestic remedies
30.28
time limit for ECHR applications
30.24
Special needs, children 21.31–21.33
Speedy hearing
habeas corpus proceedings
3.80–3.82
lawfulness of detention 16.47
pre–trial detention 7.5–7.8,
7.33–7.40
right to liberty 7.5–7.8
suspected terrorists 7.8–7.10
Sperm donors 19.21–19.22
Spouses, witnesses 9.7–9.11
Standard of proof 8.48–8.49
civil proceedings 13.63
police misconduct 15.91–15.93
torture 14.44
Stare decisis. *See* Precedent
State duties
information and advice 5.23–5.27
preventing breaches of Convention
rights 5.13–5.17
privacy 3.123–3.124
protection of Convention rights
4.88–4.93, 5.7–5.12
resources for preventing breaches
of Convention rights 5.30–5.32
right to life 3.6–3.7
State pension, prisoners 16.83
State religion, indoctrination 3.133,
27.8
State responsibility
acts of private individuals 2.16,
2.75, 14.60

State responsibility *continued*
  delegation of obligations 2.16
  education 20.10
  eviction 22.27–22.29
  health advice 14.70–14.71
  meaning, Convention case law
    2.12–2.17
  negative obligations 5.33–5.45
  protection from arbitrary detention
    3.32, 3.37
  protection from torture [etc.]
    14.57–14.60
  protection of vulnerable
    individuals 20.12–20.14
  relations between individuals
    5.11–5.12
  trial within reasonable time 13.83
State servants. *See* Public officials
Statement of compatibility, new
  legislation 1.11–1.13
States
  parties, civil rights and obligations
    12.6
  vicarious liability 15.94–15.95
Status
See also Locus standi
  discrimination 29.11–29.14
  prohibition 3.183–3.187
  individuals, lawful detention
    3.30–3.32
Statutory instruments, remedial
  orders 1.55
Statutory rights, compensation, UK
  12.22
Statutory sickness benefit
  23.14–23.15
Statutory widows' pensions 23.16
Staying criminal proceedings 2.42
Stonehenge 27.18
Stop and search
  police powers 15.72–15.79
  prevention of terrorism
    15.76–15.79
Strasbourg bodies
See also Committee of Ministers;
    European Commission of
    Human Rights; European Court
    of Human Rights

case law
  effect on UK law 1.44–1.47
  state responsibility 2.12–2.17
case load 30.2
reconstitution by Protocol 11 30.2
Streets, freedom of assembly
  25.10–25.13
Strict liability of states, public
  officials 14.57–14.60,
  15.94–15.95
Strict liability offences, burden of
  proof 8.47
Strikes 28.34–28.35
Striking down, subordinate
  legislation 1.1, 1.36
Striking out, applications to ECHR
  30.36
Subordinate legislation
  interpretation 1.14–1.19, 1.36
  striking down 1.1, 1.36
  ultra vires 1.36
Subsidiarity doctrine 1.47, 4.88–4.93
Succession to home 22.7
Sufficient interest
  public interest groups 2.37
  relation to victim 2.36–2.38
  victims 2.18–2.35
Suicide of prisoner 16.3, 16.6
Supergrasses, evidence 9.50
Surrogacy, parent and child
  19.21–19.22
Surveillance
  effective remedies 3.179
  police powers 15.6–15.8
  privacy 3.112
  solitary confinement 16.17
Suspect groups, discrimination 29.17
Suspected terrorists 15.62
  compulsory questioning 9.71–9.74
  speedy hearing 7.8–7.10
Suspension
  from employment 28.3
  from schools 21.42–21.45
  state pension, prisoners 16.83
Suspicious deaths
  criminal investigations
    14.19–14.20
  investigation 14.9

Taking of life
  civil proceedings 14.8
  criminal sanctions 14.6
Tapping. *See* Telephone tapping
Tariff,.discretionary life sentences
    16.42
Tax burdens
  effects of marriage 19.33
  restrictions on right of property
    26.21
Tax payments
  restrictions on right of property
    26.21
  whether refusal justified by
    religion or belief 27.14
Tax proceedings
  civil rights and obligations
    12.16–12.17
  fair trial 12.15–12.17
  whether criminal proceedings
    6.15–6.17
Telephone tapping
  employees 28.40–28.41
  police powers 15.16–15.19
Telephone use, prisoners 16.78
Telephones
  metering 15.24
  privacy 3.121–3.122
Television, licensing 3.146,
    24.10–24.13
Tenants
See also Landlord and tenant
  interests 22.15
Termination of medical treatment
    14.68
Terrorism
See also Anti-terrorist legislation;
    Prevention of terrorism;
    Suspected terrorists
  meaning 3.52
  reasonable suspicion 15.62
UK derogation from Convention,
    right to liberty 3.73
Testing legality, arrests and detention
    7.28–7.32
Third parties, criminal cases
    9.38–9.41

Third states 8.55–8.56
Threats of reprisals to witnesses
    9.19–9.22
Threats of torture
  breaches of Convention rights 3.13
  non-official sources 18.19–18.20
Thresholds, legal aid, ECHR 30.41
Time for preparation of defence case
    7.72–7.75
Time limits
  applications to ECHR 30.14
  criminal appeals 10.11
Time running
  ECHR applications 30.21–30.24
  trial within reasonable time
    7.34–7.35
Tort actions by members of armed
    forces, Crown immunity 13.17
Torture
  meaning 6.3, 14.43, 14.44–14.47
  prohibition 3.10–3.14, 14.41–14.47
  standard of proof 14.44
Trade unions 3.160–3.161
See also Employment
  anti-union employers 28.35
  ballots 28.35
  collective bargaining 28.31–28.33
  ILO Conventions 28.27
  joining rights 3.151–3.167,
    28.25–28.27
  membership rules 28.26
  protection of members' interest
    28.31–28.33
  representative actions 2.31–2.32,
    2.37
  right to be heard 28.31–28.33
Trafalgar Square, ban on meetings
    25.26
Translations 3.87, 8.37–8.41
Transsexuals 19.25, 19.37,
    19.60–19.63
Treaties, interpretation 4.5–4.8
Trial in absentia 8.23–8.24
Trial within reasonable time
    7.33–7.40, 13.78–13.83
Tribunals
  meaning 13.41–13.43
  public authorities 2.7

Tribunals *continued*
    responsibility for developing law
        2.76–2.78

UK. *See* United Kingdom
Ultra vires
    public officials 14.57–14.60,
        15.94–15.95
    subordinate legislation 1.36
Unborn children. *See* Abortion;
    Foetus
Uncles and nephews 19.28
Undercover agents, criminal cases
    9.30–9.35
Unemployed persons, conditions on
    benefits 28.24
Unfair dismissal
    industrial tribunal cases 28.3–28.4
    limitation of actions 13.26
Unfit defendants, presence at trial
    8.21–8.22
Uniforms
    prisoners 16.58, 16.73, 16.76
    schools 21.48
Unincorporated bodies,
    representative actions 2.31–2.32
Unintentional killing 14.23
United Kingdom
    death penalty 14.39–14.40
    derogation from Convention 1.60
        right to liberty 3.73, 4.82
        suspected terrorists 7.9–7.10
    incorporation of Convention 30.1
    Legal Aid Board, ECHR cases
        30.40
    reservation, right to education
        3.196, 21.2–21.3
United Nations Convention on the
    Rights of the Child 20.1, 20.21
United Nations Guidelines for the
    Prevention of Juvenile
    Delinquency 20.28
United Nations human rights
    instruments 4.24–4.24
United Nations Rules for the
    Protection of Juveniles Deprived
    of their Liberty 20.28
United Nations Standard Minimum

    Rules for the Administration of
        Juvenile Justice 20.23–20.24
United States
    death row phenomenon 18.14,
        18.16
    Supreme Court, case law, effect on
        UK law 1.48
Unlawful acts, public authorities 1.1,
    1.39–1.41
Unlawfully obtained evidence
    9.42–9.45
    New Zealand 9.45
Unsound mind, meaning 17.5
Urgent applications, ECHR
    30.37–30.39
Urine samples, evidence 9.75
Use of force
    absolute necessity 14.7, 14.22,
        14.27–14.31
    arrests 14.22, 14.24
    insurrection 14.22
    police custody 15.81–15.87
    prevention of crime 14.22, 14.25
    prevention of escape 14.22, 14.24
    reasonable justification 14.7
    right to life 3.8–3.9, 14.7
    riot control 14.22
    self-defence 14.22

Vagrants, lawful detention 3.22,
    3.58–3.64
Veganism 27.5
Vertical family relationships 3.114
Very essence test, proportionality
    4.54–4.55
Vexatious litigation 13.8
Vicarious liability, states 14.57–14.60,
    15.94–15.95
Victims
See also Indirect victims
    applications to ECHR 30.6–30.8
    involvement in sentencing 10.7
    meaning 2.18–2.35
    privacy 2.27–2.28
    protection 9.36–9.41
    relation to sufficient interest
        2.36–2.38
    sufficient interest 2.18–2.35

Video, freedom of expression 3.143,
24.6
Video news films, protection of
sources 24.43
Vienna Convention on the Law of
Treaties 1969 1.26, 4.5–4.8
Violence. *See* Corporal punishment;
Domestic violence; Use of force
Voluntary arbitration 13.13
Voluntary groups. *See* Associations
Voluntary surrender
lawful detention 3.28, 15.53–15.55
persons of unsound mind 17.11
Vulnerable individuals
degrading treatment/punishment
14.54
protection by state 20.12–20.14
protection from torture [etc.] 14.43

Waiver
Convention rights 4.97–4.98
presence at trial 8.21
right of access to courts
13.12–13.13
right to public hearing 13.47
Wales, application of HRA 1.68
War crimes 3.107, 6.28
War injuries annuities 23.16
Waste treatment 22.34
Wasted costs orders 13.71
Welfare assistance, distinguished
from social insurance
23.17–23.21
Welfare benefits
assessment boards 12.41
civil rights and obligations 12.26
conditions, unemployed persons
28.24
deprivation of property 23.9–23.10
discrimination 23.23
effects of marriage 19.33
emergency assistance 23.6, 23.11
industrial accidents 23.16
possessions 23.4–23.8, 26.10
procedural fairness 23.12–23.12
property 23.4–23.8
property rights 23.3–23.3
sexual discrimination 23.8
unemployed persons, conditions

28.24
whether civil rights 23.1–23.2,
23.13–23.21
whether contributions-based
23.17–23.21
Withdrawal of medical treatment
14.68
Within the jurisdiction, meaning 2.20
Witnesses
See also Evidence
civil proceedings 13.62
compellability 9.7–9.11
criminal cases 9.1–9.3
death or illness 9.12–9.16
defence evidence 9.55–9.59
defendants 9.60
examination by accused 3.87
experts 9.52–9.54
family members 9.7–9.11
fear of reprisals 9.19–9.22
protection 9.36–9.41
spouses 9.7–9.11
Women
See also Sexual discrimination
discrimination 1.73, 29.1
Words, freedom of expression 3.143,
24.6
Work during legal detention
3.18–3.19, 16.37, 28.16, and
28.17
Workplace rights. *See* Employment;
Forced or compulsory labour;
Right to join trade unions
World Council of Churches,
proselytism 27.19
World Development Movement,
representative actions 2.37
Wrongful detention
compensation 3.84–3.86, 3.176,
16.48
damages 2.58–2.59
persons of unsound mind 17.12

Young persons
homosexual acts 6.34–6.35
in detention, education 16.84
life sentences 10.6, 16.36,
16.41–16.42, 16.45–16.46
preventive detention 16.36, 16.41

LAG Legal Action Group

Working with lawyers and advisers to promote equal access to justice

Legal Action magazine

The only monthly magazine published specifically for legal aid practitioners and the advice sector. Future articles will examine the application and impact of the Human Rights Act 1998 across a wide range of issues.

1999 annual subscription: £73
Concessionary rates available for students and trainees – call the LAG office for details.

Books

LAG's catalogue includes a range of titles covering:

- community care
- crime
- debt
- education
- family
- housing
- human rights
- immigration
- personal injury
- practice & procedure
- welfare benefits
- LAG policy

Community Care Law Reports

The only law reports devoted entirely to community care issues. Compiled by an expert team and published quarterly, each issue contains:

- editorial review
- community care law update
- law reports
- guidance
- cumulative index
- full tables

Training

Accredited with the Law Society, the Bar Council and the Institute of Legal Executives, LAG has been providing pioneering courses in continuing professional development for many years. Where relevant, courses will examine the practical impact of the Human Rights Act on specific areas of practice.

Conferences

LAG runs major conferences to examine issues at the cutting-edge of legal services policy and to inform practitioners of their implications.

For further information about any of Legal Action Group's activities please contact:

Legal Action Group
242 Pentonville Road
London
N1 9UN
DX 130400 London (Pentonville Road)
Telephone: 0171 833 2931
Fax: 0171 837 6094
e-mail: lag@lag.org.uk